Mastering Go

Third Edition

Harness the power of Go to build professional utilities and concurrent servers and services

Mihalis Tsoukalos

Packt>

BIRMINGHAM – MUMBAI

Mastering Go
Third Edition

Producer: Dr. Shailesh Jain
Acquisition Editor – Peer Reviews: Saby Dsilva
Project Editor: Amisha Vathare
Content Development Editor: Edward Doxey
Copy Editor: Safis Editing
Technical Editor: Aniket Shetty
Proofreader: Safis Editing
Indexer: Rekha Nair
Presentation Designer: Pranit Padwal

First published: April 2018

Second edition: August 2019

Third edition: August 2021

Production reference: 1200821

Published by Packt Publishing Ltd.
Livery Place
35 Livery Street
Birmingham
B3 2PB, UK.

ISBN 978-1-80107-931-0

`www.packt.com`

Contributors

About the author

Mihalis Tsoukalos is a UNIX Systems Engineer who enjoys technical writing. He is the author of *Go Systems Programming* and *Mastering Go*, both first and second editions. He holds a BSc in Mathematics from the University of Patras and an MSc in IT from University College London, UK. He has written more than 300 technical articles for magazines including *Sys Admin*, *MacTech*, *Linux User and Developer*, *Usenix ;login:*, *Linux Format*, and *Linux Journal*. His research interests include time series, databases, and indexing.

You can reach him at `https://www.mtsoukalos.eu/` and `@mactsouk`.

As writing a book is a team effort, I would like to thank the people at Packt Publishing for helping me write this book. This includes Amit Ramadas for answering all my questions, Shailesh Jain for convincing me to write the third edition of Mastering Go, Edward Doxey for the helpful comments and suggestions, and Derek Parker, the technical reviewer, for his good work.

Last, I would like to thank you, the reader of the book, for choosing this book. I hope you find it helpful.

About the reviewer

Derek Parker is a Software Engineer at Red Hat. He is the creator of the Delve debugger for Go and a contributor to the Go compiler, linker, and standard library. Derek is an open-source contributor and maintainer and has worked on everything from front-end JavaScript to low-level assembly code.

I would like to thank my wife, Erica, and our two incredible children for lending me the time to work on this project.

Table of Contents

Preface

The book you are reading right now is *Mastering Go, Third Edition*, which is all about helping you become a better Go developer! If you have the second edition of *Mastering Go*, do not throw it away—Go has not changed that much, and the second edition is still useful. However, *Mastering Go, Third Edition* is better than the second edition in many aspects.

There exist many exciting new topics in this edition, including writing RESTful services, working with the WebSocket protocol, and using GitHub Actions and GitLab Actions for Go projects, as well as an entirely new chapter on generics and the development of lots of practical utilities. Additionally, I tried to make this book smaller than the second edition and structure it in a more natural way to make it both easier and faster to read, especially if you are a busy professional.

I also tried to include the right amount of theory and hands-on content—but, only you, the reader, can tell whether I succeed! Try to do the exercises located at the end of each chapter and do not hesitate to contact me about ways or ideas that can make future editions of this book even better!

Who this book is for

This book is for intermediate Go programmers who want to take their Go knowledge to the next level. It will also be helpful for experienced developers in other programming languages who want to learn Go without going over programming basics.

What this book covers

Chapter 1, A Quick Introduction to Go, begins by talking about the history of Go, the important characteristics of Go, and the advantages of Go, before describing the `godoc` and `go doc` utilities and explaining how we can compile and execute Go programs. Afterward, the chapter talks about printing output and getting user input, working with command-line arguments, and using log files. Lastly, we develop a basic version of a phone book application that we are going to keep improving in forthcoming chapters.

Chapter 2, Basic Go Data Types, discusses the basic data types of Go, both numeric and non-numeric, as well as arrays and slices that allow you to group data of the same data type. It also considers Go pointers, constants, and working with dates and times. The last part of the chapter is about generating random numbers and populating the phone book application with random data.

Chapter 3, Composite Data Types, begins with maps, before going into structures and the `struct` keyword. Additionally, it talks about regular expressions, pattern matching, and working with CSV files. Lastly, we improve the phone book application by adding data persistency to it.

Chapter 4, Reflection and Interfaces, is about reflection, interfaces and type methods, which are functions attached to data types. The chapter also includes the use of the `sort.Interface` interface for sorting slices, the use of the empty interface, type assertions, type switches, and the `error` data type. Additionally, we discuss how Go can mimic some object-oriented concepts before improving the phone book application.

Chapter 5, Go Packages and Functions, is all about packages, modules, and functions, which are the main elements of packages. Among other things, we create a Go package for interacting with a PostgreSQL database, create documentation for it, and explain the use of the sometimes tricky `defer` keyword. This chapter also includes information about the use of GitLab Runners and GitHub Actions for automation and how to create a Docker image for a Go binary.

Chapter 6, Telling a UNIX System What to Do, is about systems programming, which includes subjects such as working with command-line arguments, handling UNIX signals, file input and output, the `io.Reader` and `io.Writer` interfaces, and the use of the `viper` and `cobra` packages. Additionally, we talk about working with JSON, XML, and YAML files, create a handy command-line utility for discovering cycles in a UNIX filesystem, and discuss embedding files in Go binaries as well as the `os.ReadDir()` function, the `os.DirEntry` type, and the `io/fs` package. Lastly, we update the phone book application to use JSON data and convert it into a proper command-line utility with the help of the `cobra` package.

Chapter 7, Go Concurrency, discusses goroutines, channels, and pipelines. We learn about the differences between processes, threads, and goroutines, the `sync` package, and the way the Go scheduler operates. Additionally, we explore the use of the `select` keyword and we discuss the various "types" of Go channels as well as shared memory, mutexes, the `sync.Mutex` type, and the `sync.RWMutex` type. The rest of the chapter talks about the `context` package, the `semaphore` package, worker pools, how to time out goroutines, and how to detect race conditions.

Chapter 8, Building Web Services, discusses the `net/http` package, the development of web servers and web services, exposing metrics to Prometheus, visualizing metrics in Grafana, creating web clients and creating file servers. We also convert the phone book application into a web service and create a command-line client for it.

Chapter 9, Working with TCP/IP and WebSocket, is about the `net` package, TCP/IP, and the TCP and UDP protocols, as well as UNIX sockets and the WebSocket protocol. We develop lots of network servers and clients in this chapter.

Chapter 10, Working with REST APIs, is all about working with REST APIs and RESTful services. We learn how to define REST APIs and develop powerful concurrent RESTful servers as well as command-line utilities that act as clients to RESTful services. Lastly, we introduce Swagger for creating documentation for REST APIs and learn how to upload and download binary files.

Chapter 11, Code Testing and Profiling, discusses code testing, code optimization, and code profiling as well as cross-compilation, benchmarking Go code, creating example functions, the use of `go:generate`, and finding unreachable Go code.

Chapter 12, Working with gRPC, is all about working with gRPC in Go. gRPC is an alternative to RESTful services that was developed by Google. This chapter teaches you how to define the methods and the messages of a gRPC service, how to translate them into Go code, and how to develop a server and a client for that gRPC service.

Chapter 13, Go Generics, is about generics and how to use the new syntax to write generic functions and define generic data types. Generics is coming to Go 1.18, which, according to the Go development cycle, is going to be officially released during February 2022.

Appendix A, Go Garbage Collector, talks about the operation of the Go garbage collector and illustrates how this Go component can affect the performance of your code.

To get the most out of this book

This book requires a UNIX computer with a relatively recent Go version installed, which includes any machine running macOS X, macOS, or Linux. Most of the presented code also runs on Microsoft Windows machines without any changes.

To get the most out of this book, you should try to apply the knowledge of each chapter in your own programs as soon as possible and see what works and what does not! As I told you before, try to solve the exercises found at the end of each chapter or create your own programming problems.

Download the example code files

The code bundle for the book is hosted on GitHub at `https://github.com/mactsouk/mastering-Go-3rd`. We also have other code bundles from our rich catalog of books and videos available at `https://github.com/PacktPublishing/`. Check them out!

Download the color images

We also provide a PDF file that has color images of the screenshots/diagrams used in this book. You can download it here: `https://static.packt-cdn.com/downloads/9781801079310_ColorImages.pdf`.

Conventions used

There are a number of text conventions used throughout this book.

`CodeInText`: Indicates code words in text, folder names, filenames, file extensions, pathnames, and user input. For example, "The star of this chapter will be the `net/http` package, which offers functions that allow you to develop powerful web servers and web clients."

A block of code is set as follows:

```
package main

import (
    "fmt"
    "math/rand"
    "os"
    "path/filepath"
    "strconv"
```

```
    "time"
)
```

When we wish to draw your attention to a particular part of a code block, the relevant lines or items are highlighted:

```
package main

import (
    "fmt"
    "math/rand"
    "os"
    "path/filepath"
    "strconv"
    "time"
)
```

Any command-line input or output is written as follows:

```
$ go run www.go
Using default port number:  :8001
Served: localhost:8001
```

Bold: Indicates a new term, an important word, or words that you see on the screen, for example, in menus or dialog boxes. For example: "The UNIX logging service has support for two properties named **logging level** and **logging facility**."

> Warnings or important notes appear like this.

> Tips and tricks appear like this.

Get in touch

Feedback from our readers is always welcome.

General feedback: Email `feedback@packtpub.com`, and mention the book's title in the subject of your message. If you have questions about any aspect of this book, please email us at `questions@packtpub.com`.

Errata: Although we have taken every care to ensure the accuracy of our content, mistakes do happen. If you have found a mistake in this book we would be grateful if you would report this to us. Please visit `http://www.packtpub.com/submit-errata`, selecting your book, clicking on the Errata Submission Form link, and entering the details.

Piracy: If you come across any illegal copies of our works in any form on the internet, we would be grateful if you would provide us with the location address or website name. Please contact us at `copyright@packtpub.com` with a link to the material.

If you are interested in becoming an author: If there is a topic that you have expertise in and you are interested in either writing or contributing to a book, please visit `http://authors.packtpub.com`.

Share your thoughts

Once you've read *Mastering Go, Third Edition*, we'd love to hear your thoughts! Scan the QR code below to go straight to the Amazon review page for this book and share your feedback.

https://packt.link/r/1-801-07931-5

Your review is important to us and the tech community and will help us make sure we're delivering excellent quality content.

1

A Quick Introduction to Go

Imagine that you are a developer and you want to create a command-line utility. Similarly, imagine that you have a REST API and you want to create a RESTful server that implements that REST API. The first thought that will come to your mind will most likely be which programming language to use.

The most common answer to this question is to use the programming language you know best. However, this book is here to help you consider Go for all these and many more tasks and projects. In this chapter, we begin by explaining what Go is, and continue with the history of Go, and how to run Go code. We will explain some core characteristics of Go, such as how to define variables, control the flow of your programs, and get user input, and we will apply some of these concepts by creating a command-line phone book application.

We will cover the following topics:

- Introducing Go
- Hello World!
- Running Go code
- Important characteristics of Go
- Developing the `which(1)` utility in Go
- Logging information
- Overview of Go generics
- Developing a basic phone book application

Introducing Go

Go is an open-source systems programming language initially developed as an internal Google project that went public back in 2009. The spiritual fathers of Go are Robert Griesemer, Ken Thomson, and Rob Pike.

> Although the official name of the language is Go, it is sometimes (wrongly) referred to as *Golang*. The official reason for this is that `go.org` was not available for registration and `golang.org` was chosen instead. The practical reason for this is that when you are querying a search engine for Go-related information, the word *Go* is usually interpreted as a verb. Additionally, the official Twitter hashtag for Go is *#golang*.

Although Go is a general-purpose programming language, it is primarily used for writing system tools, command-line utilities, web services, and software that work over networks. Go can also be used for teaching programming and is a good candidate as your first programming language because of its lack of verbosity and clear ideas and principles. Go can help you develop the following kinds of applications:

- Professional web services
- Networking tools and servers such as Kubernetes and Istio
- Backend systems
- System utilities
- Powerful command-line utilities such as `docker` and `hugo`
- Applications that exchange data in JSON format
- Applications that process data from relational databases, NoSQL databases, or other popular data storage systems
- Compilers and interpreters for programming languages you design
- Database systems such as CockroachDB and key/value stores such as etcd

There are many things that Go does better than other programming languages, including the following:

- The default behavior of the Go compiler can catch a large set of silly errors that might result in bugs.
- Go uses fewer parentheses than C, C++, or Java, and no semicolons, which makes the look of Go source code more human-readable and less error-prone.
- Go comes with a rich and reliable standard library.
- Go has support for concurrency out of the box through goroutines and channels.
- Goroutines are really lightweight. You can easily run thousands of goroutines on any modern machine without any performance issues.
- Unlike C, Go supports functional programming.
- Go code is backward compatible, which means that newer versions of the Go compiler accept programs that were created using a previous version of the language without any modifications. This compatibility guarantee is limited to major versions of Go. For example, there is no guarantee that a Go 1.x program will compile with Go 2.x.

Now that we know what Go can do and what Go is good at, let's discuss the history of Go.

The history of Go

As mentioned earlier, Go started as an internal Google project that went public back in 2009. Griesemer, Thomson, and Pike designed Go as a language for professional programmers who want to build reliable, robust, and efficient software that is easy to manage. They designed Go with simplicity in mind, even if simplicity meant that Go was not going to be a programming language for everyone.

The figure that follows shows the programming languages that directly or indirectly influenced Go. As an example, Go syntax looks like C whereas the package concept was inspired by Modula-2.

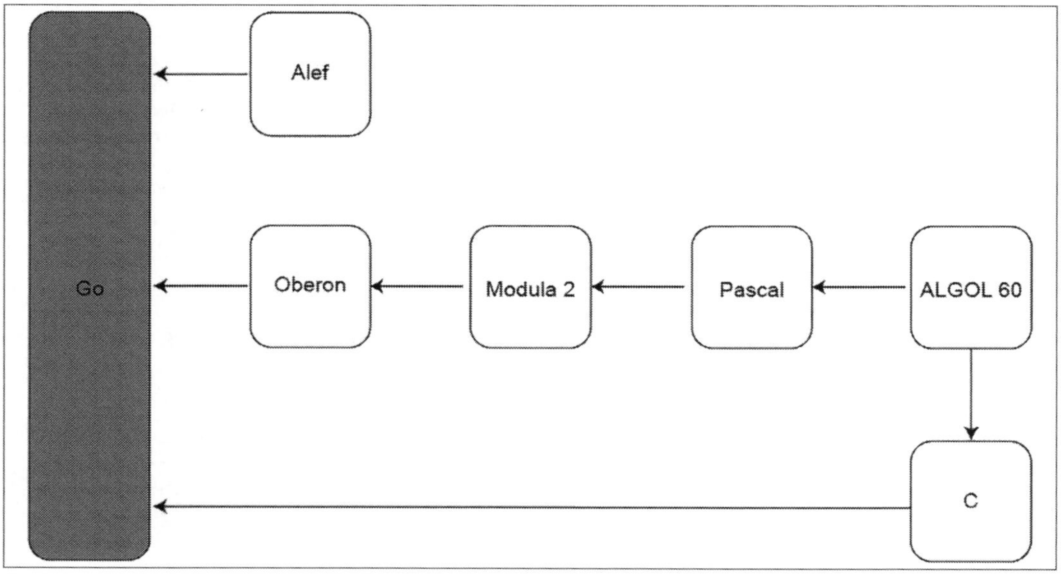

Figure 1.1: The programming languages that influenced Go

The deliverable was a programming language, its tools, and its standard library. What you get with Go, apart from its syntax and tools, is a pretty rich standard library and a type system that tries to save you from easy mistakes such as implicit type conversions, unused variables and unused packages. The Go compiler catches most of these easy mistakes and refuses to compile until you do something about them. Additionally, the Go compiler can find difficult to catch mistakes such as race conditions.

If you are going to install Go for the first time, you can start by visiting `https://golang.org/dl/`. However, there is a big chance that your UNIX variant has a ready-to-install package for the Go programming language, so you might want to get Go by using your favorite package manager.

Why UNIX and not Windows?

You might ask why we're talking about UNIX all the time and not discussing Microsoft Windows as well. There are two main reasons for this. The first reason is that most Go programs will work on Windows machines without any code changes because **Go is portable by design**—this means that you should not worry about the operating system you are using.

However, you might need to make small changes to the code of some system utilities for them to work in Windows. Additionally, there are still going to be some libraries that only work on Windows machines and some that only work on non-Windows machines. The second reason is that many services written in Go are executed in a Docker environment—**Docker images use the Linux operating system**, which means that you should program your utilities having the Linux operating system in mind.

> As far as user experience is concerned, UNIX and Linux are very similar. The main difference is that Linux is open-source software whereas UNIX is proprietary software.

The advantages of Go

Go comes with some important advantages for developers, starting with the fact that it was designed and is currently maintained by real programmers. Go is also easy to learn, especially if you are already familiar with programming languages such as C, Python, or Java. On top of that, Go code is good-looking, at least to me, which is great, especially when you are programming applications for a living and you have to look at code on a daily basis. Go code is also easy to read and offers support for Unicode out of the box, which means that you can make changes to existing Go code easily. Lastly, Go has reserved only 25 keywords, which makes it much easier to remember the language. Can you do that with C++?

Go also comes with concurrency capabilities using a simple concurrency model that is implemented using **goroutines** and **channels**. Go manages OS threads for you and has a powerful runtime that allows you to spawn lightweight units of work (*goroutines*) that communicate with each other using *channels*. Although Go comes with a rich standard library, there are really handy Go packages such as `cobra` and `viper` that allow Go to develop complex command-line utilities such as `docker` and `hugo`. This is greatly supported by the fact that Go's executable binaries are *statically linked*, which means that once they are generated, they do not depend on any shared libraries and include all required information.

Due to its simplicity, Go code is predictable and does not have strange side effects, and although Go supports **pointers**, it does not support pointer arithmetic like C, unless you use the `unsafe` package, which is the root of many bugs and security holes. Although Go is not an object-oriented programming language, Go interfaces are very versatile and allow you to mimic some of the capabilities of object-oriented languages such as **polymorphism**, **encapsulation**, and **composition**.

Additionally, the latest Go versions offer support for **generics**, which simplifies your code when working with multiple data types. Last but not least, Go comes with support for **garbage collection**, which means that no manual memory management is needed.

Although Go is a very practical and competent programming language, it is not perfect:

- Although this is a personal preference rather than an actual technical shortcoming, Go has no direct support for object-oriented programming, which is a popular programming paradigm.
- Although goroutines are lightweight, they are not as powerful as OS threads. Depending on the application you are trying to implement, there might exist some rare cases where goroutines will not be appropriate for the job. However, in most cases, designing your application with goroutines and channels in mind will solve your problems.
- Although garbage collection is fast enough most of the time and for almost all kinds of applications, there are times when you need to handle memory allocation manually—Go cannot do that. In practice, this means that Go will not allow you to perform any memory management manually.

However, there are many cases where you can choose Go, including the following:

- Creating complex command-line utilities with multiple commands, sub-commands, and command-line parameters
- Building highly concurrent applications
- Developing servers that work with APIs and clients that interact by exchanging data in myriad formats including JSON, XML, and CSV
- Developing WebSocket servers and clients
- Developing gRCP servers and clients
- Developing robust UNIX and Windows system tools
- Learning programming

In the following sections, we will cover a number of concepts and utilities in order to build a solid foundation of knowledge, before building a simplified version of the `which(1)` utility. At the end of the chapter, we'll develop a naive phone book application that will keep evolving as we explain more Go features in the chapters that follow.

But first, we'll present the `go doc` command, which allows you to find information about the Go standard library, its packages, and their functions. Then, we'll show how to execute Go code using the `Hello World!` program as an example.

The go doc and godoc utilities

The Go distribution comes with a plethora of tools that can make your life as a programmer easier. Two of these tools are the `go doc` subcommand and `godoc` utility, which allow you to see the documentation of existing Go functions and packages without needing an internet connection. However, if you prefer viewing the Go documentation online, you can visit `https://pkg.go.dev/`. As `godoc` is not installed by default, you might need to install it by running `go get golang.org/x/tools/cmd/godoc`.

The `go doc` command can be executed as a normal command-line application that displays its output on a terminal, and `godoc` as a command-line application that starts a web server. In the latter case, you need a web browser to look at the Go documentation. The first utility is similar to the UNIX `man(1)` command, but for Go functions and packages.

> The number after the name of a UNIX program or system call refers to the section of the manual a manual page belongs to. Although most of the names can be found only once in the manual pages, which means that putting the section number is not required, there are names that can be located in multiple sections because they have multiple meanings, such as `crontab(1)` and `crontab(5)`. Therefore, if you try to retrieve the manual page of a name with multiple meanings without stating its section number, you will get the entry that has the smallest section number.

So, in order to find information about the `Printf()` function of the `fmt` package, you should execute the following command:

```
$ go doc fmt.Printf
```

Similarly, you can find information about the entire `fmt` package by running the following command:

```
$ go doc fmt
```

The second utility requires executing `godoc` with the `-http` parameter:

```
$ godoc -http=:8001
```

The numeric value in the preceding command, which in this case is `8001`, is the port number the HTTP server will listen to. As we have omitted the IP address, `godoc` is going to listen to all network interfaces.

> You can choose any port number that is available provided that you have the right privileges. However, note that port numbers `0-1023` are restricted and can only be used by the root user, so it is better to avoid choosing one of those and pick something else, provided that it is not already in use by a different process.

You can omit the equals sign in the presented command and put a space character in its place. So, the following command is completely equivalent to the previous one:

```
$ godoc -http :8001
```

After that, you should point your web browser to the `http://localhost:8001/` URL in order to get the list of available Go packages and browse their documentation. If you are using Go for the first time, you will find the Go documentation very handy for learning the parameters and the return values of the functions you want to use—as you progress in your Go journey, you will use the Go documentation for learning the gory details of the functions and variables that you want to use.

Hello World!

The following is the Go version of the Hello World program. Please type it and save it as `hw.go`:

```
package main

import (
    "fmt"
)

func main() {
    fmt.Println("Hello World!")
}
```

Each Go source code begins with a `package` declaration. In this case, the name of the package is `main`, which has a special meaning in Go. The `import` keyword allows you to include functionality from existing packages. In our case, we only need some of the functionality of the `fmt` package that belongs to the standard Go library. Packages that are not part of the standard Go library are imported using their full internet path. The next important thing if you are creating an executable application is a `main()` function. Go considers this the entry point to the application and begins the execution of the application with the code found in the `main()` function of the `main` package.

`hw.go` is a Go program that runs on its own. Two characteristics make `hw.go` an autonomous source file that can generate an executable binary: the name of the package, which should be `main`, and the presence of the `main()` function—we discuss Go functions in more detail in the next subsection but we will learn even more about functions and methods, which are functions attached to specific data types, in *Chapter 5, Go Packages and Functions*.

Introducing functions

Each Go function definition begins with the `func` keyword followed by its name, signature and implementation. As happens with the `main` package, you can name your functions anything you want—there is a global Go rule that also applies to function and variable names and is valid for all packages except `main`: **everything that begins with a lowercase letter is considered private and is accessible in the current package only**. We will learn more about that rule in *Chapter 5, Go Packages and Functions*. The only exception to this rule is package names, which can begin with either lowercase or uppercase letters. Having said that, I am not aware of a Go package that begins with an uppercase letter!

You might now ask how functions are organized and delivered. Well, the answer is in packages—the next subsection sheds some light on that.

Introducing packages

Go programs are organized in packages—even the smallest Go program should be delivered as a package. The `package` keyword helps you define the name of a new package, which can be anything you want with just one exception: if you are creating an executable application and not just a package that will be shared by other applications or packages, you should name your package `main`. You will learn more about developing Go packages in *Chapter 5, Go Packages and Functions*.

> Packages can be used by other packages. In fact, reusing existing packages is a good practice that saves you from having to write lots of code or implement existing functionality from scratch.

The `import` keyword is used for importing other Go packages in your Go programs in order to use some or all of their functionality. A Go package can either be a part of the rich Standard Go library or come from an external source. Packages of the standard Go library are imported by name (`os`) without the need for a hostname and a path, whereas external packages are imported using their full internet paths, like `github.com/spf13/cobra`.

Running Go code

You now need to know how to execute `hw.go` or any other Go application. As will be explained in the two subsections that follow, there are two ways to execute Go code: as a compiled language using `go build` or as a scripting language using `go run`. So, let us find out more about these two ways of running Go code.

Compiling Go code

In order to compile Go code and create a binary executable file, you need to use the `go build` command. What `go build` does is create an executable file for you to distribute and execute manually. This means that the `go build` command requires an additional step for running your code.

The generated executable is automatically named after the source code filename without the `.go` file extension. Therefore, because of the `hw.go` source file, the executable will be called `hw`. In case this is not what you want, `go build` supports the `-o` option, which allows you to change the filename and the path of the generated executable file. As an example, if you want to name the executable file as `helloWorld`, you should execute `go build -o helloWorld hw.go` instead. If no source files are provided, `go build` looks for a `main` package in the current directory.

After that, you need to execute the generated executable binary file on your own. In our case, this means executing either `hw` or `helloWorld`. This is shown in the next output:

```
$ go build hw.go
$ ./hw
Hello World!
```

Now that we know how to compile Go code, let us continue with using Go as a scripting language.

Using Go like a scripting language

The `go run` command builds the named Go package, which in this case is the `main` package implemented in a single file, creates a temporary executable file, executes that file, and deletes it once it is done—to our eyes, this looks like using a scripting language. In our case, we can do the following:

```
$ go run hw.go
Hello World!
```

If you want to test your code, then using `go run` is a better choice. However, if you want to create and distribute an executable binary, then `go build` is the way to go.

Important formatting and coding rules

You should know that Go comes with some strict formatting and coding rules that help the developer avoid beginner mistakes and bugs—once you learn these few rules and Go idiosyncrasies as well as the implications they have for your code, you will be free to concentrate on the actual functionality of your code. Additionally, the Go compiler is here to help you follow these rules with its expressive error messages and warnings. Last, Go offers standard tooling (`gofmt`) that can format your code for you so you never have to think about it.

The following is a list of important Go rules that will help you while reading this chapter:

- Go code is delivered in packages and you are free to use the functionality found in existing packages. However, if you are going to import a package, you should use some of this functionality—there are some exceptions to this rule that mainly have to with initializing connections, but they are not important for now.
- You either use a variable or you do not declare it at all. This rule helps you avoid errors such as misspelling an existing variable or function name.
- There is only one way to format curly braces in Go.
- Coding blocks in Go are embedded in curly braces even if they contain just a single statement or no statements at all.

- Go functions can return multiple values.
- You cannot automatically convert between different data types, even if they are of the same kind. As an example, you cannot implicitly convert an integer to a floating point.

Go has more rules but these rules are the most important ones and will keep you going for most of the book. You are going to see all these rules in action in this chapter as well as other chapters. For now, let's consider the only way to format curly braces in Go because this rule applies everywhere.

Look at the following Go program named `curly.go`:

```
package main

import (
    "fmt"
)

func main()
{
    fmt.Println("Go has strict rules for curly braces!")
}
```

Although it looks just fine, if you try to execute it, you will be fairly disappointed, because the code will not compile and therefore you will get the following syntax error message:

```
$ go run curly.go
# command-line-arguments
./curly.go:7:6: missing function body
./curly.go:8:1: syntax error: unexpected semicolon or newline before {
```

The official explanation for this error message is that Go requires the use of semicolons as statement terminators in many contexts, and the compiler automatically inserts the required semicolons when it thinks that they are necessary. Therefore, putting the opening curly brace (`{`) in its own line will make the Go compiler insert a semicolon at the end of the previous line (`func main()`), which is the main cause of the error message. The correct way to write the previous code is the following:

```
package main

import (
    "fmt"
```

```
)

func main() {
    fmt.Println("Go has strict rules for curly braces!")
}
```

After learning about this global rule, let us continue by presenting some important characteristics of Go.

Important characteristics of Go

This big section discusses important and essential Go features including variables, controlling program flow, iterations, getting user input, and Go concurrency. We begin by discussing variables, variable declaration, and variable usage.

Defining and using variables

Imagine that you wanted to perform some basic mathematical calculations with Go. In that case, you need to define variables to keep your input and your results.

Go provides multiple ways to declare new variables in order to make the variable declaration process more natural and convenient. You can declare a new variable using the `var` keyword followed by the variable name, followed by the desired data type (we will cover data types in detail in *Chapter 2, Basic Go Data Types*). If you want, you can follow that declaration with `=` and an initial value for your variable. If there is an initial value given, you can omit the data type and the compiler will guess it for you.

This brings us to a very important Go rule: **if no initial value is given to a variable, the Go compiler will automatically initialize that variable to the zero value of its data type**.

There is also the `:=` notation, which can be used instead of a `var` declaration. `:=` defines a new variable by inferring the data of the value that follows it. The official name for `:=` is **short assignment statement** and it is very frequently used in Go, especially for getting the return values from functions and `for` loops with the `range` keyword.

The short assignment statement can be used in place of a `var` declaration with an implicit type. You rarely see the use of `var` in Go; the `var` keyword is mostly used for declaring global or local variables without an initial value. The reason for the former is that every statement that exists outside of the code of a function must begin with a keyword such as `func` or `var`.

This means that the short assignment statement cannot be used outside of a function environment because it is not available there. Last, you might need to use `var` when you want to be explicit about the data type. For example, when you want `int8` or `int32` instead of `int`.

Therefore, although you can declare local variables using either `var` or `:=`, only `const` (when the value of a variable is not going to change) and `var` work for **global variables**, which are variables that are defined outside of a function and are not embedded in curly braces. Global variables can be accessed from anywhere in a package without the need to explicitly pass them to a function and can be changed unless they were defined as constants using the `const` keyword.

Printing variables

Programs tend to display information, which means that they need to print data or send it somewhere for other software to store or process it. For printing data on the screen, Go uses the functionality of the `fmt` package. If you want Go to take care of the printing, then you might want to use the `fmt.Println()` function. However, there are times that you want to have full control over how data is going to get printed. In such cases, you might want to use `fmt.Printf()`.

`fmt.Printf()` is similar to the C `printf()` function and requires the use of control sequences that specify the data type of the variable that is going to get printed. Additionally, the `fmt.Printf()` function allows you to format the generated output, which is particularly convenient for floating point values because it allows you to specify the digits that will be displayed in the output (`%.2f` displays 2 digits after the decimal point). Lastly, the `\n` character is used for printing a newline character and therefore creating a new line, as `fmt.Printf()` does not automatically insert a newline—this is not the case with `fmt.Printf()`, which inserts a newline.

The following program illustrates how you can declare new variables, how to use them, and how to print them—type the following code into a plain text file named `variables.go`:

```
package main

import (
    "fmt"
    "math"
)

var Global int = 1234
var AnotherGlobal = -5678
```

```
func main() {
    var j int
    i := Global + AnotherGlobal
    fmt.Println("Initial j value:", j)
    j = Global
    // math.Abs() requires a float64 parameter
    //so we type cast it appropriately
    k := math.Abs(float64(AnotherGlobal))
    fmt.Printf("Global=%d, i=%d, j=%d k=%.2f.\n", Global, i, j, k)
}
```

Personally, I prefer to make global variables stand out by either beginning them with an uppercase letter or using all capital letters.

This program contains the following:

- A global `int` variable named `Global`.
- A second global variable named `AnotherGlobal`—Go automatically infers its data type from its value, which in this case is an integer.
- A local variable named `j` that is of type `int`, which, as you will learn in the next chapter, is a special data type. `j` does not have an initial value, which means that Go automatically assigns the zero value of its data type, which in this case is `0`.
- Another local variable named `i`—Go infers its data type from its value. As it is the sum of two `int` values, it is also an `int`.
- As `math.Abs()` requires a `float64` parameter, you cannot pass `AnotherGlobal` to it because `AnotherGlobal` is an `int` variable. The `float64()` type cast converts the value of `AnotherGlobal` to `float64`. Note that `AnotherGlobal` continues to be `int`.
- Lastly, `fmt.Printf()` formats and prints our output.

Running `variables.go` produces the following output:

```
Initial j value: 0
Global=1234, i=-4444, j=1234 k=5678.00.
```

This example demonstrated another important Go rule that was also mentioned previously: Go does not allow **implicit data conversions** like C.

As you saw in `variables.go` when using the `math.Abs()` function that expects a `float64` value, an `int` value cannot be used when a `float64` value is expected even if this particular conversion is straightforward and error-free. The Go compiler refuses to compile such statements. You should convert the `int` value to a `float64` explicitly using `float64()` for things to work properly.

For conversions that are not straightforward (for example, `string` to `int`), there exist specialized functions that allow you to catch issues with the conversion in the form of an `error` variable that is returned by the function.

Controlling program flow

So far, we have seen Go variables but how do we change the flow of a Go program based on the value of a variable or some other condition? Go supports the `if/else` and `switch` control structures. Both control structures can be found in most modern programming languages, so if you have already programmed in another programming language, you should already be familiar with `if` and `switch`. `if` statements use no parenthesis for embedding the conditions that need to be examined because Go does not use parentheses in general. As expected, `if` has support for `else` and `else if` statements.

To demonstrate the use of `if`, let's use a very common pattern in Go that is used almost everywhere. This pattern says that if the value of an `error` variable as returned from a function is `nil`, then everything is OK with the function execution. Otherwise, there is an error condition somewhere that needs special care. This pattern is usually implemented as follows:

```
err := anyFunctionCall()
if err != nil {
    // Do something if there is an error
}
```

`err` is the variable that holds the `error` value as returned from a function and `!=` means that the value of the `err` variable is not `nil`. You will see similar code multiple times in Go programs.

> Lines beginning with `//` are single-line comments. If you put `//` in the middle of a line, then everything after `//` is considered a comment. This rule does not apply if `//` is inside a string value.

The switch statement has two different forms. In the first form, the switch statement has an expression that is being evaluated, whereas in the second form, the switch statement has no expression to evaluate. In that case, expressions are evaluated in each case statement, which increases the flexibility of switch. The main benefit you get from switch is that when used properly, it simplifies complex and hard-to-read if-else blocks.

Both if and switch are illustrated in the following code, which is designed to process user input given as a command-line argument—please type it and save it as control.go. For learning purposes, we present the code of control.go in pieces in order to explain it better:

```
package main

import (
    "fmt"
    "os"
    "strconv"
)
```

This first part contains the expected preamble with the imported packages. The implementation of the main() function starts next:

```
func main() {
    if len(os.Args) != 2 {
        fmt.Println("Please provide a command line argument")
        return
    }
    argument := os.Args[1]
```

This part of the program makes sure that you have a single command-line argument to process, which is accessed as os.Args[1], before continuing. We will cover this in more detail later, but you can refer to *Figure 1.2* for more information about the os.Args slice.

```
    // With expression after switch
    switch argument {
    case "0":
        fmt.Println("Zero!")
    case "1":
        fmt.Println("One!")
    case "2", "3", "4":
        fmt.Println("2 or 3 or 4")
```

```
        fallthrough
    default:
        fmt.Println("Value:", argument)
    }
```

Here you see a `switch` block with four branches. The first three require exact `string` matches and the last one matches everything else. The order of the `case` statements is important because only the first match is executed. The `fallthrough` keyword tells Go that after this branch is executed, it will continue with the next branch, which in this case is the `default` branch:

```
    value, err := strconv.Atoi(argument)
    if err != nil {
        fmt.Println("Cannot convert to int:", argument)
        return
    }
```

As command-line arguments are initialized as string values, we need to convert user input into an integer value using a separate call, which in this case is a call to `strconv.Atoi()`. If the value of the `err` variable is `nil`, then the conversion was successful, and we can continue. Otherwise, an error message is printed onscreen and the program exits.

The following code shows the second form of `switch`, where the condition is evaluated at each `case` branch:

```
    // No expression after switch
    switch {
    case value == 0:
        fmt.Println("Zero!")
    case value > 0:
        fmt.Println("Positive integer")
    case value < 0:
        fmt.Println("Negative integer")
    default:
        fmt.Println("This should not happen:", value)
    }
}
```

This gives you more flexibility but requires more thinking when reading the code. In this case, the `default` branch should not be executed, mainly because any valid integer value would be caught by the other three branches. Nevertheless, the `default` branch is there, which is a good practice because it can catch unexpected values.

Running `control.go` generates the next output:

```
$ go run control.go 10
Value: 10
Positive integer
$ go run control.go 0
Zero!
Zero!
```

Each one of the two `switch` blocks in `control.go` creates one line of output.

Iterating with for loops and range

This section is all about iterating in Go. Go supports `for` loops as well as the `range` keyword for iterating over all the elements of arrays, slices, and (as you will see in *Chapter 3, Composite Data Types*) maps. An example of Go simplicity is the fact that Go provides support for the `for` keyword only, instead of including direct support for `while` loops. However, depending on how you write a `for` loop, it can function as a `while` loop or an infinite loop. Moreover, `for` loops can implement the functionality of JavaScript's `forEach` function when combined with the `range` keyword.

> You need to put curly braces around a `for` loop even if it contains a single statement or no statements at all.

You can also create `for` loops with variables and conditions. A `for` loop can be exited with a `break` keyword and you can skip the current iteration with the `continue` keyword. When used with `range`, `for` loops allow you to visit all the elements of a slice or an array without knowing the size of the data structure. As you will see in *Chapter 3, Composite Data Types*, `for` and `range` allow you to iterate over the elements of a map in a similar way.

The following program illustrates the use of `for` on its own and with the `range` keyword—type it and save it as `forLoops.go` in order to execute it afterward:

```
package main

import "fmt"

func main() {
    // Traditional for loop
```

```
    for i := 0; i < 10; i++ {
        fmt.Print(i*i, " ")
    }
    fmt.Println()
}
```

The previous code illustrates a traditional `for` loop that uses a local variable named `i`. This prints the squares of `0`, `1`, `2`, `3`, `4`, `5`, `6`, `7`, `8`, and `9` onscreen. The square of `10` is not printed because it does not satisfy the `10 < 10` condition.

The following code is idiomatic Go:

```
    i := 0
    for ok := true; ok; ok = (i != 10) {
        fmt.Print(i*i, " ")
        i++
    }
    fmt.Println()
```

You might use it, but it is sometimes hard to read, especially for people that are new to Go. The following code shows how a `for` loop can simulate a `while` loop, which is not supported directly:

```
    // For loop used as while loop
    i := 0
    for {
        if i == 10 {
            break
        }
        fmt.Print(i*i, " ")
        i++
    }
    fmt.Println()
```

The `break` keyword in the `if` condition exits the loop early and acts as the loop exit condition.

Lastly, given a slice named `aSlice`, you iterate over all its elements with the help of `range`, which returns two ordered values: the index of the current element in the slice and its value. If you want to ignore either of these return values, which is not the case here, you can use _ in the place of the value that you want to ignore. If you just need the index, you can leave out the second value from `range` entirely without using _.

```
    // This is a slice but range also works with arrays
    aSlice := []int{-1, 2, 1, -1, 2, -2}
    for i, v := range aSlice {
        fmt.Println("index:", i, "value: ", v)
    }
```

If you run `forLoops.go`, you get the following output:

```
$ go run forLoops.go
0 1 4 9 16 25 36 49 64 81
0 1 4 9 16 25 36 49 64 81
0 1 4 9 16 25 36 49 64 81
index: 0 value:  -1
index: 1 value:  2
index: 2 value:  1
index: 3 value:  -1
index: 4 value:  2
index: 5 value:  -2
```

The previous output illustrates that the first three `for` loops are equivalent and therefore produce the same output. The last six lines show the index and the value of each element found in `aSlice`.

Now that we know about `for` loops, let us see how to get user input.

Getting user input

Getting user input is an important part of every program. This section presents two ways of getting user input, which are reading from standard input and using the command-line arguments of the program.

Reading from standard input

The `fmt.Scanln()` function can help you read user input while the program is already running and store it to a `string` variable, which is passed as a pointer to `fmt.Scanln()`. The `fmt` package contains additional functions for reading user input from the console (`os.Stdin`), from files or from argument lists.

The following code illustrates reading from standard input—type it and save it as `input.go`:

```
package main

import (
    "fmt"
)

func main() {
    // Get User Input
    fmt.Printf("Please give me your name: ")
    var name string
    fmt.Scanln(&name)
    fmt.Println("Your name is", name)
}
```

While waiting for user input, it is good to let the user know what kind of information they have to give, which is the purpose of the `fmt.Printf()` call. The reason for not using `fmt.Println()` instead is that `fmt.Println()` automatically adds a newline character at the end, which is not what we want here.

Executing `input.go` generates the following kind of output and user interaction:

```
$ go run input.go
Please give me your name: Mihalis
Your name is Mihalis
```

Working with command-line arguments

Although typing user input when needed might look like a nice idea, this is not usually how real software works. Usually, user input is given in the form of command-line arguments to the executable file. By default, command-line arguments in Go are stored in the `os.Args` slice. Go also offers the `flag` package for parsing command-line arguments, but there are better and more powerful alternatives.

The figure that follows shows the way command-line arguments work in Go, which is the same as in the C programming language. It is important to know that the `os.Args` slice is properly initialized by Go and is available to the program when referenced. The `os.Args` slice contains `string` values:

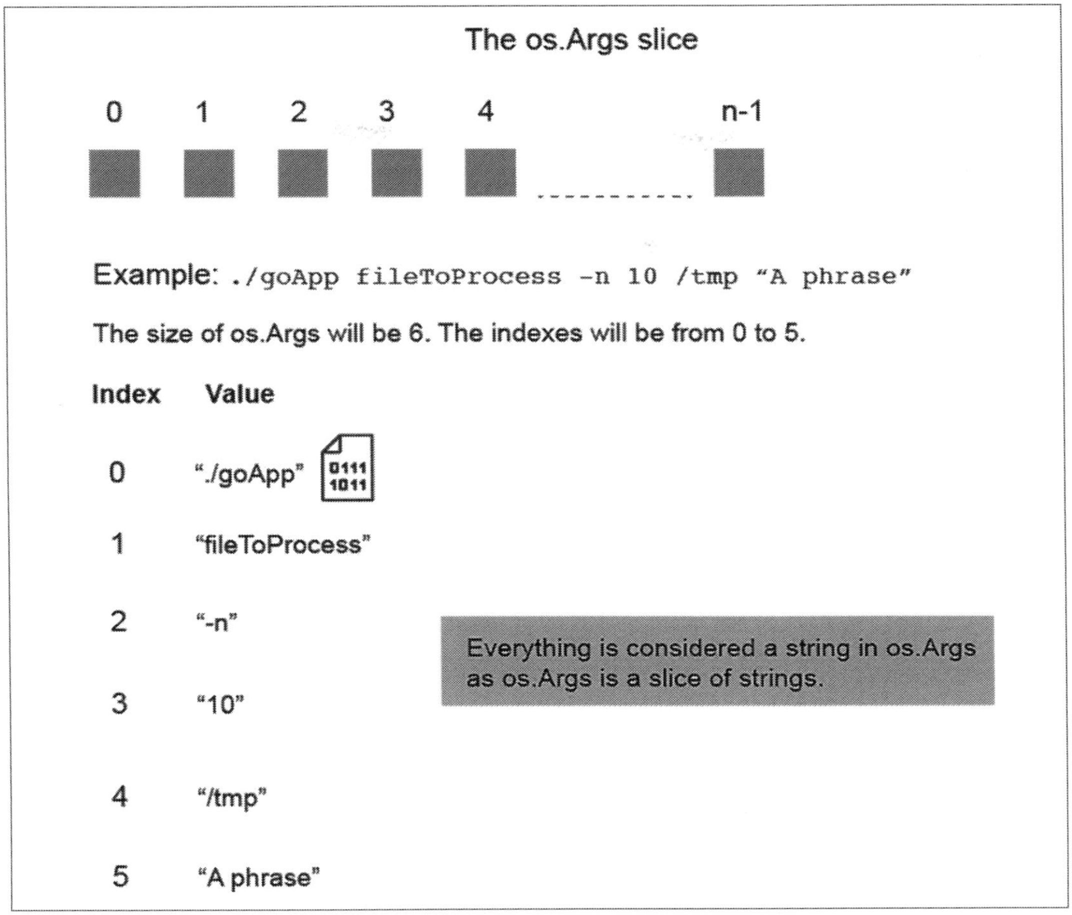

Figure 1.2: How the os.Args slice works

The first command-line argument stored in the `os.Args` slice is always the name of the executable. If you are using `go run`, you will get a temporary name and path, otherwise, it will be the path of the executable as given by the user. The remaining command-line arguments are what comes after the name of the executable—the various command-line arguments are automatically separated by space characters unless they are included in double or single quotes.

The use of `os.Args` is illustrated in the code that follows, which is to find the minimum and the maximum numeric values of its input while ignoring invalid input such as characters and strings. Type the code and save it as `cla.go` (or any other filename you want):

```
package main

import (
    "fmt"
    "os"
    "strconv"
)
```

As expected, `cla.go` begins with its preamble. The `fmt` package is used for printing output whereas the `os` package is required because `os.Args` is a part of it. Lastly, the `strconv` package contains functions for converting strings to numeric values. Next, we make sure that we have at least one command-line argument:

```
func main() {
    arguments := os.Args
    if len(arguments) == 1 {
        fmt.Println("Need one or more arguments!")
        return
    }
```

Remember that the first element in `os.Args` is always the path of the executable file so `os.Args` is never totally empty. Next, the program checks for errors in the same way we have looked at in previous examples. You will learn more about errors and error handling in *Chapter 2, Basic Go Data Types*:

```
    var min, max float64
    for i := 1; i < len(arguments); i++ {
        n, err := strconv.ParseFloat(arguments[i], 64)
        if err != nil {
            continue
        }
```

In this case, we use the `error` variable returned by `strconv.ParseFloat()` to make sure that the call to `strconv.ParseFloat()` was successful and we have a valid numeric value to process. Otherwise, we should continue to the next command-line argument. The `for` loop is used for iterating over all available command-line arguments except the first one, which uses an index value of `0`. This is another popular technique for working with all command-line arguments.

The following code is used for properly initializing the value of `min` and `max` after the first command-line argument has been processed:

```
        if i == 1 {
            min = n
            max = n
            continue
        }
```

We are using `i == 1` as the test of if this is the first iteration. In this case, it is, so we are processing the first command-line argument. The next code checks whether the current value is our new minimum or maximum—this is where the logic of the program is implemented:

```
        if n < min {
            min = n
        }
        if n > max {
            max = n
        }
    }
    fmt.Println("Min:", min)
    fmt.Println("Max:", max)
}
```

The last part of the program is about printing your findings, which are the minimum and the maximum numeric values of all valid command-line arguments. The output you get from `cla.go` depends on its input:

```
$ go run cla.go a b 2 -1
Min: -1
Max: 2
```

In this case, `a` and `b` are invalid, and the only valid input are `-1` and `2`, which are the minimum value and the maximum value, respectively.

```
$ go run cla.go a 0 b -1.2 10.32
Min: -1.2
Max: 10.32
```

In this case, `a` and `b` are invalid input and therefore ignored.

```
$ go run cla.go
Need one or more arguments!
```

In the final case, as `cla.go` has no input to process, it prints a help message. If you execute the program with no valid input values, for example `go run cla.go a b c`, then both `Min` and `Max` values are going to be zero.

The next subsection shows a technique for differentiating between different data types using `error` variables.

Using error variables to differentiate between input types

Now let me show you a technique that uses `error` variables to differentiate between various kinds of user input. For this technique to work, you should go from more specific cases to more generic ones. If we are talking about numeric values, you should first examine whether a string is a valid integer before examining whether the same string is a floating-point value because every valid integer is also a valid floating-point value.

This is illustrated in the next code excerpt:

```
var total, nInts, nFloats int
invalid := make([]string, 0)
for _, k := range arguments[1:] {
    // Is it an integer?
    _, err := strconv.Atoi(k)
    if err == nil {
        total++
        nInts++
        continue
    }
```

First, we create three variables for keeping a count of the total number of valid values examined, the total number of integer values found, and the total number of floating-point values found, respectively. The `invalid` variable, which is a slice, is used for keeping all non-numeric values.

Once again, we need to iterate over all the command-line arguments except the first one, which has an index value of `0`, because this is the path of the executable file. We ignore the path of the executable using `arguments[1:]` instead of just `arguments`—selecting a continuous part of a slice is discussed in the next chapter.

The call to `strconv.Atoi()` determines whether we are processing a valid `int` value or not. If so, we increase the `total` and `nInts` counters:

```
        // Is it a float
        _, err = strconv.ParseFloat(k, 64)
        if err == nil {
            total++
            nFloats++
            continue
        }
```

Similarly, if the examined string represents a valid floating-point value, the call to `strconv.ParseFloat()` is going to be successful and the program will update the relevant counters. Lastly, if a value is not numeric, it is added to the `invalid` slice with a call to `append()`:

```
        // Then it is invalid
        invalid = append(invalid, k)
    }
```

This is a common practice for keeping unexpected input in applications. The previous code can be found as `process.go` in the GitHub repository of the book—not presented here is extra code that warns you when your invalid input is more than the valid one. Running `process.go` produces the next kind of output:

```
$ go run process.go 1 2 3
#read: 3 #ints: 3 #floats: 0
```

In this case, we process `1`, `2`, and `3`, which are all valid integer values.

```
$ go run process.go 1 2.1 a
#read: 2 #ints: 1 #floats: 1
```

In this case, we have a valid integer, `1`, a floating-point value, `2.1`, and an invalid value, `a`.

```
$ go run process.go a 1 b
#read: 1 #ints: 1 #floats: 0
Too much invalid input: 2
a
b
```

If the invalid input is more than the valid one, then `process.go` prints an extra error message.

The next subsection discusses the concurrency model of Go.

Understanding the Go concurrency model

This section is a quick introduction to the Go concurrency model. The Go concurrency model is implemented using goroutines and channels. A **goroutine** is the smallest executable Go entity. In order to create a new goroutine, you have to use the `go` keyword followed by a predefined function or an anonymous function—both methods are equivalent as far as Go is concerned.

> Note that you can only execute functions or anonymous functions as goroutines.

A **channel** in Go is a mechanism that, among other things, allows goroutines to communicate and exchange data. If you are an amateur programmer or you're hearing about goroutines and channels for the first time, do not panic. Goroutines and channels, as well as pipelines and sharing data among goroutines, will be explained in much more detail in *Chapter 7, Go Concurrency*.

Although it is easy to create goroutines, there are other difficulties when dealing with concurrent programming including goroutine synchronization and sharing data between goroutines—this is a Go mechanism for avoiding side effects when running goroutines. As `main()` runs as a goroutine as well, you do not want `main()` to finish before the other goroutines of the program because when `main()` exits, the entire program along with any goroutines that have not finished yet will terminate. Although goroutines are do not share any variables, they can share memory. The good thing is that there are various techniques for the `main()` function to wait for goroutines to exchange data through channels or, less frequently in Go, using shared memory.

Type the following Go program, which synchronizes goroutines using `time.Sleep()` calls (this is not the right way to synchronize goroutines—we will discuss the proper way to synchronize goroutines in *Chapter 7, Go Concurrency*), into your favorite editor and save it as `goRoutines.go`:

```
package main

import (
    "fmt"
    "time"
)

func myPrint(start, finish int) {
```

```
    for i := start; i <= finish; i++ {
        fmt.Print(i, " ")
    }
    fmt.Println()
    time.Sleep(100 * time.Microsecond)
}

func main() {
    for i := 0; i < 5; i++ {
        go myPrint(i, 5)
    }
    time.Sleep(time.Second)
}
```

The preceding naively implemented example creates 4 goroutines and prints some values on the screen using the `myPrint()` function—the `go` keyword is used for creating goroutines. Running `goRoutines.go` generates the next output:

```
$ go run goRoutines.go
2 3 4 5
0 4 1 2 3 1 2 3 4 4 5
5
3 4 5
5
```

However, if you run it multiple times, you'll most likely get a different output each time:

```
1 2 3 4 5
4 2 5 3 4 5
3 0 1 2 3 4 5

4 5
```

This happens because goroutines are initialized in random order and start running in random order. The Go scheduler is responsible for the execution of goroutines just like the OS scheduler is responsible for the execution of the OS threads. *Chapter 7, Go Concurrency*, discusses Go concurrency in more detail and presents the solution to that randomness issue with the use of a `sync.WaitGroup` variable—however, keep in mind that Go concurrency is everywhere, which is the main reason for including this section here. Therefore, as some error messages generated by the compiler talk about goroutines, you should not think that these goroutines were created by you.

The next section shows a practical example, which is developing a Go version of the `which(1)` utility, which locates a program file in the user's `PATH` value.

Developing the which(1) utility in Go

Go can work with your operating system through a set of packages. A good way of learning a new programming language is by trying to implement simple versions of traditional UNIX utilities. In this section, you'll see a Go version of the `which(1)` utility, which will help you understand the way Go interacts with the underlying OS and reads environment variables.

The presented code, which will implement the functionality of `which(1)`, can be divided into three logical parts. The first part is about reading the input argument, which is the name of the executable file that the utility will be searching for. The second part is about reading the `PATH` environment variable, splitting it, and iterating over the directories of the `PATH` variable. The third part is about looking for the desired binary file in these directories and determining whether it can be found or not, whether it is a regular file, and whether it is an executable file. If the desired executable file is found, the program terminates with the help of the `return` statement. Otherwise, it will terminate after the `for` loop ends and the `main()` function exits.

Now let us see the code, beginning with the logical preamble that usually includes the package name, the `import` statements, and other definitions with a global scope:

```
package main

import (
    "fmt"
    "os"
    "path/filepath"
)
```

The `fmt` package is used for printing onscreen, the `os` package is for interacting with the underlying operating system, and the `path/filepath` package is used for working with the contents of the `PATH` variable that is read as a long string, depending on the number of directories it contains.

The second logical part of the utility is the following:

```
func main() {
    arguments := os.Args
    if len(arguments) == 1 {
```

```
        fmt.Println("Please provide an argument!")
        return
    }
    file := arguments[1]

    path := os.Getenv("PATH")
    pathSplit := filepath.SplitList(path)
    for _, directory := range pathSplit {
```

First, we read the command-line arguments of the program (`os.Args`) and save the first command-line argument into the `file` variable. Then, we get the contents of the `PATH` environment variable and split it using `filepath.SplitList()`, which offers a **portable** way of separating a list of paths. Lastly, we iterate over all the directories of the `PATH` variable using a `for` loop with `range` as `filepath.SplitList()` returns a slice.

The rest of the utility contains the following code:

```
        fullPath := filepath.Join(directory, file)
        // Does it exist?
        fileInfo, err := os.Stat(fullPath)
        if err == nil {
            mode := fileInfo.Mode()
            // Is it a regular file?
            if mode.IsRegular() {
                // Is it executable?
                if mode&0111 != 0 {
                    fmt.Println(fullPath)
                    return
                }
            }
        }
    }
}
```

We construct the full path that we examine using `filepath.Join()` that is used for concatenating the different parts of a path using an **OS-specific** separator—this makes `filepath.Join()` work in all supported operating systems. In this part, we also get some lower-level information about the file—remember that in UNIX everything is a file, which means that we want to make sure that we are dealing with a regular file that is also executable.

> In this first chapter, we are including the entire code of the presented source files. However, starting from *Chapter 2, Basic Go Types*, this will not be the case. This serves two purposes: the first one is that you get to see the code that really matters and the second one is that we save book space.

Executing `which.go` generates the following kind of output:

```
$ go run which.go which
/usr/bin/which
$ go run which.go doesNotExist
```

The last command could not find the `doesNotExist` executable—according to the UNIX philosophy and the way UNIX pipes work, utilities generate no output onscreen if they have nothing to say. However, an exit code of `0` means success whereas a **non-zero** exit code usually means failure.

Although it is useful to print error messages onscreen, there are times that you need to keep all error messages together and be able to search them when it is convenient for you. In this case, you need to use one or more log files.

Logging information

All UNIX systems have their own log files for writing logging information that comes from running servers and programs. Usually, most system log files of a UNIX system can be found under the `/var/log` directory. However, the log files of many popular services, such as Apache and Nginx, can be found elsewhere, depending on their configuration.

> Logging and putting logging information in log files is a practical way of examining data and information from your software asynchronously either locally or at a central log server or using server software such as Elasticsearch, Beats, and Grafana Loki.

Generally speaking, using a log file to write some information used to be considered a better practice than writing the same output on screen for two reasons: firstly, because the output does not get lost as it is stored on a file, and secondly, because you can search and process log files using UNIX tools, such as `grep(1)`, `awk(1)`, and `sed(1)`, which cannot be done when messages are printed on a terminal window. However, this is not true anymore.

As we usually run our services via `systemd`, programs should log to `stdout` so `systemd` can put logging data in the journal. `https://12factor.net/logs` offers more information about app logs. Additionally, in cloud native applications, we are encouraged to simply log to `stderr` and let the container system redirect the `stderr` stream to the desired destination.

The UNIX logging service has support for two properties named **logging level** and **logging facility**. The logging level is a value that specifies the severity of the log entry. There are various logging levels, including `debug`, `info`, `notice`, `warning`, `err`, `crit`, `alert`, and `emerg`, in reverse order of severity. The `log` package of the standard Go library does not support working with logging levels. The logging facility is like a category used for logging information. The value of the logging facility part can be one of `auth`, `authpriv`, `cron`, `daemon`, `kern`, `lpr`, `mail`, `mark`, `news`, `syslog`, `user`, `UUCP`, `local0`, `local1`, `local2`, `local3`, `local4`, `local5`, `local6`, or `local7` and is defined inside `/etc/syslog.conf`, `/etc/rsyslog.conf`, or another appropriate file depending on the server process used for system logging on your UNIX machine. This means that if a logging facility is not defined correctly, it will not be handled; therefore, the log messages you send to it might get ignored and therefore lost.

The `log` package sends log messages to standard error. Part of the `log` package is the `log/syslog` package, which allows you to send log messages to the `syslog` server of your machine. Although by default `log` writes to standard error, the use of `log.SetOutput()` modifies that behavior. The list of functions for sending logging data includes `log.Printf()`, `log.Print()`, `log.Println()`, `log.Fatalf()`, `log.Fatalln()`, `log.Panic()`, `log.Panicln()` and `log.Panicf()`.

> Logging is for application code, not library code. If you are developing libraries, do not put logging in them.

In order to write to system logs, you need to call the `syslog.New()` function with the appropriate parameters. Writing to the main system log file is as easy as calling `syslog.New()` with the `syslog.LOG_SYSLOG` option. After that you need to tell your Go program that all logging information goes to the new logger—this is implemented with a call to the `log.SetOutput()` function. The process is illustrated in the following code—type it on your favorite plain text editor and save it as `systemLog.go`:

```
package main

import (
    "log"
    "log/syslog"
```

```
)

func main() {
    sysLog, err := syslog.New(syslog.LOG_SYSLOG, "systemLog.go")

    if err != nil {
        log.Println(err)
        return
    } else {
        log.SetOutput(sysLog)
        log.Print("Everything is fine!")
    }
}
```

After the call to `log.SetOutput()`, all logging information goes to the `syslog` logger variable that sends it to `syslog.LOG_SYSLOG`. Custom text for the log entries coming from that program is specified as the second parameter to the `syslog.New()` call.

> Usually, you want to store logging data on user-defined files because they group relevant information, which makes them easier to process and inspect.

Running `systemLog.go` generates no output—however, if you look at the system logs of a macOS Big Sur machine, for example, you will find entries like the following inside `/var/log/system.log`:

```
Dec  5 16:20:10 iMac systemLog.go[35397]: 2020/12/05 16:20:10
Everything is fine!
Dec  5 16:43:18 iMac systemLog.go[35641]: 2020/12/05 16:43:18
Everything is fine!
```

The number inside the brackets is the process ID of the process that wrote the log entry—in our case, `35397` and `35641`.

Similarly, if you execute `journalctl -xe` on a Linux machine, you can see entries similar to the next:

```
Dec 05 16:33:43 thinkpad systemLog.go[12682]: 2020/12/05 16:33:43
Everything is fine!
Dec 05 16:46:01 thinkpad systemLog.go[12917]: 2020/12/05 16:46:01
Everything is fine!
```

The output on your own operating system might be slightly different but the general idea is the same.

Bad things happen all the time, even to good people and good software. So, the next subsection covers the Go way of dealing with bad situations in your programs.

log.Fatal() and log.Panic()

The `log.Fatal()` function is used when something erroneous has happened and you just want to exit your program as soon as possible after reporting that bad situation. The call to `log.Fatal()` terminates a Go program at the point where `log.Fatal()` was called after printing an error message. In most cases, this custom error message can be `Not enough arguments`, `Cannot access file`, or similar. Additionally, it returns back a non-zero exit code, which in UNIX indicates an error.

There are situations where a program is about to fail for good and you want to have as much information about the failure as possible—`log.Panic()` implies that something really unexpected and unknown, such as not being able to find a file that was previously accessed or not having enough disk space, has happened. Analogous to the `log.Fatal()` function, `log.Panic()` prints a custom message and immediately terminates the Go program.

Have in mind that `log.Panic()` is equivalent to a call to `log.Print()` followed by a call to `panic()`. `panic()` is a built-in function that stops the execution of the current function and begins panicking. After that, it returns to the caller function. On the other hand, `log.Fatal()` calls `log.Print()` and then `os.Exit(1)`, which is an immediate way of terminating the current program.

Both `log.Fatal()` and `log.Panic()` are illustrated in the `logs.go` file, which contains the next Go code:

```
package main

import (
    "log"
    "os"
)

func main() {
    if len(os.Args) != 1 {
        log.Fatal("Fatal: Hello World!")
    }
    log.Panic("Panic: Hello World!")
}
```

If you call `logs.go` without any command-line arguments, it calls `log.Panic()`. Otherwise, it calls `log.Fatal()`. This is illustrated in the next output from an Arch Linux system:

```
$ go run logs.go
2020/12/03 18:39:26 Panic: Hello World!
panic: Panic: Hello World!

goroutine 1 [running]:
log.Panic(0xc00009ef68, 0x1, 0x1)
        /usr/lib/go/src/log/log.go:351 +0xae
main.main()
        /home/mtsouk/Desktop/mGo3rd/code/ch01/logs.go:12 +0x6b
exit status 2
$ go run logs.go 1
2020/12/03 18:39:30 Fatal: Hello World!
exit status 1
```

So, the output of `log.Panic()` includes additional low-level information that, hopefully, will help you to resolve difficult situations that happened in your Go code.

Writing to a custom log file

Most of the time, and especially on applications and services that are deployed to production, you just need to write your logging data in a log file of your choice. This can be for many reasons, including writing debugging data without messing with the system log files, or keeping your own logging data separate from system logs in order to transfer it or store it in a database or software like Elasticsearch. This subsection teaches you how to write to a custom log file that is usually application-specific.

> Writing to files and file I/O are both covered in *Chapter 6, Telling a UNIX System What to Do*—however, saving information to files is very handy when troubleshooting and debugging Go code, which is why this is covered in the first chapter of the book.

The path of the log file that is used is hardcoded into the code using a global variable named `LOGFILE`. For the purposes of this chapter and for preventing your file system from getting full in case something goes wrong, that log file resides inside the `/tmp` directory, which is not the usual place for storing data because usually, the `/tmp` directory is emptied after each system reboot.

Additionally, at this point, this will save you from having to execute `customLog.go` with root privileges and from putting unnecessary files into your precious system directories.

Type the following code and save it as `customLog.go`:

```
package main

import (
    "fmt"
    "log"
    "os"
    "path"
)

func main() {
    LOGFILE := path.Join(os.TempDir(), "mGo.log")
    f, err := os.OpenFile(LOGFILE, os.O_APPEND|os.O_CREATE|os.O_WRONLY,
0644)
// The call to os.OpenFile() creates the log file for writing,
// if it does not already exist, or opens it for writing
// by appending new data at the end of it (os.O_APPEND)

    if err != nil {
        fmt.Println(err)
        return
    }
    defer f.Close()
```

The `defer` keyword tells Go to execute the statement just before the current function returns. This means that `f.Close()` is going to be executed just before `main()` returns. We'll go into more detail on `defer` in *Chapter 5, Go Packages and Functions.*

```
    iLog := log.New(f, "iLog ", log.LstdFlags)
    iLog.Println("Hello there!")
    iLog.Println("Mastering Go 3rd edition!")
}
```

The last three statements create a new log file based on an opened file (`f`) and write two messages to it using `Println()`.

> If you ever decide to use the code of `customLog.go` in a real application, you should change the path stored in `LOGFILE` into something that makes more sense.

Running `customLog.go` generates no output. However, what is really important is what has been written in the custom log file:

```
$ cat /tmp/mGo.log
iLog 2020/12/05 17:31:07 Hello there!
iLog 2020/12/05 17:31:07 Mastering Go 3rd edition!
```

Printing line numbers in log entries

In this subsection, you'll learn how to print the filename as well as the line number in the source file where the statement that wrote a log entry is located.

The desired functionality is implemented with the use of `log.Lshortfile` in the parameters of `log.New()` or `SetFlags()`. The `log.Lshortfile` flag adds the filename as well as the line number of the Go statement that printed the log entry in the log entry itself. If you use `log.Llongfile` instead of `log.Lshortfile`, then you get the full path of the Go source file—usually, this is not necessary, especially when you have a really long path.

Type the following code and save it as `customLogLineNumber.go`:

```
package main

import (
    "fmt"
    "log"
    "os"
    "path"
)

func main() {
    LOGFILE := path.Join(os.TempDir(), "mGo.log")
    f, err := os.OpenFile(LOGFILE, os.O_APPEND|os.O_CREATE|os.O_WRONLY,
0644)

    if err != nil {
        fmt.Println(err)
```

```
        return
    }
    defer f.Close()

    LstdFlags := log.Ldate | log.Lshortfile
    iLog := log.New(f, "LNum ", LstdFlags)
    iLog.Println("Mastering Go, 3rd edition!")

    iLog.SetFlags(log.Lshortfile | log.LstdFlags)
    iLog.Println("Another log entry!")
}
```

In case you are wondering, you are allowed to change the format of the log entries during program execution—this means that when there is a reason, you can print more analytical information in the log entries. This is implemented with multiple calls to `iLog.SetFlags()`.

Running `customLogLineNumber.go` generates no output but writes the following entries in the file path that is specified by the value of the `LOGFILE` global variable:

```
$ cat /tmp/mGo.log
LNum 2020/12/05 customLogLineNumber.go:24: Mastering Go, 3rd edition!
LNum 2020/12/05 17:33:23 customLogLineNumber.go:27: Another log entry!
```

You will most likely get a different output on your own machine, which is the expected behavior.

Overview of Go generics

This section discusses Go generics, which is a forthcoming Go feature. Currently, generics and Go are under discussion by the Go community. However, one way or another, it is good to know how generics work, its philosophy, and what the generics discussions are about.

> Go generics has been one of the most requested additions to the Go programming language. At the time of writing, it is said that generics is going to be part of Go 1.18.

The main idea behind generics in Go, as well as any other programming language that supports generics, is not having to write special code for supporting multiple data types when performing the same task.

Currently, Go supports multiple data types in functions such as `fmt.Println()` using the empty interface and reflection—both interfaces and reflection are discussed in *Chapter 4, Reflection and Interfaces*.

However, demanding every programmer to write lots of code and implement lots of functions and methods for supporting multiple custom data types is not the optimal solution—generics comes into play for providing an alternative to the use of interfaces and reflection for supporting multiple data types. The following code showcases how and where generics can be useful:

```
package main

import (
    "fmt"
)

func Print[T any](s []T) {
    for _, v := range s {
        fmt.Print(v, " ")
    }
    fmt.Println()
}

func main() {
    Ints := []int{1, 2, 3}
    Strings := []string{"One", "Two", "Three"}
    Print(Ints)
    Print(Strings)
}
```

In this case, we have a function named `Print()` that uses generics through a generics variable, which is specified by the use of `[T any]` after the function name and before the function parameters. Due to the use of `[T any]`, `Print()` can accept any slice of any data type and work with it. However, `Print()` does not work with input other than slices and that is fine because if your application supports slices of different data types, this function can still save you from having to implement **multiple** functions for supporting each distinct slice. This is the general idea behind generics.

> In *Chapter 4, Reflection and Interfaces*, you will learn about the *empty interface* and how it can be used for accepting data of any data type. However, the empty interface requires extra code for working with specific data types.

We end this section by stating some useful facts about generics:

- You do not need to use generics in your programs all the time.
- You can continue working with Go as before even if you use generics.
- You can fully replace generics code with non-generics code. The question is are you willing to write the extra code required for this?
- I believe that generics should be used when they can create simpler code and designs. It is better to have **repetitive straightforward** code than optimal abstractions that slow down your applications.
- There are times that you need to limit the data types that are supported by a function that uses generics—this is not a bad thing as all data types do not share the same capabilities. Generally speaking, generics can be useful when processing data types that share some characteristics.

You need time to get used to generics and use generics at its full potential. Take your time. We will cover generics in more depth in *Chapter 13, Go Generics*.

Developing a basic phone book application

In this section, to utilize the skills you've picked up so far, we will develop a basic phone book application in Go. Despite its limitations, the presented application is a command-line utility that searches a slice of structures that is statically defined (*hardcoded*) in the Go code. The utility offers support for two commands named `search` and `list` that search for a given surname and return its full record if the surname is found, and lists all available records, respectively.

The implementation has many shortcomings, including the following:

- If you want to add or delete any data, you need to change the source code
- You cannot present the data in a sorted form, which might be OK when you have 3 entries but might not work with more than 40 entries
- You cannot export your data or load it from an external file
- You cannot distribute the phone book application as a binary file because it uses hardcoded data

> The chapters that follow enhance the functionality of the phone book application in order to be fully functional, versatile, and powerful.

The code of `phoneBook.go` can be briefly described as follows:

- There exists a new user-defined data type for holding the records of the phone book that is a Go structure with three fields named `Name`, `Surname`, and `Tel`. Structures group a set of values into a **single data type**, which allows you to pass and receive this set of values as a single entity.
- There exists a global variable that holds the data of the phone book, which is a slice of structures named `data`.
- There exist two functions that help you implement the functionality of the `search` and `list` commands.
- The contents of the `data` global variable are defined in the `main()` function using multiple `append()` calls. You can change, add, or delete the contents of the `data` slice according to your needs.
- Lastly, the program can only serve one task at a time. This means that to perform multiple queries, you have to run the program multiple times.

Let us now see `phoneBook.go` in more detail, beginning with its preamble:

```
package main

import (
    "fmt"
    "os"
)
```

After that, we have a section where we declare a Go structure named `Entry` as well as a global variable named `data`:

```
type Entry struct {
    Name    string
    Surname string
    Tel     string
}

var data = []Entry{}
```

After that, we define and implement two functions for supporting the functionality of the phone book:

```
func search(key string) *Entry {
    for i, v := range data {
        if v.Surname == key {
```

```
            return &data[i]
        }
    }
    return nil
}

func list() {
    for _, v := range data {
        fmt.Println(v)
    }
}
```

The `search()` function performs a linear search on the `data` slice. Linear search is slow, but it does the job for now considering that the phone book does not contain lots of entries. The `list()` function just prints the contents of the `data` slice using a `for` loop with `range`. As we are not interested in displaying the index of the element that we print, we ignore it using the _ character and just print the structure that holds the actual data.

Lastly, we have the implementation of the `main()` function. The first part of it is as follows:

```
func main() {
    arguments := os.Args
    if len(arguments) == 1 {
        exe := path.Base(arguments[0])
        fmt.Printf("Usage: %s search|list <arguments>\n", exe)
        return
    }
```

The `exe` variable holds the path to the executable file—it is a nice and professional touch to print the name of the executable binary in the instructions of the program.

```
    data = append(data, Entry{"Mihalis", "Tsoukalos", "2109416471"})
    data = append(data, Entry{"Mary", "Doe", "2109416871"})
    data = append(data, Entry{"John", "Black", "2109416123"})
```

In this part, we check whether we were given any command arguments. If not (`len(arguments) == 1`), the program prints a message and exits by calling `return`. Otherwise, it puts the desired data in the `data` slice before continuing.

The rest of the `main()` function implementation is as follows:

```
    // Differentiate between the commands
    switch arguments[1] {
    // The search command
    case "search":
        if len(arguments) != 3 {
            fmt.Println("Usage: search Surname")
            return
        }
        result := search(arguments[2])
        if result == nil {
            fmt.Println("Entry not found:", arguments[2])
            return
        }
        fmt.Println(*result)
    // The list command
    case "list":
        list()
    // Response to anything that is not a match
    default:
        fmt.Println("Not a valid option")
    }
}
```

This code uses a `case` block, which is really handy when you want to write readable code and avoid using multiple and nested `if` blocks. That `case` block differentiates between the two supported commands by examining the value of `arguments[1]`. If the given command is not recognized, the `default` branch is executed instead. For the `search` command, `arguments[2]` is also examined.

Working with `phoneBook.go` looks as follows:

```
$ go build phoneBook.go
$ ./phoneBook list
{Mihalis Tsoukalos 2109416471}
{Mary Doe 2109416871}
{John Black 2109416123}
$ ./phoneBook search Tsoukalos
{Mihalis Tsoukalos 2109416471}
$ ./phoneBook search Tsouk
Entry not found: Tsouk
$ ./phoneBook
Usage: ./phoneBook search|list <arguments>
```

The first command lists the contents of the phone book whereas the second command searches for a given surname (`Tsoukalos`). The third command searches for something that does not exist in the phone book and the last command builds `phoneBook.go` and runs the generated executable without any arguments, which prints the instructions of the program.

Despite its shortcomings, `phoneBook.go` has a clean design that you can easily extend and works as expected, which is a great starting point. The phone book application will keep improving in the chapters that follow as we learn more advanced concepts.

Exercises

- Our version of `which(1)` stops after finding the first occurrence of the desired executable. Make the necessary changes to `which.go` in order to find all possible occurrences of the desired executable.
- The current version of `which.go` processes the first command-line argument only. Make the necessary changes to `which.go` in order to accept and search the `PATH` variable for multiple executable binaries.
- Read the documentation of the `fmt` package at `https://golang.org/pkg/fmt/`.

Summary

If you are using Go for the first time, the information in this chapter will help you understand the advantages of Go, how Go code looks, and some important characteristics of Go such as variables, iterations, flow control, and the Go concurrency model. If you already know Go, then this chapter is a good reminder of where Go excels and the kinds of software where it is advised to use Go. Lastly, we built a basic phone book application with the techniques that we have learned so far.

The next chapter discusses the basic data types of Go in more detail.

Additional resources

- The official Go website: `https://golang.org/`
- The Go Playground: `https://play.golang.org/`
- The `log` package: `https://golang.org/pkg/log/`
- Elasticsearch Beats: `https://www.elastic.co/beats/`
- Grafana Loki: `https://grafana.com/oss/loki/`
- Microsoft Visual Studio: `https://visualstudio.microsoft.com/`
- The Standard Go library: `https://golang.org/pkg/`

2

Basic Go Data Types

Data is stored and used in variables and all Go variables should have a data type that is determined either implicitly or explicitly. Knowing the built-in data types of Go allows you to understand how to manipulate simple data values and construct more complex data structures when simple data types are not enough or not efficient for a given job.

This chapter is all about the basic data types of Go and the data structures that allow you to **group data of the same data type**. But let us begin with something more practical: imagine that you want to read data as command-line arguments of a utility. How can you be sure that what you have read was what you expected? How can you handle error situations? What about reading not just numbers and strings but dates and times from the command line? Do you have to write your own parser for working with dates and times?

This chapter will answer all these questions and many more by implementing the following three utilities:

- A command-line utility that parses dates and times
- A utility that generates random numbers and random strings
- A new version of the phone book application that contains randomly generated data

This chapter covers:

- The `error` data type
- Numeric data types

- Non-numeric data types
- Go constants
- Grouping similar data
- Pointers
- Generating random numbers
- Updating the phone book application

We begin this chapter with the `error` data type, because errors play a key role in Go.

The error data type

Go provides a special data type for representing error conditions and error messages named `error`—in practice, this means that Go treats errors as values. In order to program successfully in Go, you should be aware of the error conditions that might occur with the functions and methods you are using and handle them accordingly.

As you already know from the previous chapter, Go follows the next convention about `error` values: if the value of an `error` variable is `nil`, then there was no error. As an example, let us consider `strconv.Atoi()`, which is used for converting a `string` value into an `int` value (`Atoi` stands for ASCII to Int). As specified by its signature, `strconv.Atoi()` returns `(int, error)`. Having an `error` value of `nil` means that the conversion was successful and that you can use the `int` value if you want. Having an `error` value that is not `nil` means that the conversion was unsuccessful and that the `string` input is not a valid `int` value.

> If you want to learn more about `strconv.Atoi()`, you should execute `go doc strconv.Atoi` in your terminal window.

You might wonder what happens if you want to create your own error messages. Is this possible? Should you wish to return a custom error, you can use `errors.New()` from the `errors` package. This usually happens inside a function other than `main()` because `main()` does not return anything to any other function. Additionally, a good place to define your custom errors is inside the Go packages you create.

> You will most likely work with errors in your programs without needing the functionality of the `errors` package. Additionally, you do not need to define custom error messages unless you are creating big applications or packages.

If you want to format your error messages in the way `fmt.Printf()` works, you can use the `fmt.Errorf()` function, which simplifies the creation of custom error messages—the `fmt.Errorf()` function returns an `error` value just like `errors.New()`.

And now we should talk about something important: you should have a global error handling tactic in each application that should not change. In practice, this means the following:

- All error messages should be handled at the same level, which means that all errors should either be returned to the calling function or be handled at the place they occurred.
- It should be clearly documented how to handle critical errors. This means that there will be situations where a critical error should terminate the program and other times where a critical error might just create a warning message onscreen.
- It is considered a good practice to send all error messages to the *log service* of your machine because this way the error messages can be examined at a later time. However, this is not always true, so exercise caution when setting this up—for example, cloud native apps do not work that way.

> The `error` data type is actually defined as an *interface*—interfaces are covered in *Chapter 4, Reflection and Interfaces.*

Type the following code in your favorite text editor and save it as `error.go` in the directory where you put the code for this chapter. Using `ch02` as the directory name is a good idea.

```
package main

import (
    "errors"
    "fmt"
    "os"
    "strconv"
)
```

The first part is the preamble of the program—`error.go` uses the `fmt`, `os`, `strconv`, and `errors` packages.

```
// Custom error message with errors.New()
func check(a, b int) error {
```

```
    if a == 0 && b == 0 {
        return errors.New("this is a custom error message")
    }
    return nil
}
```

The preceding code implements a function named `check()` that returns an `error` value. If both input parameters of `check()` are equal to `0`, the function returns a custom error message using `errors.New()`—otherwise it returns `nil`, which means that everything is OK.

```
// Custom error message with fmt.Errorf()
func formattedError(a, b int) error {
    if a == 0 && b == 0 {
        return fmt.Errorf("a %d and b %d. UserID: %d", a, b,
os.Getuid())
    }
    return nil
}
```

The previous code implements `formattedError()`, which is a function that returns a formatted error message using `fmt.Errorf()`. Among other things, the error message prints the user ID of the user that executed the program with a call to `os.Getuid()`. When you want to create a custom error message, using `fmt.Errorf()` gives you more control over the output.

```
func main() {
    err := check(0, 10)
    if err == nil {
        fmt.Println("check() ended normally!")
    } else {
        fmt.Println(err)
    }

    err = check(0, 0)
    if err.Error() == "this is a custom error message" {
        fmt.Println("Custom error detected!")
    }

    err = formattedError(0, 0)
    if err != nil {
        fmt.Println(err)
    }
```

```
    i, err := strconv.Atoi("-123")
    if err == nil {
        fmt.Println("Int value is", i)
    }

    i, err = strconv.Atoi("Y123")
    if err != nil {
        fmt.Println(err)
    }
}
```

The previous code is the implementation of the `main()` function where you can see the use of the `if err != nil` statement multiple times as well as the use of `if err == nil`, which is used to make sure that everything was OK before executing the desired code.

Running `error.go` produces the next output:

```
$ go run error.go
check() ended normally!
Custom error detected!
a 0 and b 0. UserID: 501
Int value is -123
strconv.Atoi: parsing "Y123": invalid syntax
```

Now that you know about the `error` data type, how to create custom errors, and how to use `error` values, we'll continue with the basic data types of Go that can be logically divided into two main categories: numeric data types and non-numeric data types. Go also supports the `bool` data type, which can have a value of `true` or `false` only.

Numeric data types

Go supports integer, floating-point, and complex number values in various versions depending on the memory space they consume—this saves memory and computing time. Integer data types can be either signed or unsigned, which is not the case for floating point numbers.

The table that follows lists the numeric data types of Go.

Data Type	Description
`int8`	8-bit signed integer
`int16`	16-bit signed integer
`int32`	32-bit signed integer
`int64`	64-bit signed integer
`int`	32- or 64-bit signed integer
`uint8`	8-bit unsigned integer
`uint16`	16-bit unsigned integer
`uint32`	32-bit unsigned integer
`uint64`	64-bit unsigned integer
`uint`	32- or 64-bit unsigned integer
`float32`	32-bit floating-point number
`float64`	64-bit floating-point number
`complex64`	Complex number with `float32` parts
`Complex128`	Complex number with `float64` parts

The `int` and `uint` data types are special as they are the most efficient sizes for signed and unsigned integers on a given platform and can be either 32 or 64 bits each—their size is defined by Go itself. The `int` data type is the most widely used data type in Go due to its versatility.

The code that follows illustrates the use of numeric data types—you can find the entire program as `numbers.go` inside the `ch02` directory of the book GitHub repository.

```
func main() {
    c1 := 12 + 1i
    c2 := complex(5, 7)
    fmt.Printf("Type of c1: %T\n", c1)
    fmt.Printf("Type of c2: %T\n", c2)
```

The previous code creates two complex variables in two different ways—both ways are perfectly valid and equivalent. Unless you are into mathematics, you will most likely not use complex numbers in your programs. However, the existence of complex numbers shows how modern Go is.

```
    var c3 complex64 = complex64(c1 + c2)
    fmt.Println("c3:", c3)
    fmt.Printf("Type of c3: %T\n", c3)
```

```
    cZero := c3 - c3
    fmt.Println("cZero:", cZero)
```

The previous code continues to work with complex numbers by adding and subtracting two pairs of them. Although `cZero` is equal to zero, it is still a complex number and a `complex64` variable.

```
    x := 12
    k := 5
    fmt.Println(x)
    fmt.Printf("Type of x: %T\n", x)

    div := x / k
    fmt.Println("div", div)
```

In this part, we define two integer variables named `x` and `k`—their data type is identified by Go based on their initial values. Both are of type `int`, which is what Go prefers to use for storing integer values. Additionally, when you divide two integer values, you get an integer result even when the division is not perfect. This means that if this is not what you want, you should take extra care—this is shown in the next code excerpt:

```
    var m, n float64
    m = 1.223
    fmt.Println("m, n:", m, n)

    y := 4 / 2.3
    fmt.Println("y:", y)

    divFloat := float64(x) / float64(k)
    fmt.Println("divFloat", divFloat)
    fmt.Printf("Type of divFloat: %T\n", divFloat)
}
```

The previous code works with `float64` values and variables. As `n` does not have an initial value, it is **automatically assigned** with the zero value of its data type, which is `0` for the `float64` data type.

Additionally, the code presents a technique for dividing integer values and getting a floating-point result, which is the use of `float64()`: `divFloat := float64(x) / float64(k)`. This is a type conversion where two integers (`x` and `k`) are converted to `float64` values. As the division between two `float64` values is a `float64` value, we get the result in the desired data type.

Running `numbers.go` creates the following output:

```
$ go run numbers.go
Type of c1: complex128
Type of c2: complex128
c3: (17+8i)
Type of c3: complex64
cZero: (0+0i)
12
Type of x: int
div 2
m, n: 1.223 0
y: 1.7391304347826086
divFloat 2.4
Type of divFloat: float64
```

The output shows that both `c1` and `c2` are `complex128` values, which is the preferred complex data type for the machine on which the code was executed. However, `c3` is a `complex64` value because it was created using `complex64()`. The value of `n` is `0` because the `n` variable was not initialized, which means that Go automatically assigned the zero value of its data type to `n`.

After learning about numeric data types, it is time to learn about non-numeric data types, which is the subject of the next section.

Non-numeric data types

Go has support for **Strings**, **Characters**, **Runes**, **Dates**, and **Times**. However, Go does not have a dedicated `char` data type. We begin by explaining the string-related data types.

> For Go, dates and times are the same thing and are represented by the same data type. However, it is up to you to determine whether a time and date variable contains valid information or not.

Strings, Characters, and Runes

Go supports the `string` data type for representing strings. A Go string is just a collection of bytes and can be accessed as a whole or as an array. A single byte can store any ASCII character—however, multiple bytes are usually needed for storing a single Unicode character.

Nowadays, supporting Unicode characters is a common requirement—Go is designed with Unicode support in mind, which is the main reason for having the rune data type. A rune is an `int32` value that is used for representing a single Unicode code point, which is an integer value that is used for representing single Unicode characters or, less frequently, providing formatting information.

> Although a rune is an `int32` value, you cannot compare a rune with an `int32` value. Go considers these two data types as totally different.

You can create a new byte slice from a given string by using a `[]byte("A String")` statement. Given a byte slice variable `b`, you can convert it into a string using the `string(b)` statement. When working with byte slices that contain Unicode characters, the number of bytes in a byte slice is not always connected to the number of characters in the byte slice, because most Unicode characters require more than one byte for their representation. As a result, when you try to print each single byte of a byte slice using `fmt.Println()` or `fmt.Print()`, the output is not text presented as characters but integer values. If you want to print the contents of a byte slice as text, you should either print it using `string(byteSliceVar)` or using `fmt.Printf()` with `%s` to tell `fmt.Printf()` that you want to print a string. You can initialize a new byte slice with the desired string by using a statement such as `[]byte("My Initialization String")`.

> We will cover byte slices in more detail in the *Byte slices* section.

You can define a rune using single quotes: `r := '€'` and you can print the integer value of the bytes that compose it as `fmt.Println(r)`—in this case, the integer value is `8364`. Printing it as a single Unicode character requires the use of the `%c` control string in `fmt.Printf()`.

As strings can be accessed as arrays, you can iterate over the runes of the string using a `for` loop or point to a specific character if you know its place in the string. The length of the string is the same as the number of characters found in the string, which is usually not true for byte slices because Unicode characters usually require more than one byte.

The following Go code illustrates the use of strings and runes and how you can work with strings in your code. You can find the entire program as `text.go` in the `ch02` directory of the GitHub repository of the book.

The first part of the program defines a string literal that contains a Unicode character. Then it accesses its first character as if the string was an array.

```
func main() {
    aString := "Hello World! €"
    fmt.Println("First character", string(aString[0]))
```

The next part is about working with runes.

```
    // Runes
    // A rune
    r := '€'
    fmt.Println("As an int32 value:", r)
    // Convert Runes to text
    fmt.Printf("As a string: %s and as a character: %c\n", r, r)

    // Print an existing string as runes
    for _, v := range aString {
        fmt.Printf("%x ", v)
    }
    fmt.Println()
```

First, we define a rune named `r`. What makes this a rune is the use of single quotes around the € character. The rune is an `int32` value and is printed as such by `fmt.Println()`. The `%c` control string in `fmt.Printf()` prints a rune as a character.

Then we iterate over `aString` as a slice or an array using a `for` loop with `range` and print the contents of `aString` as runes.

```
    // Print an existing string as characters
    for _, v := range aString {
        fmt.Printf("%c", v)
    }
    fmt.Println()
}
```

Lastly, we iterate over `aString` as a slice or an array using a `for` loop with `range` and print the contents of `aString` as characters.

Running `text.go` produces the following output:

```
$ go run text.go
First character H
As an int32 value: 8364
```

```
As a string: %!s(int32=8364) and as a character: €
48 65 6c 6c 6f 20 57 6f 72 6c 64 21 20 20ac
Hello World! €
```

The first line of the output shows that we can access a `string` as an array whereas the second line verifies that a rune is an integer value. The third line shows what to expect when you print a `rune` as a `string` and as a character—the correct way is to print it as a character. The fifth line shows how to print a string as runes and the last line shows the output of processing a string as characters using `range` and a `for` loop.

Converting from int to string

You can convert an integer value into a string in two main ways: using `string()` and using a function from the `strconv` package. However, the two methods are fundamentally different. The `string()` function converts an integer value into a Unicode code point, which is a single character, whereas functions such as `strconv.FormatInt()` and `strconv.Itoa()` convert an integer value into a string value with the same representation and the same number of characters.

This is illustrated in the `intString.go` program—its most important statements are the following. You can find the entire program in the GitHub repository of the book.

```
input := strconv.Itoa(n)
input = strconv.FormatInt(int64(n), 10)
input = string(n)
```

Running `intString.go` generates the following kind of output:

```
$ go run intString.go 100
strconv.Itoa() 100 of type string
strconv.FormatInt() 100 of type string
string() d of type string
```

The data type of the output is always `string`, however, `string()` converted `100` into `d` because the ASCII representation of `d` is `100`.

The unicode package

The `unicode` standard Go package contains various handy functions for working with Unicode code points. One of them, which is called `unicode.IsPrint()`, can help you to identify the parts of a string that are printable using runes.

The following code excerpt illustrates the functionality of the `unicode` package:

```
for i := 0; i < len(sL); i++ {
    if unicode.IsPrint(rune(sL[i])) {
        fmt.Printf("%c\n", sL[i])
    } else {
        fmt.Println("Not printable!")
    }
}
```

The `for` loop iterates over the contents of a string defined as a list of runes (`"\x99\x00ab\x50\x00\x23\x50\x29\x9c"`) while `unicode.IsPrint()` examines whether the character is printable or not—if it returns `true` then a rune is printable.

You can find this code excerpt inside the `unicode.go` source file at the `ch02` directory in the GitHub repository of the book. Running `unicode.go` produces the following output:

```
Not printable!
Not printable!
a
b
P
Not printable!
#
P
)
Not printable!
```

This utility is very handy for filtering your input or filtering data before printing it on screen, storing it in log files, transferring it on a network, or storing it in a database.

The strings package

The `strings` standard Go package allows you to manipulate UTF-8 strings in Go and includes many powerful functions. Many of these functions are illustrated in the `useStrings.go` source file, which can be found in the `ch02` directory of the book GitHub repository.

> If you are working with text and text processing, you definitely need to learn all the gory details and functions of the `strings` package, so make sure that you experiment with all these functions and create many examples that will help you to clarify things.

The most important parts of `useStrings.go` are the following:

```
import (
    "fmt"
    s "strings"
    "unicode"
)

var f = fmt.Printf
```

As we are going to use the `strings` package multiple times, we create a convenient alias for it named `s`. We do the same for the `fmt.Printf()` function where we create a global alias using a variable named `f`. These two shortcuts make code less populated with long, repeated lines of code. You can use it when learning Go but this is not recommended in any kind of production software, as it makes code less readable.

The first code excerpt is the following.

```
f("EqualFold: %v\n", s.EqualFold("Mihalis", "MIHAlis"))
f("EqualFold: %v\n", s.EqualFold("Mihalis", "MIHAli"))
```

The `strings.EqualFold()` function compares two strings without considering their case and returns `true` when they are the same and `false` otherwise.

```
f("Index: %v\n", s.Index("Mihalis", "ha"))
f("Index: %v\n", s.Index("Mihalis", "Ha"))
```

The `strings.Index()` function checks whether the string of the second parameter can be found in the string that is given as the first parameter and returns the index where it was found for the first time. On an unsuccessful search, it returns `-1`.

```
    f("Prefix: %v\n", s.HasPrefix("Mihalis", "Mi"))
    f("Prefix: %v\n", s.HasPrefix("Mihalis", "mi"))
    f("Suffix: %v\n", s.HasSuffix("Mihalis", "is"))
    f("Suffix: %v\n", s.HasSuffix("Mihalis", "IS"))
```

The `strings.HasPrefix()` function checks whether the given string, which is the first parameter, begins with the string that is given as the second parameter. In the previous code, the first call to `strings.HasPrefix()` returns `true`, whereas the second returns `false`.

Similarly, the `strings.HasSuffix()` function checks whether the given string ends with the second string. Both functions take into account the case of the input string and the case of the second parameter.

```
t := s.Fields("This is a string!")
f("Fields: %v\n", len(t))
t = s.Fields("ThisIs a\tstring!")
f("Fields: %v\n", len(t))
```

The handy `strings.Fields()` function splits the given string around one or more white space characters as defined by the `unicode.IsSpace()` function and returns a slice of substrings found in the input string. If the input string contains white characters only, it returns an empty slice.

```
f("%s\n", s.Split("abcd efg", ""))
f("%s\n", s.Replace("abcd efg", "", "_", -1))
f("%s\n", s.Replace("abcd efg", "", "_", 4))
f("%s\n", s.Replace("abcd efg", "", "_", 2))
```

The `strings.Split()` function allows you to split the given string according to the desired separator string—the `strings.Split()` function returns a **string slice**. Using `""` as the second parameter of `strings.Split()` allows you to process a string character by character.

The `strings.Replace()` function takes four parameters. The first parameter is the string that you want to process. The second parameter contains the string that, if found, will be replaced by the third parameter of `strings.Replace()`. The last parameter is the maximum number of replacements that are allowed to happen. If that parameter has a negative value, then there is no limit to the number of replacements that can take place.

```
f("SplitAfter: %s\n", s.SplitAfter("123++432++", "++"))

trimFunction := func(c rune) bool {
    return !unicode.IsLetter(c)
}
f("TrimFunc: %s\n", s.TrimFunc("123 abc ABC \t .", trimFunction))
```

The `strings.SplitAfter()` function splits its first parameter string into substrings based on the separator string that is given as the second parameter to the function. The separator string is included in the returned slice.

The last lines of code define a **trim function** named `trimFunction` that is used as the second parameter to `strings.TrimFunc()` in order to filter the given input based on the return value of the trim function—in this case, the trim function keeps all letters and nothing else due to the `unicode.IsLetter()` call.

Running `useStrings.go` produces the next output:

```
To Upper: HELLO THERE!
To Lower: hello there
THis WiLL Be A Title!
EqualFold: true
EqualFold: false
Prefix: true
Prefix: false
Suffix: true
Suffix: false
Index: 2
Index: -1
Count: 2
Count: 0
Repeat: ababababab
TrimSpace: This is a line.
TrimLeft: This is a      line.
TrimRight:      This is a        line.
Compare: 1
Compare: 0
Compare: -1
Fields: 4
Fields: 3
[a b c d   e f g]
_a_b_c_d_ _e_f_g_
_a_b_c_d efg
_a_bcd efg
Join: Line 1+++Line 2+++Line 3
SplitAfter: [123++ 432++ ]
TrimFunc: abc ABC
```

Visit the documentation page of the `strings` package at `https://golang.org/pkg/strings/` for the complete list of available functions. You will see the functionality of the `strings` package in other places in this book.

Enough with strings and text; the next section is about working with dates and times in Go.

Times and dates

Often, we need to work with date and time information to store the time an entry was last used in a database or the time an entry was inserted into a database, which brings us to another interesting topic: working with dates and times in Go.

The king of working with times and dates in Go is the `time.Time` data type, which represents an instant in time with *nanosecond precision*. Each `time.Time` value is associated with a location (time zone).

If you are a UNIX person, you might already know about the UNIX epoch time and wonder how to get it in Go. The `time.Now().Unix()` function returns the popular UNIX epoch time, which is the number of seconds that have elapsed since 00:00:00 UTC, January 1, 1970. If you want to convert the UNIX time to the equivalent `time.Time` value, you can use the `time.Unix()` function. If you are not a UNIX person, then you might not have heard about the UNIX epoch time before but now you know what it is!

> The `time.Since()` function calculates the time that has passed since a given time and returns a `time.Duration` variable—the `duration` data type is defined as `type Duration int64`. Although a `Duration` is, in reality, an `int64` value, you cannot compare or convert a `duration` to an `int64` value implicitly because **Go does not allow implicit data type conversions**.

The single most important topic about Go and dates and times is the way Go parses a string in order to convert it into a date and a time. The reason that this is important is usually such input is given as a string and not as a valid date variable. The function used for parsing is `time.Parse()` and its full signature is `Parse(layout, value string) (Time, error)`, where `layout` is the parse string and `value` is the input that is being parsed. The `time.Time` value that is returned is a moment in time with nanosecond precision and contains both date and time information.

The next table shows the most widely used strings for parsing dates and times.

Parse Value	Meaning (examples)
`05`	12-hour value (12pm, 07am)
`15`	24-hour value (23, 07)
`04`	Minutes (55, 15)
`05`	Seconds (5, 23)
`Mon`	Abbreviated day of week (Tue, Fri)
`Monday`	Day of week (Tuesday, Friday)
`02`	Day of month (15, 31)
`2006`	Year with 4 digits (2020, 2004)
`06`	Year with the last 2 digits (20, 04)
`Jan`	Abbreviated month name (Feb, Mar)
`January`	Full month name (July, August)
`MST`	Time zone (EST, UTC)

The previous table shows that if you want to parse the `30 January 2020` string and convert it into a Go date variable, you should match it against the `02 January 2006` string—you cannot use anything else in its place when matching a string with the `30 January 2020` format. Similarly, if you want to parse the `15 August 2020 10:00` string, you should match it against the `02 January 2006 15:04` string. The documentation of the `time` package (`https://golang.org/pkg/time/`) contains even more detailed information about parsing dates and times—however, the ones presented here should be more than enough for regular use.

A utility for parsing dates and times

On a rare occasion, a situation can happen when we do not know anything about our input. If you do not know the exact format of your input, then you need to try matching your input against multiple Go strings without being sure that you are going to succeed in the end. This is the approach that the example uses. The Go matching strings for dates and times can be tried in any order.

If you are matching a string that only contains the date, then your time will be set to `00:00` by Go and will most likely be incorrect. Similarly, when matching the time only, your date will be incorrect and should not be used.

> The formatting strings can be also used for printing dates and times in the desired format. So in order to print the current date in the `01-02-2006` format, you should use `time.Now().Format("01-02-2006")`.

The code that follows illustrates how to work with epoch time in Go and showcases the parsing process—create a text file, type the following code, and save it as `dates.go`.

```
package main

import (
	"fmt"
	"os"
	"time"
)
```

This is the expected preamble of the Go source file.

```
func main() {
	start := time.Now()

	if len(os.Args) != 2 {
		fmt.Println("Usage: dates parse_string")
		return
	}
	dateString := os.Args[1]
```

This is how we get user input that is stored in the `dateString` variable. If the utility gets no input, there is no point in continuing its operation.

```
	// Is this a date only?
	d, err := time.Parse("02 January 2006", dateString)
	if err == nil {
		fmt.Println("Full:", d)
		fmt.Println("Time:", d.Day(), d.Month(), d.Year())
	}
```

The first test is for matching a date only using the `02 January 2006` format. If the match is successful, you can access the individual fields of a variable that holds a valid date using `Day()`, `Month()`, and `Year()`.

```
// Is this a date + time?
d, err = time.Parse("02 January 2006 15:04", dateString)
if err == nil {
    fmt.Println("Full:", d)
    fmt.Println("Date:", d.Day(), d.Month(), d.Year())
    fmt.Println("Time:", d.Hour(), d.Minute())
}
```

This time we try to match a string using `"02 January 2006 15:04"`, which contains a date and a time value. If the match is successful, you can access the fields of a valid time using `Hour()` and `Minute()`.

```
// Is this a date + time with month represented as a number?
d, err = time.Parse("02-01-2006 15:04", dateString)
if err == nil {
    fmt.Println("Full:", d)
    fmt.Println("Date:", d.Day(), d.Month(), d.Year())
    fmt.Println("Time:", d.Hour(), d.Minute())
}
```

This time we try to match against the `"02-01-2006 15:04"` format, which contains both a date and a time. Note that it is compulsory that the string that is being examined contains the `-` and the `:` characters as specified in the `time.Parse()` call and that `"02-01-2006 15:04"` is different from `"02/01/2006 1504"`.

```
// Is it time only?
d, err = time.Parse("15:04", dateString)
if err == nil {
    fmt.Println("Full:", d)
    fmt.Println("Time:", d.Hour(), d.Minute())
}
```

The last match is for time only using the `"15:04"` format. Note that the `:` should exist in the string that is being examined.

```
t := time.Now().Unix()
fmt.Println("Epoch time:", t)
// Convert Epoch time to time.Time
d = time.Unix(t, 0)
fmt.Println("Date:", d.Day(), d.Month(), d.Year())
fmt.Printf("Time: %d:%d\n", d.Hour(), d.Minute())
```

```
    duration := time.Since(start)
    fmt.Println("Execution time:", duration)
}
```

The last part of `dates.go` shows how to work with UNIX epoch time. You get the current date and time in epoch time using `time.Now().Unix()` and you can convert that to a `time.Time` value using a call to `time.Unix()`.

Lastly, you can calculate the time duration between the current time and a time in the past using a call to `time.Since()`.

Running `dates.go` creates the following kind of output, depending on its input:

```
$ go run dates.go
Usage: dates parse_string
$ go run dates.go 14:10
Full: 0000-01-01 14:10:00 +0000 UTC
Time: 14 10
Epoch time: 1607964956
Date: 14 December 2020
Time: 18:55
Execution time: 163.032µs
$ go run dates.go "14 December 2020"
Full: 2020-12-14 00:00:00 +0000 UTC
Time: 14 December 2020
Epoch time: 1607964985
Date: 14 December 2020
Time: 18:56
Execution time: 180.029µs
```

> If a command-line argument such as `14 December 2020` contains space characters, you should put it in double quotes for the UNIX shell to treat it as a single command-line argument. Running `go run dates.go 14 December 2020` does not work.

Now that we know how to work with dates and times, it is time to learn more about time zones.

Working with different time zones

The presented utility accepts a date and a time and converts them into different time zones. This can be particularly handy when you want to preprocess log files from different sources that use different time zones in order to convert these different time zones into a common one.

Once again, you need `time.Parse()` in order to convert a valid input into a `time.Time` value before doing the conversions. This time the input string contains the time zone and is parsed by the `"02 January 2006 15:04 MST"` string.

In order to convert the parsed date and time into New York time, the program uses the following code:

```
    loc, _ = time.LoadLocation("America/New_York")
    fmt.Printf("New York Time: %s\n", now.In(loc))
```

This technique is used multiple times in `convertTimes.go`.

Running `convertTimes.go` generates the following output:

```
$ go run convertTimes.go "14 December 2020 19:20 EET"
Current Location: 2020-12-14 19:20:00 +0200 EET
New York Time: 2020-12-14 12:20:00 -0500 EST
London Time: 2020-12-14 17:20:00 +0000 GMT
Tokyo Time: 2020-12-15 02:20:00 +0900 JST
$ go run convertTimes.go "14 December 2020 20:00 UTC"
Current Location: 2020-12-14 22:00:00 +0200 EET
New York Time: 2020-12-14 15:00:00 -0500 EST
London Time: 2020-12-14 20:00:00 +0000 GMT
Tokyo Time: 2020-12-15 05:00:00 +0900 JST
$ go run convertTimes.go "14 December 2020 25:00 EET"
parsing time "14 December 2020 25:00": hour out of range
```

In the last execution of the program, the code has to parse `25` as the hour of the day, which is wrong and generates the `hour out of range` error message.

Go constants

Go supports **constants**, which are variables that cannot change their values. Constants in Go are defined with the help of the `const` keyword. Generally speaking, constants can be either **global or local variables**.

However, you might need to rethink your approach if you find yourself defining too many constant variables with a local scope. The main benefit you get from using constants in your programs is the guarantee that their value will not change during program execution. Strictly speaking, the value of a constant variable is defined at compile time, not at runtime—this means that it is included in the binary executable. Behind the scenes, Go uses Boolean, string, or number as the type for storing constant values because this gives Go more flexibility when dealing with constants.

The next subsection discusses the constant generator iota, which is a handy way of creating sequences of constants.

The constant generator iota

The **constant generator iota** is used for declaring a sequence of related values that use incrementing numbers without the need to explicitly type each one of them.

The concepts related to the `const` keyword, including the constant generator iota, are illustrated in the `constants.go` file.

```
package main

import (
    "fmt"
)

type Digit int
type Power2 int

const PI = 3.1415926

const (
    C1 = "C1C1C1"
    C2 = "C2C2C2"
    C3 = "C3C3C3"
)
```

In this part, we declare two new types named `Digit` and `Power2` that will be used in a while, and four new constants named `PI`, `C1`, `C2`, and `C3`.

> A Go **type** is a way of defining a new **named type** that uses the same underlying type as an existing type. This is mainly used for differentiating between different types that might use the same kind of data. The `type` keyword can be used for defining *structures* and *interfaces*.

```
func main() {
    const s1 = 123
    var v1 float32 = s1 * 12
    fmt.Println(v1)
    fmt.Println(PI)

    const (
        Zero Digit = iota
        One
        Two
        Three
        Four
    )
```

The previous code defines a constant named `s1`. Here you also see the definition of a *constant generator iota* based on `Digit`, which is equivalent to the next declaration of four constants:

```
const (
    Zero = 0
    One = 1
    Two = 2
    Three = 3
    Four = 4
)
```

> Although we are defining constants inside `main()`, constants can be normally found outside of `main()` or any other function or method.

The last part of `constants.go` is as follows.

```
    fmt.Println(One)
    fmt.Println(Two)
```

```
    const (
        p2_0 Power2 = 1 << iota
        _
        p2_2
        _
        p2_4
        _
        p2_6
    )

    fmt.Println("2^0:", p2_0)
    fmt.Println("2^2:", p2_2)
    fmt.Println("2^4:", p2_4)
    fmt.Println("2^6:", p2_6)
}
```

There is another constant generator iota here that is a little different than the previous one. Firstly, you can see the use of the underscore character in a `const` block with a constant generator iota, which allows you to skip unwanted values. Secondly, the value of `iota` always increments and can be used in expressions, which is what occurred in this case.

Now let us see what really happens inside the `const` block. For `p2_0`, `iota` has the value of `0` and `p2_0` is defined as `1`. For `p2_2`, `iota` has the value of `2` and `p2_2` is defined as the result of the expression `1 << 2`, which is `00000100` in binary representation. The decimal value of `00000100` is `4`, which is the result and the value of `p2_2`. Analogously, the value of `p2_4` is `16` and the value of `p2_6` is `64`.

Running `constants.go` produces the next output:

```
$ go run constants.go
1476
3.1415926
1
2
2^0: 1
2^2: 4
2^4: 16
2^6: 64
```

Having data is good but what happens when you have lots of similar data? Do you need to have lots of variables to hold this data or is there a better way to do so? Go answers these questions by introducing arrays and slices.

Grouping similar data

There are times when you want to keep multiple values of the same data type under a single variable and access them using an index number. The simplest way to do that in Go is by using arrays or slices.

Arrays are the most widely used data structures and can be found in almost all programming languages due to their simplicity and speed of access. Go provides an alternative to arrays that is called a slice. The subsections that follow help you understand the differences between arrays and slices so that you know which data structure to use and when.

> The quick answer is that you can use slices instead of arrays almost anywhere in Go but we are also demonstrating arrays because they can still be useful and because slices are implemented by Go using arrays!

Arrays

Arrays in Go have the following characteristics and limitations:

- When defining an array variable, you must define its size. Otherwise, you should put `[...]` in the array declaration and let the Go compiler find out the length for you. So you can create an array with 4 `string` elements either as `[4]string{"Zero", "One", "Two", "Three"}` or as `[...]string{"Zero", "One", "Two", "Three"}`. If you put nothing in the square brackets, then a slice is going to be created instead. The (valid) indexes for that particular array are `0`, `1`, `2`, and `3`.
- You cannot change the size of an array after you have created it.
- When you pass an array to a function, what is happening is that Go creates a copy of that array and passes that copy to that function—therefore any changes you make to an array inside a function are lost when the function returns.

As a result, arrays in Go are not very powerful, which is the main reason that Go has introduced an additional data structure named **slice** that is similar to an array but is dynamic in nature and is explained in the next subsection. However, data in both arrays and slices is accessed the same way.

Slices

Slices in Go are more powerful than arrays mainly because they are dynamic, which means that they can grow or shrink after creation if needed. Additionally, any changes you make to a slice inside a function also affect the original slice. But how does this happen? Strictly speaking, *all parameters in Go are passed by value*—there is no other way to pass parameters in Go.

In reality, a slice value is a *header* that contains **a pointer to an underlying array** where the elements are actually stored, the length of the array, and its capacity—the capacity of a slice is explained in the next subsection. Note that the slice value does not include its elements, just a pointer to the underlying array. So, when you pass a slice to a function, Go makes a copy of that header and passes it to the function. This copy of the slice header includes the pointer to the underlying array. That slice header is defined in the `reflect` package (`https://golang.org/pkg/reflect/#SliceHeader`) as follows:

```
type SliceHeader struct {
    Data uintptr
    Len  int
    Cap  int
}
```

A side effect of passing the slice header is that it is faster to pass a slice to a function because Go does not need to make a copy of the slice and its elements, just the slice header.

You can create a slice using `make()` or like an array without specifying its size or using `[...]`. If you do not want to initialize a slice, then using `make()` is better and faster. However, if you want to initialize it at the time of creation, then `make()` cannot help you. As a result, you can create a slice with three `float64` elements as `aSlice := []float64{1.2, 3.2, -4.5}`. Creating a slice with space for three `float64` elements with `make()` is as simple as executing `make([]float64, 3)`. Each element of that slice has a value of `0`, which is the zero value of the `float64` data type.

Both slices and arrays can have many dimensions—creating a slice with two dimensions with `make()` is as simple as writing `make([][]int, 2)`. This returns a slice with two dimensions where the first dimension is `2` (rows) and the second dimension (columns) is unspecified and should be **explicitly specified** when adding data to it.

If you want to define and initialize a slice with two dimensions at the same time, you should execute something similar to `twoD := [][]int{{1, 2, 3}, {4, 5, 6}}`.

You can find the length of an array or a slice using `len()`. As you will find out in the next subsection, slices have an additional property named *capacity*. You can add new elements to a full slice using the `append()` function. `append()` automatically allocates the required memory space.

The example that follows clarifies many things about slices—feel free to experiment with it. Type the following code and save it as `goSlices.go`.

```
package main

import "fmt"

func main() {
    // Create an empty slice
    aSlice := []float64{}
    // Both length and capacity are 0 because aSlice is empty
    fmt.Println(aSlice, len(aSlice), cap(aSlice))

    // Add elements to a slice
    aSlice = append(aSlice, 1234.56)
    aSlice = append(aSlice, -34.0)
    fmt.Println(aSlice, "with length", len(aSlice))
```

The `append()` commands add two new elements to `aSlice`. You should save the return value of `append()` to an existing variable or a new one.

```
    // A slice with length 4
    t := make([]int, 4)
    t[0] = -1
    t[1] = -2
    t[2] = -3
    t[3] = -4
    // Now you will need to use append
    t = append(t, -5)
    fmt.Println(t)
```

Once a slice has no place left for more elements, you should add new elements to it using `append()`.

```
    // A 2D slice
    // You can have as many dimensions as needed
    twoD := [][]int{{1, 2, 3}, {4, 5, 6}}
```

```
    // Visiting all elements of a 2D slice
    // with a double for loop
    for _, i := range twoD {
            for _, k := range i {
                fmt.Print(k, " ")
            }
            fmt.Println()
    }
```

The previous code shows how to create a 2D slice variable named `twoD` and initialize it at the same time.

```
    make2D := make([][]int, 2)
    fmt.Println(make2D)
    make2D[0] = []int{1, 2, 3, 4}
    make2D[1] = []int{-1, -2, -3, -4}
    fmt.Println(make2D)
}
```

The previous part shows how to create a 2D slice with `make()`. What makes the `make2D` a 2D slice is the use of `[][]int` in `make()`.

Running `goSlices.go` produces the next output:

```
$ go run goSlices.go
[] 0 0
[1234.56 -34] with length 2
[-1 -2 -3 -4 -5]
1 2 3
4 5 6
[[] []]
[[1 2 3 4] [-1 -2 -3 -4]]
```

About slice length and capacity

Both arrays and slices support the `len()` function for finding out their length. However, slices also have an additional property called **capacity** that can be found using the `cap()` function.

> The capacity of a slice is really important when you want to select a part of a slice or when you want to reference an array using a slice. Both subjects will be discussed over the next few sections.

The capacity shows how much a slice can be expanded without the need to allocate more memory and change the underlying array. Although after slice creation the capacity of a slice is handled by Go, a developer can define the capacity of a slice at creation time using the `make()` function—after that the capacity of the slice doubles each time the length of the slice is about to become bigger than its current capacity. The first argument of `make()` is the type of the slice and its dimensions, the second is its initial length and the third, which is optional, is the capacity of the slice. Although the data type of a slice cannot change after creation, the other two properties can change.

> Writing something like `make([]int, 3, 2)` generates an error message because at any given time the capacity of a slice (2) cannot be smaller than its length (3).

But what happens when you want to append a slice or an array to an existing slice? Should you do that element by element? Go supports the `...` operator, which is used for exploding a slice or an array into multiple arguments before appending it to an existing slice.

The figure that follows illustrates with a graphical representation how length and capacity work in slices.

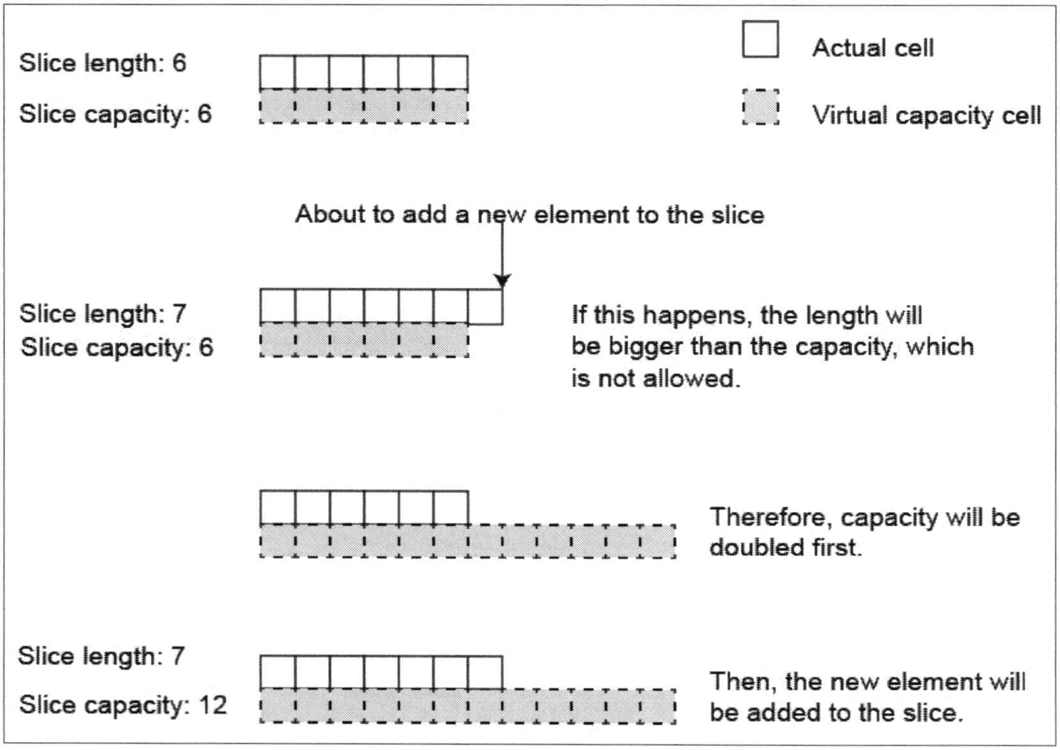

Figure 2.1: How slice length and capacity are related

For those of you that prefer code, here is a small Go program that showcases the length and capacity properties of slices. Type it and save it as `capLen.go`.

```
package main

import "fmt"

func main() {
    // Only length is defined. Capacity = length
    a := make([]int, 4)
```

In this case, the capacity of a is the same as its length, which is 4.

```
    fmt.Println("L:", len(a), "C:", cap(a))
    // Initialize slice. Capacity = Length
    b := []int{0, 1, 2, 3, 4}
    fmt.Println("L:", len(b), "C:", cap(b))
```

Once again, the capacity of slice b is the same as its length, which is 5.

```
    // Same length and capacity
    aSlice := make([]int, 4, 4)
    fmt.Println(aSlice)
```

This time the capacity of slice aSlice is the same as its length, not because Go decided to do so but because we specified it.

```
    // Add an element
    aSlice = append(aSlice, 5)
```

When you add a new element to slice aSlice, its capacity is doubled and becomes 8.

```
    fmt.Println(aSlice)
    // The capacity is doubled
    fmt.Println("L:", len(aSlice), "C:", cap(aSlice))
    // Now add four elements
    aSlice = append(aSlice, []int{-1, -2, -3, -4}...)
```

The ... operator expands []int{-1, -2, -3, -4} into multiple arguments and append() appends each argument one by one to aSlice.

```
    fmt.Println(aSlice)
    // The capacity is doubled
    fmt.Println("L:", len(aSlice), "C:", cap(aSlice))
}
```

Running capLen.go produces the next output:

```
$ go run capLen.go
L: 4 C: 4
L: 5 C: 5
[0 0 0 0]
```

```
[0 0 0 0 5]
L: 5 C: 8
[0 0 0 0 5 -1 -2 -3 -4]
L: 9 C: 16
```

> Setting the correct capacity of a slice, if known in advance, will make your programs faster because Go will not have to allocate a new underlying array and have all the data copied over.

Working with slices is good but what happens when you want to work with a continuous part of an existing slice? Is there a practical way to select a part of a slice? Fortunately, the answer is yes—the next subsection sheds some light on selecting a *continuous part* of a slice.

Selecting a part of a slice

Go allows you to select parts of a slice, provided that all desired elements are next to each other. This can be pretty handy when you select a range of elements and you do not want to give their indexes one by one. In Go you select a part of a slice by defining two indexes, the first one is the beginning of the selection whereas the second one is the end of the selection, without including the element at that index, separated by `:`.

> If you want to process all the command-line arguments of a utility apart from the first one, which is its name, you can assign it to a new variable (`arguments := os.Args`) for ease of use and use the `arguments[1:]` notation to skip the first command-line argument.

However, there is a variation where you can add a third parameter that controls the capacity of the resulting slice. So, using `aSlice[0:2:4]` selects the first 2 elements of a slice (at indexes `0` and `1`) and creates a new slice with a maximum capacity of `4`. The resulting capacity is defined as the result of the `4-0` subtraction where `4` is the maximum capacity and `0` is the first index—if the first index is omitted, it is automatically set to `0`. In this case, the capacity of the result slice will be `4` because `4-0` equals `4`.

If we would have used `aSlice[2:4:4]`, we would have created a new slice with the `aSlice[2]` and `aSlice[3]` elements and with a capacity of `4-2`. Lastly, **the resulting capacity cannot be bigger** than the capacity of the original slice because in that case, you would need a different underlying array.

Type the following code using your favorite editor and save it as `partSlice.go`.

```
package main
import "fmt"

func main() {
    aSlice := []int{0, 1, 2, 3, 4, 5, 6, 7, 8, 9}
    fmt.Println(aSlice)
    l := len(aSlice)

    // First 5 elements
    fmt.Println(aSlice[0:5])
    // First 5 elements
    fmt.Println(aSlice[:5])
```

In this first part, we define a new slice named `aSlice` that has 10 elements. Its capacity is the same as its length. Both `0:5` and `:5` notations select the first 5 elements of the slice, which are the elements found at indexes `0`, `1`, `2`, `3`, and `4`.

```
    // Last 2 elements
    fmt.Println(aSlice[l-2 : l])
    // Last 2 elements
    fmt.Println(aSlice[l-2:])
```

Given the length of the slice (`l`), we can select the last two elements of the slice either as `l-2 : l` or as `l-2:`.

```
    // First 5 elements
    t := aSlice[0:5:10]
    fmt.Println(len(t), cap(t))
    // Elements at indexes 2,3,4
    // Capacity will be 10-2
    t = aSlice[2:5:10]
    fmt.Println(len(t), cap(t))
```

Initially, the capacity of `t` will be `10-0`, which is `10`. In the second case, the capacity of `t` will be `10-2`.

```
    // Elements at indexes 0,1,2,3,4
    // New capacity will be 6-0
    t = aSlice[:5:6]
    fmt.Println(len(t), cap(t))
}
```

The capacity of `t` is now `6-0` and its length is going to be `5` because we have selected the first 5 elements of slice `aSlice`.

Running `partSlice.go` generates the next output:

```
$ go run partSlice.go
[0 1 2 3 4 5 6 7 8 9]
```

The previous line is the output of `fmt.Println(aSlice)`.

```
[0 1 2 3 4]
[0 1 2 3 4]
```

The previous two lines are generated from `fmt.Println(aSlice[0:5])` and `fmt.Println(aSlice[:5])`.

```
[8 9]
[8 9]
```

Analogously, the previous two lines are generated from `fmt.Println(aSlice[l-2 : l])` and `fmt.Println(aSlice[l-2:])`.

```
5 10
3 8
5 6
```

The last three lines print the length and the capacity of `aSlice[0:5:10]`, `aSlice[2:5:10]` and `aSlice[:5:6]`.

Byte slices

A **byte slice** is a slice of the `byte` data type (`[]byte`). Go knows that most `byte` slices are used to store strings and so makes it easy to switch between this type and the `string` type. There is nothing special in the way you can access a byte slice compared to the other types of slices. What is special is that Go uses *byte slices* for performing file I/O operations because they allow you to determine with precision the amount of data you want to read or write to a file. This happens because bytes are a universal unit among computer systems.

> As Go does not have a `char` data type, it uses `byte` and `rune` for storing character values. A single `byte` can only store a single ASCII character whereas a `rune` can store Unicode characters. However, a rune can occupy multiple bytes.

The small program that follows illustrates how you can convert a `byte` slice into a `string` and vice versa, which you need for most File I/O operations—type it and save it as `byteSlices.go`.

```
package main

import "fmt"

func main() {
    // Byte slice
    b := make([]byte, 12)
    fmt.Println("Byte slice:", b)
```

An empty byte slice contains zeros—in this case, 12 zeros.

```
    b = []byte("Byte slice €")
    fmt.Println("Byte slice:", b)
```

In this case, the size of `b` is the size of the string `"Byte slice €"`, without the double quotes—`b` now points to a different memory location than before, which is where `"Byte slice €"` is stored. This is how you convert a `string` into a `byte` slice.

As Unicode characters like € need more than one byte for their representation, the length of the `byte` slice might not be the same as the length of the string that it stores.

```
    // Print byte slice contents as text
    fmt.Printf("Byte slice as text: %s\n", b)
    fmt.Println("Byte slice as text:", string(b))
```

The previous code shows how to print the contents of a byte slice as text using two techniques. The first one is by using the `%s` control string and the second one using `string()`.

```
    // Length of b
    fmt.Println("Length of b:", len(b))
}
```

The previous code prints the real length of the byte slice.

Running `byteSlices.go` produces the next output:

```
$ go run byteSlices.go
Byte slice: [0 0 0 0 0 0 0 0 0 0 0 0]
Byte slice: [66 121 116 101 32 115 108 105 99 101 32 226 130 172]
Byte slice as text: Byte slice €
Byte slice as text: Byte slice €
Length of b: 14
```

The last line of the output proves that although the `b` byte slice has 12 characters, it has a size of `14`.

Deleting an element from a slice

There is no default function for deleting an element from a slice, which means that if you need to delete an element from a slice, you must write your own code. Deleting an element from a slice can be tricky, so this subsection presents two techniques for doing so. The first technique virtually divides the original slice into two slices, split at the index of the element that needs to be deleted. Neither of the two slices includes the element that is going to be deleted. After that, we concatenate these two slices and creates a new one. The second technique copies the last element at the place of the element that is going to be deleted and creates a new slice by excluding the last element from the original slice.

The next figure shows a graphical representation of the two techniques for deleting an element from a slice.

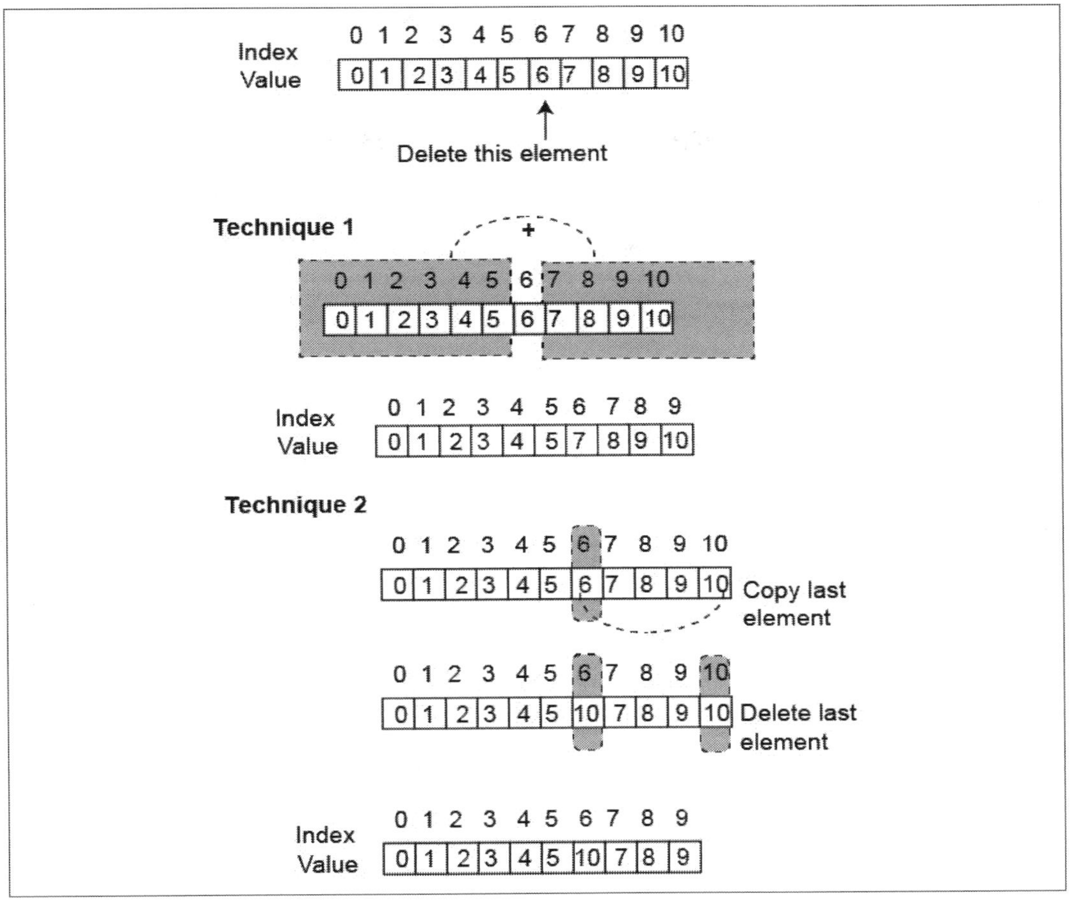

Figure 2.2: Deleting an element from a slice

The following program shows the two techniques that can be used for deleting an element from a slice. Create a text file by typing the following code—save it as `deleteSlice.go`.

```
package main

import (
    "fmt"
    "os"
    "strconv"
)

func main() {
    arguments := os.Args
    if len(arguments) == 1 {
        fmt.Println("Need an integer value.")
        return
    }

    index := arguments[1]
    i, err := strconv.Atoi(index)
    if err != nil {
        fmt.Println(err)
        return
    }
    fmt.Println("Using index", i)

    aSlice := []int{0, 1, 2, 3, 4, 5, 6, 7, 8}
    fmt.Println("Original slice:", aSlice)

    // Delete element at index i
    if i > len(aSlice)-1 {
        fmt.Println("Cannot delete element", i)
        return
    }

    // The ... operator auto expands aSlice[i+1:] so that
    // its elements can be appended to aSlice[:i] one by one
    aSlice = append(aSlice[:i], aSlice[i+1:]...)
    fmt.Println("After 1st deletion:", aSlice)
```

Here we logically divide the original slice into two slices. The two slices are split at the index of the element that needs to be deleted. After that, we concatenate these two slices with the help of `...`. Next, we see the second technique in action.

```
    // Delete element at index i
    if i > len(aSlice)-1 {
        fmt.Println("Cannot delete element", i)
        return
    }

    // Replace element at index i with last element
    aSlice[i] = aSlice[len(aSlice)-1]
    // Remove last element
    aSlice = aSlice[:len(aSlice)-1]
    fmt.Println("After 2nd deletion:", aSlice)
}
```

We replace the element that we want to delete with the last element using the `aSlice[i] = aSlice[len(aSlice)-1]` statement and then we remove the last element with the `aSlice = aSlice[:len(aSlice)-1]` statement.

Running `deleteSlice.go` produces the following kind of output, depending on your input:

```
$ go run deleteSlice.go 1
Using index 1
Original slice: [0 1 2 3 4 5 6 7 8]
After 1st deletion: [0 2 3 4 5 6 7 8]
After 2nd deletion: [0 8 3 4 5 6 7]
```

As the slice has 9 elements, you can delete the element at index value `1`.

```
$ go run deleteSlice.go 10
Using index 10
Original slice: [0 1 2 3 4 5 6 7 8]
Cannot delete element 10
```

As the slice has only 9 elements, you cannot delete an element with an index value of `10` from the slice.

How slices are connected to arrays

As mentioned before, behind the scenes, each slice is implemented using an **underlying array**. The length of the underlying array is the same as the capacity of the slice and there exist pointers that connect the slice elements to the appropriate array elements.

You can understand that by connecting an existing array with a slice, Go allows you to reference an array or a part of an array using a slice. This has some strange capabilities including the fact that the changes to the slice affect the referenced array! However, when the capacity of the slice changes, the connection to the array ceases to exist! This happens because when the capacity of a slice changes, so does the underlying array, and the connection between the slice and the original array does not exist anymore.

Type the following code and save it as `sliceArrays.go`.

```
package main

import (
	"fmt"
)

func change(s []string) {
	s[0] = "Change_function"
}
```

This is a function that changes the first element of a slice.

```
func main() {
	a := [4]string{"Zero", "One", "Two", "Three"}
	fmt.Println("a:", a)
```

Here we define an array named a with 4 elements.

```
	var S0 = a[0:1]
	fmt.Println(S0)
	S0[0] = "S0"
```

Here we connect `S0` with the first element of the array a and we print it. Then we change the value of `S0[0]`.

```
	var S12 = a[1:3]
	fmt.Println(S12)
```

```
S12[0] = "S12_0"
S12[1] = "S12_1"
```

In this part, we associate `S12` with `a[1]` and `a[2]`. Therefore `S12[0]` = `a[1]` and `S12[1]` = `a[2]`. Then, we change the values of both `S12[0]` and `S12[1]`. These two changes will also change the contents of a. Put simply, `a[1]` takes the new value of `S12[0]` and `a[2]` takes the new value of `S12[1]`.

```
fmt.Println("a:", a)
```

And we print variable a, which has not changed at all in a direct way. However, due to the connections of a with `S0` and `S12`, the contents of a have changed!

```
// Changes to slice -> changes to array
change(S12)
fmt.Println("a:", a)
```

As the slice and the array are connected, any changes you make to the slice will also affect the array even if the changes take place inside a function.

```
// capacity of S0
fmt.Println("Capacity of S0:", cap(S0), "Length of S0:", len(S0))

// Adding 4 elements to S0
S0 = append(S0, "N1")
S0 = append(S0, "N2")
S0 = append(S0, "N3")
a[0] = "-N1"
```

As the capacity of `S0` changes, it is no longer connected to the same underlying array (a).

```
// Changing the capacity of S0
// Not the same underlying array anymore!
S0 = append(S0, "N4")

fmt.Println("Capacity of S0:", cap(S0), "Length of S0:", len(S0))
// This change does not go to S0
a[0] = "-N1-"

// This change does not go to S12
a[1] = "-N2-"
```

However, array a and slice S12 are still connected because the capacity of S12 has not changed.

```
    fmt.Println("S0:", S0)
    fmt.Println("a: ", a)
    fmt.Println("S12:", S12)
}
```

Lastly, we print the final versions of a, S0, and S12.

Running sliceArrays.go produces the following output:

```
$ go run sliceArrays.go
a: [Zero One Two Three]
[Zero]
[One Two]
a: [S0 S12_0 S12_1 Three]
a: [S0 Change_function S12_1 Three]
Capacity of S0: 4 Length of S0: 1
Capacity of S0: 8 Length of S0: 5
S0: [-N1 N1 N2 N3 N4]
a:  [-N1- -N2- N2 N3]
S12: [-N2- N2]
```

Let us now discuss the use of the copy() function in the next subsection.

The copy() function

Go offers the copy() function for copying an existing array to a slice or an existing slice to another slice. However, the use of copy() can be tricky because the destination slice is not auto-expanded if the source slice is bigger than the destination slice. Additionally, if the destination slice is bigger than the source slice, then copy() does not empty the elements from the destination slice that did not get copied. This is better illustrated in the figure that follows.

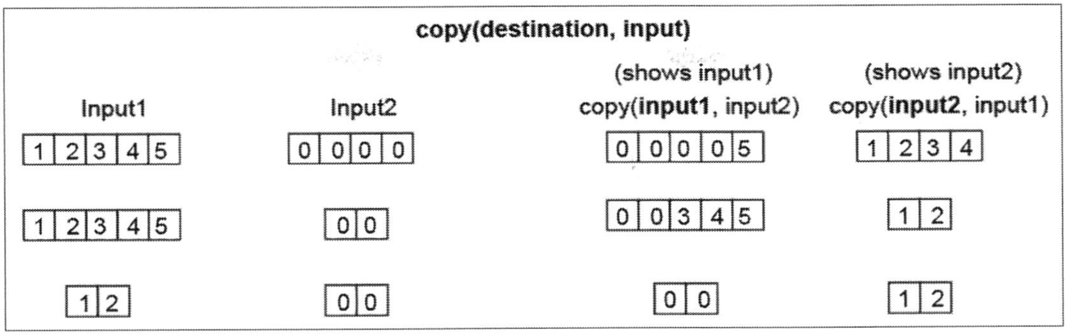

Figure 2.3: The use of the copy() function

The following program illustrates the use of `copy()`—type it in your favorite text editor and save it as `copySlice.go`.

```
package main

import "fmt"

func main() {
    a1 := []int{1}
    a2 := []int{-1, -2}
    a5 := []int{10, 11, 12, 13, 14}
    fmt.Println("a1", a1)
    fmt.Println("a2", a2)
    fmt.Println("a5", a5)
    // copy(destination, input)
    // len(a2) > len(a1)
    copy(a1, a2)
    fmt.Println("a1", a1)
    fmt.Println("a2", a2)
```

Here we run the `copy(a1, a2)` command. In this case, the `a2` slice is bigger than `a1`. After `copy(a1, a2)`, `a2` remains the same, which makes perfect sense as `a2` is the input slice, whereas the first element of `a2` is copied to the first element of `a1` because `a1` has space for a single element only.

```
    // len(a5) > len(a1)
    copy(a1, a5)
    fmt.Println("a1", a1)
    fmt.Println("a5", a5)
```

In this case, a5 is bigger than a1. Once again, after copy(a1, a5), a5 remains the same whereas a5[0] is copied to a1[0].

```
    // len(a2) < len(a5) -> OK
    copy(a5, a2)
    fmt.Println("a2", a2)
    fmt.Println("a5", a5)
}
```

In this last case, a2 is shorter than a5. This means that the entire a2 is copied into a5. As the length of a2 is 2, only the first 2 elements of a5 change.

Running copySlice.go produces the next output:

```
$ go run copySlice.go
a1 [1]
a2 [-1 -2]
a5 [10 11 12 13 14]
a1 [-1]
a2 [-1 -2]
```

The copy(a1, a2) statement does not alter the a2 slice, just a1. As the size of a1 is 1, only the first element from a2 is copied.

```
a1 [10]
a5 [10 11 12 13 14]
```

Similarly, copy(a1, a5) alters a1 only. As the size of a1 is 1, only the first element from a5 is copied to a1.

```
a2 [-1 -2]
a5 [-1 -2 12 13 14]
```

Last, copy(a5, a2) alters a5 only. As the size of a5 is 5, only the first two elements from a5 are altered and become the same as the first two elements of a2, which has a size of 2.

Sorting slices

There are times when you want to present your information sorted and you want Go to do the job for you. In this subsection, we'll see how to sort slices of various standard data types using the functionality offered by the sort package.

The `sort` package can sort slices of built-in data types without the need to write any extra code. Additionally, Go provides the `sort.Reverse()` function for sorting in the reverse order than the default. However, what is really interesting is that `sort` allows you to write your own sorting functions for custom data types by implementing the `sort.Interface` interface—you will learn more about the `sort.Interface` interface and interfaces in general in *Chapter 4, Reflection and Interfaces*.

So, you can sort a slice of integers saved as `sInts` by typing `sort.Ints(sInts)`. When sorting a slice of integers in reverse order using `sort.Reverse()`, you need to pass the desired slice to `sort.Reverse()` using `sort.IntSlice(sInts)` because the `IntSlice` type implements the `sort.Interface` internally, which allows you to sort in a different way than usual. The same applies to the other standard Go data types.

Create a text file with the code that illustrates the use of `sort` and name it `sortSlice.go`.

```
package main

import (
    "fmt"
    "sort"
)

func main() {
    sInts := []int{1, 0, 2, -3, 4, -20}
    sFloats := []float64{1.0, 0.2, 0.22, -3, 4.1, -0.1}
    sStrings := []string{"aa", "a", "A", "Aa", "aab", "AAa"}

    fmt.Println("sInts original:", sInts)
    sort.Ints(sInts)
    fmt.Println("sInts:", sInts)
    sort.Sort(sort.Reverse(sort.IntSlice(sInts)))
    fmt.Println("Reverse:", sInts)
```

As `sort.Interface` knows how to sort integers, it is trivial to sort them in reverse order. Sorting in reverse order is as simple as calling the `sort.Reverse()` function.

```
    fmt.Println("sFloats original:", sFloats)
    sort.Float64s(sFloats)
    fmt.Println("sFloats:", sFloats)
    sort.Sort(sort.Reverse(sort.Float64Slice(sFloats)))
    fmt.Println("Reverse:", sFloats)
```

```
    fmt.Println("sStrings original:", sStrings)
    sort.Strings(sStrings)
    fmt.Println("sStrings:", sStrings)
    sort.Sort(sort.Reverse(sort.StringSlice(sStrings)))
    fmt.Println("Reverse:", sStrings)
}
```

The same rules apply when sorting floating point numbers and strings.

Running `sortSlice.go` produces the next output:

```
$ go run sortSlice.go
sInts original: [1 0 2 -3 4 -20]
sInts: [-20 -3 0 1 2 4]
Reverse: [4 2 1 0 -3 -20]
sFloats original: [1 0.2 0.22 -3 4.1 -0.1]
sFloats: [-3 -0.1 0.2 0.22 1 4.1]
Reverse: [4.1 1 0.22 0.2 -0.1 -3]
sStrings original: [aa a A Aa aab AAa]
sStrings: [A AAa Aa a aa aab]
Reverse: [aab aa a Aa AAa A]
```

The output illustrates how the original slices were sorted in both normal and reverse order.

Pointers

Go has support for pointers but not for pointer arithmetic, which is the cause of many bugs and errors in programming languages like C. A **pointer** is the memory address of a variable. You need to **dereference** a pointer in order to get its value—dereferencing is performed using the * character in front of the pointer variable. Additionally, you can get the memory address of a normal variable using an `&` in front of it.

The next diagram shows the difference between a pointer to an `int` and an `int` variable.

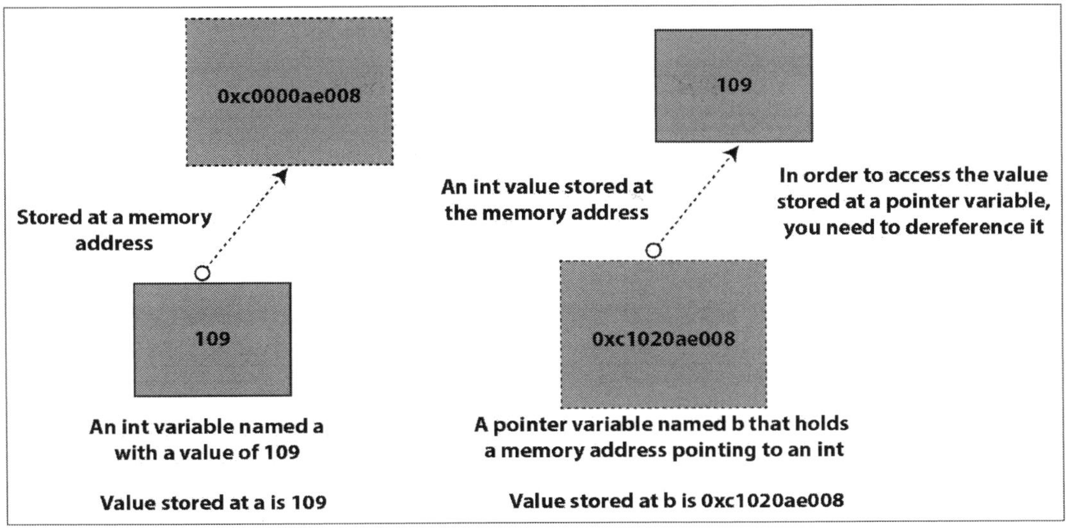

Figure 2.4: An int variable and a pointer to an int

If a pointer variable points to an existing regular variable, then any changes you make to the stored value using the pointer variable will modify the regular variable.

> The format and the values of memory addresses might be different between different machines, different operating systems, and different architectures.

You might ask, what is the point of using pointers since there is no support for pointer arithmetic. The main benefit you get from pointers is that passing a variable to a function as a pointer (we can call that *by reference*) does not discard any changes you make to the value of that variable inside that function when the function returns. There exist times where you want that functionality because it simplifies your code, but the price you pay for that simplicity is being extra careful with what you do with a pointer variable. Remember that slices are passed to functions without the need to use a pointer—it is Go that passes the pointer to the underlying array of a slice and there is no way to change that behavior.

Apart from reasons of simplicity, there exist three more reasons for using pointers:

- Pointers allow you to share data between functions. However, when sharing data between functions and goroutines, you should be extra careful with race condition issues.
- Pointers are also very handy when you want to tell the difference between the zero value of a variable and a value that is not set (`nil`). This is particularly useful with structures because pointers (and therefore **pointers to structures**, which are fully covered in the next chapter), can have the `nil` value, which means that you can compare a pointer to a structure with the `nil` value, which is not allowed for normal structure variables.
- Having support for pointers and, more specifically, pointers to structures allows Go to support data structures such as linked lists and binary trees, which are widely used in computer science. Therefore, you are allowed to define a structure field of a `Node` structure as `Next *Node`, which is a pointer to another `Node` structure. Without pointers, this would have been difficult to implement and may be too slow.

The following code illustrates how you can use pointers in Go—create a text file named `pointers.go` and type the presented code.

```
package main

import "fmt"

type aStructure struct {
    field1 complex128
    field2 int
}
```

This is a structure with two fields named `field1` and `field2`.

```
func processPointer(x *float64) {
    *x = *x * *x
}
```

This is a function that gets a pointer to a `float64` variable as input. As we are using a pointer, all changes to the function parameter inside the function are persistent. Additionally, there is no need to return something.

```
func returnPointer(x float64) *float64 {
    temp := 2 * x
    return &temp
}
```

This is a function that requires a `float64` parameter as input and returns a pointer to a `float64`. In order to return the memory address of a regular variable, you need to use `&` (`&temp`).

```
func bothPointers(x *float64) *float64 {
    temp := 2 * *x
    return &temp
}
```

This is a function that requires a pointer to a `float64` as input and returns a pointer to a `float64` as output. The `*x` notation is used for getting the value stored in the memory address stored in `x`.

```
func main() {
    var f float64 = 12.123
    fmt.Println("Memory address of f:", &f)
```

To get the memory address of a regular variable named `f`, you should use the `&f` notation.

```
    // Pointer to f
    fP := &f
    fmt.Println("Memory address of f:", fP)
    fmt.Println("Value of f:", *fP)
    // The value of f changes
    processPointer(fP)
    fmt.Printf("Value of f: %.2f\n", f)
```

`fP` is now a pointer to the memory address of the `f` variable. Any changes to the value stored in the `fP` memory address have an effect on the `f` value as well. However, this is only true for as long as `fP` points to the memory address of the `f` variable.

```
    // The value of f does not change
    x := returnPointer(f)
    fmt.Printf("Value of x: %.2f\n", *x)
```

The value of `f` does not change because the function only uses its value.

```
    // The value of f does not change
    xx := bothPointers(fP)
    fmt.Printf("Value of xx: %.2f\n", *xx)
```

In this case, the value of `f`, as well as the value stored in the `fP` memory address, does not change because the `bothPointers()` function does not make any changes to the value stored in the `fP` memory address.

```
    // Check for empty structure
    var k *aStructure
```

The `k` variable is a pointer to an `aStructure` structure. As `k` points to nowhere, Go makes it point to `nil`, which is the **zero value for pointers**.

```
    // This is nil because currently k points to nowhere
    fmt.Println(k)
    // Therefore you are allowed to do this:
    if k == nil {
        k = new(aStructure)
    }
```

As `k` is `nil`, we are allowed to assign it to an empty `aStructure` value with `new(aStructure)` without losing any data. Now, `k` is no longer `nil` but both fields of `aStructure` have the zero values of their data types.

```
    fmt.Printf("%+v\n", k)
    if k != nil {
        fmt.Println("k is not nil!")
    }
}
```

Just make sure that `k` is not `nil`—you might consider that check redundant, but it does not hurt to double-check.

Running `pointers.go` generates the following kind of output:

```
Memory address of f: 0xc000014090
Memory address of f: 0xc000014090
Value of f: 12.123
Value of f: 146.97
Value of x: 293.93
Value of xx: 293.93
<nil>
&{field1:(0+0i) field2:0}
k is not nil!
```

We revisit pointers in the next chapter where we discuss structures. Next, we discuss generating random numbers and random strings.

Generating random numbers

Random number generation is an art as well as a research area in computer science. This is because computers are purely logical machines, and it turns out that using them to generate random numbers is extremely difficult! Go can help you with that using the functionality of the `math/rand` package. Each random number generator needs a **seed** to start producing numbers. The seed is used for initializing the entire process and is extremely important because if you always start with the same seed, you will always get the same sequence of pseudo-random numbers. This means that everybody can regenerate that sequence, and that particular sequence will not be random after all. However, this feature is really useful for testing purposes. In Go, the `rand.Seed()` function is used for initializing a random number generator.

> If you are really interested in random number generation, you should start by reading the second volume of *The Art of Computer Programming* by Donald E. Knuth (Addison-Wesley Professional, 2011).

The following function, which is part of `randomNumbers.go` found in `ch02` in the book's GitHub repository, is what generates random numbers in the `[min, max)` range.

```
func random(min, max int) int {
    return rand.Intn(max-min) + min
}
```

The `random()` function does all of the work, which is generating pseudo-random numbers in a given range from `min` to `max-1` by calling `rand.Intn()`. `rand.Intn()` generates non-negative random integers from `0` up to the value of its single parameter minus `1`.

The `randomNumbers.go` utility accepts four command-line parameters but can also work with fewer parameters by using default values. By default, `randomNumbers.go` produces 100 random integers from `0` up to and including `99`.

```
$ go run randomNumbers.go
Using default values!
39 75 78 89 39 28 37 96 93 42 60 69 50 9 69 27 22 63 4 68 56 23 54 14
93 61 19 13 83 72 87 29 4 45 75 53 41 76 84 51 62 68 37 11 83 20 63 58
12 50 8 31 14 87 13 97 17 60 51 56 21 68 32 41 79 13 79 59 95 56 24 83
53 62 97 88 67 59 49 65 79 10 51 73 48 58 48 27 30 88 19 16 16 11 35 45
72 51 41 28
```

In the next output, we define each of the parameters manually (the last parameter of the utility is the seed value):

```
$ go run randomNumbers.go 1 5 10 10
3 1 4 4 1 1 4 4 4 3
$ go run randomNumbers.go 1 5 10 10
3 1 4 4 1 1 4 4 4 3
$ go run randomNumbers.go 1 5 10 11
1 4 2 1 3 2 2 4 1 3
```

The first two times the seed value was `10`, so we got the same output. The third time the value of the seed was `11`, which generated a different output.

Generating random strings

Imagine that you want to generate random strings that can be used as difficult to guess passwords or for testing purposes. Based on random number generation, we create a utility that produces random strings. The utility is implemented as `genPass.go` and can be found in the `ch02` directory of the book's GitHub repository. The core functionality of `genPass.go` is found in the next function.

```
func getString(len int64) string {
    temp := ""
    startChar := "!"
    var i int64 = 1
    for {
        myRand := random(MIN, MAX)
        newChar := string(startChar[0] + byte(myRand))
        temp = temp + newChar
        if i == len {
            break
        }
        i++
    }
    return temp
}
```

As we only want to get printable ASCII characters, we limit the range of pseudo-random numbers that can be generated. The total number of printable characters in the ASCII table is 94. This means that the range of the pseudo-random numbers that the program can generate should be from 0 to 94, without including 94. Therefore, the values of the `MIN` and `MAX` global variables, which are not shown here, are `0` and `94`, respectively.

The `startChar` variable holds the first ASCII character that can be generated by the utility, which, in this case, is the exclamation mark, which has a decimal ASCII value of `33`. Given that the program can generate pseudo-random numbers up to `94`, the maximum ASCII value that can be generated is `93 + 33`, which is equal to `126`, which is the ASCII value of ~. All generated characters are kept in the `temp` variable, which is returned once the `for` loop exits. The `string(startChar[0] + byte(myRand))` statement converts the random integers into characters in the desired range.

The `genPass.go` utility accepts a single parameter, which is the length of the generated password. If no parameter is given, `genPass.go` produces a password with 8 characters, which is the default value of the `LENGTH` variable.

Running `genPass.go` produces the following kind of output:

```
$ go run genPass.go
Using default values...
!QrNq@;R
$ go run genPass.go 20
sZL>{F~"hQqY>r_>TX?O
```

The first program execution uses the default value for the length of the generated string whereas the second program execution creates a random string with 20 characters.

Generating secure random numbers

If you intend to use these pseudo-random numbers for security-related work, it is important that you use the `crypto/rand` package, which implements a cryptographically secure pseudo-random number generator. You do not need to define a seed when using the `crypto/rand` package.

The following function that is part of the `cryptoRand.go` source code showcases how secure random numbers are generated with the functionality of `crypto/rand`.

```
func generateBytes(n int64) ([]byte, error) {
    b := make([]byte, n)
    _, err := rand.Read(b)
    if err != nil {
        return nil, err
    }
    return b, nil
}
```

The `rand.Read()` function randomly generates numbers that occupy the entire `b` byte slice. You need to decode that byte slice using `base64.URLEncoding.EncodeToString(b)` in order to get a valid string without any control or unprintable characters. This conversion takes place in the `generatePass()` function, which is not shown here.

Running `cryptoRand.go` creates the following kind of output:

```
$ go run cryptoRand.go
Using default values!
Ce30g--D
$ go run cryptoRand.go 20
AEIePSYb13KwkDnO5Xk_
```

The output is not different from the one generated by `genPass.go`, it is just that the random numbers are generated more securely, which means that they can be used in applications where security is important.

Now that we know how to generate random numbers and random strings, we are going to revisit the phone book application and use these techniques to populate the phone book with random data.

Updating the phone book application

In this last section of the book, we are going to create a function that populates the phone book application from the previous chapter with random data, which is pretty handy when you want to put lots of data in an application for testing purposes.

> I have used this handy technique in the past in order to put sample data on Kafka topics.

The biggest change in this version of the phone book application is that the searching is based on the telephone number because it is easier to search random numbers instead of random strings. But this is a small code change in the `search()` function—this time `search()` uses `v.Tel == key` instead of `v.Surname == key` in order to try to match the `Tel` field.

The `populate()` function of `phoneBook.go` (as found in the `ch02` directory) does all the work—the implementation of `populate()` is the following.

```
func populate(n int, s []Entry) {
    for i := 0; i < n; i++ {
        name := getString(4)
        surname := getString(5)
        n := strconv.Itoa(random(100, 199))
        data = append(data, Entry{name, surname, n})
    }
}
```

The `getString()` function generates letters from `A` to `Z` and nothing else in order to make the generated strings more readable. There is no point in using special characters in names and surnames. The generated telephone numbers are in the 100 to 198 range, which is implemented using a call to `random(100, 199)`. The reason for this is that it is easier to search for a three-digit number. Feel free to experiment with the generated names, surnames, and telephone numbers.

Working with `phoneBook.go` generates the following kind of output:

```
$ go run phoneBook.go search 123
Data has 100 entries.
{BHVA QEEQL 123}
$ go run phoneBook.go search 1234
Data has 100 entries.
Entry not found: 1234
$ go run phoneBook.go list
Data has 100 entries.
{DGTB GNQKI 169}
{BQNU ZUQFP 120}
...
```

Although these randomly generated names and surnames are not perfect, they are more than enough for testing purposes. In the next chapter, we'll learn how to work with CSV data.

Exercises

- Create a function that concatenates two arrays into a new slice.
- Create a function that concatenates two arrays into a new array.
- Create a function that concatenates two slices into a new array.

Summary

In this chapter, we learned about the basic data types of Go, including numerical data types, strings, and errors. Additionally, we learned how to group similar values using arrays and slices. Lastly, we learned about the differences between arrays and slices and why slices are more versatile than arrays, as well as pointers and generating random numbers and strings in order to provide random data to the phone book application.

The next chapter discusses a couple of more complex composite data types of Go, *maps* and *structures*. Maps can use keys of different data types whereas structures can group multiple data types and create new ones that you can access as single entities. As you will see in later chapters, structures play a key role in Go.

Additional resources

- The `sort` package documentation: `https://golang.org/pkg/sort/`
- The `time` package documentation: `https://golang.org/pkg/time/`
- The `crypto/rand` package documentation: `https://golang.org/pkg/crypto/rand/`
- The `math/rand` package documentation: `https://golang.org/pkg/math/rand/`

3
Composite Data Types

Go offers support for maps and structures, which are composite data types and the main subject of this chapter. The reason that we present them separately from arrays and slices is that both maps and structures are more flexible and powerful than arrays and slices. The general idea is that if an array or a slice cannot do the job, you might need to look at maps. If a map cannot help you, then you should consider creating and using a structure.

You have already seen structures in *Chapter 1, A Quick Introduction to Go*, where we created the initial version of the phone book application. However, in this chapter we are going to learn more about structures as well as maps. This knowledge will allow us to read and save data in CSV format using structures and **create an index** for quickly searching a slice of structures, based on a given key, by using a map.

Last, we are going to apply some of these Go features to improve the phone book application we originally developed in *Chapter 1, A Quick Introduction to Go*. The new version of the phone book application loads and saves its data from disk, which means that it is no longer needed to hardcode your data.

This chapter covers:

- Maps
- Structures
- Pointers and structures
- Regular expressions and pattern matching
- Improving the phone book application

Maps can use keys of different data types whereas structures can group multiple data types and create new ones. So, without further ado, let us begin by presenting maps.

Maps

Both arrays and slices limit you to using positive integers as indexes. Maps are powerful data structures because they allow you to use indexes of various data types as keys to look up your data as long as these keys are **comparable**. A practical rule of thumb is that you should use a map when you are going to need indexes that are not positive integer numbers or when the integer indexes have big gaps.

> Although `bool` variables are comparable, it makes no sense to use a `bool` variable as the key to a Go map because it only allows for two distinct values. Additionally, although floating point values are comparable, precision issues caused by the internal representation of such values might create bugs and crashes, so you might want to avoid using floating point values as keys to Go maps.

You might ask, why do we need maps and what are their advantages? The following list will help clarify things:

- Maps are very versatile. Later in this chapter we will create a *database index* using a map, which allows us to search and access slice elements based on a given key or, in more advanced situations, a combination of keys.
- Although this is not always the case, working with maps in Go is fast, as you can access all elements of a map in **linear time**. Inserting and retrieving elements from a map is fast and does not depend on the cardinality of the map.
- Maps are easy to understand, which leads to clear designs.

You can create a new `map` variable using either `make()` or a map literal. Creating a new map with `string` keys and `int` values using `make()` is as simple as writing `make(map[string]int)` and assigning its return value to a variable. On the other hand, if you decide to create a map using a map literal, you need to write something like the following:

```
m := map[string]int {
    "key1": -1
    "key2": 123
}
```

The map literal version is faster when you want to add data to a map at the time of creation.

> You should make no assumptions about the order of the elements inside a map. Go randomizes keys when iterating over a map—this is done on purpose and is an intentional part of the language design.

You can find the length of a map, which is the number of keys in the map, using the `len()` function, which also works with arrays and slices; and you can delete a key and value pair from a map using the `delete()` function, which accepts two arguments: the name of the map and the name of the key, in that order.

Additionally, you can tell whether a key `k` exists on a map named `aMap` by the second return value of the `v, ok := aMap[k]` statement. If `ok` is set to `true`, then `k` exists, and its value is `v`. If it does not exist, `v` will be set to the zero value of its data type, which depends on the definition of the map. If you try to get the value of a key that does not exist in a map, Go will not complain about it and returns the zero value of the data type of the value.

Now, let us discuss a special case where a map variable has the `nil` value.

Storing to a nil map

You are allowed to assign a map variable to `nil`. In that case, you will not be able to use that variable until you assign it to a new map variable. Put simply, if you try to store data on a `nil` map, your program will crash. This is illustrated in the next bit of code, which is the implementation of the `main()` function of the `nilMap.go` source file that can be found in the `ch03` directory of the GitHub repository of this book.

```
func main() {
    aMap := map[string]int{}
    aMap["test"] = 1
```

This works because `aMap` points somewhere, which is the return value of `map[string]int{}`.

```
    fmt.Println("aMap:", aMap)
    aMap = nil
```

At this point aMap points to nil, which is a synonym for nothing.

```
    fmt.Println("aMap:", aMap)
    if aMap == nil {
        fmt.Println("nil map!")
        aMap = map[string]int{}
    }
```

Testing whether a map points to nil before using it is a good practice. In this case, if aMap == nil allows us to determine whether we can store a key/pair value to aMap or not—we cannot and if we try it, the program will crash. We correct that by issuing the aMap = map[string]int{} statement.

```
    aMap["test"] = 1
    // This will crash!
    aMap = nil
    aMap["test"] = 1
}
```

In this last part of the program, we illustrate how your program will crash if you try to store on a nil map—never use such code in production!

> In real-world applications, if a function accepts a map argument, then it should check that the map is not nil before working with it.

Running nilMap.go produces this output:

```
$ go run nilMap.go
aMap: map[test:1]
aMap: map[]
nil map!
panic: assignment to entry in nil map

goroutine 1 [running]:
main.main()
        /Users/mtsouk/Desktop/mGo3rd/code/ch03/nilMap.go:21 +0x225
```

The reason the program crashed is shown in the program output: panic: assignment to entry in nil map.

Iterating over maps

When `for` is combined with the `range` keyword it implements the functionality of `foreach` loops found in other programming languages and allows you to iterate over all the elements of a map without knowing its size or its keys. When `range` is applied on a map, it returns **key and value pairs** in that order.

Type the following code and save it as `forMaps.go`.

```
package main

import "fmt"

func main() {
	aMap := make(map[string]string)
	aMap["123"] = "456"
	aMap["key"] = "A value"

	// range works with maps as well
	for key, v := range aMap {
		fmt.Println("key:", key, "value:", v)
	}
```

In this case we use both the key and the value that returned from `range`.

```
	for _, v := range aMap {
		fmt.Print(" # ", v)
	}
	fmt.Println()
}
```

In this case, as we are only interested in the values returned by the map, we ignore the keys.

> As you already know, you should make no assumptions about the order that the key and value pairs of a map will be returned in from a `for` and `range` loop.

Running `forMaps.go` produces this output:

```
$ go run forMaps.go
key: key value: A value
key: 123 value: 456
 # 456 # A value
```

Having covered maps, it is time to learn about Go structures.

Structures

Structures in Go are both very powerful and very popular and are used for organizing and grouping various types of data under the same name. Structures are the more versatile data types in Go and they can even be associated with functions, which are called methods.

> Structures, as well as other user-defined data types, are usually defined outside the `main()` function or any other package function so that they have a global scope and are available to the entire Go package. Therefore, unless you want to make clear that a type is only useful within the current local scope and is not expected to be used elsewhere, you should write the definitions of new data types outside functions.

Defining new structures

When you define a new structure, you group a set of values into a single data type, which allows you to pass and receive this set of values as a single entity. A structure has **fields**, and each field has its own data type, which can even be another structure or slice of structures. Additionally, as a structure is a new data type, it is defined using the `type` keyword followed by the name of the structure and ending with the `struct` keyword, which signifies that we are defining a new structure.

The following code defines a new structure named `Entry`:

```
type Entry struct {
    Name    string
    Surname string
    Year    int
}
```

> The `type` keyword allows you to define new data types or create aliases for existing ones. Therefore, you are allowed to say `type myInt int` and define a new data type called `myInt` that is an alias for `int`. However, Go considers `myInt` and `int` as totally different data types that you cannot compare directly even though they hold the same kind of values. Each structure defines a new data type, hence the use of the `type` keyword.

For reasons that will become evident in *Chapter 5, Go Packages and Functions*, the fields of a structure usually begin with an uppercase letter—this depends on what you want to do with the fields. The `Entry` structure has three fields named `Name`, `Surname`, and `Year`. The first two fields are of the `string` data type, whereas the last field holds an `int` value.

These three fields can be accessed with the dot notation as `V.Name`, `V.Surname`, and `V.Year`, where `V` is the name of the variable holding the instance of the `Entry` structure. A **structure literal** named `p1` can be defined as `p1 := aStructure{"fmt", 12, -2}`.

There exist two ways to work with structure variables. The first one is as **regular variables** and the second one is as **pointer variables** that point to the memory address of a structure. Both ways are equally good and are usually embedded into separate functions because they allow you to initialize some or all of the fields of structure variables properly and/or do any other tasks you want before using the structure variable. As a result, there exist two main ways to create a new structure variable using a function. The first one returns a regular structure variable whereas the second one returns a pointer to a structure. Each one of these two ways has two variations. The first variation returns a structure instance that is initialized by the Go compiler, whereas the second variation returns a structure instance that is initialized by the user.

The order in which you put the fields in the definition of a structure type is significant for the **type identity** of the defined structure. Put simply, two structures with the same fields will not be considered identical in Go if their fields are not in the same order.

Using the new keyword

Additionally, you can create new structure instances using the `new()` keyword: `pS := new(Entry)`. The `new()` keyword has the following properties:

- It allocates the proper memory space, which depends on the data type, and then it zeroes it

- It always **returns a pointer** to the allocated memory
- It works for all data types except *channel* and *map*

All these techniques are illustrated in the code that follows. Type the following code in your favorite text editor and save it as `structures.go`.

```
package main

import "fmt"

type Entry struct {
	Name    string
	Surname string
	Year    int
}

// Initialized by Go
func zeroS() Entry {
	return Entry{}
}
```

Now is a good time to remind you of an important Go rule: **If no initial value is given to a variable, the Go compiler automatically initializes that variable to the zero value of its data type**. For structures, this means that a structure variable without an initial value is initialized to the zero values of each one of the data types of its fields. Therefore, the `zeroS()` function returns a zero-initialized `Entry` structure.

```
// Initialized by the user
func initS(N, S string, Y int) Entry {
	if Y < 2000 {
		return Entry{Name: N, Surname: S, Year: 2000}
	}
	return Entry{Name: N, Surname: S, Year: Y}
}
```

In this case the user initializes the new structure variable. Additionally, the `initS()` function checks whether the value of the `Year` field is smaller than `2000` and acts accordingly. If it is smaller than `2000`, then the value of the `Year` field becomes `2000`. This condition is specific to the requirements of the application you are developing—what this shows is that the place where you initialize a structure is good for checking your input.

```
// Initialized by Go - returns pointer
func zeroPtoS() *Entry {
    t := &Entry{}
    return t
}
```

The `zeroPtoS()` function returns a pointer to a zero-initialized structure.

```
// Initialized by the user - returns pointer
func initPtoS(N, S string, Y int) *Entry {
    if len(S) == 0 {
        return &Entry{Name: N, Surname: "Unknown", Year: Y}
    }
    return &Entry{Name: N, Surname: S, Year: Y}
}
```

The `initPtoS()` function also returns a pointer to a structure but also checks the length of the user input. Again, this checking is application-specific.

```
func main() {
    s1 := zeroS()
    p1 := zeroPtoS()
    fmt.Println("s1:", s1, "p1:", *p1)

    s2 := initS("Mihalis", "Tsoukalos", 2020)
    p2 := initPtoS("Mihalis", "Tsoukalos", 2020)
    fmt.Println("s2:", s2, "p2:", *p2)

    fmt.Println("Year:", s1.Year, s2.Year, p1.Year, p2.Year)

    pS := new(Entry)
    fmt.Println("pS:", pS)
}
```

The `new(Entry)` call returns a **pointer** to an `Entry` structure. Generally speaking, when you have to initialize lots of structure variables, it is considered a good practice to create a function for doing so as this is less error-prone.

Running `structures.go` creates the following output:

```
s1: {  0} p1: {  0}
s2: {Mihalis Tsoukalos 2020} p2: {Mihalis Tsoukalos 2020}
Year: 0 2020 0 2020
pS: &{  0}
```

As the zero value of a string is the empty string, `s1`, `p1`, and `pS` do not show any data for the `Name` and `Surname` fields.

The next subsection shows how to group structures of the same data type and use them as the elements of a slice.

Slices of structures

You can create slices of structures in order to group and handle multiple structures under a single variable name. However, accessing a field of a given structure requires knowing the exact place of the structure in the slice.

For now, have a look at the following figure to better understand how a slice of structures works and how you can access the fields of a specific slice element.

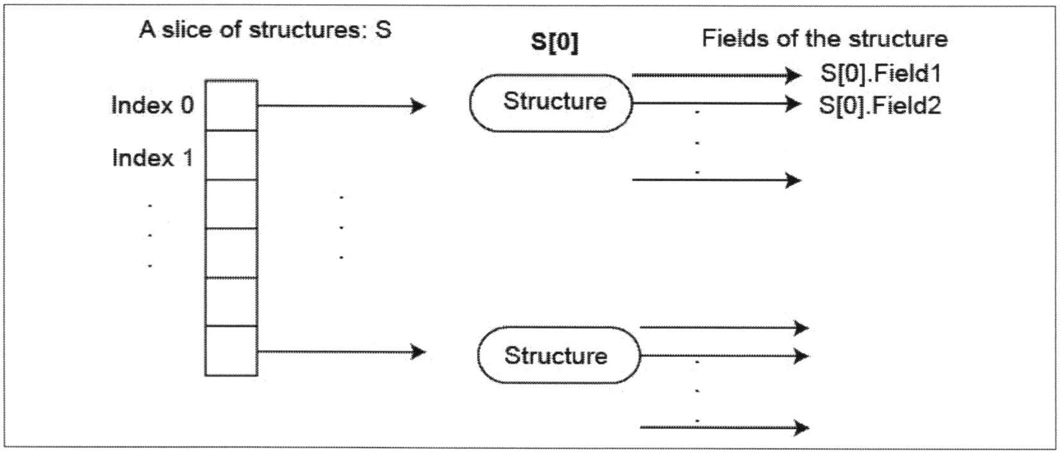

Figure 3.1: A slice of structures

So, each slice element is a structure that is accessed using a slice index. Once we select the slice element we want, we can select its field.

As the whole process can be a little perplexing, the code of this subsection sheds some light and clarifies things. Type the following code and save it as `sliceStruct.go`. You can also find it by the same name in the `ch03` directory in the GitHub repository of the book.

```
package main

import (
    "fmt"
    "strconv"
)

type record struct {
    Field1 int
    Field2 string
}

func main() {
    S := []record{}
    for i := 0; i < 10; i++ {
        text := "text" + strconv.Itoa(i)
        temp := record{Field1: i, Field2: text}
        S = append(S, temp)
    }
```

You still need `append()` to add a new structure to the slice.

```
    // Accessing the fields of the first element
    fmt.Println("Index 0:", S[0].Field1, S[0].Field2)
    fmt.Println("Number of structures:", len(S))
    sum := 0
    for _, k := range S {
        sum += k.Field1
    }
    fmt.Println("Sum:", sum)
}
```

Running `sliceStruct.go` produces the following output:

```
Index 0: 0 text0
Number of structures: 10
Sum: 45
```

We revisit structures in the next chapter where we discuss reflection, as well as *Chapter 6, Telling a UNIX System What to Do* where we learn how to work with JSON data using structures. For now, let us discuss regular expressions and pattern matching.

Regular expressions and pattern matching

Pattern matching is a technique for searching a string for some set of characters based on a specific search pattern that is based on regular expressions and grammars.

A **regular expression** is a sequence of characters that defines a search pattern. Every regular expression is compiled into a recognizer by building a generalized transition diagram called a **finite automaton**. A finite automaton can be either deterministic or nondeterministic. Nondeterministic means that more than one transition out of a state can be possible for the same input. A **recognizer** is a program that takes a string `x` as input and is able to tell whether `x` is a sentence of a given language.

A **grammar** is a set of production rules for strings in a formal language—the production rules describe how to create strings from the alphabet of the language that are valid according to the syntax of the language. A grammar does not describe the meaning of a string or what can be done with it in whatever context—it only describes its form. What is important here is to realize that grammars are at the heart of regular expressions because without a grammar, you cannot define or use a regular expression.

So, you might wonder why we're talking about regular expressions and pattern matching in this chapter. The reason is simple. In a while, you will learn how to store and read CSV data from plain text files, and you should be able to tell whether the data you are reading is valid or not.

About Go regular expressions

We begin this subsection by presenting some common *match patterns* used for constructing regular expressions.

Expression	Description
`.`	Matches any character
`*`	Means any number of times—cannot be used on its own
`?`	Zero or one time—cannot be used on its own
`+`	Means one or more times—cannot be used on its own
`^`	This denotes the beginning of the line
`^`	This denotes the end of the line
`[]`	`[]` is for grouping characters
`[A-Z]`	This means all characters from capital `A` to capital `Z`
`\d`	Any digit in `0-9`
`\D`	A non-digit
`\w`	Any word character: `[0-9A-Za-z_]`
`\W`	Any non-word character
`\s`	A whitespace character
`\S`	A non-whitespace character

The characters presented in the previous table are used for constructing and defining the grammar of the regular expression. The Go package responsible for defining regular expressions and performing pattern matching is called `regexp`. We use the `regexp.MustCompile()` function to create the regular expression and the `Match()` function to see whether the given string is a match or not.

The `regexp.MustCompile()` function parses the given regular expression and returns a `regexp.Regexp` variable that can be used for matching—`regexp.Regexp` is the representation of a **compiled regular expression**. The function panics if the expression cannot be parsed, which is good because you will know that your expression is invalid early in the process. The `re.Match()` method returns `true` if the given **byte slice** matches the `re` regular expression, which is a `regexp.Regexp` variable, and `false` otherwise.

> Creating separate functions for pattern matching can be handy because it allows you to reuse the functions without worrying about the context of the program.

Keep in mind that although regular expressions and pattern matching look convenient and handy at first, they are the root of lots of bugs. My advice is to use the simplest regular expression that can solve your problem. However, if you can avoid using regular expressions at all, it would be much better in the long run!

Matching names and surnames

The presented utility matches names and surnames, that is, strings that begin with an uppercase letter and continue with lowercase letters. The input should not contain any numbers or other characters.

The source code of the utility can be found in `nameSurRE.go`, which is located in the `ch03` directory. The function that supports the desired functionality is named `matchNameSur()` and is implemented as follows:

```
func matchNameSur(s string) bool {
    t := []byte(s)
    re := regexp.MustCompile(`^[A-Z][a-z]*$`)
    return re.Match(t)
}
```

The logic of the function is in the `` `^[A-Z][a-z]*$` `` regular expression, where `^` denotes the beginning of a line and `$` denotes the end of a line. What the regular expression does is match anything that begins with an uppercase letter (`[A-Z]`) and continues with any number of lowercase letters (`[a-z]*`). This means that `Z` is a match, but `ZA` is not a match because the second letter is uppercase. Similarly, `Jo+` is not a match because it contains a + character.

Running `nameSurRE.go` with various types of input produces the following output:

```
$ go run nameSurRE.go Z
true
$ go run nameSurRE.go ZA
false
$ go run nameSurRE.go Mihalis
True
```

This technique can help you check user input.

Matching integers

The presented utility matches both signed and unsigned integers—this is implemented in the way we define the regular expression. If we only want unsigned integers, then we should remove the `[-+]?` from the regular expression or replace it with `[+]?`.

The source code of the utility can be found in `intRE.go`, which is in the `ch03` directory. The `matchInt()` function that supports the desired functionality is implemented as follows:

```
func matchInt(s string) bool {
	t := []byte(s)
	re := regexp.MustCompile(`^[-+]?\d+$`)
	return re.Match(t)
}
```

As before, the logic of the function is found in the regular expression that is used for matching integers, which is `` `^[-+]?\d+$` ``. In plain English, what we say here is that we want to match something that begins with `-` or `+`, which is optional (`?`), and ends with any number of digits (`\d+`)—it is required that we have at least one digit before the end of the string that is examined (`$`).

Running `intRE.go` with various types of input produces the following output:

```
$ go run intRE.go 123
true
$ go run intRE.go /123
false
$ go run intRE.go +123.2
false
$ go run intRE.go +
false
$ go run intRE.go -123.2
false
```

Later in this book, you will learn how to test Go code by writing testing functions—for now, we will do most of the testing manually.

Matching the fields of a record

This example takes a different approach as we read an entire record and split it prior to doing any checking. Additionally, we make an extra check to make sure that the record we are processing contains the right number of fields. Each record should contain three fields: name, surname, and telephone number.

The full code of the utility can be found in `fieldsRE.go`, which is located in the `ch03` directory. The function that supports the desired functionality is implemented as follows:

```
func matchRecord(s string) bool {
    fields := strings.Split(s, ",")
    if len(fields) != 3 {
        return false
    }

    if !matchNameSur(fields[0]) {
        return false
    }

    if !matchNameSur(fields[1]) {
        return false
    }
    return matchTel(fields[2])
}
```

What the `matchRecord()` function does first is to separate the fields of the record based on the `,` character and then send each individual field to an appropriate function for further checking after making sure that the record has the right number of fields, which is a common practice. The field splitting is done using `strings.Split(s, ",")`, which returns a slice with as many elements as there are fields of the record.

If the checks of the first two fields are successful, then the function returns the return value of `matchTel(fields[2])` because it is that last check that determines the final result.

Running `fieldsRE.go` with various types of input produces the following output:

```
$ go run fieldsRE.go Name,Surname,2109416471
true
$ go run fieldsRE.go Name,Surname,OtherName
false
```

```
$ go run fieldsRE.go One,Two,Three,Four
false
```

The first record is correct and therefore the `true` value is returned, which is not true for the second running where the phone number field is not correct. The last one failed because it contains four fields instead of three.

Improving the phone book application

It is time to update the phone book application. The new version of the phone book utility has the following improvements:

- Support for the `insert` and `delete` commands
- Ability to read data from a file and write it before it exits
- Each entry has a last visited field that is updated
- Has a database index that is implemented using a Go map
- Uses regular expressions to verify the phone numbers read

Working with CSV files

Most of the time you do not want to lose your data or have to begin without any data every time you execute your application. There exist many techniques for doing so—the easiest one is by saving your data locally. A very easy to work with format is CSV, which is what is explained here and used in the phone book application later on. The good thing is that Go provides a dedicated package for working with CSV data named `encoding/csv` (`https://golang.org/pkg/encoding/csv/`). For the presented utility, both the input and output files are given as command-line arguments.

> There exist two very popular Go interfaces named `io.Reader` and `io.Write` that are to do with reading from files and writing to files. Almost all reading and writing operations in Go use these two interfaces. The use of the same interface for readers allows readers to share some common characteristics but most importantly allows you to **create your own readers** and use them anywhere that Go expects an `io.Reader` reader. The same applies to writers that satisfy the `io.Write` interface. You will learn more about interfaces in *Chapter 4, Reflection and Interfaces*.

The main tasks that need to be implemented are the following:

- Loading CSV data from disk and putting it into a slice of structures
- Saving data to disk using CSV format

The `encoding/csv` package contains functions that can help you read and write CSV files. As we are dealing with small CSV files, we use `csv.NewReader(f).ReadAll()` to read the entire input file all at once. For bigger data files or if we wanted to check the input or make any changes to the input as we read it, it would have been better to read it line by line using `Read()` instead of `ReadAll()`.

Go assumes that the CSV file uses the comma character (`,`) for separating the different fields of each line. Should we wish to change that behavior, we should change the value of the `Comma` variable of the CSV reader or the writer depending on the task we want to perform. We change that behavior in the output CSV file, which separates its fields using the tab character.

> For reasons of compatibility, it is better if the input and output CSV files are using the same field delimiter. We are just using the tab character as the field delimiter in the output file in order to illustrate the use of the `Comma` variable.

As working with CSV files is a new topic, there is a separate utility named `csvData.go` in the `ch03` directory of the GitHub repository of this book that illustrates the techniques for reading and writing CSV files. The source code of `csvData.go` is presented in chunks. First, we present the preamble of `csvData.go` that contains the `import` section as well as the `Record` structure and the `myData` global variable, which is a slice of `Record`.

```
package main

import (
    "encoding/csv"
    "fmt"
    "os"
)

type Record struct {
    Name       string
    Surname    string
    Number     string
```

```
    LastAccess string
}

var myData = []Record{}
```

Then we present the `readCSVFile()` function, which reads the plain text file with the CSV data.

```
func readCSVFile(filepath string) ([][]string, error) {
    _, err := os.Stat(filepath)
    if err != nil {
        return nil, err
    }

    f, err := os.Open(filepath)
    if err != nil {
        return nil, err
    }
    defer f.Close()

    // CSV file read all at once
    // lines data type is [][]string
    lines, err := csv.NewReader(f).ReadAll()
    if err != nil {
        return [][]string{}, err
    }

    return lines, nil
}
```

Note that we check whether the given file path exists and is associated with a regular file inside the function. There is no right or wrong decision about where to perform that checking—you just have to be consistent. The `readCSVFile()` function returns a `[][]string` slice that contains all the lines we have read. Additionally, have in mind that `csv.NewReader()` does separate the fields of each input line, which is the main reason for needing a slice with two dimensions to store the input.

After that, we illustrate the writing to a CSV file technique with the help of the `saveCSVFile()` function.

```
func saveCSVFile(filepath string) error {
    csvfile, err := os.Create(filepath)
    if err != nil {
```

```
        return err
    }
    defer csvfile.Close()

    csvwriter := csv.NewWriter(csvfile)
    // Changing the default field delimiter to tab
    csvwriter.Comma = '\t'
    for _, row := range myData {
        temp := []string{row.Name, row.Surname, row.Number, row.
LastAccess}
        _ = csvwriter.Write(temp)
    }
    csvwriter.Flush()
    return nil
}
```

Note that change in the default value of `csvwriter.Comma`.

Last, we can see the implementation of the `main()` function.

```
func main() {
    if len(os.Args) != 3 {
        fmt.Println("csvData input output!")
        return
    }

    input := os.Args[1]
    output := os.Args[2]
    lines, err := readCSVFile(input)
    if err != nil {
        fmt.Println(err)
        return
    }

    // CSV data is read in columns - each line is a slice
    for _, line := range lines {
        temp := Record{
            Name:       line[0],
            Surname:    line[1],
            Number:     line[2],
            LastAccess: line[3],
        }
        myData = append(myData, temp)
```

```
        fmt.Println(temp)

    }

    err = saveCSVFile(output)
    if err != nil {
        fmt.Println(err)
        return
    }
}
```

The `main()` function puts what you have read with `readCSVFile()` in the `myData` slice—remember that `lines` is a slice with two dimensions and that each row in `lines` is already separated into fields.

In this case, each line of input contains four fields. The contents of the CSV data file used as input are as follows:

```
$ cat ~/csv.data
Dimitris,Tsoukalos,2101112223,1600665563
Mihalis,Tsoukalos,2109416471,1600665563
Jane,Doe,0800123456,1608559903
```

Running `csvData.go` produces the following kind of output:

```
$ go run csvData.go ~/csv.data /tmp/output.data
{Dimitris Tsoukalos 2101112223 1600665563}
{Mihalis Tsoukalos 2109416471 1600665563}
{Jane Doe 0800123456 1608559903}
```

The contents of the output CSV file are the following:

```
$ cat /tmp/output.data
Dimitris	Tsoukalos	2101112223	1600665563
Mihalis	Tsoukalos	2109416471	1600665563
Jane	Doe	0800123456	1608559903
```

The `output.data` file uses tab characters for separating the different fields of each record. The `csvData.go` utility can be handy for converting between different types of CSV files.

Adding an index

This subsection explains how the database index is implemented with the help of a map. Indexing in databases is based on one or more keys that are unique. In practice, we index something that is unique and that we want to access quickly. In the database case, primary keys are unique by default and cannot be present in more than one record. In our case, phone numbers are used as primary keys, which means that the index is built based on the phone number field of the structure.

> As a rule of thumb, you index a field that is going to be used for searching. There is no point in creating an index that is not going to be used for querying.

Let us now see what this means in practice. Imagine that we have a slice named `S` with the following kind of data:

```
S[0]={0800123123, ...}
S[1]={0800123000, ...}
S[2]={2109416471, ...}
.
.
.
```

So, each slice element is a structure that can contain much more data apart from the telephone number. How can we create an index for it? The index, which is named `Index`, is going to have the following data and format:

```
Index["0800123123"] = 0
Index["0800123000"] = 1
Index["2109416471"] = 2
.
.
.
```

This means that if we want to look for the telephone number `0800123000`, we should see whether `0800123000` exists as a key in `Index`. If it is there, then we know that the value of `0800123000`, which is `Index["0800123000"]`, is the index of the slice element that contains the desired record. So, as we know which slice element to access, we do not have to search the entire slice. With that in mind, let us update the application.

The improved version of the phone book application

It would be a shame to create a phone book application that has its entries hardcoded in the code. This time, the entries of the address book are read from an external file that contains data in CSV format. Similarly, the new version saves its data into the same CSV file, which you can read afterward.

Each entry of the phone book application is based on the following structure:

```
type Entry struct {
	Name       string
	Surname    string
	Tel        string
	LastAccess string
}
```

The key to the entries is the `Tel` field and therefore its values. In practice, this means that if you try to add an entry that uses an existing `Tel` value, the process fails. This also means that the application searches the phone book using the `Tel` values. Databases use primary keys to identify between unique records—the phone book application has a small database implemented as a slice of `Entry` structures. Last, phone numbers are saved without any - characters in them. The utility removes all - characters from phone numbers, if there are any, before saving them.

> Personally, I prefer to explore the various parts of a bigger application by creating smaller programs that when combined implement some or all of the functionality of the bigger program. This helps me understand how the bigger application needs to be implemented. This makes it much easier for me to connect all the dots afterward and develop the final product.

As this is a real application implemented as a command-line utility, it should support commands for data manipulation and searching. The updated functionality of the utility is explained in the following list:

- Data insertion using the `insert` command
- Data deletion using the `delete` command
- Data searching using the `search` command
- Listing of the available records through the `list` command

To make the code simpler, the path of the CSV data file is hardcoded. Additionally, the CSV file is automatically read when the utility is executed but it is automatically updated when the `insert` and the `delete` commands are executed.

> Although Go supports CSV, **JSON** is a far more popular format that is used for data exchange in web services. However, working with CSV data is simpler than working with data in JSON format. Working with JSON data is explored in *Chapter 6, Telling a UNIX System What to Do.*

As explained earlier, this version of the phone book application has support for *indexing* to find the desired records faster without needing to make a linear search to the slice that holds your phone book data. The indexing technique that is used is not very fancy, but it makes searching really fast: provided that the searching process is based on phone numbers, we are going to create a map that associates each phone number with the index number of the record that contains that phone number in the slice of structures. This way, a simple and fast map lookup tells us whether a phone number already exists or not. If the phone number exists, we can access its record directly without having to search the entire slice of structures for it. The only downside of this technique, and every indexing technique, is that you must keep the map up to date all the time.

The previous process is called a high-level design of the application. For such a simple application, you do not have to be too analytic about the capabilities of the application—stating the supported commands and the location of the CSV data file is enough. However, for a RESTful server that implements a REST API, the design phase or the dependencies of the program are as important as the development phase itself.

The entire code of the updated phone book utility can be found in `ch03` as `phoneBook.go`—as always, we are referring to the GitHub repository of the book. This is the last time we make this clarification—from now on, we will only tell you the name of the source file unless there is a specific reason to do otherwise.

The most interesting parts of the `phoneBook.go` file are presented here, starting from the implementation of the `main()` function, which is presented in two parts. The first part is about getting a command to execute and having a valid CSV file to work with.

```
func main() {
    arguments := os.Args
    if len(arguments) == 1 {
```

```
        fmt.Println("Usage: insert|delete|search|list <arguments>")
        return
    }

    // If the CSVFILE does not exist, create an empty one
    _, err := os.Stat(CSVFILE)
    // If error is not nil, it means that the file does not exist
    if err != nil {
        fmt.Println("Creating", CSVFILE)
        f, err := os.Create(CSVFILE)
        if err != nil {
            f.Close()
            fmt.Println(err)
            return
        }
        f.Close()
    }
```

If the file path specified by the `CSVFILE` global variable does not already exist, we have to create it for the rest of the program to use it. This is determined by the return value of the `os.Stat(CSVFILE)` call.

```
    fileInfo, err := os.Stat(CSVFILE)
    // Is it a regular file?
    mode := fileInfo.Mode()
    if !mode.IsRegular() {
        fmt.Println(CSVFILE, "not a regular file!")
        return
    }
```

Not only must the `CSVFILE` exist but it should be a regular UNIX file, which is determined by the call to `mode.IsRegular()`. If it is not a regular file, the utility prints an error message and exits.

```
    err = readCSVFile(CSVFILE)
    if err != nil {
        fmt.Println(err)
        return
    }
```

This is the place where we read the `CSVFILE`, even if it is empty. The contents of `CSVFILE` are kept in the `data` global variable that is defined as `[]Entry{}`, which is a slice of `Entry` variables.

```
    err = createIndex()
    if err != nil {
        fmt.Println("Cannot create index.")
        return
    }
```

This is where we create the index by calling `createIndex()`. The index is kept in the `index` global variable that is defined as `map[string]int`.

The second part of `main()` is about running the right command and understanding whether the command was executed successfully or not.

```
    // Differentiating between the commands
    switch arguments[1] {
    case "insert":
        if len(arguments) != 5 {
            fmt.Println("Usage: insert Name Surname Telephone")
            return
        }
        t := strings.ReplaceAll(arguments[4], "-", "")
        if !matchTel(t) {
            fmt.Println("Not a valid telephone number:", t)
            return
        }
```

You need to remove any - characters from the telephone number before storing it using `strings.ReplaceAll()`. If there are not any - characters, then no substitution takes place.

```
        temp := initS(arguments[2], arguments[3], t)
        // If it was nil, there was an error
        if temp != nil {
            err := insert(temp)
            if err != nil {
                fmt.Println(err)
                return
            }
        }
    case "delete":
```

```
        if len(arguments) != 3 {
            fmt.Println("Usage: delete Number")
            return
        }
        t := strings.ReplaceAll(arguments[2], "-", "")
        if !matchTel(t) {
            fmt.Println("Not a valid telephone number:", t)
            return
        }
        err := deleteEntry(t)
        if err != nil {
            fmt.Println(err)
        }
    case "search":
        if len(arguments) != 3 {
            fmt.Println("Usage: search Number")
            return
        }
        t := strings.ReplaceAll(arguments[2], "-", "")
        if !matchTel(t) {
            fmt.Println("Not a valid telephone number:", t)
            return
        }
        temp := search(t)
        if temp == nil {
            fmt.Println("Number not found:", t)
            return
        }
        fmt.Println(*temp)
    case "list":
        list()
    default:
        fmt.Println("Not a valid option")
    }
}
```

In this relatively big `switch` block, we can see what is executed for each given command. So, we have the following:

- For the `insert` command, we execute the `insert()` function
- For the `list` command, we execute the `list()` function, which is the only function that requires any arguments

- For the `delete` command, we execute the `deleteEntry()` function
- For the `search` command, we execute the `search()` function

Anything else is handled by the `default` branch. The index is created and updated using the `createIndex()` function, which is implemented as follows:

```
func createIndex() error {
    index = make(map[string]int)
    for i, k := range data {
        key := k.Tel
        index[key] = i
    }
    return nil
}
```

Put simply, you access the entire `data` slice and put the index and value pairs of the slice in a map using the value as the key for the map and the slice index as the value of the map.

The `delete` command is implemented as follows:

```
func deleteEntry(key string) error {
    i, ok := index[key]
    if !ok {
        return fmt.Errorf("%s cannot be found!", key)
    }
    data = append(data[:i], data[i+1:]...)
    // Update the index - key does not exist any more
    delete(index, key)

    err := saveCSVFile(CSVFILE)
    if err != nil {
        return err
    }
    return nil
}
```

The operation of the `deleteEntry()` function is simple. First, you search the index for the telephone number in order to find the place of the entry in the slice with the data—if it does not exist, then you simply create an error message with `fmt.Errorf("%s cannot be found!", key)` and the function returns. If the telephone number can be found, then you delete that relevant entry from the `data` slice with `append(data[:i], data[i+1:]...)`.

Then, you must update the index—taking care of the index is the price you have to pay for the extra speed that the index gives you. Also, after you delete an entry, you should save the updated data by calling `saveCSVFile(CSVFILE)` for changes to take effect.

> Strictly speaking, as the current version of the phone book application processes one request at a time, you do not need to update the index because it is created from scratch each time you use the application. On database management systems, indexes are also saved on disk in order to avoid the major cost of creating them from scratch.

The `insert` command is implemented as follows:

```
func insert(pS *Entry) error {
    // If it already exists, do not add it
    _, ok := index[(*pS).Tel]
    if ok {
        return fmt.Errorf("%s already exists", pS.Tel)
    }
    data = append(data, *pS)
    // Update the index
    _ = createIndex()

    err := saveCSVFile(CSVFILE)
    if err != nil {
        return err
    }
    return nil
}
```

The index here helps you determine whether the telephone number you are trying to add already exists or not—as stated earlier, if you try to add an entry that uses an existing `Tel` value, the process fails. If this test passes, you add the new record in that `data` slice, update the index, and save the data to the CSV file.

The `search` command, which uses the index, is implemented as follows:

```
func search(key string) *Entry {
    i, ok := index[key]
    if !ok {
        return nil
    }
```

```
    data[i].LastAccess = strconv.FormatInt(time.Now().Unix(), 10)
    return &data[i]
}
```

Due to the index, searching for a telephone number is straightforward—the code just looks in the `index` for the desired telephone number. If it is present, the code returns that record—otherwise, the code returns `nil`, which is possible because the function returns a pointer to an `Entry` variable. Before returning the record, the `search()` function updates the `LastAccess` field of the structure that is about to be returned in order to know the last time it was accessed.

The initial contents of the CSV data file used as input are as follows:

```
$ cat ~/csv.data
Dimitris,Tsoukalos,2101112223,1600665563
Mihalis,Tsoukalos,2109416471,1600665563
Mihalis,Tsoukalos,2109416771,1600665563
Efipanios,Savva,2101231234,1600665582
```

As long at the telephone number is unique, the name and surname fields can exist multiple times. Running `phoneBook.go` produces the following kind of output:

```
$ go run phoneBook.go list
{Dimitris Tsoukalos 2101112223 1600665563}
{Mihalis Tsoukalos 2109416471 1600665563}
{Mihalis Tsoukalos 2109416771 1600665563}
{Efipanios Savva 2101231234 1600665582}
$ go run phoneBook.go delete 2109416771
$ go run phoneBook.go search 2101231234
{Efipanios Savva 2101231234 1608559833}
$ go run phoneBook.go search 210-1231-234
{Efipanios Savva 2101231234 1608559840}
```

Due to our code, `210-1231-234` is converted to `2101231234`.

```
$ go run phoneBook.go delete 210-1231-234
$ go run phoneBook.go search 210-1231-234
Number not found: 2101231234
$ go run phoneBook.go insert Jane Doe 0800-123-456
$ go run phoneBook.go insert Jane Doe 0800-123-456
0800123456 already exists
$ go run phoneBook.go search 2101112223
{Dimitris Tsoukalos 2101112223 1608559928}
```

The contents of the CSV file after the previous commands are the following:

```
$ cat ~/csv.data
Dimitris,Tsoukalos,2101112223,1600665563
Mihalis,Tsoukalos,2109416471,1600665563
Jane,Doe,0800123456,1608559903
```

You can see that the utility converted `0800-123-456` into `0800123456`, which is the desired behavior.

Despite being much better than the previous version, the new version of the phone book utility is still not perfect. Here is a list of things that can be improved:

- Ability to sort its output based on the telephone number
- Ability to sort its output based on the surname
- Ability to use JSON records and JSON slices for the data instead of CSV files

The phone book application will keep improving, starting from the next chapter, where sorting slices with structure elements is implemented.

Exercises

- Write a Go program that converts an existing array into a map.
- Write a Go program that converts an existing map into two slices—the first slice contains the keys of the map whereas the second slice contains the values. The values at index `n` of the two slices should correspond to a key and value pair that can be found in the original map.
- Make the necessary changes to `nameSurRE.go` to be able to process multiple command-line arguments.
- Change the code of `intRE.go` to process multiple command-line arguments and display totals of `true` and `false` results at the end.
- Make changes to `csvData.go` to separate the fields of a record based on the `#` character.
- Write a Go utility that converts `os.Args` into a slice of structures with fields for storing the index and the value of each command-line argument—you should define the structure that is going to be used on your own.
- Make the necessary changes to `phoneBook.go` in order to create the index based on the `LastAccess` field. Is this practical? Does it work? Why?
- Make changes to `csvData.go` in order to separate the fields of a record with a character that is given as a command-line argument.

Summary

In this chapter we discussed the composite data types of Go, which are maps and structures. Additionally, we talked about working with CSV files as well as about using regular expressions and pattern matching in Go. We can now keep our data in proper structures, validate it using regular expressions, when this is possible, and store it in CSV files to achieve data persistency.

The next chapter is about type methods, which are functions attached to a data type, reflection, and interfaces. All these things will allow us to improve the phone book application.

Additional resources

- The `encoding/csv` documentation: `https://golang.org/pkg/encoding/csv/`
- The `runtime` package documentation: `https://golang.org/pkg/runtime/`

4

Reflection and Interfaces

Do you remember the phone book application from the previous chapter? You might wonder what happens if you want to sort user-defined data structures, such as phone book records, based on your own criteria, such as a surname or first name. What happens when you want to sort different datasets that share some common behavior without having to implement sorting from scratch for each one of the different data types using multiple functions? Now imagine that you have a utility like the phone book application that can process two different formats of CSV data files based on the given input file. Each kind of CSV record is stored in a different Go structure, which means that each kind of CSV record might be sorted differently. How do you implement that without having to write two different command-line utilities? Lastly, imagine that you want to write a utility that sorts really unusual data. For example, imagine that you want to sort a slice that holds various kinds of 3D shapes based on their volume. Can this be performed easily and in a way that makes sense?

The answer to all these questions and concerns is the use of *interfaces*. However, interfaces are not just about data manipulation and sorting. Interfaces are about expressing abstractions and identifying and defining behaviors that can be shared among different data types. Once you have implemented an interface for a data type, a new world of functionality becomes available to the variables and the values of that type, which can save you time and increase your productivity. Interfaces work with *methods on types* or *type methods*, which are like functions attached to given data types, which in Go are usually structures. Remember that once you implement the required type methods of an interface, that interface is **satisfied implicitly**, which is also the case with the *empty interface* that is explained in this chapter.

Another handy Go feature is *reflection*, which allows you to examine the structure of a data type at execution time. However, as reflection is an advanced Go feature, you do not need to use it on a regular basis.

This chapter covers:

- Reflection
- Type methods
- Interfaces
- Working with two different CSV file formats
- Object-oriented programming in Go
- Updating the phone book application

Reflection

We begin this chapter with reflection, which is an advanced Go feature, not because it is an easy subject but because it is going to help you understand how Go works with different data types, including interfaces, and why they are needed.

You might be wondering how you can find out the names of the fields of a structure at execution time. In such cases, you need to use reflection. Apart from enabling you to print the fields and the values of a structure, reflection also allows you to explore and manipulate unknown structures like the ones created from decoding JSON data.

The two main questions that I asked myself when I was introduced to reflection for the first time were the following:

- Why was reflection included in Go?
- When should I use reflection?

To answer the first question, reflection allows you to **dynamically** learn the type of an arbitrary object along with information about its structure. Go provides the `reflect` package for working with reflection. Remember when we said in a previous chapter that `fmt.Println()` is clever enough to understand the data types of its parameters and act accordingly? Well, behind the scenes, the `fmt` package uses reflection to do that.

As far as the second question is concerned, reflection allows you to handle and work with data types that do not exist at the time at which you write your code but might exist in the future, which is when we use an existing package with user-defined data types.

Additionally, reflection might come in handy when you have to work with data types that do not implement a common interface and therefore have an uncommon or unknown behavior—this does not mean that they have bad or erroneous behavior, just uncommon behavior such as a user-defined structure.

> The introduction of *generics* in Go might make the use of reflection less frequent in some cases, because with generics you can work with different data types more easily and without the need to know their exact data types in advance. However, nothing beats reflection for fully exploring the structure and the data types of a variable. We talk about reflection compared to generics in *Chapter 13, Go Generics*.

The most useful parts of the `reflect` package are two data types named `reflect.Value` and `reflect.Type`. Now, `reflect.Value` is used for storing values of any type, whereas `reflect.Type` is used for representing Go types. There exist two functions named `reflect.TypeOf()` and `reflect.ValueOf()` that return the `reflect.Type` and `reflect.Value` values, respectively. Note that `reflect.TypeOf()` returns the actual type of variable—if we are examining a structure, it returns the name of the structure.

As structures are really important in Go, the `reflect` package offers the `reflect.NumField()` method for listing the number of fields in a structure as well as the `Field()` method for getting the `reflect.Value` value of a specific field of a structure.

The `reflect` package also defines the `reflect.Kind` data type, which is used for representing the *specific* data type of a variable: `int`, `struct`, etc. The documentation of the `reflect` package lists all possible values of the `reflect.Kind` data type. The `Kind()` function returns the kind of a variable.

Last, the `Int()` and `String()` methods return the integer and string value of a `reflect.Value`, respectively.

> Reflection code can look unpleasant and hard to read sometimes. Therefore, according to the Go philosophy, you should rarely use reflection unless it is absolutely necessary because despite its cleverness, it does not create clean code.

Learning the internal structure of a Go structure

The next utility shows how to use reflection to discover the internal structure and fields of a Go structure variable. Type it and save it as `reflection.go`.

```
package main

import (
	"fmt"
	"reflect"
)

type Secret struct {
	Username string
	Password string
}

type Record struct {
	Field1 string
	Field2 float64
	Field3 Secret
}

func main() {
	A := Record{"String value", -12.123, Secret{"Mihalis",
"Tsoukalos"}}
```

We begin by defining a `Record` structure variable that contains another structure value (`Secret{"Mihalis", "Tsoukalos"}`).

```
	r := reflect.ValueOf(A)
	fmt.Println("String value:", r.String())
```

This returns the `reflect.Value` of the `A` variable.

```
	iType := r.Type()
```

Using `Type()` is how we get the data type of a variable—in this case variable `A`.

```
	fmt.Printf("i Type: %s\n", iType)
	fmt.Printf("The %d fields of %s are\n", r.NumField(), iType)

	for i := 0; i < r.NumField(); i++ {
```

The previous for loop allows you to visit all the fields of a structure and examine their characteristics.

```
        fmt.Printf("\t%s ", iType.Field(i).Name)
        fmt.Printf("\twith type: %s ", r.Field(i).Type())
        fmt.Printf("\tand value _%v_\n", r.Field(i).Interface())
```

The previous fmt.Printf() statements return the name, the data type, and the value of the fields.

```
        // Check whether there are other structures embedded in Record
        k := reflect.TypeOf(r.Field(i).Interface()).Kind()
        // Need to convert it to string in order to compare it
        if k.String() == "struct" {
```

In order to check the data type of a variable with a string, we need to convert the data type into a string variable first.

```
            fmt.Println(r.Field(i).Type())
        }

        // Same as before but using the internal value
        if k == reflect.Struct {
```

You can also use the internal representation of a data type during checking. However, this makes less sense than using a string value.

```
            fmt.Println(r.Field(i).Type())
        }
    }
}
```

Running reflection.go produces the following output:

```
$ go run reflection.go
String value: <main.Record Value>
i Type: main.Record
The 3 fields of main.Record are
        Field1  with type: string       and value _String value_
        Field2  with type: float64      and value _-12.123_
        Field3  with type: main.Secret  and value _{Mihalis Tsoukalos}_
main.Secret
main.Secret
```

`main.Record` is the full unique name of the structure as defined by Go—`main` is the package name and `Record` is the `struct` name. This happens so that Go can differentiate between the elements of different packages.

The presented code does not modify any values of the structure. If you were to make changes to the values of the structure fields, you would use the `Elem()` method and pass the structure as a pointer to `ValueOf()`—remember that pointers allow you to make changes to the actual variable. There exist methods that allow you to modify an existing value. In our case, we are going to use `SetString()` for modifying a `string` field and `SetInt()` for modifying an `int` field.

This technique is illustrated in the next subsection.

Changing structure values using reflection

Learning about the internal structure of a Go structure is handy, but what is more practical is being able to change values in the Go structure, which is the subject of this subsection.

Type the following Go code and save it as `setValues.go`—it can also be found in the GitHub repository of the book.

```
package main

import (
    "fmt"
    "reflect"
)

type T struct {
    F1 int
    F2 string
    F3 float64
}

func main() {
    A := T{1, "F2", 3.0}
```

`A` is the variable that is examined in this program.

```
    fmt.Println("A:", A)

    r := reflect.ValueOf(&A).Elem()
```

With the use of `Elem()` and a pointer to variable `A`, variable `A` can be modified if needed.

```
    fmt.Println("String value:", r.String())
    typeOfA := r.Type()
    for i := 0; i < r.NumField(); i++ {
        f := r.Field(i)
        tOfA := typeOfA.Field(i).Name
        fmt.Printf("%d: %s %s = %v\n", i, tOfA, f.Type(),
f.Interface())

        k := reflect.TypeOf(r.Field(i).Interface()).Kind()
        if k == reflect.Int {
            r.Field(i).SetInt(-100)
        } else if k == reflect.String {
            r.Field(i).SetString("Changed!")
        }
    }
```

We are using `SetInt()` for modifying an integer value and `SetString()` for modifying a `string` value. Integer values are set to `-100` and string values are set to `Changed!`.

```
    fmt.Println("A:", A)
}
```

Running `setValues.go` creates the next output:

```
$ go run setValues.go
A: {1 F2 3}
String value: <main.T Value>
0: F1 int = 1
1: F2 string = F2
2: F3 float64 = 3
A: {-100 Changed! 3}
```

The first line of output shows the initial version of `A` whereas the last line shows the final version of `A` with the modified fields. The main use of such code is *dynamically* changing the values of the fields of a structure.

The three disadvantages of reflection

Without a doubt, reflection is a powerful Go feature. However, as with all tools, reflection should be used sparingly for three main reasons:

- The first reason is that extensive use of reflection will make your programs hard to read and maintain. A potential solution to this problem is good documentation, but developers are notorious for not having the time to write proper documentation.
- The second reason is that the Go code that uses reflection makes your programs slower. Generally speaking, Go code that works with a particular data type is always faster than Go code that uses reflection to dynamically work with any Go data type. Additionally, such dynamic code makes it difficult for tools to refactor or analyze your code.
- The last reason is that reflection errors cannot be caught at build time and are reported at runtime as panics, which means that reflection errors can potentially crash your programs. This can happen months or even years after the development of a Go program! One solution to this problem is extensive testing before a dangerous function call. However, this adds even more Go code to your programs, which makes them even slower.

Now that we know about reflection and what it can do for us, it is time to begin the discussion about type methods, which are necessary for using interfaces.

Type methods

A **type method** is a function that is attached to a specific data type. Although type methods (or methods on types) are in reality functions, they are defined and used in a slightly different way.

> The methods on types feature gives some object-oriented capabilities to Go, which is very handy and is used extensively in Go. Additionally, interfaces require type methods to work.

Defining new type methods is as simple as creating new functions, provided that you follow certain rules that associate the function with a data type.

Creating type methods

So, imagine that you want to do calculations with 2x2 matrices. A very natural way of implementing that is by defining a new data type and defining type methods for adding, subtracting, and multiplying 2x2 matrices using that new data type. To make it even more interesting and generic, we are going to create a command-line utility that accepts the elements of two 2x2 matrices as command-line arguments, which are eight integer values in total, and performs all three calculations between them using the defined type methods.

Having a data type called `ar2x2`, you can create a type method named `FunctionName` for it as follows:

```
func (a ar2x2) FunctionName(parameters) <return values> {
    ...
}
```

The `(a ar2x2)` part is what makes the `FunctionName()` function a type method because it associates `FunctionName()` with the `ar2x2` data type. **No other data type can use that function**. However, you are free to implement `FunctionName()` for other data types or as a regular function. If you have a `ar2x2` variable named `varAr`, you can invoke `FunctionName()` as `varAr.FunctionName(...)`, which looks like selecting the field of a structure variable.

You are not obligated to develop type methods if you do not want to. In fact, each type method can be **rewritten as a regular function**. Therefore, `FunctionName()` can be rewritten as follows:

```
func FunctionName(a ar2x2, parameters...) <return values> {
    ...
}
```

Have in mind that under the hood, the Go compiler does turn methods into regular function calls with the `self` value as the first parameter. However, **interfaces require the use of type methods** to work.

> The expressions used for selecting a field of a structure or a type method of a data type, which would replace the ellipsis after the variable name above, are called **selectors**.

Performing calculations between matrices of a given size is one of the rare cases where using an array instead of a slice makes more sense because you do not have to modify the size of the matrices. Some might argue that using a slice instead of an array pointer is a better practice—you are allowed to use what makes more sense to you.

Most of the time, and when there is such a need, the results of a type method are saved in the variable that invoked the type method—in order to implement that for the `ar2x2` data type, we pass a pointer to the array that invoked the type method, like `func (a *ar2x2)`.

The next subsection illustrates type methods in action.

Using type methods

This subsection shows the use of type methods using the `ar2x2` data type as an example. The `Add()` function and the `Add()` method use the exact same algorithm for adding two matrices. The only difference between them is the way they are being called and the fact that the function returns an array whereas the method saves the result to the calling variable.

Although adding and subtracting matrices is a straightforward process—you just add or subtract each element of the first matrix with the element of the second matrix that is located at the same position—matrix multiplication is a more complex process. This is the main reason that both addition and subtraction use `for` loops, which means that the code can also work with bigger matrices, whereas multiplication uses static code that cannot be applied to bigger matrices without major changes.

> If you are defining type methods for a structure, you should make sure that the names of the type methods do not conflict with any field name of the structure because the Go compiler will reject such ambiguities.

Type the following code and save it as `methods.go`.

```
package main

import (
	"fmt"
	"os"
	"strconv"
)
```

```
type ar2x2 [2][2]int

// Traditional Add() function
func Add(a, b ar2x2) ar2x2 {
	c := ar2x2{}
	for i := 0; i < 2; i++ {
		for j := 0; j < 2; j++ {
			c[i][j] = a[i][j] + b[i][j]
		}
	}
	return c
}
```

Here, we have a traditional function that adds two `ar2x2` variables and returns their result.

```
// Type method Add()
func (a *ar2x2) Add(b ar2x2) {
	for i := 0; i < 2; i++ {
		for j := 0; j < 2; j++ {
			a[i][j] = a[i][j] + b[i][j]
		}
	}
}
```

Here we have a type method named `Add()` that is attached to the `ar2x2` data type. The result of the addition is not returned. What happens is that the `ar2x2` variable that called the `Add()` method is going to be modified and hold the result—this is the reason for using a pointer when defining the type method. If you do not want that behavior, you should modify the signature and the implementation of the type method to fit your needs.

```
// Type method Subtract()
func (a *ar2x2) Subtract(b ar2x2) {
	for i := 0; i < 2; i++ {
		for j := 0; j < 2; j++ {
			a[i][j] = a[i][j] - b[i][j]
		}
	}
}
```

The previous method subtracts `ar2x2 b` from `ar2x2 a` and the result is saved in `a`.

```
// Type method Multiply()
func (a *ar2x2) Multiply(b ar2x2) {
    a[0][0] = a[0][0]*b[0][0] + a[0][1]*b[1][0]
    a[1][0] = a[1][0]*b[0][0] + a[1][1]*b[1][0]
    a[0][1] = a[0][0]*b[0][1] + a[0][1]*b[1][1]
    a[1][1] = a[1][0]*b[0][1] + a[1][1]*b[1][1]
}
```

As we are working with small arrays, we do the multiplications without using `for` loops.

```
func main() {
    if len(os.Args) != 9 {
        fmt.Println("Need 8 integers")
        return
    }

    k := [8]int{}
    for index, i := range os.Args[1:] {
        v, err := strconv.Atoi(i)
        if err != nil {
            fmt.Println(err)
            return
        }
        k[index] = v
    }
    a := ar2x2{{k[0], k[1]}, {k[2], k[3]}}
    b := ar2x2{{k[4], k[5]}, {k[6], k[7]}}
```

The `main()` function gets the input and creates two 2x2 matrices. After that, it performs the desired calculations with these two matrices.

```
    fmt.Println("Traditional a+b:", Add(a, b))
    a.Add(b)
    fmt.Println("a+b:", a)
    a.Subtract(a)
    fmt.Println("a-a:", a)

    a = ar2x2{{k[0], k[1]}, {k[2], k[3]}}
```

We calculate `a+b` using two different ways: using a regular function and using a type method. As both `a.Add(b)` and `a.Subtract(a)` change the value of `a`, we have to initialize `a` before using it again.

```
	a.Multiply(b)
	fmt.Println("a*b:", a)

	a = ar2x2{{k[0], k[1]}, {k[2], k[3]}}
	b.Multiply(a)
	fmt.Println("b*a:", b)
}
```

Last, we calculate `a*b` and `b*a` to show that they are different because the commutative property does not apply to matrix multiplication.

Running `methods.go` produces the next output:

```
$ go run methods.go 1 2 0 0 2 1 1 1
Traditional a+b: [[3 3] [1 1]]
a+b: [[3 3] [1 1]]
a-a: [[0 0] [0 0]]
a*b: [[4 6] [0 0]]
b*a: [[2 4] [1 2]]
```

The input here is two 2x2 matrices, `[[1 2] [0 0]]` and `[[2 1] [1 1]]`, and the output is their calculations.

Now that we know about type methods, it is time to begin exploring interfaces as interfaces cannot be implemented without type methods.

Interfaces

An **interface** is a Go mechanism for defining behavior that is implemented using a set of methods. Interfaces play a key role in Go and can simplify the code of your programs when they have to deal with multiple data types that perform the same task—recall that `fmt.Println()` works for almost all data types. But remember, interfaces should not be unnecessarily complex. If you decide to create your own interfaces, then you should begin with a common behavior that you want to be used by multiple data types.

Interfaces work with **methods on types** (or **type methods**), which are like functions attached to given data types, which in Go are usually structures (although we can use any data type we want).

As you already know, once you implement the required type methods of an interface, that interface is **satisfied implicitly**.

The **empty interface** is defined as just `interface{}`. As the empty interface has no methods, it means that it is already **implemented by all data types**.

> Once you implement the methods of an interface for a data type, that interface is satisfied **automatically** for that data type.

In a more formal way, a Go interface type defines (or describes) the **behavior** of other types by specifying a set of *methods* that need to be implemented for supporting that behavior. For a data type to satisfy an interface, it needs to implement **all the type methods** required by that interface. Therefore, interfaces are **abstract types** that specify a set of methods that need to be implemented so that another type can be considered an instance of the interface. So, an interface is two things: **a set of methods and a type**. Have in mind that small and well-defined interfaces are usually the most popular ones.

> As a rule of thumb, only create a new interface when you want to share a common behavior between two or more concrete data types. This is basically **duck typing**.

The biggest **advantage** you get from interfaces is that if needed, you can pass a variable of a data type that implements a particular interface to any function that expects a parameter of that specific interface, which saves you from having to write separate functions for each supported data type. However, Go offers an alternative to this with the recent addition of generics.

Interfaces can also be used for providing a kind of polymorphism in Go, which is an object-oriented concept. *Polymorphism* offers a way of accessing objects of different types in the same uniform way when they share a common behavior.

Lastly, interfaces can be used for *composition*. In practice, this means that you can combine existing interfaces and create new ones that offer the combined behavior of the interfaces that were brought together. The next figure shows interface composition in a graphical way.

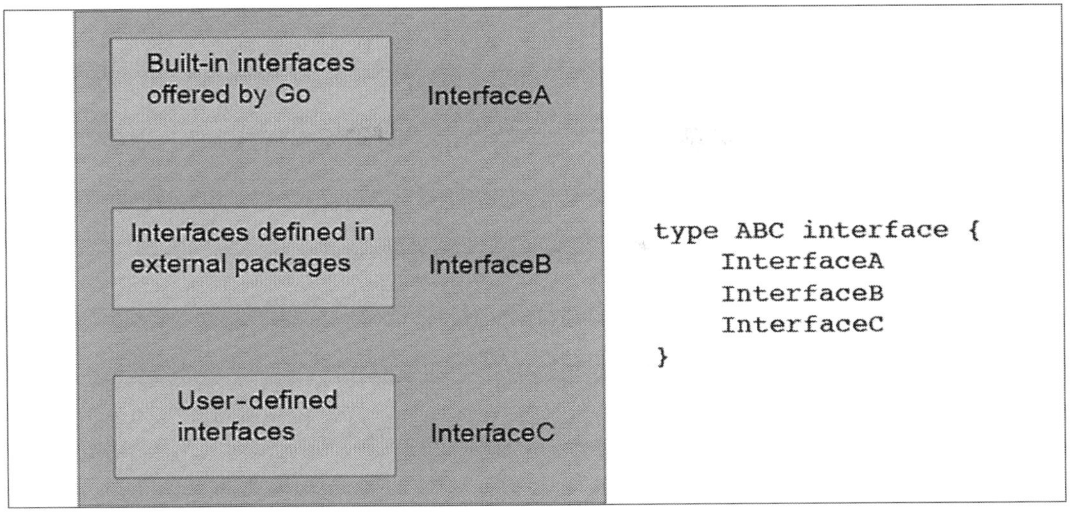

Figure 4.1: Interface composition

Put simply, the previous figure illustrates that because of its definition, satisfying interface `ABC` requires satisfying `InterfaceA`, `InterfaceB`, and `InterfaceC`. Additionally, any `ABC` variable can be used instead of an `InterfaceA` variable, an `InterfaceB` variable, or an `InterfaceC` variable because it supports all these three behaviors. Last, only `ABC` variables can be used where an `ABC` variable is expected. There is nothing prohibiting you from including additional methods in the definition of the `ABC` interface if the combination of existing interfaces does not describe the desired behavior accurately.

> When you combine existing interfaces, it is better that the interfaces do not contain methods with the same name.

What you should keep in mind is that there is no need for an interface to be impressive and require the implementation of a large number of methods. In fact, the fewer methods an interface has, the more generic and widely used it can be, which improves its usefulness and therefore its usage.

The subsection that follows illustrates the use of `sort.Interface`.

The sort.Interface interface

The `sort` package contains an interface named `sort.Interface` that allows you to sort slices according to your needs and your data, provided that you implement `sort.Interface` for the custom data types stored in your slices. The `sort` package defines the `sort.Interface` as follows:

```
type Interface interface {
    // Len is the number of elements in the collection.
    Len() int
    // Less reports whether the element with
    // index i should sort before the element with index j.
    Less(i, j int) bool
    // Swap swaps the elements with indexes i and j.
    Swap(i, j int)
}
```

What we can understand from the definition of `sort.Interface` is that in order to implement `sort.Interface`, we need to implement the following three type methods:

- `Len() int`
- `Less(i, j int) bool`
- `Swap(i, j int)`

The `Len()` method returns the length of the slice that will be sorted and helps the interface to process all slice elements whereas the `Less()` method, which compares and sorts elements in pairs, defines how elements are going to be compared and therefore sorted. The return value of `Less()` is `bool`, which means that `Less()` only cares about whether the element at index `i` is bigger or not than the element at index `j` in the way that the two elements are being compared. Lastly, the `Swap()` method is used for swapping two elements of the slice, which is required for the sorting algorithm to work.

The following code, which can be found as `sort.go`, illustrates the use of `sort.Interface`.

```
package main

import (
    "fmt"
    "sort"
)
```

```
type S1 struct {
    F1 int
    F2 string
    F3 int
}

// We want to sort S2 records based on the value of F3.F1,
// Which is equivalent to S1.F1 as F3 is an S1 structure
type S2 struct {
    F1 int
    F2 string
    F3 S1
}
```

The `S2` structure includes a field named `F3` that is of the `S1` data type, which is also a structure.

```
type S2slice []S2
```

You need to have a slice because all sorting operations work on slices. It is for this slice, which should be a new data type that in this case is called `S2slice`, that you are going to implement the three type methods of the `sort.Interface`.

```
// Implementing sort.Interface for S2slice
func (a S2slice) Len() int {
    return len(a)
}
```

Here is the implementation of `Len()` for the `S2slice` data type. It is usually that simple.

```
// What field to use when comparing
func (a S2slice) Less(i, j int) bool {
    return a[i].F3.F1 < a[j].F3.F1
}
```

Here is the implementation of `Less()` for the `S2slice` data type. This method defines the way elements get sorted. In this case, by using a field of the embedded data structure (`F3.F1`).

```
func (a S2slice) Swap(i, j int) {
    a[i], a[j] = a[j], a[i]
}
```

This is the implementation of the `Swap()` type method that defines the way to swap slice elements during sorting. It is usually that simple.

```
func main() {
    data := []S2{
        S2{1, "One", S1{1, "S1_1", 10}},
        S2{2, "Two", S1{2, "S1_1", 20}},
        S2{-1, "Two", S1{-1, "S1_1", -20}},
    }
    fmt.Println("Before:", data)
    sort.Sort(S2slice(data))
    fmt.Println("After:", data)

    // Reverse sorting works automatically
    sort.Sort(sort.Reverse(S2slice(data)))
    fmt.Println("Reverse:", data)
}
```

Once you have implemented `sort.Interface`, you'll see that `sort.Reverse()`, which is used for reverse sorting your slice, works automatically.

Running `sort.go` generates the following output:

```
$ go run sort.go
Before: [{1 One {1 S1_1 10}} {2 Two {2 S1_1 20}} {-1 Two {-1 S1_1
-20}}]
After: [{-1 Two {-1 S1_1 -20}} {1 One {1 S1_1 10}} {2 Two {2 S1_1 20}}]
Reverse: [{2 Two {2 S1_1 20}} {1 One {1 S1_1 10}} {-1 Two {-1 S1_1
-20}}]
```

The first line shows the elements of the slice as initially stored. The second line shows the sorted version whereas the last line shows the reverse sorted version.

The empty interface

As mentioned before, the **empty interface** is defined as just `interface{}` and is already implemented by **all data types**. Therefore, variables of any data type can be put in the place of a parameter of the empty interface data type. Therefore, a function with an `interface{}` parameter can accept variables of any data type in this place. However, if you intend to work with `interface{}` function parameters without examining their data type inside the function, you should process them with statements that work on all data types, otherwise your code may crash or misbehave.

The program that follows defines two structures named `S1` and `S2` but just a single function named `Print()` for printing both of them. This is allowed because `Print()` requires an `interface{}` parameter that can accept both `S1` and `S2` variables. The `fmt.Println(s)` statement inside `Print()` can work with both `S1` and `S2`.

> If you create a function that accepts one or more `interface{}` parameters and you run a statement that can only be applied to a limited number of data types, things will not work out well. As an example, not all `interface{}` parameters can be multiplied by 5 or be used in `fmt.Printf()` with the `%d` control string.

The source code of `empty.go` is as follows:

```
package main

import "fmt"

type S1 struct {
    F1 int
    F2 string
}

type S2 struct {
    F1 int
    F2 S1
}

func Print(s interface{}) {
    fmt.Println(s)
}

func main() {
    v1 := S1{10, "Hello"}
    v2 := S2{F1: -1, F2: v1}
    Print(v1)
    Print(v2)
```

Although `v1` and `v2` are of different data types, `Print()` can work with both of them.

```
    // Printing an integer
    Print(123)
    // Printing a string
    Print("Go is the best!")
}
```

`Print()` can also work with integers and strings.

Running `empty.go` produces the following output:

```
{10 Hello}
{-1 {10 Hello}}
123
Go is the best!
```

Using the empty interface is easy as soon as you realize that you can pass any type of variable in the place of an `interface{}` parameter and you can return any data type as an `interface{}` return value. However, with great power comes great responsibility—you should be very careful with `interface{}` parameters and their return values, because in order to use their real values you have to be sure about their underlying data type. We'll discuss this in the next section.

Type assertions and type switches

A **type assertion** is a mechanism for working with the underlying concrete value of an interface. This mainly happens because interfaces are virtual data types without their own values—interfaces just define behavior and do not hold data of their own. But what happens when you do not know the data type before attempting a type assertion? How can you differentiate between the supported data types and the unsupported ones? How can you choose a different action for each supported data type? The answer is by using *type switches*. **Type switches** use `switch` blocks for data types and allow you to differentiate between type assertion values, which are data types, and process each data type the way you want. On the other hand, in order to use the empty interface in type switches, you need to use **type assertions**.

> You can have type switches for all kinds of interfaces and data types in general.

Therefore, the real work begins once you enter the function, because this is where you need to define the supported data types and the actions that take place for each supported data type.

Type assertions use the `x.(T)` notation, where `x` is an interface type and `T` is a type, and help you extract the value that is hidden behind the empty interface. For a type assertion to work, `x` should not be `nil` and the dynamic type of `x` should be identical to the `T` type.

The following code can be found as `typeSwitch.go`:

```
package main

import "fmt"

type Secret struct {
    SecretValue string
}

type Entry struct {
    F1 int
    F2 string
    F3 Secret
}

func Teststruct(x interface{}) {
    // type switch
    switch T := x.(type) {
    case Secret:
        fmt.Println("Secret type")
    case Entry:
        fmt.Println("Entry type")
    default:
        fmt.Printf("Not supported type: %T\n", T)
    }
}
```

This is a type switch that supports the `Secret` and `Entry` data types.

```
func Learn(x interface{}) {
    switch T := x.(type) {
    default:
        fmt.Printf("Data type: %T\n", T)
    }
}
```

The `Learn()` function prints the data type of its input parameter.

```
func main() {
    A := Entry{100, "F2", Secret{"myPassword"}}
    Teststruct(A)
    Teststruct(A.F3)
```

```
    Teststruct("A string")

    Learn(12.23)
    Learn('€')
}
```

The last part of the code calls the desired functions to explore variable `A`. Running `typeSwitch.go` produces the following output:

```
$ go run typeSwitch.go
Entry type
Secret type
Not supported type: string
Data type: float64
Data type: int32
```

As you can see, we have managed to execute different code based on the data type of the variable passed to `TestStruct()` and `Learn()`.

Strictly speaking, type assertions allow you to perform two main tasks:

- Checking whether an interface value keeps a particular type. When used this way, a type assertion returns two values: the underlying value and a `bool` value. The underlying value is what you might want to use. However, it is the value of the `bool` variable that tells you whether the type assertion was successful or not and therefore whether you can use the underlying value or not. Checking whether a variable named `aVar` is of the `int` type requires the use of the `aVar.(int)` notation, which returns two values. If successful, it returns the real `int` value of `aVar` and `true`. Otherwise, it returns `false` as the second value, which means that the type assertion was not successful and that the real value could not be extracted.
- Using the concrete value stored in an interface or assigning it to a new variable. This means that if there is a `float64` variable in an interface, a type assertion allows you to get that value.

> The functionality offered by the `reflect` package helps Go identify the underlying data type and the real value of an `interface{}` variable.

So far, we have seen a variation of the first case where we extract the data type stored in an empty interface variable. Now, we are going to learn how to extract the real value stored in an empty interface variable.

As explained, trying to extract the concrete value from an interface using a type assertion can have two outcomes:

- If you use the correct concrete data type, you get the underlying value without any issues
- If you use an incorrect concrete data type, your program will panic

All these are illustrated in `assertions.go`, which contains the next code as well as lots of code comments that explain the process.

```
package main

import (
    "fmt"
)

func returnNumber() interface{} {
    return 12
}

func main() {
    anInt := returnNumber()
```

The `returnNumber()` function returns an `int` value that is wrapped in an empty interface.

```
    number := anInt.(int)
    number++
    fmt.Println(number)
```

In the previous code, we get the `int` value wrapped in an empty interface variable (`anInt`).

```
    // The next statement would fail because there
    // is no type assertion to get the value:
    // anInt++

    // The next statement fails but the failure is under
    // control because of the ok bool variable that tells
    // whether the type assertion is successful or not
    value, ok := anInt.(int64)
    if ok {
        fmt.Println("Type assertion successful: ", value)
```

```
    } else {
        fmt.Println("Type assertion failed!")
    }

    // The next statement is successful but
    // dangerous because it does not make sure that
    // the type assertion is successful.
    // It just happens to be successful
    i := anInt.(int)
    fmt.Println("i:", i)

    // The following will PANIC because anInt is not bool
    _ = anInt.(bool)
}
```

The last statement panics the program because the `anInt` variable does not hold a `bool` value. Running `assertions.go` generates the next output:

```
$ go run assertions.go
13
Type assertion failed!
i: 12
panic: interface conversion: interface {} is int, not bool

goroutine 1 [running]:
main.main()
        /Users/mtsouk/Desktop/mGo3rd/code/ch04/assertions.go:39 +0x192
```

The reason for the panic is written onscreen: `panic: interface conversion: interface {} is int, not bool`. What else can the Go compiler do to help you?

Next we discuss the `map[string]interface{}` map and its use.

The map[string]interface{} map

You have a utility that processes its command-line arguments; if everything goes as expected, then you get the supported types of command-line arguments and everything goes smoothly. But what happens when something unexpected occurs? In that case, the `map[string]interface{}` map is here to help and this subsection shows how!

Remember that the biggest advantage you get from using a `map[string]interface{}` map or any map that stores an `interface{}` value in general, is that you still have your data in its original state and data type. If you use `map[string]string` instead, or anything similar, then any data you have is going to be converted into a `string`, which means that you are going to lose information about the original data type and the structure of the data you are storing in the map.

Nowadays, web services work by exchanging JSON records. If you get a JSON record in a supported format, then you can process it as expected and everything will be fine. However, there are times when you might get an erroneous record or a record in an unsupported JSON format. In these cases, using `map[string]interface{}` for storing these unknown JSON records (*arbitrary data*) is a good choice because `map[string]interface{}` is good at storing JSON records of an unknown type. We are going to illustrate that using a utility named `mapEmpty.go` that processes arbitrary JSON records given as command-line arguments. We process the input JSON record in two ways that are similar but not identical. There is no real difference between the `exploreMap()` and `typeSwitch()` functions apart from the fact that `typeSwitch()` generates a much richer output. The code of `mapEmpty.go` is as follows:

```
package main

import (
    "encoding/json"
    "fmt"
    "os"
)

var JSONrecord = `{
    "Flag": true,
    "Array": ["a","b","c"],
    "Entity": {
      "a1": "b1",
      "a2": "b2",
      "Value": -456,
      "Null": null
    },
    "Message": "Hello Go!"
  }`
```

This global variable holds the default value of `JSONrecord`, in case there is no user input.

```
func typeSwitch(m map[string]interface{}) {
    for k, v := range m {
        switch c := v.(type) {
        case string:
            fmt.Println("Is a string!", k, c)
        case float64:
            fmt.Println("Is a float64!", k, c)
        case bool:
            fmt.Println("Is a Boolean!", k, c)
        case map[string]interface{}:
            fmt.Println("Is a map!", k, c)
            typeSwitch(v.(map[string]interface{}))
        default:
            fmt.Printf("...Is %v: %T!\n", k, c)
        }
    }
    return
}
```

The `typeSwitch()` function uses a type switch for differentiating between the values in its input map. If a map is found, then we *recursively* call `typeSwitch()` on the new map in order to examine it even more.

The `for` loop allows you to examine all the elements of the `map[string]interface{}` map.

```
func exploreMap(m map[string]interface{}) {
    for k, v := range m {
        embMap, ok := v.(map[string]interface{})
        // If it is a map, explore deeper
        if ok {
            fmt.Printf("{\"%v\": \n", k)
            exploreMap(embMap)
            fmt.Printf("}\n")
        } else {
            fmt.Printf("%v: %v\n", k, v)
        }
    }
}
```

The `exploreMap()` function inspects the contents of its input map. If a map is found, then we call `exploreMap()` on the new map *recursively* in order to examine it on its own.

```
func main() {
    if len(os.Args) == 1 {
        fmt.Println("*** Using default JSON record.")
    } else {
        JSONrecord = os.Args[1]
    }

    JSONMap := make(map[string]interface{})
    err := json.Unmarshal([]byte(JSONrecord), &JSONMap)
```

As you will learn in *Chapter 6, Telling a UNIX System What To Do*, `json.Unmarshal()` processes JSON data and converts it into a Go value. Although this value is usually a Go structure, in this case we are using a map as specified by the `map[string]interface{}` variable. Strictly speaking, the second parameter of `json.Unmarshal()` is of the empty interface data type, which means that its data type can be anything.

```
    if err != nil {
        fmt.Println(err)
        return
    }
    exploreMap(JSONMap)
    typeSwitch(JSONMap)
}
```

> `map[string]interface{}` is extremely handy for storing JSON records when you do not know their schema in advance. In other words, `map[string]interface{}` is good at storing arbitrary JSON data of unknown schema.

Running `mapEmpty.go` produces the following output:

```
$ go run mapEmpty.go
*** Using default JSON record.
Message: Hello Go!
Flag: true
Array: [a b c]
```

```
{"Entity":
Value: -456
Null: <nil>
a1: b1
a2: b2
}
Is a Boolean! Flag true
...Is Array: []interface {}!
Is a map! Entity map[Null:<nil> Value:-456 a1:b1 a2:b2]
Is a string! a2 b2
Is a float64! Value -456
...Is Null: <nil>!
Is a string! a1 b1
Is a string! Message Hello Go!
$ go run mapEmpty.go '{"Array": [3, 4], "Null": null, "String": "Hello
Go!"}'
Array: [3 4]
Null: <nil>
String: Hello Go!
...Is Array: []interface {}!
...Is Null: <nil>!
Is a string! String Hello Go!
$ go run mapEmpty.go '{"Array":"Error"'
unexpected end of JSON input
```

The first run is without any command-line parameters, which means that it uses the default value of `JSONrecord` and therefore outputs the hardcoded data. The other two executions use user data. First, valid data, and then data that does not represent a valid JSON record. The error message in the third execution is generated by `json.Unmarshal()` as it cannot understand the schema of the JSON record.

The error data type

As promised, we are revisiting the `error` data type because it is an interface defined as follows:

```
type error interface {
    Error() string
}
```

So, in order to satisfy the `error` interface you just need to implement the `Error() string` type method. This does not change the way we use errors to find out whether the execution of a function or method was successful or not but shows how important interfaces are in Go as they are being used transparently all the time. However, the crucial question is *when* you should implement the `error` interface on your own instead of using the default one. The answer to that question is when you want to give more context to an error condition.

Now, let us talk about the `error` interface in a more practical situation. When there is nothing more to read from a file, Go returns an `io.EOF` error, which, strictly speaking, is not an error condition but a logical part of reading a file. If a file is totally empty, you still get `io.EOF` when you try to read it. However, this might cause problems in some situations and you might need to have a way of differentiating between a totally empty file and a file that has been read fully and there is nothing more to read. One way of dealing with that issue is with the help of the `error` interface.

> The code example that is presented here is connected to File I/O. Putting it here might generate some questions about reading files in Go—however, I feel that this is the appropriate place to put it because it is connected to errors and error handling more than it is connected to file reading.

The code of `errorInt.go` without the `package` and `import` blocks is as follows:

```
type emptyFile struct {
    Ended bool
    Read  int
}
```

This is a new data type that is used in the program.

```
// Implement error interface
func (e emptyFile) Error() string {
    return fmt.Sprintf("Ended with io.EOF (%t) but read (%d) bytes",
e.Ended, e.Read)
}
```

This is the implementation of the `error` interface for `emptyFile`.

```
// Check values
func isFileEmpty(e error) bool {
    // Type assertion
    v, ok := e.(emptyFile)
```

This is a type assertion for getting an `emptyFile` structure from the `error` variable.

```
    if ok {
        if v.Read == 0 && v.Ended == true {
            return true
        }
    }
    return false
}
```

This is a method for checking whether a file is empty or not. The `if` condition translates as: if you have read 0 bytes (`v.Read == 0`) and you have reached the end of the file (`v.Ended == true`), then the file is empty.

If you are dealing with multiple `error` variables, you should add a type switch to the `isFileEmpty()` function after the type assertion.

```
func readFile(file string) error {
    var err error
    fd, err := os.Open(file)
    if err != nil {
        return err
    }
    defer fd.Close()

    reader := bufio.NewReader(fd)
    n := 0
    for {
        line, err := reader.ReadString('\n')
        n += len(line)
```

We read the input file line by line—you are going to learn more about File I/O in *Chapter 6, Telling a UNIX System What to Do*.

```
        if err == io.EOF {
            // End of File: nothing more to read
            if n == 0 {
                return emptyFile{true, n}
            }
```

If we have reached the end of a file (`io.EOF`) and we have read `0` characters, then we are dealing with an empty file. This kind of context is added to the `emptyFile` structure and returned as an `error` value.

```
            break
        } else if err != nil {
            return err
        }
    }
    return nil
}

func main() {
    flag.Parse()
    if len(flag.Args()) == 0 {
        fmt.Println("usage: errorInt <file1> [<file2> ...]")
        return
    }

    for _, file := range flag.Args() {
        err := readFile(file)
        if isFileEmpty(err) {
            fmt.Println(file, err)
```

This is where we check the error message of the `readFile()` function. The order we do the checking in is important because only the first match is executed. This means that we have to go from more specific cases to more generic conditions.

```
        } else if err != nil {
            fmt.Println(file, err)
        } else {
            fmt.Println(file, "is OK.")
        }
    }
}
```

Running `errorInt.go` produces the next output:

```
$ go run errorInt.go /etc/hosts /tmp/doesNotExist /tmp/empty /tmp /tmp/
Empty.txt
/etc/hosts is OK.
/tmp/doesNotExist open /tmp/doesNotExist: no such file or directory
/tmp/empty open /tmp/empty: permission denied
/tmp read /tmp: is a directory
/tmp/Empty.txt Ended with io.EOF (true) but read (0) bytes
```

The first file (`/etc/hosts`) was read without any issues, whereas the second file (`/tmp/doesNotExist`) could not be found. The third file (`/tmp/empty`) was there but we did not have the required file permissions to read it, whereas the fourth file (`/tmp`) was in reality a directory. The last file (`/tmp/Empty.txt`) was there but was empty, which is the error situation that we wanted to catch.

Writing your own interfaces

After learning about using existing interfaces, we will write another command-line utility that sorts 3D shapes according to their volumes. This task requires learning the following tasks:

- Creating new interfaces
- Combining existing interfaces
- Implementing `sort.Interface` for 3D shapes

Creating your own interfaces is easy. For reasons of simplicity, we include our own interface in the `main` package. However, this is rarely the case as we usually want to share our interfaces, which means that interfaces are usually included in Go packages other than `main`.

The following code excerpt defines a new interface:

```
type Shape2D interface {
    Perimeter() float64
}
```

This interface has the following properties:

- It is called `Shape2D`
- It requires the implementation of a single method named `Perimeter()` that returns a `float64` value

Apart from being user-defined, there is nothing special about that interface compared to the built-in Go interfaces—you can use it as you do all other existing interfaces. So, in order for a data type to satisfy the `Shape2D` interface, it needs to implement a type method named `Perimeter()` that returns a `float64` value.

Using a Go interface

The code that follows presents the simplest way of using an interface, which is by calling its method directly, as if it was a function, to get a result. Although this is allowed, it is rarely the case as we usually create functions that accept interface parameters in order for these functions to be able to work with multiple data types.

The code uses a handy technique for quickly finding out whether a given variable is of a given data type that was presented earlier in `assertions.go`. In this case, we examine whether a variable is of the `Shape2D` interface by using the `interface{}(a).(Shape2D)` notation, where a is the variable that is being examined and `Shape2D` is the data type against the variable being checked.

The next program is called `Shape2D.go`—its most interesting parts are the following:

```
type Shape2D interface {
    Perimeter() float64
}
```

This is the definition of the `Shape2D` interface that requires the implementation of the `Perimeter()` type method.

```
type circle struct {
    R float64
}

func (c circle) Perimeter() float64 {
    return 2 * math.Pi * c.R
}
```

This is where the `circle` type implements the `Shape2D` interface with the implementation of the `Perimeter()` type method.

```
func main() {
    a := circle{R: 1.5}
    fmt.Printf("R %.2f -> Perimeter %.3f \n", a.R, a.Perimeter())

    _, ok := interface{}(a).(Shape2D)
    if ok {
        fmt.Println("a is a Shape2D!")
    }
}
```

As stated before, the `interface{}(a).(Shape2D)` notation checks whether the a variable satisfies the `Shape2D` interface without using its underlying value (`circle{R: 1.5}`).

Running `Shape2D.go` creates the next output:

```
R 1.50 -> Perimeter 9.425
a is a Shape2D!
```

Implementing sort.Interface for 3D shapes

In this section we will create a utility for sorting various 3D shapes based on their volume, which clearly illustrates the power and versatility of Go interfaces. This time, we will use a single slice for storing all kinds of structures that all satisfy a given interface. The fact that Go considers interfaces as data types allows us to create slices with elements that satisfy a given interface without getting any error messages.

This kind of scenario can be useful in various cases because it illustrates how to store elements with different data types that all satisfy a common interface on the same slice and how to sort them using `sort.Interface`. Put simply, the presented utility sorts different structures with different numbers and names of fields that all share a common behavior through an interface implementation. The dimensions of the shapes are created using random numbers, which means that each time you execute the utility, you get a different output.

The name of the interface is `Shape3D` and requires the implementation of the `Vol() float64` type method. This interface is satisfied by the `Cube`, `Cuboid`, and `Sphere` data types. The `sort.Interface` interface is implemented for the `shapes` data type, which is defined as a slice of `Shape3D` elements.

All floating-point numbers are randomly generated using the `rF64(min, max float64) float64` function. As floating-point numbers have a lot of decimal points, printing is implemented using a separate function named `PrintShapes()` that uses an `fmt.Printf("%.2f ", v)` statement to specify the number of decimal points that are displayed onscreen—in this case, we print the first two decimal points of each floating-point value.

> As you might recall, once you have implemented `sort.Interface`, you can also sort your data in reverse order using `sort.Reverse()`.

Type the following code on your favorite editor and save it as `sortShapes.go`. The code illustrates how to sort 3D shapes based on their volume.

```
package main

import (
	"fmt"
	"math"
	"math/rand"
	"sort"
```

```
    "time"
)

const min = 1
const max = 5

func rF64(min, max float64) float64 {
    return min + rand.Float64()*(max-min)
}
```

The `rF64()` function generates `float64` random values.

```
type Shape3D interface {
    Vol() float64
}
```

The definition of the `Shape3D` interface.

```
type Cube struct {
    x float64
}

type Cuboid struct {
    x float64
    y float64
    z float64
}

type Sphere struct {
    r float64
}

func (c Cube) Vol() float64 {
    return c.x * c.x * c.x
}
```

`Cube` implementing the `Shape3D` interface.

```
func (c Cuboid) Vol() float64 {
    return c.x * c.y * c.z
}
```

`Cuboid` implementing the `Shape3D` interface.

```
func (c Sphere) Vol() float64 {
    return 4 / 3 * math.Pi * c.r * c.r * c.r
}
```

`Sphere` implementing the `Shape3D` interface.

```
type shapes []Shape3D
```

This is the data type that uses `sort.Interface`.

```
// Implementing sort.Interface
func (a shapes) Len() int {
    return len(a)
}

func (a shapes) Less(i, j int) bool {
    return a[i].Vol() < a[j].Vol()
}

func (a shapes) Swap(i, j int) {
    a[i], a[j] = a[j], a[i]
}
```

The previous three functions implement `sort.Interface`.

```
func PrintShapes(a shapes) {
    for _, v := range a {
        switch v.(type) {
        case Cube:
            fmt.Printf("Cube: volume %.2f\n", v.Vol())
        case Cuboid:
            fmt.Printf("Cuboid: volume %.2f\n", v.Vol())
        case Sphere:
            fmt.Printf("Sphere: volume %.2f\n", v.Vol())
        default:
            fmt.Println("Unknown data type!")
        }
    }
    fmt.Println()
}
```

```
func main() {
    data := shapes{}
    rand.Seed(time.Now().Unix())
```

The `PrintShapes()` function is used for customizing the output.

```
    for i := 0; i < 3; i++ {
        cube := Cube{rF64(min, max)}
        cuboid := Cuboid{rF64(min, max), rF64(min, max), rF64(min,
max)}
        sphere := Sphere{rF64(min, max)}
        data = append(data, cube)
        data = append(data, cuboid)
        data = append(data, sphere)
    }
    PrintShapes(data)

    // Sorting
    sort.Sort(shapes(data))
    PrintShapes(data)

    // Reverse sorting
    sort.Sort(sort.Reverse(shapes(data)))
    PrintShapes(data)
}
```

The following code produces shapes with randomly generated dimensions using the `rF64()` function.

Running `sortShapes.go` produces the following output:

```
Cube: volume 105.27
Cuboid: volume 34.88
Sphere: volume 212.31
Cube: volume 55.76
Cuboid: volume 28.84
Sphere: volume 46.50
Cube: volume 52.41
Cuboid: volume 36.90
Sphere: volume 257.03
```

This is the unsorted output of the program:

```
Cuboid: volume 28.84
Cuboid: volume 34.88
Cuboid: volume 36.90
Sphere: volume 46.50
Cube: volume 52.41
...
Sphere: volume 257.03
```

This is the sorted output of the program from smaller to bigger shapes:

```
Sphere: volume 257.03
...
Cuboid: volume 28.84
```

This is the reversed sorted output of the program from bigger to smaller shapes.

The next section shows a technique for differentiating between two CSV file formats in your programs.

Working with two different CSV file formats

In this section we are going to implement a separate command-line utility that works with two different CSV formats. The reason we are doing this is that there are times when you will need your utilities to be able to work with multiple data formats.

Remember that the records of each CSV format are stored using their own Go structure under a different variable name. As a result, we need to implement `sort.Interface` for both CSV formats and therefore for both slice variables.

The two supported formats are the following:

- *Format 1*: name, surname, telephone number, time of last access
- *Format 2*: name, surname, area code, telephone number, time of last access

As the two CSV formats that are going to be used have a different number of fields, the utility determines the format that is being used by the number of fields found in the first record that was read and acts accordingly. After that, the data will be sorted using `sort.Sort()`—the data type of the slice that keeps the data helps Go determine the sort implementation that is going to be used without any help from the developer.

> The main benefit you get from functions that work with empty interface variables is that you can add support for additional data types easily at a later time without the need to implement additional functions and without breaking existing code.

What follows is the implementation of the most important functions of the utility beginning with `readCSVFile()` because the logic of the utility is found in the `readCSVFile()` function.

```
func readCSVFile(filepath string) error {
.
.
.
```

The code that has to do with reading the input file and making sure that it exists is omitted for brevity.

```
    var firstLine bool = true
    var format1 = true
```

The first line of the CSV file determines its format—therefore, we need a flag variable for specifying whether we are dealing with the first line (`firstLine`) or not. Additionally, we need a second variable for specifying the format we are working with (`format1` is that variable).

```
    for _, line := range lines {
        if firstLine {
            if len(line) == 4 {
                format1 = true
            } else if len(line) == 5 {
                format1 = false
```

The first format has four fields whereas the second format has five fields.

```
            } else {
                return errors.New("Unknown File Format!")
            }
            firstLine = false
        }
```

If the first line of the CSV file has neither four nor five fields, then we have an error, and the function returns with a custom error message.

```
        if format1 {
            if len(line) == 4 {
                temp := F1{
                    Name:       line[0],
                    Surname:    line[1],
                    Tel:        line[2],
                    LastAccess: line[3],
                }
                d1 = append(d1, temp)
            }
```

If we are working with `format1`, we add data to the `d1` global variable.

```
        } else {
            if len(line) == 5 {
                temp := F2{
                    Name:       line[0],
                    Surname:    line[1],
                    Areacode:   line[2],
                    Tel:        line[3],
                    LastAccess: line[4],
                }
                d2 = append(d2, temp)
            }
```

If we are working with `format2`, we add data to the `d2` global variable.

```
        }
    }
    return nil
}
```

The `sortData()` function accepts an empty interface parameter. The code of the function determines the data type of the slice that is passed as an empty interface to that function using a type switch. After that, a type assertion allows you to use the actual data stored under the empty interface parameter. Its full implementation is as follows:

```
func sortData(data interface{}) {
    // type switch
```

```
    switch T := data.(type) {
    case Book1:
        d := data.(Book1)
        sort.Sort(Book1(d))
        list(d)
    case Book2:
        d := data.(Book2)
        sort.Sort(Book2(d))
        list(d)
    default:
        fmt.Printf("Not supported type: %T\n", T)
    }
}
```

The type switch does the job of determining the data type we are working with, which can be either `Book1` or `Book2`. If you want to look at the implementation of `sort.Interface`, you should view the `sortCSV.go` source code file.

Lastly, `list()` prints the data of the data variable used using the technique found in `sortData()`. Although the code that handles `Book1` and `Book2` is the same as in `sortData()`, you still need a type assertion to get the data from the empty interface variable.

```
func list(d interface{}) {
    switch T := d.(type) {
    case Book1:
        data := d.(Book1)
        for _, v := range data {
            fmt.Println(v)
        }
    case Book2:
        data := d.(Book2)
        for _, v := range data {
            fmt.Println(v)
        }
    default:
        fmt.Printf("Not supported type: %T\n", T)
    }
}
```

Running `sortCSV.go` produces the following kind of output:

```
$ go run sortCSV.go /tmp/csv.file
{Jane Doe 0800123456 1609310777}
{Dimitris Tsoukalos 2109416871 1609310731}
{Dimitris Tsoukalos 2109416971 1609310734}
{Mihalis Tsoukalos 2109416471 1609310706}
{Mihalis Tsoukalos 2109416571 1609310717}
```

The program correctly found out the format of `/tmp/csv.file` and worked with it even though it supports two CSV formats. Trying to work with an unsupported format generates the next output:

```
$ go run sortCSV.go /tmp/differentFormat.csv
Unknown File Format!
```

This means that the code successfully understands that we are dealing with an unsupported format.

The next section explores the limited object-oriented capabilities of Go.

Object-oriented programming in Go

As Go does not support all object-oriented features, it cannot replace an object-oriented programming language fully. However, it can **mimic some object-oriented concepts**.

First of all, a Go structure with its type methods is like an object with its methods. Second, interfaces are like abstract data types that define behaviors and objects of the same class, which is similar to **polymorphism**. Third, Go supports **encapsulation**, which means it supports hiding data and functions from the user by making them private to the structure and the current Go package. Lastly, combining interfaces and structures is like **composition** in object-oriented terminology.

> If you really want to develop applications using the object-oriented methodology, then choosing Go might not be your best option. As I am not really into **Java**, I would suggest looking at **C++** or **Python** instead. The general rule here is to choose the best tool for your job.

You have already seen some of these points earlier in this chapter—the next chapter discusses how to define private fields and functions. The example that follows, which is named `objO.go`, illustrates composition and polymorphism as well as embedding an anonymous structure into an existing one to get all its fields.

```
package main

import (
    "fmt"
)

type IntA interface {
    foo()
}

type IntB interface {
    bar()
}

type IntC interface {
    IntA
    IntB
}
```

The `IntC` interface combines interfaces `IntA` and `IntB`. If you implement `IntA` and `IntB` for a data type, then this data type implicitly satisfies `IntC`.

```
func processA(s IntA) {
    fmt.Printf("%T\n", s)
}
```

This function works with data types that satisfy the `IntA` interface.

```
type a struct {
    XX int
    YY int
}

// Satisfying IntA
func (varC c) foo() {
    fmt.Println("Foo Processing", varC)
}
```

Structure `c` satisfying `IntA` as it implements `foo()`.

```
// Satisfying IntB
func (varC c) bar() {
    fmt.Println("Bar Processing", varC)
}
```

Structure c satisfying IntB. As structure c satisfies both IntA and IntB, it implicitly satisfies IntC, which is a composition of the IntA and IntB interfaces.

```
type b struct {
    AA string
    XX int
}

// Structure c has two fields
type c struct {
    A a
    B b
}
```

This structure has two fields named A and B that are of the a and b data types, respectively.

```
// Structure compose gets the fields of structure a
type compose struct {
    field1 int
    a
}
```

This new structure uses an anonymous structure (a), which means that it gets the fields of that anonymous structure.

```
// Different structures can have methods with the same name
func (A a) A() {
    fmt.Println("Function A() for A")
}

func (B b) A() {
    fmt.Println("Function A() for B")
}

func main() {
    var iC c = c{a{120, 12}, b{"-12", -12}}
```

Here we define a c variable that is composed of an a structure and a b structure.

```
    iC.A.A()
    iC.B.A()
```

Here we access a method of the a structure (`A.A()`) and a method of the `b` structure (`B.A()`).

```
    // The following will not work
    // iComp := compose{field1: 123, a{456, 789}}
    // iComp := compose{field1: 123, XX: 456, YY: 789}
    iComp := compose{123, a{456, 789}}
    fmt.Println(iComp.XX, iComp.YY, iComp.field1)
```

When using an anonymous structure inside another structure, as we do with `a{456, 789}`, you can access the fields of the anonymous structure, which is the `a{456, 789}` structure, directly as `iComp.XX` and `iComp.YY`.

```
    iC.bar()
    processA(iC)
}
```

Although `processA()` works with `IntA` variables, it can also work with `IntC` variables because the `IntC` interface satisfies `IntA`!

All the code in `objO.go` is pretty simplistic compared to the code of a real object-oriented programming language that supports abstract classes and inheritance. However, it is more than adequate for generating types and elements with a structure in them, as well as for having different data types with the same method names.

Running `objO.go` produces the next output:

```
$ go run objO.go
Function A() for A
Function A() for B
456 789 123
Bar Processing {{120 12} {-12 -12}}
main.c
```

The first two lines of the output show that two different structures can have a method with the same name. The third line proves that when using an anonymous structure inside one other structure, you can access the fields of the anonymous structure directly. The fourth line is the output of the `iC.bar()` call, where `iC` is a `c` variable accessing a method from the `IntB` interface. The last line is the output of `processA(iC)` that requires an `IntA` parameter and prints the real data type of its parameter, which in this case is `main.c`.

Evidently, although Go is not an object-oriented programming language, it can mimic some of the characteristics of object-oriented programming. Moving on, the last section of this chapter is about updating the phone book application by reading an environment variable and sorting its output.

Updating the phone book application

The functionality that is added to this new version of the phone book utility is the following:

- The CSV file path can be optionally given as an environment variable named `PHONEBOOK`
- The `list` command sorts the output based on the surname field

Although we could have given the path of the CSV file as a command-line argument instead of the value of an environment variable, it would have complicated the code, especially if that argument was made optional. More advanced Go packages such as `viper`, which is presented in *Chapter 6, Telling a UNIX System What to Do*, simplify the process of parsing command-line arguments with the use of command-line options such as `-f` followed by a file path or `--filepath`.

> The current default value of `CSVFILE` is set to my home directory on a macOS Big Sur machine—you should change that default value to fit your needs or use a proper value for the `PHONEBOOK` environment variable.

Last, if the `PHONEBOOK` environment variable is not set, then the utility uses a default value for the CSV file path. Generally speaking, not having to recompile your software for user-defined data is considered a good practice.

Setting up the value of the CSV file

The value of the CSV file is set in the `setCSVFILE()` function, which is defined as follows:

```
func setCSVFILE() error {
	filepath := os.Getenv("PHONEBOOK")
	if filepath != "" {
		CSVFILE = filepath
	}
```

Here is where we read the PHONEBOOK environment variable. The rest of the code is about making sure that we can use that file path or the default one if PHONEBOOK is not set.

```
	_, err := os.Stat(CSVFILE)
	if err != nil {
		fmt.Println("Creating", CSVFILE)
		f, err := os.Create(CSVFILE)
		if err != nil {
			f.Close()
			return err
		}
		f.Close()
	}
```

If the specified file does not exist, it is created using `os.Create()`.

```
	fileInfo, err := os.Stat(CSVFILE)
	mode := fileInfo.Mode()
	if !mode.IsRegular() {
		return fmt.Errorf("%s not a regular file", CSVFILE)
	}
```

Then, we make sure that the specified path belongs to a regular file that can be used for saving data.

```
	return nil
}
```

In order to simplify the implementation of the `main()` function, we moved the code related to the existence of and access to the CSV file path to `setCSVFILE()`.

The first time we set the PHONEBOOK environment variable and executed the phone book application, we got the following output—you should get something similar.

```
$ export PHONEBOOK="/tmp/csv.file"
$ go run phoneBook.go list
Creating /tmp/csv.file
```

As `/tmp/csv.file` does not exist, `phoneBook.go` creates it from scratch. This verifies that the Go code of the `setCSVFILE()` function works as expected.

Now that we know where to get and write our data, it is time to learn how to sort it using `sort.Interface`, which is the subject of the subsection that follows.

Using the sort package

The first thing to decide when trying to sort data is the field that is going to be used for sorting. After that, we need to decide what we are going to do when two or more records have the same value in the main field used for sorting.

The code related to sorting using `sort.Interface` is the following:

```
type PhoneBook []Entry
```

You need to have a separate data type—`sort.Interface` is implemented for this data type.

```
var data = PhoneBook{}
```

As you have a separate data type for implementing `sort.Interface`, the data type of the `data` variable needs to change and become `PhoneBook`. Then `sort.Interface` is implemented for `PhoneBook`.

```
// Implement sort.Interface
func (a PhoneBook) Len() int {
    return len(a)
}
```

The `Len()` function has a standard implementation.

```
// First based on surname. If they have the same
// surname take into account the name.
func (a PhoneBook) Less(i, j int) bool {
    if a[i].Surname == a[j].Surname {
        return a[i].Name < a[j].Name
    }
```

The `Less()` function is the place to define how you are going to sort the elements of the slice. What we say here is that if the entries that are compared, which are Go structures, have the same `Surname` field value, then compare these entries using their `Name` field values.

```
    return a[i].Surname < a[j].Surname
}
```

If the entries have different values in the `Surname` field, then compare them using the `Surname` field.

```
func (a PhoneBook) Swap(i, j int) {
    a[i], a[j] = a[j], a[i]
}
```

The `Swap()` function has a standard implementation. After implementing the desired interface, we need to tell our code to sort the data, which happens in the implementation of the `list()` function:

```
func list() {
    sort.Sort(PhoneBook(data))
    for _, v := range data {
        fmt.Println(v)
    }
}
```

Now that we know how sorting is implemented, it is time to use the utility. First, we add some entries:

```
$ go run phoneBook.go insert Mihalis Tsoukalos 2109416471
$ go run phoneBook.go insert Mihalis Tsoukalos 2109416571
$ go run phoneBook.go insert Dimitris Tsoukalos 2109416871
$ go run phoneBook.go insert Dimitris Tsoukalos 2109416971
$ go run phoneBook.go insert Jane Doe 0800123456
```

Last, we print the contents of the phone book using the `list` command:

```
$ go run phoneBook.go list
{Jane Doe 0800123456 1609310777}
{Dimitris Tsoukalos 2109416871 1609310731}
{Dimitris Tsoukalos 2109416971 1609310734}
{Mihalis Tsoukalos 2109416471 1609310706}
{Mihalis Tsoukalos 2109416571 1609310717}
```

As `Dimitris` comes before `Mihalis` alphabetically, all relevant entries come first as well, which means that our sorting works as expected.

Exercises

- Create a slice of structures using a structure that you created and sort the elements of the slice using a field from the structure
- Integrate the functionality of `sortCSV.go` in `phonebook.go`

- Add support for a `reverse` command to `phonebook.go` in order to list its entries in reverse order
- Use the empty interface and a function that allows you to differentiate between two different structures that you create

Summary

In this chapter, we learned about *interfaces*, which are like contracts, and also about *type methods*, type assertion, and reflection. Although reflection is a very powerful Go feature, it might slow down your Go programs because it adds a layer of complexity at runtime. Furthermore, your Go programs could crash if you use reflection carelessly.

The last section of this chapter discussed writing Go code that follows the principles of object-oriented programming. If you are going to remember just one thing from this chapter, it should be that Go is not an object-oriented programming language, but it can mimic some of the functionality offered by object-programming languages, such as Java, Python, and C++.

The next chapter discusses Go packages, functions, and automation using GitHub and GitLab CI/CD systems.

Additional resources

- The documentation of the `reflect` package: `https://golang.org/pkg/reflect/`
- The documentation of the `sort` package: `https://golang.org/pkg/sort/`
- Working with errors in Go 1.13: `https://blog.golang.org/go1.13-errors`
- The implementation of the `sort` package: `https://golang.org/src/sort/`

5

Go Packages and Functions

The main focus of this chapter is Go **packages**, which are Go's way of organizing, delivering, and using code. The most common component of packages is **functions**, which are pretty flexible and powerful and are used for data processing and manipulation. Go also supports **modules**, which are packages with version numbers. This chapter will also explain the operation of `defer`, which is used for cleaning up and releasing resources.

Regarding the visibility of package elements, Go follows a simple rule that states that functions, variables, data types, structure fields, and so forth that begin with an uppercase letter are **public**, whereas functions, variables, types, and so on that begin with a lowercase letter are **private**. This is the reason why `fmt.Println()` is named `Println()` instead of just `println()`. The same rule applies not only to the name of a `struct` variable but to the fields of a `struct` variable—in practice, this means that you can have a `struct` variable with both private and public fields. However, this rule does not affect package names, which are allowed to begin with either uppercase or lowercase letters.

In summary, this chapter covers:

- Go packages
- Functions
- Developing your own packages
- Using GitHub to store Go packages
- A package for working with a database
- Modules

- Creating better packages
- Creating documentation
- GitLab Runners and Go
- GitHub Actions and Go
- Versioning utilities

Go packages

Everything in Go is delivered in the form of packages. A Go package is a Go source file that begins with the `package` keyword, followed by the name of the package.

> Note that packages can have structure. For example, the `net` package has several subdirectories, named `http`, `mail`, `rpc`, `smtp`, `textproto`, and `url`, which should be imported as `net/http`, `net/mail`, `net/rpc`, `net/smtp`, `net/textproto`, and `net/url`, respectively.

Apart from the packages of the Go standard library, there are external packages that can be imported using their full address and that should be downloaded on the local machine, before their first use. One such example is `https://github.com/spf13/cobra`, which is stored in GitHub.

Packages are mainly used for grouping related functions, variables, and constants so that you can transfer them easily and use them in your own Go programs. Note that apart from the `main` package, Go packages are not autonomous programs and cannot be compiled into executable files on their own. As a result, if you try to execute a Go package as if it were an autonomous program, you are going to be disappointed:

```
$ go run aPackage.go
go run: cannot run non-main package
```

Instead, packages need to be called directly or indirectly from a `main` package in order to be used, as we have shown in previous chapters.

Downloading Go packages

In this subsection, you will learn how to download external Go packages using `https://github.com/spf13/cobra` as an example. The `go get` command for downloading the `cobra` package is as follows:

```
$ go get github.com/spf13/cobra
```

Note that you can download the package without using `https://` in its address. The results can be found inside the `~/go` directory—the full path is `~/go/src/github.com/spf13/cobra`. As the `cobra` package comes with a binary file that helps you structure and create command-line utilities, you can find that binary file inside `~/go/bin` as `cobra`.

The following output, which was created with the help of the `tree(1)` utility, shows a high-level view with 3 levels of detail of the structure of `~/go` on my machine:

```
$ tree ~/go -L 3
/Users/mtsouk/go
├── bin
│   ├── cobra
│   ├── go-outline
│   ├── gocode
│   ├── gocode-gomod
│   ├── godef
│   ├── golint
│   ├── gopkgs
│   └── goreturns
├── pkg
│   ├── darwin_amd64
│   │   ├── github.com
│   │   ├── golang.org
│   │   ├── gonum.org
│   │   └── google.golang.org
│   ├── mod
│   │   ├── 9fans.net
│   │   ├── cache
│   │   ├── cloud.google.com
│   │   ├── github.com
│   │   ├── go.opencensus.io@v0.22.4
│   │   ├── golang.org
│   │   └── google.golang.org
│   └── sumdb
│       └── sum.golang.org
└── src
    ├── github.com
    │   ├── sirupsen
    │   └── spf13
    └── golang.org
        └── x

23 directories, 8 files
```

> The x path, which is displayed last, is used by the Go team.

Basically, there are three main directories under ~/go with the following properties:

- The bin directory: This is where binary tools are placed.
- The pkg directory: This is where reusable packages are put. The darwin_amd64 directory, which can be found on macOS machines only, contains compiled versions of the installed packages. On a Linux machine, you can find a linux_amd64 directory instead of darwin_amd64.
- The src directory: This is where the source code of the packages is located. The underlying structure is based on the URL of the package you are looking for. So, the URL for the github.com/spf13/viper package is ~/go/src/github.com/spf13/viper. If a package is downloaded as a module, then it will be located under ~/go/pkg/mod.

> Starting with Go 1.16, `go install` is the recommended way of building and installing packages in module mode. The use of `go get` is deprecated, but this chapter uses `go get` because it's commonly used online and is worth knowing about. However, most of the chapters in this book use `go mod init` and `go mod tidy` for downloading external dependencies for your own source files.

If you want to upgrade an existing package, you should execute go get with the -u option. Additionally, if you want to see what is happening behind the scenes, add the -v option to the go get command—in this case, we are using the viper package as an example, but we abbreviate the output:

```
$ go get -v github.com/spf13/viper
github.com/spf13/viper (download)
...
github.com/spf13/afero (download)
get "golang.org/x/text/transform": found meta tag get.
metaImport{Prefix:"golang.org/x/text", VCS:"git", RepoRoot:"https://
go.googlesource.com/text"} at //golang.org/x/text/transform?go-get=1
get "golang.org/x/text/transform": verifying non-authoritative meta tag
...
github.com/fsnotify/fsnotify
github.com/spf13/viper
```

What you can basically see in the output is the dependencies of the initial package being downloaded before the desired package—most of the time, you do not want to know that.

We will continue this chapter by looking at the most important package element: *functions*.

Functions

The main elements of packages are functions, which are the subject of this section.

> Type methods and functions are implemented in the same way and sometimes, the terms functions and type methods are used interchangeably.

A piece of advice: functions must be as independent from each other as possible and must do one job (and only one job) well. So, if you find yourself writing functions that do multiple things, you might want to consider replacing them with multiple functions instead.

You should already know that all function definitions begin with the `func` keyword, followed by the function's signature and its implementation, and that functions accept none, one, or more arguments and return none, one, or more values back. The single-most popular Go function is `main()`, which is used in every executable Go program—the `main()` function accepts no parameters and returns nothing, but it is the starting point of every Go program. Additionally, when the `main()` function ends, the entire program ends as well.

Anonymous functions

Anonymous functions can be defined inline without the need for a name, and they are usually used for implementing things that require a small amount of code. In Go, a function can return an anonymous function or take an anonymous function as one of its arguments. Additionally, anonymous functions can be attached to Go variables. Note that anonymous functions are called **lambdas** in functional programming terminology. Similar to that, a **closure** is a specific type of anonymous function that carries or *closes over* variables that are in the same lexical scope as the anonymous function that was defined.

It is considered a good practice for anonymous functions to have a small implementation and a local focus. If an anonymous function does not have a local focus, then you might need to consider making it a regular function. When an anonymous function is suitable for a job, it is extremely convenient and makes your life easier; just do not use too many anonymous functions in your programs without having a good reason to. We will look at anonymous functions in action in a while.

Functions that return multiple values

As you already know from functions such as `strconv.Atoi()`, functions can return multiple distinct values, which saves you from having to create a dedicated structure for returning and receiving multiple values from a function. However, if you have a function that returns more than 3 values, you should reconsider that decision and maybe redesign it to use a single structure or slice for grouping and returning the desired values as a single entity—this makes handling the returned values simpler and easier. Functions, anonymous functions, and functions that return multiple values are all illustrated in `functions.go`, as shown in the following code:

```
package main

import "fmt"

func doubleSquare(x int) (int, int) {
    return x * 2, x * x
}
```

This function returns two `int` values, without the need for having separate variables to keep them—the returned values are created on the fly. Note the compulsory use of **parentheses** when a function returns more than one value.

```
// Sorting from smaller to bigger value
func sortTwo(x, y int) (int, int) {
    if x > y {
        return y, x
    }
    return x, y
}
```

The preceding function returns two `int` values as well.

```
func main() {
    n := 10
    d, s := doubleSquare(n)
```

The previous statement reads the two return values of `doubleSquare()` and saves them in `d` and `s`.

```
    fmt.Println("Double of", n, "is", d)
    fmt.Println("Square of", n, "is", s)

    // An anonymous function
    anF := func(param int) int {
        return param * param
    }
```

The `anF` variable holds an **anonymous function** that requires a single parameter as input and returns a single value. The only difference between an anonymous function and a regular one is that the name of the anonymous function is `func()` and that there is no `func` keyword.

```
    fmt.Println("anF of", n, "is", anF(n))

    fmt.Println(sortTwo(1, -3))
    fmt.Println(sortTwo(-1, 0))
}
```

The last two statements print the return values of `sortTwo()`. Running `functions.go` produces the following output:

```
Double of 10 is 20
Square of 10 is 100
anF of 10 is 100
-3 1
-1 0
```

The subsection that follows illustrates functions that have named return values.

The return values of a function can be named

Unlike C, Go allows you to name the return values of a Go function. Additionally, when such a function has a `return` statement without any arguments, the function automatically returns the current value of each named return value, in the order in which they were declared in the function signature.

The following function is included in `namedReturn.go`:

```
func minMax(x, y int) (min, max int) {
    if x > y {
```

```
        min = y
        max = x
        return min, max
```

This `return` statement returns the values stored in the `min` and `max` variables—both `min` and `max` are defined in the **function signature** and not in the function body.

```
    }

    min = x
    max = y
    return
}
```

This `return` statement is equivalent to `return min, max`, which is based on the function signature and the use of named return values.

Running `namedReturn.go` produces the following output:

```
$ go run namedReturn.go 1 -2
-2 1
-2 1
```

Functions that accept other functions as parameters

Functions can accept other functions as parameters. The best example of a function that accepts another function as an argument can be found in the `sort` package. You can provide the `sort.Slice()` function with another function as an argument that specifies the way sorting is implemented. The signature of `sort.Slice()` is `func Slice(slice interface{}, less func(i, j int) bool)`. This means the following:

- The `sort.Slice()` function does not return any data.
- The `sort.Slice()` function requires two arguments, a slice of type `interface{}` and another function—the slice variable is modified inside `sort.Slice()`.
- The function parameter of `sort.Slice()` is named `less` and should have the `func(i, j int) bool` signature—there is no need for you to name the anonymous function. The name `less` is required because all function parameters should have a name.
- The `i` and `j` parameters of `less` are indexes of the `slice` parameter.

Similarly, there is another function in the sort package named `sort.SliceIsSorted()` that is defined as `func SliceIsSorted(slice interface{}, less func(i, j int) bool) bool`. `sort.SliceIsSorted()` returns a `bool` value and checks whether the `slice` parameter is sorted according to the rules of the second parameter, which is a function.

> You are not obliged to use an anonymous function in either `sort.Slice()` or `sort.SliceIsSorted()`. You can define a regular function with the required signature and use that. However, using an anonymous function is more convenient.

The use of both `sort.Slice()` and `sort.SliceIsSorted()` is illustrated in the Go program that follows—the name of the source file is `sorting.go`:

```
package main

import (
    "fmt"
    "sort"
)

type Grades struct {
    Name    string
    Surname string
    Grade   int
}

func main() {
    data := []Grades{{"J.", "Lewis", 10}, {"M.", "Tsoukalos", 7},
        {"D.", "Tsoukalos", 8}, {"J.", "Lewis", 9}}

    isSorted := sort.SliceIsSorted(data, func(i, j int) bool {
        return data[i].Grade < data[j].Grade
    })
```

The `if else` block that follows checks the `bool` value of `sort.SliceIsSorted()` to determine whether the slice is sorted:

```
    if isSorted {
        fmt.Println("It is sorted!")
    } else {
        fmt.Println("It is NOT sorted!")
    }
```

```
    sort.Slice(data,
        func(i, j int) bool { return data[i].Grade < data[j].Grade })
    fmt.Println("By Grade:", data)
}
```

The call to `sort.Slice()` sorts the data according to the anonymous function that is passed as the second argument to `sort.Slice()`.

Running `sorting.go` produces the following output:

```
It is NOT sorted!
By Grade: [{M. Tsoukalos 7} {D. Tsoukalos 8} {J. Lewis 9} {J. Lewis
10}]
```

Functions can return other functions

Apart from accepting functions as arguments, functions can also return anonymous functions, which can be handy when the returned function is not always the same but depends on the function's input or other external parameters. This is illustrated in `returnFunction.go`:

```
package main

import "fmt"

func funRet(i int) func(int) int {
    if i < 0 {
        return func(k int) int {
            k = -k
            return k + k
        }
    }

    return func(k int) int {
        return k * k
    }
}
```

The signature of `funRet()` declares that the function returns another function with the `func(int) int` signature. The implementation of the function is unknown, but it is going to be defined at runtime. Functions are returned using the `return` keyword. The developer should take care and save the returned function.

```
func main() {
    n := 10
    i := funRet(n)
    j := funRet(-4)
```

Note that `n` and `-4` are only used for determining the anonymous functions that are going to be returned from `funRet()`.

```
    fmt.Printf("%T\n", i)
    fmt.Printf("%T %v\n", j, j)
    fmt.Println("j", j, j(-5))
```

The first statement prints the signature of the function whereas the second statement prints the function signature and its memory address. The last statement also returns the memory address of `j`, because `j` is a pointer to the anonymous function and the value of `j(-5)`.

```
    // Same input parameter but DIFFERENT
    // anonymous functions assigned to i and j
    fmt.Println(i(10))
    fmt.Println(j(10))
}
```

Although both `i` and `j` are called with the same input (`10`), they are going to return different values because they store different anonymous functions.

Running `returnFunction.go` generates the following output:

```
func(int) int
func(int) int 0x10a8d40
j 0x10a8d40 10
100
-20
```

The first line of the output shows the data type of the `i` variable that holds the return value of `funRet(n)`, which is `func(int) int` as it holds a function. The second line of output shows the data type of `j`, as well as the memory address where the anonymous function is stored. The third line shows the memory address of the anonymous function stored in the `j` variable, as well as the return value of `j(-5)`. The last two lines are the return values of `i(10)` and `j(10)`, respectively.

So, in this subsection, we learned about functions returning functions. This makes Go a functional programming language, albeit not a pure one, and allows Go to benefit from the functional programming paradigm.

We are now going to examine variadic functions, which are functions with a variable number of parameters.

Variadic functions

Variadic functions are functions that can accept a variable number of parameters—you already know about `fmt.Println()` and `append()`, which are both variadic functions that are widely used. In fact, most functions found in the `fmt` package are variadic.

The general ideas and rules behind variadic functions are as follows:

- Variadic functions use the *pack operator*, which consists of a `...`, followed by a data type. So, for a variadic function to accept a variable number of `int` values, the pack operator should be `...int`.
- The pack operator can only be used once in any given function.
- The variable that holds the pack operation is a slice and, therefore, is accessed as a slice inside the variadic function.
- The variable name that is related to the pack operator is always last in the list of function parameters.
- When calling a variadic function, you should put a list of values separated by `,` in the place of the variable with the *pack operator* or a slice with the *unpack operator*.

This list contains all the rules that you need to know in order to define and use variadic functions.

The pack operator can also be used with an empty interface. In fact, most functions in the `fmt` package use `...interface{}` to accept a variable number of arguments of all data types. You can find the source code of the latest implementation of `fmt` at `https://golang.org/src/fmt/`.

However, there is a situation that needs special care here—I made that mistake when I was learning Go. If you try to pass `os.Args`, which is a slice of strings (`[]string`), as `...interface{}` to a variadic function), your code will not compile and will generate an error message similar to `cannot use os.Args (type []string) as type []interface {} in argument to <function_name>`. This happens because the two data types (`[]string` and `[]interface{}`) do not have the same representations in memory—this applies to all data types. In practice, this means that you cannot write `os.Args...` to pass each individual value of the `os.Args` slice to a variadic function.

On the other hand, if you just use `os.Args`, it will work, but this passes the entire slice as a *single entity* instead of its individual values! This means that the `everything(os.Args, os.Args)` statement works but does not do what you want.

The solution to this problem is converting the slice of strings—or any other slice—into a slice of `interface{}`. One way to do that is by using the code that follows:

```
empty := make([]interface{}, len(os.Args[1:]))
for i, v := range os.Args {
    empty[i] = v
}
```

Now, you are allowed to use `empty...` as an argument to the variadic function. This is the only subtle point related to variadic functions and the pack operator.

> As there is no standard library function to perform that conversion for you, you have to write your own code. Note that the conversion takes time because the code must visit all slice elements. The more elements the slice has, the more time the conversion will take. This topic is also discussed at `https://github.com/golang/go/wiki/InterfaceSlice`.

We are now ready to see variadic functions in action. Type the following Go code using your favorite text editor and save it as `variadic.go`:

```
package main

import (
    "fmt"
    "os"
)
```

As variadic functions are built into the grammar of the language, you do not need anything extra to support variadic functions.

```
func addFloats(message string, s ...float64) float64 {
```

This is a variadic function that accepts a `string` and an unknown number of `float64` values. It prints the `string` variable and calculates the sum of the `float64` values.

```
    fmt.Println(message)
    sum := float64(0)
    for _, a := range s {
        sum = sum + a
    }
```

This `for` loop accesses the pack operator as a slice, so there is nothing special here.

```
    s[0] = -1000
    return sum
}
```

You can also access individual elements of the s slice.

```
func everything(input ...interface{}) {
    fmt.Println(input)
}
```

This is another variadic function that accepts an unknown number of `interface{}` values.

```
func main() {
    sum := addFloats("Adding numbers...", 1.1, 2.12, 3.14, 4, 5, -1,
10)
```

You can put the arguments of a variadic function inline.

```
    fmt.Println("Sum:", sum)
    s := []float64{1.1, 2.12, 3.14}
```

But you usually use a slice variable with the unpack operator.

```
    sum = addFloats("Adding numbers...", s...)
    fmt.Println("Sum:", sum)
    everything(s)
```

The previous code works because the content of s is not unpacked.

```
    // Cannot directly pass []string as []interface{}
    // You have to convert it first!
    empty := make([]interface{}, len(os.Args[1:]))
```

You can convert `[]string` into `[]interface{}` in order to use the unpack operator.

```
    for i, v := range os.Args[1:] {
        empty[i] = v
    }
    everything(empty...)
```

And now, we can unpack the contents of empty.

```
    arguments := os.Args[1:]
    empty = make([]interface{}, len(arguments))
    for i := range arguments {
        empty[i] = arguments[i]
    }
```

This is a slightly different way of converting []string into []interface{}.

```
    everything(empty...)
    // This will work!
    str := []string{"One", "Two", "Three"}
    everything(str, str, str)
}
```

The previous statement works because you are passing the entire str variable three times—not its contents. So, the slice contains three elements—each element is equal to the contents of the str variable.

Running variadic.go produces the following output:

```
$ go run variadic.go
Adding numbers...
Sum: 24.36
Adding numbers...
Sum: 6.36
[[-1000 2.12 3.14]]
[]
[]
[[One Two Three] [One Two Three] [One Two Three]]
```

The last line of the output shows that we have passed the str variable three times to the everything() function as three separate entities.

Variadic functions come in very handy when you want to have an unknown number of parameters in a function. The next subsection discusses the use of defer, which we have already used multiple times.

The defer keyword

So far, we have seen defer in ch03/csvData.go, as well as in the implementations of the phone book application. But what does defer do? The defer keyword postpones the execution of a function until the surrounding function returns.

Usually, `defer` is used in file I/O operations to keep the function call that closes an opened file close to the call that opened it, so that you do not have to remember to close a file that you have opened just before the function exits.

It is very important to remember that **deferred functions** are executed in **last in, first out** (**LIFO**) order after the surrounding function has been returned. Putting it simply, this means that if you `defer` function `f1()` first, function `f2()` second, and function `f3()` third in the same surrounding function, then when the surrounding function is about to return, function `f3()` will be executed first, function `f2()` will be executed second, and function `f1()` will be the last one to get executed.

In this section, we will discuss the dangers of `defer`, when used carelessly using a simple program. The code for `defer.go` is as follows.

```
package main

import (
    "fmt"
)

func d1() {
    for i := 3; i > 0; i-- {
        defer fmt.Print(i, " ")
    }
}
```

In `d1()`, `defer` is executed inside the function body with just a `fmt.Print()` call. Remember that these calls to `fmt.Print()` are executed just before function `d1()` returns.

```
func d2() {
    for i := 3; i > 0; i-- {
        defer func() {
            fmt.Print(i, " ")
        }()
    }
    fmt.Println()
}
```

In `d2()`, `defer` is attached to an anonymous function that does not accept any parameters. In practice, this means that the anonymous function should get the value of `i` on its own—this is dangerous because the current value of `i` depends on when the anonymous function is executed.

> The anonymous function is a **closure**, and that is why it has access to variables that would normally be out of scope.

```
func d3() {
    for i := 3; i > 0; i-- {
        defer func(n int) {
            fmt.Print(n, " ")
        }(i)
    }
}
```

In this case, the current value of `i` is passed to the anonymous function as a parameter that initializes the `n` function parameter. This means that there are no ambiguities about the value that `i` has.

```
func main() {
    d1()
    d2()
    fmt.Println()
    d3()
    fmt.Println()
}
```

The task of `main()` is to call `d1()`, `d2()`, and `d3()`.

Running `defer.go` produces the following output:

```
$ go run defer.go
1 2 3
0 0 0
1 2 3
```

You will most likely find the generated output complicated and challenging to understand, which proves that the operation and the results of the use of `defer` can be tricky if your code is not clear and unambiguous. Let me explain the results so that you get a better idea of how tricky `defer` can be if you do not pay close attention to your code.

Let's start with the first line of the output (`1 2 3`) that is generated by the `d1()` function. The values of `i` in `d1()` are `3`, `2`, and `1` in that order. The function that is deferred in `d1()` is the `fmt.Print()` statement; as a result, when the `d1()` function is about to return, you get the three values of the `i` variable of the `for` loop in reverse order. This is because deferred functions are executed in LIFO order.

Now, let me explain the second line of the output that is produced by the `d2()` function. It is really strange that we got three zeros instead of `1 2 3` in the output; however, there is a reason for that. After the `for` loop ended, the value of `i` is `0`, because it is that value of `i` that made the `for` loop terminate. However, the tricky point here is that the deferred anonymous function is evaluated after the `for` loop ends because it has no parameters, which means that it is evaluated three times for an `i` value of `0`, hence the generated output. This kind of confusing code is what might lead to the creation of nasty bugs in your projects, so try to avoid it.

Finally, we will talk about the third line of the output, which is generated by the `d3()` function. Due to the parameter of the anonymous function, each time the anonymous function is deferred, it gets and therefore uses the current value of `i`. As a result, each execution of the anonymous function has a different value to process without any ambiguities, hence the generated output.

After that, it should be clear that the best approach to using `defer` is the third one, which is exhibited in the `d3()` function, because you intentionally pass the desired variable in the anonymous function in an easy-to-read way. Now that we have learned about `defer`, it is time to discuss something completely different: how to develop your own packages.

Developing your own packages

At some point, you are going to need to develop your own packages to organize your code and distribute it if needed. As stated at the beginning of this chapter, everything that begins with an uppercase letter is considered public and can be accessed from outside its package, whereas all other elements are considered private. The only exception to this Go rule is package names—it is a best practice to use lowercase package names, even though uppercase package names are allowed.

Compiling a Go package can be done manually, if the package exists on the local machine, but it is also done automatically after you download the package from the internet, so there is no need to worry about it. Additionally, if the package you are downloading contains any errors, you will learn about them at downloading time.

However, if you want to compile a package that has been saved in the `post05.go` file (a combination of *PostgreSQL* and *Chapter 05*) on your own, you can use the following command:

```
$ go build  -o post.a post05.go
```

So, the previous command compiles the `post05.go` file and saves its output in the `post.a` file:

```
$ file post.a
post.a: current ar archive
```

The `post.a` file is an `ar` archive.

> The main reason for compiling Go packages on your own is to check for syntax or other kinds of errors in your code. Additionally, you can build Go packages as plugins (`https://golang.org/pkg/plugin/`) or shared libraries. Discussing more about these is beyond the scope of this book.

The init() function

Each Go package can optionally have a private function named `init()` that is automatically executed at the beginning of execution time—`init()` runs when the package is initialized at the beginning of program execution. The `init()` function has the following characteristics:

- `init()` takes no arguments.
- `init()` returns no values.
- The `init()` function is optional.
- The `init()` function is called implicitly by Go.
- You can have an `init()` function in the `main` package. In that case, `init()` is executed *before* the `main()` function. In fact, all `init()` functions are always executed prior to the `main()` function.
- A source file can contain multiple `init()` functions—these are executed in the order of declaration.
- The `init()` function or functions of a package are executed only once, even if the package is imported multiple times.
- Go packages can contain multiple files. Each source file can contain one or more `init()` functions.

The fact that the `init()` function is a private function by design means that it cannot be called from outside the package in which it is contained. Additionally, as the user of a package has no control over the `init()` function, you should think carefully before using an `init()` function in public packages or changing any global state in `init()`.

There are some exceptions where the use of `init()` makes sense:

- For initializing network connections that might take time prior to the execution of package functions or methods.
- For initializing connections to one or more servers prior to the execution of package functions or methods.
- For creating required files and directories.
- For checking whether required resources are available or not.

As the order of execution can be perplexing sometimes, in the next subsection, we will explain the order of execution in more detail.

Order of execution

This subsection illustrates how Go code is executed. As an example, if a `main` package imports package `A` and package `A` depends on package `B`, then the following will take place:

- The process starts with `main` package.
- The `main` package imports package `A`.
- Package `A` imports package `B`.
- The global variables, if any, in package `B` are initialized.
- The `init()` function or functions of package `B`, if they exist, run. This is the first `init()` function that gets executed.
- The global variables, if any, in package `A` are initialized.
- The `init()` function or functions of package `A`, if there are any, run.
- The global variables in the `main` package are initialized.
- The `init()` function or functions of `main` package, if they exist, run.
- The `main()` function of the `main` package begins execution.

> Notice that if the `main` package imports package `B` on its own, nothing is going to happen because everything related to package `B` is triggered by package `A`. This is because package `A` imports package `B` first.

The following diagram shows what is happening behind the scenes regarding the order of execution of Go code:

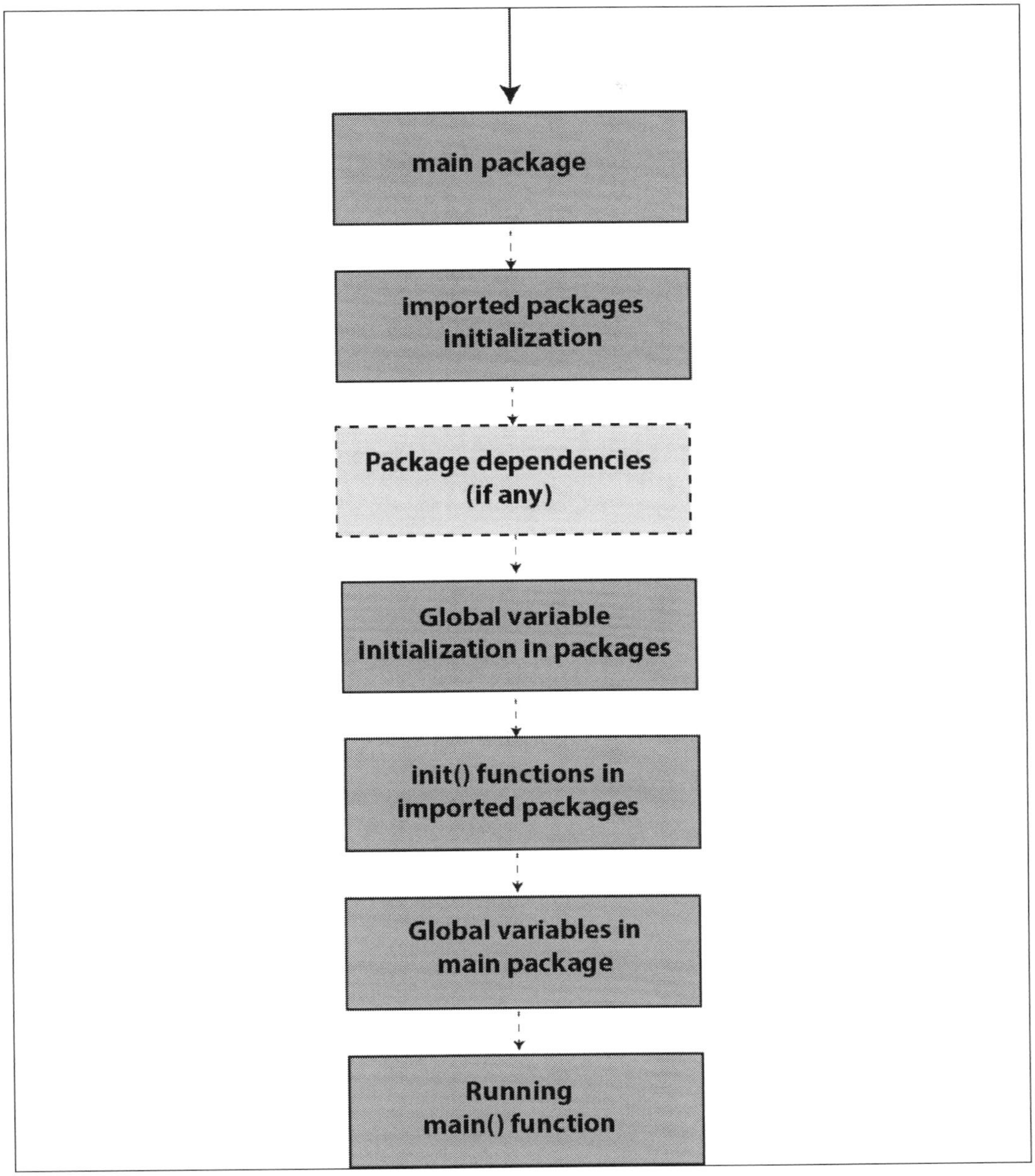

Figure 5.1: Order of execution in Go

You can learn more about the order of execution in Go by reading the Go Language Specification document at `https://golang.org/ref/spec#Order_of_evaluation` and about package initialization at `https://golang.org/ref/spec#Package_initialization`.

Using GitHub to store Go packages

This section will teach you how to create a GitHub repository where you can keep your Go package and make it available to the world.

First, you need to create the GitHub repository on your own. The easiest way to create a new GitHub repository is by visiting the GitHub website and going to the *Repositories* tab, where you can see your existing repositories and create new ones. Press the **New** button and type in the necessary information for creating a new GitHub repository. If you made your repository public, everyone will be able to see it—if it is a private repository, only the people you choose are going to be able to look into it.

> Having a clear `README.md` file in your GitHub repository that explains the way the Go package works is considered a very good practice.

Next, you need to clone the repository on your local computer. I usually clone it using the `git(1)` utility. As the name of the repository is `post05` and my GitHub username is `mactsouk`, the `git clone` command looks as follows:

```
$ git clone git@github.com:mactsouk/post05.git
```

Type `cd post05` and you are done! After that, you just have to write the code of the Go package and remember to `git commit` and `git push` the code to the GitHub repository.

The look of such a repository, after it has been used for a while, can be seen in *Figure 5.2*—you are going to learn more about the `post05` repository in a while:

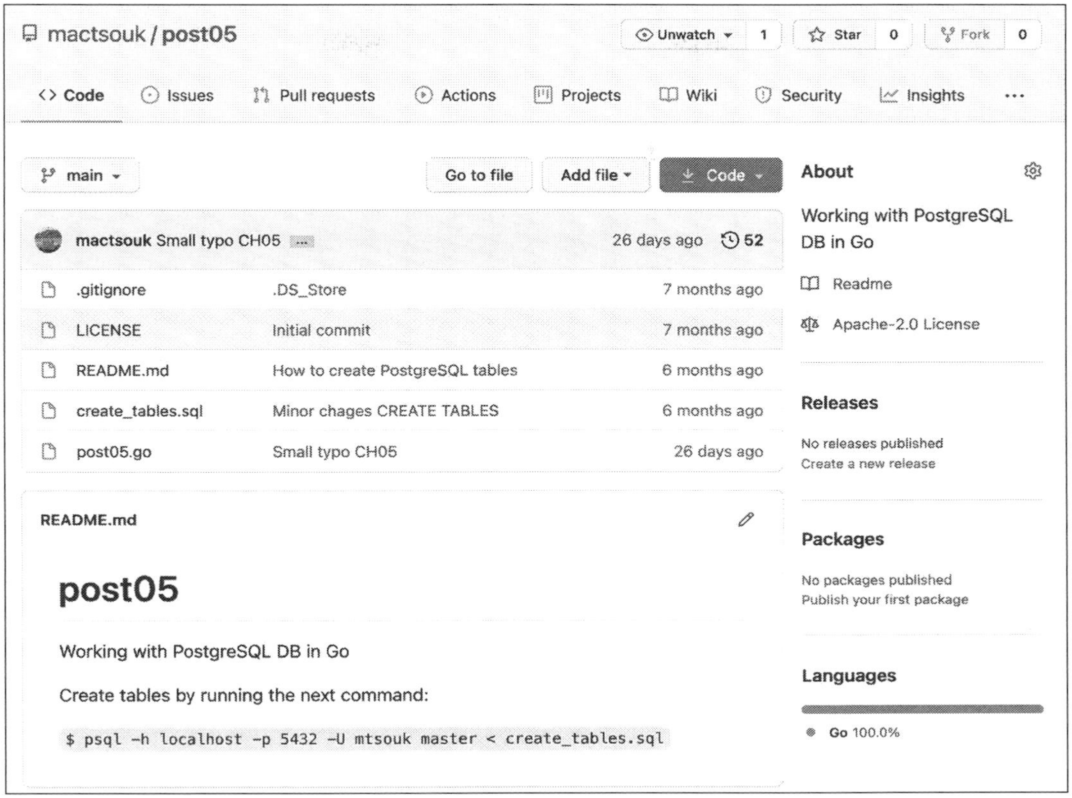

Figure 5.2: A GitHub repository with a Go package

> Using GitLab instead of GitHub for hosting your code does not require making any changes to the way you work.

If you want to use that package, you just need to `go get` the package using its URL and include it in your `import` block—we will see this when we actually use it in a program.

The next section presents a Go package that allows you to work with a database.

A package for working with a database

This section will develop a Go package for working with a given database schema stored on a Postgres database, with the end goal of demonstrating how to develop, store, and use a package. When interacting with specific schemas and tables in your application, you usually create separate packages with all the database-related functions—this also applies to NoSQL databases.

Go offers a generic package (`https://golang.org/pkg/database/sql/`) for working with databases. However, each database requires a specific package that acts as the driver and allows Go to connect and work with this specific database.

The steps for creating the desired Go package are as follows:

- Downloading the necessary external Go packages for working with PostgreSQL.
- Creating package files.
- Developing the required functions.
- Using the Go package for developing utilities.
- Using CI/CD tools for automation (this is optional).

You might be wondering why we would create such a package for working with a database and not write the actual commands in our programs when needed. The reasons for this include the following:

- A Go package can be shared by all team members that work with the application.
- A Go package allows people to use the database in ways that are documented.
- The specialized functions you put in your Go package fit your needs a lot better.
- People do not need full access to the database—they just use the package functions and the functionality they offer.
- If you ever make changes to the database, people do not need to know about them, as long as the functions of the Go package remain the same.

Put simply, the functions you create can interact with a specific database schema, along with its tables and data—it would be almost impossible to work with an unknown database schema without knowing how the tables are connected to each other.

> Apart from all these technical reasons, it is really fun to create Go packages that are shared among multiple developers!

Let's now continue by learning more about the database and its tables.

Getting to know your database

You most likely need to download an additional package for working with a database server such as Postgres, MySQL, or MongoDB. In this case, we are using *PostgreSQL* and therefore need to download a Go package that allows us to communicate with PostgreSQL. There are two main Go packages for connecting to PostgreSQL—we are going to use the `github.com/lib/pq` package here, but it is up to you to decide which package to use.

> There is another Go package for working with PostgreSQL called `jackc/pgx` that can be found at `https://github.com/JackC/pgx`.

You can download that package as follows:

```
$ go get github.com/lib/pq
```

To make things simpler, the PostgreSQL server is executed from a Docker image using a `docker-compose.yml` file, which has the following contents:

```
version: '3'

services:
  postgres:
    image: postgres
    container_name: postgres
    environment:
      - POSTGRES_USER=mtsouk
      - POSTGRES_PASSWORD=pass
      - POSTGRES_DB=master
    volumes:
      - ./postgres:/var/lib/postgresql/data/
```

```
    networks:
      - psql
    ports:
      - "5432:5432"

volumes:
  postgres:

networks:
  psql:
    driver: bridge
```

The default port number the PostgreSQL server listens to is `5432`. As we connect to that PostgreSQL server from the same machine, the hostname that is going to be used is `localhost` or, if you prefer an IP address, `127.0.0.1`. If you are using a different PostgreSQL server, then you should change the connection details in the code that follows accordingly.

> In PostgreSQL, a schema is a namespace that contains named database objects such as tables, views, and indexes. PostgreSQL automatically creates a schema called `public` for every new database.

The following Go utility, which is named `getSchema.go`, verifies that you can connect successfully to a PostgreSQL database and get a list of the available databases and tables in the given database and the `public` schema—all connection information is provided as command-line arguments:

```
package main

import (
	"database/sql"
	"fmt"
	"os"
	"strconv"

	_ "github.com/lib/pq"
)
```

The `lib/pq` package, which is the interface to the PostgreSQL database, is not used directly by the code. Therefore, you need to import the `lib/pq` package with _ in order to prevent the Go compiler from creating an error message related to importing a package and not "using" it.

Most of the time, you do not need to import a package with _, but this is one of the exceptions. This kind of import is usually because the imported package has side effects, such as registering itself as the database handler for the `sql` package:

```
func main() {
	arguments := os.Args
	if len(arguments) != 6 {
		fmt.Println("Please provide: hostname port username password
db")
		return
	}
```

Having a good help message for the information required by such a utility is very handy.

```
	host := arguments[1]
	p := arguments[2]
	user := arguments[3]
	pass := arguments[4]
	database := arguments[5]
```

This is where we collect the details of the database connection.

```
	// Port number SHOULD BE an integer
	port, err := strconv.Atoi(p)
	if err != nil {
		fmt.Println("Not a valid port number:", err)
		return
	}

	// connection string
	conn := fmt.Sprintf("host=%s port=%d user=%s password=%s dbname=%s
sslmode=disable", host, port, user, pass, database)
```

This is how you define the connection string with the details for the connection to the PostgreSQL database server. The connection string should be passed to the `sql.Open()` function for establishing the connection. So far, we have no connection.

```
	// open PostgreSQL database
	db, err := sql.Open("postgres", conn)
	if err != nil {
		fmt.Println("Open():", err)
		return
	}
	defer db.Close()
```

The `sql.Open()` function opens the database connection and keeps it open until the program ends, or until you execute `Close()` in order to properly close the database connection.

```
// Get all databases
rows, err := db.Query(`SELECT "datname" FROM "pg_database"
WHERE datistemplate = false`)
if err != nil {
    fmt.Println("Query", err)
    return
}
```

In order to execute a `SELECT` query, you need to create it first. As the presented `SELECT` query contains no parameters, which means that it does not change based on variables, you can pass it to the `Query()` function and execute it. The *live* outcome of the `SELECT` query is kept in the `rows` variable, which is a **cursor**. You do not get all the results from the database, as a query might return millions of records, but you get them one by one—this is the point of using a cursor.

```
for rows.Next() {
    var name string
    err = rows.Scan(&name)
    if err != nil {
        fmt.Println("Scan", err)
        return
    }
    fmt.Println("*", name)
}
defer rows.Close()
```

The previous code shows how to process the results of a `SELECT` query, which can be from nothing to lots of rows. As the `rows` variable is a cursor, you advance from row to row by calling `Next()`. After that, you need to assign the values returned from the `SELECT` query into Go variables, in order to use them. This happens with a call to `Scan()`, which requires pointer parameters. If the `SELECT` query returns multiple values, you need to put multiple parameters in `Scan()`. Lastly, you must call `Close()` with `defer` for the `rows` variable in order to close the statement and free various types of used resources.

```
// Get all tables from __current__ database
query := `SELECT table_name FROM information_schema.tables WHERE
    table_schema = 'public' ORDER BY table_name`
rows, err = db.Query(query)
```

```
    if err != nil {
        fmt.Println("Query", err)
        return
    }
```

We are going to execute another `SELECT` query in the current database, as provided by the user. The definition of the `SELECT` query is kept in the `query` variable for simplicity and for creating easy to read code. The contents of the `query` variable are passed to the `db.Query()` method.

```
    // This is how you process the rows that are returned from SELECT
    for rows.Next() {
        var name string
        err = rows.Scan(&name)
        if err != nil {
            fmt.Println("Scan", err)
            return
        }
        fmt.Println("+T", name)
    }
    defer rows.Close()
}
```

Once again, we need to process the rows returned by the `SELECT` statement using the `rows` cursor and the `Next()` method.

Running `getSchema.go` generates the following kind of output:

```
$ go run getSchema.go localhost 5432 mtsouk pass go
* postgres
* master
* go
+T userdata
+T users
```

But what is the output telling us? Lines beginning with * show PostgreSQL databases, whereas lines beginning with `+T` show database tables—this is our decision. Therefore, this specific PostgreSQL installation contains three databases named `postgres`, `master`, and `go`. The `public` schema of the `go` database, which is specified by the last command-line argument, contains two tables named `userdata` and `users`.

The main advantage of the `getSchema.go` utility is that it is generic and can be used for learning more about PostgreSQL servers, which is the main reason that it requires so many command-line arguments to work.

Now that we know how to access and query a PostgreSQL database using Go, the next task should be creating a GitHub or GitLab repository for keeping and distributing the Go package we are about to develop.

Storing the Go package

The first action we should take is creating a repository for storing the Go package. In our case, we are going to use a GitHub repository to keep the package. It is not a bad idea to keep the GitHub repository **private** during development, before exposing it to the rest of the world, especially when you are creating something critical.

> Keeping the GitHub repository private does not affect the development process, but it might make sharing the Go package more difficult, so in some cases, it would be good to make it public.

For simplicity, we will use a public Go repository for the Go module, which is named `post05`—its full URL is `https://github.com/mactsouk/post05`.

In order to use that package on your machines, you should `go get` it first. However, during development, you should begin with `git clone git@github.com:mactsouk/post05.git` to get the contents of the GitHub repository and make changes to it.

The design of the Go package

The following diagram shows the database schema that the Go package works on. Remember that when working with a specific database and schema, you need to "include" the schema information in your Go code. Put simply, the Go code should know about the schema it works on:

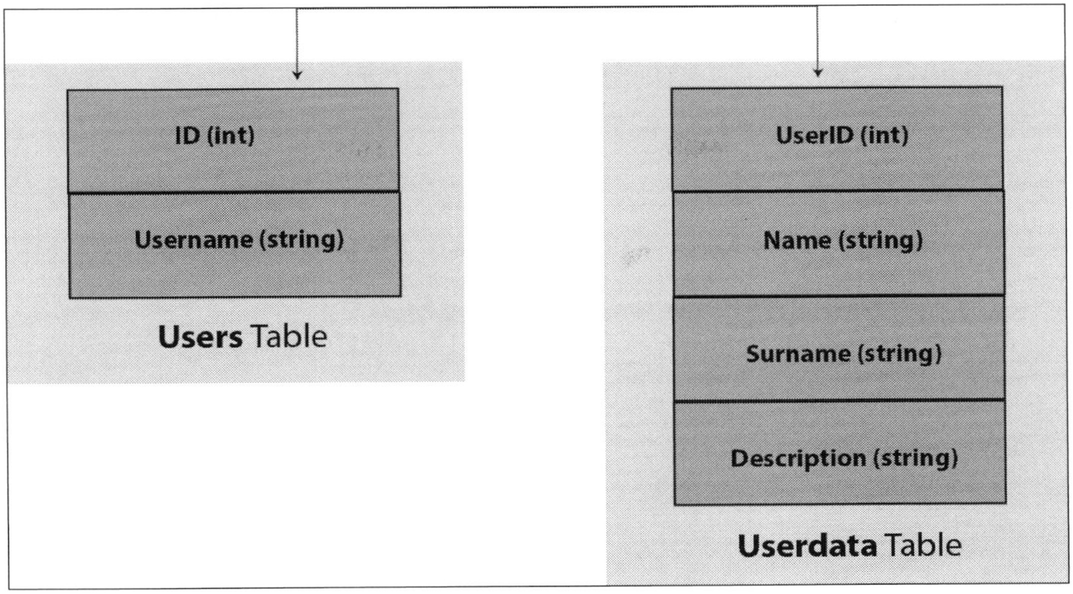

Figure 5.3: The two database tables the Go package works on

This is a simple schema that allows us to keep user data and update it. What connects the two tables is the **user ID**, which should be unique. Additionally, the `Username` field on the `Users` table should also be unique as two or more users cannot share the same username.

This schema already exists in the PostgreSQL database server, which means that the Go code assumes that the relevant tables are in the right place and are stored in the correct PostgreSQL database. Apart from the `Users` table, there is also a table named `Userdata` that holds information about each user. Once a record is entered in the `Users` table, it cannot be changed. What can change, however, is the data stored in the `Userdata` table.

If you want to create the Users database and the two tables in a database called go, you can execute the following statements, which are saved in a file named create_tables.sql with the psgl utility:

```
DROP DATABASE IF EXISTS go;
CREATE DATABASE go;

DROP TABLE IF EXISTS Users;
DROP TABLE IF EXISTS Userdata;

\c go;

CREATE TABLE Users (
    ID SERIAL,
    Username VARCHAR(100) PRIMARY KEY
);

CREATE TABLE Userdata (
    UserID Int NOT NULL,
    Name VARCHAR(100),
    Surname VARCHAR(100),
    Description VARCHAR(200)
);
```

The command-line utility for working with Postgres is called psql. The psql command for executing the code of create_tables.sql is as follows:

```
$ psql -h localhost -p 5432 -U mtsouk master < create_tables.sql
```

Now that we have the necessary infrastructure up and running, let's begin discussing the Go package. The tasks that the Go package should perform to make our lives easier are as follows:

- Create a new user
- Delete an existing user
- Update an existing user
- List all users

Each of these tasks should have one or more Go functions or methods to support it, which is what we are going to implement in the Go package:

- A function to initiate the Postgres connection—the connection details should be given by the user and the package should be able to use them. However, the helper function to initiate the connection can be private.
- There should exist default values in some of the connection details.
- A function that checks whether a given username exists—this is a helper function that might be private.
- A function that inserts a new user into the database.
- A function that deletes an existing user from the database.
- A function for updating an existing user.
- A function for listing all users.

Now that we know the overall structure and functionality of the Go package, we should begin implementing it.

The implementation of the Go package

In this subsection, we will implement the Go package for working with the Postgres database and the given database schema. We will present each function separately—if you combine all these functions, then you have the functionality of the entire package.

> During package development, you should regularly commit your changes to the GitHub or GitLab repository.

The first element that you need in your Go package is one or more **structures** that can hold data from the database tables. Most of the times, you need as many structures as there are database tables—we will begin with that and see how it goes. Therefore, we will define the following structures:

```
type User struct {
    ID       int
    Username string
}

type Userdata struct {
    ID          int
    Name        string
```

```
    Surname     string
    Description string
}
```

If you think about this, you should see that there is no point in creating two separate Go structures. This is because the `User` structure holds no real data, and there is no point in passing multiple structures to the functions that process data for the `Users` and `Userdata` PostgreSQL tables. Therefore, we can create a single Go structure for holding all the data that has been defined, as follows:

```
type Userdata struct {
    ID          int
    Username    string
    Name        string
    Surname     string
    Description string
}
```

I have decided to name the structure after the database table for simplicity—however, in this case, this is not completely accurate as the `Userdata` structure has more fields than the `Userdata` database table. The thing is that we do not need everything from the `Userdata` database table.

The preamble of the package is as follows:

```
package post05

import (
    "database/sql"
    "errors"
    "fmt"
    "strings"

    _ "github.com/lib/pq"
)
```

For the first time in this book, you will see a package name different than `main`, which in this case is `post05`. As the package communicates with PostgreSQL, we import the `github.com/lib/pq` package and we use _ in front of the package's path. As we discussed earlier, this happens because the imported package is registering itself as the database handler for the `sql` package, but it is not being directly used in the code. It is only being used through the `sql` package.

Next, you should have variables to hold the connection details. In the case of the `post05` package, this can be implemented with the following global variables:

```
// Connection details
var (
    Hostname = ""
    Port     = 2345
    Username = ""
    Password = ""
    Database = ""
)
```

Apart from the `Port` variable, which has an initial value, the other global variables have the default value of their data type, which is `string`. All these variables must be properly initialized by the Go code that uses the `post05` package and should be accessible from outside the package, which means that their first letter should be in uppercase.

The `openConnection()` function, which is **private** and only accessed within the scope of the package, is defined as:

```
func openConnection() (*sql.DB, error) {
    // connection string
    conn := fmt.Sprintf("host=%s port=%d user=%s password=%s dbname=%s
sslmode=disable", Hostname, Port, Username, Password, Database)

    // open database
    db, err := sql.Open("postgres", conn)
    if err != nil {
        return nil, err
    }
    return db, nil
}
```

You have already seen the previous code in the `getSchema.go` utility. You create the connection string and you pass it to `sql.Open()`.

Now, let's consider the `exists()` function, which is also private:

```
// The function returns the User ID of the username
// -1 if the user does not exist
func exists(username string) int {
    username = strings.ToLower(username)

    db, err := openConnection()
```

```
    if err != nil {
        fmt.Println(err)
        return -1
    }
    defer db.Close()

    userID := -1
    statement := fmt.Sprintf(`SELECT "id" FROM "users" where username =
'%s'`, username)
    rows, err := db.Query(statement)
```

This is where we define the query that shows whether the provided username exists in the database or not. As all our data is kept in the database, we need to interact with the database all the time.

```
    for rows.Next() {
        var id int
        err = rows.Scan(&id)
        if err != nil {
            fmt.Println("Scan", err)
            return -1
        }
```

If the `rows.Scan(&id)` call is executed without any errors, then we know that a result has been returned, which is the desired user ID.

```
        userID = id
    }
    defer rows.Close()
    return userID
}
```

The last part of `exists()` sets or closes the query to free resources and returns the ID value of the username that is given as a parameter to `exists()`.

> During development, I include many `fmt.Println()` statements in the package code for debugging purposes. However, I have removed most of them in the final version of the Go package and replaced them with `error` values. These `error` values are passed to the program that uses the functionality of the package, which is responsible for deciding what to do with the error messages and error conditions. You can also use logging for this—the output can go to standard output or even `/dev/null` when not needed.

Here is the implementation of the `AddUser()` function:

```
// AddUser adds a new user to the database
// Returns new User ID
// -1 if there was an error
func AddUser(d Userdata) int {
    d.Username = strings.ToLower(d.Username)
```

All usernames are converted into lowercase in order to avoid duplicates. This is a design decision.

```
    db, err := openConnection()
    if err != nil {
        fmt.Println(err)
        return -1
    }
    defer db.Close()

    userID := exists(d.Username)
    if userID != -1 {
        fmt.Println("User already exists:", Username)
        return -1
    }

    insertStatement := `insert into "users" ("username") values ($1)`
```

This is how we construct a query that accepts parameters. The presented query requires one value that is named `$1`.

```
    _, err = db.Exec(insertStatement, d.Username)
```

This is how you pass the desired value, which is `d.Username`, into the `insertStatement` variable.

```
    if err != nil {
        fmt.Println(err)
        return -1
    }

    userID = exists(d.Username)
    if userID == -1 {
        return userID
    }
```

```
	insertStatement = `insert into "userdata" ("userid", "name", 
"surname", "description") values ($1, $2, $3, $4)`
```

The presented query needs 4 values that are named `$1`, `$2`, `$3`, and `$4`.

```
	_, err = db.Exec(insertStatement, userID, d.Name, d.Surname, 
d.Description)
	if err != nil {
		fmt.Println("db.Exec()", err)
		return -1
	}
```

As we need to pass 4 variables to `insertStatement`, we will put 4 values in the `db.Exec()` call.

```
	return userID
}
```

This is the end of the function that adds a new user to the database. The implementation of the `DeleteUser()` function is as follows.

```
// DeleteUser deletes an existing user
func DeleteUser(id int) error {
	db, err := openConnection()
	if err != nil {
		return err
	}
	defer db.Close()

	// Does the ID exist?
	statement := fmt.Sprintf(`SELECT "username" FROM "users" where id = 
%d`, id)
	rows, err := db.Query(statement)
```

Here, we double-check whether the given user ID exists or not in the `users` table.

```
	var username string
	for rows.Next() {
		err = rows.Scan(&username)
		if err != nil {
			return err
		}
	}
```

```
    defer rows.Close()

    if exists(username) != id {
        return fmt.Errorf("User with ID %d does not exist", id)
    }
```

If the previously returned username exists and has the same user ID as the parameter to `DeleteUser()`, then you can continue the deletion process, which contains two steps: first, deleting the relevant user data from the `userdata` table, and, second, deleting the data from the `users` table.

```
    // Delete from Userdata
    deleteStatement := `delete from "userdata" where userid=$1`
    _, err = db.Exec(deleteStatement, id)
    if err != nil {
        return err
    }

    // Delete from Users
    deleteStatement = `delete from "users" where id=$1`
    _, err = db.Exec(deleteStatement, id)
    if err != nil {
        return err
    }

    return nil
}
```

Now, let's examine the implementation of the `ListUsers()` function.

```
func ListUsers() ([]Userdata, error) {
    Data := []Userdata{}
    db, err := openConnection()
    if err != nil {
        return Data, err
    }
    defer db.Close()
```

Once again, we need to open a connection to the database before executing a database query.

```
    rows, err := db.Query(`SELECT
        "id","username","name","surname","description"
```

```
        FROM "users","userdata"
        WHERE users.id = userdata.userid`)
    if err != nil {
        return Data, err
    }

    for rows.Next() {
        var id int
        var username string
        var name string
        var surname string
        var description string
        err = rows.Scan(&id, &username, &name, &surname, &description)
        temp := Userdata{ID: id, Username: username, Name: name,
Surname: surname, Description: description}
```

At this point, we will store the data we've received from the `SELECT` query into a `Userdata` structure. This is added to the slice that is going to be returned from the `ListUsers()` function. This process continues until there is nothing left to read.

```
        Data = append(Data, temp)
        if err != nil {
            return Data, err
        }
    }
    defer rows.Close()
    return Data, nil
}
```

After updating the contents of `Data` using `append()`, we end the query, and the function returns the list of available users, as stored in `Data`.

Lastly, let's examine the `UpdateUser()` function:

```
// UpdateUser is for updating an existing user
func UpdateUser(d Userdata) error {
    db, err := openConnection()
    if err != nil {
        return err
    }
    defer db.Close()

    userID := exists(d.Username)
```

```
    if userID == -1 {
        return errors.New("User does not exist")
    }
```

First, we need to make sure that the given username exists in the database—the update process is based on the username.

```
    d.ID = userID
    updateStatement := `update "userdata" set "name"=$1, "surname"=$2,
"description"=$3 where "userid"=$4`
    _, err = db.Exec(updateStatement, d.Name, d.Surname, d.Description,
d.ID)
    if err != nil {
        return err
    }

    return nil
}
```

The update statement stored in `updateStatement` that is executed using the desired parameters with the help of `db.Exec()` updates the user data.

Now that we know the details of how to implement each function in the `post05` package, it is time to begin using that package!

Testing the Go package

In order to test the package, we must develop a command-line utility called `postGo.go`.

> As `postGo.go` uses an external package, even if we develop that package, you should not forget to download the latest version of that external package using `go get` or `go get -u`.

As `postGo.go` is used for testing purposes only, we hardcoded most of the data apart from the username of the user we put into the database. All usernames are randomly generated.

The code of `postGo.go` is as follows:

```
package main

import (
    "fmt"
    "math/rand"
    "time"

    "github.com/mactsouk/post05"
)
```

As the `post05` package works with Postgres, there is no need to import `lib/pq` here:

```
var MIN = 0
var MAX = 26

func random(min, max int) int {
    return rand.Intn(max-min) + min
}

func getString(length int64) string {
    startChar := "A"
    temp := ""
    var i int64 = 1
    for {
        myRand := random(MIN, MAX)
        newChar := string(startChar[0] + byte(myRand))
        temp = temp + newChar
        if i == length {
            break
        }
        i++
    }
    return temp
}
```

Both the `random()` and `getString()` functions are helper functions for generating random strings that are used as usernames.

```
func main() {
    post05.Hostname = "localhost"
    post05.Port = 5432
    post05.Username = "mtsouk"
    post05.Password = "pass"
    post05.Database = "go"
```

This is where you define the connection parameters to the Postgres server, as well as the database you are going to work in (go). As all these variables are in the post05 package, they are accessed as such.

```
    data, err := post05.ListUsers()
    if err != nil {
        fmt.Println(err)
        return
    }
    for _, v := range data {
        fmt.Println(v)
    }
```

We begin by listing existing users.

```
    SEED := time.Now().Unix()
    rand.Seed(SEED)
    random_username := getString(5)
```

Then, we generate a random string that is used as the username. All randomly generated usernames are 5 characters long because of the getString(5) call. You can change that value if you want.

```
    t := post05.Userdata{
        Username:    random_username,
        Name:        "Mihalis",
        Surname:     "Tsoukalos",
        Description: "This is me!"}

    id := post05.AddUser(t)
    if id == -1 {
        fmt.Println("There was an error adding user", t.Username)
    }
```

The previous code adds a new user to the database—the user data, including the username, is kept in a `post05.Userdata` structure. That `post05.Userdata` structure is passed to the `post05.AddUser()` function, which returns the user ID of the new user.

```
    err = post05.DeleteUser(id)
    if err != nil {
        fmt.Println(err)
    }
```

Here, we delete the user that we created using the user ID value returned by `post05.AddUser(t)`.

```
    // Trying to delete it again!
    err = post05.DeleteUser(id)
    if err != nil {
        fmt.Println(err)
    }
```

If you try to delete the same user again, the process fails because the user does not exist.

```
    id = post05.AddUser(t)
    if id == -1 {
        fmt.Println("There was an error adding user", t.Username)
    }
```

Here, we add the same user again—however, as user ID values are generated by Postgres, this time, the user is going to have a different user ID value than before.

```
    t = post05.Userdata{
        Username:    random_username,
        Name:        "Mihalis",
        Surname:     "Tsoukalos",
        Description: "This might not be me!"}
```

Here, we update the `Description` field of the `post05.Userdata` structure before passing it to `post05.UpdateUser()`, in order update the information stored in the database.

```
    err = post05.UpdateUser(t)
    if err != nil {
        fmt.Println(err)
    }
}
```

Working with postGo.go creates the following kind of output:

```
$ go run postGo.go
{4 mhmxz Mihalis Tsoukalos This might not be me!}
{6 wsdlg Mihalis Tsoukalos This might not be me!}
User with ID 7 does not exist
```

The previous output confirms that postGo.go works as expected as it can connect to the database, add a new user, and delete an existing one. This also means that the post05 package works as expected. Now that we know how to create Go packages, let's briefly discuss Go modules.

Modules

A Go module is like a Go package with a version—however, Go modules can consist of multiple packages. Go uses **semantic versioning** for versioning modules. This means that versions begin with the letter v, followed by the major.minor.patch version numbers. Therefore, you can have versions such as v1.0.0, v1.0.5, and v2.0.2. The v1, v2, and v3 parts signify the major version of a Go package that is usually not backward compatible. This means that if your Go program works with v1, it will not necessarily work with v2 or v3—it might work, but you cannot count on it. The second number in a version is about features. Usually, v1.1.0 has more features than v1.0.2 or v1.0.0, while being compatible with all older versions. Lastly, the third number is just about bug fixes without having any new features. Note that semantic versioning is also used for Go versions.

> Go modules were introduced in Go v1.11 but were finalized in Go v1.13.

If you want to learn more about modules, visit and read https://blog.golang.org/using-go-modules, which has five parts, as well as https://golang.org/doc/modules/developing. Just remember that **a Go module is similar but not identical to a regular Go package with a version**, and that a module can consist of multiple packages.

Creating better packages

This section provides handy advice that can help you develop better Go packages. Here are several good rules to follow to create high-class Go packages:

- The first unofficial rule of a successful package is that its elements must be connected in some way. Thus, you can create a package for supporting cars, but it would not be a good idea to create a single package for supporting cars and bicycles and airplanes. Put simply, it is better to split the functionality of a package unnecessarily into multiple packages than to add too much functionality to a single Go package.
- A second practical rule is that you should use your own packages first for a reasonable amount of time before giving them to the public. This helps you discover silly bugs and make sure that your packages operate as expected. After that, give them to some fellow developers for additional testing before making them publicly available. Additionally, you should always write tests for any package you intend others to use.
- Next, make sure your package has a clear and useful API so that any consumer can be productive with it quickly.
- Try and limit the public API of your packages to only what is absolutely necessary. Additionally, give your functions descriptive but not very long names.
- Interfaces, and in future Go versions, **generics**, can improve the usefulness of your functions, so when you think it is appropriate, use an interface instead of a single type as a function parameter or return type.
- When updating one of your packages, try not to break things and create incompatibilities with older versions unless it is absolutely necessary.
- When developing a new Go package, try to use multiple files in order to group similar tasks or concepts.
- Do not create a package that already exists from scratch. Make changes to the existing package and maybe create your own version of it.
- Nobody wants a Go package that prints logging information on the screen. It would be more professional to have a flag for turning on logging when needed. The Go code of your packages should be in harmony with the Go code of your programs. This means that if you look at a program that uses your packages and your function names stand out in the code in a bad way, it would be better to change the names of your functions. As the name of a package is used almost everywhere, try to use concise and expressive package names.

- It is more convenient if you put new Go type definitions near where they are used the first time because nobody, including yourself, wants to search source files for definitions of new data types.
- Try to create test files for your packages, because packages with test files are considered more professional than ones without them; small details make all the difference and give people confidence that you are a serious developer! Notice that writing tests for your packages is not optional and that you should avoid using packages that do not include tests. You will learn more about testing in *Chapter 11, Code Testing and Profiling*.

Always remember that apart from the fact that the actual Go code in a package should be bug-free, the next most important element of a successful package is its documentation, as well as some code examples that clarify its use and showcase the idiosyncrasies of the functions of the package. The next section discusses creating documentation in Go.

Generating documentation

This section discusses how to create **documentation** for your Go code using the code of the `post05` package as an example. The new package is renamed and is now called `document`.

Go follows a simple rule regarding documentation: in order to document a function, a method, a variable, or even the package itself, you can write comments, as usual, that should be located directly before the element you want to document, without any empty lines in between. You can use one or more single-line comments, which are lines beginning with `//`, or *block* comments, which begin with `/*` and end with `*/`—everything in-between is considered a comment.

> It is highly recommended that each Go package you create has a block comment preceding the `package` declaration that introduces developers to the package, and also explains what the package does.

Instead of presenting the entire code of the `post05` package, we will only present the important part, which means that function implementations are going to be `return` statements only. The new version of `post05.go` is called `document.go` and comes with the following code and comments:

```
/*
The package works on 2 tables on a PostgreSQL data base server.
```

```
The names of the tables are:

    * Users
    * Userdata

The definitions of the tables in the PostgreSQL server are:

    CREATE TABLE Users (
        ID SERIAL,
        Username VARCHAR(100) PRIMARY KEY
    );

    CREATE TABLE Userdata (
        UserID Int NOT NULL,
        Name VARCHAR(100),
        Surname VARCHAR(100),
        Description VARCHAR(200)
    );

    This is rendered as code

This is not rendered as code

*/
package document
```

This is the first block of documentation that is located right before the name of the package. This is the appropriate place to document the functionality of the package, as well as other essential information. In this case, we are presenting the SQL create commands that fully describe the database tables we are going to work on. Another important element is specifying the database server this package interacts with. Other information that you can put at the beginning of a package is the author, the license, and the version of the package.

If a line in a block comment begins with a tab, then it is rendered differently in the graphical output, which is good for differentiating between various kinds of information in the documentation:

```
// BUG(1): Function ListUsers() not working as expected
// BUG(2): Function AddUser() is too slow
```

The `BUG` keyword is special when writing documentation. Go knows that bugs are part of the code and therefore should be documented as well. You can write any message you want after a `BUG` keyword, and you can place them anywhere you want—preferably close to the bugs they describe.

```
import (
    "database/sql"
    "fmt"
    "strings"
)
```

The `github.com/lib/pq` package was removed from the `import` block to make the file size smaller.

```
/*
This block of global variables holds the connection details to the
Postgres server
    Hostname: is the IP or the hostname of the server
    Port: is the TCP port the DB server listens to
    Username: is the username of the database user
    Password: is the password of the database user
    Database: is the name of the Database in PostgreSQL
*/
var (
    Hostname = ""
    Port     = 2345
    Username = ""
    Password = ""
    Database = ""
)
```

The previous code shows a way of documenting lots of variables at once—in this case, global variables. The good thing with this way is that you do not have to put a comment before each global variable and make the code less readable. The only downside of this method is that you should remember to update the comments, should you wish to make any changes to the code. However, documenting multiple variables at once might not end up rendering correctly in web-based `godoc` pages. For that reason, you might want to document each field directly.

```
// The Userdata structure is for holding full user data
// from the Userdata table and the Username from the
// Users table
type Userdata struct {
```

```
    ID          int
    Username    string
    Name        string
    Surname     string
    Description string
}
```

The previous excerpt shows how to document a Go structure—this is especially useful when you have lots of structures in a source file and you want to have a quick look at them.

```
// openConnection() is for opening the Postgres connection
// in order to be used by the other functions of the package.
func openConnection() (*sql.DB, error) {
    var db *sql.DB
    return db, nil
}
```

When documenting a function, it is good to begin the first line of the comments with the function name. Apart from that, you can write any information that you consider important in the comments.

```
// The function returns the User ID of the username
// -1 if the user does not exist
func exists(username string) int {
    fmt.Println("Searching user", username)
    return 0
}
```

In this case, we will explain the return values of the `exists()` function as they have a special meaning.

```
// AddUser adds a new user to the database
//
// Returns new User ID
// -1 if there was an error
func AddUser(d Userdata) int {
    d.Username = strings.ToLower(d.Username)
    return -1
}

/*
    DeleteUser deletes an existing user if the user exists.
```

```
    It requires the User ID of the user to be deleted.
*/
func DeleteUser(id int) error {
    fmt.Println(id)
    return nil
}
```

You can use block comments anywhere you want, not only at the beginning of a package.

```
// ListUsers lists all users in the database
// and returns a slice of Userdata.
func ListUsers() ([]Userdata, error) {
    // Data holds the records returned by the SQL query
    Data := []Userdata{}
    return Data, nil
}
```

When you request the documentation of the `Userdata` structure, Go automatically presents the functions that use `Userdata` as input or output, or both.

```
// UpdateUser is for updating an existing user
// given a Userdata structure.
// The user ID of the user to be updated is found
// inside the function.
func UpdateUser(d Userdata) error {
    fmt.Println(d)
    return nil
}
```

We are not done yet because we need to see the documentation somehow. There are two ways to see the documentation of the package. The first one involves using `go get`, which also means creating a GitHub repository of the package, as we did with `post05`. However, as this is for testing purposes, we are going to do things the easy way: we are going to copy it in `~/go/src` and access it from there. As the package is called `document`, we are going to create a directory with the same name inside `~/go/src`. After that, we are going to copy `document.go` in `~/go/src/document` and we are done—for more complex packages, the process is going to be more complex as well. In such cases, it would be better to `go get` the package from its repository.

Either way, the `go doc` command is going to work just fine with the `document` package:

```
$ go doc document
package document // import "document"

The package works on 2 tables on a PostgreSQL data base server.

The names of the tables are:

    * Users
    * Userdata

The definitions of the tables in the PostgreSQL server are:

        CREATE TABLE Users (
            ID SERIAL,
            Username VARCHAR(100) PRIMARY KEY
        );

        CREATE TABLE Userdata (
            UserID Int NOT NULL,
            Name VARCHAR(100),
            Surname VARCHAR(100),
            Description VARCHAR(200)
        );

        This is rendered as code
```

```
This is not rendered as code

var Hostname = "" ...
func AddUser(d Userdata) int
func DeleteUser(id int) error
func UpdateUser(d Userdata) error
type Userdata struct{ ... }
    func ListUsers() ([]Userdata, error)

BUG: Function ListUsers() not working as expected

BUG: Function AddUser() is too slow
```

If you want to see information about a specific function, you should use `go doc`, as follows:

```
$ go doc document ListUsers
package document // import "document"

func ListUsers() ([]Userdata, error)
    ListUsers lists all users in the database and returns a slice of
Userdata.
```

Additionally, we can use the web version of the Go documentation, which can be accessed after running the `godoc` utility and going to the `Third Party` section—by default, the web server initiated by `godoc` listens to port number `6060` and can be accessed at `http://localhost:6060`.

A part of the documentation page for the `document` package is shown in *Figure 5.4*:

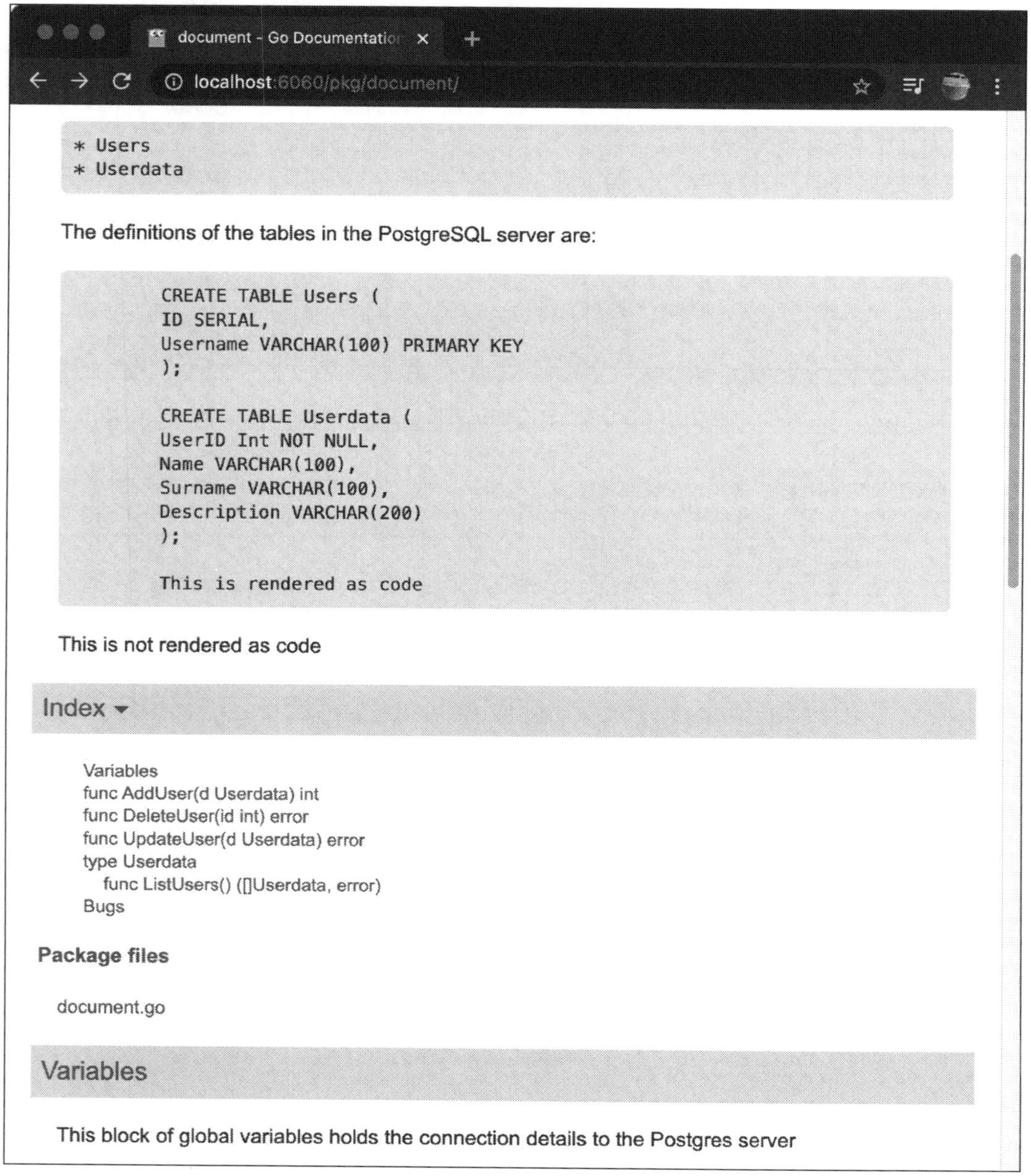

Figure 5.4: Viewing the documentation of a user-developed Go package

> Go automatically puts the bugs at the end of the text and graphical output.

In my personal opinion, rendering the documentation is much better when using the graphical interface, making it better when you do not know what you are looking for. On the other hand, using `go doc` from the command line is much faster and allows you to process the output using traditional UNIX command-line tools.

The next section will briefly present the CI/CD systems of GitLab and GitHub, starting with GitLab Runners, which can be helpful for automating package development and deployment.

GitLab Runners and Go

When developing Go packages and documentation, you want to be able to test the results and find out bugs as quickly as possible. When everything works as expected, you might want to publish your results to the world automatically, without spending more time on this. One of the best solutions for this is using a CI/CD system for automating tasks. This section will briefly illustrate the use of GitLab Runners for automating Go projects.

> In order to follow this section, you need to have a GitLab account, create a dedicated GitLab repository, and store the relevant files there.

We will begin with a GitLab repository that contains the following files:

- `hw.go`: This is a sample program that is used to make sure that everything works.
- `.gitignore`: It is not necessary to have such a file, but it is very handy for ignoring some files and directories.
- `usePost05.go`: This is a sample Go file that uses an external package—please refer to the `https://gitlab.com/mactsouk/runners-go/` repository for its contents.
- `README.md`: This file is automatically displayed on the repository web page and is usually used for explaining the purpose of the repository.

There is also a directory called `.git` that contains information and metadata about the repository.

The initial version of the configuration file

The first version of the configuration file is for making sure that everything is fine with our GitLab setup. The name of the configuration file is `.gitlab-ci.yml` and is a YAML file that should be located in the root directory of the GitLab repository. This initial version of the `.gitlab-ci.yml` configuration file compiles `hw.go` and creates a binary file, which is executed in a different stage than the one it was created in. This means that we should create an artifact for keeping and transferring that binary file:

```
$ cat .gitlab-ci.yml
image: golang:1.15.7

stages:
    - download
    - execute

compile:
    stage: download
    script:
        - echo "Getting System Info"
        - uname -a
        - mkdir bin
        - go version
        - go build -o ./bin/hw hw.go
    artifacts:
        paths:
            - bin/

execute:
    stage: execute
    script:
        - echo "Executing Hello World!"
        - ls -l bin
        - ./bin/hw
```

The important thing about the previous configuration file is that we are using an image that comes with Go already installed, which saves us from having to install it from scratch and allows us to specify the Go version we want to use.

However, if you ever want to install extra software, you can do that based on the Linux distribution being used. After saving the file, you need to push the changes to GitLab for the pipeline to start running. In order to see the results, you should click on the **CI/CD** option on the left bar of the GitLab UI.

Figure 5.5 shows information about a specific workflow based on the aforementioned YAML file. Everything that is in green is a good thing, whereas red is used in error situations. If you want to learn more information about a specific stage, you can press its button and see a more detailed output:

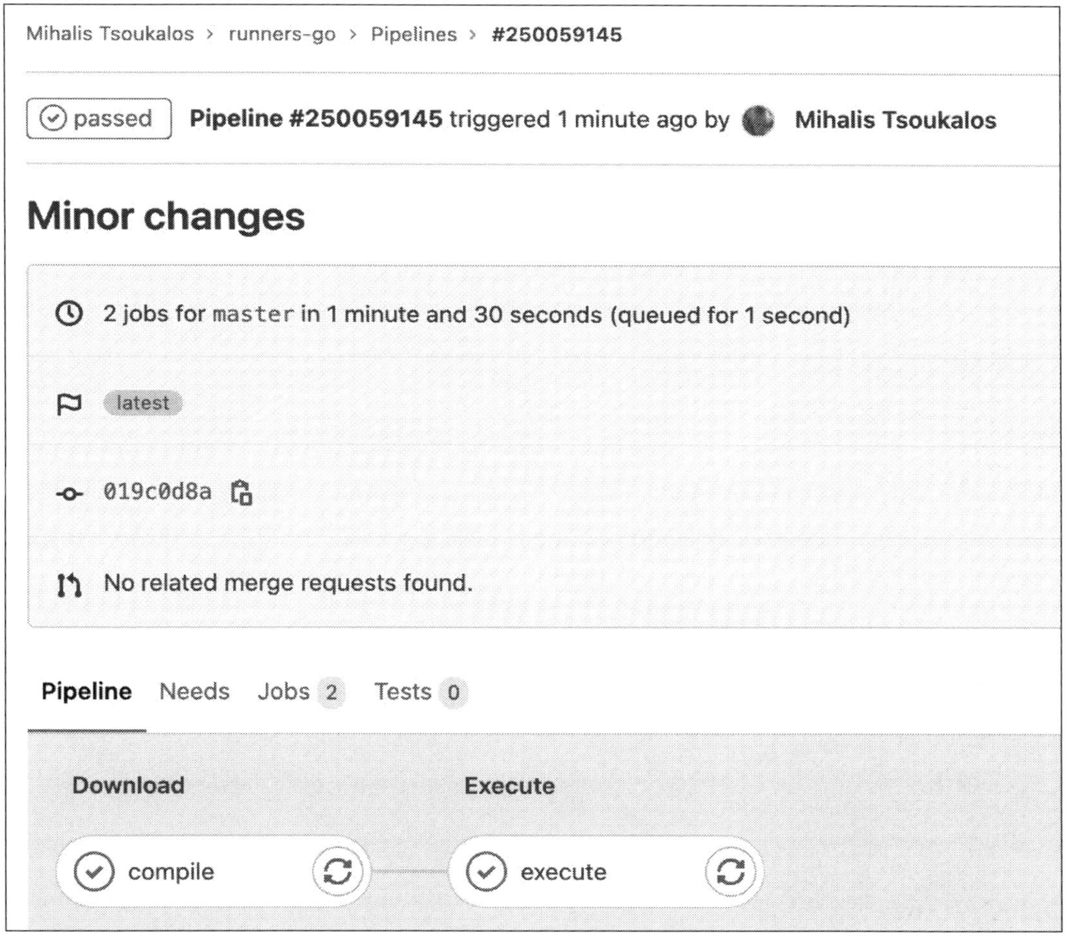

Figure 5.5: Looking at the progress of a GitLab pipeline

As everything looks fine, we are ready to create the final version of `.gitlab-ci.yml`. Note that if there is an error in the workflow, you will most likely receive an email the email address you used when registering for GitLab. If everything is fine, no email will be sent.

The final version of the configuration file

The final version of the CI/CD configuration file compiles `usePost05.go`, which imports `post05`. This is used for illustrating how external packages are downloaded. The contents of `.gitlab-ci.yml` is as follows:

```
image: golang:1.15.7

stages:
    - download
    - execute

compile:
    stage: download
    script:
        - echo "Compiling usePost05.go"
        - mkdir bin
        - go get -v -d ./...
```

The `go get -v -d ./...` command is the Go way of downloading all the package dependencies of a project. After that, you are free to build your project and generate your executable file:

```
        - go build -o ./bin/usePost05 usePost05.go
    artifacts:
        paths:
            - bin/
```

The `bin` directory, along with its contents, will be available to the `execute` state:

```
execute:
    stage: execute
    script:
        - echo "Executing usePost05"
        - ls -l bin
        - ./bin/usePost05
```

Pushing it to GitLab automatically triggers its execution. This is illustrated in *Figure 5.6*, which shows in more detail the progress of the `compile` stage:

```
Fetching changes with git depth set to 50...
Initialized empty Git repository in /builds/mactsouk/runners-go/.git/
Created fresh repository.
Checking out 8ba14df7 as master...
Skipping Git submodules setup
Executing "step_script" stage of the job script
$ echo "Compiling usePost05.go"
Compiling usePost05.go
$ mkdir bin
$ go get -v -d ./...
github.com/mactsouk/post05 (download)
github.com/lib/pq (download)
$ go build -o ./bin/usePost05 usePost05.go
Uploading artifacts for successful job                                00:03
Uploading artifacts...
bin/: found 2 matching files and directories
Uploading artifacts as "archive" to coordinator... ok  id=1001258536 responseStatus=201 Created t
oken=_JMwiwyt
Cleaning up file based variables                                      00:01
Job succeeded
```

Figure 5.6: Seeing a detailed view of a stage

What we can see here is that all the required packages are being downloaded and that `usePost05.go` is compiled without any issues. As we do not have a PostgreSQL instance available, we cannot try interacting with PostgreSQL, but we can execute `usePost05.go` and see the values of the `Hostname` and `Port` global variables. This is illustrated in *Figure 5.7*:

```
Downloading artifacts                                                 00:01
Downloading artifacts for compile (1001263660)...
Downloading artifacts from coordinator... ok       id=1001263660 responseStatus=200 OK token=Skr
LxVpx
Executing "step_script" stage of the job script                       00:01
$ echo "Executing usePost05"
Executing usePost05
$ ls -l bin
total 5752
-rwxr-xr-x. 1 root root 5883134 Feb  2 07:23 usePost05
$ ./bin/usePost05
2345
localhost
Cleaning up file based variables                                      00:01
Job succeeded
```

Figure 5.7: Seeing more details about the execute stage

So far, we have seen how to use GitLab Runners to automate Go package development and testing. Next, we are going to create a CI/CD scenario in GitHub using GitHub Actions as another method of automating software publication.

GitHub Actions and Go

This section will use GitHub Actions to push a Docker image that contains a Go executable file in Docker Hub.

> In order to follow this section, you must have a GitHub account, create a dedicated GitHub repository, and store the related files there.

We will begin with a GitHub repository that contains the following files:

- `.gitignore`: This is an optional file that's used for ignoring files and directories during `git push` operations.
- `usePost05.go`: This is the same file as before.
- `Dockerfile`: This file is used for creating a Docker image with the Go executable. Please refer to `https://github.com/mactsouk/actions-with-go` for its contents.
- `README.md`: As before, this is a Markdown file that contains information about the repository.

In order to set up GitHub Actions, we need to create a directory named `.github` and then create another directory named `workflows` in it. The `.github/workflows` directory contains YAML files with the pipeline configuration.

Figure 5.8 shows the overview screen of the workflows of the selected GitHub repository:

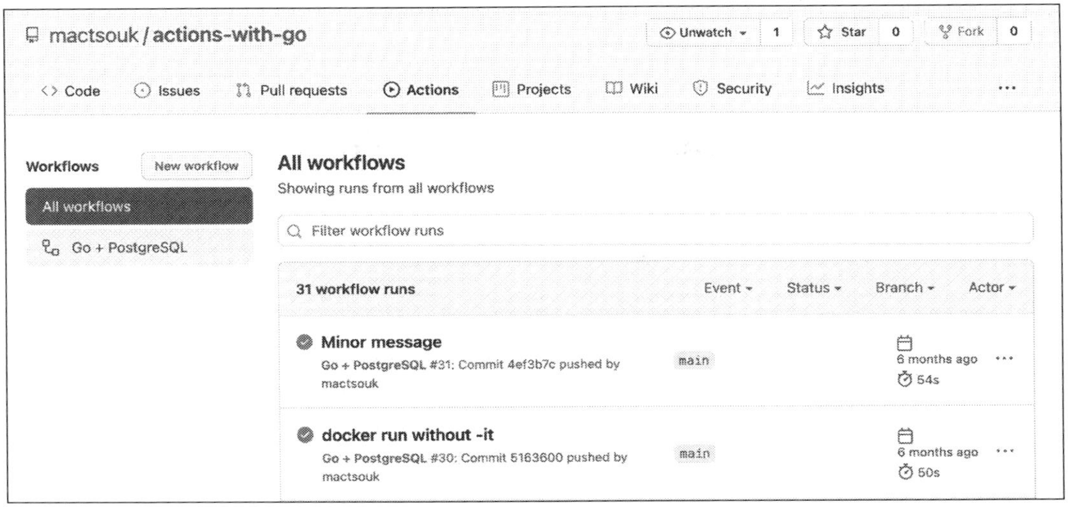

Figure 5.8: Displaying the Workflows associated with a given GitHub repository

To push an image to Docker Hub, you need to log in. As this process requires using a password, which is sensitive information, the next subsection illustrates how to store secrets in GitHub.

Storing secrets in GitHub

The credentials for connecting to Docker Hub are stored in GitHub using the secrets feature that exists in almost all CI/CD systems. However, the exact implementation might differ.

> You can also use HashiCorp Vault as a central point for storing passwords and other sensitive data. Unfortunately, presenting HashiCorp Vault is beyond the scope of this book.

In your GitHub repository, go to the **Settings** tab and select **Secrets** from the left column. You will see your existing secrets, if any, and an **Add new secret** link, which you need to click on. Do this process twice to store your Docker Hub username and password.

Figure 5.9 shows the secrets associated with the GitHub repository used in this section—the presented secrets hold the username and password that were used for connecting to Docker Hub:

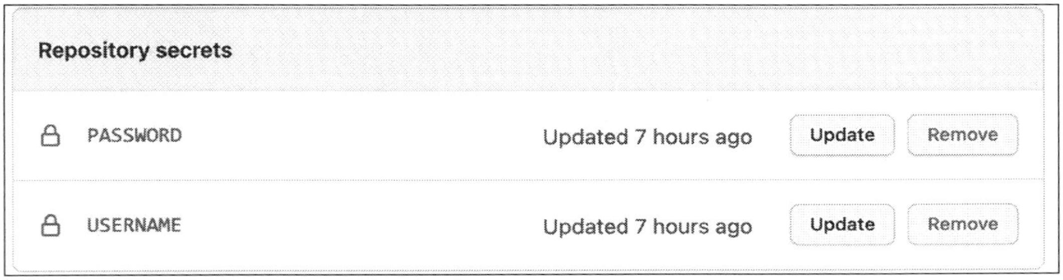

Figure 5.9: The secrets of the mactsouk/actions-with-go repository

The final version of the configuration file

The final version of the configuration file compiles the Go code, puts it in a Docker image, as described by `Dockerfile`, connects with Docker Hub using the specified credentials, and pushes the Docker image to Docker Hub using the provided data. This is a very common way of automation when creating Docker images. The contents of `go.yml` is as follows:

```
name: Go + PostgreSQL

on: [push]
```

This line in the configuration file specifies that this pipeline is triggered on push operations only.

```
jobs:
  build:
    runs-on: ubuntu-18.04
```

This is the Linux image that is going to be used. As the Go binary is built inside a Docker image, we do not need to install Go on the Linux VM.

```
    steps:
    # Checks-out your repository under $GITHUB_WORKSPACE, so your job
can access it
    - uses: actions/checkout@v2
    - uses: actions/setup-go@v2
      with:
        stable: 'false'
        go-version: '1.15.7'
```

```
    - name: Publish Docker Image
      env:
          USERNAME: ${{ secrets.USERNAME }}
          PASSWORD: ${{ secrets.PASSWORD }}
```

This is how you access the secrets that were stored previously and how you store them.

```
          IMAGE_NAME: gopost
      run: |
        docker images
        docker build -t "$IMAGE_NAME" .
        docker images
        echo "$PASSWORD" | docker login --username "$USERNAME"
  --password-stdin
        docker tag "${IMAGE_NAME}" "$USERNAME/${IMAGE_NAME}:latest"
        docker push "$USERNAME/${IMAGE_NAME}:latest"
        echo "* Running Docker Image"
        docker run ${IMAGE_NAME}:latest
```

This time, most of the work is performed by the `docker build` command because the Go executable is built inside a Docker image. The following screenshot shows some of the output of the pipeline defined by `go.yml`:

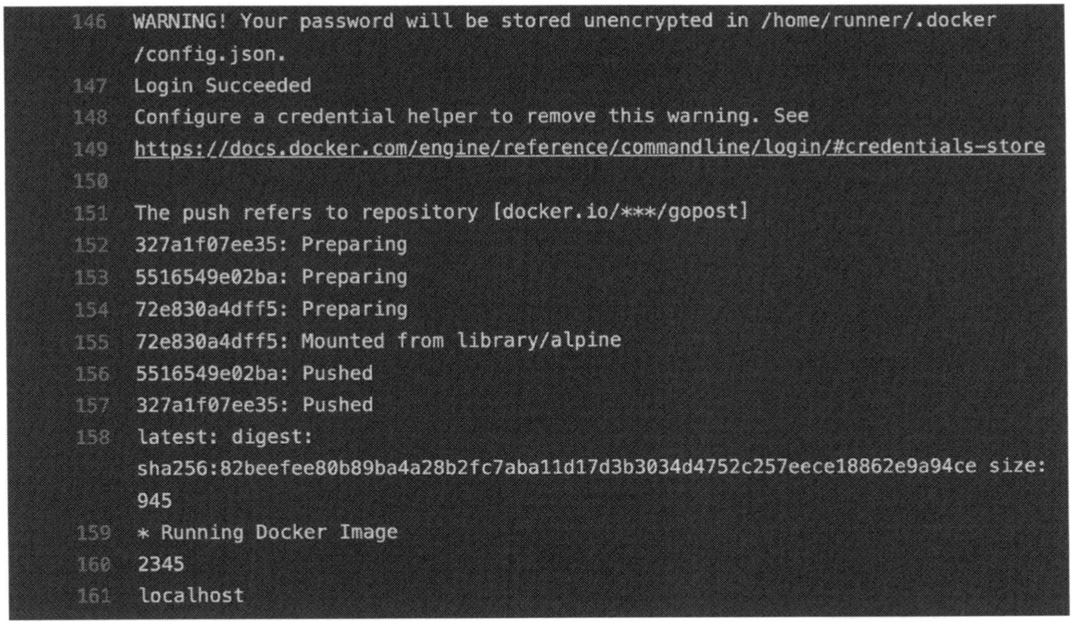

Figure 5.10: The pipeline for pushing Docker images to Docker Hub

Automation saves you development time, so try to automate as many things as possible, especially when you're making your software available to the world.

Versioning utilities

One of the most difficult tasks is to automatically and uniquely version command-line utilities, especially when using a CI/CD system. This section presents a technique that uses a GitHub value to version a command-line utility on your local machine.

> You can apply the same technique to GitLab—just search for the available GitLab variables and values and choose one that fits your needs.

This technique is used by both the `docker` and `kubectl` utilities, among others:

```
$ docker version
Client: Docker Engine - Community
 Cloud integration: 1.0.4
 Version:           20.10.0
 API version:       1.41
 Go version:        go1.13.15
 Git commit:        7287ab3
 Built:             Tue Dec  8 18:55:43 2020
 OS/Arch:           darwin/amd64
...
```

The previous output shows that `docker` uses the Git commit value for versioning—we are going to use a slightly different value that is longer than the one used by `docker`.

The utility that is used, which is saved as `gitVersion.go`, is implemented as follows:

```
package main

import (
    "fmt"
    "os"
)

var VERSION string
```

`VERSION` is the variable that is going to be set at runtime using the Go linker.

```
func main() {
    if len(os.Args) == 2 {
        if os.Args[1] == "version" {
            fmt.Println("Version:", VERSION)
        }
    }
}
```

The previous code says that if there is a command-line argument and its value is `version`, print the version message with the help of the `VERSION` variable.

What we need to do is tell the Go linker that we are going to define the value of the `VERSION` variable. This happens with the help of the `-ldflags` flag, which stands for linker flags—this passes values to the `cmd/link` package, which allows us to change values in imported packages at build time. The `-X` value that is used requires a key/value pair, where the key is a variable name and the value is the value that we want to set for that key. In our case, the key has the `main.Variable` form because we change the value of a variable in the `main` package. As the name of the variable in `gitVersion.go` is `VERSION`, the key is `main.VERSION`.

But first, we need to decide on the GitHub value that we are going to use as the version string. The `git rev-list HEAD` command returns a full list of commits for the current repository from the latest to the oldest. We only need the last one—the most recent—which we can get using `git rev-list -1 HEAD` or `git rev-list HEAD | head -1`. So, we need to assign that value to an environment variable and pass that environment variable to the Go compiler. As this value changes each time you make a commit and you always want to have the latest value, you should reevaluate it each time you execute `go build`—this will be shown in a while.

In order to provide `gitVersion.go` with the value of the desired environment variable, we should execute it as follows:

```
$ export VERSION=$(git rev-list -1 HEAD)
$ go build -ldflags "-X main.VERSION=$VERSION" gitVersion.go
```

> This works on both `bash` and `zsh` shells. If you are using a different shell, you should make sure that you are defining an environment variable the right way.

If you want to execute the two commands at the same time, you can do the following:

```
$ export VERSION=$(git rev-list -1 HEAD) && go build -ldflags "-X main.
VERSION=$VERSION" gitVersion.go
```

Running the generated executable, which is called `gitVersion`, produces the next output:

```
$ ./gitVersion version
Version: 99745c8fbaff94790b5818edf55f15d309f5bfeb
```

Your output is going to be different because your GitHub repository is going to be different. As GitHub generates random and unique values, you won't have the same version number twice!

Exercises

- Can you write a function that sorts three `int` values? Try to write two versions of the function: one with named returned values and another without named return values. Which one do you think is better?
- Rewrite the `getSchema.go` utility so that it works with the `jackc/pgx` package.
- Rewrite the `getSchema.go` utility so that it works with MySQL databases.
- Use GitLab CI/CD to push Docker images to Docker Hub.

Summary

This chapter presented two primary topics: functions and packages. Functions are first-class citizens in Go, which makes them powerful and handy. Remember that everything that begins with an uppercase letter is public. The only exception to this rule is package names. Private variables, functions, data type names, and structure fields can be strictly used and called internally in a package, whereas public ones are available to everyone. Additionally, we learned more about the `defer` keyword. Also, memorize that Go packages are not like Java classes—a Go package can be as big as it needs to be. Regarding Go modules, keep in mind that a Go module is multiple packages with a version.

Finally, this chapter discussed creating documentation, GitHub Actions and GitLab Runners, how the two CI/CD systems can help you automate boring processes and how to assign unique version numbers to your utilities.

The next chapter discusses system programming in general, as well as file I/O in more detail.

Additional resources

- New module changes in Go 1.16: `https://blog.golang.org/go116-module-changes`
- How do you structure your Go apps? Talk by Kat Zien from GopherCon UK 2018: `https://www.youtube.com/watch?v=1rxDzs0zgcE`
- PostgreSQL: `https://www.postgresql.org/`
- PostgreSQL Go package: `https://github.com/lib/pq`
- PostgreSQL Go package: `https://github.com/jackc/pgx`
- HashiCorp Vault: `https://www.vaultproject.io/`
- The documentation of database/sql: `https://golang.org/pkg/database/sql/`
- You can learn more about GitHub Actions environment variables at `https://docs.github.com/en/actions/reference/environment-variables`
- GitLab CI/CD variables: `https://docs.gitlab.com/ee/ci/variables/`
- The documentation of the `cmd/link` package: `https://golang.org/cmd/link/`
- `golang.org` moving to `go.dev`: `https://go.dev/blog/tidy-web`

6

Telling a UNIX System What to Do

This chapter teaches you about **systems programming** in Go. Systems programming involves working with files and directories, process control, signal handling, network programming, system files, configuration files, and file input and output (I/O). If you recall from *Chapter 1, A Quick Introduction to Go*, the reason for writing system utilities with Linux in mind is that often Go software is executed in a Docker environment—Docker images use the Linux operating system, which means that you might need to **develop your utilities with the Linux operating system in mind**. However, as Go code is portable, most system utilities work on Windows machines without any changes or with minor modifications. Among other things, this chapter implements two utilities, one that finds cycles in UNIX file systems and another that converts JSON data to XML data and vice versa. Additionally, in this chapter we are going to improve the phone book application with the help of the `cobra` package.

> **Important note**: Starting with Go 1.16, the `GO111MODULE` environment variable defaults to `on`—this affects the use of Go packages that do not belong to the Go standard library. In practice, this means that you must put your code under `~/go/src`. You can go back to the previous behavior by setting `GO111MODULE` to `auto`, but you do not want to do that—modules are the future. The reason for mentioning this in this chapter is that both `viper` and `cobra` prefer to be treated as Go modules instead of packages, which changes the development process but not the code.

This chapter covers:

- `stdin`, `stdout`, and `stderr`
- UNIX processes
- Handling UNIX signals
- File input and output
- Reading plain text files
- Writing to a file
- Working with JSON
- Working with XML
- Working with YAML
- The `viper` package
- The `cobra` package
- Finding cycles in a UNIX file system
- New to Go 1.16
- Updating the phone book application

stdin, stdout, and stderr

Every UNIX operating system has three files open all the time for its processes. Remember that UNIX considers everything, even a printer or your mouse, as a file. UNIX uses **file descriptors**, which are positive integer values, as an internal representation for accessing open files, which is much prettier than using long paths. So, by default, all UNIX systems support three special and standard filenames: `/dev/stdin`, `/dev/stdout`, and `/dev/stderr`, which can also be accessed using file descriptors `0`, `1`, and `2`, respectively. These three file descriptors are also called **standard input**, **standard output**, and **standard error**, respectively. Additionally, file descriptor `0` can be accessed as `/dev/fd/0` on a macOS machine and as both `/dev/fd/0` and `/dev/pts/0` on a Debian Linux machine.

Go uses `os.Stdin` for accessing standard input, `os.Stdout` for accessing standard output, and `os.Stderr` for accessing standard error. Although you can still use `/dev/stdin`, `/dev/stdout`, and `/dev/stderr` or the related file descriptor values for accessing the same devices, it is better, safer, and more portable to stick with `os.Stdin`, `os.Stdout`, and `os.Stderr`.

UNIX processes

As Go servers, utilities, and Docker images are mainly executed on Linux, it is good to know about Linux processes and threads.

Strictly speaking, a **process** is an execution environment that contains instructions, user data and system data parts, and other types of resources that are obtained during runtime. On the other hand, a **program** is a binary file that contains instructions and data that are used for initializing the instruction and user data parts of a process. Each running UNIX process is uniquely identified by an unsigned integer, which is called the **process ID** of the process.

There are three process categories: **user processes**, **daemon processes**, and **kernel processes**. User processes run in user space and usually have no special access rights. Daemon processes are programs that can be found in the user space and run in the background without the need for a terminal. Kernel processes are executed in kernel space only and can fully access all kernel data structures.

The C way of creating new processes involves the calling of the `fork(2)` system call. The return value of `fork(2)` allows the programmer to differentiate between a parent and a child process. Although you can fork a new process in Go using the `exec` package, Go does not allow you to control threads—Go offers **goroutines**, which the user can create on top of threads that are created and handled by the Go runtime.

Handling UNIX signals

UNIX signals offer a very handy way of *interacting asynchronously with your applications*. However, UNIX signal handling requires the use of Go channels that are used exclusively for this task. So, it would be good to talk a little about the concurrency model of Go, which requires the use of goroutines and channels for signal handling.

A **goroutine** is the smallest executable Go entity. In order to create a new goroutine you **have to** use the `go` keyword followed by a predefined function or an anonymous function—the methods are equivalent. A **channel** in Go is a mechanism that among other things allows goroutines to communicate and exchange data. If you are an amateur programmer or are hearing about goroutines and channels for the first time, do not panic. Goroutines and channels are explained in much more detail in *Chapter 7, Go Concurrency*.

> In order for a goroutine or a function to terminate the entire Go application, it should call `os.Exit()` instead of `return`. However, most of the time, you should exit a goroutine or a function using `return` because you just want to exit that specific goroutine or function and not stop the entire application.

The presented program handles `SIGINT`, which is called `syscall.SIGINT` in Go, and `SIGINFO` separately and uses a `default` case in a `switch` block for handling the remaining cases (other signals). The implementation of that `switch` block allows you to differentiate between the various signals according to your needs.

There exists a *dedicated channel* that receives all signals, as defined by the `signal.Notify()` function. Go channels can have a capacity—the capacity of this particular channel is `1` in order to be able to receive and keep one signal at a time. This makes perfect sense as a signal can terminate a program and there is no need to try to handle another signal at the same time. There is usually an anonymous function that is executed as a goroutine and performs the signal handling and nothing else. The main task of that goroutine is to listen to the channel for data. Once a signal is received, it is sent to that channel, read by the goroutine, and stored into a variable—at this point the channel can receive more signals. That variable is processed by a `switch` statement.

> Some signals cannot be caught, and the operating system cannot ignore them. So, the `SIGKILL` and `SIGSTOP` signals cannot be blocked, caught, or ignored and the reason for this is that they allow privileged users as well as the UNIX kernel to terminate any process they desire.

Create a text file by typing the following code—a good filename for it would be `signals.go`.

```
package main

import (
    "fmt"
    "os"
    "os/signal"
    "syscall"
    "time"
)
func handleSignal(sig os.Signal) {
    fmt.Println("handleSignal() Caught:", sig)
}
```

`handleSignal()` is a separate function for handling signals. However, you can also handle signals **inline**, in the branches of a `switch` statement.

```
func main() {
    fmt.Printf("Process ID: %d\n", os.Getpid())
    sigs := make(chan os.Signal, 1)
```

We create a channel with data of type `os.Signal` because all channels must have a type.

```
    signal.Notify(sigs)
```

The previous statement means *handle all signals that can be handled.*

```
    start := time.Now()
    go func() {
        for {
            sig := <-sigs
```

Wait until you read data (`<-`) from the `sigs` channel and store it in the `sig` variable.

```
            switch sig {
```

Depending on the read value, act accordingly. This is how you differentiate between signals.

```
            case syscall.SIGINT:
                duration := time.Since(start)
                fmt.Println("Execution time:", duration)
```

For the handling of `syscall.SIGINT`, we calculate the time that has passed since the beginning of the program execution, and print it on screen.

```
            case syscall.SIGINFO:
                handleSignal(sig)
```

The code of the `syscall.SIGINFO` case calls the `handleSignal()` function—it is up to the developer to decide on the details of the implementation. On Linux machines, you should replace `syscall.SIGINFO` with another signal such as `syscall.SIGUSR1` or `syscall.SIGUSR2` because `syscall.SIGINFO` **is not available on Linux** (`https://github.com/golang/go/issues/1653`).

```
                // do not use return here because the goroutine exits
                // but the time.Sleep() will continue to work!
                os.Exit(0)
            default:
                fmt.Println("Caught:", sig)
            }
```

If there is not a match, the `default` case handles the rest of the values and just prints a message.

```
        }
    }()

    for {
        fmt.Print("+")
        time.Sleep(10 * time.Second)
    }
}
```

The endless `for` loop at the end of the `main()` function is for emulating the operation of a real program. Without an endless `for` loop, the program exits almost immediately.

Running `signals.go` and interacting with it creates the following kind of output:

```
$ go run signals.go
Process ID: 74252
+Execution time: 9.989863093s
+Caught: user defined signal 1
+signal: killed
```

The second line of output was generated by pressing *Ctrl* + *C* on the keyboard, which on UNIX machines sends the `syscall.SIGINT` signal to the program. The third line of output was caused by executing `kill -USR1 74252` on a different terminal. The last line in the output was generated by the `kill -9 74252` command. As the `KILL` signal, which is also represented by the number `9`, cannot be handled, it terminates the program, and the shell prints the `killed` message.

Handling two signals

If you want to handle a limited number of signals, instead of all of them, you should replace the `signal.Notify(sigs)` statement with the next statement:

```
signal.Notify(sigs, syscall.SIGINT, syscall.SIGINFO)
```

After that you need to make the appropriate changes to the code of the goroutine responsible for signal handling in order to identify and handle `syscall.SIGINT` and `syscall.SIGINFO`—the current version (`signals.go`) already handles both of them.

Now, we need to learn how to read and write files in Go.

File I/O

This section discusses file I/O in Go, which includes the use of the `io.Reader` and `io.Writer` interfaces, buffered and unbuffered I/O, as well as the `bufio` package.

> The `io/ioutil` package (`https://golang.org/pkg/io/ioutil/`) is deprecated in Go version 1.16. Existing Go code that uses the functionality of `io/ioutil` will continue to work but it is better to stop using that package.

The io.Reader and io.Writer interfaces

This subsection presents the definitions of the popular `io.Reader` and `io.Writer` interfaces because these two interfaces are the basis of file I/O in Go—the former allows you to read from a file whereas the latter allows you to write to a file. The definition of the `io.Reader` interface is the following:

```
type Reader interface {
    Read(p []byte) (n int, err error)
}
```

This definition, which should be revisited when we want one of our data types to satisfy the `io.Reader` interface, tells us the following:

- The `Reader` interface requires the implementation of a single method
- The parameter of `Read()` is a byte slice
- The return values of `Read()` are an integer and an error

The `Read()` method takes a byte slice as input, which is going to be filled with data **up to its length**, and returns the number of bytes read as well as an `error` variable.

The definition of the `io.Writer` interface is the following:

```
type Writer interface {
    Write(p []byte) (n int, err error)
}
```

The previous definition, which should be revisited when we want one of our data types to satisfy the `io.Writer` interface and to write to a file, reveals the following information:

- The interface requires the implementation of a single method
- The parameter of `Write()` is a byte slice
- The return values of `Write()` are an integer and an `error` value

The `Write()` method takes a byte slice, which contains the data that you want to write, as input and returns the number of bytes written and an `error` variable.

Using and misusing io.Reader and io.Writer

The code that follows showcases the use of `io.Reader` and `io.Writer` for custom data types, which in this case are two Go structures named `S1` and `S2`.

For the `S1` structure, the presented code implements both interfaces in order to read user data from the terminal and print data to the terminal, respectively. Although this is redundant as we already have `fmt.Scanln()` and `fmt.Printf()`, it is a good exercise that shows how versatile and flexible both interfaces are. In a different situation, you could have used `io.Writer` for writing to a log service, or keeping a second backup copy of the written data, or anything else that fits your needs. However, this is also an example of interfaces allowing you to do crazy or, if you prefer, unusual things—it is up to the developer to create the desired functionality using the appropriate Go concepts and features!

The `Read()` method is using `fmt.Scanln()` to get user input from the terminal whereas the `Write()` method is printing the contents of its buffer parameter as many times as the value of the `F1` field of the structure using `fmt.Printf()`!

For the `S2` structure, the presented code implements the `io.Reader` interface only in the traditional way. The `Read()` method reads the `text` field of the `S2` structure, which is a byte slice. When there is nothing left to read, the `Read()` method returns the expected `io.EOF` error, which in reality is not an error but an expected situation. Along with the `Read()` method there exist two helper methods, named `eof()`, which declares that there is nothing more to read, and `readByte()`, which reads the `text` field of the `S2` structure byte by byte. After the `Read()` method is done, the `text` field of the `S2` structure, which is used as a buffer, is emptied.

With this implementation, the `io.Reader` for `S2` can be used for reading in a traditional way, which in this case is with `bufio.NewReader()` and multiple `Read()` calls—the number of `Read()` calls depends on the size of the buffer that is used, which in this case is a byte slice with 2 places for data.

Type the following code and save it as `ioInterface.go`:

```
package main

import (
    "bufio"
    "fmt"
    "io"
)
```

The previous part shows that we are using the `io` and `bufio` packages for working with files.

```
type S1 struct {
    F1 int
    F2 string
}

type S2 struct {
    F1   S1
    text []byte
}
```

These are the two structures we are going to work with.

```
// Using pointer to S1 for changes to be persistent when the method
exits
func (s *S1) Read(p []byte) (n int, err error) {
    fmt.Print("Give me your name: ")
    fmt.Scanln(&p)
    s.F2 = string(p)
    return len(p), nil
}
```

In the preceding code, we are implementing the `io.Reader()` interface for `S1`.

```
func (s *S1) Write(p []byte) (n int, err error) {
    if s.F1 < 0 {
        return -1, nil
    }

    for i := 0; i < s.F1; i++ {
        fmt.Printf("%s ", p)
    }
```

```
    fmt.Println()
    return s.F1, nil
}
```

The previous method implements the `io.Writer` interface for `S1`.

```
func (s S2) eof() bool {
    return len(s.text) == 0
}

func (s *S2) readByte() byte {
    // this function assumes that eof() check was done before
    temp := s.text[0]
    s.text = s.text[1:]
    return temp
}
```

The previous function is an implementation of `bytes.Buffer.ReadByte` from the standard library.

```
func (s *S2) Read(p []byte) (n int, err error) {
    if s.eof() {
        err = io.EOF
        return
    }

    l := len(p)
    if l > 0 {
        for n < l {
```

The previous functions read from the given buffer until the buffer is empty. This is where we implement `io.Reader` for `S2`.

```
            p[n] = s.readByte()
            n++
            if s.eof() {
                s.text = s.text[0:0]
                break
            }
        }
    }
    return
}
```

When all data is read, the relevant structure field is emptied. The previous method implements `io.Reader` for `S2`. However, the operation of `Read()` is supported by `eof()` and `readByte()`, which are also user-defined.

Recall that Go allows you to name the return values of a function—in that case, a `return` statement without any additional arguments automatically returns the current value of each named return variable in the order they appear in the function signature. The `Read()` method uses that feature.

```
func main() {
	s1var := S1{4, "Hello"}
	fmt.Println(s1var)
```

We initialize an `S1` variable that is named `s1var`.

```
	buf := make([]byte, 2)
	_, err := s1var.Read(buf)
```

The previous line is reading for the `s1var` variable using a buffer with `2` bytes.

```
	if err != nil {
		fmt.Println(err)
		return
	}
	fmt.Println("Read:", s1var.F2)
	_, _ = s1var.Write([]byte("Hello There!"))
```

In the previous line, we call the `Write()` method for `s1var` in order to write the contents of a byte slice.

```
	s2var := S2{F1: s1var, text: []byte("Hello world!!")}
```

In the previous code, we initialize an `S2` variable that is named `s2var`.

```
	// Read s2var.text
	r := bufio.NewReader(&s2var)
```

We now create a reader for `s2var`.

```
	for {
		n, err := r.Read(buf)
		if err == io.EOF {
			break
```

We keep reading from `s2var` until there is an `io.EOF` condition.

```
        } else if err != nil {
            fmt.Println("*", err)
            break
        }
        fmt.Println("**", n, string(buf[:n]))
    }
}
```

Running `ioInterface.go` produces the next output:

```
$ go run ioInterface.go
{4 Hello}
```

The first line of the output shows the contents of the `s1var` variable.

```
Give me your name: Mike
```

Calling the `Read()` method of the `s1var` variable.

```
Read: Mike
Hello There! Hello There! Hello There! Hello There!
```

The previous line is the output of `s1var.Write([]byte("Hello There!"))`.

```
** 2 He
** 2 ll
** 2 o
** 2 wo
** 2 rl
** 2 d!
** 1 !
```

The last part of the output illustrates the reading process using a buffer with a size of 2. The next section discusses buffered and unbuffered operations.

Buffered and unbuffered file I/O

Buffered file I/O happens when there is a buffer for temporarily storing data before reading data or writing data. Thus, instead of reading a file byte by byte, you read many bytes at once. You put the data in a buffer and wait for someone to read it in the desired way.

Unbuffered file I/O happens when there is no buffer to temporarily store data before actually reading or writing it—this can affect the performance of your programs.

The next question that you might ask is how to decide when to use buffered and when to use unbuffered file I/O. When dealing with critical data, unbuffered file I/O is generally a better choice because buffered reads might result in out-of-date data and buffered writes might result in data loss when the power of your computer is interrupted. However, most of the time, there is no definitive answer to that question. This means that you can use whatever makes your tasks easier to implement. However, keep in mind that **buffered readers can also improve performance** by reducing the number of system calls needed to read from a file or socket, so there can be a real performance impact on what the programmer decides to use.

There is also the `bufio` package. As the name suggests, `bufio` is about buffered I/O. Internally, the `bufio` package implements the `io.Reader` and `io.Writer` interfaces, which it wraps in order to create the `bufio.Reader` and `bufio.Writer` objects, respectively. The `bufio` package is very popular for working with plain text files and you are going to see it in action in the next section.

Reading text files

In this section you will learn how to read plain text files, as well as using the `/dev/random` UNIX device, which offers you a way of getting random numbers.

Reading a text file line by line

The function for reading a file line by line is found in `byLine.go` and is named `lineByLine()`. The technique for reading a text file line by line is also used when reading a plain text file word by word as well as when reading a plain text file character by character because you usually process plain text files line by line. The presented utility prints every line that it reads, which makes it a simplified version of the `cat(1)` utility.

First, you create a new reader to the desired file using a call to `bufio.NewReader()`. Then, you use that reader with `bufio.ReadString()` in order to read the input file line by line. The trick is done by the parameter of `bufio.ReadString()`, which is a character that tells `bufio.ReadString()` to keep reading until that character is found. Constantly calling `bufio.ReadString()` when that parameter is the newline character (`\n`) results in reading the input file line by line.

The implementation of `lineByLine()` is as follows:

```
func lineByLine(file string) error {
    f, err := os.Open(file)
    if err != nil {
        return err
    }
    defer f.Close()

    r := bufio.NewReader(f)
```

After making sure that you can open the given file for reading (`os.Open()`), you create a new reader using `bufio.NewReader()`.

```
    for {
        line, err := r.ReadString('\n')
```

`bufio.ReadString()` returns two values: the string that was read and an `error` variable.

```
        if err == io.EOF {
            break
        } else if err != nil {
            fmt.Printf("error reading file %s", err)
            break
        }
        fmt.Print(line)
```

The use of `fmt.Print()` instead of `fmt.Println()` for printing the input line shows that the newline character is included in each input line.

```
    }
    return nil
}
```

Running `byLine.go` generates the following kind of output:

```
$ go run byLine.go ~/csv.data
Dimitris,Tsoukalos,2101112223,1600665563
Mihalis,Tsoukalos,2109416471,1600665563
Jane,Doe,0800123456,1608559903
```

The previous output shows the contents of `~/csv.data` presented line by line with the help of `byLine.go`. The next subsection shows how to read a plain text file word by word.

Reading a text file word by word

Reading a plain text file word by word is the single most useful function that you want to perform on a file because you usually want to process a file on a per-word basis—it is illustrated in this subsection using the code found in `byWord.go`. The desired functionality is implemented in the `wordByWord()` function. The `wordByWord()` function uses **regular expressions** to separate the words found in each line of the input file. The regular expression defined in the `regexp.MustCompile("[^\\s]+")` statement states that we use whitespace characters to separate one word from another.

The implementation of the `wordByWord()` function is as follows:

```
func wordByWord(file string) error {
	f, err := os.Open(file)
	if err != nil {
		return err
	}
	defer f.Close()

	r := bufio.NewReader(f)
	for {
		line, err := r.ReadString('\n')
		if err == io.EOF {
			break
		} else if err != nil {
			fmt.Printf("error reading file %s", err)
			return err
		}

		r := regexp.MustCompile("[^\\s]+")
```

This is the place where you define the regular expression you want to use.

```
		words := r.FindAllString(line, -1)
```

This is where you apply the regular expression to split the line variable into fields.

```
        for i := 0; i < len(words); i++ {
            fmt.Println(words[i])
        }
```

This for loop just prints the fields of the words slice. If you want to know the number of words found in the input line, you can just find the value of the len(words) call.

```
    }
    return nil
}
```

Running byWord.go produces the following kind of output:

```
$ go run byWord.go ~/csv.data
Dimitris,Tsoukalos,2101112223,1600665563
Mihalis,Tsoukalos,2109416471,1600665563
Jane,Doe,0800123456,1608559903
```

As ~/csv.data does not contain any whitespace characters, each line is considered a single word!

Reading a text file character by character

In this subsection, you learn how to read a text file character by character, which is a pretty rare requirement unless you want to develop a text editor. You take each line that you read and split it using a for loop with range, which returns two values. You discard the first, which is the location of the current character in the line variable, and you use the second. However, that value is a rune, which means that you have to convert it into a character using string().

The implementation of charByChar() is as follows:

```
func charByChar(file string) error {
    f, err := os.Open(file)
    if err != nil {
        return err
    }
    defer f.Close()

    r := bufio.NewReader(f)
    for {
        line, err := r.ReadString('\n')
```

```
        if err == io.EOF {
            break
        } else if err != nil {
            fmt.Printf("error reading file %s", err)
            return err
        }

        for _, x := range line {
            fmt.Println(string(x))
        }
```

Note that, due to the `fmt.Println(string(x))` statement, each character is printed in a distinct line, which means that the output of the program is going to be large. If you want a more compressed output, you should use the `fmt.Print()` function instead.

```
    }
    return nil
}
```

Running `byCharacter.go` and filtering it with `head(1)`, without any parameters, produces the following kind of output:

```
$ go run byCharacter.go ~/csv.data | head
D
...
,
T
```

The use of the `head(1)` utility without any parameters limits the output to just 10 lines.

The next section is about reading from `/dev/random`, which is a UNIX system file.

Reading from /dev/random

In this subsection, you learn how to read from the `/dev/random` system device. The purpose of the `/dev/random` system device is to generate random data, which you might use for testing your programs or, in this case, as the seed for a random number generator. Getting data from `/dev/random` can be a little bit tricky, and this is the main reason for specifically discussing it here.

The code of `devRandom.go` is the following:

```
package main

import (
    "encoding/binary"
    "fmt"
    "os"
)
```

You need `encoding/binary` because you are reading binary data from `/dev/random` that you convert into an integer value.

```
func main() {
    f, err := os.Open("/dev/random")
    defer f.Close()

    if err != nil {
        fmt.Println(err)
        return
    }

    var seed int64
    binary.Read(f, binary.LittleEndian, &seed)
    fmt.Println("Seed:", seed)
}
```

There are two representations named **little endian** and **big endian** that have to do with the **byte order** in the internal representation. In our case, we are using little endian. The *endian-ness* has to do with the way different computing systems order multiple bytes of information.

> A real-world example of endian-ness is how different languages read text in different ways: European languages tend to be read from left to right, whereas Arabic texts are read from right to left.

In a big endian representation, bytes are read from left to right, while little endian reads bytes from right to left. For the `0x01234567` value, which requires 4 bytes for storing, the big endian representation is `01 | 23 | 45 | 67` whereas the little endian representation is `67 | 45 | 23 | 01`.

Running devRandom.go creates the following kind of output:

```
$ go run devRandom.go
Seed: 422907465220227415
```

This means that the /dev/random device is a good place for getting random data including a seed value for your random number generator.

Reading a specific amount of data from a file

This subsection teaches you how to read a specific amount of data from a file. The presented utility can come in handy when you want to see a small part of a file. The numeric value that is given as a command-line argument specifies the size of the buffer that is going to be used for reading. The most important code of readSize.go is the implementation of the readSize() function:

```
func readSize(f *os.File, size int) []byte {
	buffer := make([]byte, size)
	n, err := f.Read(buffer)
```

All the magic happens in the definition of the buffer variable because this is where we define the maximum amount of data that we want to read. Therefore, each time you invoke readSize(), the function is going to read from f at most size characters.

```
	// io.EOF is a special case and is treated as such
	if err == io.EOF {
		return nil
	}

	if err != nil {
		fmt.Println(err)
		return nil
	}
	return buffer[0:n]
}
```

The remaining code is about error conditions; io.EOF is a special and expected condition that should be treated separately and return the read characters as a byte slice to the caller function.

Running `readSize.go` produces the following kind of output:

```
$ go run readSize.go 12 readSize.go
package main
```

In this case, we read 12 characters from `readSize.go` itself because of the `12` parameter.

Now that we know how to read files, it is time to learn how to write to files.

Writing to a file

So far, we have seen ways to read files. This subsection shows how to write data to files in four different ways and how to append data to an existing file. The code of `writeFile.go` is as follows:

```
package main

import (
    "bufio"
    "fmt"
    "io"
    "os"
)

func main() {
    buffer := []byte("Data to write\n")
    f1, err := os.Create("/tmp/f1.txt")
```

`os.Create()` returns an `*os.File` value associated with the file path that is passed as a parameter. Note that if the file already exists, `os.Create()` truncates it.

```
    if err != nil {
        fmt.Println("Cannot create file", err)
        return
    }
    defer f1.Close()
    fmt.Fprintf(f1, string(buffer))
```

The `fmt.Fprintf()` function, which requires a `string` variable, helps you write data to your own files using the format you want. The only requirement is having an `io.Writer` to write to. In this case, a valid `*os.File` variable, which satisfies the `io.Writer` interface, does the job.

```
    f2, err := os.Create("/tmp/f2.txt")
    if err != nil {
        fmt.Println("Cannot create file", err)
        return
    }
    defer f2.Close()
    n, err := f2.WriteString(string(buffer))
```

The `os.WriteString()` method writes the contents of a string to a valid `*os.File` variable.

```
    fmt.Printf("wrote %d bytes\n", n)

    f3, err := os.Create("/tmp/f3.txt")
```

Here we create a temporary file on our own. Later on in this chapter you are going to learn about using `os.CreateTemp()` for creating temporary files.

```
    if err != nil {
        fmt.Println(err)
        return
    }
    w := bufio.NewWriter(f3)
```

This function returns a `bufio.Writer`, which satisfies the `io.Writer` interface.

```
    n, err = w.WriteString(string(buffer))
    fmt.Printf("wrote %d bytes\n", n)
    w.Flush()

    f := "/tmp/f4.txt"
    f4, err := os.Create(f)
    if err != nil {
        fmt.Println(err)
        return
    }
    defer f4.Close()

    for i := 0; i < 5; i++ {
        n, err = io.WriteString(f4, string(buffer))
        if err != nil {
            fmt.Println(err)
            return
        }
```

```
        fmt.Printf("wrote %d bytes\n", n)
    }

    // Append to a file
    f4, err = os.OpenFile(f, os.O_APPEND|os.O_CREATE|os.O_WRONLY, 0644)
```

`os.OpenFile()` provides a *better way* to create or open a file for writing. `os.O_APPEND` is saying that if the file already exists, you should append to it instead of truncating it. `os.O_CREATE` is saying that if the file does not already exist, it should be created. Last, `os.O_WRONLY` is saying that the program should open the file for writing only.

```
    if err != nil {
        fmt.Println(err)
        return
    }
    defer f4.Close()

    // Write() needs a byte slice
    n, err = f4.Write([]byte("Put some more data at the end.\n"))
```

The `Write()` method gets its input from a byte slice, which is the Go way of writing. All previous techniques used strings, which is not the best way, especially when working with binary data. However, using strings instead of byte slices is more practical as it is more convenient to manipulate `string` values than the elements of a byte slice, especially when working with Unicode characters. On the other hand, using `string` values increases allocation and can cause a lot of garbage collection pressure.

```
    if err != nil {
        fmt.Println(err)
        return
    }
    fmt.Printf("wrote %d bytes\n", n)
}
```

Running `writeFile.go` generates some information output about the bytes written on disk. What is really interesting is seeing the files created in the `/tmp` folder:

```
$ ls -l /tmp/f?.txt
-rw-r--r--  1 mtsouk  wheel   14 Feb 27 19:44 /tmp/f1.txt
-rw-r--r--  1 mtsouk  wheel   14 Feb 27 19:44 /tmp/f2.txt
-rw-r--r--  1 mtsouk  wheel   14 Feb 27 19:44 /tmp/f3.txt
-rw-r--r--  1 mtsouk  wheel  101 Feb 27 19:44 /tmp/f4.txt
```

The previous output shows that the same amount of information has been written in `f1.txt`, `f2.txt`, and `f3.txt`, which means that the presented writing techniques are equivalent.

The next section shows how to work with JSON data in Go.

Working with JSON

The Go standard library includes `encoding/json`, which is for working with JSON data. Additionally, Go allows you to add support for **JSON fields** in Go structures using **tags**, which is the subject of the *Structures and JSON* subsection. Tags control the encoding and decoding of JSON records to and from Go structures. But first we should talk about marshaling and unmarshaling JSON records.

Using Marshal() and Unmarshal()

Both the marshaling and unmarshaling of JSON data are important procedures for working with JSON data using Go structures. **Marshaling** is the process of converting a Go structure into a JSON record. You usually want that for transferring JSON data via computer networks or for saving it on disk. **Unmarshaling** is the process of converting a JSON record given as a byte slice into a Go structure. You usually want that when receiving JSON data via computer networks or when loading JSON data from disk files.

> The number one bug when converting JSON records into Go structures and vice versa is not making the required fields of your Go structures **exported**. When you have issues with marshaling and unmarshaling, begin your debugging process from there.

The code in `encodeDecode.go` illustrates both the marshaling and unmarshaling of JSON records using hardcoded data for simplicity:

```
package main

import (
    "encoding/json"
    "fmt"
)

type UseAll struct {
    Name    string `json:"username"`
```

```
    Surname string `json:"surname"`
    Year    int    `json:"created"`
}
```

What the previous metadata tells us is that the `Name` field of the `UseAll` structure is translated to `username` in the JSON record, and **vice versa**, the `Surname` field is translated to `surname`, and **vice versa**, and the `Year` structure field is translated to `created` in the JSON record, and **vice versa**. This information has to do with the marshaling and unmarshaling of JSON data. Other than this, you treat and use `UseAll` as a regular Go structure.

```
func main() {
    useall := UseAll{Name: "Mike", Surname: "Tsoukalos", Year: 2021}

    // Regular Structure
    // Encoding JSON data -> Convert Go Structure to JSON record with
fields
    t, err := json.Marshal(&useall)
```

The `json.Marshal()` function requires a pointer to a structure variable—its real data type is an empty interface variable—and returns a byte slice with the encoded information and an `error` variable.

```
    if err != nil {
        fmt.Println(err)
    } else {
        fmt.Printf("Value %s\n", t)
    }

    // Decoding JSON data given as a string
    str := `{"username": "M.", "surname": "Ts", "created":2020}`
```

JSON data usually comes as a string.

```
    // Convert string into a byte slice
    jsonRecord := []byte(str)
```

However, as `json.Unmarshal()` requires a byte slice, you need to convert that string into a byte slice before passing it to `json.Unmarshal()`.

```
    // Create a structure variable to store the result
    temp := UseAll{}
    err = json.Unmarshal(jsonRecord, &temp)
```

The `json.Unmarshal()` function requires the byte slice with the JSON record and a pointer to the Go structure variable that is going to store the JSON record and returns an `error` variable.

```
    if err != nil {
        fmt.Println(err)
    } else {
        fmt.Printf("Data type: %T with value %v\n", temp, temp)
    }
}
```

Running `encodeDecode.go` produces the next output:

```
$ go run encodeDecode.go
Value {"username":"Mike","surname":"Tsoukalos","created":2021}
Data type: main.UseAll with value {M. Ts 2020}
```

The next subsection illustrates how to define the JSON tags in a Go structure in more detail.

Structures and JSON

Imagine that you have a Go structure that you want to convert into a JSON record without including any empty fields—the next code illustrates how to perform that task with the use of `omitempty`:

```
// Ignoring empty fields in JSON
type NoEmpty struct {
    Name    string `json:"username"`
    Surname string `json:"surname"`
    Year    int    `json:"creationyear,omitempty"`
}
```

Last, imagine that you have some sensitive data on some of the fields of a Go structure that you do not want to include in the JSON records. You can do that by including the `"-"` special value in the desired `json:` structure tags. This is shown in the next code excerpt:

```
// Removing private fields and ignoring empty fields
type Password struct {
    Name     string `json:"username"`
    Surname  string `json:"surname,omitempty"`
```

```
    Year    int    `json:"creationyear,omitempty"`
    Pass    string `json:"-"`
}
```

So, the `Pass` field is going to be ignored when converting a `Password` structure into a JSON record using `json.Marshal()`.

These two techniques are illustrated in `tagsJSON.go`, which can be found in the `ch06` directory of the GitHub repository of this book. Running `tagsJSON.go` produces the next output:

```
$ go run tagsJSON.go
noEmptyVar decoded with value {"username":"Mihalis","surname":""}
password decoded with value {"username":"Mihalis"}
```

For the first line of output, we have the following: the value of `noEmpty`, which is converted into a `NoEmpty` structure variable named `noEmptyVar`, is `NoEmpty{Name: "Mihalis"}`. The `noEmpty` structure has the default values for the `Surname` and `Year` fields. However, as they are not specifically defined, `json.Marshal()` ignores the `Year` field because it has the `omitempty` tag but does not ignore the `Surname` field, which has the empty string value.

For the second line of output: the value of the `password` variable is `Password{Name: "Mihalis", Pass: "myPassword"}`. When the `password` variable is converted into a JSON record, the `Pass` field is not included in the output. The remaining two fields of the `Password` structure, `Surname` and `Year`, are omitted because of the `omitempty` tag. So, what is left is the `username` field.

So far, we have seen working with single JSON records. But what happens when you have multiple records to process? The next subsection answers this question and many more!

Reading and writing JSON data as streams

Imagine that you have a slice of Go structures that represent JSON records that you want to process. Should you process the records one by one? It can be done but does it look efficient? It does not! The good thing is that Go supports the processing of multiple JSON records as streams instead of individual records, which is faster and more efficient. This subsection teaches how to perform that using the `JSONstreams.go` utility, which contains the following two functions:

```
// DeSerialize decodes a serialized slice with JSON records
func DeSerialize(e *json.Decoder, slice interface{}) error {
    return e.Decode(slice)
}
```

The `DeSerialize()` function is used for reading input in the form of JSON records, decoding it, and putting it into a slice. The function writes the slice, which is of the `interface{}` data type and is given as a parameter, and gets its input from the buffer of the `*json.Decoder` parameter. The `*json.Decoder` parameter along with its buffer is defined in the `main()` function in order to avoid allocating it all the time and therefore losing the performance gains and efficiency of using this type—the same applies to the use of `*json.Encoder` that follows:

```
// Serialize serializes a slice with JSON records
func Serialize(e *json.Encoder, slice interface{}) error {
    return e.Encode(slice)
}
```

The `Serialize()` function accepts two parameters, a `*json.Encoder` and a slice of any data type, hence the use of `interface{}`. The function processes the slice and writes the output to the buffer of the `json.Encoder`—this buffer is passed as a parameter to the encoder at the time of its creation.

> Both the `Serialize()` and `DeSerialize()` functions can work with any type of JSON record due to the use of `interface{}`.

The `JSONstreams.go` utility generates random data. Running `JSONstreams.go` creates the next output:

```
$ go run JSONstreams.go
After Serialize:[{"key":"XVLBZ","value":16},{"key":"BAICM","value":89}]
After DeSerialize:
0 {XVLBZ 16}
1 {BAICM 89}
```

The input slice of structures, which is generated in `main()`, is serialized as seen in the first line of the output. After that it is deserialized into the original slice of structures.

Pretty printing JSON records

This subsection illustrates how to **pretty print** JSON records, which means printing JSON records in a pleasant and readable format without knowing the format of the Go structure that holds the JSON records. As there exist two ways to read JSON records, individually and as a stream, there exist two ways to pretty print JSON data: as single JSON records and as a stream. Therefore, we are going to implement two separate functions named `prettyPrint()` and `JSONstream()`, respectively.

The implementation of the `prettyPrint()` function is the following:

```
func PrettyPrint(v interface{}) (err error) {
    b, err := json.MarshalIndent(v, "", "\t")
    if err == nil {
        fmt.Println(string(b))
    }
    return err
}
```

All the work is done by `json.MarshalIndent()`, which **applies indent** to format the output.

Although both `json.MarshalIndent()` and `json.Marshal()` produce a JSON text result (*byte slice*), only `json.MarshalIndent()` allows applying customizable indent, whereas `json.Marshal()` generates a more compact output.

For pretty printing streams of JSON data, you should use the `JSONstream()` function:

```
func JSONstream(data interface{}) (string, error) {
  buffer := new(bytes.Buffer)
  encoder := json.NewEncoder(buffer)
  encoder.SetIndent("", "\t")
```

The `json.NewEncoder()` function returns a new `Encoder` that writes to a writer that is passed as a parameter to `json.NewEncoder()`. An `Encoder` writes JSON values to an output stream. Similarly to `json.MarshalIndent()`, the `SetIndent()` method allows you to apply a customizable indent to a stream.

```
  err := encoder.Encode(data)
  if err != nil {
    return "", err
  }
  return buffer.String(), nil
}
```

After we are done configuring the encoder, we are free to process the JSON stream using `Encode()`.

These two functions are illustrated in `prettyPrint.go`, which generates JSON records using random data. Running `prettyPrint.go` produces the following kind of output:

```
Last record: {BAICM 89}
{
        "key": "BAICM",
        "value": 89
}
[
        {
                "key": "XVLBZ",
                "value": 16
        },
        {
                "key": "BAICM",
                "value": 89
        }
]
```

The previous output shows the beautified output of a single JSON record followed by the beautified output of a slice with two JSON records—all JSON records are represented as Go structures.

The next section is about working with XML in Go.

Working with XML

This section briefly describes how to work with XML data in Go using records. The idea behind XML and Go is the same as with JSON and Go. You put tags in Go structures in order to specify the XML tags and you can still serialize and deserialize XML records using `xml.Unmarshal()` and `xml.Marshal()`, which are found in the `encoding/xml` package. However, there exist some differences that are illustrated in `xml.go`:

```
package main

import (
    "encoding/xml"
    "fmt"
)
```

```
type Employee struct {
    XMLName   xml.Name `xml:"employee"`
    ID        int      `xml:"id,attr"`
    FirstName string   `xml:"name>first"`
    LastName  string   `xml:"name>last"`
    Height    float32  `xml:"height,omitempty"`
    Address
    Comment string `xml:",comment"`
}
```

This is where the structure for the XML data is defined. However, there is additional information regarding the name and the type of each XML element. The `XMLName` field provides the name of the XML record, which in this case will be `employee`.

A field with the tag `",comment"` is a comment and it is formatted as such in the output. A field with the tag `attr` appears as an attribute to the provided field name (which is `id` in this case) in the output. The `name>first` notation tells Go to embed the `first` tag inside a tag called `name`.

Lastly, a field with the `omitempty` option is omitted from the output if it is empty. An **empty value** is any of `0`, `false`, a `nil` pointer or interface, and any array, slice, map, or string with a length of zero.

```
type Address struct {
    City, Country string
}

func main() {
    r := Employee{ID: 7, FirstName: "Mihalis", LastName: "Tsoukalos"}
    r.Comment = "Technical Writer + DevOps"
    r.Address = Address{"SomeWhere 12", "12312, Greece"}

    output, err := xml.MarshalIndent(&r, "  ", "    ")
```

As is the case with JSON, `xml.MarshalIndent()` is for beautifying the output.

```
    if err != nil {
        fmt.Println("Error:", err)
    }
    output = []byte(xml.Header + string(output))
    fmt.Printf("%s\n", output)
}
```

The output of `xml.go` is the following:

```
<?xml version="1.0" encoding="UTF-8"?>
  <employee id="7">
      <name>
          <first>Mihalis</first>
          <last>Tsoukalos</last>
      </name>
      <City>SomeWhere 12</City>
      <Country>12312, Greece</Country>
      <!--Technical Writer + DevOps-->
  </employee>
```

The previous output shows the XML version of the Go structure given as input to the program.

In the next section we develop a utility that converts JSON records to XML records and vice versa.

Converting JSON to XML and vice versa

As promised, we are going to produce a utility that converts records between the JSON and XML formats. The input is given as a command-line argument. The utility tries to guess the format of the input starting from XML. If `xml.Unmarshal()` fails, then the utility tries using `json.Unmarshal()`. If there is not a match, then the user is informed about the error condition. On the other hand, if `xml.Unmarshal()` is successful, the data is stored into an `XMLrec` variable and is then converted into a `JSONrec` variable. The same happens with `json.Unmarshal()` in the case where the `xml.Unmarshal()` call is unsuccessful.

The logic of the utility can be found in the Go structures:

```
type XMLrec struct {
    Name    string `xml:"username"`
    Surname string `xml:"surname,omitempty"`
    Year    int    `xml:"creationyear,omitempty"`
}

type JSONrec struct {
    Name    string `json:"username"`
    Surname string `json:"surname,omitempty"`
    Year    int    `json:"creationyear,omitempty"`
}
```

Both structures store the same data. However, the former (`XMLrec`) is for storing XML data whereas the latter (`JSONrec`) is for storing JSON data.

Running `JSON2XML.go` produces the next kind of output:

```
$ go run JSON2XML.go '<XMLrec><username>Mihalis</username></XMLrec>'
<XMLrec><username>Mihalis</username></XMLrec>
{"username":"Mihalis"}
```

So, we give an XML record as input, which is converted into a JSON record.

The next output illustrates the reverse process:

```
$ go run JSON2XML.go '{"username": "Mihalis"}'
{"username": "Mihalis"}
<XMLrec><username>Mihalis</username></XMLrec>
```

In the previous output the input is a JSON record, and the output is an XML record.

The next section discusses working with YAML files in Go.

Working with YAML

In this section, we briefly discuss how to work with YAML files in Go. The Go standard library does not include support for YAML files, which means that you should look at external packages for YAML support. There exist three main packages that allow you to work with YAML from Go:

- `https://github.com/kylelemons/go-gypsy`
- `https://github.com/go-yaml/yaml`
- `https://github.com/goccy/go-yaml`

Choosing one is a matter of personal preference. We are going to work with `go-yaml` in this section using the code found in `yaml.go`. Due to the use of Go modules, `yaml.go` is developed in `~/go/src/github.com/mactsouk/yaml`—you can also find it in the GitHub repository of this book. The most important part of it is the next:

```
var yamlfile = `
image: Golang
matrix:
  docker: python
  version: [2.7, 3.9]
`
```

The `yamlfile` variable contains the YAML data; you usually read the data from a file—we are just using that to save some space.

```
type Mat struct {
    DockerImage string    `yaml:"docker"`
    Version     []float32 `yaml:",flow"`
}
```

The `Mat` structure defines two fields and their associations with the YAML file. The `Version` field is a slice of `float32` values. As there is no name for the `Version` field, the name is going to be `version`. The `flow` keyword says that the marshal is using a flow style, which is useful for structs, sequences, and maps.

```
type YAML struct {
    Image  string
    Matrix Mat
}
```

The YAML structure embeds a `Mat` structure and contains a field named `Image`, which is associated with `image` in the YAML file. The `main()` function contains the expected `yaml.Unmarshal()` and `yaml.Marshal()` calls.

Once you have the source file at the desired place, run the next commands—if you need to run any extra commands, the go binary is nice enough to help you:

```
$ go mod init
$ go mod tidy
```

The `go mod init` command initializes and writes a new `go.mod` file in the current directory whereas the `go mod tidy` command synchronizes `go.mod` with the source code.

> If you want to play it safe and you are using packages that do not belong to the standard library, then developing inside `~/go/src`, committing to a GitHub repository, and using Go modules for all dependencies might be the best option. However, this does not mean that you must develop your own packages in the form of Go modules.

Running `yaml.go` produces the next output:

```
$ go run yaml.go
After Unmarshal (Structure):
{Golang {python [2.7 3.9]}}
```

```
After Marshal (YAML code):
image: Golang
matrix:
  docker: python
  version: [2.7, 3.9]
```

The previous output shows how the `{Golang {python [2.7 3.9]}}` text is converted into a YAML file and vice versa. Now that we know about working with JSON, XML, and YAML data in Go, we are ready to learn about the `viper` package.

The viper package

Flags are specially formatted strings that are passed into a program to control its behavior. Dealing with flags on your own might become very frustrating if you want to support multiple flags and options. Go offers the `flag` package for working with command-line options, parameters, and flags. Although `flag` can do many things, it is not as capable as other external Go packages. Thus, if you are developing simple UNIX system command-line utilities, you might find the `flag` package very interesting and useful. But you are not reading this book to create simple command-line utilities! Therefore, I'll skip the `flag` package and introduce you to an external package named `viper`, which is a powerful Go package that supports a plethora of options. `viper` uses the `pflag` package instead of `flag`, which is also illustrated in the code we will look at in the following sections.

All `viper` projects follow a pattern. First, you initialize `viper` and then you define the elements that interest you. After that, you get these elements and read their values in order to use them. The desired values can be taken either directly, as happens when you are using the `flag` package from the standard Go library, or indirectly using configuration files. When using formatted configuration files in the JSON, YAML, TOML, HCL, or Java properties format, `viper` does all the parsing for you, which saves you from having to write and debug lots of Go code. `viper` also allows you to extract and save values in Go structures. However, this requires that the fields of the Go structure match the keys of the configuration file.

The home page of `viper` is on GitHub (`https://github.com/spf13/viper`). Please note that you are not obliged to use every capability of `viper` in your tools—just the features that you want. The general rule is to use the features of Viper that simplify your code. Put simply, if your command-line utility requires too many command-line parameters and flags, then it would be better to use a configuration file instead.

Using command-line flags

The first example shows how to write a simple utility that accepts two values as command-line parameters and prints them on screen for verification. This means that we are going to need two command-line flags for these parameters.

Starting from **Go version 1.16**, using modules is the default behavior, which the `viper` package needs to use. So, you need to put `useViper.go`, which is the name of the source file, inside `~/go` for things to work. As my GitHub username is `mactsouk`, I had to run the following commands:

```
$ mkdir ~/go/src/github.com/mactsouk/useViper
$ cd ~/go/src/github.com/mactsouk/useViper
$ vi useViper.go
$ go mod init
$ go mod tidy
```

You can either edit `useViper.go` on your own or copy it from the GitHub repository of this book. Keep in mind that the last two commands should be executed when `useViper.go` is ready and includes all required external packages.

The implementation of `useViper.go` is as follows:

```
package main

import (
    "fmt"

    "github.com/spf13/pflag"
    "github.com/spf13/viper"
)
```

We need to import both the `pflag` and `viper` packages as we are going to use the functionality from both of them.

```
func aliasNormalizeFunc(f *pflag.FlagSet, n string) pflag.
NormalizedName {
    switch n {
    case "pass":
        n = "password"
        break
    case "ps":
        n = "password"
        break
```

```
    }
    return pflag.NormalizedName(n)
}
```

The `aliasNormalizeFunc()` function is used for creating additional aliases for a flag—in this case an alias for the `--password` flag. According to the existing code, the `--password` flag can be accessed as either `--pass` or `--ps`.

```
func main() {
    pflag.StringP("name", "n", "Mike", "Name parameter")
```

In the preceding code, we create a new flag called `name` that can also be accessed as `-n`. Its default value is `Mike` and its description that appears in the usage of the utility is `Name parameter`.

```
    pflag.StringP("password", "p", "hardToGuess", "Password")
    pflag.CommandLine.SetNormalizeFunc(aliasNormalizeFunc)
```

We create another flag named `password` that can also be accessed as `-p` and has a default value of `hardToGuess` and a description. Additionally, we register a **normalization function** for generating aliases for the `password` flag.

```
    pflag.Parse()
    viper.BindPFlags(pflag.CommandLine)
```

The `pflag.Parse()` call should be used after all command-line flags are defined—its purpose is to parse the command-line flags into the defined flags.

Additionally, the `viper.BindPFlags()` call makes all flags available to the `viper` package—strictly speaking, we say that the `viper.BindPFlags()` call binds an existing set of `pflag` flags (`pflag.FlagSet`) to `viper`.

```
    name := viper.GetString("name")
    password := viper.GetString("password")
```

The previous commands show how to read the values of two `string` command-line flags.

```
    fmt.Println(name, password)

    // Reading an Environment variable
    viper.BindEnv("GOMAXPROCS")
    val := viper.Get("GOMAXPROCS")
    if val != nil {
```

```
        fmt.Println("GOMAXPROCS:", val)
    }
```

The viper package can work with environment variables. We first need to call viper.BindEnv() to tell viper the environment variable that interests us and then we can read its value by calling viper.Get(). If GOMAXPROCS is not already set, the fmt.Println() call will not get executed.

```
    // Setting an Environment variable
    viper.Set("GOMAXPROCS", 16)
    val = viper.Get("GOMAXPROCS")
    fmt.Println("GOMAXPROCS:", val)
}
```

Similarly, we can change the current value of an environment variable using viper.Set().

The good thing is that viper automatically provides usage information:

```
$ go run useViper.go --help
Usage of useViper:
  -n, --name string       Name parameter (default "Mike")
  -p, --password string   Password (default "hardToGuess")
pflag: help requested
exit status 2
```

Using useViper.go without any command-line arguments produces the next kind of output. Remember that we are inside ~/go/src/github.com/mactsouk/useViper:

```
$ go run useViper.go
Mike hardToGuess
GOMAXPROCS: 16
```

However, if we provide values for the command-line flags, the output is going to be slightly different:

```
$ go run useViper.go -n mtsouk -p hardToGuess
mtsouk hardToGuess
GOMAXPROCS: 16
```

In this second case, we used the shortcuts for the command-line flags because it is faster.

The next subsection discusses the use of JSON files for storing configuration information.

Reading JSON configuration files

The `viper` package can read JSON files to get its configuration, and this subsection illustrates how. Using text files for storing configuration details can be very helpful when writing complex applications that require lots of data and setup. This is illustrated in `jsonViper.go`.

Once again, we need to put `jsonViper.go` inside `~/go/src/github.com/mactsouk/jsonViper`—please adjust that command to fit your own GitHub username, although if you do not create a GitHub repository, you can use `mactsouk`. The code of `jsonViper.go` is as follows:

```
package main

import (
    "encoding/json"
    "fmt"
    "os"

    "github.com/spf13/viper"
)

type ConfigStructure struct {
    MacPass     string `mapstructure:"macos"`
    LinuxPass   string `mapstructure:"linux"`
    WindowsPass string `mapstructure:"windows"`
    PostHost    string `mapstructure:"postgres"`
    MySQLHost   string `mapstructure:"mysql"`
    MongoHost   string `mapstructure:"mongodb"`
}
```

There is an *important point here*: although we are using a JSON file to store the configuration, the Go structure uses `mapstructure` instead of `json` for the fields of the JSON configuration file.

```
var CONFIG = ".config.json"

func main() {
    if len(os.Args) == 1 {
        fmt.Println("Using default file", CONFIG)
    } else {
        CONFIG = os.Args[1]
    }
```

```
viper.SetConfigType("json")
viper.SetConfigFile(CONFIG)
fmt.Printf("Using config: %s\n", viper.ConfigFileUsed())
viper.ReadInConfig()
```

The previous four statements declare that we are using a JSON file, let `viper` know the path to the configuration file, print the configuration file used, and read and parse that configuration file.

Keep in mind that `viper` does not check whether the configuration file actually exists and is readable. If the file cannot be found or read, `viper.ReadInConfig()` acts like processing an empty configuration file.

```
if viper.IsSet("macos") {
    fmt.Println("macos:", viper.Get("macos"))
} else {
    fmt.Println("macos not set!")
}
```

The `viper.IsSet()` call checks whether a key named `macos` can be found in the configuration. If it is set, it reads its value using `viper.Get("macos")` and prints it on screen.

```
if viper.IsSet("active") {
    value := viper.GetBool("active")
    if value {
        postgres := viper.Get("postgres")
        mysql := viper.Get("mysql")
        mongo := viper.Get("mongodb")
        fmt.Println("P:", postgres, "My:", mysql, "Mo:", mongo)
    }
} else {
    fmt.Println("active is not set!")
}
```

In the aforementioned code, we check whether the `active` key can be found before reading its value. If its value is equal to `true` then we read the values from three more keys named `postgres`, `mysql`, and `mongodb`.

As the `active` key should hold a Boolean value, we use `viper.GetBool()` for reading it.

```
    if !viper.IsSet("DoesNotExist") {
        fmt.Println("DoesNotExist is not set!")
    }
```

As expected, trying to read a key that does not exist fails.

```
    var t ConfigStructure
    err := viper.Unmarshal(&t)
    if err != nil {
        fmt.Println(err)
        return
    }
```

The call to `viper.Unmarshal()` allows you to put the information from the JSON configuration file into a properly defined Go structure—this is optional but handy.

```
    PrettyPrint(t)
}
```

The implementation of the `PrettyPrint()` function was presented in `prettyPrint.go` earlier on in this chapter.

Now you need to download the dependencies of `jsonViper.go`:

```
$ go mod init
$ go mod tidy # This command is not always required
```

The contents of the current directory are as follows:

```
$ ls -l
total 44
-rw-r--r-- 1 mtsouk users    85 Feb 22 18:46 go.mod
-rw-r--r-- 1 mtsouk users 29678 Feb 22 18:46 go.sum
-rw-r--r-- 1 mtsouk users  1418 Feb 22 18:45 jsonViper.go
-rw-r--r-- 1 mtsouk users   189 Feb 22 18:46 myConfig.json
```

The contents of the `myConfig.json` file used for testing are as follows:

```
{
    "macos": "pass_macos",
    "linux": "pass_linux",
```

```
    "windows": "pass_windows",

    "active": true,
    "postgres": "machine1",
    "mysql": "machine2",
    "mongodb": "machine3"
}
```

Running `jsonViper.go` on the preceding JSON file produces the next output:

```
$ go run jsonViper.go myConfig.json
Using config: myConfig.json
macos: pass_macos
P: machine1 My: machine2 Mo: machine3
DoesNotExist is not set!
{
  "MacPass": "pass_macos",
  "LinuxPass": "pass_linux",
  "WindowsPass": "pass_windows",
  "PostHost": "machine1",
  "MySQLHost": "machine2",
  "MongoHost": "machine3"
}
```

The previous output is generated by `jsonViper.go` when parsing `myConfig.json` and trying to find the desired information.

The next section discusses a Go package for creating powerful and professional command-line utilities such as `docker` and `kubectl`.

The cobra package

`cobra` is a very handy and popular Go package that allows you to develop command-line utilities with commands, subcommands, and aliases. If you have ever used `hugo`, `docker`, or `kubectl` you are going to realize immediately what the `cobra` package does, as all these tools are developed using `cobra`. Commands can have one or more aliases, which is very handy when you want to please both amateur and experienced users. `cobra` also supports **persistent flags** and **local flags**, which are flags that are available to all commands and flags that are available to given commands only, respectively. Also, by default, `cobra` uses `viper` for parsing its command-line arguments.

All `cobra` projects follow the same development pattern. You use the `cobra` utility, then you create commands, and then you make the desired changes to the generated Go source code files in order to implement the desired functionality. Depending on the complexity of your utility, you might need to make lots of changes to the created files. Although `cobra` saves you lots of time, you still have to write the code that implements the desired functionality for each command.

You need to take some extra steps in order to download the `cobra` binary the right way:

```
$ GO111MODULE=on go get -u -v github.com/spf13/cobra/cobra
```

The previous command downloads the `cobra` binary and the required dependencies using Go modules even if you are using a Go version older than 1.16.

> It is not necessary to know about all of the supported environment variables such as `GO111MODULE`, but sometimes they can help you resolve tricky problems with your Go installation. So, if you want to learn about your current Go environment, you can use the `go env` command.

For the purposes of this section, we are going to need a GitHub repository—this is optional, but it is the only way for the readers of this book to have access to the presented code.

The path of the GitHub repository is `https://github.com/mactsouk/go-cobra`. The first thing to do is place the files of the GitHub repository in the right place. Everything is going to be much easier if you put it inside `~/go`; the exact place depends on the GitHub repository, because the Go compiler will not have to search for the Go files.

In our case, we are going to put it under `~/go/src/github.com/mactsouk` because `mactsouk` is my GitHub username. This requires running the next commands:

```
$ cd ~/go/src/github.com
$ mkdir mactsouk # only required if the directory is not there
$ cd mactsouk
$ git clone git@github.com:mactsouk/go-cobra.git
$ cd go-cobra
$ ~/go/bin/cobra init --pkg-name github.com/mactsouk/go-cobra
Using config file: /Users/mtsouk/.cobra.yaml
Your Cobra application is ready at
/Users/mtsouk/go/src/github.com/mactsouk/go-cobra
```

```
$ go mod init
go: creating new go.mod: module github.com/mactsouk/go-cobra
```

As the cobra package works better with modules, we define the project dependencies using Go modules. In order to specify that a Go project uses Go modules, you should execute `go mod init`. This command creates two files named `go.sum` and `go.mod`.

```
$ go run main.go
go: finding module for package github.com/spf13/cobra
go: finding module for package github.com/mitchellh/go-homedir
go: finding module for package github.com/spf13/viper
go: found github.com/mitchellh/go-homedir in github.com/mitchellh/go-homedir v1.1.0
go: found github.com/spf13/cobra in github.com/spf13/cobra v1.1.3
go: found github.com/spf13/viper in github.com/spf13/viper v1.7.1
A longer description that spans multiple lines and likely contains
examples and usage of using your application. For example:

Cobra is a CLI library for Go that empowers applications.
This application is a tool to generate the needed files
to quickly create a Cobra application.
```

All lines beginning with `go:` have to do with Go modules and will appear only once. The last lines are the default message of a `cobra` project—we are going to modify that message later on. You are now ready to begin working with the `cobra` tool.

A utility with three commands

This subsection illustrates the use of the `cobra add` command, which is used for adding new commands to a `cobra` project. The names of the commands are `one`, `two`, and `three`:

```
$ ~/go/bin/cobra add one
Using config file: /Users/mtsouk/.cobra.yaml
one created at /Users/mtsouk/go/src/github.com/mactsouk/go-cobra
$ ~/go/bin/cobra add two
$ ~/go/bin/cobra add three
```

The previous commands create three new files in the `cmd` folder named `one.go`, `two.go`, and `three.go`, which are the initial implementations of the three commands.

The first thing you should usually do is delete unwanted code from `root.go` and change the messages of the utility and each command as described in the `Short` and `Long` fields. However, if you want you can leave the source files unchanged.

The next subsection enriches the utility by adding command-line flags to the commands.

Adding command-line flags

We are going to create two global command-line flags and one command-line flag that is attached to a given command (`two`) and is not supported by the other two commands. Global command-line flags are defined in the `./cmd/root.go` file. We are going to define two global flags named `directory`, which is a string, and `depth`, which is an unsigned integer.

Both global flags are defined in the `init()` function of `./cmd/root.go`.

```
rootCmd.PersistentFlags().StringP("directory", "d", "/tmp", "Path to
use.")
rootCmd.PersistentFlags().Uint("depth", 2, "Depth of search.")
viper.BindPFlag("directory", rootCmd.PersistentFlags().
Lookup("directory"))
viper.BindPFlag("depth", rootCmd.PersistentFlags().Lookup("depth"))
```

We use `rootCmd.PersistentFlags()` to define global flags followed by the data type of the flag. The name of the first flag is `directory` and its shortcut is `d` whereas the name of the second flag is `depth` and has no shortcut—if you want to add a shortcut to it, you should use the `UintP()` method instead. After defining the two flags, we pass their control to `viper` by calling `viper.BindPFlag()`. The first flag is a `string` whereas the second one is a `uint` value. As both of them are available in the `cobra` project, we call `viper.GetString("directory")` to get the value of the `directory` flag and `viper.GetUint("depth")` to get the value of the `depth` flag.

Last, we add a command-line flag that is only available to the `two` command using the next line in the `./cmd/two.go` file:

```
twoCmd.Flags().StringP("username", "u", "Mike", "Username value")
```

The name of the flag is `username` and its shortcut is `u`. As this is a local flag available to the `two` command only, we can get its value by calling `cmd.Flags().GetString("username")` inside the `./cmd/two.go` file only.

The next subsection creates command aliases for the existing commands.

Creating command aliases

In this subsection we continue building on the code from the previous subsection by creating aliases for existing commands. This means that commands `one`, `two`, and `three` will also be accessible as `cmd1`, `cmd2`, and `cmd3` respectively.

In order to do that, you need to add an extra field named `Aliases` in the `cobra.Command` structure of each command—the data type of the `Aliases` field is `string` slice. So, for the `one` command, the beginning of the `cobra.Command` structure in `./cmd/one.go` will look as follows:

```
var oneCmd = &cobra.Command{
	Use:     "one",
	Aliases: []string{"cmd1"},
	Short:   "Command one",
```

You should make similar changes to `./cmd/two.go` and `./cmd/three.go`. Please keep in mind that the **internal name** of the `one` command is `oneCmd`—the other commands have analogous internal names.

> If you accidentally put the `cmd1` alias, or any other alias, in multiple commands, the Go compiler will not complain. However, only its first occurrence gets executed.

The next subsection enriches the utility by adding subcommands for the `one` and `two` commands.

Creating subcommands

This subsection illustrates how to create two subcommands for the command named `three`. The names of the two subcommands will be `list` and `delete`. The way to create them using the `cobra` utility is the following:

```
$ ~/go/bin/cobra add list -p 'threeCmd'
Using config file: /Users/mtsouk/.cobra.yaml
list created at /Users/mtsouk/go/src/github.com/mactsouk/go-cobra
$ ~/go/bin/cobra add delete -p 'threeCmd'
Using config file: /Users/mtsouk/.cobra.yaml
delete created at /Users/mtsouk/go/src/github.com/mactsouk/go-cobra
```

The previous commands create two new files inside `./cmd` named `delete.go` and `list.go`. The `-p` flag is followed by the **internal name** of the command you want to associate the subcommands with. The internal name of the `three` command is `threeCmd`. You can verify that these two commands are associated with the `three` command as follows:

```
$ go run main.go three delete
delete called
$ go run main.go three list
list called
```

If you run `go run main.go two list`, Go considers `list` as a command-line argument of `two` and it will not execute the code in `./cmd/list.go`. The final version of the `go-cobra` project has the following structure and contains the following files, as generated by the `tree(1)` utility:

```
$ tree
.
├── LICENSE
├── README.md
├── cmd
│   ├── delete.go
│   ├── list.go
│   ├── one.go
│   ├── root.go
│   ├── three.go
│   └── two.go
├── go.mod
├── go.sum
└── main.go

1 directory, 11 files
```

At this point you might wonder what happens when you want to create two subcommands with the same name for two different commands. In that case, you create the first subcommand and rename its file before creating the second one.

As there is no point in presenting long listings of code, you can find the code of the `go-cobra` project at `https://github.com/mactsouk/go-cobra`. The `cobra` package is also illustrated in the final section where we radically update the phone book application.

Finding cycles in a UNIX file system

This section implements a practical UNIX command-line utility that can find cycles (loops) in UNIX file systems. The idea behind the utility is that with UNIX **symbolic links**, there is a possibility to create cycles in our file system. This can perplex backup software such as `tar(1)` or utilities such as `find(1)` and can create security-related issues. The presented utility, which is called `FScycles.go`, tries to inform us about such situations.

The idea behind the solution is that we keep every visited directory path in a map and if a path appears for the second time, then we have a cycle. The map is called `visited` and is defined as `map[string]int`.

> If you are wondering why we are using a string and not a byte slice or some other kind of slice as the key for the `visited` map, it is because maps cannot have slices as keys because **slices are not comparable**.

The output of the utility depends on the root path used for initialing the search process—that path is given as a command-line argument to the utility.

The `filepath.Walk()` function does not traverse symbolic links by design in order to avoid cycles. However, in our case, we want to traverse symbolic links to directories in order to discover loops. We solve that issue in a while.

The utility uses `IsDir()`, which is a function that helps you to identify directories—we are only interested in directories because only directories and symbolic links to directories can create cycles in file systems. Last, the utility uses `os.Lstat()` because it can handle symbolic links. Additionally, `os.Lstat()` returns information about the symbolic link without following it, which is not the case with `os.Stat()`—in this case we do not want to automatically follow symbolic links.

The important code of `FScycles.go` can be found in the implementation of `walkFunction()`:

```
func walkFunction(path string, info os.FileInfo, err error) error {
    fileInfo, err := os.Stat(path)
    if err != nil {
        return nil
    }

    fileInfo, _ = os.Lstat(path)
    mode := fileInfo.Mode()
```

First, we make sure that the path actually exists, and then we call `os.Lstat()`.

```
    // Find regular directories first
    if mode.IsDir() {
        abs, _ := filepath.Abs(path)
        _, ok := visited[abs]
        if ok {
            fmt.Println("Found cycle:", abs)
            return nil
        }
        visited[abs]++
        return nil
    }
```

If a regular directory is already visited, then we have a cycle. The `visited` map keeps track of all visited directories.

```
    // Find symbolic links to directories
    if fileInfo.Mode()&os.ModeSymlink != 0 {
        temp, err := os.Readlink(path)
        if err != nil {
            fmt.Println("os.Readlink():", err)
            return err
        }

        newPath, err := filepath.EvalSymlinks(temp)
        if err != nil {
            return nil
        }
```

The `filepath.EvalSymlinks()` function is used for finding out where symbolic links point to. If that destination is another directory, then the code that follows makes sure that it is going to be visited as well using an additional call to `filepath.Walk()`.

```
        linkFileInfo, err := os.Stat(newPath)
        if err != nil {
            return err
        }

        linkMode := linkFileInfo.Mode()
        if linkMode.IsDir() {
            fmt.Println("Following...", path, "-->", newPath)
```

The `linkMode.IsDir()` statement makes sure that only directories are being followed.

```
            abs, _ := filepath.Abs(newPath)
```

The call to `filepath.Abs()` returns the absolute path of the path that is given as a parameter. The keys of the `visited` slice are values returned by `filepath.Abs()`.

```
            _, ok := visited[abs]
            if ok {
                fmt.Println("Found cycle!", abs)
                return nil
            }
            visited[abs]++
            err = filepath.Walk(newPath, walkFunction)
            if err != nil {
                return err
            }
            return nil
        }
    }
    return nil
}
```

Running `FScycles.go` produces the following kind of output:

```
$ go run FScycles.go ~
Following... /home/mtsouk/.local/share/epiphany/databases/indexeddb/v0
--> /home/mtsouk/.local/share/epiphany/databases/indexeddb
Found cycle! /home/mtsouk/.local/share/epiphany/databases/indexeddb
```

The previous output tells us that there is a cycle in the home directory of the current user—once we identify the loop, we should remove it on our own.

The remaining sections of this chapter discuss some new features that came with Go version 1.16.

New to Go 1.16

Go 1.16 came with some new features including embedding files in Go binaries as well as the introduction of the `os.ReadDir()` function, the `os.DirEntry` type, and the `io/fs` package.

As these features are related to systems programming, they are included and explored in the current chapter. We begin by presenting the embedding of files into Go binary executables.

Embedding files

This section presents a feature that first appeared in Go 1.16 that allows you to **embed static assets** into Go binaries. The allowed data types for keeping an embedded file are `string`, `[]byte`, and `embed.FS`. This means that a Go binary may contain a file that you do not have to manually download when you execute the Go binary! The presented utility embeds two different files that it can retrieve based on the given command-line argument.

The code that follows, which is saved as `embedFiles.go`, illustrates this new Go feature:

```
package main

import (
    _ "embed"
    "fmt"
    "os"
)
```

You need the `embed` package in order to embed any files in your Go binaries. As the `embed` package is not directly used, you need to put _ in front of it so that the Go compiler won't complain.

```
//go:embed static/image.png
var f1 []byte
```

You need to begin a line with `//go:embed`, which denotes a Go comment but is treated in a special way, followed by the path to the file you want to embed. In this case we embed `static/image.png`, which is a binary file. The next line should define the variable that is going to hold the data of the embedded file, which in this case is a byte slice named `f1`—using a byte slice is recommended for binary files because we are going to directly use that byte slice to save that binary file.

```
//go:embed static/textfile
var f2 string
```

In this case we save the contents of a plain text file, which is `static/textfile`, in a `string` variable named `f2`.

```
func writeToFile(s []byte, path string) error {
	fd, err := os.OpenFile(path, os.O_CREATE|os.O_WRONLY, 0644)
	if err != nil {
		return err
	}
	defer fd.Close()

	n, err := fd.Write(s)
	if err != nil {
		return err
	}
	fmt.Printf("wrote %d bytes\n", n)
	return nil
}
```

The `writeToFile()` function is used for storing a byte slice into a file and is a helper function that can be used in other cases as well.

```
func main() {
	arguments := os.Args
	if len(arguments) == 1 {
		fmt.Println("Print select 1|2")
		return
	}

	fmt.Println("f1:", len(f1), "f2:", len(f2))
```

This statement prints the lengths of the `f1` and `f2` variables to make sure that they represent the size of the embedded files.

```
	switch arguments[1] {
	case "1":
		filename := "/tmp/temporary.png"
		err := writeToFile(f1, filename)
		if err != nil {
			fmt.Println(err)
			return
		}
	case "2":
		fmt.Print(f2)
	default:
		fmt.Println("Not a valid option!")
	}
}
```

The `switch` block is responsible for returning the desired file to the user—in the case of `static/textfile`, the file contents are printed on the screen. For the binary file, we decided to store it as `/tmp/temporary.png`.

This time we are going to compile `embedFiles.go` to make things more realistic, because it is the executable binary file that holds the embedded files. We build the binary file using `go build embedFiles.go`. Running `embedFiles` produces the following kind of output:

```
$ ./embedFiles 2
f1: 75072 f2: 14
Data to write
$ ./embedFiles 1
f1: 75072 f2: 14
wrote 75072 bytes
```

The next output verifies that `temporary.png` is located at the right path (`/tmp/temporary.png`):

```
$ ls -l /tmp/temporary.png
-rw-r--r--  1 mtsouk  wheel  75072 Feb 25 15:20 /tmp/temporary.png
```

Using the embedding functionality, we can create a utility that embeds its own source code and prints it on screen when it gets executed! This is a fun way of using embedded files. The source code of `printSource.go` is the following:

```
package main
import (
    _ "embed"
    "fmt"
)

//go:embed printSource.go
var src string

func main() {
    fmt.Print(src)
}
```

As before, the file that is being embedded is defined in the `//go:embed` line. Running `printSource.go` prints the aforementioned code on screen.

ReadDir and DirEntry

This section discusses `os.ReadDir()` and `os.DirEntry`. However, it begins by discussing the deprecation of the `io/ioutil` package—the functionality of the `io/ioutil` package has been transferred to other packages. So, we have the following:

- `os.ReadDir()`, which is a new function, returns `[]DirEntry`. This means that it cannot directly replace `ioutil.ReadDir()`, which returns `[]FileInfo`. Although neither `os.ReadDir()` nor `os.DirEntry` offers any new functionality, they make things faster and simpler, which is important.
- The `os.ReadFile()` function directly replaces `ioutil.ReadFile()`.
- The `os.WriteFile()` function can directly replace `ioutil.WriteFile()`.
- Similarly, `os.MkdirTemp()` can replace `ioutil.TempDir()` without any changes. However, as the `os.TempDir()` name was already taken, the new function name is different.
- The `os.CreateTemp()` function is the same as `ioutil.TempFile()`. Although the name `os.TempFile()` was not taken, the Go people decided to name it `os.CreateTemp()` in order to be on par with `os.MkdirTemp()`.

> Both `os.ReadDir()` and `os.DirEntry` can be found as `fs.ReadDir()` and `fs.DirEntry` in the `io/fs` package for working with the file system interface found in `io/fs`.

The `ReadDirEntry.go` utility illustrates the use of `os.ReadDir()`. Additionally, we are going to see `fs.DirEntry` in combination with `fs.WalkDir()` in action in the next section—`io/fs` only supports `WalkDir()`, which uses `DirEntry` by default. Both `fs.WalkDir()` and `filepath.WalkDir()` are using `DirEntry` instead of `FileInfo`. This means that in order to see any performance improvements when walking directory trees, you need to change `filepath.Walk()` calls to `filepath.WalkDir()` calls.

The presented utility calculates the size of a directory tree using `os.ReadDir()` with the help of the next function:

```
func GetSize(path string) (int64, error) {
    contents, err := os.ReadDir(path)
    if err != nil {
        return -1, err
    }
```

```
    var total int64
    for _, entry := range contents {
        // Visit directory entries
        if entry.IsDir() {
```

If we are processing a directory, we need to keep digging.

```
            temp, err := GetSize(filepath.Join(path, entry.Name()))
            if err != nil {
                return -1, err
            }
            total += temp
            // Get size of each non-directory entry
        } else {
```

If it is a file, then we just need to get its size. This involves calling `Info()` to get general information about the file and then `Size()` to get the size of the file:

```
            info, err := entry.Info()
            if err != nil {
                return -1, err
            }
            // Returns an int64 value
            total += info.Size()
        }
    }
    return total, nil
}
```

Running `ReadDirEntry.go` produces the next output, which indicates that the utility works as expected:

```
$ go run ReadDirEntry.go /usr/bin
Total Size: 1170983337
```

Last, keep in mind that both `ReadDir` and `DirEntry` are copied from the Python programming language.

The next section introduces us to the `io/fs` package.

The io/fs package

This section illustrates the functionality of the `io/fs` package, which was first introduced in Go 1.16. As `io/fs` offers a unique kind of functionality, we begin this section by explaining what `io/fs` can do. Put simply, `io/fs` offers a **read-only** file system interface named `FS`. Note that `embed.FS` implements the `fs.FS` interface, which means that `embed.FS` can take advantage of some of the functionality offered by the `io/fs` package. This means that your applications can create their own internal file systems and work with their files.

The code example that follows, which is saved as `ioFS.go`, creates a file system using `embed` by putting all the files of the `./static` folder in there. `ioFS.go` supports the following functionality: list all files, search for a filename, and extract a file using `list()`, `search()`, and `extract()`, respectively. We begin by presenting the implementation of `list()`:

```
func list(f embed.FS) error {
    return fs.WalkDir(f, ".", walkFunction)
}
```

All the magic happens in the `walkFunction()` function, which is implemented as follows:

```
func walkFunction(path string, d fs.DirEntry, err error) error {
    if err != nil {
        return err
    }
    fmt.Printf("Path=%q, isDir=%v\n", path, d.IsDir())
    return nil
}
```

The `walkFunction()` function is pretty compact as all functionality is implemented by Go.

Then, we present the implementation of the `extract()` function:

```
func extract(f embed.FS, filepath string) ([]byte, error) {
    s, err := fs.ReadFile(f, filepath)
    if err != nil {
        return nil, err
    }
    return s, nil
}
```

The `ReadFile()` function is used for retrieving a file, which is identified by its file path, from the `embed.FS` file system as a byte slice, which is returned from the `extract()` function.

Last, we have the implementation of the `search()` function, which is based on `walkSearch()`:

```
func walkSearch(path string, d fs.DirEntry, err error) error {
    if err != nil {
        return err
    }
    if d.Name() == searchString {
```

`searchString` is a global variable that holds the search string. When a match is found, the matching path is printed on screen.

```
        fileInfo, err := fs.Stat(f, path)
        if err != nil {
            return err
        }
        fmt.Println("Found", path, "with size", fileInfo.Size())
        return nil
    }
```

Before printing a match, we make a call to `fs.Stat()` in order to get more details about it.

```
    return nil
}
```

The `main()` function specifically calls these three functions. Running `ioFS.go` produces the next kind of output:

```
$ go run ioFS.go
Path=".", isDir=true
Path="static", isDir=true
Path="static/file.txt", isDir=false
Path="static/image.png", isDir=false
Path="static/textfile", isDir=false
Found static/file.txt with size 14
wrote 14 bytes
```

Initially, the utility lists all files in the file system (lines beginning with `Path`). Then, it verifies that `static/file.txt` can be found in the file system. Last, it verifies that the writing of 14 bytes into a new file was successful as all 14 bytes have been written.

So, it turns out that Go version 1.16 introduced important additions and performance improvements.

Updating the phone book application

In this section we will change the format that the phone application uses for storing its data. This time, the phone book application uses JSON all over. Additionally, it uses the `cobra` package for implementing the supported commands. As a result, all relevant code resides on its own GitHub repository and not in the `ch06` directory of the GitHub repository of this book. The path of the GitHub repository is `https://github.com/mactsouk/phonebook`—you can `git clone` that directory if you want but try to create your own version if you have the time.

> When developing real applications, do not forget to `git commit` and `git push` your changes from time to time to ensure that you keep a history of the development phase in GitHub or GitLab. Among other things, this is a good way to keep backups!

Using cobra

First, you need to create an empty GitHub repository and clone it:

```
$ cd ~/go/src/github.com/mactsouk
$ git clone git@github.com:mactsouk/phonebook.git
$ cd phonebook
```

The output of the `git clone` command is not important, so it is omitted.

The first task after cloning the GitHub repository, which at this point is almost empty, is to run the `cobra init` command with the appropriate parameters.

```
$ ~/go/bin/cobra init --pkg-name github.com/mactsouk/phonebook
Using config file: /Users/mtsouk/.cobra.yaml
Your Cobra application is ready at
/Users/mtsouk/go/src/github.com/mactsouk/phonebook
```

Then, you should create the structure of the application using the `cobra` binary. Once you have the structure, it is easy to know what you have to implement. The structure of the application is based on the supported commands.

```
$ ~/go/bin/cobra add list
Using config file: /Users/mtsouk/.cobra.yaml
list created at /Users/mtsouk/go/src/github.com/mactsouk/phonebook
$ ~/go/bin/cobra add delete
$ ~/go/bin/cobra add insert
$ ~/go/bin/cobra add search
```

At this point the structure of the project should be the following:

```
$ tree
.
├── LICENSE
├── README.md
├── cmd
│   ├── delete.go
│   ├── insert.go
│   ├── list.go
│   ├── root.go
│   └── search.go
├── go.mod
├── go.sum
└── main.go

1 directory, 10 files
```

After that you should declare that we want to use Go modules by executing the next command:

```
$ go mod init
go: creating new go.mod: module github.com/mactsouk/phonebook
```

If needed you can run `go mod tidy` after `go mod init`. At this point executing `go run main.go` should download all required package dependencies and generate the default `cobra` output.

The next subsection discusses the storing of JSON data on disk.

Storing and loading JSON data

This functionality of the `saveJSONFile()` helper function is implemented in `./cmd/root.go` using the following function:

```
func saveJSONFile(filepath string) error {
    f, err := os.Create(filepath)
    if err != nil {
        return err
    }
    defer f.Close()

    err = Serialize(&data, f)
    if err != nil {
        return err
    }
    return nil
}
```

So, basically, all you have to do is serialize the slice of structures using `Serialize()` and save the result into a file. Next, we need to load the JSON data from the file.

The loading functionality is implemented in `./cmd/root.go` using the `readJSONFile()` helper function. All you have to do is read the data file with the JSON data and put that data into a slice of structures by deserializing it.

Implementing the delete command

The `delete` command deletes existing entries from the phone book application—it is implemented in `./cmd/delete.go`:

```
var deleteCmd = &cobra.Command{
    Use:   "delete",
    Short: "delete an entry",
    Long:  `delete an entry from the phone book application.`,
    Run: func(cmd *cobra.Command, args []string) {
        // Get key
        key, _ := cmd.Flags().GetString("key")
        if key == "" {
            fmt.Println("Not a valid key:", key)
            return
        }
```

First, we read the appropriate command-line flag (`key`) in order to be able to identify the record that is going to be deleted.

```
        // Remove data
        err := deleteEntry(key)
        if err != nil {
            fmt.Println(err)
            return
        }
    },
}
```

Then, we call the `deleteEntry()` helper function to actually delete the key. After a successful deletion, `deleteEntry()` calls `saveJSONFile()` for changes to take effect.

The next subsection discusses the `insert` command.

Implementing the insert command

The `insert` command requires user input, which means that it should support local command-line flags for doing so. As each record has three fields, the command requires three command-line flags. Then it calls the `insert()` helper function for writing the data to disk. Please refer to the `./cmd/insert.go` source file for the details of the implementation of the `insert` command.

Implementing the list command

The `list` command lists the contents in the phone book application. It requires no command-line arguments and is basically implemented with the `list()` function:

```
func list() {
    sort.Sort(PhoneBook(data))
    text, err := PrettyPrintJSONstream(data)
    if err != nil {
        fmt.Println(err)
        return
    }
    fmt.Println(text)
    fmt.Printf("%d records in total.\n", len(data))
}
```

The function sorts the data before calling `PrettyPrintJSONstream()` in order to beautify the generated output.

Implementing the search command

The `search` command is used for looking into the phone book application for a given phone number. It is implemented with the `search()` function found in `./cmd/search.go` that looks into the index map for a given key. If the key is found, then the respective record is returned.

> Apart from the JSON-related operations and changes due to the use of JSON and `cobra`, all other Go code is almost the same as the version of the phone book application from *Chapter 4, Reflection and Interfaces*.

Working with the phone book utility produces the next kind of output:

```
$ go run main.go list
[
	{
		"name": "Mastering",
		"surname": "Go",
		"tel": "333123",
		"lastaccess": "1613503772"
	}
]

1 records in total.
```

This is the output from the `list` command. Adding an entry is as simple as running the next command:

```
$ go run main.go insert -n Mike -s Tsoukalos -t 9416471
```

Running the `list` command verifies the success of the `insert` command:

```
$ go run main.go list
[
	{
		"name": "Mastering",
		"surname": "Go",
		"tel": "333123",
		"lastaccess": "1613503772"
	},
	{
```

```
                "name": "Mike",
        "surname": "Tsoukalos",
        "tel": "9416471",
        "lastaccess": "1614602404"
        }
]

2 records in total.
```

Then you can delete that entry by running `go run main.go delete --key 9416471`. As stated before, the keys of the application are the phone numbers, which means that we delete entries based on phone numbers. However, nothing prohibits you from implementing deletion based on other properties.

If a command is not found, then you are going to get the next kind of output:

```
$ go run main.go doesNotExist
Error: unknown command "doesNotExist" for "phonebook"
Run 'phonebook --help' for usage.
Error: unknown command "doesNotExist" for "phonebook"
exit status 1
```

As the `doesNotExist` command is not supported by the command-line application, `cobra` prints a descriptive error message (`unknown command`).

Exercises

- Use the functionality of `byCharacter.go`, `byLine.go`, and `byWord.go` in order to create a simplified version of the `wc(1)` UNIX utility.
- Create a full version of the `wc(1)` UNIX utility using the `viper` package for processing command-line options.
- Create a full version of the `wc(1)` UNIX utility using commands instead of command-line options with the help of the `cobra` package.
- Modify `JSONstreams.go` to accept user data or data from a file.
- Modify `embedFiles.go` in order to save the binary file at a user-selected location.
- Modify `ioFS.go` in order to get the desired command as well as the search string as a command-line argument.
- Make `ioFS.go` a `cobra` project.

- The `byLine.go` utility uses `ReadString('\n')` to read the input file. Modify the code to use `Scanner` (`https://golang.org/pkg/bufio/#Scanner`) for reading.
- Similarly, `byWord.go` uses `ReadString('\n')` to read the input file—modify the code to use `Scanner` instead.
- Modify the code of `yaml.go` in order to read the YAML data from an external file.

Summary

This chapter was all about systems programming and file I/O in Go and included topics such as signal handling, working with command-line arguments, reading and writing plain text files, working with JSON data, and creating powerful command-line utilities using `cobra`.

This is one of the most important chapters in this book because you cannot create any real-world utility without interacting with the operating system as well as the file system.

The next chapter is about concurrency in Go, with the main subjects being goroutines, channels, and data sharing.

Additional resources

- The `viper` package: `https://github.com/spf13/viper`
- The `cobra` package: `https://github.com/spf13/cobra`
- The documentation of `encoding/json`: `https://golang.org/pkg/encoding/json`
- The documentation of `io/fs`: `https://golang.org/pkg/io/fs/`
- Endian-ness: `https://en.wikipedia.org/wiki/Endianness`
- Go 1.16 release notes: `https://golang.org/doc/go1.16`

7
Go Concurrency

The key component of the Go concurrency model is the **goroutine**, which is the minimum executable entity in Go. Everything in Go is executed as a goroutine, either transparently or consciously. Each executable Go program has at least one goroutine, which is used for running the `main()` function of the `main` package. Each goroutine is executed on a single OS thread according to the instructions of the **Go scheduler**, which is responsible for the execution of goroutines. The OS scheduler does not dictate how many threads the Go runtime is going to create because the Go runtime will spawn enough threads to ensure that `GOMAXPROCS` threads are available to run Go code.

However, goroutines cannot directly communicate with each other. Data sharing in Go is implemented using either **channels** or **shared memory**. Channels act as the glue that connects multiple goroutines. Remember that although goroutines can process data and execute commands, they cannot communicate *directly* with each other, but they can communicate in other ways, including channels, local sockets, and shared memory. On the other hand, channels cannot process data or execute code but can send data to goroutines, receive data from goroutines, or have a special purpose.

When you combine multiple channels and goroutines you can create data flows, which in Go terminology are also called pipelines. So, you might have a goroutine that reads data from a database and sends it to a channel and a second goroutine that reads from that channel, processes that data, and sends it to another channel in order to be read from another goroutine, before making modifications to the data and storing it to a different database.

This chapter covers:

- Processes, threads, and goroutines
- The Go scheduler
- Goroutines
- Channels
- Race conditions
- The `select` keyword
- Timing out a goroutine
- Go channels revisited
- Shared memory and shared variables
- Closured variables and the go statement
- The `context` package
- The `semaphore` package

Processes, threads, and goroutines

A **process** is an OS representation of a running program, while a **program** is a binary file on disk that contains all the information necessary for creating an OS process. The binary file is written in a specific format (ELF on Linux) and contains all the instructions the CPU is going to run as well as a plethora of other useful sections. That program is loaded into memory and the instructions are executed, creating a running process. So, a **process** carries with it additional resources such as memory, opened file descriptions, and user data as well as other types of resources that are obtained during runtime.

A **thread** is a smaller and lighter entity than a process. Processes consist of one or more threads that have their own flow of control and stack. A quick and simplistic way to differentiate a thread from a process is to consider a process as the running binary file and a thread as a subset of a process.

A **goroutine** is the minimum Go entity that can be executed concurrently. The use of the word *minimum* is very important here, as goroutines are not autonomous entities like UNIX processes—goroutines live in OS threads that live in OS processes. The good thing is that goroutines are lighter than threads, which, in turn, are lighter than processes—running thousands or hundreds of thousands of goroutines on a single machine is not a problem. Among the reasons that goroutines are lighter than threads is because they have a smaller stack that can grow, they have a faster startup time, and they can communicate with each other through channels with low latency.

In practice, this means that a process can have multiple threads as well as lots of goroutines, whereas a goroutine needs the environment of a process to exist. So, to create a goroutine, you need to have a process with at least one thread. The OS takes care of the process and thread scheduling, while Go creates the necessary threads and the developer creates the desired number of goroutines.

Now that you know the basics of processes, programs, threads, and goroutines, let us talk a little bit about the **Go scheduler**.

The Go scheduler

The OS kernel scheduler is responsible for the execution of the threads of a program. Similarly, the Go runtime has its own scheduler, which is responsible for the execution of the goroutines using a technique known as **m:n scheduling**, where `m` goroutines are executed using `n` OS threads using multiplexing. The Go scheduler is the Go component responsible for the way and the order in which the goroutines of a Go program get executed. This makes the Go scheduler a really important part of the Go programming language. The Go scheduler is executed as a goroutine.

> Be aware that as the Go scheduler only deals with the goroutines of a single program, its operation is much simpler, cheaper, and faster than the operation of the kernel scheduler.

Go uses the **fork-join concurrency** model. The fork part of the model, which should not be confused with the `fork(2)` system call, states that a child branch can be created at any point of a program. Analogously, the join part of the Go concurrency model is where the child branch ends and joins with its parent. Keep in mind that both `sync.Wait()` statements and channels that collect the results of goroutines are join points, whereas each new goroutine creates a child branch.

The **fair scheduling strategy**, which is pretty straightforward and has a simple implementation, shares all load evenly among the available processors. At first, this might look like the perfect strategy because it does not have to take many things into consideration while keeping all processors equally occupied. However, it turns out that this is not exactly the case because most distributed tasks usually depend on other tasks. Therefore, some processors are underutilized, or equivalently, some processors are utilized more than others. A goroutine is a task, whereas everything after the calling statement of a goroutine is a **continuation**. In the **work-stealing** strategy used by the Go scheduler, a (logical) processor that is underutilized looks for additional work from other processors.

When it finds such jobs, it steals them from the other processor or processors, hence the name. Additionally, the work-stealing algorithm of Go queues and steals continuations. A stalling join, as is suggested by its name, is a point where a thread of execution stalls at a join and starts looking for other work to do.

Although both task stealing and continuation stealing have stalling joins, continuations happen more often than tasks; therefore, the Go scheduling algorithm works with continuations rather than tasks.

The main disadvantage of continuation stealing is that it requires extra work from the compiler of the programming language. Fortunately, Go provides that extra help and therefore uses continuation stealing in its work-stealing algorithm. One of the benefits of continuation stealing is that you get the same results when using function calls instead of goroutines or a single thread with multiple goroutines. This makes perfect sense, as only one thing is executed at any given point in both cases.

The Go scheduler works using three main kinds of entities: OS threads (**M**), which are related to the OS in use; goroutines (**G**); and logical processors (**P**). The number of processors that can be used by a Go program is specified by the value of the `GOMAXPROCS` environment variable—at any given time, there are at most `GOMAXPROCS` processors. Now, let us return to the `m:n` scheduling algorithm used in Go. Strictly speaking, at any time, you have `m` goroutines that are executed, and therefore scheduled to run, on `n` OS threads using, at most, `GOMAXPROCS` number of logical processors. You will learn more about `GOMAXPROCS` shortly.

The next figure shows that there are two different kinds of queues: a global run queue and a local run queue attached to each logical processor. Goroutines from the global queue are assigned to the queue of a logical processor in order to get executed at some point.

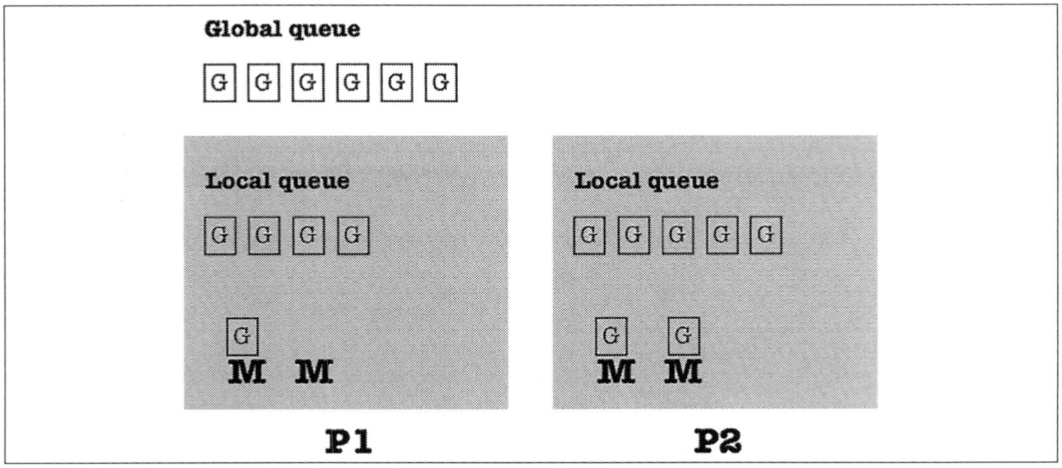

Figure 7.1: The operation of the Go scheduler

Each logical processor can have multiple threads, and the stealing occurs between the local queues of the available logical processors. Finally, keep in mind that the Go scheduler is allowed to create more OS threads when needed. OS threads are pretty expensive in terms of resources, which means that dealing too much with OS threads might slow down your Go applications.

Next, we discuss the meaning and the use of `GOMAXPROCS`.

The GOMAXPROCS environment variable

The `GOMAXPROCS` environment variable allows you to set the number of OS threads (**CPUs**) that can execute user-level Go code **simultaneously**. Starting with Go version 1.5, the default value of `GOMAXPROCS` should be the number of logical cores available in your machine. There is also the `runtime.GOMAXPROCS()` function, which allows you to set and get the value of `GOMAXPROCS` programmatically.

If you decide to assign a value to `GOMAXPROCS` that is smaller than the number of the cores in your machine, you might affect the performance of your program. However, using a `GOMAXPROCS` value that is larger than the number of the available cores does not necessarily make your Go programs run faster.

As mentioned earlier in this subsection, you can programmatically set and get the value of the `GOMAXPROCS` environment variable—this is illustrated in `maxprocs.go`, which will also show additional capabilities of the `runtime` package. The `main()` function is implemented as follows:

```
func main() {
    fmt.Print("You are using ", runtime.Compiler, " ")
    fmt.Println("on a", runtime.GOARCH, "machine")
    fmt.Println("Using Go version", runtime.Version())
```

The `runtime.Compiler` variable holds the compiler toolchain used for building the running binary. The two most well-known values are `gc` and `gccgo`. The `runtime.GOARCH` variable holds the current architecture and `runtime.Version()` returns the current version of the Go compiler. This information is not necessary for using `runtime.GOMAXPROCS()` but it is good to have a better knowledge of your system.

```
    fmt.Printf("GOMAXPROCS: %d\n", runtime.GOMAXPROCS(0))
}
```

What happens with the `runtime.GOMAXPROCS(0)` call? `runtime.GOMAXPROCS()` always returns the previous value of *the maximum number of CPUs that can be executing simultaneously*. When the parameter of `runtime.GOMAXPROCS()` is equal to or bigger than 1, then `runtime.GOMAXPROCS()` also changes the current setting. As we are using 0, our call does not alter the current setting.

Running `maxprocs.go` produces the next output:

```
You are using gc on a amd64 machine
Using Go version go1.16.2
GOMAXPROCS: 8
```

You can change the value of `GOMAXPROCS` on the fly using the next technique:

```
$ export GOMAXPROCS=100; go run maxprocs.go
You are using gc on a amd64 machine
Using Go version go1.16.2
GOMAXPROCS: 100
```

The previous command temporarily changes the value of `GOMAXPROCS` to `100` and runs `maxprocs.go`.

Apart from testing the performance of your code using fewer cores, you will most likely not need to change `GOMAXPROCS`. The next subsection will explain the similarities and the differences between concurrency and parallelism.

Concurrency and parallelism

It is a common misconception that **concurrency** is the same thing as **parallelism**—this is just not true! Parallelism is the simultaneous execution of multiple entities of some kind, whereas concurrency is a way of structuring your components so that they can be executed independently when possible.

It is only when you build software components concurrently that you can safely execute them in parallel, when and if your OS and your hardware permit it. The Erlang programming language did this a long time ago—long before CPUs had multiple cores and computers had lots of RAM.

In a valid concurrent design, adding concurrent entities makes the whole system run faster because more things can be executed in parallel. So, the desired parallelism comes from a better concurrent expression and implementation of the problem. The developer is responsible for taking concurrency into account during the design phase of a system and will benefit from a potential parallel execution of the components of the system. So, the developer should not think about parallelism but about breaking things into independent components that solve the initial problem when combined.

Even if you cannot run your functions in parallel on your machine, a valid concurrent design still improves the design and the maintainability of your programs.

In other words, concurrency is better than parallelism! Let us now talk about goroutines before looking into channels, which are the main components of the Go concurrency model.

Goroutines

You can define, create, and execute a new goroutine using the go keyword followed by a function name or an **anonymous function**. The go keyword makes the function call return immediately, while the function starts running in the background as a goroutine and the rest of the program continues its execution. You cannot control or make any assumptions about the **order** in which your goroutines are going to be executed because that depends on the scheduler of the OS, the Go scheduler, and the load of the OS.

Creating a goroutine

In this subsection, we learn how to create goroutines. The program that illustrates the technique is called `create.go`. The implementation of the `main()` function is as follows:

```
func main() {
    go func(x int) {
        fmt.Printf("%d ", x)
    }(10)
```

This is how you run an anonymous function as a goroutine. The `(10)` at the end is how you pass a parameter to an anonymous function. The previous anonymous function just prints a value onscreen.

```
    go printme(15)
```

This is how you execute a function as a goroutine. As a general rule of thumb, the functions that you execute as goroutines **do not return any values directly**. Exchanging data with goroutines happens via the use of shared memory or channels or some other mechanism.

```
    time.Sleep(time.Second)
    fmt.Println("Exiting...")
}
```

As a Go program does not wait for its goroutines to end before exiting, we need to delay it manually, which is the purpose of the `time.Sleep()` call. We will correct that shortly in order to wait for all goroutines to finish before exiting.

Running `create.go` produces the next output:

```
$ go run create.go
10 * 15
Exiting...
```

The `10` part in the output is from the anonymous function, whereas the `* 15` part is from the `go printme(15)` statement. However, if you run `create.go` more than once, you might get a different output because the two goroutines are not always executed in the same order:

```
$ go run create.go
* 15
10 Exiting...
```

The next subsection shows how to run a variable number of goroutines.

Creating multiple goroutines

In this subsection, you learn how to create a variable number of goroutines. The program that illustrates the technique is called `multiple.go`. The number of goroutines is given as a command-line argument to the program. The important code from the implementation of the `main()` function is the following:

```
fmt.Printf("Going to create %d goroutines.\n", count)
for i := 0; i < count; i++ {
```

There is nothing prohibiting you from using a `for` loop to create multiple goroutines, especially when you want to create lots of them.

```
    go func(x int) {
        fmt.Printf("%d ", x)
    }(i)
}
time.Sleep(time.Second)
fmt.Println("\nExiting...")
```

Once again, `time.Sleep()` delays the termination of the `main()` function.

Running `multiple.go` generates the next kind of output:

```
$ go run multiple.go 15
Going to create 15 goroutines.
3 0 8 4 5 6 7 11 9 12 14 13 1 2 10
Exiting...
```

If you run `multiple.go` many times, you are going to get different output. So, there is still room for improvement. The next subsection shows how to remove the call to `time.Sleep()` and make your programs wait for the goroutines to finish.

Waiting for your goroutines to finish

It is not enough to create multiple goroutines—you also need to wait for them to finish before the `main()` function ends. Therefore, this subsection shows a technique that improves the code of `multiple.go`—the improved version is called `varGoroutines.go`. But first, we need to explain how this works.

The synchronization process begins by defining a `sync.WaitGroup` variable and using the `Add()`, `Done()` and `Wait()` methods. If you look at the source code of the `sync` Go package, and more specifically at the `waitgroup.go` file, you see that the `sync.WaitGroup` type is nothing more than a structure with two fields:

```
type WaitGroup struct {
	noCopy noCopy
	state1 [3]uint32
}
```

Each call to `sync.Add()` increases a counter in the `state1` field, which is an array with three `uint32` elements. Notice that it is really important to call `sync.Add()` before the `go` statement in order to prevent any race conditions—we are going to learn about race conditions in the *Race conditions* section. When each goroutine finishes its job, the `sync.Done()` function should be executed in order to decrease the same counter by one. Behind the scenes, `sync.Done()` runs a `Add(-1)` call. The `Wait()` method waits until that counter becomes `0` in order to return. The return of `Wait()` inside the `main()` function means that `main()` is going to return and the program ends.

> You can call `Add()` with a positive integer value other than `1` in order to avoid calling `Add(1)` multiple times. This can be handy when you know the number of goroutines you are going to create in advance. `Done()` does not support that functionality.

The important part of `varGoroutines.go` is the following:

```
var waitGroup sync.WaitGroup
fmt.Printf("%#v\n", waitGroup)
```

This is where you create a `sync.WaitGroup` variable that you are going to use. The `fmt.Printf()` call prints the contents of the `sync.WaitGroup` structure—you do not usually do that but it is good for learning more about the `sync.WaitGroup` structure.

```
for i := 0; i < count; i++ {
    waitGroup.Add(1)
```

We call `Add(1)` just before we create the goroutine in order to avoid race conditions.

```
    go func(x int) {
        defer waitGroup.Done()
```

The `Done()` call is going to be executed just before the anonymous function returns because of the `defer` keyword.

```
        fmt.Printf("%d ", x)
    }(i)
}

fmt.Printf("%#v\n", waitGroup)
waitGroup.Wait()
```

The `Wait()` function is going to wait for the counter in the `waitGroup` variable to become `0` before it returns, which is what we want to achieve.

```
fmt.Println("\nExiting...")
```

When the `Wait()` function returns, the `fmt.Println()` statement is going to be executed. No need to call `time.Sleep()` anymore!

Running `varGoroutines.go` produces the next output:

```
$ go run varGoroutines.go 15
Going to create 15 goroutines.
sync.WaitGroup{noCopy:sync.noCopy{}, state1:[3]uint32{0x0, 0x0, 0x0}}
sync.WaitGroup{noCopy:sync.noCopy{}, state1:[3]uint32{0x0, 0x0, 0xf}}
14 8 9 10 11 5 0 4 1 2 3 6 13 12 7
Exiting...
```

The value in the third place of the `state1` slice is `0xf`, which is `15` in the decimal system, because we called `Add(1)` fifteen times.

> Remember that using more goroutines in a program is not a panacea for performance, as more goroutines, in addition to the various calls to `sync.Add()`, `sync.Wait()`, and `sync.Done()`, might slow down your program due to the extra housekeeping that needs to be done by the Go scheduler.

What if the number of Add() and Done() calls differ?

When the number of `sync.Add()` calls and `sync.Done()` calls are equal, everything is going to be fine in your programs. However, this subsection tells you what happens when these two numbers do not agree with each other.

Depending on whether command-line parameters exist or not, the presented program acts differently. Without any command-line parameters, the number of `Add()` calls is smaller than the number of `Done()` calls. With at least one command-line parameter, the number of `Done()` calls is smaller than the number of `Add()` calls. You can look at the Go code of `addDone.go` on your own. What is important is the output it generates. Running `addDone.go` without command-line arguments produces the next error message:

```
$ go run addDone.go
Going to create 20 goroutines.
sync.WaitGroup{noCopy:sync.noCopy{}, state1:[3]uint32{0x0, 0x0, 0x0}}
sync.WaitGroup{noCopy:sync.noCopy{}, state1:[3]uint32{0x0, 0x0, 0x13}}
19 14 15 16 17 18 10 8 9 11 12 1 0 2 5 6 3 4 7 13
Exiting...
panic: sync: negative WaitGroup counter

goroutine 19 [running]:
sync.(*WaitGroup).Add(0xc000014094, 0xffffffffffffffff)
        /usr/local/Cellar/go/1.16/libexec/src/sync/waitgroup.go:74
+0x147
sync.(*WaitGroup).Done(0xc000014094)
        /usr/local/Cellar/go/1.16/libexec/src/sync/waitgroup.go:99
+0x34
main.main.func1(0xc000014094, 0xd)
        /Users/mtsouk/ch07/addDone.go:26 +0xdb
created by main.main
        /Users/mtsouk/ch07/addDone.go:23 +0x1c6
exit status 2
```

The cause of the error message can be found in the output: `panic: sync: negative WaitGroup counter`—caused by more calls to `Done()` than calls to `Add()`. Note that sometimes `addDone.go` does not produce any error messages and terminates just fine. This is an issue with concurrent programs in general—they do not always crash or misbehave as the order of execution can change, which might change the behavior of the program. This makes debugging even more difficult.

Running `addDone.go` with one command-line argument produces the next error message:

```
$ go run addDone.go 1
Going to create 20 goroutines.
sync.WaitGroup{noCopy:sync.noCopy{}, state1:[3]uint32{0x0, 0x0, 0x0}}
sync.WaitGroup{noCopy:sync.noCopy{}, state1:[3]uint32{0x0, 0x0, 0x15}}
19 5 6 7 8 9 0 1 3 14 11 12 13 4 17 10 2 15 16 18 fatal error: all
goroutines are asleep - deadlock!

goroutine 1 [semacquire]:
sync.runtime_Semacquire(0xc000014094)
        /usr/local/Cellar/go/1.16/libexec/src/runtime/sema.go:56 +0x45
sync.(*WaitGroup).Wait(0xc000014094)
        /usr/local/Cellar/go/1.16/libexec/src/sync/waitgroup.go:130
+0x65
main.main()
        /Users/mtsouk/ch07/addDone.go:38 +0x2b6
exit status 2
```

Once again, the reason for the crash is printed on screen: `fatal error: all goroutines are asleep - deadlock!`. This means that the program should **wait indefinitely** for a goroutine to finish, that is, for a `Done()` call that is never going to happen.

Creating multiple files with goroutines

As a practical example of the use of goroutines, this subsection presents a command-line utility that creates multiple files populated with randomly generated data—such files can be used for testing file systems or generating data used for testing. The crucial code of `randomFiles.go` is the following:

```
var waitGroup sync.WaitGroup
for i := start; i <= end; i++ {
    waitGroup.Add(1)
    filepath := fmt.Sprintf("%s/%s%d", path, filename, i)
```

```
    go func(f string) {
        defer waitGroup.Done()
        createFile(f)
    }(filepath)
}
waitGroup.Wait()
```

We first create a `sync.WaitGroup` variable in order to wait for all goroutines to finish the right way. Each file is created by a single goroutine only. What is important here is that each file has a unique filename—this is implemented with the `filepath` variable that contains the value of the `for` loop counter. Multiple `createFile()` functions executed as goroutines create the files. This is a simple yet very efficient way of creating multiple files.

Running `randomFiles.go` generates the next output:

```
$ go run randomFiles.go
Usage: randomFiles firstInt lastInt filename directory
```

So, the utility requires four parameters, which are the first and last value of the `for` loop as well as the filename and the directory where the files are going to be written. So, let us run the utility with the correct number of parameters:

```
$ go run randomFiles.go 2 5 masterGo /tmp
/tmp/masterGo5 created!
/tmp/masterGo3 created!
/tmp/masterGo2 created!
/tmp/masterGo4 created!
```

Everything looks fine, and four files have been created according to our instructions! Now that we know about goroutines, let us continue with channels.

Channels

A **channel** is a communication mechanism that, among other things, allows goroutines to exchange data. Firstly, each channel allows the exchange of a particular data type, which is also called the element type of the channel, and secondly, for a channel to operate properly, you need someone to receive what is sent via the channel. You should declare a new channel using `make()` and the `chan` keyword (`make(chan int)`), and you can close a channel using the `close()` function. You can declare the size of a channel by writing something like `make(chan int, 1)`.

A **pipeline** is a virtual method for connecting goroutines and channels so that the output of one goroutine becomes the input of another goroutine using channels to transfer your data. One of the benefits that you get from using pipelines is that there is a constant data flow in your program, as no goroutine or channel has to wait for everything to be completed in order to start their execution. Additionally, you use fewer variables and therefore less memory space because you do not have to save everything as a variable. Finally, the use of pipelines simplifies the design of the program and improves its maintainability.

Writing to and reading from a channel

Writing the value `val` to channel `ch` is as easy as writing `ch <- val`. The arrow shows the direction of the value, and you will have no problem with this statement as long as both `var` and `ch` are of the same data type.

You can read a single value from a channel named `c` by executing `<-c`. In this case, the direction is from the channel to the outer world. You can save that value into a variable using `aVar := <-c`.

Both channel reading and writing are illustrated in `channels.go`, which comes with the following code:

```
package main

import (
    "fmt"
    "sync"
)

func writeToChannel(c chan int, x int) {
    c <- x
    close(c)
}
```

This function just writes a value to the channel and immediately closes it.

```
func printer(ch chan bool) {
    ch <- true
}
```

This function just sends the `true` value to a `bool` channel.

```
func main() {
    c := make(chan int, 1)
```

This channel is **buffered** with a size of `1`. This means that as soon as we fill that buffer, we can close the channel and the goroutine is going to continue its execution and return. A channel that is **unbuffered** has a different behavior: when you try to send a value to that channel, it blocks forever because it is waiting for someone to fetch that value. In this case, we definitely want a buffered channel in order to avoid any blocking.

```
var waitGroup sync.WaitGroup
waitGroup.Add(1)
go func(c chan int) {
    defer waitGroup.Done()
    writeToChannel(c, 10)
    fmt.Println("Exit.")
}(c)

fmt.Println("Read:", <-c)
```

Here, we read from the channel and print the value without storing it in a separate variable.

```
_, ok := <-c
if ok {
    fmt.Println("Channel is open!")
} else {
    fmt.Println("Channel is closed!")
}
```

The previous code shows a technique for **determining whether a channel is closed or not**. In this case, we are ignoring the read value—if the channel was open, then the read value would be **discarded**.

```
waitGroup.Wait()

var ch chan bool = make(chan bool)
for i := 0; i < 5; i++ {
    go printer(ch)
}
```

Here, we make an unbuffered channel, and we create five goroutines *without any synchronization* as we do not use any `Add()` calls.

```
// Range on channels
// IMPORTANT: As the channel c is not closed,
```

```
    // the range loop does not exit on its own.
    n := 0
    for i := range ch {
```

The range keyword works with channels! However, a range loop on a channel only exits when the channel is closed or using the break keyword.

```
        fmt.Println(i)
        if i == true {
            n++
        }
        if n > 2 {
            fmt.Println("n:", n)
            close(ch)
            break
        }
    }
```

We close the ch channel when a condition is met and exit the for loop using break.

```
    for i := 0; i < 5; i++ {
        fmt.Println(<-ch)
    }
}
```

When trying to read from a closed channel, we get the zero value of its data type, so this for loop works just fine and does not cause any issues.

Running channels.go generates the next output:

```
Exit.
Read: 10
```

After writing the value 10 to the channel using writeToChannel(c, 10), we read that value back.

```
Channel is closed!
true
true
true
```

The for loop with the range exits after three iterations—each iteration prints true on screen.

```
n: 3
false
false
false
false
false
```

These five `false` values are printed by the last `for` loop of the program.

Although everything looks fine with `channels.go`, there is a logical issue with it, which we will explain and resolve in the *Race conditions* section. Additionally, if we run `channels.go` multiple times, it might crash. However, most of the time it does not, which makes debugging even more challenging.

Receiving from a closed channel

Reading from a closed channel returns the zero value of its data type. However, if you try to write to a closed channel, your program is going to crash in a bad way (**panic**). These two situations are explored in `readCloseCh.go` and more specifically in the implementation of the `main()` function:

```
func main() {
    willClose := make(chan complex64, 10)
```

If you make that an unbuffered channel, the program is going to crash.

```
    // Write some data to the channel
    willClose <- -1
    willClose <- 1i
```

We write two values to the `willClose` channel.

```
    // Read data and empty channel
    <-willClose
    <-willClose
    close(willClose)
```

Then, we read and discard these two values and we close the channel.

```
    // Read again - this is a closed channel
    read := <-willClose
    fmt.Println(read)
}
```

The last value that we read from the channel is the zero value of a `complex64` data type. Running `readCloseCh.go` generates the next output:

```
(0+0i)
```

So, we got back the zero value of the `complex64` data type. Now let us continue and discuss how to work with functions that accept channels as parameters.

Channels as function parameters

When using a channel as a *function parameter*, you can specify its direction; that is, whether it is going to be used for sending or receiving data. In my opinion, if you know the purpose of a channel in advance, you should use this capability because it makes your programs more robust. You will not be able to send data accidentally to a channel from which you should only receive data or receive data from a channel to which you should only be sending data. As a result, if you declare that a channel function parameter is going to be used for reading only and you try to write to it, you get an error message that will most likely save you from nasty bugs in the future.

All these are illustrated in `channelFunc.go`—the implementation of the functions that accept channel parameters are the following:

```
func printer(ch chan<- bool) {
    ch <- true
}
```

This function accepts a channel parameter that is available for writing only.

```
func writeToChannel(c chan<- int, x int) {
    fmt.Println("1", x)
    c <- x
    fmt.Println("2", x)
}
```

The channel parameter of this function is available for reading only.

```
func f2(out <-chan int, in chan<- int) {
    x := <-out
    fmt.Println("Read (f2):", x)
    in <- x
    return
}
```

The last function accepts two channel parameters. However, `out` is available for reading whereas `in` is offered for writing. If you try to perform an operation on a channel parameter that is not allowed, the Go compiler is going to complain. This happens even if the function is not being used.

The subject of the next section is race conditions—read it carefully in order to avoid undefined behaviors and unpleasant situations when working with multiple goroutines.

Race conditions

A data race condition is a situation where two or more running elements, such as threads and goroutines, try to take control of or modify a shared resource or shared variable of a program. Strictly speaking, a data race occurs when two or more instructions access the same memory address, where at least one of them performs a write (change) operation. If all operations are read operations, then there is no race condition. In practice, this means that you might get different output if you run your program multiple times, and that is a bad thing.

Using the `-race` flag when running or building Go source files executes the Go race detector, which makes the compiler create a modified version of a typical executable file. This modified version can record all accesses to shared variables as well as all synchronization events that take place, including calls to `sync.Mutex` and `sync.WaitGroup`, which are presented later on in this chapter. After analyzing the relevant events, the race detector prints a report that can help you identify potential problems so that you can correct them.

The Go race detector

You can run the race detector tool with `go run -race`. If we test `channels.go` using `go run -race`, we are going to get the following output:

```
$ go run -race channels.go
Exit.
Read: 10
Channel is closed!
true
true
true
n: 3
==================
WARNING: DATA RACE
```

```
Write at 0x00c00006e010 by main goroutine:
  runtime.closechan()
      /usr/local/Cellar/go/1.16.2/libexec/src/runtime/chan.go:355 +0x0
  main.main()
      /Users/mtsouk/ch07/channels.go:54 +0x46c

Previous read at 0x00c00006e010 by goroutine 12:
  runtime.chansend()
      /usr/local/Cellar/go/1.16.2/libexec/src/runtime/chan.go:158 +0x0
  main.printer()
      /Users/mtsouk/ch07/channels.go:14 +0x47

Goroutine 12 (running) created at:
  main.main()
      /Users/mtsouk/ch07/channels.go:40 +0x2b4
==================
false
false
false
false
false
Found 1 data race(s)
exit status 66
```

Therefore, although `channels.go` looks fine, there is a race condition waiting to happen. Let us now discuss where the problem with `channels.go` lies based on the previous output.

There is a closing of a channel at `channels.go` on line 54, and there is a write to the same channel on line 14 that looks to be the root of the race condition situation. Line 54 is `close(ch)`, whereas line 14 is `ch <- true`. The issue is that we cannot be sure about what is going to happen and *in which order*—this is the race condition. If you execute `channels.go` without the race detector, it might work but if you try it multiple times, you might get a `panic: send on closed channel` error message—this mainly has to do with the order the Go scheduler is going to run the goroutines of the program. So, if the closing of the channel happens first, then writing to that channel is going to fail—**race condition**!

Fixing `channels.go` requires changing the code and more specifically the implementation of the `printer()` function. The corrected version of `channels.go` is named `chRace.go` and comes with the next code:

```
func printer(ch chan<- bool, times int) {
    for i := 0; i < times; i++ {
        ch <- true
    }
    close(ch)
}
```

The first thing to notice here is that instead of using multiple goroutines for writing to the desired channel, we use a single goroutine. A single goroutine writing to a channel followed by the closing of that channel cannot create any race conditions because things happen sequentially.

```
func main() {
    // This is an unbuffered channel
    var ch chan bool = make(chan bool)

    // Write 5 values to channel with a single goroutine
    go printer(ch, 5)

    // IMPORTANT: As the channel c is closed,
    // the range loop is going to exit on its own.
    for val := range ch {
        fmt.Print(val, " ")
    }
    fmt.Println()

    for i := 0; i < 15; i++ {
        fmt.Print(<-ch, " ")
    }
    fmt.Println()
}
```

Running `go run -race chRace.go` produces the next output, which means that there is not a race condition any more:

```
true true true true true
false false false false false false false false false false false false
false false false
```

The next section is about the important and powerful `select` keyword.

The select keyword

The `select` keyword is really important because it allows you to listen to multiple channels at the same time. A `select` block can have multiple cases and an optional `default` case, which mimics the `switch` statement. It is good for `select` blocks to have a timeout option just in case. Last, a `select` without any cases (`select{}`) waits forever.

In practice, this means that `select` allows a goroutine to **wait on multiple** communication operations. So, `select` gives you the power to listen to multiple channels using a single `select` block. As a consequence, you can have nonblocking operations on channels, provided that you have implemented your `select` blocks appropriately.

A `select` statement is not evaluated sequentially, as all of its channels are examined simultaneously. If none of the channels in a select statement are ready, the `select` statement blocks (*waits*) until one of the channels is ready. **If multiple channels of a `select` statement are ready, then the Go runtime makes a random selection from the set of these ready channels**.

The code in `select.go` presents a simple use of `select` running in a goroutine that has three cases. But first, let us see how the goroutine that contains `select` runs:

```
    wg.Add(1)
    go func() {
        gen(0, 2*n, createNumber, end)
        wg.Done()
    }()
```

The previous code tells us that for `wg.Done()` to get executed, `gen()` should return first. So, let us see the implementation of `gen()`:

```
func gen(min, max int, createNumber chan int, end chan bool) {
    time.Sleep(time.Second)
    for {
        select {
        case createNumber <- rand.Intn(max-min) + min:
        case <-end:
            fmt.Println("Ended!")
            // return
```

The right thing to do here is add the return statement for gen() to finish. But let us imagine that you have forgotten to add the return statement. This means that the function is not going to finish after the select branch associated with the end channel parameter is executed—createNumber is not going to end the function as it has no return statement. Therefore, the select block keeps waiting for more. The solution can be found in the code that follows:

```
        case <-time.After(4 * time.Second):
            fmt.Println("time.After()!")
            return
        }
    }
}
```

So, what is really happening in the code of the entire select block? This particular select statement has three cases. As stated earlier, select does not require a default branch. You can consider the third branch of the select statement as a clever default branch. This happens because time.After() waits for the specified duration (4 * time.Second) to elapse and then prints a message and properly ends gen() with return. This unblocks the select statement in case all of the other channels are blocked for some reason. Although omitting return from the second branch is a bug, this shows that having an exit strategy is always a good thing.

Running select.go produces the next output:

```
$ go run select.go 10
Going to create 10 random numbers.
13 0 2 8 12 4 13 15 14 19 Ended!
time.After()!
Exiting...
```

We are going to see select in action in the remainder of the chapter, starting from the next section, which discusses how to time out goroutines. What you should remember is that select allows us to listen to multiple channels from a single point.

Timing out a goroutine

There are times that goroutines take more time than expected to finish—in such situations, we want to time out the goroutines so that we can unblock the program. This section presents two such techniques.

Timing out a goroutine – inside main()

This subsection presents a simple technique for timing out a goroutine. The relevant code can be found in the `main()` function of `timeOut1.go`:

```
func main() {
    c1 := make(chan string)
    go func() {
        time.Sleep(3 * time.Second)
        c1 <- "c1 OK"
    }()
```

The `time.Sleep()` call is used for emulating the time it normally takes for a function to finish its operation. In this case, the anonymous function that is executed as a goroutine takes about three seconds before writing a message to the `c1` channel.

```
    select {
    case res := <-c1:
        fmt.Println(res)
    case <-time.After(time.Second):
        fmt.Println("timeout c1")
    }
```

The purpose of the `time.After()` call is to wait for the desired time before being executed—if another branch is executed, the waiting time resets. In this case, we are not interested in the actual value returned by `time.After()` but in the fact that the `time.After()` branch was executed, which means that the waiting time has passed. In this case, as the value passed to the `time.After()` function is smaller than the value used in the `time.Sleep()` call that was executed previously, you will most likely get a timeout message. The reason for saying "most likely" is that Linux is not a real-time OS and sometimes the OS scheduler plays strange games, especially when it has to deal with a high load and has to schedule lots of tasks.

```
    c2 := make(chan string)
    go func() {
        time.Sleep(3 * time.Second)
        c2 <- "c2 OK"
    }()

    select {
    case res := <-c2:
        fmt.Println(res)
    case <-time.After(4 * time.Second):
```

```
        fmt.Println("timeout c2")
    }
}
```

The preceding code both executes a goroutine that takes about three seconds to execute because of the `time.Sleep()` call and defines a timeout period of four seconds in `select` using `time.After(4 * time.Second)`. If the `time.After(4 * time.Second)` call returns after you get a value from the `c2` channel found in the first case of the `select` block, then there will be no timeout; otherwise, you get a timeout. However, in this case, the value of the `time.After()` call provides enough time for the `time.Sleep()` call to return, so you will most likely not get a timeout message here.

Let us now verify our thoughts. Running `timeOut1.go` produces the next output:

```
$ go run timeOut1.go
timeout c1
c2 OK
```

As expected, the first goroutine timed out whereas the second one did not. The subsection that follows presents another timeout technique.

Timing out a goroutine – outside main()

This subsection illustrates another technique for timing out goroutines. The `select` statement can be found in a separate function. Additionally, the timeout period is given as a command-line argument.

The interesting part of `timeOut2.go` is in the implementation of `timeout()`:

```
func timeout(t time.Duration) {
    temp := make(chan int)
    go func() {
        time.Sleep(5 * time.Second)
        defer close(temp)
    }()

    select {
    case <-temp:
        result <- false
    case <-time.After(t):
        result <- true
    }
}
```

In `timeout()`, the time duration that is used in the `time.After()` call is a function parameter, which means that it can vary. Once again, the `select` block holds the logic of the time out. Any timeout period bigger than 5 seconds will most likely give the goroutine enough time to finish. If `timeout()` writes `false` to the `result` channel, then there was no timeout, whereas if it writes `true`, there was a timeout. Running `timeOut2.go` produces the next output:

```
$ go run timeOut2.go 100
Timeout period is 100ms
Time out!
```

The timeout period is 100 milliseconds, which means that the goroutine did not have enough time to finish, hence the timeout message.

```
$ go run timeOut2.go 5500
Timeout period is 5.5s
OK
```

This time the timeout is 5,500 milliseconds, which means that the goroutine had enough time to finish.

The next section revisits and presents advanced concepts related to channels.

Go channels revisited

So far, we have seen basic usages of channels—this section presents the definition and the usage of `nil` channels, signal channels, and buffered channels.

It helps to remember that the zero value of the channel type is `nil`, and that if you send a message to a closed channel, the program panics. However, if you try to read from a closed channel, you get the zero value of the type of that channel. So, **after closing a channel, you can no longer write to it, but you can still read from it**. To be able to close a channel, the channel must not be receive-only.

Additionally, a `nil` channel always blocks, which means that both reading and writing from `nil` channels blocks. This property of channels can be very useful when you want to disable a branch of a `select` statement by assigning the `nil` value to a channel variable. Finally, if you try to **close** a `nil` channel, your program is going to panic. This is best illustrated in the `closeNil.go` program:

```
package main

func main() {
var c chan string
```

The previous statement defines a `nil` channel named `c` of type `string`.

```
close(c)
}
```

Running `closeNil.go` generates the following output:

```
panic: close of nil channel

goroutine 1 [running]:
main.main()
        /Users/mtsouk/ch07/closeNil.go:5 +0x2a
exit status 2
```

The previous output shows the message you are going to get if you try to close a `nil` channel.

Let us now discuss buffer channels.

Buffered channels

The topic of this subsection is buffered channels. These channels allow us to put jobs in a queue quickly in order to be able to deal with more requests and process requests later on. Moreover, you can use buffered channels as semaphores in order to limit the throughput of your application.

The presented technique works as follows: all incoming requests are forwarded to a channel, which processes them one by one. When the channel is done processing a request, it sends a message to the original caller saying that it is ready to process a new one. So, the capacity of the buffer of the channel restricts the number of simultaneous requests that it can keep.

The file that implements the technique is named `bufChannel.go` and contains the next code:

```
package main

import (
    "fmt"
)

func main() {
    numbers := make(chan int, 5)
```

The `numbers` channel cannot store more than five integers—this is a buffer channel with a capacity of `5`.

```
    counter := 10

    for i := 0; i < counter; i++ {
        select {
        // This is where the processing takes place
        case numbers <- i * i:
            fmt.Println("About to process", i)
        default:
        fmt.Print("No space for ", i, " ")
        }
```

We begin putting data into `numbers`—however, when the channel is full, it is not going to store more data and the `default` branch is going to be executed.

```
    }
    fmt.Println()

    for {
        select {
        case num := <-numbers:
            fmt.Print("*", num, " ")
        default:
            fmt.Println("Nothing left to read!")
            return
        }
    }
}
```

Similarly, we try to read data from `numbers` using a `for` loop. When all data from channel is read, the `default` branch is going to be executed and terminate the program with its `return` statement.

Running `bufChannel.go` produces the next output:

```
$ go run bufChannel.go
About to process 0
. . .
About to process 4
No space for 5 No space for 6 No space for 7 No space for 8 No space
for 9
*0 *1 *4 *9 *16 Nothing left to read!
```

Let us now discuss nil channels.

nil channels

nil channels **always block**! Therefore, you should use them when you want that behavior on purpose! The code that follows illustrates nil channels:

```
package main

import (
    "fmt"
    "math/rand"
    "sync"
    "time"
)

var wg sync.WaitGroup
```

We are making wg a global variable in order to be available from anywhere in the code and avoid passing it to every function that needs it.

```
func add(c chan int) {
    sum := 0
    t := time.NewTimer(time.Second)

    for {
        select {
        case input := <-c:
            sum = sum + input
        case <-t.C:
            c = nil
            fmt.Println(sum)
            wg.Done()
        }
    }
}
```

The send() function keeps sending random numbers to the c channel. Do not confuse channel c, which is a channel function parameter, with channel t.C, which is part of timer t—you can change the name of the c variable but not the name of the C field. When the time of timer t expires, the timer sends a value to the t.C channel.

This triggers the execution of the relevant branch of the `select` statement, which assigns the value `nil` to channel `c`, prints the value of the `sum` variable and `wg.Done()` is executed, which is going to unblock `wg.Wait()` found in the `main()` function. Additionally, as `c` becomes `nil`, it stops/blocks `send()` from sending any data to it.

```
func send(c chan int) {
	for {
		c <- rand.Intn(10)
	}
}

func main() {
	c := make(chan int)
	rand.Seed(time.Now().Unix())
	wg.Add(1)
	go add(c)
	go send(c)
	wg.Wait()
}
```

Running `nilChannel.go` produces the next output:

```
$ go run nilChannel.go
11168960
```

Since the number of times that the first branch of the `select` statement in `add()` is going to be executed is not fixed, you will get different results each time you execute `nilChannel.go`.

The next subsection discusses worker pools.

Worker pools

A **worker pool** is a set of threads that process jobs assigned to them. The Apache web server and the `net/http` package of Go more or less work this way: the main process accepts all incoming requests, which are forwarded to worker processes to get served. Once a worker process has finished its job, it is ready to serve a new client. As Go does not have threads, the presented implementation is going to use goroutines instead of threads. Additionally, threads do not usually die after serving a request because the cost of ending a thread and creating a new one is too high, whereas goroutines do die after finishing their job. Worker pools in Go are implemented with the help of buffered channels, because they allow you to limit the number of goroutines running at the same time.

The presented utility implements a simple task: it processes integers and prints their square values using a single goroutine for serving each request. The code of `wPools.go` is as follows:

```
package main

import (
    "fmt"
    "os"
    "runtime"
    "strconv"
    "sync"
    "time"
)

type Client struct {
    id      int
    integer int
}
```

The `Client` structure is used for keeping track of the requests that the program is going to process.

```
type Result struct {
    job    Client
    square int
}
```

The `Result` structure is used for keeping the data of each `Client` as well as the results generated by the client. Put simply, the `Client` structure holds the input data of each request, whereas `Result` holds the results of a request—if you want to process complex data, you should modify these structures.

```
var size = runtime.GOMAXPROCS(0)
var clients = make(chan Client, size)
var data = make(chan Result, size)
```

The `clients` and `data` **buffered channels** are used to get new client requests and write the results, respectively. If you want your program to run faster, you can increase the value of `size`.

```
func worker(wg *sync.WaitGroup) {
    for c := range clients {
```

```
        square := c.integer * c.integer
        output := Result{c, square}
        data <- output
        time.Sleep(time.Second)
    }
    wg.Done()
}
```

The `worker()` function processes requests by reading the `clients` channel. Once the processing is complete, the result is written to the `data` channel. The delay that is introduced with `time.Sleep()` is not necessary, but it gives you a better sense of the way that the generated output is printed.

```
func create(n int) {
    for i := 0; i < n; i++ {
        c := Client{i, i}
        clients <- c
    }
    close(clients)
}
```

The purpose of the `create()` function is to create all requests properly and then send them to the `clients` **buffered channel** for processing. Note that the `clients` channel is read by `worker()`.

```
func main() {
    if len(os.Args) != 3 {
        fmt.Println("Need #jobs and #workers!")
        return
    }

    nJobs, err := strconv.Atoi(os.Args[1])
    if err != nil {
        fmt.Println(err)
        return
    }

    nWorkers, err := strconv.Atoi(os.Args[2])
    if err != nil {
        fmt.Println(err)
        return
    }
```

In the preceding code, you read the command-line parameters that define the number of jobs and workers. If the number of workers is bigger than the size of the `clients` buffered channel, then the number of goroutines that are going to be created is equal to the size of the `clients` channel. Similarly, if the number of jobs is greater than the number of workers, the jobs are served in smaller chunks.

```
    go create(nJobs)
```

The `create()` call mimics the client requests that you are going to process.

```
    finished := make(chan interface{})
```

The `finished` channel is used for blocking the program and, therefore, needs no particular data type.

```
    go func() {
        for d := range data {
            fmt.Printf("Client ID: %d\tint: ", d.job.id)
            fmt.Printf("%d\tsquare: %d\n", d.job.integer, d.square)
        }
        finished <- true
```

The `finished <- true` statement is used for unblocking the program as soon as the `for range` loop ends. The `for range` loop ends when the `data` channel is closed, which happens after `wg.Wait()`, which means after all workers have finished.

```
    }()

    var wg sync.WaitGroup
    for i := 0; i < nWorkers; i++ {
        wg.Add(1)
        go worker(&wg)
    }
    wg.Wait()
    close(data)
```

The purpose of the previous `for` loop is to generate the required number of `worker()` goroutines to process all requests.

```
    fmt.Printf("Finished: %v\n", <-finished)
}
```

The `<-finished` statement in `fmt.Printf()` blocks until the `finished` channel is closed.

Running `wPools.go` creates the next kind of output:

```
$ go run wPools.go 10 4
Client ID: 1    int: 1  square: 1
Client ID: 0    int: 0  square: 0
Client ID: 2    int: 2  square: 4
Client ID: 3    int: 3  square: 9
Client ID: 4    int: 4  square: 16
Client ID: 5    int: 5  square: 25
Client ID: 6    int: 6  square: 36
Client ID: 7    int: 7  square: 49
Client ID: 8    int: 8  square: 64
Client ID: 9    int: 9  square: 81
Finished: true
```

The previous output shows that all requests were processed. This technique allows you to serve a given number of requests that saves you from server overload. The price you pay for that is having to write more code.

The next subsection introduces signal channels and shows a technique for using them to define the order of execution for a small number of goroutines.

Signal channels

A signal channel is one that is used just for signaling. Put simply, you can use a signal channel when you want to inform another goroutine about something. Signal channels should not be used for data transferring. You are going to see signal channels in action in the next subsection where we specify the order of execution of goroutines.

Specifying the order of execution for your goroutines

This subsection shows a technique for specifying the order of execution of goroutines with the help of *signal channels*. However, have in mind that this technique works best when you are dealing with a small number of goroutines. The presented code example has four goroutines that we want to execute in the desired order—first, goroutine for function `A()`, then function `B()`, then `C()`, and finally, `D()`.

The code of `defineOrder.go` without the `package` statement and `import` block is the following:

```
var wg sync.WaitGroup

func A(a, b chan struct{}) {
    <-a
    fmt.Println("A()!")
    time.Sleep(time.Second)
    close(b)
}
```

Function `A()` is going to be blocked until channel a, which is passed as a parameter, is closed. Just before it ends, it closes channel `b`, which is passed as a parameter. This is going to unblock the next goroutine, which is going to be function `B()`.

```
func B(a, b chan struct{}) {
    <-a
    fmt.Println("B()!")
    time.Sleep(3 * time.Second)
    close(b)
}
```

Similarly, function `B()` is going to be blocked until channel `a`, which is passed as a parameter, is closed. Just before `B()` ends, it closes channel `b`, which is passed as a parameter. As before, this is going to unblock the next function.

```
func C(a, b chan struct{}) {
    <-a
    fmt.Println("C()!")
    close(b)
}
```

As it happened with functions `A()` and `B()`, the execution of function `C()` is blocked by channel `a`. Just before it ends, it closes channel `b`.

```
func D(a chan struct{}) {
    <-a
    fmt.Println("D()!")
    wg.Done()
}
```

This is the last function that is going to be executed. Therefore, although it is blocked, it does not close any channels before exiting. Additionally, being the last function means that it can be executed more than once, which is not true for functions `A()`, `B()` and `C()` because **a channel can be closed only once**.

```
func main() {
    x := make(chan struct{})
    y := make(chan struct{})
    z := make(chan struct{})
    w := make(chan struct{})
```

We need to have as many channels as the number of functions we want to execute as goroutines.

```
    wg.Add(1)
    go func() {
        D(w)
    }()
```

This proves that the order of execution dictated by the Go code does not matter as `D()` is going to be executed last.

```
    wg.Add(1)
    go func() {
        D(w)
    }()

    go A(x, y)

    wg.Add(1)
    go func() {
        D(w)
    }()

    go C(z, w)
    go B(y, z)
```

Although we run `C()` before `B()`, `C()` is going to finish after `B()` has finished.

```
    wg.Add(1)
    go func() {
        D(w)
    }()
```

```
    // This triggers the process
    close(x)
```

The closing of the first channel is what triggers the execution of the goroutines because this unblocks `A()`.

```
    wg.Wait()
}
```

Running `defineOrder.go` produces the next output:

```
$ go run defineOrder.go
A()!
B()!
C()!
D()! D()! D()! D()!
```

So, the four functions, which are executed as goroutines, are executed in the desired order, and, in the case of the last function, the desired number of times. The next section talks about shared memory and shared variables, which is a very handy way of making goroutines communicate with each other.

Shared memory and shared variables

Shared memory and shared variables are huge topics in concurrent programming and the most common ways for UNIX threads to communicate with each other. The same principles apply to Go and goroutines, which is what this section is about. A **mutex** variable, which is an abbreviation of *mutual exclusion variable*, is mainly used for thread synchronization and for protecting shared data when multiple writes can occur at the same time. A **mutex works like a buffered channel with a capacity of one**, which allows at most one goroutine to access a shared variable at any given time. This means that there is no way for two or more goroutines to be able to update that variable simultaneously. Go offers the `sync.Mutex` and `sync.RWMutex` data types.

A **critical section** of a concurrent program is the code that cannot be executed simultaneously by all processes, threads, or, in this case, goroutines. It is the code that needs to be protected by mutexes. Therefore, identifying the critical sections of your code makes the whole programming process so much simpler that you should pay particular attention to this task. A critical section cannot be embedded into another critical section when both critical sections use the same `sync.Mutex` or `sync.RWMutex` variable.

Put simply, avoid at almost any cost spreading mutexes across functions because that makes it really hard to see whether you are embedding or not.

The sync.Mutex type

The `sync.Mutex` type is the Go implementation of a *mutex*. Its definition, which can be found in the `mutex.go` file of the `sync` directory, is as follows—you do not need to know the definition of `sync.Mutex` in order to use it:

```
type Mutex struct {
    state int32
    sema  uint32
}
```

The definition of `sync.Mutex` is nothing special. All of the interesting work is done by the `sync.Lock()` and `sync.Unlock()` functions, which can lock and unlock a `sync.Mutex` variable, respectively. Locking a mutex means that nobody else can lock it until it has been released using the `sync.Unlock()` function. All these are illustrated in `mutex.go`, which contains the next code:

```
package main

import (
    "fmt"
    "os"
    "strconv"
    "sync"
    "time"
)

var m sync.Mutex
var v1 int

func change(i int) {
    m.Lock()
```

This function makes changes to the value of `v1`. The critical section begins here.

```
    time.Sleep(time.Second)
    v1 = v1 + 1
    if v1 == 10 {
        v1 = 0
```

```
        fmt.Print("* ")
    }
    m.Unlock()
```

This is the end of the critical section. Now, another goroutine can lock the mutex.

```
}
func read() int {
    m.Lock()
    a := v1
    m.Unlock()
    return a
}
```

This function is used for reading the value of `v1`—therefore it should use a mutex to make the process concurrently safe. Most specifically, we want to make sure that nobody is going to change the value of `v1` while we are reading it. The rest of the program contains the implementation of the `main()` function—feel free to see the entire code of `mutex.go` in the GitHub repository of the book.

Running `mutex.go` produces the next output:

```
$ go run -race mutex.go 10
0 -> 1-> 2-> 3-> 4-> 5-> 6-> 7-> 8-> 9* -> 0-> 0
```

The previous output shows that due to the use of a mutex, goroutines cannot access shared data and therefore there are no hidden race conditions.

The next subsection shows what could happen if we forget to unlock a mutex.

What happens if you forget to unlock a mutex?

Forgetting to unlock a `sync.Mutex` mutex creates a panic situation even in the simplest kind of a program. The same applies to the `sync.RWMutex` mutex, which is presented in the next section.

Let us now see a code example to understand this unpleasant situation a lot better—this is part of `forgetMutex.go`.

```
var m sync.Mutex
var w sync.WaitGroup

func function() {
    m.Lock()
```

```
    fmt.Println("Locked!")
}
```

Here, we lock a mutex without releasing it afterwards. This means that if we run `function()` as a goroutine more than once, all instances after the first one are going to be blocked waiting to `Lock()` the shared mutex. In our case, we run two goroutines—feel free to see the entire code of `forgetMutex.go` for more details. Running `forgetMutex.go` generates the next output:

```
Locked!
fatal error: all goroutines are asleep - deadlock!

goroutine 1 [semacquire]:
sync.runtime_Semacquire(0x118d3e8)
        /usr/local/Cellar/go/1.16.2/libexec/src/runtime/sema.go:56
+0x45
sync.(*WaitGroup).Wait(0x118d3e0)
        /usr/local/Cellar/go/1.16.2/libexec/src/sync/waitgroup.go:130
+0x65
main.main()
        /Users/mtsouk/ch07/forgetMutex.go:29 +0x95

goroutine 18 [semacquire]:
sync.runtime_SemacquireMutex(0x118d234, 0x0, 0x1)
        /usr/local/Cellar/go/1.16.2/libexec/src/runtime/sema.go:71
+0x47
sync.(*Mutex).lockSlow(0x118d230)
        /usr/local/Cellar/go/1.16.2/libexec/src/sync/mutex.go:138
+0x105
sync.(*Mutex).Lock(...)
        /usr/local/Cellar/go/1.16.2/libexec/src/sync/mutex.go:81
main.function()
        /Users/mtsouk/ch07/forgetMutex.go:12 +0xac
main.main.func1()
        /Users/mtsouk/ch07/forgetMutex.go:20 +0x4c
created by main.main
        /Users/mtsouk/ch07/forgetMutex.go:18 +0x52
exit status 2
```

As expected, the program crashes because of the deadlock. To avoid such situations, always remember to unlock any mutexes created in your program.

Let us now discuss sync.RWMutex, which is an improved version of sync.Mutex.

The sync.RWMutex type

The sync.RWMutex data type is an improved version of sync.Mutex and is defined in the rwmutex.go file of the sync directory of the Go Standard library as follows:

```
type RWMutex struct {
    w           Mutex
    writerSem   uint32
    readerSem   uint32
    readerCount int32
    readerWait  int32
}
```

In other words, sync.RWMutex is based on sync.Mutex with the necessary additions and improvements. So, you might ask, how does sync.RWMutex improve sync.Mutex? Although a single function is allowed to perform write operations with a sync.RWMutex mutex, you can have **multiple readers** owning a sync.RWMutex mutex—this means that read operations are usually faster with sync.RWMutex. However, there is one important detail that you should be aware of: until **all of the readers** of a sync.RWMutex mutex unlock that mutex, you cannot lock it for writing, which is the small price you have to pay for the performance improvement you get for allowing multiple readers.

The functions that can help you to work with sync.RWMutex are RLock() and RUnlock(), which are used for locking and unlocking the mutex for reading purposes, respectively. The Lock() and Unlock() functions used in sync.Mutex should still be used when you want to lock and unlock a sync.RWMutex mutex for writing purposes. Finally, it should be apparent that you should not make changes to any shared variables inside an RLock() and RUnlock() block of code.

All these are illustrated in rwMutex.go—the important code is the following:

```
var Password *secret
var wg sync.WaitGroup

type secret struct {
    RWM      sync.RWMutex
    password string
}
```

This is the shared variable of the program—you can share any type of variable you want.

```
func Change(pass string) {
     fmt.Println("Change() function")
     Password.RWM.Lock()
```

This is the beginning of the critical section.

```
     fmt.Println("Change() Locked")
     time.Sleep(4 * time.Second)
     Password.password = pass
     Password.RWM.Unlock()
```

This is the end of the critical section.

```
     fmt.Println("Change() UnLocked")
}
```

The `Change()` function makes changes to the shared variable `Password` and therefore needs to use the `Lock()` function, which can be held by a single writer only.

```
func show () {
     defer wg.Done()
     Password.RWM.RLock()
     fmt.Println("Show function locked!")
     time.Sleep(2 * time.Second)
     fmt.Println("Pass value:", Password.password)
     defer Password.RWM.RUnlock()
}
```

The `show()` function reads the shared variable `Password` and therefore is allowed to use the `RLock()` function, which can be held by multiple readers. Inside `main()`, three `show()` functions are executed as goroutines before a call to the `Change()` function, which also runs as a goroutine. The key point here is that no race conditions are going to happen. Running `rwMutex.go` produces the next output:

```
$ go run rwMutex.go
Change() function
```

The `Change()` function is executed but cannot acquire the mutex because it is already taken by one or more `show()` goroutines.

```
Show function locked!
Show function locked!
```

The previous output verifies that two `show()` goroutines have successfully taken the mutex for reading.

```
Change() function
```

Here, we can see a second `Change()` function **running and waiting** to get the mutex.

```
Pass value: myPass
Pass value: myPass
```

This is the output from the two `show()` goroutines.

```
Change() Locked
Change() UnLocked
```

Here we see that one `Change()` goroutine finishes its job.

```
Show function locked!
Pass value: 54321
```

After that another `show()` goroutine finishes.

```
Change() Locked
Change() UnLocked
Current password value: 123456
```

Last, the second `Change()` goroutine finishes. The last output line is for making sure that the password value has changed—please look at the full code of `rwMutex.go` for more details.

The next subsection discusses the use of the `atomic` package for avoiding race conditions.

The atomic package

An **atomic operation** is an operation that is completed in a single step relative to other threads or, in this case, to other goroutines. This means that **an atomic operation cannot be interrupted in the middle of it**. The Go Standard library offers the `atomic` package, which, in some simple cases, can help you to avoid using a mutex. With the `atomic` package, you can have atomic counters accessed by multiple goroutines without synchronization issues and without worrying about race conditions. However, mutexes are more versatile than atomic operations.

As illustrated in the code that follows, when using an atomic variable, **all reading and writing operations of an atomic variable** must be done using the functions provided by the `atomic` package in order to avoid race conditions.

The code in `atomic.go` is as follows, which is made smaller by hardcoding some values:

```
package main

import (
    "fmt"
    "sync"
    "sync/atomic"
)

type atomCounter struct {
    val int64
}
```

This is a structure for holding the desired `int64` atomic variable.

```
func (c *atomCounter) Value() int64 {
    return atomic.LoadInt64(&c.val)
}
```

This is a helper function that returns the current value of an `int64` atomic variable using `atomic.LoadInt64()`.

```
func main() {
    X := 100
    Y := 4
    var waitGroup sync.WaitGroup
    counter := atomCounter{}
    for i := 0; i < X; i++ {
```

We are creating lots of goroutines that change the shared variable—as stated before, the use of the `atomic` package for working with the shared variable offers a simple way of avoiding race conditions when changing the value of the shared variable.

```
        waitGroup.Add(1)
        go func(no int) {
            defer waitGroup.Done()
            for i := 0; i < Y; i++ {
```

```
                atomic.AddInt64(&counter.val, 1)
            }
```

The `atomic.AddInt64()` function changes the value of the `val` field of the `counter` structure variable in a safe way.

```
        }(i)
    }

    waitGroup.Wait()
    fmt.Println(counter.Value())
}
```

Running `atomic.go` while checking for race conditions produces the next kind of output:

```
$ go run -race atomic.go
400
```

So, the atomic variable is modified by multiple goroutines without any issues.

The next subsection shows how to share memory using goroutines.

Sharing memory using goroutines

This subsection illustrates how to share data using **a dedicated goroutine**. Although shared memory is the traditional way that threads communicate with each other, Go comes with built-in synchronization features that allow a single goroutine to own a shared piece of data. This means that other goroutines must send messages to this single goroutine that owns the shared data, which prevents the corruption of the data. Such a goroutine is called a **monitor goroutine**. In Go terminology, this is *sharing by communicating instead of communicating by sharing*.

> Personally, I prefer to use a **monitor goroutine** instead of traditional shared memory techniques because the implementation with the monitor goroutine is safer, closer to the Go philosophy, and easier to understand.

The logic of the program can be found in the implementation of the `monitor()` function. More specifically, the `select` statement orchestrates the operation of the entire program. When you have a read request, the `read()` function attempts to read from the `readValue` channel, which is controlled by the `monitor()` function.

This returns the current value of the `value` variable. On the other hand, when you want to change the stored value, you call `set()`. This writes to the `writeValue` channel, which is also handled by the same `select` statement. As a result, no one can deal with the shared variable without using the `monitor()` function, which is in charge.

The code of `monitor.go` is as follows:

```
package main

import (
    "fmt"
    "math/rand"
    "os"
    "strconv"
    "sync"
    "time"
)

var readValue = make(chan int)
var writeValue = make(chan int)

func set(newValue int) {
    writeValue <- newValue
}
```

This function sends data to the `writeValue` channel.

```
func read() int {
    return <-readValue
}
```

When the `read()` function is called, it reads from the `readValue` channel—this reading happens inside the `monitor()` function.

```
func monitor() {
    var value int
    for {
        select {
        case newValue := <-writeValue:
            value = newValue
            fmt.Printf("%d ", value)
```

```
        case readValue <- value:
        }
    }
}
```

The monitor() function contains the logic of the program with the endless for loop and the select statement. The first case receives data from the writeValue channel, sets the value variable accordingly, and prints that new value. The second case sends the value of the value variable to the readValue channel. As all traffic goes through monitor() and its select block, there is no way to have a race condition because there is a single instance of monitor() running.

```
func main() {
    if len(os.Args) != 2 {
        fmt.Println("Please give an integer!")
        return
    }
    n, err := strconv.Atoi(os.Args[1])
    if err != nil {
        fmt.Println(err)
        return
    }

    fmt.Printf("Going to create %d random numbers.\n", n)
    rand.Seed(time.Now().Unix())
    go monitor()
```

It is important that the monitor() function is executed first because that is the goroutine that orchestrates the flow of the program.

```
    var wg sync.WaitGroup

    for r := 0; r < n; r++ {
        wg.Add(1)
        go func() {
            defer wg.Done()
            set(rand.Intn(10 * n))
        }()
    }
```

When the `for` loop ends, it means that we have created the desired number of random numbers.

```
    wg.Wait()
    fmt.Printf("\nLast value: %d\n", read())
}
```

Last, we wait for all `set()` goroutines to finish before printing the last random number.

Running `monitor.go` produces the following output:

```
$ go run monitor.go 10
Going to create 10 random numbers.
98 22 5 84 20 26 45 36 0 16
Last value: 16
```

So, 10 random numbers are created by 10 goroutines and all these goroutines send their output to the `monitor()` function that is also executed as a goroutine. Apart from receiving the results, the `monitor()` function prints them on screen, so all this output is generated by `monitor()`.

The next section discusses the go statement in more detail.

Closured variables and the go statement

In this section, we are going to talk about **closured variables**, which are variables inside closures, and the go statement. Notice that closured variables in goroutines are evaluated when the goroutine actually runs and when the go statement is executed in order to create a new goroutine. This means that closured variables are going to be replaced by their values when the Go scheduler decides to execute the relevant code. This is illustrated in the `main()` function of `goClosure.go`:

```
func main() {
    for i := 0; i <= 20; i++ {
        go func() {
            fmt.Print(i, " ")
        }()
    }
    time.Sleep(time.Second)
    fmt.Println()
}
```

Running `goClosure.go` produces the next output:

```
$ go run goClosure.go
3 7 21 21 21 21 21 21 21 21 21 21 21 21 21 21 21 21 21 21 21
```

The program mostly prints the number `21`, which is the last value of the variable of the `for` loop and not the other numbers. As `i` is a **closured variable**, it is **evaluated at the time of execution**. As the goroutines begin but wait for the Go scheduler to allow them to get executed, the `for` loop ends, so the value of `i` that is being used is `21`. Lastly, the same issue also applies to Go channels, so be careful.

Running `goClosure.go` with the Go race detector reveals the issue:

```
$ go run -race goClosure.go
2 ==================
WARNING: DATA RACE
Read at 0x00c00013a008 by goroutine 7:
  main.main.func1()
      /Users/mtsouk/ch07/goClosure.go:11 +0x3c

Previous write at 0x00c00013a008 by main goroutine:
  main.main()
      /Users/mtsouk/ch07/goClosure.go:9 +0xa4

Goroutine 7 (running) created at:
  main.main()
      /Users/mtsouk/ch07/goClosure.go:10 +0x7e
==================
2 3 5 5 7 8 9 10 9 11 12 13 14 17 18 18 18 19 20 21
Found 1 data race(s)
exit status 66
```

Now, let us correct `goClosure.go` and present it to you—the new name is `goClosureCorrect.go` and its `main()` function is as follows:

```
func main() {
    for i := 0; i <= 20; i++ {
        i := i
        go func() {
            fmt.Print(i, " ")
        }()
    }
```

This is one way of correcting the issue. The valid yet bizarre `i := i` statement **creates a new instance of the variable** for the goroutine that holds the correct value.

```
    time.Sleep(time.Second)
    fmt.Println()

    for i := 0; i <= 20; i++ {
        go func(x int) {
            fmt.Print(x, " ")
        }(i)
    }
```

This is a totally different way of correcting the race condition: pass the current value of `i` to the anonymous function as a parameter and everything is OK.

```
    time.Sleep(time.Second)
    fmt.Println()
}
```

Testing `goClosureCorrect.go` with the race detector generates the expected output:

```
$ go run -race goClosureCorrect.go
0 1 2 4 3 5 6 9 8 7 10 11 13 12 14 16 15 17 18 20 19
0 1 2 3 4 5 6 7 8 10 9 12 13 11 14 15 16 17 18 19 20
```

The next section presents the functionality of the `context` package.

The context package

The main purpose of the `context` package is to define the `Context` type and support *cancellation*. Yes, you heard that right; there are times when, for some reason, you want to abandon what you are doing. However, it would be very helpful to be able to include some extra information about your cancellation decisions. The `context` package allows you to do exactly that.

If you take a look at the source code of the `context` package, you will realize that its implementation is pretty simple—even the implementation of the `Context` type is pretty simple, yet the `context` package is very important.

The `Context` type is an interface with four methods named `Deadline()`, `Done()`, `Err()`, and `Value()`. The good news is that you do not need to implement all of these functions of the `Context` interface—you just need to modify a `Context` variable using methods such as `context.WithCancel()`, `context.WithDeadline()`, and `context.WithTimeout()`.

> All three of these functions return a derived `Context` (the child) and a `CancelFunc()` function. Calling the `CancelFunc()` function removes the parent's reference to the child and stops any associated timers. As a side effect, this means that the Go garbage collector is free to garbage collect the child goroutines that no longer have associated parent goroutines. For garbage collection to work correctly, the parent goroutine needs to keep a reference to each child goroutine. If a child goroutine ends without the parent knowing about it, then a memory leak occurs until the parent is canceled as well.

The example that follows showcases the use of the `context` package. The program contains four functions, including the `main()` function. Functions `f1()`, `f2()`, and `f3()` each require just one parameter, which is a time delay, because everything else they need is defined inside their function body. In this example, we use `context.Background()` to initialize an empty `Context`. The other function that can create an empty `Context` is `context.TODO()`, which is presented later on in this chapter.

```
package main

import (
    "context"
    "fmt"
    "os"
    "strconv"
    "time"
)

func f1(t int) {
    c1 := context.Background()
    c1, cancel := context.WithCancel(c1)
    defer cancel()
```

The `WithCancel()` method returns a copy of parent context with a new `Done` channel. Notice that the `cancel` variable, which is a function, is one of the return values of `context.CancelFunc()`. The `context.WithCancel()` function uses an existing `Context` and creates a child with cancellation. The `context.WithCancel()` function also returns a `Done` channel that can be closed, either when the `cancel()` function is called, as shown in the preceding code, or when the `Done` channel of the parent context is closed.

```
    go func() {
        time.Sleep(4 * time.Second)
        cancel()
```

```
    }()

    select {
    case <-c1.Done():
        fmt.Println("f1() Done:", c1.Err())
        return
    case r := <-time.After(time.Duration(t) * time.Second):
        fmt.Println("f1():", r)
    }
    return
}
```

The `f1()` function creates and executes a goroutine. The `time.Sleep()` call simulates the time it would take a real goroutine to do its job. In this case it is 4 seconds, but you can put any time period you want. If the `c1` context calls the `Done()` function in less than 4 seconds, the goroutine will not have enough time to finish.

```
func f2(t int) {
    c2 := context.Background()
    c2, cancel := context.WithTimeout(c2, time.Duration(t)*time.Second)
    defer cancel()
```

The `cancel` variable in `f2()` comes from `context.WithTimeout()`, which requires two parameters: a `Context` parameter and a `time.Duration` parameter. When the timeout period expires the `cancel()` function is called automatically.

```
    go func() {
        time.Sleep(4 * time.Second)
        cancel()
    }()

    select {
    case <-c2.Done():
        fmt.Println("f2() Done:", c2.Err())
        return
    case r := <-time.After(time.Duration(t) * time.Second):
        fmt.Println("f2():", r)
    }
    return
}

func f3(t int) {
```

```
    c3 := context.Background()
    deadline := time.Now().Add(time.Duration(2*t) * time.Second)
    c3, cancel := context.WithDeadline(c3, deadline)
    defer cancel()
```

The `cancel` variable in `f3()` comes from `context.WithDeadline()`. `context.WithDeadline()` requires two parameters: a `Context` variable and a time in the future that signifies the deadline of the operation. When the deadline passes, the `cancel()` function is called automatically.

```
    go func() {
        time.Sleep(4 * time.Second)
        cancel()
    }()

    select {
    case <-c3.Done():
        fmt.Println("f3() Done:", c3.Err())
        return
    case r := <-time.After(time.Duration(t) * time.Second):
        fmt.Println("f3():", r)
    }
    return
}
```

The logic of `f3()` is the same as in `f1()` and `f2()`—the `select` block orchestrates the process.

```
func main() {
    if len(os.Args) != 2 {
        fmt.Println("Need a delay!")
        return
    }

    delay, err := strconv.Atoi(os.Args[1])
    if err != nil {
        fmt.Println(err)
        return
    }
    fmt.Println("Delay:", delay)

    f1(delay)
```

```
    f2(delay)
    f3(delay)
}
```

The three functions are executed in sequence by the `main()` function.

Running `useContext.go` produces the next kind of output:

```
$ go run useContext.go 3
Delay: 3
f1(): 2021-03-18 13:10:24.739381 +0200 EET m=+3.001331808
f2(): 2021-03-18 13:10:27.742732 +0200 EET m=+6.004804424
f3(): 2021-03-18 13:10:30.742793 +0200 EET m=+9.004988055
```

The long lines of the output are the return values of `time.After()`, which show the times that `After()` sent the current time on the returned channel. All of them denote a normal operation of the program.

If you define a bigger delay, then the output is going to be similar to the following:

```
$ go run useContext.go 13
Delay: 13
f1() Done: context canceled
f2() Done: context canceled
f3() Done: context canceled
```

The point here is that the operation of the program is canceled when there are delays in its execution.

The next subsection shows a different use of the `context` package.

Using context as a key/value store

In this subsection, we pass values in a `Context` and use it as a key-value store. In this case, we do not pass values into contexts in order to provide further information about why they were canceled. The `keyVal.go` program illustrates the use of the `context.TODO()` function as well as the use of the `context.WithValue()` function.

All these and many more are found in `keyVal.go`, which is as follows.

```
package main

import (
    "context"
```

```
    "fmt"
)

type aKey string

func searchKey(ctx context.Context, k aKey) {
    v := ctx.Value(k)
    if v != nil {
        fmt.Println("found value:", v)
        return
    } else {
        fmt.Println("key not found:", k)
    }
}
```

The `searchKey()` function retrieves a value from a `Context` variable using `Value()` and checks whether that value exists or not.

```
func main() {
    myKey := aKey("mySecretValue")
    ctx := context.WithValue(context.Background(), myKey, "mySecret")
```

The `context.WithValue()` function that is used in `main()` offers a way to associate a value with a `Context`. The next two statements search an existing context (`ctx`) for the values of two keys.

```
    searchKey(ctx, myKey)
    searchKey(ctx, aKey("notThere"))
    emptyCtx := context.TODO()
```

This time we create a context using `context.TODO()` instead of `context.Background()`. Although both functions return a non-`nil`, empty `Context`, their purposes differ. You should never pass a `nil` context—use the `context.TODO()` function to create a suitable context. Additionally, use the `context.TODO()` function when you are not sure about the `Context` that you want to use. The `context.TODO()` function signifies that we intend to use an operation context, without being sure about it yet.

```
    searchKey(emptyCtx, aKey("notThere"))
}
```

Running `keyVal.go` creates the following output:

```
$ go run keyVal.go
found value: mySecret
key not found: notThere
key not found: notThere
```

The first call to `searchKey()` is successful whereas the next two calls cannot find the desired key in the context. So, contexts allow us to store key and value pairs and search for keys.

We are not completely done with `context` as the next chapter is going to use it to time-out HTTP interactions on the client side of the connection. The last section of this chapter discusses the `semaphore` package, which is not part of the Standard library.

The semaphore package

This last section of this chapter presents the `semaphore` package, which is provided by the Go team. A **semaphore** is a construct that can limit or control the access to a shared resource. As we are talking about Go, a semaphore can limit the access of goroutines to a shared resource but originally, semaphores were used for limiting access to threads. Semaphores can have *weights* that limit the number of threads or goroutines that can have access to a resource.

The process is supported via the `Acquire()` and `Release()` methods, which are defined as follows:

```
func (s *Weighted) Acquire(ctx context.Context, n int64) error
func (s *Weighted) Release(n int64)
```

The second parameter of `Acquire()` defines the weight of the semaphore.

As we are going an external package, we need to put the code inside `~/go/src` in order to use Go modules: `~/go/src/github.com/mactsouk/semaphore`. Now, let us present the code of `semaphore.go`, which shows an implementation of a *worker pool* using semaphores:

```
package main

import (
    "context"
    "fmt"
```

```
    "os"
    "strconv"
    "time"

    "golang.org/x/sync/semaphore"
)

var Workers = 4
```

This variable specifies the maximum number of goroutines that can be executed by this program.

```
var sem = semaphore.NewWeighted(int64(Workers))
```

This is where we define the semaphore with a weight identical to the maximum number of goroutines that can be executed concurrently. This means that no more than `Workers` goroutines can acquire the semaphore at the same time.

```
func worker(n int) int {
    square := n * n
    time.Sleep(time.Second)
    return square
}
```

The `worker()` function is run as part of a goroutine. However, as we are using a semaphore, there is no need to return the results to a channel.

```
func main() {
    if len(os.Args) != 2 {
        fmt.Println("Need #jobs!")
        return
    }

    nJobs, err := strconv.Atoi(os.Args[1])
    if err != nil {
        fmt.Println(err)
        return
    }
```

The previous code reads the number of jobs that we want to run.

```
    // Where to store the results
    var results = make([]int, nJobs)
```

```
    // Needed by Acquire()
    ctx := context.TODO()

    for i := range results {
        err = sem.Acquire(ctx, 1)
        if err != nil {
            fmt.Println("Cannot acquire semaphore:", err)
            break
        }
```

In this part, we try to acquire the semaphore as many times as the number of jobs defined by `nJobs`. If `nJobs` is bigger than `Workers`, then the `Acquire()` call is going to block and wait for `Release()` calls in order to unblock.

```
        go func(i int) {
            defer sem.Release(1)
            temp := worker(i)
            results[i] = temp
        }(i)
    }
```

This is where we run the goroutines that do the job and write the results to the `results` slice. As each goroutine writes to a different slice element, there are not any race conditions.

```
    err = sem.Acquire(ctx, int64(Workers))
    if err != nil {
        fmt.Println(err)
    }
```

This is a clever trick: we acquire all of the tokens so that the `sem.Acquire()` call blocks until all workers/goroutines have finished. This is similar in functionality to a `Wait()` call.

```
    for k, v := range results {
        fmt.Println(k, "->", v)
    }
}
```

The last part of the program is about printing the results. After writing the code, we need to run the next commands in order to get the required Go modules:

```
$ go mod init
$ go mod tidy
$ mod download golang.org/x/sync
```

Apart from the first command, these commands were indicated by the output of `go mod init`, so you do not have to remember anything.

Lastly, running `semaphore.go` produces the next output:

```
$ go run semaphore.go 6
0 -> 0
1 -> 1
2 -> 4
3 -> 9
4 -> 16
5 -> 25
```

Each line in the output shows the input value and the output value separated by `->`. The use of the semaphore keeps things in order.

Exercises

- Try to implement a concurrent version of `wc(1)` that uses a buffered channel.
- Try to implement a concurrent version of `wc(1)` that uses shared memory.
- Try to implement a concurrent version of `wc(1)` that uses semaphores.
- Try to implement a concurrent version of `wc(1)` that saves its output to a file.
- Modify `wPools.go` so that each worker implements the functionality of `wc(1)`.

Summary

This important chapter was about Go concurrency, goroutines, channels, the `select` keyword, shared memory, and mutexes, as well as timing out goroutines and the use of the `context` package. All this knowledge is going to allow you to write powerful concurrent Go applications. Feel free to experiment with the concepts and the examples of this chapter to better understand goroutines, channels, and shared memory.

The next chapter is all about web services and working with the HTTP protocol in Go. Among other things, we are going to convert the phone book application into a web service.

Additional resources

- The documentation page of `sync` is at `https://golang.org/pkg/sync/`
- Learn about `semaphore` at `https://pkg.go.dev/golang.org/x/sync/semaphore`
- Learn more about the Go scheduler by reading a series of posts starting with `https://www.ardanlabs.com/blog/2018/08/scheduling-in-go-part1.html`
- The implementation of the Go scheduler: `https://golang.org/src/runtime/proc.go`

8

Building Web Services

The core subject of this chapter is working with HTTP using the `net/http` package—remember that all web services require a web server in order to operate. Additionally, in this chapter, we are going to convert the phone book application into a web application that accepts HTTP connections and create a command-line client to work with it. Lastly, we'll illustrate how to create an **FTP** (**File Transfer Protocol**) server and how to export metrics from Go applications to Prometheus and work with the `runtime/metrics` package to get implementation-defined metrics exported by the Go runtime.

In more detail, this chapter covers:

- The `net/http` package
- Creating a web server
- Updating the phone book application
- Exposing metrics to Prometheus
- Developing web clients
- Creating a client for the phone book service
- Creating file servers
- Timing out HTTP connections

The net/http package

The `net/http` package offers functions that allow you to develop web servers and clients. For example, `http.Get()` and `http.NewRequest()` are used by clients for making HTTP requests, whereas `http.ListenAndServe()` is used for starting web servers by specifying the IP address and the TCP port the server listens to. Additionally, `http.HandleFunc()` defines supported URLs as well as the functions that are going to handle these URLs.

The next three subsections describe three important data structures of the `net/http` package—you can use these descriptions as a reference while reading this chapter.

The http.Response type

The `http.Response` structure embodies the response from an HTTP request—both `http.Client` and `http.Transport` return `http.Response` values once the response headers have been received. Its definition can be found at `https://golang.org/src/net/http/response.go`:

```
type Response struct {
    Status     string // e.g. "200 OK"
    StatusCode int    // e.g. 200
    Proto      string // e.g. "HTTP/1.0"
    ProtoMajor int    // e.g. 1
    ProtoMinor int    // e.g. 0
    Header Header
    Body io.ReadCloser
    ContentLength int64
    TransferEncoding []string
    Close bool
    Uncompressed bool
    Trailer Header
    Request *Request
    TLS *tls.ConnectionState
}
```

You do not have to use all the structure fields, but it is good to know that they exist. However, some of them, such as `Status`, `StatusCode`, and `Body`, are more important than others. The Go source file, as well as the output of `go doc http.Response`, contains more information about the purpose of each field, which is also the case with most `struct` data types found in the standard Go library.

The http.Request type

The `http.Request` structure represents an HTTP request as constructed by a client in order to be sent or received by an HTTP server. The public fields of `http.Request` are as follows:

```
type Request struct {
     Method string
     URL *url.URL
     Proto  string
     ProtoMajor int
     ProtoMinor int
     Header Header
     Body io.ReadCloser
     GetBody func() (io.ReadCloser, error)
     ContentLength int64
     TransferEncoding []string
     Close bool
     Host string
     Form url.Values
     PostForm url.Values
     MultipartForm *multipart.Form
     Trailer Header
     RemoteAddr string
     RequestURI string
     TLS *tls.ConnectionState
     Cancel <-chan struct{}
     Response *Response
}
```

The `Body` field holds the body of the request. After reading the body of a request, you are allowed to call `GetBody()`, which returns a new copy of the body—this is optional.

Let us now present the `http.Transport` structure.

The http.Transport type

The definition of `http.Transport`, which gives you more control over your HTTP connections, is fairly long and complex:

```
type Transport struct {
     Proxy func(*Request) (*url.URL, error)
```

```
    DialContext func(ctx context.Context, network, addr string) (net.
Conn, error)
    Dial func(network, addr string) (net.Conn, error)
    DialTLSContext func(ctx context.Context, network, addr string)
(net.Conn, error)
    DialTLS func(network, addr string) (net.Conn, error)
    TLSClientConfig *tls.Config
    TLSHandshakeTimeout time.Duration
    DisableKeepAlives bool
    DisableCompression bool
    MaxIdleConns int
    MaxIdleConnsPerHost int
    MaxConnsPerHost int
    IdleConnTimeout time.Duration
    ResponseHeaderTimeout time.Duration
    ExpectContinueTimeout time.Duration
    TLSNextProto map[string]func(authority string, c *tls.Conn)
RoundTripper
    ProxyConnectHeader Header
    GetProxyConnectHeader func(ctx context.Context, proxyURL *url.URL,
target string) (Header, error)
    MaxResponseHeaderBytes int64
    WriteBufferSize int
    ReadBufferSize int
    ForceAttemptHTTP2 bool
}
```

Note that `http.Transport` is pretty low-level, whereas `http.Client`, which is also used in this chapter, implements a high-level HTTP client—each `http.Client` contains a `Transport` field. If its value is `nil`, then `DefaultTransport` is used. You do not need to use `http.Transport` in all of your programs and you are not required to deal with all of its fields each time you use it. If you want to learn more about `DefaultTransport`, type `go doc http.DefaultTransport`.

Let us now learn how to develop a web server.

Creating a web server

This section presents a simple web server developed in Go in order to better understand the principles behind such applications.

> Although a web server programmed in Go can do many things efficiently and securely, if what you really need is a powerful web server that supports modules, multiple websites, and virtual hosts, then you would be better off using a web server such as **Apache**, **Nginx**, or **Caddy** that is written in Go.

You might ask why the presented web server uses HTTP instead of **secure HTTP (HTTPS)**. The answer to this question is simple: most Go web servers are deployed as Docker images and are hidden behind web servers such as Caddy and Nginx that provide the secure HTTP operation part using the appropriate security credentials. It does not make any sense to use the secure HTTP protocol along with the required security credentials without knowing how and under which domain name the application is going to be deployed. This is a common practice in microservices as well as regular web applications that are deployed in Docker images.

The `net/http` package offers functions and data types that allow you to develop powerful web servers and clients. The `http.Set()` and `http.Get()` methods can be used to make HTTP and HTTPS requests, whereas `http.ListenAndServe()` is used for creating web servers given the user-specified handler function or functions that handle incoming requests. As most web services require support for multiple endpoints, you end up needing multiple discrete functions for handling incoming requests, which also leads to the better design of your services.

The simplest way to define the supported endpoints, as well as the handler function that responds to each client request, is with the use of `http.HandleFunc()`, which can be called multiple times.

After this quick and somewhat theoretical introduction, it is time to begin talking about more practical topics, beginning with the implementation of a simple web server as illustrated in `wwwServer.go`:

```
package main

import (
    "fmt"
    "net/http"
    "os"
    "time"
)
```

```
func myHandler(w http.ResponseWriter, r *http.Request) {
    fmt.Fprintf(w, "Serving: %s\n", r.URL.Path)
    fmt.Printf("Served: %s\n", r.Host)
}
```

This is a handler function that sends a message back to the client using the `w http.ResponseWriter`, which is also an interface that implements `io.Writer` and is used for sending the server response.

```
func timeHandler(w http.ResponseWriter, r *http.Request) {
    t := time.Now().Format(time.RFC1123)
    Body := "The current time is:"
    fmt.Fprintf(w, "<h1 align=\"center\">%s</h1>", Body)
    fmt.Fprintf(w, "<h2 align=\"center\">%s</h2>\n", t)

    fmt.Fprintf(w, "Serving: %s\n", r.URL.Path)
    fmt.Printf("Served time for: %s\n", r.Host)
}
```

This is another handler function called `timeHandler` that returns back the current time in HTML format. All `fmt.Fprintf()` calls send data back to the HTTP client whereas the output of `fmt.Printf()` is printed on the terminal the web server runs on. The first argument of `fmt.Fprintf()` is the `w http.ResponseWriter`, which implements `io.Writer` and therefore can accept data.

```
func main() {
    PORT := ":8001"
```

This is where you define the port number your web server listens to.

```
    arguments := os.Args
    if len(arguments) != 1 {
        PORT = ":" + arguments[1]
    }
    fmt.Println("Using port number: ", PORT)
```

If you do not want to use the predefined port number (`8001`), then you should provide `wwwServer.go` with your own port number as a command-line argument.

```
    http.HandleFunc("/time", timeHandler)
    http.HandleFunc("/", myHandler)
```

So, the web server supports the `/time` URL as well as `/`. The `/` path **matches every URL** not matched by other handlers. The fact that we associate `myHandler()` with `/` makes `myHandler()` the default handler function.

```
    err := http.ListenAndServe(PORT, nil)
    if err != nil {
        fmt.Println(err)
        return
    }
}
```

The `http.ListenAndServe()` call begins the HTTP server using the predefined port number. As there is no hostname given in the `PORT` string, the web server is going to listen to all available network interfaces. The port number and the hostname should be separated with a colon (`:`), which should be there even if there is no hostname—in that case the server listens to all available network interfaces and, therefore, all supported hostnames. This is the reason that the value of `PORT` is `:8001` instead of just `8001`.

Part of the `net/http` package is the `ServeMux` type (`go doc http.ServeMux`), which is an **HTTP request multiplexer** that provides a slightly different way of defining handler functions and endpoints than the default one, which is used in `wwwServer.go`. So, if we do not create and configure our own `ServeMux` variable, then `http.HandleFunc()` uses `DefaultServeMux`, which is the default `ServeMux`. So, in this case we are going to implement the web service using the **default Go router**—this is the reason that the second parameter of `http.ListenAndServe()` is `nil`.

Running `wwwServer.go` and interacting with it using `curl(1)` produces the next output:

```
$ go run wwwServer.go
Using port number:  :8001
Served: localhost:8001
Served time for: localhost:8001
Served: localhost:8001
```

Note that as `wwwServer.go` does not terminate automatically, you need to stop it on your own.

On the `curl(1)` side, the interaction looks as follows:

```
$ curl localhost:8001
Serving: /
```

In this first case, we visit the / path of the web server and we are being served by `myHandler()`.

```
$ curl localhost:8001/time
<h1 align="center">The current time is:</h1><h2 align="center">Mon, 29 Mar 2021 08:26:27 EEST</h2>
Serving: /time
```

In this case we visit `/time` and we get HTML output back from `timeHandler()`.

```
$ curl localhost:8001/doesNotExist
Serving: /doesNotExist
```

In this last case, we visit `/doesNotExist`, which does not exist. As this cannot be matched by any other path, it is served by the default handler, which is the `myHandler()` function.

The next section is about making the phone book application a web application!

Updating the phone book application

This time the phone book application is going to work as a web service. The two main tasks that need to be performed are defining the API along with the endpoints and implementing the API. A third task that needs to be determined concerns **data exchange** between the application server and its clients. There exist four main approaches regarding data exchange:

- Using plain text
- Using HTML
- Using JSON
- Using a hybrid approach that combines plain text and JSON data

As JSON is explored in *Chapter 10, Working with REST APIs*, and HTML might not be the best option for a service because you need to separate the data from the HTML tags and parse the data, we are going to use the first approach. Therefore, the service is going to work with **plain text data**. We begin by defining the API that supports the operation of the phone book application.

Defining the API

The API has support for the following URLs:

- `/list`: This lists all available entries.
- `/insert/name/surname/telephone/`: This inserts a new entry. Later on, we are going to see how to extract the desired information from a URL that contains user data.
- `/delete/telephone/`: This deletes an entry based on the value of `telephone`.
- `/search/telephone/`: This searches for an entry based on the value of `telephone`.
- `/status`: This is an extra URL that returns the number of entries in the phone book.

> The list of endpoints does not follow standard REST conventions—all these are going to be presented in *Chapter 10, Working with REST APIs*.

This time we not using the default Go router, which means that we define and configure our own `http.NewServeMux()` variable. This changes the way we provide handler functions: a handler function with the `func(http.ResponseWriter, *http.Request)` signature has to be converted into an `http.HandlerFunc` **type** and be used by the `ServeMux` type and its own `Handle()` method. Therefore, when using a different `ServeMux` than the default one, we should do that conversion explicitly by calling `http.HandlerFunc()`, which makes the `http.HandlerFunc` **type** act as an **adapter** that allows the use of ordinary functions as HTTP handlers provided that they have the required signature. This is not a problem when using the default Go router (`DefaultServeMux`) because the `http.HandleFunc()` **function** does that conversion automatically and internally.

> To make things clearer, the `http.HandlerFunc` **type** has support for a **method** named `HandlerFunc()`—both the type and method are defined in the `http` package. The similarly named the `http.HandleFunc()` **function** (without an `r`) is used with the default Go router.

As an example, for the `/time` endpoint and the `timeHandler()` handler function, you should call `mux.Handle()` as `mux.Handle("/time", http.HandlerFunc(timeHandler))`. If you were using `http.HandleFunc()` and as a consequence `DefaultServeMux`, then you should have called `http.HandleFunc("/time", timeHandler)` instead.

The subject of the next subsection is the implementation of the HTTP endpoints.

Implementing the handlers

The new version of the phone book is going to be created on a dedicated GitHub repository for storing and sharing it: `https://github.com/mactsouk/www-phone`. After creating the repository, you need to do the following:

```
$ cd ~/go/src/github.com/mactsouk # Replace with your own path
$ git clone git@github.com:mactsouk/www-phone.git
$ cd www-phone
$ touch handlers.go
$ touch www-phone.go
```

The `www-phone.go` file holds the code that defines the operation of the web server. Usually, handlers are put in a separate package, but for reasons of simplicity, we decided to put handlers in a separate file within the same package named `handlers.go`. The contents of the `handlers.go` file, which contains all functionality related to the serving of the clients, are the following:

```
package main

import (
    "fmt"
    "log"
    "net/http"
    "strings"
)
```

All required packages for `handlers.go` are imported even if some of them are already imported by `www-phone.go`. Note that the name of the package is `main`, which is also the case for `www-phone.go`.

```
const PORT = ":1234"
```

This is the default port number the HTTP server listens to.

```
func defaultHandler(w http.ResponseWriter, r *http.Request) {
    log.Println("Serving:", r.URL.Path, "from", r.Host)
    w.WriteHeader(http.StatusOK)
    Body := "Thanks for visiting!\n"
    fmt.Fprintf(w, "%s", Body)
}
```

This is the default handler, which serves all requests that are not a match for any of the other handlers.

```
func deleteHandler(w http.ResponseWriter, r *http.Request) {
    // Get telephone
    paramStr := strings.Split(r.URL.Path, "/")
```

This is the handler function for the `/delete` path, which begins by splitting the URL in order to read the desired information.

```
    fmt.Println("Path:", paramStr)
    if len(paramStr) < 3 {
        w.WriteHeader(http.StatusNotFound)
        fmt.Fprintln(w, "Not found: "+r.URL.Path)
        return
    }
```

If we do not have enough parameters, we should send an error message back to the client with the desired HTTP code, which in this case is `http.StatusNotFound`. You can use any HTTP code you want as long as it makes sense. The `WriteHeader()` method sends back a header with the provided status code before writing the body of the response.

```
    log.Println("Serving:", r.URL.Path, "from", r.Host)
```

This is where the HTTP server sends data to log files—this mainly happens for debugging reasons.

```
    telephone := paramStr[2]
```

As the delete process is based on the telephone number, all that is required is a valid telephone number. This is where the parameter is read after splitting the provided URL.

```
	err := deleteEntry(telephone)
	if err != nil {
		fmt.Println(err)
		Body := err.Error() + "\n"
		w.WriteHeader(http.StatusNotFound)
		fmt.Fprintf(w, "%s", Body)
		return
	}
```

Once we have a telephone number, we call `deleteEntry()` in order to delete it. The return value of `deleteEntry()` determines the result of the operation and, therefore, the response to the client.

```
	Body := telephone + " deleted!\n"
	w.WriteHeader(http.StatusOK)
	fmt.Fprintf(w, "%s", Body)
}
```

At this point, we know that the delete operation was successful so we send a proper message to the client as well as the `http.StatusOK` status code. Type `go doc http.StatusOK` for the list of codes.

```
func listHandler(w http.ResponseWriter, r *http.Request) {
	log.Println("Serving:", r.URL.Path, "from", r.Host)
	w.WriteHeader(http.StatusOK)
	Body := list()
	fmt.Fprintf(w, "%s", Body)
}
```

The `list()` helper function that is used in the `/list` path cannot fail. Therefore, `http.StatusOK` is always returned when serving `/list`. However, sometimes the return value of `list()` can be empty.

```
func statusHandler(w http.ResponseWriter, r *http.Request) {
	log.Println("Serving:", r.URL.Path, "from", r.Host)
	w.WriteHeader(http.StatusOK)
	Body := fmt.Sprintf("Total entries: %d\n", len(data))
	fmt.Fprintf(w, "%s", Body)
}
```

The preceding code defines the handler function for the `/status` URL. It just returns information about the total number of entries found in the phone book. It can be used for verifying that the web service works fine.

```
func insertHandler(w http.ResponseWriter, r *http.Request) {
	// Split URL
	paramStr := strings.Split(r.URL.Path, "/")
	fmt.Println("Path:", paramStr)
```

As happened with `delete`, we need to split the given URL in order to extract the information. In this case, we need three elements as we are trying to insert a new entry into the phone book application.

```
	if len(paramStr) < 5 {
		w.WriteHeader(http.StatusNotFound)
		fmt.Fprintln(w, "Not enough arguments: "+r.URL.Path)
		return
	}
```

Needing to extract three elements from the URL means that we require `paramStr` to have at least four elements in it, hence the `len(paramStr) < 5` condition.

```
	name := paramStr[2]
	surname := paramStr[3]
	tel := paramStr[4]

	t := strings.ReplaceAll(tel, "-", "")
	if !matchTel(t) {
		fmt.Println("Not a valid telephone number:", tel)
		return
	}
```

In the previous part, we get the desired data and make sure that the telephone number contains digits only—this happens with the use of the `matchTel()` helper function.

```
	temp := &Entry{Name: name, Surname: surname, Tel: t}
	err := insert(temp)
```

As the `insert()` helper function requires an `*Entry` value, we create one before calling it.

```
	if err != nil {
		w.WriteHeader(http.StatusNotModified)
```

```
        Body := "Failed to add record\n"
        fmt.Fprintf(w, "%s", Body)
    } else {
        log.Println("Serving:", r.URL.Path, "from", r.Host)
        Body := "New record added successfully\n"
        w.WriteHeader(http.StatusOK)
        fmt.Fprintf(w, "%s", Body)
    }

    log.Println("Serving:", r.URL.Path, "from", r.Host)
}
```

This is the end of the handler for `/insert`. The last part of the implementation of `insertHandler()` deals with the return value of `insert()`. If there was not an error, then `http.StatusOK` is returned to the client. In the opposite case, `http.StatusNotModified` is returned to signify that there was not a change in the phone book. It is the job of the client to examine the status code of the interaction but it is the job of the server to send an appropriate status code back to the client.

```
func searchHandler(w http.ResponseWriter, r *http.Request) {
    // Get Search value from URL
    paramStr := strings.Split(r.URL.Path, "/")
    fmt.Println("Path:", paramStr)

    if len(paramStr) < 3 {
        w.WriteHeader(http.StatusNotFound)
        fmt.Fprintln(w, "Not found: "+r.URL.Path)
        return
    }

    var Body string
    telephone := paramStr[2]
```

At this point, we extract the telephone number from the URL as we did with `/delete`.

```
    t := search(telephone)
    if t == nil {
        w.WriteHeader(http.StatusNotFound)
        Body = "Could not be found: " + telephone + "\n"
    } else {
        w.WriteHeader(http.StatusOK)
```

```
        Body = t.Name + " " + t.Surname + " " + t.Tel + "\n"
    }

    fmt.Println("Serving:", r.URL.Path, "from", r.Host)
    fmt.Fprintf(w, "%s", Body)
}
```

The last function of `handlers.go` ends here and is about the `/search` endpoint. The `search()` helper function checks whether the given input exists in the phone book records or not and acts accordingly. Additionally, the implementation of the `main()` function, which can be found in `www-phone.go`, is the following:

```
func main() {
    err := readCSVFile(CSVFILE)
    if err != nil {
        fmt.Println(err)
        return
    }

    err = createIndex()
    if err != nil {
        fmt.Println("Cannot create index.")
        return
    }
```

This first part of `main()` has to do with the initialization of the phone book application.

```
    mux := http.NewServeMux()
    s := &http.Server{
        Addr:         PORT,
        Handler:      mux,
        IdleTimeout:  10 * time.Second,
        ReadTimeout:  time.Second,
        WriteTimeout: time.Second,
    }
```

Here, we store the parameters of the HTTP server in the `http.Server` structure and use our own `http.NewServeMux()` instead of the default one.

```
    mux.Handle("/list", http.HandlerFunc(listHandler))
    mux.Handle("/insert/", http.HandlerFunc(insertHandler))
    mux.Handle("/insert", http.HandlerFunc(insertHandler))
```

```
    mux.Handle("/search", http.HandlerFunc(searchHandler))
    mux.Handle("/search/", http.HandlerFunc(searchHandler))
    mux.Handle("/delete/", http.HandlerFunc(deleteHandler))
    mux.Handle("/status", http.HandlerFunc(statusHandler))
    mux.Handle("/", http.HandlerFunc(defaultHandler))
```

This is the list of the supported URLs. Note that `/search` and `/search/` are both handled by the same handler function even though `/search` is going to fail as it does not include the required argument. On the other hand, `/delete/` is handled in a special way—this is going to be shown when testing the application. As we are using `http.NewServeMux()` and not the default Go router, we need to use `http.HandlerFunc()` when defining the handler functions.

```
    fmt.Println("Ready to serve at", PORT)
    err = s.ListenAndServe()
    if err != nil {
        fmt.Println(err)
        return
    }
}
```

The `ListenAndServe()` method starts the HTTP server using the parameters defined previously in the `http.Server` structure. The rest of `www-phone.go` contains helper functions related to the operation of the phone book. Note that it is important to save and update the contents of the phone book application as often as possible because this is a live application, and you might lose data if it crashes.

The next command allows you to execute the application—you need to provide both files in `go run`:

```
$ go run www-phone.go handlers.go
Ready to serve at :1234
2021/03/29 17:13:49 Serving: /list from localhost:1234
2021/03/29 17:13:53 Serving: /status from localhost:1234
Path: [ search 2109416471]
Serving: /search/2109416471 from localhost:1234
Path: [ search]
2021/03/29 17:28:34 Serving: /list from localhost:1234
Path: [ search 2101112223]
Serving: /search/2101112223 from localhost:1234
Path: [ delete 2109416471]
2021/03/29 17:29:24 Serving: /delete/2109416471 from localhost:1234
Path: [ insert Mike Tsoukalos 2109416471]
```

```
2021/03/29 17:29:56 Serving: /insert/Mike/Tsoukalos/2109416471 from
localhost:1234
2021/03/29 17:29:56 Serving: /insert/Mike/Tsoukalos/2109416471 from
localhost:1234
Path: [ insert Mike Tsoukalos 2109416471]
2021/03/29 17:30:18 Serving: /insert/Mike/Tsoukalos/2109416471 from
localhost:1234
```

On the client side, which is `curl(1)`, we have the next output:

```
$ curl localhost:1234/list
Dimitris Tsoukalos 2101112223
Jane Doe 0800123456
Mike Tsoukalos 2109416471
```

Here, we get all entries from the phone book application by visiting `/list`.

```
$ curl localhost:1234/status
Total entries: 3
```

Next, we visit `/status` and get back the expected output.

```
$ curl localhost:1234/search/2109416471
Mike Tsoukalos 2109416471
```

The previous command searches for an existing phone number—the server responds with its full record.

```
$ curl localhost:1234/delete/2109416471
2109416471 deleted!
```

The previous output shows that we have deleted the record with telephone number `2109416471`. In REST, this requires a `DELETE` method, but for reasons of simplicity we leave the details for *Chapter 10, Working with REST APIs*.

Now, let us try and visit `/delete` instead of `/delete/`:

```
$ curl localhost:1234/delete
<a href="/delete/">Moved Permanently</a>.
```

The presented message was generated by the Go router and tells us that we should try `/delete/` instead as `/delete` was moved permanently. This is the kind of message that we get by not specifically defining both `/delete` and `/delete/` in the routes.

Now, let us insert a new record:

```
$ curl localhost:1234/insert/Mike/Tsoukalos/2109416471
New record added successfully
```

In REST, this requires a `POST` method, but again, we will leave that for *Chapter 10, Working with REST APIs*.

If we try to insert the same record again, the response is going to be as follows:

```
$ curl localhost:1234/insert/Mike/Tsoukalos/2109416471
Failed to add record
```

Everything looks like it is working OK. We can now put the phone application online and interact with it using multiple HTTP requests as the `http` package uses multiple goroutines for interacting with clients—in practice, this means that the phone book application **runs concurrently**!

Later in this chapter we are going to create a command-line client for the phone book server. Additionally, *Chapter 11, Code Testing and Profiling*, shows how to test your code.

The next section shows how to expose metrics to Prometheus and how to build Docker images for server applications.

Exposing metrics to Prometheus

Imagine that you have an application that writes files to disk and you want to get metrics for that application to better understand how the writing of multiple files has an effect on the general performance—you need to gather performance data for understanding the behavior of your application. Although the presented application uses the *gauge* type of metric only because it is what is appropriate for the information that is sent to Prometheus, Prometheus accepts many types of data. The list of supported data types for metrics is the following:

- *Counter*: This is a cumulative value that is used for representing increasing counters—the value of a counter can stay the same, go up, or be reset to zero but cannot decrease. Counters are usually used for representing cumulative values such as the number of requests served so far, the total number of errors, etc.
- *Gauge*: This is a single numerical value that is allowed to increase or decrease. Gauges are usually used for representing values that can go up or down such as the number of requests, time durations, etc.

- *Histogram*: A histogram is used for sampling observations and creating counts and buckets. Histograms are usually used for counting request durations, response times, etc.
- *Summary*: A summary is like a histogram but can also calculate quantiles over sliding windows that work with times.

Both histograms and summaries are useful and handy for performing statistical calculations and properties. Usually, a counter or a gauge is all that you need for storing your system metrics.

This section shows how you can collect and expose a system to Prometheus. For reasons of simplicity, the presented application is going to generate random values. We begin by explaining the use of the `runtime/metrics` package, which provides Go runtime-related metrics.

The runtime/metrics package

The `runtime/metrics` package makes metrics exported by the Go runtime available to the developer. Each metric name is specified by a path. As an example, the number of live goroutines is accessed as `/sched/goroutines:goroutines`. However, if you want to collect all available metrics, you should use `metrics.All()`—this saves you from having to write lots of code in order to collect all metrics manually.

Metrics are saved using the `metrics.Sample` data type. The definition of the `metrics.Sample` data structure is as follows:

```
type Sample struct {
    Name string
    Value Value
}
```

The `Name` value must correspond to the name of one of the metric descriptions returned by `metrics.All()`. If you already know the metric description, there is no need to use `metrics.All()`.

The use of the `runtime/metrics` package is illustrated in `metrics.go`. The presented code gets the value of `/sched/goroutines:goroutines` and prints it on screen:

```
package main

import (
    "fmt"
    "runtime/metrics"
```

```
	"sync"
	"time"
)

func main() {
	const nGo = "/sched/goroutines:goroutines"
```

The nGo variable holds the path of the metric we want to collect.

```
	// A slice for getting metric samples
	getMetric := make([]metrics.Sample, 1)
	getMetric[0].Name = nGo
```

After that we create a slice of type metrics.Sample in order to keep the metric value. The initial size of the slice is 1 because we are only collecting values for a single metric. We set the Name value to /sched/goroutines:goroutines as stored in nGo.

```
	var wg sync.WaitGroup
	for i := 0; i < 3; i++ {
		wg.Add(1)
		go func() {
			defer wg.Done()
			time.Sleep(4 * time.Second)
		}()
```

Here we manually create three goroutines to have relevant data to collect.

```
		// Get actual data
		metrics.Read(getMetric)
		if getMetric[0].Value.Kind() == metrics.KindBad {
			fmt.Printf("metric %q no longer supported\n", nGo)
		}
```

The metrics.Read() function collects the desired metrics based on the data in the getMetric slice.

```
		mVal := getMetric[0].Value.Uint64()
		fmt.Printf("Number of goroutines: %d\n", mVal)
	}
```

After reading the desired metric, we convert it into a numeric value (unsigned int64 here) in order to use it in our program.

```
    wg.Wait()

    metrics.Read(getMetric)
    mVal := getMetric[0].Value.Uint64()
    fmt.Printf("Before exiting: %d\n", mVal)
}
```

The last lines of the code verify that after all goroutines have finished, the value of the metric is going to be `1`, which is the goroutine used for running the `main()` function.

Running `metrics.go` produces the next output:

```
$ go run metrics.go
Number of goroutines: 2
Number of goroutines: 3
Number of goroutines: 4
Before exiting: 1
```

We have created 3 goroutines and we already have a goroutine for running the `main()` function. Therefore, the maximum number of goroutines is indeed 4.

The subsections that follow illustrate how to make any metric you collect available to Prometheus.

Exposing metrics

Collecting metrics is a totally different task from exposing them for Prometheus to collect them. This subsection shows how to make the metrics available for collection.

The code of `samplePro.go` is as follows:

```
package main

import (
    "fmt"
    "net/http"

    "math/rand"
    "time"

    "github.com/prometheus/client_golang/prometheus"
    "github.com/prometheus/client_golang/prometheus/promhttp"
)
```

We need to use two external packages for communicating with Prometheus.

```
var PORT = ":1234"

var counter = prometheus.NewCounter(
    prometheus.CounterOpts{
        Namespace: "mtsouk",
        Name:      "my_counter",
        Help:      "This is my counter",
    })
```

This is how we define a new `counter` variable and specify the desired options. The `Namespace` field is very important as it allows you to group metrics in sets.

```
var gauge = prometheus.NewGauge(
    prometheus.GaugeOpts{
        Namespace: "mtsouk",
        Name:      "my_gauge",
        Help:      "This is my gauge",
    })
```

This is how we define a new `gauge` variable and specify the desired options.

```
var histogram = prometheus.NewHistogram(
    prometheus.HistogramOpts{
        Namespace: "mtsouk",
        Name:      "my_histogram",
        Help:      "This is my histogram",
    })
```

This is how we define a new `histogram` variable and specify the desired options.

```
var summary = prometheus.NewSummary(
    prometheus.SummaryOpts{
        Namespace: "mtsouk",
        Name:      "my_summary",
        Help:      "This is my summary",
    })
```

This is how we define a new `summary` variable and specify the desired options. However, as you are going to see, defining a metric variable is not enough. You also need to register it.

```
func main() {
    rand.Seed(time.Now().Unix())

    prometheus.MustRegister(counter)
    prometheus.MustRegister(gauge)
    prometheus.MustRegister(histogram)
    prometheus.MustRegister(summary)
```

In these four statements, you register the four metric variables. Now Prometheus knows about them.

```
    go func() {
        for {
            counter.Add(rand.Float64() * 5)
            gauge.Add(rand.Float64()*15 - 5)
            histogram.Observe(rand.Float64() * 10)
            summary.Observe(rand.Float64() * 10)
            time.Sleep(2 * time.Second)
        }
    }()
```

This goroutine runs for as long as the web server runs with the help of the endless `for` loop. In this goroutine, the metrics are updated every 2 seconds due to the use of the `time.Sleep(2 * time.Second)` statement—in this case using random values.

```
    http.Handle("/metrics", promhttp.Handler())
    fmt.Println("Listening to port", PORT)
    fmt.Println(http.ListenAndServe(PORT, nil))
}
```

As you already know, each URL is handled by a handler function that you usually implement on your own. However, in this case we are using the `promhttp.Handler()` handler function that comes with the `github.com/prometheus/client_golang/prometheus/promhttp` package—this saves us from having to write our own code. However, we still need to register the `promhttp.Handler()` handler function using `http.Handle()` before we start the web server. Note that the metrics are found under the `/metrics` path—Prometheus knows how to find that.

With `samplePro.go` running, getting the list of metrics that belong to the `mtsouk` namespace is as simple as running the next `curl(1)` command:

```
$ curl localhost:1234/metrics --silent | grep mtsouk
# HELP mtsouk_my_counter This is my counter
```

```
# TYPE mtsouk_my_counter counter
mtsouk_my_counter 19.948239343027772
```

This is the output from a `counter` variable. If the `| grep mtsouk` part is omitted, then you are going to get the list of all available metrics.

```
# HELP mtsouk_my_gauge This is my gauge
# TYPE mtsouk_my_gauge gauge
mtsouk_my_gauge 29.335329668135287
```

This is the output from a gauge variable.

```
# HELP mtsouk_my_histogram This is my histogram
# TYPE mtsouk_my_histogram histogram
mtsouk_my_histogram_bucket{le="0.005"} 0
mtsouk_my_histogram_bucket{le="0.01"} 0
mtsouk_my_histogram_bucket{le="0.025"} 0
. . .
mtsouk_my_histogram_bucket{le="5"} 4
mtsouk_my_histogram_bucket{le="10"} 9
mtsouk_my_histogram_bucket{le="+Inf"} 9
mtsouk_my_histogram_sum 44.52262035556937
mtsouk_my_histogram_count 9
```

This is the output from a `histogram` variable. Histograms contain *buckets*, hence the large number of output lines.

```
# HELP mtsouk_my_summary This is my summary
# TYPE mtsouk_my_summary summary
mtsouk_my_summary_sum 19.407554729772105
mtsouk_my_summary_count 9
```

The last lines of the output are for the `summary` data type.

So, the metrics are there and ready to be pulled by Prometheus—in practice, this means that every production Go application can export metrics that can be used for measuring its performance and discovering its bottlenecks. However, we are not done yet as we need to learn about building Docker images for Go applications.

Creating a Docker image for a Go server

This section shows how to create a Docker image for a Go application. The main benefit you get from this is that you can deploy it in a Docker environment without worrying about compiling it and having the required resources—everything is included in the Docker image.

Still, you might ask, "*why not use a normal Go binary instead of a Docker image?*" The answer is simple: Docker images can be put in `docker-compose.yml` files and can be deployed using Kubernetes. The same is not true about Go binaries.

You usually start with a base Docker image that already includes Go and you create the desired binary in there. The key point here is that `samplePro.go` uses an external package that should be downloaded in the Docker image before building the executable binary.

The process must start with `go mod init` and `go mod tidy`. The contents of the Dockerfile, which can be found as `dFilev2` in the GitHub repository of the book, are as follows:

```
# WITH Go Modules

FROM golang:alpine AS builder
RUN apk update && apk add --no-cache git
```

As `golang:alpine` uses the latest Go version, which does not come with `git`, we install it manually.

```
RUN mkdir $GOPATH/src/server
ADD ./samplePro.go $GOPATH/src/server
```

If you want to use Go modules, you should put your code in `$GOPATH/src`.

```
WORKDIR $GOPATH/src/server
RUN go mod init
RUN go mod tidy
RUN go mod download
RUN mkdir /pro
RUN go build -o /pro/server samplePro.go
```

We download dependencies using various `go mod` commands. The building of the binary file is the same as before.

```
FROM alpine:latest

RUN mkdir /pro
COPY --from=builder /pro/server /pro/server
EXPOSE 1234
WORKDIR /pro
CMD ["/pro/server"]
```

In this second stage, we put the binary file into the desired location (`/pro`) and expose the desired port, which in this case is `1234`. The port number depends on the code in `samplePro.go`.

Building a Docker image using `dFilev2` is as simple as running the next command:

```
$ docker build -f dFilev2 -t go-app116 .
```

Once the Docker image has been created, there is no difference in the way you should use it in a `docker-compose.yml` file—a relevant entry in a `docker-compose.yml` file would look as follows:

```
goapp:
  image: goapp
  container_name: goapp-int
  restart: always
  ports:
    - 1234:1234
  networks:
    - monitoring
```

The name of the Docker image is `goapp` whereas the internal name of the container would be `goapp-int`. So, if a different container from the `monitoring` network wants to access that container, it should use the `goapp-int` hostname. Last, the only open port is port number `1234`.

The next section illustrates how to expose metrics to Prometheus.

Exposing the desired metrics

This section illustrates how to expose metrics from the `runtime/metrics` package to Prometheus. In our case we use `/sched/goroutines:goroutines` and `/memory/classes/total:bytes`. You already know about the former, which is the total number of goroutines. The latter metric is the amount of memory mapped by the Go runtime into the current process as read-write.

> As the presented code uses an external package, it should be put inside `~/go/src` and Go modules should be enabled using `go mod init`.

The Go code of `prometheus.go` is as follows:

```
package main

import (
    "log"
    "math/rand"
    "net/http"
    "runtime"
    "runtime/metrics"
    "time"

    "github.com/prometheus/client_golang/prometheus"
    "github.com/prometheus/client_golang/prometheus/promhttp"
)
```

The first external package is the Go client library for Prometheus and the second package is for using the default handler function (`promhttp.Handler()`).

```
var PORT = ":1234"

var n_goroutines = prometheus.NewGauge(
    prometheus.GaugeOpts{
        Namespace: "packt",
        Name:      "n_goroutines",
        Help:      "Number of goroutines"})

var n_memory = prometheus.NewGauge(
    prometheus.GaugeOpts{
        Namespace: "packt",
        Name:      "n_memory",
        Help:      "Memory usage"})
```

Here, we define the two Prometheus metrics.

```
func main() {
    rand.Seed(time.Now().Unix())
    prometheus.MustRegister(n_goroutines)
    prometheus.MustRegister(n_memory)
```

```
    const nGo = "/sched/goroutines:goroutines"
    const nMem = "/memory/classes/heap/free:bytes"
```

This is where you define the metrics you want to read from the `runtime/metrics` package.

```
    getMetric := make([]metrics.Sample, 2)
    getMetric[0].Name = nGo
    getMetric[1].Name = nMem

    http.Handle("/metrics", promhttp.Handler())
```

This is where you register the handler function for the `/metrics` path. We use `promhttp.Handler()`.

```
    go func() {
        for {
            for i := 1; i < 4; i++ {
                go func() {
                    _ = make([]int, 1000000)
                    time.Sleep(time.Duration(rand.Intn(10)) * time.
Second)
                }()
            }
```

Note that such a program should definitely have **at least two goroutines**: one for running the HTTP server and another one for collecting the metrics. Usually, the HTTP server is on the goroutine that runs the `main()` function and the metric collection happens in a user-defined goroutine.

The external `for` loop makes sure that the goroutine runs forever whereas the internal `for` loop creates additional goroutines so that the value of the `/sched/goroutines:goroutines` metric changes all the time.

```
            runtime.GC()
            metrics.Read(getMetric)
            goVal := getMetric[0].Value.Uint64()
            memVal := getMetric[1].Value.Uint64()
            time.Sleep(time.Duration(rand.Intn(15)) * time.Second)
```

```
            n_goroutines.Set(float64(goVal))
            n_memory.Set(float64(memVal))
        }
    }()
```

The `runtime.GC()` function tells the Go garbage collector to run and is called for changing the `/memory/classes/heap/free:bytes` metric. The two `Set()` calls update the values of the metrics.

> You can read more about the operation of the Go garbage collector in *Appendix A*.

```
    log.Println("Listening to port", PORT)
    log.Println(http.ListenAndServe(PORT, nil))
}
```

The last statement runs the web server using the default Go router. Running `prometheus.go` from a directory inside `~/go/src/github.com/mactsouk` requires executing the next commands:

```
$ cd ~/go/src/github.com/mactsouk/Prometheus # use any path inside ~/
go/src
$ go mod init
$ go mod tidy
$ go mod download
$ go run prometheus.go
2021/04/01 12:18:11 Listening to port :1234
```

Although `prometheus.go` generates no output apart from the previous line, the next subsection illustrates how to read the desired metrics from it using `curl(1)`.

Reading metrics

You can get a list of the metrics from `prometheus.go` using `curl(1)` in order to make sure that the application works as expected. I always test the operation of such an application with `curl(1)` or some other similar utility such as `wget(1)` before trying to get the metrics with Prometheus.

```
$ curl localhost:1234/metrics --silent | grep packt
# HELP packt_n_goroutines Number of goroutines
```

```
# TYPE packt_n_goroutines gauge
packt_n_goroutines 5
# HELP packt_n_memory Memory usage
# TYPE packt_n_memory gauge
packt_n_memory 794624
```

The previous command assumes that `curl(1)` is executed on the same machine as the server and that the server listens to TCP port number `1234`. Next, we must enable Prometheus to pull the metrics. The easiest way for a Prometheus Docker image to be able to see the Go application with the metrics is to execute both as Docker images. There is an important point here: the `runtime/metrics` package was first introduced with Go version 1.16. This means that to build a Go source file that uses `runtime/metrics`, we need to use Go version 1.16 or newer, which means that we need to use modules for building the Docker image. Therefore, we are going to use the following Dockerfile:

```
FROM golang:alpine AS builder
```

This is the name of the base Docker image that is used for building the binary. `golang:alpine` always contains the latest Go version as long as you update it regularly.

```
RUN apk update && apk add --no-cache git
```

As `golang:alpine` does not come with `git`, we need to install it manually.

```
RUN mkdir $GOPATH/src/server
ADD ./prometheus.go $GOPATH/src/server
WORKDIR $GOPATH/src/server
RUN go mod init
RUN go mod tidy
RUN go mod download
```

The previous commands download the required dependencies before trying to build the binary.

```
RUN mkdir /pro
RUN go build -o /pro/server prometheus.go

FROM alpine:latest

RUN mkdir /pro
COPY --from=builder /pro/server /pro/server
```

```
EXPOSE 1234
WORKDIR /pro
CMD ["/pro/server"]
```

Building the desired Docker image, which is going to be named `goapp`, is as simple as running the next command:

```
$ docker build -f Dockerfile -t goapp .
```

As usual, the output of `docker images` verifies the successful creation of the `goapp` Docker image—in my case the relevant entry looks as follows:

```
goapp          latest        a1f0cd4bd8f5   5 seconds ago   16.9MB
```

Let us now discuss how to configure Prometheus to pull the desired metrics.

Putting the metrics in Prometheus

To be able to pull the metrics, Prometheus needs a proper configuration file. The configuration file that is going to be used is as follows:

```
# prometheus.yml
scrape_configs:
  - job_name: GoServer
    scrape_interval: 5s
    static_configs:
      - targets: ['goapp:1234']
```

We tell Prometheus to connect to a host named `goapp` using port number `1234`. Prometheus pulls data every 5 seconds, according to the value of the `scrape_interval` field. You should put `prometheus.yml` in the `prometheus` directory, which should be in the same directory as the `docker-compose.yml` file that is presented next.

Prometheus as well as Grafana and the Go application are going to run as Docker containers using the next `docker-compose.yml` file:

```
version: "3"

services:
  goapp:
    image: goapp
    container_name: goapp
    restart: always
```

```
      ports:
        - 1234:1234
      networks:
        - monitoring
```

This is the part that deals with the Go application that collects the metrics. The Docker image name, as well as the internal hostname of the Docker container, is `goapp`. You should define the port number that is going to be open for connections. In this case both the internal and external port numbers are `1234`. The internal one is mapped to the external one. Additionally, you should put all Docker images under the same network, which in this case is called `monitoring` and is defined in a while.

```
    prometheus:
      image: prom/prometheus:latest
      container_name: prometheus
      restart: always
      user: "0"
      volumes:
        - ./prometheus/:/etc/prometheus/
```

This is how you pass your own copy of `prometheus.yml` to the Docker image to be used by Prometheus. So, `./prometheus/prometheus.yml` from the local machine can be accessed as `/etc/prometheus/prometheus.yml` from within the Docker image.

```
        - ./prometheus_data/:/prometheus/
      command:
        - '--config.file=/etc/prometheus/prometheus.yml'
```

This is where you tell Prometheus which configuration file to use.

```
        - '--storage.tsdb.path=/prometheus'
        - '--web.console.libraries=/etc/prometheus/console_libraries'
        - '--web.console.templates=/etc/prometheus/consoles'
        - '--storage.tsdb.retention.time=200h'
        - '--web.enable-lifecycle'
      ports:
        - 9090:9090
      networks:
        - monitoring
```

This is where the definition of the Prometheus part of the scenario ends. The Docker image used is called `prom/prometheus:latest` and the internal name of it is `prometheus`. Prometheus listens to port number `9090`.

```
  grafana:
    image: grafana/grafana
    container_name: grafana
    depends_on:
      - prometheus
    restart: always
    user: "0"
    ports:
      - 3000:3000
    environment:
      - GF_SECURITY_ADMIN_PASSWORD=helloThere
```

This is the current password of the `admin` user—you need that for connecting to Grafana.

```
      - GF_USERS_ALLOW_SIGN_UP=false
      - GF_PANELS_DISABLE_SANITIZE_HTML=true
      - GF_SECURITY_ALLOW_EMBEDDING=true
    networks:
      - monitoring
    volumes:
      - ./grafana_data/:/var/lib/grafana/
```

Last, we present the Grafana part. Grafana listens to port number `3000`.

```
volumes:
    grafana_data: {}
    prometheus_data: {}
```

The preceding two lines in combination with the two `volumes` fields allow both Grafana and Prometheus to save their data locally so that data is not lost each time you restart the Docker images.

```
networks:
  monitoring:
    driver: bridge
```

Internally, all three containers are known by the value of their `container_name` field. However, externally, you can connect to the open ports from your local machine as `http://localhost:port` or from another machine using `http://hostname:port`—the second way is not very secure and should be blocked by a firewall. Lastly, you need to run `docker-compose up` and you are done! The Go application begins exposing data and Prometheus begins collecting it.

The next figure shows the Prometheus UI (`http://hostname:9090`) displaying a simple plot of `packt_n_goroutines`:

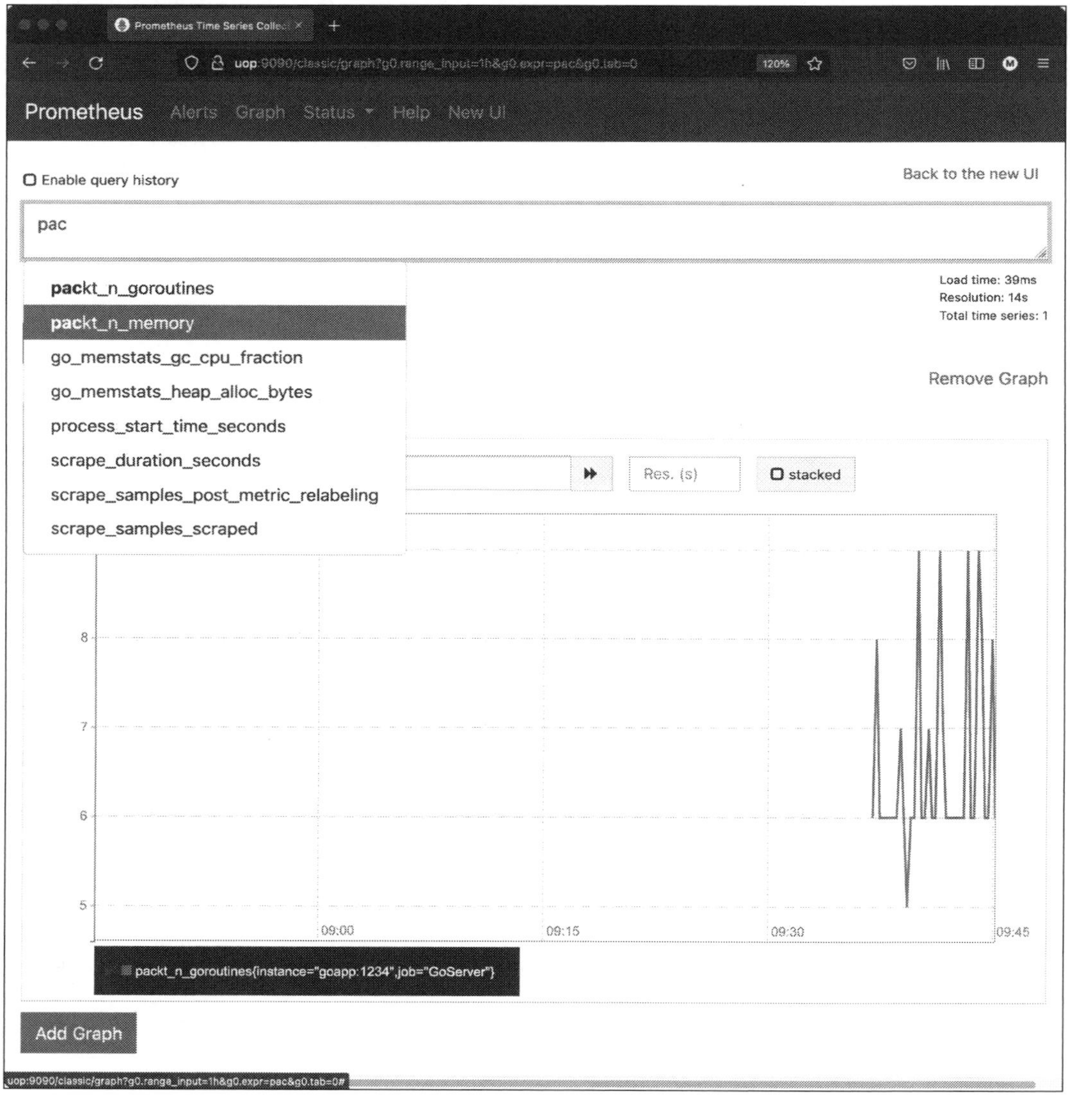

Figure 8.1: The Prometheus UI

This output, which shows the values of the metrics in a graphical way, is very handy for debugging purposes, but it is far from being truly professional as Prometheus is not a visualization tool. The next subsection shows how to connect Prometheus with Grafana and create impressive plots.

Visualizing Prometheus metrics in Grafana

There is no point in collecting metrics without doing something with them, and by something, I mean visualizing them. Prometheus and Grafana work very well together so we are going to use Grafana for the visualization part. The single most important task that you should perform in Grafana is connecting it with your Prometheus instance. In Grafana terminology, you should create a Grafana *data source* that allows Grafana to get data from Prometheus.

The steps for creating a data source with our Prometheus installation are the following:

1. First go to `http://localhost:3000` to connect to Grafana.
2. The username of the administrator is `admin` whereas the password is defined in the value of the `GF_SECURITY_ADMIN_PASSWORD` parameter of the `docker-compose.yml` file.
3. Then select **Add your first data source**. From the list of data sources, select **Prometheus**, which is usually at the top of the list.
4. Put `http://prometheus:9090` in the URL field and then press the **Save & Test** button. Due to the internal network that exists between the Docker images, the Grafana container knows the Prometheus container by the `prometheus` hostname—this is the value of the `container_name` field. As you already know, you can also connect to Prometheus from your local machine using `http://localhost:9090`. We are done! The name of the data source is `Prometheus`.

After these steps, create a new dashboard from the initial Grafana screen and put a new panel on it. Select **Prometheus** as the data source of the panel, if it is not already selected. Then go to the **Metrics** drop-down menu and select the desired metrics. Click **Save** and you are done. Create as many panels as you want.

The next figure shows Grafana visualizing two metrics from Prometheus as exposed by `prometheus.go`.

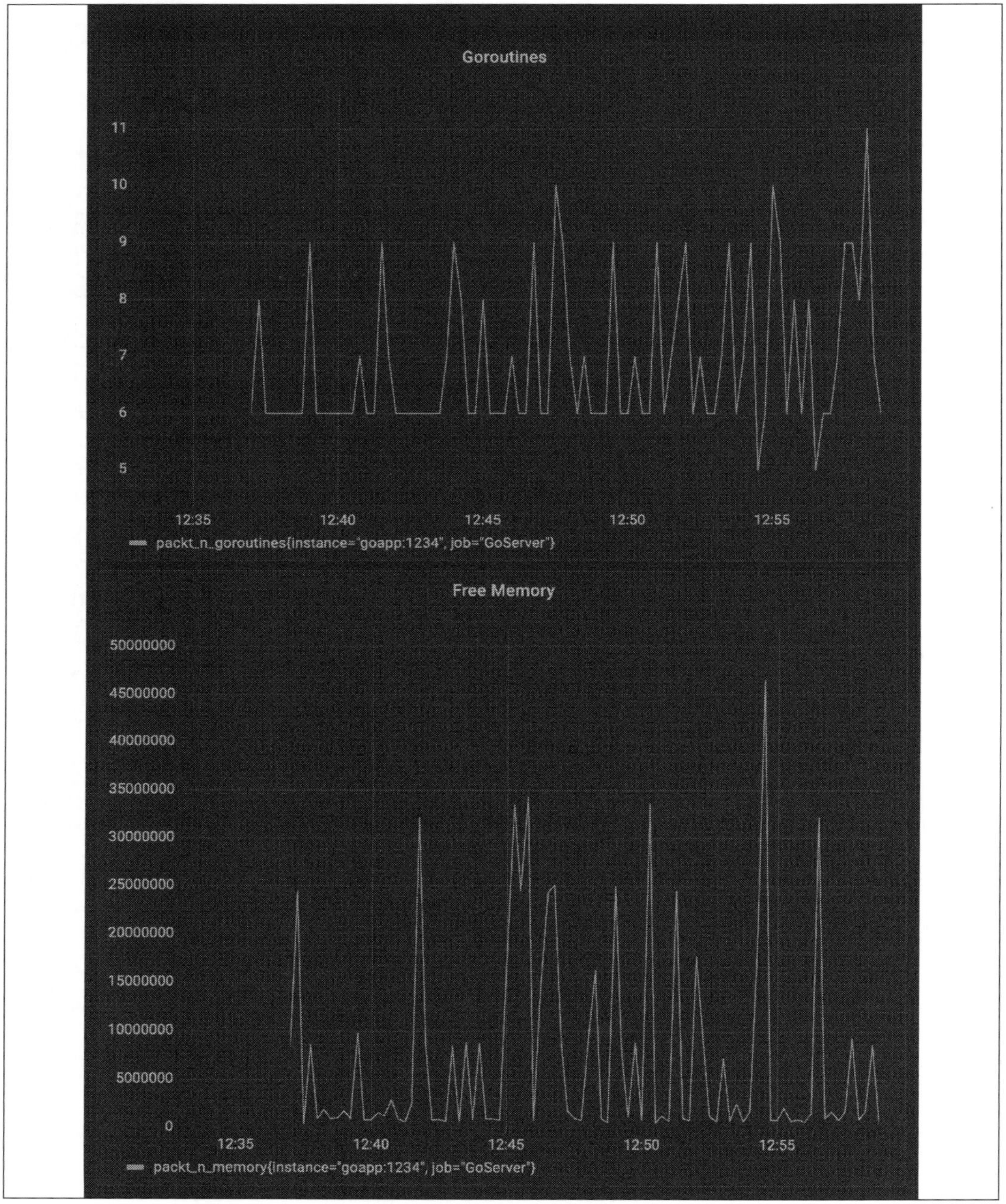

Figure 8.2: Visualizing metrics in Grafana

Grafana has many more capabilities than the ones presented here—if you are working with system metrics and want to check the performance of your Go applications, Prometheus and Grafana are good choices.

After learning about HTTP servers, the next section shows how to develop HTTP clients.

Developing web clients

This section shows how to develop HTTP clients starting with a simplistic version and continuing with a more advanced one. In this simplistic version, all of the work is done by the `http.Get()` call, which is pretty convenient when you do not want to deal with lots of options and parameters. However, this type of call gives you no flexibility over the process. Notice that `http.Get()` returns an `http.Response` value. All this is illustrated in `simpleClient.go`:

```
package main

import (
    "fmt"
    "io"
    "net/http"
    "os"
    "path/filepath"
)

func main() {
    if len(os.Args) != 2 {
        fmt.Printf("Usage: %s URL\n", filepath.Base(os.Args[0]))
        return
    }
```

The `filepath.Base()` function returns the last element of a path. When given `os.Args[0]` as its parameter, it returns the name of the executable binary file.

```
    URL := os.Args[1]
    data, err := http.Get(URL)
```

In the previous two statements we get the URL and get its data using `http.Get()`, which returns an `*http.Response` and an `error` variable. The `*http.Response` value contains all the information so you do not need to make any additional calls to `http.Get()`.

```
    if err != nil {
        fmt.Println(err)
        return
    }

    _, err = io.Copy(os.Stdout, data.Body)
```

The `io.Copy()` function reads from the `data.Body` reader, which contains the body of the server response, and writes the data to `os.Stdout`. As `os.Stdout` is always open, you do not need to open it for writing. Therefore, all data is written to standard output, which is usually the terminal window.

```
    if err != nil {
        fmt.Println(err)
        return
    }
    data.Body.Close()
}
```

Last, we close the `data.Body` reader to make the work of the garbage collection easier.

Working with `simpleClient.go` produces the next kind of output, which in this case is abbreviated:

```
$ go run simpleClient.go https://www.golang.org
<!DOCTYPE html>
<html lang="en">
<meta charset="utf-8">
<meta name="description" content="Go is an open source programming
language that makes it easy to build simple, reliable, and efficient
software.">
...
</script>
```

Although `simpleClient.go` does the job of verifying that the given URL exists and is reachable, it offers no control over the process. The next subsection develops an advanced HTTP client that processes the server response.

Using http.NewRequest() to improve the client

As the web client of the previous section is relatively simplistic and does not give you any flexibility, in this subsection, you learn how to read a URL without using the `http.Get()` function, and with more options. However, the extra flexibility comes at a cost as you must write more code.

The code of `wwwClient.go`, without the `import` block, is as follows:

```
package main

// For the import block go to the book GitHub repository

func main() {
    if len(os.Args) != 2 {
        fmt.Printf("Usage: %s URL\n", filepath.Base(os.Args[0]))
        return
    }
```

Although using `filepath.Base()` is not necessary, it makes your output more professional.

```
    URL, err := url.Parse(os.Args[1])
    if err != nil {
        fmt.Println("Error in parsing:", err)
        return
    }
```

The `url.Parse()` function parses a string into a `URL` structure. This means that if the given argument is not a valid URL, `url.Parse()` is going to notice. As usual, check the `error` variable.

```
    c := &http.Client{
        Timeout: 15 * time.Second,
    }

    request, err := http.NewRequest(http.MethodGet, URL.String(), nil)
    if err != nil {
        fmt.Println("Get:", err)
        return
    }
```

The `http.NewRequest()` function returns an `http.Request` object given a method, a URL, and an optional body. The `http.MethodGet` parameter defines that we want to retrieve the data using a `GET` HTTP method whereas `URL.String()` returns the string value of an `http.URL` variable.

```
httpData, err := c.Do(request)
if err != nil {
    fmt.Println("Error in Do():", err)
    return
}
```

The `http.Do()` function sends an HTTP request (`http.Request`) using an `http.Client` and gets an `http.Response`. So, `http.Do()` does the job of `http.Get()` in a more detailed way.

```
fmt.Println("Status code:", httpData.Status)
```

`httpData.Status` holds the HTTP status code of the response—this is really important because it allows you to understand what really happened with the request.

```
header, _ := httputil.DumpResponse(httpData, false)
fmt.Print(string(header))
```

The `httputil.DumpResponse()` function is used here to get the response from the server and is mainly used for debugging purposes. The second argument of `httputil.DumpResponse()` is a Boolean value that specifies whether the function is going to include the body or not in its output—in our case it is set to `false`, which excludes the response body from the output and only prints the header. If you want to do the same on the server side, you should use `httputil.DumpRequest()`.

```
contentType := httpData.Header.Get("Content-Type")
characterSet := strings.SplitAfter(contentType, "charset=")
if len(characterSet) > 1 {
    fmt.Println("Character Set:", characterSet[1])
}
```

Here we find out about the character set of the response by searching the value of `Content-Type`.

```
if httpData.ContentLength == -1 {
    fmt.Println("ContentLength is unknown!")
} else {
    fmt.Println("ContentLength:", httpData.ContentLength)
}
```

Here, we try to get the content length from the response by reading `httpData.ContentLength`. However, if the value is not set, we print a relevant message.

```
    length := 0
    var buffer [1024]byte
    r := httpData.Body
    for {
        n, err := r.Read(buffer[0:])
        if err != nil {
            fmt.Println(err)
                break
        }
        length = length + n
    }
    fmt.Println("Calculated response data length:", length)
}
```

In the last part of the program, we use a technique for discovering the size of the server HTTP response on our own. If we wanted to display the HTML output on our screen, we could have printed the contents of the `r` buffer variable.

Working with `wwwClient.go` and visiting `https://www.golang.org` produces the next output, which is the output of `fmt.Println("Status code:", httpData.Status)`:

```
$ go run wwwClient.go https://www.golang.org
Status code: 200 OK
```

Next, we see output of the `fmt.Print(string(header))` statement with the header data of the HTTP server response:

```
HTTP/2.0 200 OK
Alt-Svc: h3-29=":443"; ma=2592000,h3-T051=":443";
ma=2592000,h3-Q050=":443"; ma=2592000,h3-Q046=":443";
ma=2592000,h3-Q043=":443"; ma=2592000,quic=":443"; ma=2592000;
v="46,43"
Content-Type: text/html; charset=utf-8
Date: Sat, 27 Mar 2021 19:19:25 GMT
Strict-Transport-Security: max-age=31536000; includeSubDomains; preload
Vary: Accept-Encoding
Via: 1.1 google
```

The last part of the output is about the character set of the interaction (`utf-8`) and the content length of the response (`9216`) as calculated by the code:

```
Character Set: utf-8
ContentLength is unknown!
EOF
Calculated response data length: 9216
```

The next section shows how to create a client for the phone book web service we developed earlier.

Creating a client for the phone book service

In this subsection, we create a command-line utility that interacts with the phone book web service that was developed earlier in this chapter. This version of the phone book client is going to be created using the `cobra` package, which means that a dedicated GitHub or GitLab repository is required. In this case the repository can be found at `https://github.com/mactsouk/phone-cli`. The first thing to do after running `git clone` is associating that repository with the directory that is going to be used for development:

```
$ cd ~/go/src/github.com/mactsouk
$ git clone git@github.com:mactsouk/phone-cli.git
$ cd phone-cli
$ ~/go/bin/cobra init --pkg-name github.com/mactsouk/phone-cli
$ go mod init
$ go mod tidy
$ go mod download
```

Next, we have to create the commands for the utility. The structure of the utility is implemented using the next `cobra` commands:

```
$ ~/go/bin/cobra add search
$ ~/go/bin/cobra add insert
$ ~/go/bin/cobra add delete
$ ~/go/bin/cobra add status
$ ~/go/bin/cobra add list
```

So, we have a command-line utility with five commands named `search`, `insert`, `delete`, `status`, and `list`. After that, we need to implement the commands and define their local parameters in order to interact with the phone book server.

Now let us see the implementations of the commands, starting from the implementation of the `init()` function of the `root.go` file because this is where the global command-line parameters are defined:

```
func init() {
    rootCmd.PersistentFlags().StringP("server", "S", "localhost",
"Server")
    rootCmd.PersistentFlags().StringP("port", "P", "1234", "Port number")

    viper.BindPFlag("server", rootCmd.PersistentFlags().Lookup("server"))
    viper.BindPFlag("port", rootCmd.PersistentFlags().Lookup("port"))
}
```

So, we define two global parameters named `server` and `port`, which are the hostname and the port number, respectively. Both parameters have an alias and both parameters are handled by `viper`.

Let us now examine the implementation of the `status` command as found in `status.go`:

```
SERVER := viper.GetString("server")
PORT := viper.GetString("port")
```

All commands read the values of the `server` and `port` command-line parameters in order to get information about the server, and the `status` command is no exception.

```
// Create request
URL := "http://" + SERVER + ":" + PORT + "/status"
```

After that we construct the full URL of the request.

```
data, err := http.Get(URL)
if err != nil {
    fmt.Println(err)
    return
}
```

Then, we send a `GET` request to the server using `http.Get()`.

```
// Check HTTP Status Code
if data.StatusCode != http.StatusOK {
    fmt.Println("Status code:", data.StatusCode)
```

```
        return
    }
```

After that we check the HTTP status code of the request to make sure that everything is OK.

```
    // Read data
    responseData, err := io.ReadAll(data.Body)
    if err != nil {
        fmt.Println(err)
        return
    }
    fmt.Print(string(responseData))
```

If everything is OK, we read the entire body of the server response, which is a `byte` slice, and print it on screen as a string. The implementation of `list` is almost identical to the implementation of `status`. The only differences are that the implementation is found in `list.go` and that the full URL is constructed as follows:

```
    URL := "http://" + SERVER + ":" + PORT + "/list"
```

After that, let us see how the `delete` command is implemented in `delete.go`:

```
    SERVER := viper.GetString("server")
    PORT := viper.GetString("port")
    number, _ := cmd.Flags().GetString("tel")
    if number == "" {
        fmt.Println("Number is empty!")
        return
    }
```

Apart from reading the values of the `server` and `port` global parameters, we read the value of the `tel` parameter. If `tel` has no value, the command returns.

```
    // Create request
    URL := "http://" + SERVER + ":" + PORT + "/delete/" + number
```

Once again, we construct the full URL of the request before connecting to the server.

```
    // Send request to server
    data, err := http.Get(URL)
    if err != nil {
        fmt.Println(err)
        return
    }
```

Then, we send the request to the server.

```
// Check HTTP Status Code
if data.StatusCode != http.StatusOK {
    fmt.Println("Status code:", data.StatusCode)
    return
}
```

If there was an error in the server response, the `delete` command terminates.

```
// Read data
responseData, err := io.ReadAll(data.Body)
if err != nil {
    fmt.Println(err)
    return
}
fmt.Print(string(responseData))
```

If everything was fine, the server response text is printed on the screen.

The `init()` function of `delete.go` contains the definition of the local `tel` command-line parameter:

```
func init() {
    rootCmd.AddCommand(deleteCmd)
    deleteCmd.Flags().StringP("tel", "t", "", "Telephone number to
delete")
}
```

This is a local flag available to the `delete` command only. Next, let us learn more about the `search` command and how it is implemented in `search.go`. The implementation is the same as in `delete` except for the full request URL:

```
URL := "http://" + SERVER + ":" + PORT + "/search/" + number
```

The `search` command also supports the `tel` command-line parameter for getting the telephone number to search for—this is defined in the `init()` function of `search.go`.

The last command that is presented is the `insert` command, which supports three local command-line parameters that are defined in the `init()` function in `insert.go`:

```
func init() {
    rootCmd.AddCommand(insertCmd)
    insertCmd.Flags().StringP("name", "n", "", "Name value")
```

```
    insertCmd.Flags().StringP("surname", "s", "", "Surname value")
    insertCmd.Flags().StringP("tel", "t", "", "Telephone value")
}
```

These three parameters are needed for getting the required user input. Note that the alias for `surname` is a **lowercase** `s` whereas the alias for `server`, which is defined in `root.go`, is an **uppercase** `S`. Commands and their aliases are user-defined—use common sense when selecting command names and aliases.

The command is implemented using the next code:

```
SERVER := viper.GetString("server")
PORT := viper.GetString("port")
```

First, we read the `server` and `port` global parameters.

```
number, _ := cmd.Flags().GetString("tel")
if number == "" {
    fmt.Println("Number is empty!")
    return
}
name, _ := cmd.Flags().GetString("name")
if number == "" {
    fmt.Println("Name is empty!")
    return
}
surname, _ := cmd.Flags().GetString("surname")
if number == "" {
    fmt.Println("Surname is empty!")
    return
}
```

Then, we get the values of the three local command-line parameters. If any one of them has an empty value, the command returns without sending the request to the server.

```
URL := "http://" + SERVER + ":" + PORT + "/insert/"
URL = URL + "/" + name + "/" + surname + "/" + number
```

Here, we create the server request in two steps for readability.

```
data, err := http.Get(URL)
if err != nil {
    fmt.Println("**", err)
```

```
    return
}
```

Then, we send the request to the server.

```
if data.StatusCode != http.StatusOK {
    fmt.Println("Status code:", data.StatusCode)
    return
}
```

Checking the HTTP status code is considered a good practice. Therefore, if everything is OK with the server response, we continue by reading the data. Otherwise, we print the status code, and we exit.

```
responseData, err := io.ReadAll(data.Body)
if err != nil {
    fmt.Println("*", err)
    return
}
fmt.Print(string(responseData))
```

After reading the body of the server response, which is stored in a `byte` slice, we print it on screen as a string using `string(responseData)`.

The client application generates the next kind of output:

```
$ go run main.go list
Dimitris Tsoukalos 2101112223
Jane Doe 0800123456
Mike Tsoukalos 2109416471
```

This is the output of the `list` command.

```
$ go run main.go status
Total entries: 3
```

The output of the `status` command informs us about the number of entries in the phone book.

```
$ go run main.go search --tel 0800123456
Jane Doe 0800123456
```

The previous output shows the use of the `search` command when successfully finding a number.

```
$ go run main.go search --tel 0800
Status code: 404
```

The previous output shows the use of the `search` command when not finding a number.

```
$ go run main.go delete --tel 2101112223
2101112223 deleted!
```

This is the output of the `delete` command.

```
$ go run main.go insert -n Michalis -s Tsoukalos -t 2101112223
New record added successfully
```

This is the operation of the `insert` command. If you try to insert the same number more than once, the server output is going to be `Status code: 304`.

The next section shows how to create an FTP server using `net/http`.

Creating file servers

Although a file server is not a web server per se, it is closely connected to web services because it is being implemented using similar Go packages. Additionally, file servers are frequently used for supporting the functionality of web servers and web services.

Go offers the `http.FileServer()` handler for doing so, as well as `http.ServeFile()`. The biggest difference between these two is that `http.FileServer()` is an `http.Handler` whereas `http.ServeFile()` is not. Additionally, `http.ServeFile()` is better at serving single files whereas `http.FileServer()` is better at serving entire directory trees.

A simple code example of `http.FileServer()` is presented in `fileServer.go`:

```
package main

import (
	"fmt"
	"log"
	"net/http"
)
```

```
var PORT = ":8765"

func defaultHandler(w http.ResponseWriter, r *http.Request) {
	log.Println("Serving:", r.URL.Path, "from", r.Host)
	w.WriteHeader(http.StatusOK)
	Body := "Thanks for visiting!\n"
	fmt.Fprintf(w, "%s", Body)
}
```

This is the expected default handler of the HTTP server.

```
func main() {
	mux := http.NewServeMux()
	mux.HandleFunc("/", defaultHandler)

	fileServer := http.FileServer(http.Dir("/tmp/"))
	mux.Handle("/static/", http.StripPrefix("/static", fileServer))
```

`mux.Handle()` registers the file server as the handler for all URL paths that begin with `/static/`. However, when a match is found, we strip the `/static/` prefix before the file server tries to serve such a request because `/static/` is not part of the location where the actual files are located. As far as Go is concerned, `http.FileServer()` is just another handler.

```
	fmt.Println("Starting server on:", PORT)
	err := http.ListenAndServe(PORT, mux)
	fmt.Println(err)
}
```

Last, we start the HTTP server using `http.ListenAndServe()`.

Using `curl(1)` for visiting `/static/` produces the next kind of output, which is in HTML format:

```
$ curl http://localhost:8765/static/
<pre>
<a href="AlTest1.out">AlTest1.out</a>
<a href="adobegc.log">adobegc.log</a>
<a href="com.google.Keystone/">com.google.Keystone/</a>
<a href="data.csv">data.csv</a>
<a href="fseventsd-uuid">fseventsd-uuid</a>
<a href="powerlog/">powerlog/</a>
</pre>
```

You can also visit `http://localhost:8765/static/` in your web browser or an FTP client to browse the files and the directories of the FTP server.

The next subsection shows how to utilize `http.ServeFile()` to serve single files.

Downloading the contents of the phone book application

In this subsection we create and implement an endpoint that allows us to download the contents of a single file. The code creates **a temporary file with a different filename for each request** with the contents of the phone book application. For reasons of simplicity, the presented code supports two HTTP endpoints: one for the default router and the other for the serving of the file. As we are serving a single file, we are going to use `http.ServeFile()`, which replies to a request with the contents of the specified file or directory.

Each temporary file is kept in the file system for *30 seconds* before it is deleted. To simulate a real-world situation, the presented utility reads `data.csv`, puts it into a slice, and creates a file based on the contents of `data.csv`. The name of the utility is `getEntries.go`—its most important code is the implementation of the `getFileHandler()` function:

```
func getFileHandler(w http.ResponseWriter, r *http.Request) {
	var tempFileName string

	// Create temporary file name
	f, err := os.CreateTemp("", "data*.txt")
	tempFileName = f.Name()
```

The temporary path is created using `os.CreateTemp()` based on a given pattern and by adding a random string to the end. If the pattern includes an `*`, then the randomly generated string replaces the last `*`. The exact place where the file is created depends on the operating system being used.

```
	// Remove the file
	defer os.Remove(tempFileName)
```

We do not want to end up having lots of temporary files, so we delete the file when the handler function returns.

```
	// Save data to it
	err = saveCSVFile(tempFileName)
```

```
    if err != nil {
        fmt.Println(err)
        w.WriteHeader(http.StatusNotFound)
        fmt.Fprintln(w, "Cannot create: "+tempFileName)
        return
    }

    fmt.Println("Serving ", tempFileName)

    http.ServeFile(w, r, tempFileName)
```

This is where the temporary file is sent to the client.

```
    // 30 seconds to get the file
    time.Sleep(30 * time.Second)
}
```

The `time.Sleep()` call delays the deletion of the temporary file for 30 seconds—you can define any delay period you like.

As far as the `main()` function is concerned, `getFileHandler()` is a regular handler function used in a `mux.HandleFunc("/getContents/", getFileHandler)` statement. Therefore, each time there is a client request for `/getContents/`, the contents of a file are returned to the HTTP client.

Running `getEntries.go` and visiting `/getContents/` produces the next kind of output:

```
$ curl http://localhost:8765/getContents/
Dimitris,Tsoukalos,2101112223,1617028128
Jane,Doe,0800123456,1608559903
Mike,Tsoukalos,2109416471,1617028196
```

As we are returning plain text data, the output is presented on screen.

> *Chapter 10, Working with REST APIs,* presents a different way of creating a file server that supports both uploading and downloading files by using the `gorilla/mux` package.

The next section explains how to time out HTTP connections.

Timing out HTTP connections

This section presents techniques for timing out HTTP connections that take too long to finish and work either on the server or the client side.

Using SetDeadline()

The `SetDeadline()` function is used by `net` to set the read and write deadlines of network connections. Due to the way the `SetDeadline()` function works, you need to call `SetDeadline()` before any read or write operation. Keep in mind that Go uses deadlines to implement timeouts, so you do not need to reset the timeout every time your application receives or sends any data. The use of `SetDeadline()` is illustrated in `withDeadline.go` and more specifically in the implementation of the `Timeout()` function:

```
var timeout = time.Duration(time.Second)

func Timeout(network, host string) (net.Conn, error) {
    conn, err := net.DialTimeout(network, host, timeout)
    if err != nil {
        return nil, err
    }

    conn.SetDeadline(time.Now().Add(timeout))
    return conn, nil
}
```

The `timeout` global variable defines the timeout period used in the `SetDeadline()` call.

The previous function is used in the next code inside `main()`:

```
t := http.Transport{
    Dial: Timeout,
}

client := http.Client{
        Transport: &t,
}
```

So, `http.Transport` uses `Timeout()` in the `Dial` field and `http.Client` uses `http.Transport`. When you call the `client.Get()` method with the desired URL, which is not shown here, `Timeout` is automatically being used because of the `http.Transport` definition. So, if the `Timeout` function returns before the server response is received, we have a timeout.

Using `withDeadline.go` produces the next kind of output:

```
$ go run withDeadline.go http://www.golang.org
Timeout value: 1s
<!DOCTYPE html>
...
```

The call was successful and took less than 1 second to finish, so there was no timeout.

```
$ go run withDeadline.go http://localhost:80
Timeout value: 1s
Get "http://localhost:80": read tcp 127.0.0.1:52492->127.0.0.1:80: i/o
timeout
```

This time we have a timeout as the server took too long to answer.

Next, we show how to time out a connection using the `context` package.

Setting the timeout period on the client side

This section presents a technique for timing out network connections that take too long to finish on the **client side**. So, if the client does not receive a response from the server in the desired time, it closes the connection. The `timeoutClient.go` source file, without the `import` block, illustrates the technique.

```
package main

// For the import block go to the book code repository

var myUrl string
var delay int = 5
var wg sync.WaitGroup
```

```
type myData struct {
	r   *http.Response
	err error
}
```

In the previous code we define global variables and a structure that are going to be used in the rest of the program.

```
func connect(c context.Context) error {
	defer wg.Done()
	data := make(chan myData, 1)
	tr := &http.Transport{}
	httpClient := &http.Client{Transport: tr}
	req, _ := http.NewRequest("GET", myUrl, nil)
```

This is where you initialize the variables of the HTTP connection. The `data` channel is used in the `select` statement that follows. Additionally, the `c context.Context` parameter comes with an embedded channel that is also used in the `select` statement.

```
	go func() {
		response, err := httpClient.Do(req)
		if err != nil {
			fmt.Println(err)
			data <- myData{nil, err}
			return
		} else {
			pack := myData{response, err}
			data <- pack
		}
	}()
```

The previous goroutine is used for interacting with the HTTP server. There is nothing special here as this is a regular interaction of an HTTP client with an HTTP server.

```
	select {
	case <-c.Done():
		tr.CancelRequest(req)
		<-data
		fmt.Println("The request was canceled!")
		return c.Err()
```

The code that this `select` block executes is based on whether the context is going to time out or not. If the context times out first, then the client connection is canceled using `tr.CancelRequest(req)`.

```
    case ok := <-data:
        err := ok.err
        resp := ok.r
        if err != nil {
            fmt.Println("Error select:", err)
            return err
        }
        defer resp.Body.Close()

        realHTTPData, err := io.ReadAll(resp.Body)
        if err != nil {
            fmt.Println("Error select:", err)
            return err
        }
        fmt.Printf("Server Response: %s\n", realHTTPData)
    }
    return nil
}
```

The second `select` branch deals with the data received from the HTTP server, which is handled in the usual way.

```
func main() {
    if len(os.Args) == 1 {
        fmt.Println("Need a URL and a delay!")
        return
    }

    myUrl = os.Args[1]
    if len(os.Args) == 3 {
        t, err := strconv.Atoi(os.Args[2])
        if err != nil {
            fmt.Println(err)
            return
        }
        delay = t
    }
```

The URL is read directly because it is already a string value whereas the delay period is converted into a numeric value using `strconv.Atoi()`.

```
    fmt.Println("Delay:", delay)
    c := context.Background()
    c, cancel := context.WithTimeout(c, time.Duration(delay)*time.
Second)
    defer cancel()
```

The timeout period is defined by the `context.WithTimeout()` method. It is considered a good practice to use `context.Background()` in the `main()` function or the `init()` function of a package or in tests.

```
    fmt.Printf("Connecting to %s \n", myUrl)
    wg.Add(1)
    go connect(c)
    wg.Wait()
    fmt.Println("Exiting...")
}
```

The `connect()` function, which is also executed as a goroutine, either terminates normally or when the `cancel()` function is executed—the `cancel()` function is what calls the `Done()` method of `c`.

Working with `timeoutClient.go` and having a timeout situation generates the following kind of output:

```
$ go run timeoutClient.go http://localhost:80
Delay: 5
Connecting to http://localhost:80
Get "http://localhost:80": net/http: request canceled
The request was canceled!
Exiting...
```

The next subsection shows how to time out an HTTP request on the server side.

Setting the timeout period on the server side

This section presents a technique for timing out network connections that take too long to finish on the server side. This is much more important than the client side because a server with too many open connections might not be able to process more requests unless some of the already open connections close. This usually happens for two reasons. The first reason is software bugs, and the second reason is when a server is experiencing a **Denial of Service** (**DoS**) attack!

The `main()` function in `timeoutServer.go` shows the technique:

```
func main() {
    PORT := ":8001"
    arguments := os.Args
    if len(arguments) != 1 {
        PORT = ":" + arguments[1]
    }
    fmt.Println("Using port number: ", PORT)

    m := http.NewServeMux()
    srv := &http.Server{
        Addr:         PORT,
        Handler:      m,
        ReadTimeout:  3 * time.Second,
        WriteTimeout: 3 * time.Second,
    }
```

This is where the timeout periods are defined. Note that you can define timeout periods for both reading and writing processes. The value of the `ReadTimeout` field specifies the maximum duration allowed to read the entire client request, including the body, whereas the value of the `WriteTimeout` field specifies the maximum time duration before timing out the sending of the client response.

```
    m.HandleFunc("/time", timeHandler)
    m.HandleFunc("/", myHandler)

    err := srv.ListenAndServe()
    if err != nil {
        fmt.Println(err)
        return
    }
}
```

Apart from the parameters in the definition of `http.Server`, the rest of the code is as usual: it contains the handler functions and calls `ListenAndServe()` for starting the HTTP server.

Working with `timeoutServer.go` generates no output. However, if a client connects to it without sending any requests, the client connection is going to end after 3 seconds. The same is going to happen if it takes the client more than 3 seconds to receive the server response.

Exercises

- Put all handlers from `www-phone.go` in a different Go package and modify `www-phone.go` accordingly. You need a different repository for storing the new package.
- Modify `wwwClient.go` to save the HTML output to an external file.
- Include the functionality of `getEntries.go` in the phone book application.
- Implement a simple version of `ab(1)` using goroutines and channels. `ab(1)` is an Apache HTTP server benchmarking tool.

Summary

In this chapter, we learned how to work with HTTP, how to create Docker images from Go code, how to expose metrics to Prometheus, as well as how to develop HTTP clients and servers. We have also updated the phone book application into a web application and programmed a command-line client for it. Additionally, we learned how to time out HTTP connections and develop file servers.

We are now ready to begin developing powerful and concurrent HTTP applications—however, we are not done yet with HTTP. *Chapter 10, Working with REST APIs*, is going to connect the dots and show how to develop powerful RESTful servers and clients.

But first, we need to learn about working with TCP/IP, TCP, UDP, and WebSocket, which are the subjects of the next chapter.

Additional resources

- Caddy server: `https://caddyserver.com/`
- Nginx server: `https://nginx.org/en/`
- Histograms in Prometheus: `https://prometheus.io/docs/practices/histograms/`
- The `net/http` package: `https://golang.org/pkg/net/http/`
- Official Docker Go images: `https://hub.docker.com/_/golang/`

9
Working with TCP/IP and WebSocket

This chapter teaches you how to work with the lower-level protocols of TCP/IP, which are TCP and UDP, with the help of the `net` package so that we can develop TCP/IP servers and clients. Additionally, this chapter illustrates how to develop servers and clients for the *WebSocket* protocol, which is based on HTTP, as well as UNIX domain sockets, for programming services that work on the local machine only.

In more detail, this chapter covers:

- TCP/IP
- The `net` package
- Developing a TCP client
- Developing a TCP server
- Developing a UDP client
- Developing a UDP server
- Developing concurrent TCP servers
- Working with UNIX domain sockets
- Creating a WebSocket server
- Creating a WebSocket client

TCP/IP

TCP/IP is a family of protocols that help the internet operate. Its name comes from its two most well-known protocols: TCP and IP. TCP stands for *Transmission Control Protocol*. TCP software transmits data between machines using segments, which are also called *TCP packets*. The main characteristic of TCP is that it is a reliable protocol, which means that it makes sure that a packet was delivered without requiring any extra code from the programmer. If there is no proof of packet delivery, TCP resends that particular packet. Among other things, TCP packets can be used for establishing connections, transferring data, sending acknowledgments, and closing connections.

When a TCP connection is established between two machines, a full-duplex virtual circuit, similar to a telephone call, is created between those two machines. The two machines constantly communicate to make sure that data is sent and received correctly. If the connection fails for some reason, the two machines try to find the problem and report to the relevant application. The TCP header of each packet includes the **source port** and **destination port** fields. These two fields, plus the source and destination IP addresses, are combined to uniquely identify every single TCP connection. All these details are handled by TCP/IP as long as you provide the required details without any extra effort.

> When creating TCP/IP server processes, remember that port numbers **0-1024** have restricted access and can only be used by the root user, which means that you need administrative privileges to use a port in that range. Running a process with root privileges is a security risk and must be avoided.

IP stands for *Internet Protocol*. The main characteristic of IP is that it is not a reliable protocol by nature. IP encapsulates the data that travels over a TCP/IP network because it is responsible for delivering packets from the source host to the destination host according to the IP addresses. IP must find an addressing method for sending a packet to its destination effectively. Although there are dedicated devices, called routers, that perform IP routing, every TCP/IP device has to perform some basic routing. The first version of the IP protocol is now called **IPv4** to differentiate it from the latest version of the IP protocol, which is called **IPv6**. The main problem with IPv4 is that it is about to run out of available IP addresses, which is the main reason for creating the IPv6 protocol. This happened because an IPv4 address is represented using 32 bits only, which allows a total number of 2^{32} (4,294,967,296) different IP addresses. On the other hand, IPv6 uses 128 bits to define each one of its addresses. The format of an IPv4 address is `10.20.32.245` (four parts separated by dots), while the format of an IPv6 address is `3fce:1706:4523:3:150:f8ff:fe21:56cf` (eight parts separated by colons).

UDP (**User Datagram Protocol**) is based on IP, which means that it is also unreliable. UDP is simpler than TCP, mainly because UDP is not reliable by design. As a result, UDP messages can be lost, duplicated, or arrive out of order. Furthermore, packets can arrive faster than the recipient can process them. So, UDP is used when speed is more important than reliability.

This chapter implements both TCP and UDP software—TCP and UDP services are the basis of the internet, and it is handy to know how to develop TCP/IP servers and clients in Go. But first, let us talk about the `nc(1)` utility.

The nc(1) command-line utility

The `nc(1)` utility, which is also called `netcat(1)`, comes in very handy when you want to test TCP/IP servers and clients. Actually, `nc(1)` is a utility for everything that involves TCP and UDP as well as IPv4 and IPv6, including opening TCP connections, sending and receiving UDP messages, and acting as a TCP server.

You can use `nc(1)` as a client for a TCP service that runs on a machine with the `10.10.1.123` IP address and listens to port number `1234`, as follows:

```
$ nc 10.10.1.123 1234
```

The `-l` option tells `netcat(1)` to act as a server, which means that `netcat(1)` starts listening for incoming connections at the given port number. By default, `nc(1)` uses the TCP protocol. However, if you execute `nc(1)` with the `-u` flag, then `nc(1)` uses the UDP protocol, either as a client or as a server. Finally, the `-v` and `-vv` options tell `netcat(1)` to generate verbose output, which can come in handy when you want to troubleshoot network connections.

The net package

The `net` package of the Go Standard Library is all about TCP/IP, UDP, domain name resolution, and UNIX domain sockets. The `net.Dial()` function is used to connect to a network as a client, whereas the `net.Listen()` function is used to tell a Go program to accept incoming network connections and thus act as a server. The return value of both `net.Dial()` and `net.Listen()` is of the `net.Conn` data type, which implements the `io.Reader` and `io.Writer` interfaces—this means that you can both read and write to a `net.Conn` connection using code related to file I/O. The first parameter of both `net.Dial()`and `net.Listen()` is the network type, but this is where their similarities end.

The `net.Dial()` function is used for connecting to a remote server. The first parameter of the `net.Dial()` function defines the network protocol that is going to be used, while the second parameter defines the server address, which must also include the port number. Valid values for the first parameter are `tcp`, `tcp4` (IPv4-only), `tcp6` (IPv6-only), `udp`, `udp4` (IPv4-only), `udp6` (IPv6-only), `ip`, `ip4` (IPv4-only), `ip6` (IPv6-only), `unix` (UNIX sockets), `unixgram`, and `unixpacket`. On the other hand, valid values for `net.Listen()` are `tcp`, `tcp4`, `tcp6`, `unix`, and `unixpacket`.

> Execute the `go doc net.Listen` and `go doc net.Dial` commands for more detailed information regarding these two functions.

Developing a TCP client

This section presents two equivalent ways of developing TCP clients.

Developing a TCP client with net.Dial()

First, we are going to present the most widely used way, which is implemented in `tcpC.go`:

```
package main

import (
    "bufio"
    "fmt"
    "net"
    "os"
    "strings"
)
```

The `import` block contains packages such as `bufio` and `fmt` that also work with file I/O operations.

```
func main() {
    arguments := os.Args
    if len(arguments) == 1 {
        fmt.Println("Please provide host:port.")
        return
    }
```

First, we read the details of the TCP server we want to connect to.

```
connect := arguments[1]
c, err := net.Dial("tcp", connect)
if err != nil {
    fmt.Println(err)
    return
}
```

With the connection details, we call `net.Dial()`—its first parameter is the protocol we want to use, which in this case is `tcp`, and its second parameter is the connection details. A successful `net.Dial()` call returns an open connection (a `net.Conn` interface), which is a generic stream-oriented network connection.

```
    for {
        reader := bufio.NewReader(os.Stdin)
        fmt.Print(">> ")
        text, _ := reader.ReadString('\n')
        fmt.Fprintf(c, text+"\n")

        message, _ := bufio.NewReader(c).ReadString('\n')
        fmt.Print("->: " + message)
        if strings.TrimSpace(string(text)) == "STOP" {
            fmt.Println("TCP client exiting...")
            return
        }
    }
}
```

The last part of the TCP client keeps reading user input until the word `STOP` is given as input—in this case, the client **waits for the server response before terminating** after `STOP` because this is how the `for` loop is constructed. This mainly happens because the server might have a useful answer for us, and we do not want to miss that. All given user input is sent (written) to the open TCP connection using `fmt.Fprintf()`, whereas `bufio.NewReader()` is used for reading data from the TCP connection, just like you would do with a regular file.

Using `tcpC.go` to connect to a TCP server, which in this case is implemented with `nc(1)`, produces the next kind of output:

```
$ go run tcpC.go localhost:1234
>> Hello!
->: Hi from nc -l 1234
```

```
>> STOP
->: Bye!
TCP client exiting...
```

Lines beginning with >> denote user input, whereas lines beginning with -> signify server messages. After sending `STOP`, we wait for the server response and then the client ends the TCP connection. The previous code demonstrates how to create a proper TCP client in Go with some extra logic in it (the `STOP` keyword).

The next subsection shows a different way of creating a TCP client.

Developing a TCP client that uses net.DialTCP()

This subsection presents an alternative way to develop a TCP client. The difference lies in the Go functions that are being used for establishing the TCP connection, which are `net.DialTCP()` and `net.ResolveTCPAddr()`, and not in the functionality of the client.

The code of `otherTCPclient.go` is as follows:

```
package main

import (
    "bufio"
    "fmt"
    "net"
    "os"
    "strings"
)
```

Although we are working with TCP/IP connections, we need packages such as `bufio` because UNIX treats network connections as files, so we are basically working with I/O operations over networks.

```
func main() {
    arguments := os.Args
    if len(arguments) == 1 {
        fmt.Println("Please provide a server:port string!")
        return
    }
```

We need to read the details of the TCP server we want to connect to, including the desired port number. The utility cannot operate with default parameters when working with TCP/IP unless we are developing a very specialized TCP client.

```
    connect := arguments[1]
    tcpAddr, err := net.ResolveTCPAddr("tcp4", connect)
    if err != nil {
        fmt.Println("ResolveTCPAddr:", err)
        return
    }
```

The `net.ResolveTCPAddr()` function is specific to TCP connections, hence its name, and resolves the given address to a `*net.TCPAddr` value, which is a structure that represents the address of a TCP endpoint—in this case, the endpoint is the TCP server we want to connect to.

```
    conn, err := net.DialTCP("tcp4", nil, tcpAddr)
    if err != nil {
        fmt.Println("DialTCP:", err)
        return
    }
```

With the TCP endpoint at hand, we call `net.DialTCP()` to connect to the server. Apart from the use of `net.ResolveTCPAddr()` and `net.DialTCP()`, the rest of the code that has to do with the TCP client and TCP server interaction is exactly the same.

```
    for {
        reader := bufio.NewReader(os.Stdin)
        fmt.Print(">> ")
        text, _ := reader.ReadString('\n')
        fmt.Fprintf(conn, text+"\n")

        message, _ := bufio.NewReader(conn).ReadString('\n')
        fmt.Print("->: " + message)
        if strings.TrimSpace(string(text)) == "STOP" {
            fmt.Println("TCP client exiting...")
            conn.Close()
            return
        }
    }
}
```

Lastly, an infinite `for` loop is used for interacting with the TCP server. The TCP client reads user data, which is sent to the server. After that, it reads data from the TCP server. Once again, the `STOP` keyword ends the TCP connection on the client side using the `Close()` method.

Working with `otherTCPclient.go` and interacting with a TCP server process produces the next kind of output:

```
$ go run otherTCPclient.go localhost:1234
>> Hello!
->: Hi from nc -l 1234
>> STOP
->: Thanks for connection!
TCP client exiting...
```

The interaction is the same as with `tcpC.go`—we have just learned a different way of developing TCP clients. If you want my opinion, I prefer the implementation found in `tcpC.go` because it uses more generic functions. However, this is just personal taste.

The next section shows how to program TCP servers.

Developing a TCP server

This section presents two ways of developing a TCP server that can interact with TCP clients, just as we did with the TCP client.

Developing a TCP server with net.Listen()

The TCP server presented in this section, which uses `net.Listen()`, returns the current date and time to the client in a single network packet. In practice, this means that after accepting a client connection, the server gets the time and date from the operating system and sends that data back to the client. The `net.Listen()` function listens for connections, whereas the `net.Accept()` method waits for the next connection and returns a generic `Conn` variable with the client information. The code of `tcpS.go` is as follows:

```
package main

import (
    "bufio"
    "fmt"
```

```
    "net"
    "os"
    "strings"
    "time"
)

func main() {
    arguments := os.Args
    if len(arguments) == 1 {
        fmt.Println("Please provide port number")
        return
    }
```

The TCP server should know about the port number it is going to use—this is given as a command-line argument.

```
    PORT := ":" + arguments[1]
    l, err := net.Listen("tcp", PORT)
    if err != nil {
        fmt.Println(err)
        return
    }
    defer l.Close()
```

The `net.Listen()` function listens for connections and is what makes that particular program a server process. If the second parameter of `net.Listen()` contains a port number without an IP address or a hostname, `net.Listen()` listens to all available IP addresses of the local system, which is the case here.

```
    c, err := l.Accept()
    if err != nil {
        fmt.Println(err)
        return
    }
```

We just call `Accept()` and wait for a client connection—`Accept()` blocks until a connection comes. There is something unusual with this particular TCP server: it can only serve the first TCP client that is going to connect to it because the `Accept()` call is outside of the `for` loop and therefore is called only once. Each individual client should be specified by a different `Accept()` call.

Correcting that is left as an exercise for the reader.

```
    for {
        netData, err := bufio.NewReader(c).ReadString('\n')
        if err != nil {
            fmt.Println(err)
            return
        }
        if strings.TrimSpace(string(netData)) == "STOP" {
            fmt.Println("Exiting TCP server!")
            return
        }

        fmt.Print("-> ", string(netData))
        t := time.Now()
        myTime := t.Format(time.RFC3339) + "\n"
        c.Write([]byte(myTime))
    }
}
```

This endless `for` loop keeps interacting with the same TCP client until the word `STOP` is sent from the client. As it happened with the TCP clients, `bufio.NewReader()` is used for reading data from the network connection, whereas `Write()` is used for sending data to the TCP client.

Running `tcpS.go` and interacting with a TCP client produces the next kind of output:

```
$ go run tcpS.go 1234
-> Hello!
-> Have to leave now!
EOF
```

The server connection ended automatically with the client connection because the `for` loop concluded when `bufio.NewReader(c).ReadString('\n')` had nothing more to read. The client was `nc(1)`, which produced the next output:

```
$ nc localhost 1234
Hello!
2021-04-12T08:53:32+03:00
Have to leave now!
2021-04-12T08:53:51+03:00
```

In order to exit `nc(1)`, we need to press *Ctrl* + *D*, which is `EOF` (End Of File) in UNIX.

So, we now know how to develop a TCP server in Go. As it happened with the TCP client, there is an alternative way to develop a TCP server, which is presented in the next subsection.

Developing a TCP server that uses net.ListenTCP()

This time, this alternative version of the TCP server implements the echo service. Put simply, the TCP server sends back to the client the data that was received by the client.

The code of `otherTCPserver.go` is as follows:

```
package main

import (
    "fmt"
    "net"
    "os"
    "strings"
)

func main() {
    arguments := os.Args
    if len(arguments) == 1 {
        fmt.Println("Please provide a port number!")
        return
    }

    SERVER := "localhost" + ":" + arguments[1]
    s, err := net.ResolveTCPAddr("tcp", SERVER)
    if err != nil {
        fmt.Println(err)
        return
    }
```

The previous code gets the TCP port number value as a command-line argument, which is used in `net.ResolveTCPAddr()`—this is required to define the TCP port number the TCP server is going to listen to.

That function only works with TCP, hence its name.

```
l, err := net.ListenTCP("tcp", s)
if err != nil {
    fmt.Println(err)
    return
}
```

Similarly, `net.ListenTCP()` only works with TCP and is what makes that program a TCP server ready to accept incoming connections.

```
buffer := make([]byte, 1024)
conn, err := l.Accept()
if err != nil {
    fmt.Println(err)
    return
}
```

As before, due to the place where `Accept()` is called, this particular implementation can work with a single client only. This is used for reasons of simplicity. The concurrent TCP server that is developed later on in this chapter puts the `Accept()` call inside the endless `for` loop.

```
for {
    n, err := conn.Read(buffer)
    if err != nil {
        fmt.Println(err)
        return
    }

    if strings.TrimSpace(string(buffer[0:n])) == "STOP" {
        fmt.Println("Exiting TCP server!")
        conn.Close()
        return
    }
```

You need to use `strings.TrimSpace()` in order to remove any space characters from your input and compare the result with `STOP`, which has a special meaning in this implementation. When the `STOP` keyword is received from the client, the server closes the connection using the `Close()` method.

```
    fmt.Print("> ", string(buffer[0:n-1]), "\n")
    _, err = conn.Write(buffer)
```

```
        if err != nil {
            fmt.Println(err)
            return
        }
    }
}
```

All previous code is for interacting with the TCP client until the client decides to close the connection.

Running `otherTCPserver.go` and interacting with a TCP client produces the next kind of output:

```
$ go run otherTCPserver.go 1234
> Hello from the client!
Exiting TCP server!
```

The first line that begins with > is the client message, whereas the second line is the server output when getting the `STOP` message from the client. Therefore, the TCP server processes client requests as programmed and exits when it gets the `STOP` message, which is the expected behavior.

The next section is about developing UDP clients.

Developing a UDP client

This section demonstrates how to develop a UDP client that can interact with UDP services. The code of `udpC.go` is as follows:

```
package main

import (
    "bufio"
    "fmt"
    "net"
    "os"
    "strings"
)

func main() {
    arguments := os.Args
    if len(arguments) == 1 {
```

```
        fmt.Println("Please provide a host:port string")
        return
    }
    CONNECT := arguments[1]
```

This is how we get the UDP server details from the user.

```
    s, err := net.ResolveUDPAddr("udp4", CONNECT)
    c, err := net.DialUDP("udp4", nil, s)
```

The previous two lines declare that we are using UDP and that we want to connect to the UDP server that is specified by the return value of `net.ResolveUDPAddr()`. The actual connection is initiated using `net.DialUDP()`.

```
    if err != nil {
        fmt.Println(err)
        return
    }

    fmt.Printf("The UDP server is %s\n", c.RemoteAddr().String())
    defer c.Close()
```

This part of the program finds the details of the UDP server by calling the `RemoteAddr()` method.

```
    for {
        reader := bufio.NewReader(os.Stdin)
        fmt.Print(">> ")
        text, _ := reader.ReadString('\n')
        data := []byte(text + "\n")
        _, err = c.Write(data)
```

Data is read from the user using `bufio.NewReader(os.Stdin)` and is written to the UDP server using `Write()`.

```
        if strings.TrimSpace(string(data)) == "STOP" {
            fmt.Println("Exiting UDP client!")
            return
        }
```

If the input read from the user is the `STOP` keyword, then the connection is terminated.

```
        if err != nil {
            fmt.Println(err)
            return
        }

        buffer := make([]byte, 1024)
        n, _, err := c.ReadFromUDP(buffer)
```

Data is read from the UDP connection using the `ReadFromUDP()` method.

```
        if err != nil {
            fmt.Println(err)
            return
        }
        fmt.Printf("Reply: %s\n", string(buffer[0:n]))
    }
}
```

The `for` loop is going to keep going forever until the `STOP` keyword is received as input or the program is terminated in some other way.

Working with `udpC.go` is as simple as follows—the client side is implemented using `nc(1)`:

```
$ go run udpC.go localhost:1234
The UDP server is 127.0.0.1:1234
```

`127.0.0.1:1234` is the value of `c.RemoteAddr().String()`, which shows the details of the UDP server we have connected to.

```
>> Hello!
Reply: Hi from the server
```

Our client sent `Hello!` to the UDP server and received `Hi from the server` back.

```
>> Have to leave now :)
Reply: OK - bye from nc -l -u 1234
```

Our client sent `Have to leave now :)` to the UDP server and received `OK - bye from nc -l -u 1234` back.

```
>> STOP
Exiting UDP client!
```

Finally, after sending the `STOP` keyword to the server, the client prints `Exiting UDP client!` and terminates—the message is defined in the Go code and can be anything you want.

The next section is about programming a UDP server.

Developing a UDP server

This section shows how to develop a UDP server, which generates and returns random numbers to its clients. The code for the UDP server (`udpS.go`) is as follows:

```
package main

import (
	"fmt"
	"math/rand"
	"net"
	"os"
	"strconv"
	"strings"
	"time"
)

func random(min, max int) int {
	return rand.Intn(max-min) + min
}

func main() {
	arguments := os.Args
	if len(arguments) == 1 {
		fmt.Println("Please provide a port number!")
		return
	}
	PORT := ":" + arguments[1]
```

The UDP port number the server is going to listen to is provided as a command-line argument.

```
	s, err := net.ResolveUDPAddr("udp4", PORT)
	if err != nil {
		fmt.Println(err)
		return
	}
```

The `net.ResolveUDPAddr()` function creates a UDP endpoint that is going to be used to create the server.

```
	connection, err := net.ListenUDP("udp4", s)
	if err != nil {
		fmt.Println(err)
		return
	}
```

The `net.ListenUDP("udp4", s)` function call makes this process a server for the `udp4` protocol using the details specified by its second parameter.

```
	defer connection.Close()
	buffer := make([]byte, 1024)
```

The `buffer` variable stores a `byte` slice and is used to read data from the UDP connection.

```
	rand.Seed(time.Now().Unix())

	for {
		n, addr, err := connection.ReadFromUDP(buffer)
		fmt.Print("-> ", string(buffer[0:n-1]))
```

The `ReadFromUDP()` and `WriteToUDP()` methods are used to read data from a UDP connection and write data to a UDP connection, respectively. Additionally, due to the way UDP operates, the UDP server can serve multiple clients.

```
		if strings.TrimSpace(string(buffer[0:n])) == "STOP" {
			fmt.Println("Exiting UDP server!")
			return
		}
```

The UDP server terminates when any one of the clients sends the `STOP` message. Aside from this, the `for` loop is going to keep running forever.

```
		data := []byte(strconv.Itoa(random(1, 1001)))
		fmt.Printf("data: %s\n", string(data))
```

A `byte` slice is stored in the `data` variable and used to write the desired data to the client.

```
		_, err = connection.WriteToUDP(data, addr)
		if err != nil {
```

```
                fmt.Println(err)
                return
            }
        }
    }
```

Working with `udpS.go` is as simple as the following:

```
$ go run udpS.go 1234
-> Hello from client!
data: 395
```

Lines beginning with `->` show data coming from a client. Lines beginning with `data` show random numbers generated by the UDP server—in this case, `395`.

```
-> Going to terminate the connection now.
data: 499
```

The previous two lines show another interaction with a UDP client.

```
-> STOP
Exiting UDP server!
```

Once the UDP server receives the `STOP` keyword from the client, it closes the connection and exits.

On the client side, which uses `udpC.go`, we have the next interaction:

```
$ go run udpC.go localhost:1234
The UDP server is 127.0.0.1:1234
>> Hello from client!
Reply: 395
```

The client sends the `Hello from client!` message to the server and receives `395`.

```
>> Going to terminate the connection now.
Reply: 499
```

The client sends `Going to terminate the connection now.` to the server and receives the `499` random number.

```
>> STOP
Exiting UDP client!
```

When the client gets `STOP` as user input, it terminates the UDP connection and exits.

The next section shows how to develop a concurrent TCP server that uses goroutines for serving its clients.

Developing concurrent TCP servers

This section teaches a pattern for developing concurrent TCP servers, which are servers that are using separate goroutines to serve their clients following a successful `Accept()` call. Therefore, such servers can serve multiple TCP clients at the same time. This is how real-world production servers and services are implemented.

The code of `concTCP.go` is as follows:

```
package main

import (
	"bufio"
	"fmt"
	"net"
	"os"
	"strconv"
	"strings"
)

var count = 0

func handleConnection(c net.Conn) {
	fmt.Print(".")
```

The previous statement is not required—it just informs us that a new client has been connected.

```
	for {
		netData, err := bufio.NewReader(c).ReadString('\n')
		if err != nil {
			fmt.Println(err)
			return
		}

		temp := strings.TrimSpace(string(netData))
		if temp == "STOP" {
```

```
            break
        }
        fmt.Println(temp)
        counter := "Client number: " + strconv.Itoa(count) + "\n"
        c.Write([]byte(string(counter)))
    }
```

The `for` loop makes sure that `handleConnection()` is not going to exit automatically. Once again, the `STOP` keyword stops the current client connection—however, the server process, as well as all other active client connections, are going to keep running.

```
    c.Close()
}
```

This is the end of the function that is executed as a goroutine to serve clients. All you need in order to serve a client is a `net.Conn` parameter with the client details. After reading client data, the server sends back to the client a message indicating the number of the client that is being served so far.

```
func main() {
    arguments := os.Args
    if len(arguments) == 1 {
        fmt.Println("Please provide a port number!")
        return
    }

    PORT := ":" + arguments[1]
    l, err := net.Listen("tcp4", PORT)
    if err != nil {
        fmt.Println(err)
        return
    }
    defer l.Close()

    for {
        c, err := l.Accept()
        if err != nil {
            fmt.Println(err)
            return
        }
        go handleConnection(c)
        count++
```

```
    }
}
```

Each time a new client connects to the server, the `count` variable is increased. Each TCP client is served by a separate goroutine that executes the `handleConnection()` function. This frees the server process and allows it to accept new connections. Put simply, while multiple TCP clients are served, the TCP server is free to interact with more TCP clients. As before, new TCP clients are connected using the `Accept()` function.

Working with `concTCP.go` produces the next kind of output:

```
$ go run concTCP.go 1234
.Hello
.Hi from  nc localhost 1234
```

The first line of output is from the first TCP client, whereas the second line is from the second TCP client. This means that the concurrent TCP server works as expected. Therefore, when you want to be able to serve multiple TCP clients in your TCP services, you can use the technique and code presented as a template for developing your TCP servers.

The next section shows how to work with UNIX domain sockets, which are really fast for interactions on the local machine only.

Working with UNIX domain sockets

A *UNIX Domain Socket* or Inter-Process Communication (IPC) socket is a data communications endpoint that allows you to exchange data between processes that run **on the same machine**. You might ask, why use UNIX domain sockets instead of TCP/IP connections for processes that exchange data on the same machine? First, because UNIX domain sockets are faster than TCP/IP connections and second, because UNIX domain sockets require fewer resources than TCP/IP connections. So, you can use UNIX domain sockets when both the clients and the server are on the same machine.

A UNIX domain socket server

This section illustrates how to develop a UNIX domain socket server. Although we do not have to deal with TCP ports and network connections, the code presented is very similar to the code of the TCP server as found in `tcpS.go` and `concTCP.go`. The presented server implements the echo service.

The source code of `socketServer.go` is as follows:

```
package main

import (
    "fmt"
    "net"
    "os"
)

func echo(c net.Conn) {
```

The `echo()` function is used for serving client requests, hence the use of the `net.Conn` parameter that holds the client's details:

```
    for {
        buf := make([]byte, 128)
        n, err := c.Read(buf)
        if err != nil {
            fmt.Println("Read:", err)
            return
        }
```

We read data from the socket connection using `Read()` inside a `for` loop.

```
        data := buf[0:n]
        fmt.Print("Server got: ", string(data))
        _, err = c.Write(data)
        if err != nil {
            fmt.Println("Write:", err)
            return
        }
    }
}
```

In this second part of `echo()`, we send back to the client the data that the client sent to us. The `buf[0:n]` notation makes sure that we are going to send back the same amount of data that was read even if the size of the buffer is bigger.

This function serves all client connections—as you are going to see in a while, it is executed as a goroutine, which is the main reason that it does not return any values.

You cannot tell whether this function serves TCP/IP connections or UNIX socket domain connections, which mainly happens because UNIX treats all connections as files.

```
func main() {
    if len(os.Args) == 1 {
        fmt.Println("Need socket path")
        return
    }
    socketPath := os.Args[1]
```

This is the part where we specify the socket file that is going to be used by the server and its clients. In this case, the path to the socket file is given as a command-line argument.

```
    _, err := os.Stat(socketPath)
    if err == nil {
        fmt.Println("Deleting existing", socketPath)
        err := os.Remove(socketPath)
        if err != nil {
            fmt.Println(err)
            return
        }
    }
```

If the socket file already exists, you should **delete it** before the program continues—`net.Listen()` creates that file again.

```
    l, err := net.Listen("unix", socketPath)
    if err != nil {
        fmt.Println("listen error:", err)
        return
    }
```

What makes this a UNIX domain socket server is the use of `net.Listen()` with the `"unix"` parameter. In this case, we need to provide `net.Listen()` with the path of the socket file.

```
    for {
        fd, err := l.Accept()
        if err != nil {
            fmt.Println("Accept error:", err)
```

```
                return
            }
            go echo(fd)
        }
    }
```

Each client connection is handled by a goroutine—in this sense, this is a concurrent UNIX domain socket server that can work with multiple clients! So, if you need to serve thousands of domain socket clients on a production server, this is the way to go!

In the next section, we are going to see the server in action as it is going to interact with the UNIX domain socket client that we are going to create.

A UNIX domain socket client

This subsection shows a UNIX domain socket client implementation, which can be used to communicate with a domain socket server, such as the one developed in the previous subsection. The relevant code can be found in `socketClient.go`:

```
package main

import (
    "bufio"
    "fmt"
    "net"
    "os"
    "strings"
    "time"
)

func main() {
    if len(os.Args) == 1 {
        fmt.Println("Need socket path")
        return
    }
    socketPath := os.Args[1]
```

This is the part where we get from the user the socket file that is going to be used—the socket file should already exist and be handled by the UNIX domain socket server.

```
    c, err := net.Dial("unix", socketPath)
    if err != nil {
        fmt.Println(err)
        return
    }
    defer c.Close()
```

The `net.Dial()` function is used for connecting to the socket.

```
    for {
        reader := bufio.NewReader(os.Stdin)
        fmt.Print(">> ")
        text, _ := reader.ReadString('\n')

        _, err = c.Write([]byte(text))
```

Here, we convert user input into a `byte` slice and send it to the server using `Write()`.

```
        if err != nil {
            fmt.Println("Write:", err)
            break
        }

        buf := make([]byte, 256)

        n, err := c.Read(buf[:])
        if err != nil {
            fmt.Println(err, n)
            return
        }
        fmt.Print("Read:", string(buf[0:n]))
```

This `fmt.Print()` statement prints as many characters from the `buf` slice as the number of characters read from the `Read()` method using the `buf[0:n]` notation.

```
        if strings.TrimSpace(string(text)) == "STOP" {
            fmt.Println("Exiting UNIX domain socket client!")
            return
        }
```

If the word `STOP` is given as input, then the client returns and therefore closes the connection to the server. Generally speaking, it is always good to have a way of gracefully exiting such a utility.

```
            time.Sleep(5 * time.Second)
        }
    }
```

The `time.Sleep()` call is used to delay the `for` loop and emulate the operation of a real program.

Working with both `socketServer.go` and `socketClient.go`, provided that the server is executed first, generates the next kind of output:

```
$ go run socketServer.go /tmp/packt.socket
Server got: Hello!
Server got: STOP
Read: EOF
```

Although the client connection ended, the server continues to run and waits for more client requests.

On the client side, we have the following:

```
$ go run socketClient.go /tmp/packt.socket
>> Hello!
Read: Hello!
>> STOP
Read: STOP
Exiting UNIX domain socket client!
```

In the previous two sections, we learned how to create UNIX domain socket clients and servers that are faster than TCP/IP servers but work on the same machine only.

The sections that follow concern the WebSocket protocol.

Creating a WebSocket server

The WebSocket protocol is a computer communications protocol that provides **full-duplex** (transmission of data in two directions simultaneously) communication channels over a single TCP connection. The WebSocket protocol is defined in RFC 6455 (`https://tools.ietf.org/html/rfc6455`) and uses `ws://` and `wss://` instead of `http://` and `https://`, respectively. Therefore, the client should begin a WebSocket connection by using a URL that starts with `ws://`.

In this section, we are going to develop a small yet fully functional WebSocket server using the `gorilla/websocket` (`https://github.com/gorilla/websocket`) module. The server implements the **Echo service**, which means that it automatically returns its input to the client.

The `golang.org/x/net/websocket` package offers another way of developing WebSocket clients and servers. However, according to its documentation, `golang.org/x/net/websocket` lacks some features and it is advised that you use `https://godoc.org/github.com/gorilla/websocket`, the one used here, or `https://godoc.org/nhooyr.io/websocket` instead.

The advantages of the WebSocket protocol include the following:

- A WebSocket connection is a full-duplex, bidirectional communications channel. This means that a server does not need to wait to read from a client to send data to the client and vice versa.
- WebSocket connections are raw TCP sockets, which means that they do not have the overhead required to establish an HTTP connection.
- WebSocket connections can also be used for sending HTTP data. However, plain HTTP connections cannot work as WebSocket connections.
- WebSocket connections live until they are killed, so there is no need to reopen them all the time.
- WebSocket connections can be used for real-time web applications.
- Data can be sent from the server to the client at any time, without the client even requesting it.
- WebSocket is part of the HTML5 specification, which means that it is supported by all modern web browsers.

Before showing the server implementation, it would be good for you to know that the `websocket.Upgrader` method of the `gorilla/websocket` package **upgrades** an HTTP server connection to the WebSocket protocol and allows you to define the parameters of the upgrade. After that, your HTTP connection is a WebSocket connection, which means that you will not be allowed to execute statements that work with the HTTP protocol.

The next subsection shows the implementation of the server.

The implementation of the server

This subsection presents the implementation of the WebSocket server that implements the `echo` service, which can be really handy when testing network connections.

The GitHub repository used for keeping the code can be found at `https://github.com/mactsouk/ws`. If you want to follow along with this section, you should download that repository and put it inside `~/go/src`—in my case, it was put inside `~/go/src/github.com/mactsouk`, in the `ws` folder.

> The GitHub repository contains a `Dockerfile` file for producing a Docker image from the WebSocket server source file.

The implementation of the WebSocket server can be found in `ws.go`, which contains the next code:

```
package main

import (
	"fmt"
	"log"
	"net/http"
	"os"
	"time"

	"github.com/gorilla/websocket"
)
```

This is the external package used for working with the WebSocket protocol.

```
var PORT = ":1234"

var upgrader = websocket.Upgrader{
	ReadBufferSize:  1024,
	WriteBufferSize: 1024,
	CheckOrigin: func(r *http.Request) bool {
		return true
	},
}
```

This is where the parameters of `websocket.Upgrader` are defined. They are going to be used shortly.

```
func rootHandler(w http.ResponseWriter, r *http.Request) {
	fmt.Fprintf(w, "Welcome!\n")
```

```
    fmt.Fprintf(w, "Please use /ws for WebSocket!")
}
```

This is a regular HTTP handler function.

```
func wsHandler(w http.ResponseWriter, r *http.Request) {
    log.Println("Connection from:", r.Host)

    ws, err := upgrader.Upgrade(w, r, nil)
    if err != nil {
        log.Println("upgrader.Upgrade:", err)
        return
    }
    defer ws.Close()
```

A WebSocket server application calls the `Upgrader.Upgrade` method in order to get a WebSocket connection from an HTTP request handler. Following a successful call to `Upgrader.Upgrade`, the server begins working with the WebSocket connection and the WebSocket client.

```
    for {
        mt, message, err := ws.ReadMessage()
        if err != nil {
            log.Println("From", r.Host, "read", err)
            break
        }
        log.Print("Received: ", string(message))
        err = ws.WriteMessage(mt, message)
        if err != nil {
            log.Println("WriteMessage:", err)
            break
        }
    }
}
```

The `for` loop in `wsHandler()` handles all incoming messages for `/ws`—you can use any technique you want. Additionally, in the presented implementation, **only the client** is allowed to close an existing WebSocket connection unless there is a network issue, or the server process is killed.

Last, remember that in a WebSocket connection, you cannot use `fmt.Fprintf()` statements for sending data to the WebSocket client—if you use any of these, or any other call that can implement the same functionality, the WebSocket connection fails and you are not going to be able to send or receive any data. Therefore, the only way to send and receive data in a WebSocket connection implemented with `gorilla/websocket` is through `WriteMessage()` and `ReadMessage()` calls, respectively. Of course, you can always implement the desired functionality on your own by working with raw network data, but implementing this goes beyond the scope of this book.

```
func main() {
    arguments := os.Args
    if len(arguments) != 1 {
        PORT = ":" + arguments[1]
    }
```

If there is not a command-line argument, use the default port number stored in `PORT`.

```
    mux := http.NewServeMux()
    s := &http.Server{
        Addr:         PORT,
        Handler:      mux,
        IdleTimeout:  10 * time.Second,
        ReadTimeout:  time.Second,
        WriteTimeout: time.Second,
    }
```

These are the details of the HTTP server that also handles WebSocket connections.

```
    mux.Handle("/", http.HandlerFunc(rootHandler))
    mux.Handle("/ws", http.HandlerFunc(wsHandler))
```

The endpoint used for WebSocket can be anything you want—in this case, it is `/ws`. Additionally, you can have multiple endpoints that work with the WebSocket protocol.

```
    log.Println("Listening to TCP Port", PORT)
    err := s.ListenAndServe()
    if err != nil {
        log.Println(err)
        return
    }
}
```

The code presented uses `log.Println()` instead of `fmt.Println()` for printing messages—as this is a server process, using `log.Println()` is a much better choice than `fmt.Println()` because logging information is sent to files that can be examined at a later time. However, during development, you might prefer `fmt.Println()` calls and avoid writing to your log files because you can see your data on screen immediately without having to look elsewhere.

The server implementation is short, yet fully functional. The single most important call in the code is `Upgrader.Upgrade` because this is what upgrades an HTTP connection to a WebSocket connection.

Getting and running the code from GitHub requires the following steps—most of the steps have to do with module initialization and downloading the required packages:

```
$ cd ~/go/src/github.com/mactsouk/
$ git clone https://github.com/mactsouk/ws.git
$ cd ws
$ go mod init
$ go mod tidy
$ go mod download
$ go run ws.go
```

To test that server, you need to have a client. As we have not developed our own client so far, we are going to test the WebSocket server using two other means.

Using websocat

`websocat` is a command-line utility that can help you test WebSocket connections. However, as `websocat` is not installed by default, you need to install it on your machine using your package manager of choice. You can use it as follows, provided that there is a WebSocket server at the desired address:

```
$ websocat ws://localhost:1234/ws
Hello from websocat!
```

This is what we type and send to the server.

```
Hello from websocat!
```

This is what we get back from the WebSocket server, which implements the `echo` service—different WebSocket servers implement different functionality.

```
Bye!
```

Again, the previous line is user input given to `websocat`.

```
Bye!
```

And the last line is the data sent back from the server. The connection was closed by pressing *Ctrl* + *D* on the `websocat` client.

Should you wish for a more verbose output from `websocat`, you can execute it with the `-v` flag:

```
$ websocat -v ws://localhost:1234/ws
[INFO  websocat::lints] Auto-inserting the line mode
[INFO  websocat::stdio_threaded_peer] get_stdio_peer (threaded)
[INFO  websocat::ws_client_peer] get_ws_client_peer
[INFO  websocat::ws_client_peer] Connected to ws
Hello from websocat!
Hello from websocat!
Bye!
Bye!
[INFO  websocat::sessionserve] Forward finished
[INFO  websocat::ws_peer] Received WebSocket close message
[INFO  websocat::sessionserve] Reverse finished
[INFO  websocat::sessionserve] Both directions finished
```

In both cases, the output from our WebSocket server should be similar to the following:

```
$ go run ws.go
2021/04/10 20:54:30 Listening to TCP Port :1234
2021/04/10 20:54:42 Connection from: localhost:1234
2021/04/10 20:54:57 Received: Hello from websocat!
2021/04/10 20:55:03 Received: Bye!
2021/04/10 20:55:03 From localhost:1234 read websocket: close 1005 (no status)
```

The next subsection illustrates how to test the WebSocket server using HTML and JavaScript.

Using JavaScript

The second way of testing the WebSocket server is by creating a web page with some HTML and JavaScript code. This technique gives you more control over what is happening, but requires more code and familiarity with HTML and JavaScript.

The HTML page with the JavaScript code that makes it act like a WebSocket client is the following:

```
<!DOCTYPE html>
<meta charset="utf-8">

<html lang="en">
  <head>
    <meta charset="UTF-8" />
    <meta name="viewport" content="width=device-width, initial-
scale=1.0" />
    <meta http-equiv="X-UA-Compatible" content="ie=edge" />
    <title>Testing a WebSocket Server</title>
  </head>
  <body>
    <h2>Hello There!</h2>

    <script>
        let ws = new WebSocket("ws://localhost:1234/ws");
```

This is the single most important JavaScript statement because this is where you specify the address of the WebSocket server, the port number, and the endpoint you want to connect to.

```
        console.log("Trying to connect to server.");

        ws.onopen = () => {
            console.log("Connected!");
            ws.send("Hello From the Client!")
        };
```

The `ws.onopen` event is used for making sure that the WebSocket connection is open, whereas the `send()` method is used for sending messages to the WebSocket server.

```
        ws.onmessage = function(event) {
          console.log(`[message] Data received from server: ${event.
data}`);
          ws.close(1000, "Work complete");
        };
```

The `onmessage` event is triggered each time the WebSocket server sends a new message—however, in our case, the connection is closed as soon as the first message from the server is received.

Lastly, the `close()` JavaScript method is used for closing a WebSocket connection—in our case, the `close()` call is included in the `onmessage` event. Calling `close()` triggers the `onclose` event, which contains the code that follows:

```
        ws.onclose = event => {
            if (event.wasClean) {
              console.log(`[close] Connection closed cleanly,
code=${event.code} reason=${event.reason}`);
            }
            console.log("Socket Closed Connection: ", event);
        };

        ws.onerror = error => {
            console.log("Socket Error: ", error);
        };

    </script>
  </body>
</html>
```

You can see the output of the JavaScript code by visiting the JavaScript console on your favorite web browser, which in this case is Google Chrome. The following screenshot shows the generated output.

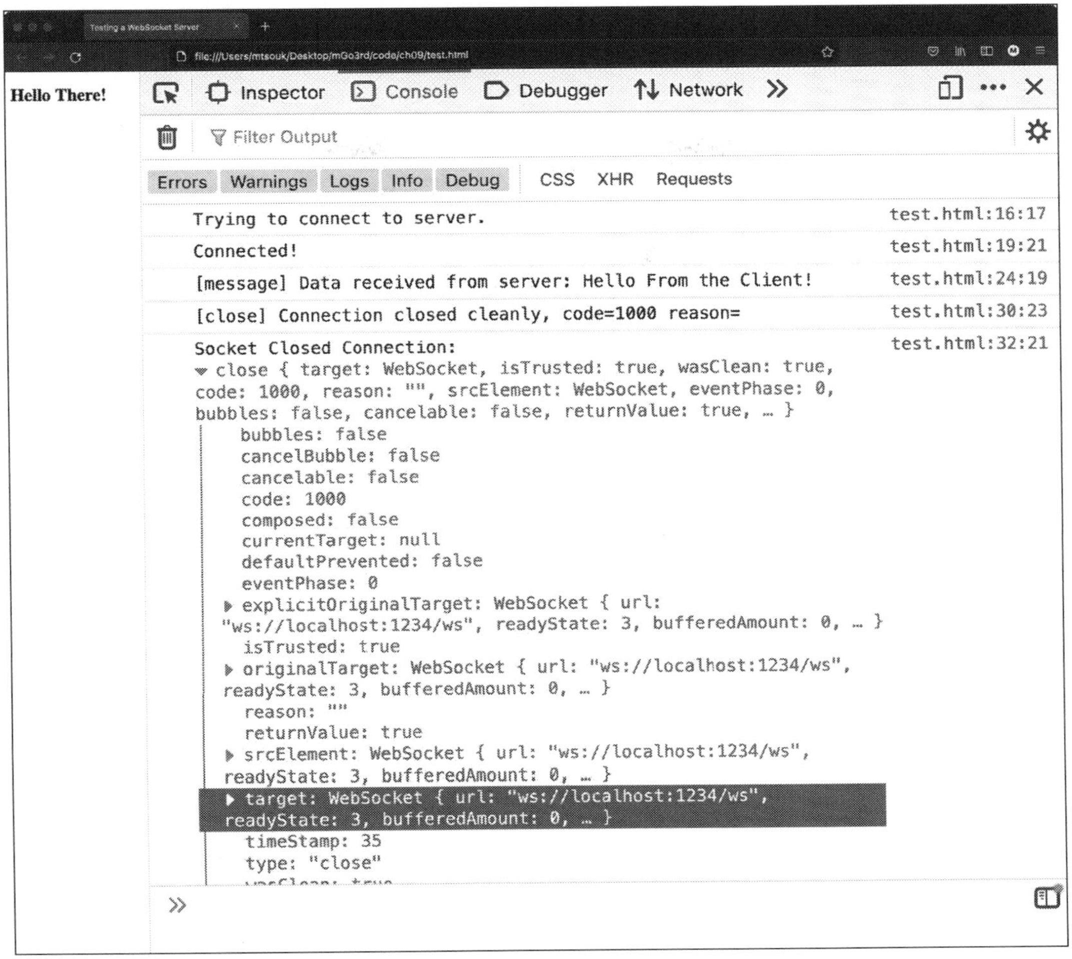

Figure 9.1: Interacting with the WebSocket server using JavaScript

For the WebSocket interaction defined in `test.html`, the WebSocket server generated the following output in the command line:

```
2021/04/10 21:43:22 Connection from: localhost:1234
2021/04/10 21:43:22 Received: Hello From the Client!
2021/04/10 21:43:22 From localhost:1234 read websocket: close 1000
(normal): Work complete
```

Both ways verify that the WebSocket server works as expected: the client can connect to the server, the server sends data that is received by the client, and the client closes the connection with the server successfully. So, it is time to develop our own WebSocket client in Go.

Creating a WebSocket client

This subsection shows how to program a WebSocket client in Go. The client reads user data that sends it to the server and reads the server response. The `client` directory of `https://github.com/mactsouk/ws` contains the implementation of the WebSocket client—I find it more convenient to include both implementations in the same repository.

As with the WebSocket server, the `gorilla/websocket` package is going to help us develop the WebSocket client.

> We are going to see `gorilla` in the next chapter when working with RESTful services.

The code of `./client/client.go` is as follows:

```go
package main

import (
	"bufio"
	"fmt"
	"log"
	"net/url"
	"os"
	"os/signal"
	"syscall"
	"time"
```

```
	"github.com/gorilla/websocket"
)

var SERVER = ""
var PATH = ""
var TIMESWAIT = 0
var TIMESWAITMAX = 5
var in = bufio.NewReader(os.Stdin)
```

The `in` variable is just a shortcut for `bufio.NewReader(os.Stdin)`.

```
func getInput(input chan string) {
	result, err := in.ReadString('\n')
	if err != nil {
		log.Println(err)
		return
	}
	input <- result
}
```

The `getInput()` function, which is executed as a goroutine, gets user input that is transferred to the `main()` function via the `input` channel. Each time the program reads some user input, the old goroutine ends and a new `getInput()` goroutine begins in order to get new input.

```
func main() {
	arguments := os.Args
	if len(arguments) != 3 {
		fmt.Println("Need SERVER + PATH!")
		return
	}

	SERVER = arguments[1]
	PATH = arguments[2]
	fmt.Println("Connecting to:", SERVER, "at", PATH)

	interrupt := make(chan os.Signal, 1)
	signal.Notify(interrupt, os.Interrupt)
```

The WebSocket client handles UNIX interrupts with the help of the `interrupt` channel. When the appropriate signal is caught (`syscall.SIGINT`), the WebSocket connection with the server is closed with the help of the `websocket.CloseMessage` message. This is how professional tools work!

```
input := make(chan string, 1)
go getInput(input)

URL := url.URL{Scheme: "ws", Host: SERVER, Path: PATH}
c, _, err := websocket.DefaultDialer.Dial(URL.String(), nil)
if err != nil {
    log.Println("Error:", err)
    return
}
defer c.Close()
```

The WebSocket connection begins with a call to `websocket.DefaultDialer.Dial()`. Everything that goes to the `input` channel is transferred to the WebSocket server using the `WriteMessage()` method.

```
done := make(chan struct{})
go func() {
    defer close(done)
    for {
        _, message, err := c.ReadMessage()
        if err != nil {
            log.Println("ReadMessage() error:", err)
            return
        }
        log.Printf("Received: %s", message)
    }
}()
```

Another goroutine, which this time is implemented using an anonymous Go function, is responsible for reading data from the WebSocket connection using the `ReadMessage()` method.

```
for {
    select {
    case <-time.After(4 * time.Second):
        log.Println("Please give me input!", TIMESWAIT)
        TIMESWAIT++
        if TIMESWAIT > TIMESWAITMAX {
```

```
                syscall.Kill(syscall.Getpid(), syscall.SIGINT)
            }
```

The `syscall.Kill(syscall.Getpid(), syscall.SIGINT)` statement sends the interrupt signal to the program using Go code. According to the logic of `client.go`, the interrupt signal makes the program close the WebSocket connection with the server and terminate its execution. This only happens if the current number of timeout periods is bigger than a predefined global value.

```
        case <-done:
            return
        case t := <-input:
            err := c.WriteMessage(websocket.TextMessage, []byte(t))
            if err != nil {
                log.Println("Write error:", err)
                return
            }
            TIMESWAIT = 0
```

If you get user input, the current number of the timeout periods (`TIMESWAIT`) is reset and new input is read.

```
            go getInput(input)
        case <-interrupt:
            log.Println("Caught interrupt signal - quitting!")
            err := c.WriteMessage(websocket.CloseMessage, websocket.
FormatCloseMessage(websocket.CloseNormalClosure, ""))
```

Just before we close the client connection, we send `websocket.CloseMessage` to the server in order to do the closing the right way.

```
            if err != nil {
                log.Println("Write close error:", err)
                return
            }
            select {
            case <-done:
            case <-time.After(2 * time.Second):
            }
            return
        }
    }
}
```

As `./client/client.go` is in a separate directory to `ws.go`, we need to run the next commands in order to collect the required dependencies and run it:

```
$ cd client
$ go mod init
$ go mod tidy
$ go mod download
```

Interacting with the WebSocket server produces the next kind of output:

```
$ go run client.go localhost:1234 ws
Connecting to: localhost:1234 at ws
Hello there!
2021/04/10 21:30:33 Received: Hello there!
```

The previous two lines show user input as well as the server response.

```
2021/04/10 21:30:37 Please give me input! 0
2021/04/10 21:30:41 Please give me input! 1
2021/04/10 21:30:45 Please give me input! 2
2021/04/10 21:30:49 Please give me input! 3
2021/04/10 21:30:53 Please give me input! 4
2021/04/10 21:30:57 Please give me input! 5
2021/04/10 21:30:57 Caught interrupt signal - quitting!
2021/04/10 21:30:57 ReadMessage() error: websocket: close 1000 (normal)
```

The last lines show how the automatic timeout process works.

The WebSocket server generated the following output for the previous interaction:

```
2021/04/10 21:30:29 Connection from: localhost:1234
2021/04/10 21:30:33 Received: Hello there!
2021/04/10 21:30:57 From localhost:1234 read websocket: close 1000
(normal)
```

However, if a WebSocket server cannot be found at the address provided, the WebSocket client produces the next output:

```
$ go run client.go localhost:1234 ws
Connecting to: localhost:1234 at ws
2021/04/09 10:29:23 Error: dial tcp [::1]:1234: connect: connection
refused
```

The `connection refused` message indicates that there is no process listening to port `1234` at `localhost`.

WebSocket gives you an alternative way of creating services. As a rule of thumb, WebSocket is better when we want to exchange lots of data, and we want the connection to remain open all the time and exchange data in full-duplex. However, if you are not sure about what to use, begin with a TCP/IP service and see how it goes before upgrading it to the WebSocket protocol.

Exercises

- Develop a concurrent TCP server that generates random numbers in a predefined range.
- Develop a concurrent TCP server that generates random numbers in a range that is given by the TCP client. This can be used as a way of randomly picking values from a set.
- Add UNIX signal processing to the concurrent TCP server developed in this chapter to gracefully stop the server process when a given signal is received.
- Develop a UNIX domain socket server that generates random numbers. After that, program a client for that server.
- Develop a WebSocket server that creates a variable number of random integers that are sent to the client. The number of random integers is specified by the client at the initial client message.

Summary

This chapter was all about the `net` package, TCP/IP, TCP, UDP, UNIX sockets, and WebSocket, which implement pretty low-level connections. TCP/IP is what governs the internet. Additionally, WebSocket is handy when you must transfer lots of data. Lastly, UNIX domain sockets are preferred when the data exchange between the server and its various clients takes place on the same machine. Go can help you create all kinds of concurrent servers and clients. You are now ready to begin developing and deploying your own services!

The next chapter is about REST APIs, exchanging JSON data over HTTP, and developing RESTful clients and servers—Go is widely used for developing RESTful clients and servers.

Additional resources

- The WebSocket protocol: `https://tools.ietf.org/rfc/rfc6455.txt`
- Wikipedia WebSocket: `https://en.wikipedia.org/wiki/WebSocket`
- Gorilla WebSocket package: `https://github.com/gorilla/websocket`
- Gorilla WebSocket docs: `https://www.gorillatoolkit.org/pkg/websocket`
- The `websocket` package: `https://pkg.go.dev/golang.org/x/net/websocket`

10

Working with REST APIs

The subject of this chapter is the development and use of simple RESTful servers and clients using the Go programming language. **REST** is an acronym for **REpresentational State Transfer** and is primarily an architecture for designing web services. Although web services exchange information in HTML, RESTful services usually use JSON format, which is well supported by Go. REST is not tied to any operating system or system architecture and is not a protocol; however, to implement a RESTful service, you need to use a protocol such as HTTP. When developing RESTful servers, you need to create the appropriate Go structures and perform the necessary marshaling and unmarshaling operations for the exchange of JSON data.

This truly important and practical chapter covers:

- An introduction to REST
- Developing RESTful servers and clients
- Creating a functional RESTful server
- Creating a RESTful client
- Uploading and downloading binary files
- Using Swagger for REST API documentation

An introduction to REST

Most modern web applications work by exposing their APIs and allowing clients to use these APIs to interact and communicate with them. Although REST is not tied to HTTP, most web services use HTTP as their underlying protocol. Additionally, although REST can work with any data format, usually REST means *JSON over HTTP* because most of the time, data is exchanged in JSON format in RESTful services. There are also times where data is exchanged in plain text format, usually when the exchanged data is simple and there is no need for using JSON records. Due to the way a RESTful service works, it should have an architecture that follows the next principles:

- Client-server design
- Stateless implementation—this means that each interaction does not depend on others
- Cacheable
- Uniform interface
- Layered system

According to the HTTP protocol, you can perform the following operations on an HTTP server:

- `POST`, which is used for creating new resources.
- `GET`, which is used for reading (*getting*) existing resources.
- `PUT`, which is used for updating existing resources. As a convention, a `PUT` request should contain the full and updated version of an existing resource.
- `DELETE`, which is used for deleting existing resources.
- `PATCH`, which is used for updating existing resources. A `PATCH` request only contains the modifications to an existing resource.

The important thing here is that everything you do, especially when it is out of the ordinary, must be well documented. As a reference, have in mind that the HTTP methods supported by Go are defined as constants in the `net/http` package:

```
const (
    MethodGet     = "GET"
    MethodHead    = "HEAD"
    MethodPost    = "POST"
    MethodPut     = "PUT"
    MethodPatch   = "PATCH" // RFC 5789
```

```
    MethodDelete  = "DELETE"
    MethodConnect = "CONNECT"
    MethodOptions = "OPTIONS"
    MethodTrace   = "TRACE"
)
```

There also exist conventions regarding the returning **HTTP status code** of each client request. The most popular HTTP status codes as well as their meanings are the following:

- `200` means that everything went well, and the specified action was executed successfully.
- `201` means that the desired resource was *created*.
- `202` means that the request was *accepted* and is currently being processed. This is usually used when an action takes too much time to complete.
- `301` means that the requested resource has been moved permanently—the new URI should be part of the response. This is rarely used in RESTful services because usually you use *API versioning*.
- `400` means that there was a *bad request* and that you should change your initial request before sending it again.
- `401` means that the client tried to access a protected request without authorization.
- `403` means that the client does not have the required permissions for accessing a resource even though the client is properly authorized. In UNIX terminology, `403` means that the user does not have the required privileges to perform an action.
- `404` means that the resource was not found.
- `405` means that the client used a method that is not allowed by the type of resource.
- `500` means internal server error—it probably indicates a server failure.

If you want to learn more about the HTTP protocol, you should visit RFC 7231 at `https://datatracker.ietf.org/doc/html/rfc7231`.

As I am writing this chapter, I am developing a small RESTful client for a project I am working on. The client connects to a given server and gets a list of usernames. For each username, I must get a list of login and logout times by hitting another endpoint.

What I can tell you from my experience is that most of the code is not about interacting with the RESTful server but about taking care of the data, transforming it to the desired format, and storing it in a MySQL database—the two most tricky tasks that I needed to perform were getting a date and time in UNIX epoch format and truncating the information about the minutes and seconds from that epoch time, as well as inserting a new record into a database table after making sure that the record was not already stored in that database. So, expect the logic of the program to be responsible for most of the code, which is true not only for RESTful services but for all services.

The first section of this chapter contains general yet essential information about programming RESTful servers and clients.

Developing RESTful servers and clients

This section is going to develop a RESTful server and a client for that server using the functionality of the Go standard library to understand how things really work behind the scenes. The functionality of the server is described in the following list of endpoints:

- `/add`: This endpoint is for adding new entries to the server
- `/delete`: This endpoint is used for deleting an existing entry
- `/get`: This endpoint is for getting information about an entry that already exists
- `/time`: This endpoint returns the current date and time and is mainly used for testing the operation of the RESTful server
- `/`: This endpoint is used for serving any request that is not a match to any other endpoint

This is my preferred way of structuring the RESTful service. An alternative way of defining the endpoints would be the following:

- `/users/` with the `GET` method: Get a list of all users
- `/users/:id` with the `GET` method: Get information about the user with the given ID value
- `/users/:id` with the `DELETE` method: Delete the user with the given ID
- `/users/` with the `POST` method: Create a new user
- `/users/:id` with either the `PATCH` or the `PUT` method: Update the user with the given ID value

The implementation of the alternative way is left as an exercise for the reader—it should not be that difficult to implement it given that the Go code for the handlers is going to be the same and you only have to redefine the part where we specify the handling of the endpoints. The next subsection presents the implementation of the RESTful server.

A RESTful server

The purpose of the presented implementation is to understand how things work behind the scenes because the principles behind REST services remain the same. The logic behind each handler function is simple: read user input and decide whether the given input and HTTP method are the desired ones. The principles of each client interaction are also simple: the server should send appropriate error messages and HTTP codes back to the client so that everyone knows what really happened. Lastly, everything should be documented to communicate in a common language.

The code of the server, which is saved as `rServer.go`, is the following:

```
package main

import (
    "encoding/json"
    "fmt"
    "io"
    "log"
    "net/http"
    "os"
    "time"
)

type User struct {
    Username string `json:"user"`
    Password string `json:"password"`
}
```

This is a structure that holds user data. The use of JSON tags is crucial.

```
var user User
```

This global variable holds user data—this is the input for the `/add`, `/get`, and `/delete` endpoints and their simplistic implementations. As this global variable is shared by the entire program, our code is not **concurrently safe**, which is fine for a RESTful server used as a proof of concept.

The real-world RESTful server that is implemented in the *Creating a functional RESTful server* section is going to be concurrently safe.

```
// PORT is where the web server listens to
var PORT = ":1234"
```

A RESTful server is just an HTTP server, so we define the TCP port number the server listens to.

```
// DATA is the map that holds User records
var DATA = make(map[string]string)
```

The preceding is another global variable that contains the data of the service.

```
func defaultHandler(w http.ResponseWriter, r *http.Request) {
    log.Println("Serving:", r.URL.Path, "from", r.Host)
    w.WriteHeader(http.StatusNotFound)
    Body := "Thanks for visiting!\n"
    fmt.Fprintf(w, "%s", Body)
}
```

This is the default handler. On a production server, the default handler might print instructions about the operation of the server as well as the list of available endpoints.

```
func timeHandler(w http.ResponseWriter, r *http.Request) {
    log.Println("Serving:", r.URL.Path, "from", r.Host)
    t := time.Now().Format(time.RFC1123)
    Body := "The current time is: " + t + "\n"
    fmt.Fprintf(w, "%s", Body)
}
```

This is another simple handler that returns the current date and time—such simple handlers are usually used for testing the health of the server and are usually removed in the production version.

```
func addHandler(w http.ResponseWriter, r *http.Request) {
    log.Println("Serving:", r.URL.Path, "from", r.Host, r.Method)
    if r.Method != http.MethodPost {
        http.Error(w, "Error:", http.StatusMethodNotAllowed)
        fmt.Fprintf(w, "%s\n", "Method not allowed!")
        return
    }
```

This is the first time that you are seeing the `http.Error()` function. The `http.Error()` function sends a reply to the client request that includes the specified error message, which should be in plain text, as well as the desired HTTP code. However, you still need to write the data you want to send back to the client using an `fmt.Fprintf()` statement.

```
	d, err := io.ReadAll(r.Body)
	if err != nil {
		http.Error(w, "Error:", http.StatusBadRequest)
		return
	}
```

We try to read all data from the client at once using `io.ReadAll()` and we make sure that we read the data without any errors by checking the value of the `error` variable returned by `io.ReadAll(r.Body)`.

```
	err = json.Unmarshal(d, &user)
	if err != nil {
		log.Println(err)
		http.Error(w, "Error:", http.StatusBadRequest)
		return
	}
```

After reading the data from the client, we put it into the `user` global variable. Where you want to store the data and what to do with it is decided by the server. There is no rule on how to interpret the data. However, the client should communicate with the server according to the wishes of the server.

```
	if user.Username != "" {
		DATA[user.Username] = user.Password
		log.Println(DATA)
		w.WriteHeader(http.StatusOK)
```

If the given `Username` field is not empty, add the new structure to the `DATA` map. Data persistence is not implemented—each time you restart the RESTful server, `DATA` is initialized from scratch.

```
	} else {
		http.Error(w, "Error:", http.StatusBadRequest)
		return
	}
}
```

If the value of the username field is empty, then we cannot add it to the DATA map and the operation fails with an http.StatusBadRequest code.

```
func getHandler(w http.ResponseWriter, r *http.Request) {
	log.Println("Serving:", r.URL.Path, "from", r.Host, r.Method)
	if r.Method != http.MethodGet {
		http.Error(w, "Error:", http.StatusMethodNotAllowed)
		fmt.Fprintf(w, "%s\n", "Method not allowed!")
		return
	}
```

For the /get endpoint we need to use http.MethodGet, so we have to make sure that this condition is met (if r.Method != http.MethodGet).

```
	d, err := io.ReadAll(r.Body)
	if err != nil {
		http.Error(w, "ReadAll - Error", http.StatusBadRequest)
		return
	}
```

Again, we need to make sure that we can read the data from the client request without issues.

```
	err = json.Unmarshal(d, &user)
	if err != nil {
		log.Println(err)
		http.Error(w, "Unmarshal - Error", http.StatusBadRequest)
		return
	}
	fmt.Println(user)
```

Then, we use the client data and put it into a User structure (the user global variable).

```
	_, ok := DATA[user.Username]
	if ok && user.Username != "" {
		log.Println("Found!")
		w.WriteHeader(http.StatusOK)
		fmt.Fprintf(w, "%s\n", d)
```

If the desired user record is found, we send it back to the client using the data stored in the d variable—remember that d was initialized in the io.ReadAll(r.Body) call and already contains a JSON record that is marshaled.

```
    } else {
        log.Println("Not found!")
        w.WriteHeader(http.StatusNotFound)
        http.Error(w, "Map - Resource not found!", http.StatusNotFound)
    }
    return
}
```

Otherwise, we inform the client that the desired record was not found.

```
func deleteHandler(w http.ResponseWriter, r *http.Request) {
    log.Println("Serving:", r.URL.Path, "from", r.Host, r.Method)
    if r.Method != http.MethodDelete {
        http.Error(w, "Error:", http.StatusMethodNotAllowed)
        fmt.Fprintf(w, "%s\n", "Method not allowed!")
        return
    }
```

The `DELETE` HTTP method looks like a rational choice when deleting a resource, hence the `r.Method != http.MethodDelete` test.

```
    d, err := io.ReadAll(r.Body)
    if err != nil {
        http.Error(w, "ReadAll - Error", http.StatusBadRequest)
        return
    }
```

Again, we read the client input and store it in the `d` variable.

```
    err = json.Unmarshal(d, &user)
    if err != nil {
        log.Println(err)
        http.Error(w, "Unmarshal - Error", http.StatusBadRequest)
        return
    }
    log.Println(user)
```

It is considered a good practice to keep additional logging information when deleting resources.

```
    _, ok := DATA[user.Username]
    if ok && user.Username != "" {
        if user.Password == DATA[user.Username] {
```

For the delete process, we make sure that both the given username and password values are the same as the ones that exist in the DATA map before deleting the relevant entry.

```
            delete(DATA, user.Username)
            w.WriteHeader(http.StatusOK)
            fmt.Fprintf(w, "%s\n", d)
            log.Println(DATA)
        }
    } else {
        log.Println("User", user.Username, "Not found!")
        w.WriteHeader(http.StatusNotFound)
        http.Error(w, "Delete - Resource not found!", http.
StatusNotFound)
    }
    log.Println("After:", DATA)
```

After the deletion process, we print the contents of the DATA map to make sure that everything went as expected—you usually do not do that on a production server.

```
    return
}

func main() {
    arguments := os.Args
    if len(arguments) != 1 {
        PORT = ":" + arguments[1]
    }
```

The previous code presents a technique for defining the TCP port number of a web server while having a default value at hand. So, if there are no command-line arguments, the default value is used. Otherwise, the value given as a command-line argument is used.

```
    mux := http.NewServeMux()
    s := &http.Server{
        Addr:         PORT,
        Handler:      mux,
        IdleTimeout:  10 * time.Second,
        ReadTimeout:  time.Second,
        WriteTimeout: time.Second,
    }
```

Above are the details and the options for the web server.

```
    mux.Handle("/time", http.HandlerFunc(timeHandler))
    mux.Handle("/add", http.HandlerFunc(addHandler))
    mux.Handle("/get", http.HandlerFunc(getHandler))
    mux.Handle("/delete", http.HandlerFunc(deleteHandler))
    mux.Handle("/", http.HandlerFunc(defaultHandler))
```

The previous code defines the endpoints of the web server—nothing special here as a RESTful server implements an HTTP server behind the scenes.

```
    fmt.Println("Ready to serve at", PORT)
    err := s.ListenAndServe()
    if err != nil {
        fmt.Println(err)
        return
    }
}
```

The last step is about running the web server with the predefined options, which is common practice. After that, we test the RESTful server using the `curl(1)` utility, which is very handy when you do not have a client and you want to test the operation of a RESTful server—the good thing is that `curl(1)` can send and receive JSON data.

```
$ curl localhost:1234/
Thanks for visiting!
```

The first interaction with the RESTful server is for making sure that the server works as expected. The next interaction is for adding a new user to the server—the details of the user are in the `{"user": "mtsouk", "password" : "admin"}` JSON record:

```
$ curl -H 'Content-Type: application/json' -d '{"user": "mtsouk",
"password" : "admin"}' http://localhost:1234/add -v
*   Trying ::1...
* TCP_NODELAY set
* Connected to localhost (::1) port 1234 (#0)
```

The previous output shows that `curl(1)` has successfully connected to the server (`localhost`) using the desired TCP port (`1234`).

```
> POST /add HTTP/1.1
> Host: localhost:1234
> User-Agent: curl/7.64.1
```

```
> Accept: */*
> Content-Type: application/json
> Content-Length: 40
```

The previous output shows that `curl(1)` is going to send data using the `POST` method and the length of the data is `40` bytes.

```
>
* upload completely sent off: 40 out of 40 bytes
< HTTP/1.1 200 OK
< Date: Tue, 27 Apr 2021 09:41:38 GMT
< Content-Length: 0
```

The previous output tells us that the data was sent and that the **body** of the server response is `0` bytes.

```
<
* Connection #0 to host localhost left intact
* Closing connection 0
```

The last part of the output tells us that after sending the data to the server, the connection was closed.

> When working with a RESTful server, we need to add `-H 'Content-Type: application/json'` to `curl(1)` to specify that we are going to work using the JSON format. The `-d` option is used for passing data to a server and is equivalent to the `--data` option, whereas the `-v` option generates more verbose output if we need more details to understand what is going on.

If we try to add the same user, the RESTful server is not going to complain:

```
$ curl -H 'Content-Type: application/json' -d '{"user": "mtsouk",
"password" : "admin"}' http://localhost:1234/add
```

Although this behavior might not be perfect, it is good if it is documented. This is not allowed on a production server, but it is acceptable when experimenting.

```
$ curl -H 'Content-Type: application/json' -d '{"user": "mihalis",
"password" : "admin"}' http://localhost:1234/add
```

With the preceding command, we add another user as specified by `{"user": "mihalis", "password" : "admin"}`.

```
$ curl -H -d '{"user": "admin"}' http://localhost:1234/add
curl: (3) URL using bad/illegal format or missing URL
Error:
Method not allowed!
```

The previous output shows an erroneous interaction where `-H` is not followed by a value. Although the request is sent to the server, it is rejected because `/add` does not use the default HTTP method.

```
$ curl -H 'Content-Type: application/json' -d '{"user": "admin",
"password" : "admin"}' http://localhost:1234/get
Error:
Method not allowed!
```

This time, the `curl` command is correct, but the HTTP method used is not set correctly. Therefore, the request is not served.

```
$ curl -X GET -H 'Content-Type: application/json' -d '{"user": "admin",
"password" : "admin"}' http://localhost:1234/get
Map - Resource not found!
$ curl -X GET -H 'Content-Type: application/json' -d '{"user":
"mtsouk", "password" : "admin"}' http://localhost:1234/get
{"user": "mtsouk", "password" : "admin"}
```

The previous two interactions use `/get` to get information about an existing user. However, only the second user is found.

```
$ curl -H 'Content-Type: application/json' -d '{"user": "mtsouk",
"password" : "admin"}' http://localhost:1234/delete -X DELETE
{"user": "mtsouk", "password" : "admin"}
```

The last interaction successfully deletes the user specified by `{"user": "mtsouk", "password" : "admin"}`.

The output generated by the server process for all previous interactions would look like the following:

```
$ go run rServer.go
Ready to serve at :1234
2021/04/27 12:41:31 Serving: / from localhost:1234
2021/04/27 12:41:38 Serving: /add from localhost:1234 POST
2021/04/27 12:41:38 map[mtsouk:admin]
2021/04/27 12:41:41 Serving: /add from localhost:1234 POST
2021/04/27 12:41:41 map[mtsouk:admin]
```

```
2021/04/27 12:41:58 Serving: /add from localhost:1234 POST
2021/04/27 12:41:58 map[mihalis:admin mtsouk:admin]
2021/04/27 12:43:02 Serving: /add from localhost:1234 GET
2021/04/27 12:43:13 Serving: /get from localhost:1234 POST
2021/04/27 12:43:30 Serving: /get from localhost:1234 GET
{admin admin}
2021/04/27 12:43:30 Not found!
2021/04/27 12:43:30 http: superfluous response.WriteHeader call from
main.getHandler (rServer.go:101)
2021/04/27 12:43:41 Serving: /get from localhost:1234 GET
{mtsouk admin}
2021/04/27 12:43:41 Found!
2021/04/27 12:44:00 Serving: /delete from localhost:1234 DELETE
2021/04/27 12:44:00 {mtsouk admin}
2021/04/27 12:44:00 map[mihalis:admin]
2021/04/27 12:44:00 After: map[mihalis:admin]
```

So far, we have a working RESTful server that has been tested with the help of the `curl(1)` utility. The next section is about developing a command-line client for the RESTful server.

A RESTful client

This subsection illustrates the development of a client for the RESTful server developed previously. However, in this case, the client acts as a testing program that tries the capabilities of the RESTful server—later in this chapter, you are going to learn how to write proper clients using `cobra`. So, the code of the client, which can be found in `rClient.go`, is as follows:

```
package main

import (
    "bytes"
    "encoding/json"
    "fmt"
    "io"
    "net/http"
    "os"
    "time"
)

type User struct {
```

```
    Username string `json:"user"`
    Password string `json:"password"`
}
```

This same structure is found in the server implementation and is used for exchanging data.

```
var u1 = User{"admin", "admin"}
var u2 = User{"tsoukalos", "pass"}
var u3 = User{"", "pass"}
```

Here, we predefine three `User` variables that are going to be used during testing.

```
const addEndPoint = "/add"
const getEndPoint = "/get"
const deleteEndPoint = "/delete"
const timeEndPoint = "/time"
```

The previous constants define the endpoints that are going to be used.

```
func deleteEndpoint(server string, user User) int {
    userMarshall, _ := json.Marshal(user)
    u := bytes.NewReader(userMarshall)

    req, err := http.NewRequest("DELETE", server+deleteEndPoint, u)
```

We prepare a request that is going to access `/delete` using the `DELETE` HTTP method.

```
    if err != nil {
        fmt.Println("Error in req: ", err)
        return http.StatusInternalServerError
    }
    req.Header.Set("Content-Type", "application/json")
```

This is the correct way to specify that we want to use **JSON data** when interacting with the server.

```
    c := &http.Client{
        Timeout: 15 * time.Second,
    }

    resp, err := c.Do(req)
    defer resp.Body.Close()
```

Then, we send the request and wait for the server response using the `Do()` method with a 15-second timeout.

```
    if err != nil {
        fmt.Println("Error:", err)
    }
    if resp == nil {
        return http.StatusNotFound
    }

    data, err := io.ReadAll(resp.Body)
    fmt.Print("/delete returned: ", string(data))
```

The reason for putting that `fmt.Print()` here is that we want to know the server response even if there is an error in the interaction.

```
    if err != nil {
        fmt.Println("Error:", err)
    }
    return resp.StatusCode
}
```

The `resp.StatusCode` value specifies the result from the `/delete` endpoint.

```
func getEndpoint(server string, user User) int {
    userMarshall, _ := json.Marshal(user)
    u := bytes.NewReader(userMarshall)

    req, err := http.NewRequest("GET", server+getEndPoint, u)
```

We are going to access `/get` using the `GET` HTTP method.

```
    if err != nil {
        fmt.Println("Error in req: ", err)
        return http.StatusInternalServerError
    }
    req.Header.Set("Content-Type", "application/json")
```

We specify that we are going to interact with the server using the JSON format using `Header.Set()`.

```
    c := &http.Client{
        Timeout: 15 * time.Second,
    }
```

We define a timeout period for the HTTP client in case the server is too busy responding.

```
    resp, err := c.Do(req)
    defer resp.Body.Close()

    if err != nil {
        fmt.Println("Error:", err)
    }
    if resp == nil {
        return http.StatusNotFound
    }
```

The previous code sends the client request to the server using `c.Do(req)` and saves the server response in `resp` and the error value in `err`. If the value of `resp` is `nil`, then the server response was empty, which is an error condition.

```
    data, err := io.ReadAll(resp.Body)
    fmt.Print("/get returned: ", string(data))
    if err != nil {
        fmt.Println("Error:", err)
    }
    return resp.StatusCode
}
```

The value of `resp.StatusCode`, which is specified and transferred by the RESTful server, determines if the interaction was successful in an HTTP sense (logically) or not.

```
func addEndpoint(server string, user User) int {
    userMarshall, _ := json.Marshal(user)
    u := bytes.NewReader(userMarshall)

    req, err := http.NewRequest("POST", server+addEndPoint, u)
```

We are going to access `/add` using the `POST` HTTP method. You can use `http.MethodPost` instead of `POST`. As stated earlier in this chapter, there exist relevant global variables in `http` for the remaining HTTP methods (`http.MethodGet`, `http.MethodDelete`, `http.MethodPut`, etc.) and it is recommended that you use them because this is the portable way.

```
    if err != nil {
        fmt.Println("Error in req: ", err)
```

```
        return http.StatusInternalServerError
    }
    req.Header.Set("Content-Type", "application/json")
```

As before, we specify that we are going to interact with the server using the JSON format.

```
    c := &http.Client{
        Timeout: 15 * time.Second,
    }
```

Once again, we define a timeout period for the client in case the server is too busy responding.

```
    resp, err := c.Do(req)
    defer resp.Body.Close()

    if resp == nil || (resp.StatusCode == http.StatusNotFound) {
        return resp.StatusCode
    }

    return resp.StatusCode
}
```

The `addEndpoint()` function is for testing the `/add` endpoint using the `POST` method and the `/add` endpoint.

```
func timeEndpoint(server string) (int, string) {
    req, err := http.NewRequest("POST", server+timeEndPoint, nil)
```

We are going to access the `/time` endpoint using the `POST` HTTP method.

```
    if err != nil {
        fmt.Println("Error in req: ", err)
        return http.StatusInternalServerError, ""
    }

    c := &http.Client{
        Timeout: 15 * time.Second,
    }
```

As before, we define a timeout period for the client in case the server is too busy responding.

```
    resp, err := c.Do(req)
    defer resp.Body.Close()

    if resp == nil || (resp.StatusCode == http.StatusNotFound) {
        return resp.StatusCode, ""
    }

    data, _ := io.ReadAll(resp.Body)
    return resp.StatusCode, string(data)
}
```

The `timeEndpoint()` function is for testing the `/time` endpoint—note that this endpoint does not require any data from the client, so the client request is empty. The server is going to return a time and date string.

```
func slashEndpoint(server, URL string) (int, string) {
    req, err := http.NewRequest("POST", server+URL, nil)
```

We are going to access `/` using the `POST` HTTP method.

```
    if err != nil {
        fmt.Println("Error in req: ", err)
        return http.StatusInternalServerError, ""
    }

    c := &http.Client{
        Timeout: 15 * time.Second,
    }
```

It is considered a good practice to have a timeout period on the client side in case there are delays in the server response.

```
    resp, err := c.Do(req)
    defer resp.Body.Close()

    if resp == nil {
        return resp.StatusCode, ""
    }

    data, _ := io.ReadAll(resp.Body)
    return resp.StatusCode, string(data)
}
```

The `slashEndpoint()` function is for testing the default endpoint in the server—note that this endpoint does not require any data from the client.

Next is the implementation of the `main()` function, which uses all previous functions to visit the RESTful server endpoints:

```
func main() {
    if len(os.Args) != 2 {
        fmt.Println("Wrong number of arguments!")
        fmt.Println("Need: Server")
        return
    }
    server := os.Args[1]
```

The `server` variable holds both the server address and the port number that is going to be used.

```
    fmt.Println("/add")
    HTTPcode := addEndpoint(server, u1)
    if HTTPcode != http.StatusOK {
        fmt.Println("u1 Return code:", HTTPcode)
    } else {
        fmt.Println("u1 Data added:", u1, HTTPcode)
    }

    HTTPcode = addEndpoint(server, u2)
    if HTTPcode != http.StatusOK {
        fmt.Println("u2 Return code:", HTTPcode)
    } else {
        fmt.Println("u2 Data added:", u2, HTTPcode)
    }

    HTTPcode = addEndpoint(server, u3)
    if HTTPcode != http.StatusOK {
        fmt.Println("u3 Return code:", HTTPcode)
    } else {
        fmt.Println("u3 Data added:", u3, HTTPcode)
    }
```

All the previous code is used for testing the `/add` endpoint using various types of data.

```
    fmt.Println("/get")
    HTTPcode = getEndpoint(server, u1)
    fmt.Println("/get u1 return code:", HTTPcode)
    HTTPcode = getEndpoint(server, u2)
    fmt.Println("/get u2 return code:", HTTPcode)
    HTTPcode = getEndpoint(server, u3)
    fmt.Println("/get u3 return code:", HTTPcode)
```

All the previous code is used for testing the `/get` endpoint using various types of input. We only test for the return code because the HTTP code specifies the success or failure of the operation.

```
    fmt.Println("/delete")
    HTTPcode = deleteEndpoint(server, u1)
    fmt.Println("/delete u1 return code:", HTTPcode)
    HTTPcode = deleteEndpoint(server, u1)
    fmt.Println("/delete u1 return code:", HTTPcode)
    HTTPcode = deleteEndpoint(server, u2)
    fmt.Println("/delete u2 return code:", HTTPcode)
    HTTPcode = deleteEndpoint(server, u3)
    fmt.Println("/delete u3 return code:", HTTPcode)
```

All the previous code is used for testing the `/delete` endpoint using various types of input. Once again, we print the HTTP code of the interaction because the value of the HTTP code specifies the success or failure of the operation.

```
    fmt.Println("/time")
    HTTPcode, myTime := timeEndpoint(server)
    fmt.Print("/time returned: ", HTTPcode, " ", myTime)
    time.Sleep(time.Second)
    HTTPcode, myTime = timeEndpoint(server)
    fmt.Print("/time returned: ", HTTPcode, " ", myTime)
```

The previous code tests the `/time` endpoint—it prints the HTTP code as well as the rest of the server response.

```
    fmt.Println("/")
    URL := "/"
    HTTPcode, response := slashEndpoint(server, URL)
    fmt.Print("/ returned: ", HTTPcode, " with response: ", response)

    fmt.Println("/what")
```

```
    URL = "/what"
    HTTPcode, response = slashEndpoint(server, URL)
    fmt.Print(URL, " returned: ", HTTPcode, " with response: ",
response)
}
```

The last part of the program tries to connect to an endpoint that does not exist to verify the correct operation of the default handler function.

Running `rClient.go` while `rServer.go` is already running produces the next kind of output:

```
$ go run rClient.go http://localhost:1234
/add
u1 Data added: {admin admin} 200
u2 Data added: {tsoukalos pass} 200
u3 Return code: 400
```

The previous part is related to the testing of the `/add` endpoint. The first two users were successfully added, whereas the third user (`var u3 = User{"", "pass"}`) was not added because it does not contain all the required information.

```
/get
/get returned: {"user":"admin","password":"admin"}
/get u1 return code: 200
/get returned: {"user":"tsoukalos","password":"pass"}
/get u2 return code: 200
/get returned: Map - Resource not found!
/get u3 return code: 404
```

The previous part is related to the testing of the `/get` endpoint. The data of the first two users with the usernames `admin` and `tsoukalos` was successfully returned, whereas the user stored in the `u3` variable was not found.

```
/delete
/delete returned: {"user":"admin","password":"admin"}
/delete u1 return code: 200
/delete returned: Delete - Resource not found!
/delete u1 return code: 404
/delete returned: {"user":"tsoukalos","password":"pass"}
/delete u2 return code: 200
/delete returned: Delete - Resource not found!
/delete u3 return code: 404
```

The previous output is related to the testing of the `/delete` endpoint. The users `admin` and `tsoukalos` were deleted. However, trying to delete `admin` for the second time failed.

```
/time
/time returned: 200 The current time is: Tue, 20 Apr 2021 10:23:04 EEST
/time returned: 200 The current time is: Tue, 20 Apr 2021 10:23:05 EEST
```

Similarly, the previous part is related to the testing of the `/time` endpoint.

```
/
/ returned: 404 with response: Thanks for visiting!
/what
/what returned: 404 with response: Thanks for visiting!
```

The last part of the output is related to the operation of the default handler.

So far, both the RESTful server and the client can interact with each other. However, neither of them perform a real job. The next section shows how to develop a real-world RESTful server using `gorilla/mux` and a database backend for storing data.

Creating a functional RESTful server

This section illustrates how to develop a RESTful server in Go given a REST API. The biggest difference between the presented RESTful service and the phone book application created in *Chapter 8, Building Web Services*, is that the RESTful service in this chapter uses JSON messages everywhere, whereas the phone book application interacts and works using plain text messages. If you are thinking of using `net/http` for the implementation of the RESTful server, please do not do so! This implementation uses the `gorilla/mux` package, which is a much better choice because it supports subrouters—more about that in the *Using gorilla/mux* subsection.

The purpose of the RESTful server is to implement a login/authentication system. The purpose of the login system is to keep track of the users who are logged in, as well as their permissions. The system comes with a default administrator user named `admin`—the default password is also `admin` and you should change it. The application stores its data in a database (PostgreSQL), which means that if you restart it, the list of existing users is read from that database and is not lost.

The REST API

The API of an application helps you implement the functionality that you have in mind. However, this is a job for the client, not the server. The job of the server is to facilitate the job of its clients as much as possible by supporting a simple yet fully working functionality through a properly defined and implemented REST API. Make sure that you understand that before trying to develop and use a RESTful server.

We are going to define the endpoints that are going to be used, the HTTP codes that are going to return, as well as the allowed method or methods. Creating a RESTful server based on a REST API for production is a serious job that should not be taken lightly. Creating a *prototype* to test and validate your ideas and designs is going to save you lots of time in the long run. Always begin with a prototype.

The supported endpoints as well as the supported HTTP methods and the parameters are as follows:

- `/`: Used for catching and serving everything that is not a match. This endpoint works with all HTTP methods.
- `/getall`: Used for getting the full contents of the database. Using this requires a user with administrative privileges. This endpoint might return multiple JSON records and works with the `GET` HTTP method.
- `/getid/username`: Used for getting the ID of a user identified by their username, which is passed to the endpoint. This command should be issued by a user with administrative privileges and supports the `GET` HTTP method.
- `/username/ID`: Used for deleting or getting information about the user with an ID equal to `ID`, depending on the HTTP method used. Therefore, the actual action that is going to be performed depends on the HTTP method used. The `DELETE` method deletes the user, whereas the `GET` method returns the user information. This endpoint should be issued by a user with administrative privileges.
- `/logged`: Used for getting a list of all logged-in users. This endpoint might return multiple JSON records and requires the use of the `GET` HTTP method.
- `/update`: Used for updating the username, the password, or the admin status of a user—the ID of the user in the database remains the same. This endpoint works with the `PUT` HTTP method only and the search for the user is based on the username.
- `/login`: Used for logging in a user to the system, given a username and a password. This endpoint works with the `POST` HTTP method.
- `/logout`: Used for logging out a user, given a username and a password. This endpoint works with the `POST` HTTP method.

- `/add`: Used for adding a new user to the database. This endpoint works with the `POST` HTTP method and is issued by a user with administrative privileges.
- `/time`: This is an endpoint used mainly for testing purposes. It is the only endpoint that does not work with JSON data, does not require a valid account, and works with all HTTP methods.

Now, let us discuss the capabilities and the functionality of the `gorilla/mux` package.

Using gorilla/mux

The `gorilla/mux` package (`https://github.com/gorilla/mux`) is a popular and powerful alternative to the default Go router that allows you to match incoming requests to their respective handler. Although there exist many differences between the default Go router (`http.ServeMux`) and `mux.Router` (the `gorilla/mux` router), the main difference is that `mux.Router` supports **multiple conditions** when matching a route with a handler function. This means that you can write less code to handle some options such as the HTTP method used. Let us begin by presenting some matching examples—this functionality is not supported by the default Go router:

- `r.HandleFunc("/url", UrlHandlerFunction)`: The previous command calls the `UrlHandlerFunction` function each time `/url` is visited.
- `r.HandleFunc("/url", UrlHandlerFunction).Methods(http.MethodPut)`: This example shows how you can tell Gorilla to match a specific HTTP method (`PUT` in this case, which is defined by the use of `http.MethodPut`), which saves you from having to write code to do that manually.
- `mux.NotFoundHandler = http.HandlerFunc(handlers.DefaultHandler)`: With Gorilla, the right way to match anything that is not a match by any other path is by using `mux.NotFoundHandler`.
- `mux.MethodNotAllowedHandler = notAllowed`: If a method is not allowed for an existing route, it is handled with the help of `MethodNotAllowedHandler`. This is specific to `gorilla/mux`.
- `s.HandleFunc("/users/{id:[0-9]+}"), HandlerFunction)`: This last example shows that you can define a variable in a path using a name (`id`) and a pattern and Gorilla does the matching for you! If there is not a regular expression, then the match is going to be anything from the beginning slash to the next slash in the path.

Now, let us talk about another capability of `gorilla/mux`, which is subrouters.

The use of subrouters

The server implementation uses **subrouters**. A *subrouter* is a **nested route** that will only be examined for potential matches if the parent route matches the parameters of the subrouter. The good thing is that the parent route can contain conditions that are common among all paths that are defined under a subrouter, which includes hosts, path prefixes, and, as it happens in our case, HTTP request methods. As a result, our subrouters are divided based on the common request method of the endpoints that follow. Not only does this optimize the request matchings, but it also makes the structure of the code easier to understand.

As an example, the subrouter for the `DELETE` HTTP method is as simple as the following:

```
deleteMux := mux.Methods(http.MethodDelete).Subrouter()
deleteMux.HandleFunc("/username/{id:[0-9]+}", handlers.DeleteHandler)
```

The first statement is for defining the common characteristics of the subrouter, which in this case is the `http.MethodDelete` HTTP method, whereas the remaining statement, which in this case is the `deleteMux.HandleFunc(...)` one, is for defining the supported paths.

Yes, `gorilla/mux` might be more difficult than the default Go router, but you should understand by now the benefits of the `gorilla/mux` package for working with HTTP services.

Working with the database

In this subsection, we develop a Go package for working with the PostgreSQL database that supports the functionality of the RESTful server. The package is named `restdb` and is stored in `https://github.com/mactsouk/restdb`. Due to the use of **Go modules**, its development can take place anywhere you want in your filesystem—in this case, in the `~/code/restdb` folder. So, we run `go mod init github.com/mactsouk/restdb` to enable Go modules for the `restdb` package during its development.

> The RESTful server itself knows nothing about the PostgreSQL server. All related functionality is kept in the `restdb` package, which means that if you change the database, the handler functions do not have to know about it.

To make things easier for the readers, the database is going to run using Docker and with a configuration that can be found in `docker-compose.yml`, inside the `restdb` GitHub repository, which comes with the following contents:

```
version: '3.1'

services:
  postgres:
    image: postgres
    container_name: postgredb
    environment:
      POSTGRES_USER: mtsouk
      POSTGRES_PASSWORD: pass
      POSTGRES_DB: restapi
    volumes:
      - ./postgres:/var/lib/postgresql/data/
    ports:
      - 5432:5432

volumes:
  postgres_data:
    driver: local
```

So, the PostgreSQL server listens to port number `5432`, both internally and externally. What really matters is the external port number because this is what all clients are going to be using. The database name, the database table, and the `admin` user are created using the next `create_db.sql` SQL file:

```
DROP DATABASE IF EXISTS restapi;
CREATE DATABASE restapi;
\c restapi;

/*
Users
*/
CREATE TABLE users (
id SERIAL PRIMARY KEY,
username VARCHAR NOT NULL,
password VARCHAR NOT NULL,
lastlogin INT,
admin INT,
```

```
active INT
);

INSERT INTO users (username, password, lastlogin, admin, active) VALUES
('admin', 'admin', 1620922454, 1, 1);
```

Provided that PostgreSQL is executed using the presented `docker-compose.yml`, you can use `create_db.sql` as follows:

```
$ psql -U mtsouk postgres -h 127.0.0.1 < create_db.sql
Password for user mtsouk:
DROP DATABASE
CREATE DATABASE
You are now connected to database "restapi" as user "mtsouk".
CREATE TABLE
INSERT 0 1
```

As most commands in `restdb` work in a similar way, we are going to present the most important functions here, beginning with `ConnectPostgres()`:

```
func ConnectPostgres() *sql.DB {
    conn := fmt.Sprintf("host=%s port=%d user=%s password=%s dbname=%s
sslmode=disable",
        Hostname, Port, Username, Password, Database)
```

All of `Hostname`, `Port`, `Username`, `Password`, and `Database` are global variables defined elsewhere in the package—they contain the connection details.

```
    db, err := sql.Open("postgres", conn)
    if err != nil {
        log.Println(err)
        return nil
    }

    return db
}
```

As we need to connect to PostgreSQL all the time, we created a helper function that returns an `*sql.DB` variable that can be used for interaction with PostgreSQL.

Next, we present the `DeleteUser()` function:

```
func DeleteUser(ID int) bool {
    db := ConnectPostgres()
```

```
    if db == nil {
        log.Println("Cannot connect to PostgreSQL!")
        db.Close()
        return false
    }
    defer db.Close()
```

The preceding code is how we use `ConnectPostgres()` to get a database connection to work with.

```
    t := FindUserID(ID)
    if t.ID == 0 {
        log.Println("User", ID, "does not exist.")
        return false
    }
```

Here, we use the `FindUserID()` helper function to make sure that the user with the given user ID exists in the database. If the user does not exist, the function stops and returns `false`.

```
    stmt, err := db.Prepare("DELETE FROM users WHERE ID = $1")
    if err != nil {
        log.Println("DeleteUser:", err)
        return false
    }
```

This is the actual statement for deleting the user. We use `Prepare()` to construct the required SQL statement that we will execute using `Exec()`. The `$1` in `Prepare()` denotes a parameter that is going to be given in `Exec()`. If we wanted to have more parameters, we should have named them `$2`, `$3`, and so on.

```
    _, err = stmt.Exec(ID)
    if err != nil {
        log.Println("DeleteUser:", err)
        return false
    }

    return true
}
```

This is where the implementation of the `DeleteUser()` function ends. The `stmt.Exec(ID)` statement is what deletes a user from the database.

The `ListAllUsers()` function, which is presented next, returns a slice of `User` elements, which holds all users found in the RESTful server:

```
func ListAllUsers() []User {
	db := ConnectPostgres()
	if db == nil {
		fmt.Println("Cannot connect to PostgreSQL!")
		db.Close()
		return []User{}
	}
	defer db.Close()

	rows, err := db.Query("SELECT * FROM users \n")
	if err != nil {
		log.Println(err)
		return []User{}
	}
```

As the `SELECT` query requires no parameters, we use `Query()` to run it instead of `Prepare()` and `Exec()`. Keep in mind that this is a query that most likely returns multiple records.

```
	all := []User{}
	var c1 int
	var c2, c3 string
	var c4 int64
	var c5, c6 int

	for rows.Next() {
		err = rows.Scan(&c1, &c2, &c3, &c4, &c5, &c6)
```

This is how we read the values from a single record returned by the SQL query. First, we define multiple variables for each one of the returned values and then we pass their pointers to `Scan()`. The `rows.Next()` method keeps returning records as long as there are results.

```
		temp := User{c1, c2, c3, c4, c5, c6}
		all = append(all, temp)
	}

	log.Println("All:", all)
	return all
}
```

So, as mentioned before, a slice of `User` structures is returned from `ListAllUsers()`.

Lastly, we are going to present the implementation of `IsUserValid()`:

```
func IsUserValid(u User) bool {
	db := ConnectPostgres()
	if db == nil {
		fmt.Println("Cannot connect to PostgreSQL!")
		db.Close()
		return false
	}
	defer db.Close()
```

This is a common pattern: we call `ConnectPostgres()` and wait to get a connection to use.

```
	rows, err := db.Query("SELECT * FROM users WHERE Username = $1 \n",
u.Username)
	if err != nil {
		log.Println(err)
		return false
	}
```

Here we pass our parameter to `Query()` without using `Prepare()` and `Exec()`.

```
	temp := User{}
	var c1 int
	var c2, c3 string
	var c4 int64
	var c5, c6 int
```

Here, we create the required parameters to keep the output of the SQL query.

```
	// If there exist multiple users with the same username,
	// we will get the FIRST ONE only.
	for rows.Next() {
		err = rows.Scan(&c1, &c2, &c3, &c4, &c5, &c6)
		if err != nil {
			log.Println(err)
			return false
		}
		temp = User{c1, c2, c3, c4, c5, c6}
	}
```

Once again, the `for` loop keeps running for as long as `rows.Next()` returns new records.

```
    if u.Username == temp.Username && u.Password == temp.Password {
        return true
    }
```

This is an important point: not only should the given user exist, but the given password should be the same as the one stored in the database for a given user to be valid.

```
    return false
}
```

You can view the rest of the `restdb` implementation on your own. Most functions are like the ones presented here. The code of `restdb.go` is going to be used in the implementation of the RESTful server that is presented next. However, as you are going to see, we are going to test `restdb` first.

Testing the restdb package

The RESTful server is developed in `~/go/src/github.com/mactsouk/rest-api`—if you do not plan on making it available to the world, you do not need to create a separate GitHub repository for it. However, I do want to be able to share it with you, so the GitHub repository for the server is `https://github.com/mactsouk/rest-api`.

Before continuing with the server implementation, we use the `restdb` package to make sure that it is working as expected before using it in the RESTful server implementation. The presented utility uses functions from `restdb`; you do not have to test every possible usage of the `restdb` package—just make sure that it works and that it connects to the PostgreSQL database. For this reason, we are going to create a separate command-line utility called `useRestdb.go` that contains the next code and is in the `test-db` directory. The most important detail in that file is the use of `restdb.User` in the code because this is the structure that is needed by the `restdb` package. We cannot pass a different structure as a parameter to the functions of `restdb`.

Initializing modules and running `useRestdb.go` produces the next kind of output:

```
$ go mod init
go: creating new go.mod: module github.com/mactsouk/rest-api/test-db
go: to add module requirements and sums:
```

```
        go mod tidy
$ go mod tidy
go: finding module for package github.com/mactsouk/restdb
go: finding module for package github.com/lib/pq
go: downloading github.com/mactsouk/restdb v0.0.0-20210510205310-
63ba9fa172df
go: found github.com/lib/pq in github.com/lib/pq v1.10.1
go: found github.com/mactsouk/restdb in github.com/mactsouk/restdb
v0.0.0-20210510205310-63ba9fa172df
$ go run useRestdb.go
&{0 {host=localhost port=5432 user=mtsouk password=pass dbname=restapi
sslmode=disable 0x856110} 0 {0 0} [] map[] 0 0 0xc00007c240 false map[]
map[] 0 0 0 0 <nil> 0 0 0 0 0x4dd260}
{0   0 0 0}
mike
packt
admin
2021/05/17 09:40:23 Populating PostgreSQL
User inserted successfully.
2021/05/17 09:40:23 Found user: {9 mtsouk admin 1621233623 1 1}
mtsouk:  {9 mtsouk admin 1621233623 1 1}
2021/05/17 09:40:23 Found user: {9 mtsouk admin 1621233623 1 1}
User Deleted.
mtsouk:  {0   0 0 0}
2021/05/17 09:40:23 User 0 does not exist.
User not Deleted.
2021/05/17 09:40:23 User 0 does not exist.
User not Deleted.
```

The absence of error messages tells us that, so far, the `restdb` package works as expected: users are added and deleted from the database and queries to the database are performed. Just remember that this is a quick and dirty way of testing a package.

> All packages are improved and new functionality is added to almost all existing packages. Should you wish to update the `restdb` package, or any other external package, and use the newer version while developing your own utilities, you can issue the `go get -u -v` command in the directory where the `go.sum` and `go.mod` files of your utility reside.

Implementing the RESTful server

Now that we are sure that the `restdb` package works as expected, we are ready to explain the implementation of the RESTful server. The server code is split into two files, both belonging to the `main` package: `main.go` and `handlers.go`. The main reason for doing so is to avoid having huge code files to work with and separating the functionality of the server logically.

The most important part of `main.go`, which belongs to the `main()` function, is the following:

```
rMux.NotFoundHandler = http.HandlerFunc(DefaultHandler)
```

First, we need to define the default handler function—although this is not necessary, it is a good practice to have such a handler.

```
notAllowed := notAllowedHandler{}
rMux.MethodNotAllowedHandler = notAllowed
```

The `MethodNotAllowedHandler` handler is executed when you try to visit an endpoint using an unsupported HTTP method. The actual implementation of the handler is found in `handlers.go`.

```
rMux.HandleFunc("/time", TimeHandler)
```

The `/time` endpoint is supported by all HTTP methods, so it does not belong to any subrouter.

```
// Define Handler Functions
// Register GET
getMux := rMux.Methods(http.MethodGet).Subrouter()

getMux.HandleFunc("/getall", GetAllHandler)
getMux.HandleFunc("/getid/{username}", GetIDHandler)
getMux.HandleFunc("/logged", LoggedUsersHandler)
getMux.HandleFunc("/username/{id:[0-9]+}", GetUserDataHandler)
```

First, we define a subrouter for the `GET` HTTP method along with the supported endpoints. Remember that `gorilla/mux` is responsible for making sure that only `GET` requests are going to be served by the `getMux` subrouter.

```
// Register PUT
// Update User
putMux := rMux.Methods(http.MethodPut).Subrouter()
putMux.HandleFunc("/update", UpdateHandler)
```

After that, we define a subrouter for `PUT` requests.

```
// Register POST
// Add User + Login + Logout
postMux := rMux.Methods(http.MethodPost).Subrouter()
postMux.HandleFunc("/add", AddHandler)
postMux.HandleFunc("/login", LoginHandler)
postMux.HandleFunc("/logout", LogoutHandler)
```

Then, we define the subrouter for `POST` requests.

```
// Register DELETE
// Delete User
deleteMux := rMux.Methods(http.MethodDelete).Subrouter()
deleteMux.HandleFunc("/username/{id:[0-9]+}", DeleteHandler)
```

The last subrouter is for `DELETE` HTTP methods. The code in `gorilla/mux` is responsible for choosing the correct subrouter based on the client request.

```
go func() {
    log.Println("Listening to", PORT)
    err := s.ListenAndServe()
    if err != nil {
        log.Printf("Error starting server: %s\n", err)
        return
    }
}()
```

The HTTP server is executed as a goroutine because the program supports signal handling—refer to *Chapter 7, Go Concurrency*, for the details.

```
sigs := make(chan os.Signal, 1)
signal.Notify(sigs, os.Interrupt)
sig := <-sigs
log.Println("Quitting after signal:", sig)
time.Sleep(5 * time.Second)
s.Shutdown(nil)
```

Last, we add signal handling for gracefully terminating the HTTP server. The `sig := <-sigs` statement prevents the `main()` function from exiting unless an `os.Interrupt` signal is received.

The `handlers.go` file contains the implementations for the handler functions and is also part of the `main` package—its most important parts are the following:

```
// AddHandler is for adding a new user
func AddHandler(rw http.ResponseWriter, r *http.Request) {
	log.Println("AddHandler Serving:", r.URL.Path, "from", r.Host)
	d, err := io.ReadAll(r.Body)
	if err != nil {
		rw.WriteHeader(http.StatusBadRequest)
		log.Println(err)
		return
	}
```

This handler is for the `/add` endpoint. The server reads the client input using `io.ReadAll()`.

```
	if len(d) == 0 {
		rw.WriteHeader(http.StatusBadRequest)
		log.Println("No input!")
		return
	}
```

Then, the code makes sure that the body of the client request is not empty.

```
	// We read two structures as an array:
	// 1. The user issuing the command
	// 2. The user to be added
	var users = []restdb.User{}
	err = json.Unmarshal(d, &users)
	if err != nil {
		log.Println(err)
		rw.WriteHeader(http.StatusBadRequest)
		return
	}
```

As the `/add` endpoint requires two `User` structures, the previous code uses `json.Unmarshal()` to put them into a `[]restdb.User` variable—this means that the client should send these two JSON records using an array. The reason for using `restdb.User` is that all database-related functions work with `restdb.User` variables. Even if we had a structure with the same definition as `restdb.User`, Go would consider them as different. This is not the case with the client because the client sends data without a data type associated with it.

```
    log.Println(users)

    if !restdb.IsUserAdmin(users[0]) {
        log.Println("Issued by non-admin user:", users[0].Username)
        rw.WriteHeader(http.StatusBadRequest)
        return
    }
```

If the user issuing the command is not an admin, the request fails. `restdb.IsUserAdmin()` is implemented in the `restdb` package.

```
    result := restdb.InsertUser(users[1])
    if !result {
        rw.WriteHeader(http.StatusBadRequest)
    }
}
```

Otherwise, `restdb.InsertUser()` inserts the desired user into the database.

Last, we present the handler for the `/getall` endpoint.

```
// GetAllHandler is for getting all data from the user database
func GetAllHandler(rw http.ResponseWriter, r *http.Request) {
    log.Println("GetAllHandler Serving:", r.URL.Path, "from", r.Host)
    d, err := io.ReadAll(r.Body)
    if err != nil {
        rw.WriteHeader(http.StatusBadRequest)
        log.Println(err)
        return
    }
```

Once again, we read the data from the client using `io.ReadAll(r.Body)` and we make sure that the process is error-free by examining the `err` variable.

```
    if len(d) == 0 {
        rw.WriteHeader(http.StatusBadRequest)
        log.Println("No input!")
        return
    }

    var user = restdb.User{}
    err = json.Unmarshal(d, &user)
```

```
    if err != nil {
        log.Println(err)
        rw.WriteHeader(http.StatusBadRequest)
        return
    }
```

Here, we put the client data into a `restdb.User` variable. The `/getall` endpoint requires a single `restdb.User` record as input.

```
    if !restdb.IsUserAdmin(user) {
        log.Println("User", user, "is not an admin!")
        rw.WriteHeader(http.StatusBadRequest)
        return
    }
```

Only admin users can visit `/getall` and get back the list of all users.

```
    err = SliceToJSON(restdb.ListAllUsers(), rw)
    if err != nil {
        log.Println(err)
        rw.WriteHeader(http.StatusBadRequest)
        return
    }
}
```

The last part of the code is about getting the desired data from the database and sending it to the client using the `SliceToJSON(restdb.ListAllUsers(), rw)` call.

Feel free to put each handler into a separate Go file. The general idea is that if you have lots of handler functions, using a separate file for each handler function is a good practice.

The next section tests the RESTful server using `curl(1)` before developing a proper client.

Testing the RESTful server

This subsection shows how to test the RESTful server using the `curl(1)` utility. You should test the RESTful server as much and as extensively as possible to find bugs or unwanted behavior. As we use two files for the server implementation, we need to run it as `go run main.go handlers.go`. Additionally, do not forget to have PostgreSQL up and running. We begin by testing the `/time` handler, which works with all HTTP methods:

```
$ curl localhost:1234/time
The current time is: Mon, 17 May 2021 09:14:00 EEST
```

Next, we test the default handler:

```
$ curl localhost:1234/
/ is not supported. Thanks for visiting!
$ curl localhost:1234/doesNotExist
/doesNotExist is not supported. Thanks for visiting!
```

Last, we see what happens if we use an unsupported HTTP method with a supported endpoint—in this case, the `/getall` endpoint that works with `GET` only:

```
$ curl -s -X PUT -H 'Content-Type: application/json' localhost:1234/
getall
Method not allowed!
```

Although the `/getall` endpoint requires a valid user to operate, the fact that we are using an HTTP method that is not supported by that endpoint takes precedence and the call fails for the right reasons.

> It is important to look at the output of the RESTful server and the log entries that it generates during testing. Not all information can be sent back to a client, but the server process is allowed to print anything we want. This can be very helpful for debugging a server process such as our RESTful server.

The next subsection tests all handlers that support the `GET` HTTP method.

Testing GET handlers

First, we test the `/getall` endpoint:

```
$ curl -s -X GET -H 'Content-Type: application/json' -d '{"username":
"admin", "password" : "newPass"}' localhost:1234/getall
[{"ID":1,"Username":"admin","Password":"newPass","LastLogin":1620922454
,"Admin":1,"Active":1},{"ID":6,"Username":"mihalis","Password":"admin",
"LastLogin":1620926815,"Admin":1,"Active":0},{"ID":7,"Username":"mike",
"Password":"admin","LastLogin":1620926862,"Admin":1,"Active":0}]
```

The previous output is a list of all existing users found in the database in JSON format.

Then, we test the /logged endpoint:

```
$ curl -X GET -H 'Content-Type: application/json' -d '{"username":
"admin", "password" : "newPass"}' localhost:1234/logged
[{"ID":1,"Username":"admin","Password":"newPass","LastLogin":1620922454
,"Admin":1,"Active":1}]
```

After that, we test the /username/{id} endpoint:

```
$ curl -X GET -H 'Content-Type: application/json' -d '{"username":
"admin", "password" : "newPass"}' localhost:1234/username/7
{"ID":7,"Username":"mike","Password":"admin","LastLogin":1620926862,"Ad
min":1,"Active":0}
```

Last, we test the /getid/{username} endpoint:

```
$ curl -X GET -H 'Content-Type: application/json' -d '{"username":
"admin", "password" : "newPass"}' localhost:1234/getid/admin
User admin has ID: 1
```

So far, we can get a list of existing users and the list of logged-in users and get information about specific users—all these endpoints use the GET method. The next subsection tests all handlers that support the POST HTTP method.

Testing POST handlers

First, we test the /add endpoint by adding the packt user, which does not have admin privileges:

```
$ curl -X POST -H 'Content-Type: application/json' -d '[{"username":
"admin", "password" : "newPass", "admin":1}, {"username": "packt",
"password" : "admin", "admin":0} ]' localhost:1234/add
```

The previous call passes an array of JSON records to the server to add a new user named packt. The command is issued by the admin user.

If we try to add the same username more than once, the process is going to fail—this is revealed with the use of -v in the curl(1) command. The relevant message is HTTP/1.1 400 Bad Request.

Additionally, if we try to add a new user using the credentials of a user that is not an administrator, the server is going to generate the Command issued by non-admin user: packt message.

Then, we test the `/login` endpoint:

```
$ curl -X POST -H 'Content-Type: application/json' -d '{"username":
"packt", "password" : "admin"}' localhost:1234/login
```

The previous command is used for logging in the `packt` user.

Last, we test the `/logout` endpoint:

```
$ curl -X POST -H 'Content-Type: application/json' -d '{"username":
"packt", "password" : "admin"}' localhost:1234/logout
```

The previous command is used for logging out the `packt` user. You can use the `/logged` endpoint to verify the results of the previous two interactions.

Let us now test the only endpoint that supports the `PUT` HTTP method.

Testing the PUT handler

First, we test the `/update` endpoint as follows:

```
$ curl -X PUT -H 'Content-Type: application/json' -d '[{"username":
"admin", "password" : "newPass", "admin":1}, {"username": "admin",
"password" : "justChanged", "admin":1} ]' localhost:1234/update
```

The previous command changes the password of the `admin` user from `newPass` to `justChanged`.

Then, we try to change a user password using the credentials of a non-admin user (`packt`):

```
$ curl -X PUT -H 'Content-Type: application/json' -d '[{"Username
":"packt","Password":"admin"}, {"username": "admin", "password" :
"justChanged", "admin":1} ]' localhost:1234/update
```

The generated log message is `Command issued by non-admin user: packt`.

We might consider the fact that a non-admin user cannot even change their password a flaw—it might be, but this is the way the RESTful server is implemented. The idea is that non-admin users should not issue dangerous commands directly. Additionally, this flaw can be easily fixed as follows: generally speaking, regular users are not going to interact in this way with the server and are going to be offered a web interface for doing so. After that, an admin user can send the user request to the server. Therefore, this can be implemented in a different way that is more secure and does not give unnecessary privileges to regular users.

Lastly, we are going to test the `DELETE` HTTP method.

Testing the DELETE handler

For the `DELETE` HTTP method, we need to test the `/username/{id}` endpoint. As that endpoint does not return any output, using `-v` in `curl(1)` is going to reveal the returned HTTP status code:

```
$ curl -X DELETE -H 'Content-Type: application/json' -d '{"username":
"admin", "password" : "justChanged"}' localhost:1234/username/6 -v
```

The `HTTP/1.1 200 OK` status code verifies that the user was deleted successfully. If we try to delete the same user again, the request is going to fail, and the returned message is going to be `HTTP/1.1 404 Not Found`.

So far, we know that the RESTful server works as expected. However, `curl(1)` is far from perfect for working with the RESTful server on a daily basis. The next section shows how to develop a command-line client for the RESTful server we developed in this section.

Creating a RESTful client

Creating a RESTful client is much easier than programming a server mainly because you do not have to work with the database on the client side. The only thing that the client needs to do is send the right amount and kind of data to the server and receive back the server response. The RESTful client is going to be developed in `~/go/src/github.com/mactsouk/rest-cli`—if you do not plan to make it available to the world, you do not need to create a separate GitHub repository for it. However, for you to be able to see the code of the client, I created a GitHub repository, which is `https://github.com/mactsouk/rest-cli`.

The supported first-level `cobra` commands are the following:

- `list`: This command accesses the `/getall` endpoint and returns the list of users
- `time`: This command is for visiting the `/time` endpoint
- `update`: This command is for updating user records—the user ID cannot change
- `logged`: This command lists all logged-in users
- `delete`: This command deletes an existing user
- `login`: This command is for logging in a user

- `logout`: This command is for logging out a user
- `add`: This command is for adding a new user to the system
- `getid`: This command returns the ID of a user, identified by their username
- `search`: This command displays information about a given user, identified by their ID

> A client like the one we are about to present is much better than working with `curl(1)` because it can process the received information but, most importantly, it can interpret the HTTP return codes and preprocess data before sending it to the server. The price you pay is the extra time needed for developing and debugging the RESTful client.

There exist two main command-line flags for passing the username and the password of the user issuing the command: `user` and `pass`. As you are going to see in their implementations, they have the `-u` and `-p` shortcuts, respectively. Additionally, as the JSON record that holds user info has a small number of fields, all the fields are going to be given in a JSON record as plain text, using the `data` flag and `-d` shortcut—this is implemented in `root.go`. Each command is going to read the desired flags only and the desired fields of the input JSON record—this is implemented in the source code file of each command. Lastly, the utility is going to return JSON records, when this makes sense, or a text message related to the endpoint that was visited. Now, let us continue with the structure of the client and the implementation of the commands.

Creating the structure of the command-line client

This subsection uses the `cobra` utility to create a structure for the command-line utility. But first we are going to create a proper `cobra` project and Go module:

```
$ cd ~/go/src/github.com/mactsouk
$ git clone git@github.com:mactsouk/rest-cli.git
$ cd rest-cli
$ ~/go/bin/cobra init --pkg-name github.com/mactsouk/rest-cli
$ go mod init
$ go mod tidy
$ go run main.go
```

You do not need to execute the last command, but it makes sure that everything is fine so far. After that, we are ready to define the commands that the utility is going to support by running the following `cobra` commands:

```
$ ~/go/bin/cobra add add
$ ~/go/bin/cobra add delete
$ ~/go/bin/cobra add list
$ ~/go/bin/cobra add logged
$ ~/go/bin/cobra add login
$ ~/go/bin/cobra add logout
$ ~/go/bin/cobra add search
$ ~/go/bin/cobra add getid
$ ~/go/bin/cobra add time
$ ~/go/bin/cobra add update
```

Now that we have the desired structure, we can begin implementing the commands and maybe remove some of the comments inserted by `cobra`, which is the subject of the next subsection.

Implementing the RESTful client commands

As there is no point in presenting all code that can be found in the GitHub repository, we are going to present the most characteristic code found in some of the commands, starting with `root.go`, which is where the next global variables are defined:

```
var SERVER string
var PORT string
var data string
var username string
var password string
```

These global variables hold the values of the command-line options of the utility and are accessible from anywhere in the utility code.

```
type User struct {
    ID        int    `json:"id"`
    Username  string `json:"username"`
    Password  string `json:"password"`
    LastLogin int64  `json:"lastlogin"`
    Admin     int    `json:"admin"`
    Active    int    `json:"active"`
}
```

We define the `User` structure for sending and receiving data.

```
func init() {
    rootCmd.PersistentFlags().StringVarP(&username, "username", "u",
"username", "The username")
    rootCmd.PersistentFlags().StringVarP(&password, "password", "p",
"admin", "The password")
    rootCmd.PersistentFlags().StringVarP(&data, "data", "d", "{}",
"JSON Record")

    rootCmd.PersistentFlags().StringVarP(&SERVER, "server", "s",
"http://localhost", "RESTful server hostname")
    rootCmd.PersistentFlags().StringVarP(&PORT, "port", "P", ":1234",
"Port of RESTful Server")
}
```

We present the implementation of the `init()` function that holds the definitions of the command-line options. The values of the command-line flags are automatically stored in the variables that are passed as the first argument to `rootCmd.PersistentFlags().StringVarP()`. So, the `username` flag, which has the `-u` alias, stores its value to the `username` global variable.

Next is the implementation of the `list` command as found in `list.go`:

```
var listCmd = &cobra.Command{
    Use:   "list",
    Short: "List all available users",
    Long:  `The list command lists all available users.`,
```

This part is about the help messages that are displayed for the command. Although they are optional, it is good to have an accurate description of the command. We continue with the implementation:

```
    Run: func(cmd *cobra.Command, args []string) {
        endpoint := "/getall"
        user := User{Username: username, Password: password}
```

First, we construct a `User` variable to hold the username and the password of the user issuing the command—this variable is going to be passed to the server.

```
        // bytes.Buffer is both a Reader and a Writer
        buf := new(bytes.Buffer)
        err := user.ToJSON(buf)
```

```
    if err != nil {
        fmt.Println("JSON:", err)
        return
    }
```

We need to encode the `user` variable before passing it to the RESTful server, which is the purpose of the `ToJSON()` method. The implementation of the `ToJSON()` method is found in `root.go`.

```
    req, err := http.NewRequest(http.MethodGet,
                    SERVER+PORT+endpoint, buf)
    if err != nil {
        fmt.Println("GetAll - Error in req: ", err)
        return
    }
    req.Header.Set("Content-Type", "application/json")
```

Here, we create the request using the `SERVER` and `PORT` global variables followed by the endpoint, using the desired HTTP method (`http.MethodGet`), and declare that we are going to send JSON data using `Header.Set()`.

```
    c := &http.Client{
        Timeout: 15 * time.Second,
    }

    resp, err := c.Do(req)
    if err != nil {
        fmt.Println("Do:", err)
        return
    }
```

After that, we send our data to the server using `Do()` and get the server response.

```
    if resp.StatusCode != http.StatusOK {
        fmt.Println(resp)
        return
    }
```

If the status code of the response is not `http.StatusOK`, then the request has failed.

```
    var users = []User{}
    SliceFromJSON(&users, resp.Body)
    data, err := PrettyJSON(users)
```

```
        if err != nil {
            fmt.Println(err)
            return
        }

        fmt.Print(data)
    },
}
```

If the status code is `http.StatusOK`, then we prepare to read a slice of `User` variables. As these variables hold JSON records, we need to decode them using `SliceFromJSON()`, which is defined in `root.go`.

Last is the code of the `add` command, as found in `add.go`. The difference between `add` and `list` is that the `add` command needs to send two JSON records to the RESTful server: the first one holding the data of the user issuing the command, and the second holding the data for the user that is about to be added to the system. The `username` and `password` flags hold the data for the `Username` and `Password` fields of the first record, whereas the `data` command-line flag holds the data for the second record.

```
var addCmd = &cobra.Command{
    Use:   "add",
    Short: "Add a new user",
    Long:  `Add a new user to the system.`,
    Run: func(cmd *cobra.Command, args []string) {
        endpoint := "/add"
        u1 := User{Username: username, Password: password}
```

As before, we get the information about the user issuing the command and put it into a structure.

```
        // Convert data string to User Structure
        var u2 User
        err := json.Unmarshal([]byte(data), &u2)
        if err != nil {
            fmt.Println("Unmarshal:", err)
            return
        }
```

As the data command-line flag holds a string value, we need to convert that string value to a User structure—this is the purpose of the json.Unmarshal() call.

```
users := []User{}
users = append(users, u1)
users = append(users, u2)
```

Then we create a slice of User variables that are going to be sent to the server. The order you put the structures in that slice is important: first, the user issuing the command, and then the data of the user that is going to be created.

```
buf := new(bytes.Buffer)
err = SliceToJSON(users, buf)
if err != nil {
    fmt.Println("JSON:", err)
    return
}
```

Then we encode that slice before sending it to the RESTful server through the HTTP request.

```
req, err := http.NewRequest(http.MethodPost,
                            SERVER+PORT+endpoint, buf)
if err != nil {
    fmt.Println("GetAll - Error in req: ", err)
    return
}
req.Header.Set("Content-Type", "application/json")

c := &http.Client{
    Timeout: 15 * time.Second,
}

resp, err := c.Do(req)
if err != nil {
    fmt.Println("Do:", err)
    return
}
```

We prepare the request and send it to the server. The server is responsible for decoding the provided data and acting accordingly, in this case adding a new user to the system. The client just needs to visit the correct endpoint using the appropriate HTTP method (http.MethodPost) and check the returned status code.

```
        if resp.StatusCode != http.StatusOK {
            fmt.Println("Status code:", resp.Status)
        } else {
            fmt.Println("User", u2.Username, "added.")
        }
    },
}
```

The `add` command does not return any data back to the client—what interests us is the HTTP status code because this is what determines the success or failure of the command.

Using the RESTful client

We are now going to use the command-line utility to interact with the RESTful server. This type of utility can be used for administering a RESTful server, creating automated tasks, and carrying out CI/CD jobs. For reasons of simplicity, the client and the server reside on the same machine, and we mostly work with the default user (`admin`)—this makes the presented commands shorter. Additionally, we execute `go build` to create a binary executable to avoid using `go main.go` all the time.

First, we get the time from the server:

```
$ ./rest-cli time
The current time is: Tue, 25 May 2021 08:38:04 EEST
```

Next, we list all users. As the output depends on the contents of the database, we print a small part of the output. Note that the `list` command requires a user with admin privileges:

```
$ ./rest-cli list -u admin -p admin
[
        {
                "id": 7,
                "username": "mike",
                "password": "admin",
                "lastlogin": 1620926862,
                "admin": 1,
                "active": 0
        },
```

Next, we test the `logged` command with an invalid password:

```
$ ./rest-cli logged -u admin -p notPass
&{400 Bad Request 400 HTTP/1.1 1 1 map[Content-Length:[0] Date:[Tue,
25 May 2021 05:42:36 GMT]] 0xc000190020 0 [] false false map[]
0xc0000fc800 <nil>}
```

As expected, the command fails—this output is used for debugging purposes. After making sure that the command works as expected, you might want to print a more appropriate error message.

After that, we test the `add` command:

```
$ ./rest-cli add -u admin -p admin --data '{"Username":"newUser",
"Password":"aPass"}'
User newUser added.
```

Trying to add the same user again is going to fail:

```
$ ./rest-cli add -u admin -p admin --data '{"Username":"newUser",
"Password":"aPass"}'
Status code: 400 Bad Request
```

Next, we are going to delete `newUser`—but first, we need to find the user ID of `newUser`:

```
$ ./rest-cli getid -u admin -p admin --data '{"Username":"newUser"}'
User newUser has ID: 15
$ ./rest-cli delete -u admin -p admin --data '{"ID":15}'
User with ID 15 deleted.
```

Feel free to continue testing the RESTful client and let me know if you find any bugs!

Working with multiple REST API versions

A REST API can change and evolve over time. There exist various approaches on how to implement REST API versioning, including the following:

- Using a custom HTTP header (`version-used`) to define the used version
- Using a different subdomain for each version (`v1.servername` and `v2.servername`)
- Using a combination of `Accept` and `Content-Type` headers—this method is based on *content negotiation*

- Using a different path for each version (`/v1` and `/v2` if the RESTful server supports two REST API versions)
- Using a query parameter to reference the desired version (`..../endpoint?version=v1` or `..../endpoint?v=1`)

There is no correct answer for how to implement REST API versioning. Use what seems more natural to you and your users. What is important is to be consistent and use the same approach everywhere. Personally, I prefer to use `/v1/...` for supporting the endpoints of version 1, and `/v2/...` for supporting the endpoints of version 2, and so on.

The development of RESTful servers and clients has come to an end here. The next section illustrates how to upload and download binary files using `gorilla/mux` in case you want to add that feature.

Uploading and downloading binary files

It is not unusual to need to store binary files in a RESTful server and being able to download them afterward—for example, for developing photo libraries or document libraries. This section illustrates how to implement that functionality.

For reasons of simplicity, the example is going to be included in the `mactsouk/rest-api` GitHub repository used earlier for implementing the RESTful server. For this subsection, we are going to be using the `file` directory to store the relevant code, which is saved as `binary.go`. In reality, `binary.go` is a small RESTful server that only supports the uploading and downloading of binary files through the `/files/` endpoint.

There exist three main ways to save the files you upload:

- On the local filesystem
- On a database management system that supports the storing of binary files
- On the cloud using a cloud provider

In our case, we are storing the files on the filesystem the server runs on. More specifically, we are storing uploaded files under `/tmp/files` as we are testing things.

The code of `binary.go` is as follows:

```
package main

import (
    "errors"
```

```
    "io"
    "log"
    "net/http"
    "os"
    "time"

    "github.com/gorilla/mux"
)

var PORT = ":1234"
var IMAGESPATH = "/tmp/files"
```

The previous two global parameters hold the TCP port the server is going to listen to and the local path where uploaded files are going to be saved, respectively. Note that on most UNIX systems, `/tmp` is automatically emptied after a system reboot.

```
func uploadFile(rw http.ResponseWriter, r *http.Request) {
    filename, ok := mux.Vars(r)["filename"]
    if !ok {
        log.Println("filename value not set!")
        rw.WriteHeader(http.StatusNotFound)
        return
    }
    log.Println(filename)
    saveFile(IMAGESPATH+"/"+filename, rw, r)
}
```

The `uploadFile()` function is responsible for the uploading of new files to the predefined directory. The most important part of it is the use of `mux.Vars(r)` for getting the value of the `filename` key. Note that the parameter to `mux.Vars()` is the `http.Request` variable. If the desired key exists, then the function continues and calls `saveFile()`. Otherwise, it returns without saving any files.

```
func saveFile(path string, rw http.ResponseWriter, r *http.Request) {
    log.Println("Saving to", path)
    err := saveToFile(path, r.Body)
    if err != nil {
        log.Println(err)
        return
    }
}
```

The purpose of `saveFile()` is to save the uploaded file by calling `saveToFile()`. You might ask, why not combine both `saveFile()` and `saveToFile()` and have a single function? The answer is that this way, the code of `saveToFile()` is generic and can be reused by other utilities.

```
func saveToFile(path string, contents io.Reader) error {
    _, err := os.Stat(path)
    if err == nil {
        err = os.Remove(path)
        if err != nil {
            log.Println("Error deleting", path)
            return err
        }
    } else if !os.IsNotExist(err) {
        log.Println("Unexpected error:", err)
        return err
    }

    f, err := os.Create(path)
    if err != nil {
        log.Println(err)
        return err
    }
    defer f.Close()

    n, err := io.Copy(f, contents)
    if err != nil {
        return err
    }
    log.Println("Bytes written:", n)

    return nil
}
```

All the previous code is related to file I/O and is used for saving the contents of the `contents io.Reader` to the desired path.

```
func createImageDirectory(d string) error {
    _, err := os.Stat(d)
    if os.IsNotExist(err) {
        log.Println("Creating:", d)
        err = os.MkdirAll(d, 0755)
```

```
        if err != nil {
            log.Println(err)
            return err
        }
    } else if err != nil {
        log.Println(err)
        return err
    }

    fileInfo, _ := os.Stat(d)

    mode := fileInfo.Mode()
    if !mode.IsDir() {
        msg := d + " is not a directory!"
        return errors.New(msg)
    }
```

The purpose of `createImageDirectory()` is to create the directory where the files are going to be saved, if the directory does not already exist. If the path exists and is not a directory, then we have a problem, so the function returns a custom error message.

```
    return nil
}
func main() {
    err := createImageDirectory(IMAGESPATH)
    if err != nil {
        log.Println(err)
        return
    }

    mux := mux.NewRouter()
    putMux := mux.Methods(http.MethodPut).Subrouter()
    putMux.HandleFunc("/files/{filename:[a-zA-Z0-9][a-zA-Z0-9\\.]*[a-
zA-Z0-9]}", uploadFile)
```

Only the `PUT` HTTP method is supported for uploading files to the server. The regular expression dictates that we want filenames that begin with a single letter or digit and end with a letter or digit. This means that filenames should not begin with `.` or `..` to avoid visiting subdirectories and therefore compromising the security of the system. As we saw earlier, the code saves the filename value in a map using the `filename` key—this map is accessed by the `uploadFile()` function.

```
    getMux := mux.Methods(http.MethodGet).Subrouter()
    getMux.Handle("/files/{filename:[a-zA-Z0-9][a-zA-Z0-9\\.]*[a-
zA-Z0-9]}", http.StripPrefix("/files/", http.FileServer(http.
Dir(IMAGESPATH))))
```

The downloading part is a combination of the functionality of `gorilla/mux` and the Go handler for file servers. So, the external package offers support for regular expressions and an easy way to define that we want to use the `GET` HTTP method, whereas Go offers the functionality of `http.FileServer()` for serving the files. This mainly happens because we are serving files from the local filesystem. However, nothing prohibits us from writing our own handler function for the downloading of the binary files when we want to divert from the default behavior.

```
    s := http.Server{
        Addr:         PORT,
        Handler:      mux,
        ErrorLog:     nil,
        ReadTimeout:  5 * time.Second,
        WriteTimeout: 5 * time.Second,
        IdleTimeout:  10 * time.Second,
    }

    log.Println("Listening to", PORT)

    err = s.ListenAndServe()
    if err != nil {
        log.Printf("Error starting server: %s\n", err)
        return
    }
}
```

The last part of the utility is about beginning the server with the desired parameters. It is really surprising that `main()` is pretty short, yet it does so many useful things.

We now need to initialize the Go module functionality for `binary.go` to run:

```
$ go mod init
$ go mod tidy
$ go mod download
```

We are going to use `curl(1)` to work with `binary.go`:

```
$ curl -X PUT localhost:1234/files/packt.png --data-binary @packt.png
```

So, first we upload a file named `packt.png` to the server and the file is saved as `packt.png` on the server side. The next command saves the same file as `1.png` on the server:

```
$ curl -X PUT localhost:1234/files/1.png --data-binary @packt.png
```

Downloading `1.png` on the local machine as `downloaded.png` is as easy as running the next command:

```
$ curl -X GET localhost:1234/files/1.png --output downloaded.png
```

If you forget to use `--output`, then `curl(1)` generates the next error message:

```
Warning: Binary output can mess up your terminal. Use "--output -" to
tell
Warning: curl to output it to your terminal anyway, or consider
"--output
Warning: <FILE>" to save to a file.
```

Last, if you try to download a file that cannot be found, `curl(1)` prints the `404 page not found` message.

For the previous interactions, `binary.go` generated the following output:

```
2021/05/25 09:06:46 Creating: /tmp/files
2021/05/25 09:06:46 Listening to :1234
2021/05/25 09:10:21 packt.png
2021/05/25 09:10:21 Saving to /tmp/files/packt.png
2021/05/25 09:10:21 Bytes written: 733
```

Now that we know how to create RESTful servers, download and upload files, and define REST APIs, it is time to learn how to document REST APIs using Swagger.

Using Swagger for REST API documentation

In this section, we discuss the documentation of a REST API. We are going to use the OpenAPI Specification for documenting the REST API. The OpenAPI Specification, which is also called the Swagger Specification, is a specification for describing, producing, consuming, and visualizing RESTful web services.

Put simply, Swagger is a representation of your RESTful API. Swagger reads the appropriate **code annotations** and creates the OpenAPI file. To be able to document a REST API using Swagger, you basically have two choices. First, writing the OpenAPI Specification file on your own (manually), or adding annotations in the source code that help Swagger generate the OpenAPI Specification file for you (automatically).

We are going to use `go-swagger`, which brings to Go a way of working with the Swagger API. The extra content for creating the documentation for the REST API is put in the Go source files as Go comments. The utility reads these comments and generates the documentation! However, all comments should follow certain rules and comply with the supported grammar and conventions.

First, we need to install the `go-swagger` binary by following the instructions found at `https://goswagger.io/install.html`. As instructions and versions change from time to time, do not forget to check for updates. The instructions from the previous web page install the `swagger` binary in `/usr/local/bin`, which is the appropriate place for external binary files. However, you are free to put it elsewhere as long as the directory you put it in is in your `PATH`. After a successful installation, running Swagger on the command line should generate the next message, which states the commands that are supported by `swagger`:

```
Please specify one command of: diff, expand, flatten, generate, init,
mixin, serve, validate or version
```

You can also get extra help for each `swagger` command with the `--help` flag. For example, getting help for the `generate` command is as simple as running `swagger generate --help`:

```
$ swagger generate --help
Usage:
  swagger [OPTIONS] generate <command>

generate go code for the swagger spec file

Application Options:
  -q, --quiet                  silence logs
      --log-output=LOG-FILE    redirect logs to file

Help Options:
  -h, --help                   Show this help message
```

```
Available commands:
  cli         generate a command line client tool from the swagger spec
  client      generate all the files for a client library
  markdown    generate a markdown representation from the swagger spec
  model       generate one or more models from the swagger spec
  operation   generate one or more server operations from the swagger
spec
  server      generate all the files for a server application
  spec        generate a swagger spec document from a go application
  support     generate supporting files like the main function and the
api builder
```

Next, we learn how to document the REST API by adding Swagger-related metadata to a source file.

Documenting the REST API

This section teaches you how to document an existing REST API. For reasons of simplicity, we are going to use a relatively short file that contains handler functions. So, we create a new folder named `swagger` in the `https://github.com/mactsouk/rest-api` repository for storing the Go file with the extra Swagger information—in our case, we are going to create a new copy of `handlers.go` inside the `swagger` directory and modify it. Have in mind that as far as Go is concerned, the new version is still a valid Go package that can be compiled and used without any issues—it just contains extra Swagger-related information in Go comments.

There is no point in displaying the entire code of the new version of `handlers.go`, which is contained in a Go package named `handlers`—we just present the most important parts of it, beginning with the preamble of the source file:

```
// Package handlers for the RESTful Server
//
// Documentation for REST API
//
//  Schemes: http
//  BasePath: /
//  Version: 1.0.7
//
//  Consumes:
//  - application/json
//
//  Produces:
```

```
//   - application/json
//
// swagger:meta
```

We declare that we are communicating with data in JSON format (`Consumes` and `Produces`), define the version, and put in some comments that describe the general purpose of the package. The `swagger:meta` tag is what informs the `swagger` binary that this is a source file with metadata about an API. Just make sure that you do not forget that particular tag. Then, we present the documentation for the `User` structure, which is essential for the operation of the service and is going to be used *indirectly* by extra structures that we need to define for the purposes of documentation generation.

```
// User defines the structure for a Full User Record
//
// swagger:model
type User struct {
    // The ID for the user
    // in: body
    //
    // required: false
    // min: 1
    ID int `json:"id"`
```

The user ID is provided by the database, which makes it a not-required field, and has a minimum value of 1.

```
    // The Username of the user
    // in: body
    //
    // required: true
    Username string `json:"username"`
```

The `Username` field is required.

```
    // The Password of the user
    //
    // required: true
    Password string `json:"password"`
```

Similarly, the `Password` field is required.

```
    // The Last Login time of the User
    //
```

```
    // required: true
    // min: 0
    LastLogin int64 `json:"lastlogin"`

    // Is the User Admin or not
    //
    // required: true
    Admin int `json:"admin"`

    // Is the User Logged In or Not
    //
    // required: true
    Active int `json:"active"`
}
```

At the end of the day, you need to add comments for all the fields of the structure.

Next, we document the `/delete` endpoint along with its handler function:

```
// swagger:route DELETE /delete/{id} DeleteUser deleteID
// Delete a user given their ID.
// The command should be issued by an admin user
```

In this first part, we say that this endpoint works with the `DELETE` HTTP method, uses the `/delete` path, requires a parameter named `id`, and is going to be displayed as `DeleteUser` on screen. The last part (`deleteID`) allows us to define the details of the `id` parameter, which is going to be presented in a while.

```
//
// responses:
// 200: noContent
// 404: ErrorMessage
```

In the preceding code, we define the two possible responses of the endpoint. Both are going to be implemented later.

```
// DeleteHandler is for deleting users based on user ID
func DeleteHandler(rw http.ResponseWriter, r *http.Request) {
}
```

The handler implementation for `/delete` is omitted for brevity.

After that, we are going to document the `/logged` endpoint along with its handler function:

```
// swagger:route GET /logged logged getUserInfo
// Returns a list of logged in users
//
// responses:
// 200: UsersResponse
// 400: BadRequest
```

This time, the first response of the handler function is called `UsersResponse` and is going to be presented in a while. If you recall, this handler returns a slice of `User` elements.

```
// LoggedUsersHandler returns the list of all logged in users
func LoggedUsersHandler(rw http.ResponseWriter, r *http.Request) {

}
```

Lastly, we need to define Go structures to represent the various inputs and results of an interaction—this is mainly needed for Swagger to work (you usually put these definitions in a separate file that is usually called `docs.go`). The two most important such Go structures are the following:

```
// swagger:parameters deleteID
type idParamWrapper struct {
	// The user id to be deleted
	// in: path
	// required: true
	ID int `json:"id"`
}
```

This one is for the `/delete` endpoint and defines the `ID` variable, which is given in the path, hence the `in: path` line. Notice the use of `swagger:parameters` followed by `deleteID`, which is what associates that particular structure with the documentation of the `/delete` handler function.

```
// A User
// swagger:parameters getUserInfo loggedInfo
type UserInputWrapper struct {
	// A list of users
	// in: body
	Body User
}
```

This time, the structure is associated with two endpoints, hence the use of both `getUserInfo` and `loggedInfo`. Each endpoint should be associated with a unique name.

These helper structures are defined once and are the (small) price you have to pay for the automatic generation of the documentation. The next subsection shows how to create the OpenAPI file given the modified version of `handlers.go`.

Generating the documentation file

Now that we have the Go file with the Swagger metadata, we are ready to generate the OpenAPI file:

```
$ swagger generate spec --scan-models -o ./swagger.yaml
```

What the previous command does is tell `swagger` to generate a Swagger spec document from a Go application that resides in the directory where we run `swagger`. The `--scan-models` option tells `swagger` to include models that were annotated with `swagger:model`. The result of the previous command is a file named `swagger.yaml`, as specified by the `-o` option. Part of the contents of that file is as follows—there is no point in trying to understand everything in the presented output:

```
  /delete/{id}:
    delete:
      description: |-
        Delete a user given their ID
        The command should be issued by an admin user
      operationId: deleteID
      parameters:
      - description: The user id to be deleted
        format: int64
        in: path
        name: id
        required: true
        type: integer
        x-go-name: ID
      responses:
        "200":
          $ref: '#/responses/noContent'
        "404":
          $ref: '#/responses/ErrorMessage'
      tags:
      - DeleteUser
```

The previous part is related to the `/delete` endpoint. The output says that the `/delete` endpoint requires a single parameter, which is the user ID of the user that is about to get deleted. The server returns HTTP code `200` on success and `404` on failure.

Feel free to have a look at the full version of `swagger.yaml`. However, we are not done yet. We need to be able to serve that generated file using a web server. The process is illustrated in the next subsection.

Serving the documentation file

Before we begin the discussion about serving the Swagger file, we first need to discuss the use of *middleware functions* using a simple yet fully functional example. The reason for doing so is simple: the `swagger` tool generates a YAML file that needs to be properly rendered before being presented on screen. So, we use ReDoc (`https://github.com/Redocly/redoc`) to do that. However, we need the `middleware` package for hosting ReDoc sites—although the job is done transparently by the `middleware` package, it is good to know what middleware functions are and what they do. Middleware functions are functions with a short amount of code that get a request, do something with it, and pass it to another middleware or to the last handler function. `gorilla/mux` allows you to attach one or more middleware functions to a router using `Router.Use()`. If a match is found, the relevant middleware functions are executed in the order they were added to the router (or subrouter).

The important code in `middleware.go` is the following:

```
mux := mux.NewRouter()
mux.Use(middleWare)

putMux := mux.Methods(http.MethodPut).Subrouter()
putMux.HandleFunc("/time", timeHandler)

getMux := mux.Methods(http.MethodGet).Subrouter()
getMux.HandleFunc("/add", addHandler)
getMux.Use(anotherMiddleWare)
```

As `middleWare()` was added to the main router (`mux.Use(middleWare)`), it is always executed *before* any subrouter middleware function. Additionally, `middleWare()` is executed with all requests, whereas `anotherMiddleWare()` is executed for the `getMux` subrouter only.

Now that you have a sense of middleware functions, it is time to continue with the serving of `swagger.yaml`. As stated before, serving `swagger.yaml` requires the addition of a handler that we are going to find in an external package, which saves us from having to write everything from scratch. As we try to keep things simple, we are going to serve `swagger.yaml` on its own in `./swagger/serve/swagger.go` using the `/docs` path. The code that follows illustrates the technique by presenting the implementation of the `main()` function:

```
func main() {
    mux := mux.NewRouter()

    getMux := mux.Methods(http.MethodGet).Subrouter()
    opts := middleware.RedocOpts{SpecURL: "/swagger.yaml"}
```

This is where we define the options of a middleware function that is going to be used when serving `/swagger.yaml`. As discussed earlier, this middleware function renders the YAML code.

```
    sh := middleware.Redoc(opts, nil)
```

This is how we define a handler function that is based on the middleware function. This middleware function does not require the use of the `Use()` method.

```
    getMux.Handle("/docs", sh)
```

And now, we must associate the previous handler with `/docs` and we are done!

```
    getMux.Handle("/swagger.yaml", http.FileServer(http.Dir("./")))

    s := http.Server{
    . . .
    }

    log.Println("Listening to", PORT)
    err := s.ListenAndServe()
    if err != nil {
        log.Printf("Error starting server: %s\n", err)
        return
    }
}
```

The rest of the code is for defining the parameters of the server and for starting the server.

The figure that follows shows the rendered `swagger.yaml` as displayed in a Firefox browser.

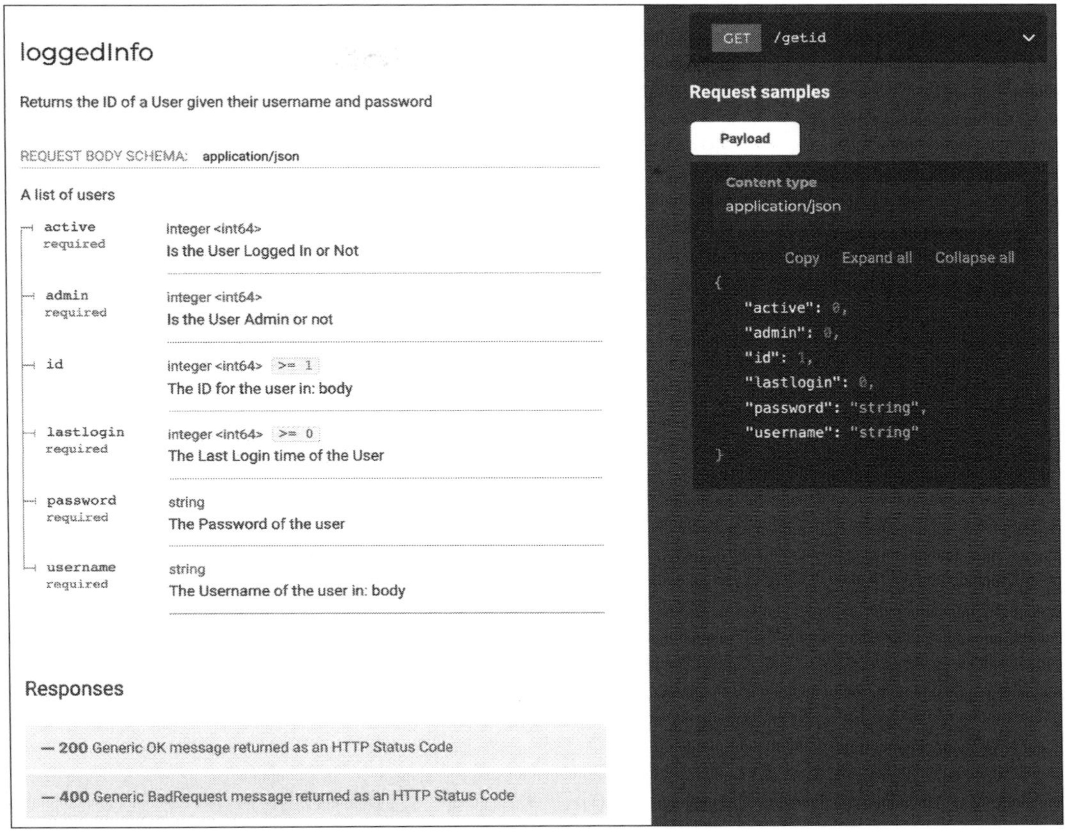

Figure 10.1: Creating documentation for the RESTful API

Figure 10.1 shows information about the `/getid` endpoint, the required payload, and the expected responses.

Unfortunately, further discussion about Swagger and `go-swagger` is beyond the scope of this book—as usual, you need to experiment with the tools to create the desired results. The point here is that having a RESTful service without proper documentation is not going to be very pleasing for potential developers.

Exercises

- Include the functionality of `binary.go` in your own RESTful server
- Change the `restdb` package to support SQLite instead of PostgreSQL
- Change the `restdb` package to support MySQL instead of PostgreSQL
- Put the handler functions from `handlers.go` into separate files

Summary

Go is widely used for developing RESTful clients and servers and this chapter illustrated how to program professional RESTful clients and servers in Go, and how to document a REST API using Swagger. Remember that defining a proper REST API and implementing a server and clients for it is a process that takes time and requires small adjustments and modifications.

The next chapter is about code testing, benchmarking, profiling, cross-compilation, and creating example functions. Among other things, we are going to write code for testing the HTTP handlers developed in this chapter as well as creating random input for testing purposes.

Additional resources

- You can find more about `gorilla/mux` at `https://github.com/gorilla/mux` and at `https://www.gorillatoolkit.org/pkg/mux`
- The `go-querystring` library is for encoding Go structures into URL query parameters: `https://github.com/google/go-querystring`
- You can find more about Swagger at `https://swagger.io/`
- Go Swagger 2.0: `https://goswagger.io/`
- The OpenAPI Specification: `https://www.openapis.org/`
- If you want to validate JSON input, have a look at the Go `validator` package at `https://github.com/go-playground/validator`
- You might find the `jq(1)` command-line utility pretty handy when working with JSON records: `https://stedolan.github.io/jq/` and `https://jqplay.org/`
- You can view OpenAPI files online at `https://editor.swagger.io/`

11

Code Testing and Profiling

The topics of this chapter are both practical and important, especially if you are interested in improving the performance of your Go programs and discovering bugs. This chapter primarily addresses code *optimization*, code *testing*, and code *profiling*.

Code optimization is the process where one or more developers try to make certain parts of a program run faster, be more efficient, or use fewer resources. Put simply, code optimization is about eliminating the bottlenecks of a program that matter. Code testing is about making sure that your code does what you want it to do. In this chapter, we are experiencing the Go way of code testing. The best time to write testing code is during development, as this can help to reveal bugs in the code as early as possible. Code profiling relates to measuring certain aspects of a program to get a detailed understanding of the way the code works. The results of code profiling may help you to decide which parts of your code need to change.

Have in mind that when writing code, we should focus on its **correctness** as well as other desirable properties such as readability, simplicity, and maintainability, not its **performance**. Once we are sure that the code is correct, then we might need to focus on its performance. A good trick on performance is to execute the code on machines that are going to be a bit slower than the ones that are going to be used in production.

This chapter covers:

- Optimizing code
- Benchmarking code
- Profiling code

- The `go tool trace` utility
- Tracing a web server
- Testing Go code
- Cross-compilation
- Using `go:generate`
- Creating example functions

Optimizing code

Code optimization is both an art and a science. This means that there is no deterministic way to help you optimize your code and that you should use your brain and try many things if you want to make your code faster. However, the general principle regarding code optimization is **first make it correct, then make it fast**. Always remember what Donald Knuth said about optimization:

> "*The real problem is that programmers have spent far too much time worrying about efficiency in the wrong places and at the wrong times; premature optimization is the root of all evil (or at least most of it) in programming.*"

Also, remember what the late Joe Armstrong, one of the developers of Erlang, said about optimization:

> "*Make it work, then make it beautiful, then if you really, really have to, make it fast. 90 percent of the time, if you make it beautiful, it will already be fast. So really, just make it beautiful!*"

If you are really into code optimization, you might want to read *Compilers: Principles, Techniques, and Tools* by Alfred V. Aho, Monica S. Lam, Ravi Sethi, and Jeffrey D. Ullman (Pearson Education Limited, 2014), which focuses on compiler construction. Additionally, all volumes in *The Art of Computer Programming* series by Donald Knuth (Addison-Wesley Professional, 1998) are great resources for all aspects of programming if you have the time to read them.

The section that follows is about benchmarking Go code, which helps you determine what is faster and what is slower in your code—this makes it a perfect place to begin.

Benchmarking code

Benchmarking measures the performance of a function or program, allowing you to compare implementations and to understand the performance impact of code changes. Using that information, you can easily reveal the part of the code that needs to be rewritten to improve its performance. It goes without saying that you should not benchmark Go code on a busy machine that is currently being used for other, more important, purposes unless you have a very good reason to do so! Otherwise, you might interfere with the benchmarking process and get inaccurate results, but most importantly, you might generate performance issues on the machine.

> Most of the time, the load of the operating system plays a key role in the performance of your code. Let me tell you a story here: a Java utility I developed for a project performs lots of computations and finishes in 6,242 seconds when running on its own. It took about a day for four instances of the same Java command-line utility to run on the same Linux machine! If you think about it, running them one after the other would have been faster than running them at the same time!

Go follows certain conventions regarding benchmarking. The most important convention is that the name of a benchmark function must begin with `Benchmark`. After the `Benchmark` word, we can put an underscore or an uppercase letter. Therefore, both `BenchmarkFunctionName()` and `Benchmark_functionName()` are valid benchmark functions whereas `Benchmarkfunctionname()` is not. The same rule applies to testing functions that begin with `Test`. Although we are allowed to put the testing and benchmarking code on the same file with the other code, it should be avoided. By convention such functions are put in files that end with `_test.go`. Once the benchmarking or the testing code is correct, the `go test` subcommand does all the dirty work for you, which includes scanning all `*_test.go` files for special functions, generating a proper temporary `main` package, calling these special functions, getting the results, and generating the final output.

Starting from Go 1.17, we can shuffle the execution order of **both tests and benchmarks** with the help of the `shuffle` parameter (`go test -shuffle=on`). The `shuffle` parameter accepts a value, which is the seed for the random number generator, and can be useful when you want to replay an execution order. Its default value is `off`. The logic behind that capability is that sometimes the order in which tests and benchmarks are executed affects their results.

Rewriting the main() function for better testing

There exists a clever way that you can rewrite each `main()` function in order to make testing and benchmarking a lot easier. The `main()` function has a restriction, which is that you cannot call it from test code—this technique presents a solution to that problem using the code found in `main.go`. The `import` block is omitted to save space.

```
func main() {
	err := run(os.Args, os.Stdout)
	if err != nil {
		fmt.Printf("%s\n", err)
		return
	}
}
```

As we cannot have an executable program without a `main()` function, we have to create a minimalistic one. What `main()` does is to call `run()`, which is our own customized version of `main()`, send `os.Args` to it, and collect the return value of `run()`.

```
func run(args []string, stdout io.Writer) error {
	if len(args) == 1 {
		return errors.New("No input!")
	}

	// Continue with the implementation of run()
	// as you would have with main()

	return nil
}
```

As discussed before, the `run()` function, or any other function that is called by `main()` in the same way, replaces `main()` with the additional benefit of being able to be called by test functions. Put simply, the `run()` function contains the code that would have been located in `main()`—the only difference is that `run()` returns an error variable, which is not possible with `main()`, which can only return exit codes to the operating system. You might say that this creates a slightly bigger stack because of the extra function call but the benefits are more important than this additional memory usage. Although you can omit the second parameter (`stdout io.Writer`), which is used for redirecting the generated output, the first one is important because it allows you to pass the command-line arguments to `run()`.

Running `main.go` produces the next output:

```
$ go run main.go
No input!
$ go run main.go some input
```

There is nothing special in the way `main.go` operates. The good thing is that you can call `run()` from anywhere you want, including the code you write for testing, and pass the desired parameters to `run()`! It is good to have that technique in mind because it might save you.

The subject of the next subsection is benchmarking buffered writing.

Benchmarking buffered writing and reading

In this section, we are going to test whether the size of the buffer plays a key role in the performance of write operations. This also gives us the opportunity to discuss **table tests** as well as the use of the `testdata` folder, which is reserved by Go for storing files that are going to be used during benchmarking—both table tests and the `testdata` folder can also be used in testing functions.

> Benchmark functions use `testing.B` variables whereas testing functions use `testing.T` variables. It is easy to remember.

The code of `table_test.go` is the following:

```
package table

import (
    "fmt"
    "os"
    "path"
    "strconv"
    "testing"
)

var ERR error
var countChars int
```

```
func benchmarkCreate(b *testing.B, buffer, filesize int) {
    filename := path.Join(os.TempDir(), strconv.Itoa(buffer))
    filename = filename + "-" + strconv.Itoa(filesize)
    var err error
    for i := 0; i < b.N; i++ {
        err = Create(filename, buffer, filesize)
    }
    ERR = err
```

And now some **important information** regarding benchmarking: each benchmark function is executed for **at least** one second by default—this duration also includes the execution time of the functions that are called by a benchmark function. If the benchmark function returns in a time that is less than one second, the value of `b.N` is increased, and the function runs again as many times in total as the value of `b.N`. The first time the value of `b.N` is 1, then it becomes 2, then 5, then 10, then 20, then 50, and so on. This happens because the faster the function, the more times Go needs to run it to get *accurate results*.

The reason for storing the return value of `Create()` in a variable named `err` and using another global variable named `ERR` afterward is tricky. We want to prevent the compiler from doing any optimizations that might exclude the function that we want to measure from being executed because its results are never used.

```
    err = os.Remove(filename)
    if err != nil {
        fmt.Println(err)
    }
    ERR = err
}
```

Neither the signature nor the name of `benchmarkCreate()` makes it a benchmark function. This is a helper function that allows you to call `Create()`, which creates a new file on disk and its implementation can be found in `table.go`, with the proper parameters. Its implementation is valid and it can be used by benchmark functions.

```
func BenchmarkBuffer4Create(b *testing.B) {
    benchmarkCreate(b, 4, 1000000)
}

func BenchmarkBuffer8Create(b *testing.B) {
    benchmarkCreate(b, 8, 1000000)
}
```

```
func BenchmarkBuffer16Create(b *testing.B) {
    benchmarkCreate(b, 16, 1000000)
}
```

These are three correctly defined benchmark functions that all call `benchmarkCreate()`. Benchmark functions require a single `*testing.B` variable and return no values. In this case, the numbers at the end of the function name indicate the size of the buffer.

```
func BenchmarkRead(b *testing.B) {
    buffers := []int{1, 16, 96}
    files := []string{"10.txt", "1000.txt", "5k.txt"}
```

This is the code that defines the array structures that are going to be used in the table tests. This saves us from having to implement `3x3 = 9` separate benchmark functions.

```
    for _, filename := range files {
        for _, bufSize := range buffers {
            name := fmt.Sprintf("%s-%d", filename, bufSize)
            b.Run(name, func(b *testing.B) {
                for i := 0; i < b.N; i++ {
                    t := CountChars("./testdata/"+filename, bufSize)
                    countChars = t
                }
            })
        }
    }
}
```

The `b.Run()` method, which allows you to run one or more **sub-benchmarks** within a benchmark function, accepts two parameters. First, the name of the sub-benchmark, which is displayed onscreen, and second, the function that implements the sub-benchmark. This is the proper way to run multiple benchmarks with the use of table tests. Just remember to define a proper name for each sub-benchmark because this is going to be displayed onscreen.

Running the benchmarks generates the next output:

```
$ go test -bench=. *.go
```

There are two important points here: first, the value of the `-bench` parameter specifies the benchmark functions that are going to be executed. The `.` value used is a regular expression that matches all valid benchmark functions. The second point is that if you omit the `-bench` parameter, no benchmark functions are going to be executed.

```
goos: darwin
goarch: amd64
cpu: Intel(R) Core(TM) i7-4790K CPU @ 4.00GHz
BenchmarkBuffer4Create-8              78212       12862 ns/op
BenchmarkBuffer8Create-8             145448        7929 ns/op
BenchmarkBuffer16Create-8            222421        5074 ns/op
```

The previous three lines are the results from the `BenchmarkBuffer4Create()`, `BenchmarkBuffer8Create()`, and `BenchmarkBuffer16Create()` benchmark functions respectively, and indicate their performance.

```
BenchmarkRead/10.txt-1-8              78852        17268 ns/op
BenchmarkRead/10.txt-16-8             84225        14161 ns/op
BenchmarkRead/10.txt-96-8             92056        14966 ns/op
BenchmarkRead/1000.txt-1-8             2821       395419 ns/op
BenchmarkRead/1000.txt-16-8           21147        56148 ns/op
BenchmarkRead/1000.txt-96-8           58035        20362 ns/op
BenchmarkRead/5k.txt-1-8                600      1901952 ns/op
BenchmarkRead/5k.txt-16-8              4893       239557 ns/op
BenchmarkRead/5k.txt-96-8             19892        57309 ns/op
```

The previous results are from the table tests with the 9 sub-benchmarks.

```
PASS
ok      command-line-arguments          44.756s
```

So, what does this output tell us? First, the `-8` at the end of each benchmark function signifies the number of goroutines used for its execution, which is essentially the value of the `GOMAXPROCS` environment variable. Similarly, you can see the values of `GOOS` and `GOARCH`, which show the operating system and the architecture of the machine. The second column in the output displays the number of times that the relevant function was executed. Faster functions are executed more times than slower functions. As an example, `BenchmarkBuffer4Create()` was executed `78212` times, while `BenchmarkBuffer16Create()` was executed `222421` times because it is faster! The third column in the output shows the average time of each run and is measured in nanoseconds per benchmark function execution (`ns/op`). The bigger the value of the third column, the slower the benchmark function. A large value in the third column is an indication that a function might need to be optimized.

Should you wish to include memory allocation statistics in the output, you can include `-benchmem` in the command:

```
BenchmarkBuffer4Create-8     91651   11580 ns/op   304 B/op     5 allocs/op
BenchmarkBuffer8Create-8     170814  6202 ns/op    304 B/op     5 allocs/op
```

The generated output is like the one without the `-benchmem` command-line parameter but includes two additional columns. The fourth column shows the amount of memory that was allocated on average in each execution of the benchmark function. The fifth column shows the number of allocations used to allocate the memory value of the fourth column.

So far, we have learned how to create benchmark functions to test the performance of our own functions to better understand potential bottlenecks that might need to be optimized. You might ask, *how often do we need to create benchmark functions?* The answer is simple: when something runs slower than needed and/or when you want to choose between two or more implementations.

The next subsection shows how to compare benchmark results.

The benchstat utility

Now imagine that you have benchmarking data, and you want to compare it with the results that were produced in another computer or with a different configuration. The `benchstat` utility can help you here. The utility can be found in the `golang.org/x/perf/cmd/benchstat` package and can be downloaded using `go get -u golang.org/x/perf/cmd/benchstat`. Go puts all binary files in `~/go/bin` and `benchstat` is no exception.

> The `benchstat` utility replaces the `benchcmp` utility that can be found at `https://pkg.go.dev/golang.org/x/tools/cmd/benchcmp`.

So, imagine that we have two benchmark results for `table_test.go` saved in `r1.txt` and `r2.txt`—you **should remove all lines** from the `go test` output that do not contain benchmarking results, which leaves all lines that begin with `Benchmark`. You can use `benchstat` as follows:

```
$ ~/go/bin/benchstat r1.txt r2.txt
name               old time/op  new time/op  delta
Buffer4Create-8    10.5µs ± 0%   0.8µs ± 0%   ~     (p=1.000 n=1+1)
Buffer8Create-8    6.88µs ± 0%  0.79µs ± 0%   ~     (p=1.000 n=1+1)
```

```
Buffer16Create-8    5.01µs ± 0%  0.78µs ± 0%   ~      (p=1.000 n=1+1)
Read/10.txt-1-8     15.0µs ± 0%   4.0µs ± 0%   ~      (p=1.000 n=1+1)
Read/10.txt-16-8    12.2µs ± 0%   2.6µs ± 0%   ~      (p=1.000 n=1+1)
Read/10.txt-96-8    11.9µs ± 0%   2.6µs ± 0%   ~      (p=1.000 n=1+1)
Read/1000.txt-1-8    381µs ± 0%   174µs ± 0%   ~      (p=1.000 n=1+1)
Read/1000.txt-16-8  54.0µs ± 0%  22.6µs ± 0%   ~      (p=1.000 n=1+1)
Read/1000.txt-96-8  19.1µs ± 0%   6.2µs ± 0%   ~      (p=1.000 n=1+1)
Read/5k.txt-1-8     1.81ms ± 0%  0.89ms ± 0%   ~      (p=1.000 n=1+1)
Read/5k.txt-16-8     222µs ± 0%   108µs ± 0%   ~      (p=1.000 n=1+1)
Read/5k.txt-96-8    51.5µs ± 0%  21.5µs ± 0%   ~      (p=1.000 n=1+1)
```

If the value of the `delta` column is ~, as it happens to be here, it means that there was no significant change in the results. The previous output shows no differences between the two results. Discussing more about `benchstat` is beyond the scope of the book. Type `benchstat -h` to learn more about the supported parameters.

The next subsection touches on a sensitive subject, which is **incorrectly defined benchmark functions**.

Wrongly defined benchmark functions

You should be very careful when defining benchmark functions because you might define them wrongly. Look at the Go code of the following benchmark function:

```
func BenchmarkFiboI(b *testing.B) {
	for i := 0; i < b.N; i++ {
		_ = fibo1(i)
	}
}
```

The `BenchmarkFibo()` function has a valid name and the correct signature. The bad news is that this benchmark function is **logically wrong** and is not going to produce any results. The reason for this is that as the `b.N` value grows in the way described earlier; the runtime of the benchmark function also increases because of the `for` loop. This fact prevents `BenchmarkFiboI()` from converging to a stable number, which prevents the function from completing and therefore returning any results. For analogous reasons, the next benchmark function is also wrongly implemented:

```
func BenchmarkfiboII(b *testing.B) {
	for i := 0; i < b.N; i++ {
		_ = fibo1(b.N)
	}
}
```

On the other hand, there is nothing wrong with the implementation of the following two benchmark functions:

```
func BenchmarkFiboIV(b *testing.B) {
    for i := 0; i < b.N; i++ {
        _ = fibo1(10)
    }
}

func BenchmarkFiboIII(b *testing.B) {
    _ = fibo1(b.N)
}
```

Correct benchmark functions are a tool for identifying bottlenecks on your code that you should put in your own projects, especially when working with file I/O or CPU-intensive operations—as I am writing this, I have been waiting **3 days** for a Python program to finish its operation to test the performance of the brute force method of a mathematical algorithm. Enough with benchmarking. The next section discusses code profiling.

Profiling code

Profiling is a process of dynamic program analysis that measures various values related to program execution to give you a better understanding of the program behavior. In this section, we are going to learn how to profile Go code to understand it better and improve its performance. Sometimes, code profiling can even reveal bugs in the code such an endless loop or functions that never return.

The `runtime/pprof` standard Go package is used for profiling all kinds of applications apart from HTTP servers. The high-level `net/http/pprof` package should be used when you want to profile a web application written in Go. You can see the help page of the `pprof` tool by executing `go tool pprof -help`.

This next section is going to illustrate how to profile a command-line application, and the following subsection shows the profiling of an HTTP server.

Profiling a command-line application

The code of the application is saved as `profileCla.go` and collects CPU and memory profiling data. What is interesting is the implementation of `main()` because this is where the collection of the profiling data takes place:

```
func main() {
    cpuFilename := path.Join(os.TempDir(), "cpuProfileCla.out")
```

```
	cpuFile, err := os.Create(cpuFilename)
	if err != nil {
		fmt.Println(err)
		return
	}
	pprof.StartCPUProfile(cpuFile)
	defer pprof.StopCPUProfile()
```

The previous code is about collecting CPU profiling data. `pprof.StartCPUProfile()` starts the collecting, which is stopped with the `pprof.StopCPUProfile()` call. All data is saved into a file named `cpuProfileCla.out` under the `os.TempDir()` directory—this depends on the OS used and makes the code **portable**. The use of `defer` means that `pprof.StopCPUProfile()` is going to get called just before `main()` exits.

```
	total := 0
	for i := 2; i < 100000; i++ {
		n := N1(i)
		if n {
			total = total + 1
		}
	}
	fmt.Println("Total primes:", total)

	total = 0
	for i := 2; i < 100000; i++ {
		n := N2(i)
		if n {
			total = total + 1
		}
	}
	fmt.Println("Total primes:", total)

	for i := 1; i < 90; i++ {
		n := fibo1(i)
		fmt.Print(n, " ")
	}
	fmt.Println()

	for i := 1; i < 90; i++ {
		n := fibo2(i)
		fmt.Print(n, " ")
	}
```

```
    fmt.Println()
    runtime.GC()
```

All the previous code performs lots of CPU-intensive calculations for the CPU profiler to have data to collect—this is where your actual code usually goes.

```
    // Memory profiling!
    memoryFilename := path.Join(os.TempDir(), "memoryProfileCla.out")
    memory, err := os.Create(memoryFilename)
    if err != nil {
        fmt.Println(err)
        return
    }
    defer memory.Close()
```

We create a second file for collecting memory-related profiling data.

```
    for i := 0; i < 10; i++ {
        s := make([]byte, 50000000)
        if s == nil {
            fmt.Println("Operation failed!")
        }
        time.Sleep(50 * time.Millisecond)
    }

    err = pprof.WriteHeapProfile(memory)
    if err != nil {
        fmt.Println(err)
        return
    }
}
```

The `pprof.WriteHeapProfile()` function writes the memory data into the specified file. Once again, we allocate lots of memory for the memory profiler to have data to collect.

Running `profileCla.go` is going to create two files in the folder returned by `os.TempDir()`—usually, we save them in a different folder. Feel free to change the code of `profileCla.go` and put the profiling files at a different place. So, what do we do next? We should use `go tool pprof` to process these files:

```
$ go tool pprof /path/ToTemporary/Directory/cpuProfileCla.out
(pprof) top
Showing nodes accounting for 5.65s, 98.78% of 5.72s total
```

```
Dropped 47 nodes (cum <= 0.03s)
Showing top 10 nodes out of 18
      flat  flat%   sum%        cum   cum%
     3.27s 57.17% 57.17%      3.65s 63.81%  main.N2 (inline)
```

The `top` command returns a summary of the top 10 entries.

```
(pprof) top10 -cum
Showing nodes accounting for 5560ms, 97.20% of 5720ms total
Dropped 47 nodes (cum <= 28.60ms)
Showing top 10 nodes out of 18
      flat  flat%   sum%        cum   cum%
      80ms  1.40%  1.40%     5660ms 98.95%  main.main
         0     0%  1.40%     5660ms 98.95%  runtime.main
```

The `top10 -cum` command returns the cumulative time for each function.

```
(pprof) list main.N1
list main.N1
Total: 5.72s
ROUTINE ======================== main.N1 in /Users/mtsouk/ch11/
profileCla.go
     1.72s      1.83s (flat, cum) 31.99% of Total
         .          .     35:func N1(n int) bool {
         .          .     36:   k := math.Floor(float64(n/2 + 1))
      50ms       60ms     37:   for i := 2; i < int(k); i++ {
     1.67s      1.77s     38:          if (n % i) == 0 {
```

Last, the `list` command shows information about a given function. The previous output shows that the `if (n % i) == 0` statement is responsible for most of the time it takes `N1()` to run.

We are not showing the full output of these commands for brevity. Try the profile commands on your own in your own code to see their full output. Visit `https://blog.golang.org/pprof` from the Go blog to learn more about profiling.

> You can also create PDF output of the profiling data from the shell of the Go profiler using the `pdf` command. Personally, most of the time, I begin with this command because it gives me a rich overview of the collected data.

Now, let us discuss how to profile an HTTP server, which is the subject of the next subsection.

Profiling an HTTP server

As discussed, the `net/http/pprof` package should be used when you want to collect profiling data for a Go application that runs an HTTP server. To that end, importing `net/http/pprof` **installs various handlers** under the `/debug/pprof/` path. You are going to see more on this in a short while. For now, it is enough to remember that the `net/http/pprof` package should be used to profile web applications, whereas `runtime/pprof` should be used to profile all other kinds of applications.

The technique is illustrated in `profileHTTP.go`, which comes with the following code:

```
package main

import (
	"fmt"
	"net/http"
	"net/http/pprof"
	"os"
	"time"
)
```

As discussed earlier, you should import the `net/http/pprof` package.

```
func myHandler(w http.ResponseWriter, r *http.Request) {
	fmt.Fprintf(w, "Serving: %s\n", r.URL.Path)
	fmt.Printf("Served: %s\n", r.Host)
}

func timeHandler(w http.ResponseWriter, r *http.Request) {
	t := time.Now().Format(time.RFC1123)
	Body := "The current time is:"
	fmt.Fprintf(w, "%s %s", Body, t)
	fmt.Fprintf(w, "Serving: %s\n", r.URL.Path)
	fmt.Printf("Served time for: %s\n", r.Host)
}
```

The previous two functions implement two handlers that are going to be used in our naïve HTTP server. `myHandler()` is the default handler function whereas `timeHandler()` returns the current time and date on the server.

```
func main() {
	PORT := ":8001"
	arguments := os.Args
```

```
    if len(arguments) == 1 {
        fmt.Println("Using default port number: ", PORT)
    } else {
        PORT = ":" + arguments[1]
        fmt.Println("Using port number: ", PORT)
    }

    r := http.NewServeMux()
    r.HandleFunc("/time", timeHandler)
    r.HandleFunc("/", myHandler)
```

Up to this point, there is nothing special as we just register the handler functions.

```
    r.HandleFunc("/debug/pprof/", pprof.Index)
    r.HandleFunc("/debug/pprof/cmdline", pprof.Cmdline)
    r.HandleFunc("/debug/pprof/profile", pprof.Profile)
    r.HandleFunc("/debug/pprof/symbol", pprof.Symbol)
    r.HandleFunc("/debug/pprof/trace", pprof.Trace)
```

All previous statements install the handlers for the HTTP profiler—you can access them using the hostname and port number of the web server. You do not have to use all handlers.

```
    err := http.ListenAndServe(PORT, r)
    if err != nil {
        fmt.Println(err)
        return
    }
}
```

Last, you start the HTTP server as usual.

What is next? First, you run the HTTP server (`go run profileHTTP.go`). After that, you run the next command to collect profiling data **while interacting with the HTTP server**:

```
$ go tool pprof http://localhost:8001/debug/pprof/profile
Fetching profile over HTTP from http://localhost:8001/debug/pprof/
profile
Saved profile in /Users/mtsouk/pprof/pprof.samples.cpu.004.pb.gz
Type: cpu
Time: Jun 18, 2021 at 12:30pm (EEST)
Duration: 30s, Total samples = 10ms (0.033%)
Entering interactive mode (type "help" for commands, "o" for options)
(pprof) %
```

The previous output shows the initial screen of the HTTP profiler—the available commands are the same as when profiling a command-line application.

You can either exit the shell and analyze your data later using `go tool pprof` or continue giving profiler commands. This is the general idea behind profiling HTTP servers in Go.

The next subsection discusses the web interface of the Go profiler.

The web interface of the Go profiler

The good news is that starting with Go version 1.10, `go tool pprof` comes with a web user interface that you can start as `go tool pprof -http=[host]:[port] aProfile.out`—do not forget to put the correct values to `-http`.

A part of the web interface of the profiler is seen in the next figure, which shows how program execution time was spent.

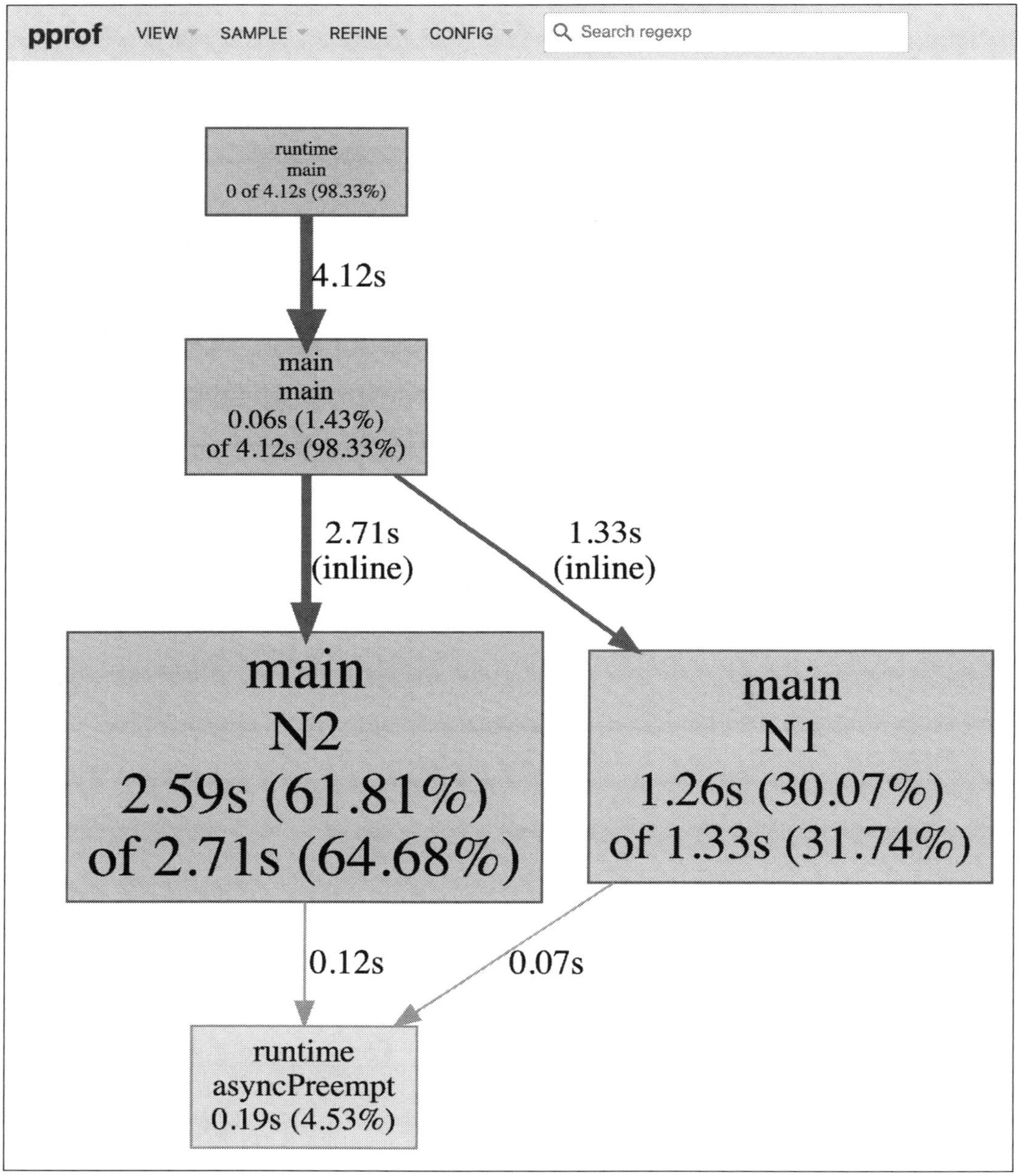

Figure 11.1: The web interface of the Go profiler

Feel free to browse the web interface and see the various options that are offered. Unfortunately, talking more about profiling is beyond the scope of this chapter. As always, if you are really interested in code profiling, experiment with it as much as possible.

The next section is about code tracing.

The go tool trace utility

Code tracing is a process that allows you to learn information such as the operation of the garbage collector, the lifetime of goroutines, the activity of each logical processor, and the number of operating system threads used. The `go tool trace` utility is a tool for viewing the data stored in trace files, which can be generated in any one of the following three ways:

- With the `runtime/trace` package
- With the `net/http/pprof` package
- With the `go test -trace` command

This section illustrates the use of the first technique using the code of `traceCLA.go`:

```
package main

import (
	"fmt"
	"os"
	"path"
	"runtime/trace"
	"time"
)
```

The `runtime/trace` package is required for collecting all kinds of tracing data—there is no point in selecting specific tracing data as all tracing data is interconnected.

```
func main() {
	filename := path.Join(os.TempDir(), "traceCLA.out")
	f, err := os.Create(filename)
	if err != nil {
		panic(err)
	}
	defer f.Close()
```

As it happened with profiling, we need to create a file to store tracing data. In this case the file is called `traceCLA.out` and is stored inside the temporary directory of your operating system.

```
    err = trace.Start(f)
    if err != nil {
        fmt.Println(err)
        return
    }
    defer trace.Stop()
```

This part is all about acquiring data for `go tool trace`, and it has nothing to do with the purpose of the program. We start the tracing process using `trace.Start()`. When we are done, we call the `trace.Stop()` function. The `defer` call means that we want to terminate tracing when the `main()` function returns.

```
    for i := 0; i < 3; i++ {
        s := make([]byte, 50000000)
        if s == nil {
            fmt.Println("Operation failed!")
        }
    }

    for i := 0; i < 5; i++ {
        s := make([]byte, 100000000)
        if s == nil {
            fmt.Println("Operation failed!")
        }
        time.Sleep(time.Millisecond)
    }
}
```

All the previous code is about allocating memory to trigger the operation of the garbage collector and generate more tracing data—you can learn more about the Go garbage collector in *Appendix A, Go Garbage Collector*. The program is executed as usual. However, when it finishes, it populates `traceCLA.out` with tracing data. After that, we should process the tracing data as follows:

```
$ go tool trace /path/ToTemporary/Directory/traceCLA.out
```

The last command automatically starts a web server and opens the web interface of the trace tool on your default web browser—you can run it on your own computer to play with the web interface of the trace tool.

The `View trace` link shows information about the goroutines of your program and the operation of the garbage collector.

Have in mind that although `go tool trace` is very handy and powerful, it cannot solve every kind of performance problem. There are times where `go tool pprof` is more appropriate, especially when we want to reveal where our code spends most of its time.

As it happens with profiling, collecting tracing data for an HTTP server is a slightly different process, which is explained in the next subsection.

Tracing a web server from a client

This section shows how to trace a web server application using `net/http/httptrace`. The package allows you to trace the phases of an HTTP request from a client. The code of `traceHTTP.go` that interacts with web servers is as follows:

```
package main

import (
    "fmt"
    "net/http"
    "net/http/httptrace"
    "os"
)
```

As expected, we need to import `net/http/httptrace` before being able to enable HTTP tracing.

```
func main() {
    if len(os.Args) != 2 {
        fmt.Printf("Usage: URL\n")
        return
    }

    URL := os.Args[1]
    client := http.Client{}

    req, _ := http.NewRequest("GET", URL, nil)
```

Up to this point, we prepare the client request to the web server as usual.

```
    trace := &httptrace.ClientTrace{
        GotFirstResponseByte: func() {
            fmt.Println("First response byte!")
        },
        GotConn: func(connInfo httptrace.GotConnInfo) {
            fmt.Printf("Got Conn: %+v\n", connInfo)
        },
        DNSDone: func(dnsInfo httptrace.DNSDoneInfo) {
            fmt.Printf("DNS Info: %+v\n", dnsInfo)
        },
        ConnectStart: func(network, addr string) {
            fmt.Println("Dial start")
        },
        ConnectDone: func(network, addr string, err error) {
            fmt.Println("Dial done")
        },
        WroteHeaders: func() {
            fmt.Println("Wrote headers")
        },
    }
```

The preceding code is all about tracing HTTP requests. The `httptrace.ClientTrace` structure defines the events that interest us, which are `GotFirstResponseByte`, `GotConn`, `DNSDone`, `ConnectStart`, `ConnectDone`, and `WroteHeaders`. When such an event occurs, the relevant code is executed. You can find more information about the supported events and their purpose in the documentation of the `net/http/httptrace` package.

```
    req = req.WithContext(httptrace.WithClientTrace(req.Context(),
trace))
    fmt.Println("Requesting data from server!")
    _, err := http.DefaultTransport.RoundTrip(req)
    if err != nil {
        fmt.Println(err)
        return
    }
```

The `httptrace.WithClientTrace()` function returns a new `context` value based on the given parent context while `http.DefaultTransport.RoundTrip()` wraps the request with the `context` value in order to keep track of the request.

Have in mind that Go HTTP tracing has been designed to trace the events of a single `http.Transport.RoundTrip`.

```
    _, err = client.Do(req)
    if err != nil {
        fmt.Println(err)
        return
    }

}
```

The last part sends the client request to the server for the tracing to begin.

Running `traceHTTP.go` generates the next output:

```
$ go run traceHTTP.go https://www.golang.org/
Requesting data from server!
DNS Info: {Addrs:[{IP:2a00:1450:4001:80e::2011 Zone:}
{IP:142.250.185.81 Zone:}] Err:<nil> Coalesced:false}
```

In this first part, we see that the IP address of the server has been resolved, which means that the client is ready to begin interacting with the HTTP server.

```
Dial start
Dial done
Got Conn: {Conn:0xc000078000 Reused:false WasIdle:false IdleTime:0s}
Wrote headers
First response byte!
Got Conn: {Conn:0xc000078000 Reused:true WasIdle:false IdleTime:0s}
Wrote headers
First response byte!
DNS Info: {Addrs:[{IP:2a00:1450:4001:80e::2011 Zone:}
{IP:142.250.185.81 Zone:}] Err:<nil> Coalesced:false}
Dial start
Dial done
Got Conn: {Conn:0xc0000a1180 Reused:false WasIdle:false IdleTime:0s}
Wrote headers
First response byte!
```

The previous output helps you understand the progress of the connection in more detail and is handy when troubleshooting. Unfortunately, talking more about tracing is beyond the scope of this book. The next subsection shows how to visit all the routes of a web server to make sure that they are properly defined.

Visiting all routes of a web server

The `gorilla/mux` package offers a `Walk` function that can be used for visiting all the registered routes of a router—this can be very handy when you want to make sure that every route is registered and is working.

The code of `walkAll.go`, which contains lots of empty handler functions because its purpose is not to test handling functions but to visit them, is as follows (nothing prohibits you from using the same technique on a fully implemented web server):

```
package main

import (
    "fmt"
    "net/http"
    "strings"

    "github.com/gorilla/mux"
)
```

As we are using an external package, the running of `walkAll.go` should take place somewhere in `~/go/src`.

```
func handler(w http.ResponseWriter, r *http.Request) {
    return
}
```

This empty handler function is shared by all endpoints for reasons of simplicity.

```
func (h notAllowedHandler) ServeHTTP(rw http.ResponseWriter, r *http.
Request) {
    handler(rw, r)
}
```

The `notAllowedHandler` handler also calls the `handler()` function.

```
type notAllowedHandler struct{}

func main() {
    r := mux.NewRouter()

    r.NotFoundHandler = http.HandlerFunc(handler)
    notAllowed := notAllowedHandler{}
```

```
    r.MethodNotAllowedHandler = notAllowed

    // Register GET
    getMux := r.Methods(http.MethodGet).Subrouter()
    getMux.HandleFunc("/time", handler)
    getMux.HandleFunc("/getall", handler)
    getMux.HandleFunc("/getid", handler)
    getMux.HandleFunc("/logged", handler)
    getMux.HandleFunc("/username/{id:[0-9]+}", handler)

    // Register PUT
    // Update User
    putMux := r.Methods(http.MethodPut).Subrouter()
    putMux.HandleFunc("/update", handler)

    // Register POST
    // Add User + Login + Logout
    postMux := r.Methods(http.MethodPost).Subrouter()
    postMux.HandleFunc("/add", handler)
    postMux.HandleFunc("/login", handler)
    postMux.HandleFunc("/logout", handler)

    // Register DELETE
    // Delete User
    deleteMux := r.Methods(http.MethodDelete).Subrouter()
    deleteMux.HandleFunc("/username/{id:[0-9]+}", handler)
```

The previous part is about defining the routes and the HTTP methods that we want to support.

```
    err := r.Walk(func(route *mux.Route, router *mux.Router, ancestors
[]*mux.Route) error {
```

This is how we call the `Walk()` method.

```
        pathTemplate, err := route.GetPathTemplate()
        if err == nil {
            fmt.Println("ROUTE:", pathTemplate)
        }
        pathRegexp, err := route.GetPathRegexp()
        if err == nil {
```

```
            fmt.Println("Path regexp:", pathRegexp)
        }
        qT, err := route.GetQueriesTemplates()
        if err == nil {
            fmt.Println("Queries templates:", strings.Join(qT, ","))
        }
        qRegexps, err := route.GetQueriesRegexp()
        if err == nil {
            fmt.Println("Queries regexps:", strings.Join(qRegexps, ","))
        }
        methods, err := route.GetMethods()
        if err == nil {
            fmt.Println("Methods:", strings.Join(methods, ","))
        }
        fmt.Println()
        return nil
    })
```

For each visited route, the program collects the desired information. Feel free to remove some of the `fmt.Println()` calls if it does not help your purpose to reduce output.

```
    if err != nil {
        fmt.Println(err)
    }

    http.Handle("/", r)
}
```

So, the general idea behind `walkAll.go` is that you assign an empty handler to each route that you have in your server and then you call `mux.Walk()` for visiting all routes. Enabling Go modules and running `walkAll.go` generates the next output:

```
$ go mod init
$ go mod tidy
$ go run walkAll.go
Queries templates:
Queries regexps:
Methods: GET

ROUTE: /time
```

```
Path regexp: ^/time$
Queries templates:
Queries regexps:
Methods: GET
```

The output shows the HTTP methods that each route supports as well as the format of the path. So, the `/time` endpoint works with `GET` and its path is `/time` because the value of `Path regexp` means that `/time` is between the beginning (`^`) and the end of the path (`$`).

```
ROUTE: /getall
Path regexp: ^/getall$
Queries templates:
Queries regexps:
Methods: GET

ROUTE: /getid
Path regexp: ^/getid$
Queries templates:
Queries regexps:
Methods: GET

ROUTE: /logged
Path regexp: ^/logged$
Queries templates:
Queries regexps:
Methods: GET

ROUTE: /username/{id:[0-9]+}
Path regexp: ^/username/(?P<v0>[0-9]+)$
Queries templates:
Queries regexps:
Methods: GET
```

In the case of `/username`, the output includes the regular expressions associated with that endpoint that is used for selecting the value of the `id` variable.

```
Queries templates:
Queries regexps:
Methods: PUT

ROUTE: /update
```

```
Path regexp: ^/update$
Queries templates:
Queries regexps:
Methods: PUT

Queries templates:
Queries regexps:
Methods: POST

ROUTE: /add
Path regexp: ^/add$
Queries templates:
Queries regexps:
Methods: POST

ROUTE: /login
Path regexp: ^/login$
Queries templates:
Queries regexps:
Methods: POST

ROUTE: /logout
Path regexp: ^/logout$
Queries templates:
Queries regexps:
Methods: POST

Queries templates:
Queries regexps:
Methods: DELETE

ROUTE: /username/{id:[0-9]+}
Path regexp: ^/username/(?P<v0>[0-9]+)$
Queries templates:
Queries regexps:
Methods: DELETE
```

Although visiting the routes of a web server is a kind of testing, it is not the official Go way of testing. The main thing to look for in such output is the absence of an endpoint, the use of the wrong HTTP method, or the absence of a parameter from an endpoint.

The next section discusses the testing of Go code in more detail.

Testing Go code

The subject of this section is the testing of Go code by **writing test functions**. Software testing is a very large subject and cannot be covered in a single section of a chapter in a book. So, this section tries to present as much practical information as possible.

Go allows you to write tests for your Go code to detect bugs. However, software testing can only show **the presence** of one or more bugs, **not the absence** of bugs. This means that you can never be 100% sure that your code has no bugs!

Strictly speaking, this section is about **automated testing**, which involves writing extra code to verify whether the real code—that is, the production code—works as expected or not. Thus, the result of a test function is either `PASS` or `FAIL`. You will see how this works shortly. Although the Go approach to testing might look simple at first, especially if you compare it with the testing practices of other programming languages, it is very efficient and effective because it does not require too much of the developer's time.

You should always put the testing code in a different source file. There is no need to create a huge source file that is hard to read and maintain. Now, let us present testing by revisiting the `matchInt()` function from *Chapter 3, Composite Data Types*.

Writing tests for ./ch03/intRE.go

In this subsection, we write tests for the `matchInt()` function, which was implemented in `intRE.go` back in *Chapter 3, Composite Data Types*. First, we create a new file named `intRE_test.go`, which is going to contain all tests. Then, we rename the package from `main` to `testRE` and remove the `main()` function—this is an optional action. After that, we must decide what we are going to test and how. The main steps in testing include writing tests for expected input, unexpected input, empty input, and edge cases. All these are going to be seen in the code. Additionally, we are going to generate random integers, convert them to strings, and use them as input for `matchInt()`. Generally speaking, a good way to test functions that works with numeric values is by using random numbers, or random values in general, as input and see how your code behaves and handles these values.

The two test functions of `intRE_test.go` are the following:

```
func Test_matchInt(t *testing.T) {
    if matchInt("") {
        t.Error(`matchInt("") != true`)
    }
```

The `matchInt("")` call should return `false`, so if it returns `true`, it means that the function does not work as expected.

```
    if matchInt("00") == false {
        t.Error(`matchInt("00") != true`)
    }
```

The `matchInt("00")` call should also return `true` because `00` is a valid integer, so if it returns `false`, it means that the function does not work as expected.

```
    if matchInt("-00") == false {
        t.Error(`matchInt("-00") != true`)
    }

    if matchInt("+00") == false {
        t.Error(`matchInt("+00") != true`)
    }
}
```

This first test function uses static input to test the correctness of `matchInt()`. As discussed earlier, a testing function accepts a single `*testing.T` parameter and returns no values.

```
func Test_with_random(t *testing.T) {
    SEED := time.Now().Unix()
    rand.Seed(SEED)
    n := strconv.Itoa(random(-100000, 19999))

    if matchInt(n) == false {
        t.Error("n = ", n)
    }
}
```

The second test function uses random but valid input to test `matchInt()`. Therefore, the given input should always pass the test. Running the two test functions with `go test` creates the next output:

```
$ go test -v *.go
=== RUN   Test_matchInt
--- PASS: Test_matchInt (0.00s)
=== RUN   Test_with_random
--- PASS: Test_with_random (0.00s)
PASS
ok      command-line-arguments    0.410s
```

So, all tests passed, which means that everything is fine with `matchInt()`.

The next subsection discusses the use of the `TempDir()` method.

The TempDir function

The `TempDir()` method works with both testing and benchmarking. Its purpose is to create a temporary directory that is going to be used during testing or benchmarking. Go automatically removes that temporary directory when the test and its subtests or the benchmarks are about to finish with the help of the `CleanUp()` method—this is arranged by Go and you do not need to use and implement `CleanUp()` on your own. The exact place where the temporary directory is going to be created depends on the operating system used. On macOS, it is under `/var/folders` whereas on Linux it is under `/tmp`. We are going to illustrate `TempDir()` in the next subsection where we also talk about `Cleanup()`.

The Cleanup() function

Although we present the `Cleanup()` method in a testing scenario, `Cleanup()` works for both testing and benchmarking. Its name reveals its purpose, which is to clean up some things that we have created when testing or benchmarking a package. However, it is us who need to tell `Cleanup()` what to do—the parameter of `Cleanup()` is a function that does the cleaning up. That function is usually implemented inline as an anonymous function, but you can also create it elsewhere and call it by its name.

The `cleanup.go` file contains a dummy function named `Foo()`—as it contains no code, there is no point in presenting it. On the other hand, all important code can be found in `cleanup_test.go`:

```
func myCleanUp() func() {
	return func() {
		fmt.Println("Cleaning up!")
	}
}
```

The `myCleanUp()` function is going to be used as a parameter to `CleanUp()` and should have that specific signature. Apart from the signature, you can put any kind of code in the implementation of `myCleanUp()`.

```
func TestFoo(t *testing.T) {
	t1 := path.Join(os.TempDir(), "test01")
	t2 := path.Join(os.TempDir(), "test02")
```

These are the paths of two directories that we are going to create.

```
    err := os.Mkdir(t1, 0755)
    if err != nil {
        t.Error("os.Mkdir() failed:", err)
        return
    }
```

We create a directory with `os.Mkdir()` and we specify its path. Therefore, it is our duty to delete that directory when it is no longer needed.

```
    defer t.Cleanup(func() {
        err = os.Remove(t1)
        if err != nil {
            t.Error("os.Mkdir() failed:", err)
        }
    })
```

After `TestFoo()` finishes, `t1` is going to be deleted by the code of the anonymous function that is passed as a parameter to `t.CleanUp()`.

```
    err = os.Mkdir(t2, 0755)
    if err != nil {
        t.Error("os.Mkdir() failed:", err)
        return
    }
}
```

We create another directory with `os.Mkdir()`—however, in this case we are not deleting that directory. Therefore, after `TestFoo()` finishes, `t2` is not going to be deleted.

```
func TestBar(t *testing.T) {
    t1 := t.TempDir()
```

Because of the use of the `t.TempDir()` method, the value (directory path) of `t1` is assigned by the operating system. Additionally, that directory path is going to be automatically deleted when the test function is about to finish.

```
    fmt.Println(t1)
    t.Cleanup(myCleanUp())
}
```

Here we use `myCleanUp()` as the parameter to `Cleanup()`. This is handy when you want to perform the same cleanup multiple times. Running the tests creates the next output:

```
$ go test -v *.go
=== RUN   TestFoo
--- PASS: TestFoo (0.00s)
=== RUN   TestBar
/var/folders/sk/ltk8cnw50lzdtr2hxcj5sv2m0000gn/T/TestBar2904465158/01
```

This is the temporary directory that was created with `TempDir()` on a macOS machine.

```
Cleaning up!
--- PASS: TestBar (0.00s)
PASS
ok      command-line-arguments          0.096s
```

Checking whether the directories created by `TempDir()` are there shows that they have been successfully deleted. On the other hand, the directory stored in the `t2` variable of `TestFoo()` has not been deleted. Running the same tests again is going to fail because the `test02` file already exists and cannot be created:

```
$ go test -v *.go
=== RUN   TestFoo
    cleanup_test.go:33: os.Mkdir() failed: mkdir /var/folders/sk/ltk8cn
w50lzdtr2hxcj5sv2m0000gn/T/test02: file exists
--- FAIL: TestFoo (0.00s)
=== RUN   TestBar
/var/folders/sk/ltk8cnw50lzdtr2hxcj5sv2m0000gn/T/TestBar2113309096/01
Cleaning up!
--- PASS: TestBar (0.00s)
FAIL
FAIL    command-line-arguments          0.097s
FAIL
```

The `/var/folders/sk/ltk8cnw50lzdtr2hxcj5sv2m0000gn/T/test02: file exists` error message shows the root of the problem. The solution is to clean up your tests.

The next subsection discusses the use of the `testing/quick` package.

The testing/quick package

There are times where you need to create testing data without human intervention. The Go standard library offers the `testing/quick` package, which can be used for **black box testing** (a software testing method that checks the functionality of an application or function without any prior knowledge of its internal working) and is somewhat related to the `QuickCheck` package found in the **Haskell** programming language—both packages implement utility functions to help you with black box testing. With the help of `testing/quick`, Go generates random values of built-in types that you can use for testing, which saves you from having to generate all these values manually.

The code of `quickT.go` is the following:

```
package quickT

type Point2D struct {
	X, Y int
}

func Add(x1, x2 Point2D) Point2D {
	temp := Point2D{}
	temp.X = x1.X + x2.X
	temp.Y = x1.Y + x2.Y
	return temp
}
```

The previous code implements a single function that adds two `Point2D` variables—this is the function that we are going to test.

The code of `quickT_test.go` is as follows:

```
package quickT

import (
	"testing"
	"testing/quick"
)

var N = 1000000

func TestWithItself(t *testing.T) {
	condition := func(a, b Point2D) bool {
```

```
        return Add(a, b) == Add(b, a)
    }

    err := quick.Check(condition, &quick.Config{MaxCount: N})
    if err != nil {
        t.Errorf("Error: %v", err)
    }
}
```

The call to `quick.Check()` **automatically generates** random numbers based on the signature of its first argument, which is a function defined earlier. There is no need to create these random numbers on your own, which makes the code easy to read and write. The actual tests happen in the `condition` function.

```
func TestThree(t *testing.T) {
    condition := func(a, b, c Point2D) bool {
        return Add(Add(a, b), c) == Add(a, b)
    }
```

This implementation is **wrong on purpose**. To correct the implementation, we should replace `Add(Add(a, b), c) == Add(a, b)` with `Add(Add(a, b), c) == Add(c, Add(a, b))`. We did that to see the output that is generated when a test fails.

```
    err := quick.Check(condition, &quick.Config{MaxCount: N})
    if err != nil {
        t.Errorf("Error: %v", err)
    }
}
```

Running the created tests generates the next output:

```
$ go test -v *.go
=== RUN   TestWithItself
--- PASS: TestWithItself (0.86s)
```

As expected, the first test was successful.

```
=== RUN   TestThree
    quickT_test.go:28: Error: #1: failed on input quickT.
Point2D{X:761545203426276355, Y:-915390795717609627}, quickT.
Point2D{X:-3981936724985737618, Y:2920823510164787684}, quickT.
Point2D{X:-8870190727513030156, Y:-7578455488760414673}
--- FAIL: TestThree (0.00s)
FAIL
```

```
FAIL    command-line-arguments  1.153s
FAIL
```

However, as expected, the second test generated an error. The good thing is that the input that caused the error is presented onscreen so that you can see the input that caused your function to fail.

The next subsection tells us how to time out tests that take too long to finish.

Timing out tests

If the `go test` tool takes too long to finish or for some reason it never ends, there is the `-timeout` parameter that can help you.

To illustrate that, we are using the code from the previous subsection as well as the `-timeout` and `-count` command-line flags. While the former specifies the maximum allowed time duration for the tests, the latter specifies the number of times the tests are going to be executed.

Running `go test -v *.go -timeout 1s` tells `go test` that all tests should take at most one second to finish—on my machine, the tests did take less than a second to finish. However, running the following generates a different output:

```
$ go test -v *.go -timeout 1s -count 2
=== RUN   TestWithItself
--- PASS: TestWithItself (0.87s)
=== RUN   TestThree
    quickT_test.go:28: Error: #1: failed on input quickT.
Point2D{X:-312047170140227400, Y:-5441930920566042029}, quickT.
Point2D{X:7855449254220087092, Y:7437813460700902767}, quickT.
Point2D{X:4838605758154930957, Y:-7621852714243790655}
--- FAIL: TestThree (0.00s)
=== RUN   TestWithItself
panic: test timed out after 1s
```

The output is longer than the presented one—the rest of the output has to do with goroutines being terminated before they have finished. The key thing here is that the `go test` command timed out the process due to the use of `-timeout 1s`.

Testing code coverage

In this section, we are going to learn how to find information about the code coverage of our programs to discover blocks of code or single code statements that are not being executed by testing functions.

Among other things, seeing the code coverage of programs can reveal issues and bugs in the code, so do not underestimate its usefulness. However, the code coverage test complements unit testing without replacing it. The only thing to remember is that you should make sure that the testing functions do try to cover all cases and therefore try to run all available code. If the testing functions do not try to cover all cases, then the issue might be with them, not the code that is being tested.

The code of `coverage.go`, which has some intentional issues in order to show how unreachable code is identified, is as follows:

```
package coverage

import "fmt"

func f1() {
    if true {
        fmt.Println("Hello!")
    } else {
        fmt.Println("Hi!")
    }
}
```

The issue with this function is that the first branch of `if` is always true and therefore the `else` branch is not going to get executed.

```
func f2(n int) int {
    if n >= 0 {
        return 0
    } else if n == 1 {
        return 1
    } else {
        return f2(n-1) + f2(n-2)
    }
}
```

There exist two issues with `f2()`. The first one is that it does not work well with negative integers and the second one is that all positive integers are handled by the first `if` branch. Code coverage can only help you with the second issue. The code of `coverage_test.go` is the following—these are regular test functions that try to run all available code:

```
package coverage

import "testing"
```

```
func Test_f1(t *testing.T) {
    f1()
}
```

This test function naively tests the operation of `f1()`.

```
func Test_f2(t *testing.T) {
    _ = f2(123)
}
```

The second test function checks the operation of `f2()` by running `f2(123)`.

First, we should run `go test` as follows—the code coverage task is done by the `-cover` flag:

```
$ go test -cover *.go
ok      command-line-arguments    0.420s    coverage: 50.0% of statements
```

The previous output shows that we have `50%` code coverage, which is not a good thing! However, we are not done yet as we can generate a test coverage report. The next command generates the code coverage report:

```
$ go test -coverprofile=coverage.out *.go
```

The contents of `coverage.out` are as follows—yours might vary a little depending on your username and the folder used:

```
$ cat coverage.out
mode: set
/Users/mtsouk/Desktop/coverage.go:5.11,6.10 1 1
/Users/mtsouk/Desktop/coverage.go:6.10,8.3 1 1
/Users/mtsouk/Desktop/coverage.go:8.8,10.3 1 0
/Users/mtsouk/Desktop/coverage.go:13.20,14.12 1 1
/Users/mtsouk/Desktop/coverage.go:14.12,16.3 1 1
/Users/mtsouk/Desktop/coverage.go:16.8,16.19 1 0
/Users/mtsouk/Desktop/coverage.go:16.19,18.3 1 0
/Users/mtsouk/Desktop/coverage.go:18.8,20.3 1 0
```

The format and the fields in each line of the coverage file are `name.go:line.column,line.column numberOfStatements count`. The **last field** is a flag that tells you whether the statements specified by `line.column,line.column` are covered or not. So, when you see `0` in the last field, it means that the code is not covered.

Last, the HTML output can be seen in your favorite web browser by running `go tool cover -html=coverage.out`. If you used a different filename than `coverage.out`, modify the command accordingly. The next figure shows the generated output—if you are reading the printed version of the book, you might not be able to see the colors. Red lines denote code that is not being executed whereas green lines show code that was executed by the tests.

Figure 11.2: Code coverage report

Some of the code is marked as `not tracked` (gray in color) because this is code that cannot be processed by the code coverage tool. The generated output clearly shows the code issues with both `f1()` and `f2()`. You just have to correct them now!

The next section discusses unreachable code and how to discover it.

Finding unreachable Go code

Sometimes, a wrongly implemented `if` or a misplaced `return` statement can create blocks of code that are unreachable, that is, blocks of code that are not going to be executed at all. As this is a **logical kind of error**, which means that it is not going to get caught by the compiler, we need to find a way of discovering it.

Fortunately, the `go vet` tool, which examines Go source code and reports suspicious constructs, can help with that—the use of `go vet` is illustrated with the help of the `cannotReach.go` source code file, which contains the next two functions:

```
func S2() {
    return
    fmt.Println("Hello!")
}
```

There is a logical error here because `S2()` returns before printing the desired message.

```
func S1() {
    fmt.Println("In S1()")
    return

    fmt.Println("Leaving S1()")
}
```

Similarly, `S1()` returns without giving the `fmt.Println("Leaving S1()")` statement a chance to be executed.

Running `go vet` on `cannotReach.go` creates the next output:

```
$ go vet cannotReach.go
# command-line-arguments
./cannotReach.go:9:2: unreachable code
./cannotReach.go:16:2: unreachable code
```

The first message points to the `fmt.Println()` statement of `S2()` and the second one to the second `fmt.Println()` statement of `S1()`. In this case, `go vet` did a great job. However, `go vet` is not particularly sophisticated and cannot catch every possible type of logical error. If you need a more advanced tool, have a look at `staticcheck` (`https://staticcheck.io/`), which can also be integrated with Microsoft Visual Studio Code (`https://code.visualstudio.com/`)—the next figure shows how Visual Studio Code signifies unreachable code with the help of `staticcheck`.

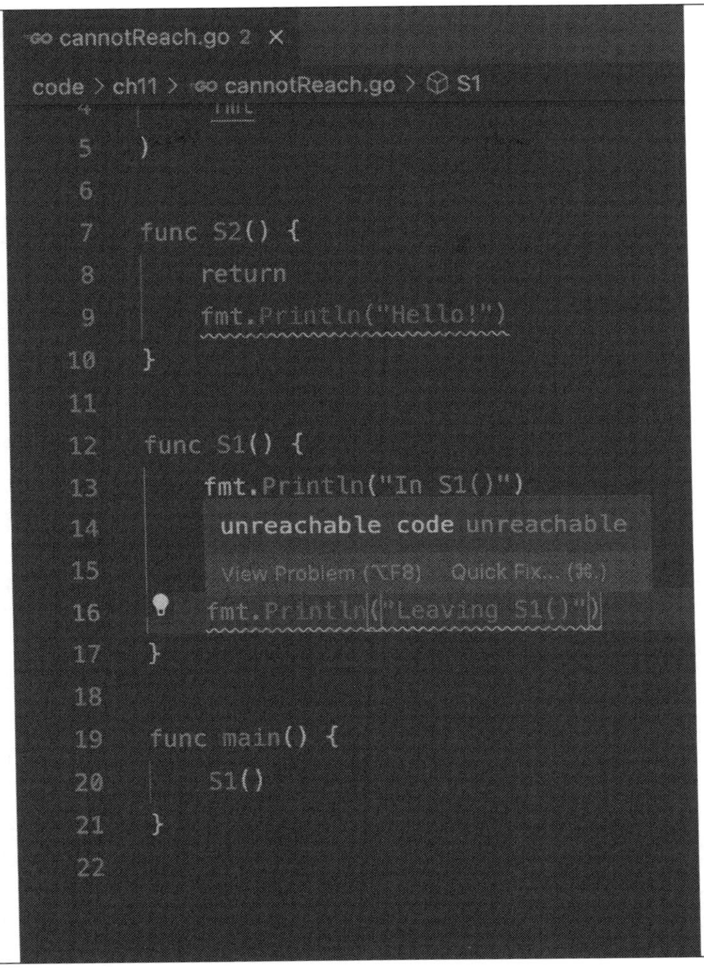

Figure 11.3: Viewing unreachable code in Visual Studio Code

As a rule of thumb, it does not hurt to include `go vet` in your workflow. You can find more information about the capabilities of `go vet` by running `go doc cmd/vet`.

The next section illustrates how to test an HTTP server with a database backend.

Testing an HTTP server with a database backend

An HTTP server is a different kind of animal because it should already run for tests to get executed. Thankfully, the `net/http/httptest` package can help—you do not need to run the HTTP server on your own as the `net/http/httptest` package does the work for you, but you need to have the database server up and running. We are going to test the REST API server we have developed in *Chapter 10, Working with REST APIs*—we are going to copy the `server_test.go` file with the test code in the `https://github.com/mactsouk/rest-api` GitHub repository of the server.

> To create `server_test.go`, we do not have to change the implementation of the REST API server.

The code of `server_test.go`, which holds the test functions for the HTTP service, is the following:

```
package main

import (
	"bytes"
	"net/http"
	"net/http/httptest"
	"strconv"
	"strings"
	"testing"
	"time"

	"github.com/gorilla/mux"
)
```

The only reason for including `github.com/gorilla/mux` is the use of `mux.SetURLVars()` later on.

```
func TestTimeHandler(t *testing.T) {
	req, err := http.NewRequest("GET", "/time", nil)
	if err != nil {
		t.Fatal(err)
	}
```

```
    rr := httptest.NewRecorder()
    handler := http.HandlerFunc(TimeHandler)
    handler.ServeHTTP(rr, req)

    status := rr.Code
    if status != http.StatusOK {
        t.Errorf("handler returned wrong status code: got %v want %v",
            status, http.StatusOK)
    }
}
```

The `http.NewRequest()` function is used for defining the HTTP request method, the endpoint, and for sending data to the endpoint when needed. The `http.HandlerFunc(TimeHandler)` call defines the handler function that is being tested.

```
func TestMethodNotAllowed(t *testing.T) {
    req, err := http.NewRequest("DELETE", "/time", nil)
    if err != nil {
        t.Fatal(err)
    }

    rr := httptest.NewRecorder()
    handler := http.HandlerFunc(MethodNotAllowedHandler)
```

We are testing `MethodNotAllowedHandler` in this test function.

```
    handler.ServeHTTP(rr, req)

    status := rr.Code
    if status != http.StatusNotFound {
        t.Errorf("handler returned wrong status code: got %v want %v",
            status, http.StatusOK)
    }
}
```

We know that this interaction is going to fail as we are testing `MethodNotAllowedHandler`. Therefore, we expect to get an `http.StatusNotFound` response code back—if we get a different code, the test function is going to fail.

```
func TestLogin(t *testing.T) {
    UserPass := []byte(`{"Username": "admin", "Password": "admin"}`)
```

Here we store the desired fields of a `User` structure in a `byte` slice. For the tests to work, the `admin` user should have `admin` as the password because this is what is used in the code—modify `server_test.go` in order to have the correct password for the `admin` user, or any other user with admin privileges, of your installation.

```
    req, err := http.NewRequest("POST", "/login", bytes.
NewBuffer(UserPass))
    if err != nil {
        t.Fatal(err)
    }
    req.Header.Set("Content-Type", "application/json")
```

The previous lines of code construct the desired request.

```
    rr := httptest.NewRecorder()
    handler := http.HandlerFunc(LoginHandler)
    handler.ServeHTTP(rr, req)
```

`NewRecorder()` returns an initialized `ResponseRecorder` that is used in `ServeHTTP()`—`ServeHTTP()` is the method that performs the request. The response is saved in the `rr` variable.

There is also a test function for the `/logout` endpoint, which is not presented here as it is almost identical to `TestLogin()`. However, running the tests in random order might create issues with testing because `TestLogin()` should always get executed before `TestLogout()`.

```
    status := rr.Code
    if status != http.StatusOK {
        t.Errorf("handler returned wrong status code: got %v want %v",
            status, http.StatusOK)
        return
    }
}
```

If the status code is `http.StatusOK`, it means that the interaction worked as expected.

```
func TestAdd(t *testing.T) {
    now := int(time.Now().Unix())
    username := "test_" + strconv.Itoa(now)
    users := `[{"Username": "admin", "Password": "admin"},
{"Username":"` + username + `", "Password": "myPass"}]`
```

For the `Add()` handler, we need to pass an array of JSON records, which is constructed here. As we do not want to create the same username every time, we append the current timestamp to the `_test` string.

```
    UserPass := []byte(users)
    req, err := http.NewRequest("POST", "/add", bytes.
NewBuffer(UserPass))
    if err != nil {
        t.Fatal(err)
    }
    req.Header.Set("Content-Type", "application/json")
```

This is where we construct the slice of JSON records (`UserPass`) and create the request.

```
    rr := httptest.NewRecorder()
    handler := http.HandlerFunc(AddHandler)
    handler.ServeHTTP(rr, req)

    // Check the HTTP status code is what we expect.
    if status := rr.Code; status != http.StatusOK {
        t.Errorf("handler returned wrong status code: got %v want %v",
            status, http.StatusOK)
        return
    }
}
```

If the server response is `http.StatusOK`, then the request is successful and the test passes.

```
func TestGetUserDataHandler(t *testing.T) {

    UserPass := []byte(`{"Username": "admin", "Password": "admin"}`)
    req, err := http.NewRequest("GET", "/username/1", bytes.
NewBuffer(UserPass))
```

Although we use `/username/1` in the request, this does not add any value in the `Vars` map. Therefore, we need to use the `SetURLVars()` function for changing the values in the `Vars` map—this is illustrated next.

```
    if err != nil {
        t.Fatal(err)
```

```
    }
    req.Header.Set("Content-Type", "application/json")

    vars := map[string]string{
        "id": "1",
    }
    req = mux.SetURLVars(req, vars)
```

The `gorilla/mux` package provides the `SetURLVars()` function for testing purposes—this function allows you to add elements to the `Vars` map. In this case, we need to set the value of the `id` key to `1`. You can add as many key/value pairs as you want.

```
    rr := httptest.NewRecorder()
    handler := http.HandlerFunc(GetUserDataHandler)
    handler.ServeHTTP(rr, req)

    if status := rr.Code; status != http.StatusOK {
        t.Errorf("handler returned wrong status code: got %v want %v",
            status, http.StatusOK)
        return
    }

expected := `{"ID":1,"Username":"admin","Password":"admin",
"LastLogin":0,"Admin":1,"Active":0}`
```

This is the record we expect to get back from our request. As we cannot guess the value of `LastLogin` in the server response, we replace it with `0`, hence the use of `0` here.

```
    serverResponse := rr.Body.String()

    result := strings.Split(serverResponse, "LastLogin")
    serverResponse = result[0] + `LastLogin":0,"Admin":1,"Active":0}`
```

As we do not want to use the value of `LastLogin` from the server response, we are changing it to `0`.

```
    if serverResponse != expected {
        t.Errorf("handler returned unexpected body: got %v but wanted
%v",
            rr.Body.String(), expected)
    }
}
```

The last part of the code contains the standard Go way of checking whether we have received the expected answer or not.

Creating tests for HTTP services is easy once you understand the presented examples. This mainly happens because most of the code is repeated among test functions.

Running the tests generates the next output:

```
$ go test -v server_test.go main.go handlers.go
=== RUN   TestTimeHandler
2021/06/17 08:59:15 TimeHandler Serving: /time from
--- PASS: TestTimeHandler (0.00s)
```

This is the output from visiting the `/time` endpoint. Its result is `PASS`.

```
=== RUN   TestMethodNotAllowed
2021/06/17 08:59:15 Serving: /time from  with method DELETE
--- PASS: TestMethodNotAllowed (0.00s)
=== RUN   TestLogin
```

This is the output from visiting the `/time` endpoint with the `DELETE` HTTP method. Its result is `PASS` because we were expecting this request to fail as it uses the wrong HTTP method.

```
2021/06/17 08:59:15 LoginHandler Serving: /login from
2021/06/17 08:59:15 Input user: {0 admin admin 0 0 0}
2021/06/17 08:59:15 Found user: {1 admin admin 1620922454 1 0}
2021/06/17 08:59:15 Logging in: {1 admin admin 1620922454 1 0}
2021/06/17 08:59:15 Updating user: {1 admin admin 1623909555 1 1}
2021/06/17 08:59:15 Affected: 1
2021/06/17 08:59:15 User updated: {1 admin admin 1623909555 1 1}
--- PASS: TestLogin (0.01s)
```

This is the output from `TestLogin()` that tests the `/login` endpoint. All lines beginning with the date and time are generated by the REST API server and show the progress of the request.

```
=== RUN   TestLogout
2021/06/17 08:59:15 LogoutHandler Serving: /logout from
2021/06/17 08:59:15 Found user: {1 admin admin 1620922454 1 1}
2021/06/17 08:59:15 Logging out: admin
2021/06/17 08:59:15 Updating user: {1 admin admin 1620922454 1 0}
2021/06/17 08:59:15 Affected: 1
```

```
2021/06/17 08:59:15 User updated: {1 admin admin 1620922454 1 0}
--- PASS: TestLogout (0.01s)
```

This is the output from `TestLogout()` that tests the `/logout` endpoint, which also has the `PASS` result.

```
=== RUN   TestAdd
2021/06/17 08:59:15 AddHandler Serving: /add from
2021/06/17 08:59:15 [{0 admin admin 0 0 0} {0 test_1623909555 myPass 0
0 0}]
--- PASS: TestAdd (0.01s)
```

This is the output from the `TestAdd()` test function. The name of the new user that is created is `test_1623909555` and it should be different each time the test is executed.

```
=== RUN   TestGetUserDataHandler
2021/06/17 08:59:15 GetUserDataHandler Serving: /username/1 from
2021/06/17 08:59:15 Found user: {1 admin admin 1620922454 1 0}
--- PASS: TestGetUserDataHandler (0.00s)
PASS
ok    command-line-arguments        (cached)
```

Last, this is the output from the `TestGetUserDataHandler()` test function that was also executed without any issues.

The next subsection discusses fuzzing, which offers a different way of testing.

Fuzzing

As software engineers, we do not worry when things go as expected but when unexpected things happen. One way to deal with the unexpected is fuzzing. *Fuzzing* (or *fuzz testing*) is a testing technique that provides invalid, unexpected, or random data on programs that require input.

The advantages of fuzzing include the following:

- Making sure that the code can handle invalid or random input
- Bugs that are discovered with fuzzing are usually severe and might indicate security risks
- Attackers often use fuzzing for locating vulnerabilities, so it is good to be prepared

Fuzzing is going to be officially included in the Go language in a future Go release, but do not expect it in 2021. It is most likely going to be officially released with Go version 1.18 or Go version 1.19. The `dev.fuzz` branch at GitHub (`https://github.com/golang/go/tree/dev.fuzz`) contains the latest implementation of fuzzing. This branch is going to exist until the relevant code is merged to the master branch. With fuzzing comes the `testing.F` data type, in the same way that we use `testing.T` for testing and `testing.B` for benchmarking. If you want to try fuzzing in Go, begin by visiting `https://blog.golang.org/fuzz-beta`.

The next section discusses a handy Go feature, which is cross-compilation.

Cross-compilation

Cross-compilation is the process of generating a binary executable file for a different architecture than the one on which we are working without having access to other machines. The main benefit that we receive from cross-compilation is that we do not need a second or third machine to create and distribute executable files for different architectures. This means that we basically need just a single machine for our development. Fortunately, Go has built-in support for cross-compilation.

To cross-compile a Go source file, we need to set the `GOOS` and `GOARCH` environment variables to the target operating system and architecture, respectively, which is not as difficult as it sounds.

> You can find a list of available values for the `GOOS` and `GOARCH` environment variables at `https://golang.org/doc/install/source`. Keep in mind, however, that not all `GOOS` and `GOARCH` combinations are valid.

The code of `crossCompile.go` is the following:

```
package main

import (
    "fmt"
    "runtime"
)

func main() {
    fmt.Print("You are using ", runtime.GOOS, " ")
    fmt.Println("on a(n)", runtime.GOARCH, "machine")
    fmt.Println("with Go version", runtime.Version())
}
```

Running it on a macOS machine with Go version 1.16.5 generates the next output:

```
$ go run crossCompile.go
You are using darwin on a(n) amd64 machine
with Go version go1.16.5
```

Compiling `crossCompile.go` **for the Linux OS** that runs on a machine with an `amd64` processor is as simple as running the next command on a macOS machine:

```
$ env GOOS=linux GOARCH=amd64 go build crossCompile.go
$ file crossCompile
crossCompile: ELF 64-bit LSB executable, x86-64, version 1
(SYSV), statically linked, Go BuildID=GHF99KZkGUrFADRlsS7l/ty-
Ka44KVhMItrIvMZ6l/rdRP5mt_yw2AEox_8uET/HqP0KyUBaOB87LY7gvVu, not
stripped
```

Transferring that file to an Arch Linux machine and running it generates the next output:

```
$ ./crossCompile
You are using linux on a(n) amd64 machine
with Go version go1.16.5
```

One thing to notice here is that the cross-compiled binary file of `crossCompile.go` prints the Go version of the machine used for compiling it—this makes perfect sense as the target machine might not even have Go installed on it.

Cross-compilation is a great Go feature that can come in handy when you want to generate multiple versions of your executables through a CI/CD system and distribute them.

The next section discusses `go:generate`.

Using go:generate

Although `go:generate` is not directly connected to testing or profiling, it is a handy and advanced Go feature and I believe that this chapter is the perfect place for discussing it as it can also help you with testing. The `go:generate` directive is associated with the `go generate` command, was added in Go 1.4 in order to help with automation, and allows you to run commands described by directives within existing files.

The `go generate` command supports the `-v`, `-n`, and `-x` flags. The `-v` flag prints the names of packages and files as they are processed whereas the `-n` flag prints the commands that would be executed. Last, the `-x` flag prints commands as they are executed—this is great for debugging `go:generate` commands.

The main reasons that you might need to use `go:generate` are the following:

- You want to download dynamic data from the Internet or some other source prior to the execution of the Go code.
- You want to execute some code prior to running the Go code.
- You want to generate a version number or other unique data before code execution.
- You want to make sure that you have sample data to work with. For example, you can put data into a database using `go:generate`.

> As using `go:generate` is not considered a good practice because it hides things from the developer and creates additional dependencies, I try to avoid it when I can, and I usually can. On the other hand, if you really need it, you are going to know it!

The use of `go:generate` is illustrated in `goGenerate.go`, which has the following content:

```
package main

import "fmt"

//go:generate ./echo.sh
```

This executes the `echo.sh` script, which should be available in the current directory.

```
//go:generate echo GOFILE: $GOFILE
//go:generate echo GOARCH: $GOARCH
//go:generate echo GOOS: $GOOS
//go:generate echo GOLINE: $GOLINE
//go:generate echo GOPACKAGE: $GOPACKAGE
```

`$GOFILE`, `$GOARCH`, `$GOOS`, `$GOLINE`, and `$GOPACKAGE` are special variables and are translated at the time of execution.

```
//go:generate echo DOLLAR: $DOLLAR
//go:generate echo Hello!
//go:generate ls -l
//go:generate ./hello.py
```

This executes the `hello.py` Python script, which should be available in the current directory.

```
func main() {
    fmt.Println("Hello there!")
}
```

The `go generate` command is not going to run the `fmt.Println()` statement or any other statements found in a Go source file. Last, have in mind that `go generate` is not executed automatically and must be run explicitly.

Working with `goGenerate.go` from within `~/go/src/` generates the next output:

```
$ go mod init
$ go mod tidy
$ go generate
Hello world!
GOFILE: goGenerate.go
GOARCH: amd64
GOOS: darwin
GOLINE: 9
GOPACKAGE: main
```

This is the output of the `$GOFILE`, `$GOARCH`, `$GOOS`, `$GOLINE`, and `$GOPACKAGE` variables, which shows the values of these variables defined at runtime.

```
DOLLAR: $
```

There is also a special variable named `$DOLLAR` for printing a dollar character in the output because `$` has a special meaning in the OS environment.

```
Hello!
total 32
-rwxr-xr-x  1 mtsouk  staff   32 Jun  2 18:18 echo.sh
-rw-r--r--  1 mtsouk  staff   45 Jun  2 16:15 go.mod
-rw-r--r--  1 mtsouk  staff  381 Jun  2 18:18 goGenerate.go
```

```
-rwxr-xr-x  1 mtsouk  staff   52 Jun  2 18:18 hello.py
drwxr-xr-x  5 mtsouk  staff  160 Jun  2 17:07 walk
```

This is the output of the `ls -l` command that shows the files found in the current directory at the time of the code execution. This can be used for testing whether some necessary files are present at the time of execution or not.

```
Hello from Python!
```

Last is the output of a naïve Python script.

Running `go generate` with `-n` shows the commands that are going to be executed:

```
$ go generate -n
./echo.sh
echo GOFILE: goGenerate.go
echo GOARCH: amd64
echo GOOS: darwin
echo GOLINE: 9
echo GOPACKAGE: main
echo DOLLAR: $
echo Hello!
ls -l
./hello.py
```

So, `go:generate` can help you work with the OS before program execution. However, as it hides things from the developer, its usage should be limited.

The last section of this chapter talks about example functions.

Creating example functions

Part of the documentation process is generating example code that showcases the use of some or all the functions and data types of a package. *Example functions* have many benefits, including the fact that they are executable tests that are executed by `go test`. Therefore, if an example function contains an `// Output:` line, the `go test` tool checks whether the calculated output matches the values found after the `// Output:` line. Although we should include example functions in Go files that end with `_test.go`, we do not need to import the `testing` Go package for example functions. Moreover, the name of each example function must begin with `Example`. Lastly, **example functions take no input parameters and return no results**.

We are going to illustrate example functions using the code of `exampleFunctions.go` and `exampleFunctions_test.go`. The content of `exampleFunctions.go` is as follows:

```
package exampleFunctions

func LengthRange(s string) int {
    i := 0
    for _, _ = range s {
        i = i + 1
    }
    return i
}
```

The previous code presents a regular package that contains a single function named `LengthRange()`. The contents of `exampleFunctions_test.go`, which includes the example functions, are the following:

```
package exampleFunctions

import "fmt"

func ExampleLengthRange() {
    fmt.Println(LengthRange("Mihalis"))
    fmt.Println(LengthRange("Mastering Go, 3rd edition!"))
    // Output:
    // 7
    // 7
}
```

What the comment lines say is that the expected output is `7` and `7`, which is obviously wrong. This is going to be seen after we run `go test`:

```
$ go test -v exampleFunctions*
=== RUN   ExampleLengthRange
--- FAIL: ExampleLengthRange (0.00s)
got:
7
26
want:
7
7
FAIL
```

```
FAIL    command-line-arguments  0.410s
FAIL
```

As expected, there is an error in the generated output—the second generated value is 26 instead of the expected 7. If we make the necessary corrections, the output is going to look as follows:

```
$ go test -v exampleFunctions*
=== RUN   ExampleLengthRange
--- PASS: ExampleLengthRange (0.00s)
PASS
ok      command-line-arguments  1.157s
```

Example functions can be a great tool both for learning the capabilities of a package and for testing the correctness of functions, so I suggest that you include both test code and example functions in your Go packages. As a bonus, your test functions **appear in the documentation of the package**, if you decide to generate package documentation.

Exercises

- Implement a simple version of `ab(1)` (`https://httpd.apache.org/docs/2.4/programs/ab.html`) on your own using goroutines and channels for testing the performance of web services.
- Write test functions for the `phoneBook.go` application from *Chapter 3, Composite Data Types*.
- Create test functions for a package that calculates numbers in the Fibonacci sequence. Do not forget to implement that package.
- Try to find the value of `os.TempDir()` in various operating systems.
- Create three different implementations of a function that copies binary files and benchmark them to find the faster one. Can you explain why this function is faster?

Summary

This chapter discussed `go:generate`, code profiling and tracing, benchmarking, and testing Go code. You might find the Go way of testing and benchmarking boring, but this happens because **Go is boring and predictable** in general and that is a good thing! Remember that writing bug-free code is important whereas writing the fastest code possible is not always that important.

Most of the time, you need to be able to write **fast enough** code. So, **spend more time writing tests than benchmarks** unless your code runs really slowly. We have also learned how to find unreachable code and how to cross-compile Go code.

Although the discussions of the Go profiler and `go tool trace` are far from complete, you should understand that with topics such as profiling and code tracing, nothing can replace experimenting and trying new techniques on your own!

The next chapter is about creating gRPC services in Go.

Additional resources

- The `generate` package: `https://golang.org/pkg/cmd/go/internal/generate/`
- Generating code: `https://blog.golang.org/generate`
- Look at the code of `testing` at `https://golang.org/src/testing/testing.go`
- About `net/http/httptrace`: `https://golang.org/pkg/net/http/httptrace/`
- Introducing HTTP Tracing by Jaana Dogan: `https://blog.golang.org/http-tracing`
- GopherCon 2019: Dave Cheney - Two Go Programs, Three Different Profiling Techniques: `https://youtu.be/nok0aYiGiYA`

12

Working with gRPC

This chapter is about working with gRPC in Go. **gRPC**, which stands for **gRPC Remote Procedure Calls**, is an alternative to RESTful services that was developed by Google. The main advantage of gRPC is that it is faster than working with REST and JSON messages. Additionally, creating clients for gRPC services is also faster due to the available tooling. Last, as gRPC uses the binary data format, it is lighter than RESTful services that work with the JSON format.

The process for creating a gRPC server and client has three main steps. The first step is creating the **interface definition language** (**IDL**) file, the second step is the development of the gRPC server, and the third step is the development of the gRPC client that can interact with the gRPC server.

This chapter covers the following topics:

- Introduction to gRPC
- Defining an interface definition language file
- Developing a gRPC server
- Developing a gRPC client

Introduction to gRPC

gRPC is an open source **remote procedure call** (**RPC**) system that was developed at Google back in 2015, is built on top of HTTP/2, allows you to create services easily, and uses *protocol buffers* as the IDL which specifies the format of the interchanged messages and the service interface.

gRPC clients and servers can be written in any programming language without the need to have clients written in the same programming language as their servers. This means that you can develop a client in Python, even if the gRPC server is implemented in Go. The list of supported programming languages includes, but is not limited to, Python, Java, C++, C#, PHP, Ruby, and Kotlin.

The advantages of gRPC include the following:

- The use of binary format for data exchange makes gRPC faster than services that work with data in plain text format
- The command-line tools provided make your work simpler and faster
- Once you have defined the functions and the messages of a gRPC service, creating servers and clients for it is simpler than RESTful services
- gRPC can be used for streaming services
- You do not have to deal with the details of data exchange because gRPC takes care of the details

> The list of advantages should not make you think that gRPC is a panacea that does not have any flaws—always use the best tool or technology for the job.

The next section discusses protocol buffers, which are the foundation of gRPC services.

Protocol buffers

A **protocol buffer** (**protobuf**) is basically a **method for serializing structured data**. A part of protobuf is the IDL. As protobuf uses binary format for data exchange, it takes up less space than plain text serialization formats. However, data needs to be encoded and decoded to be machine-usable and human-readable, respectively. Protobuf has its own data types that are translated to natively supported data types of the programming language used.

Generally speaking, the IDL file is the center of each gRPC service because it defines the format of the data that is exchanged as well as the service interface. You cannot have a gRPC service without having a protobuf file at hand. Strictly speaking, a protobuf file includes the definition of services, methods of services, and the format of the messages that are going to be exchanged—it is not an exaggeration to say that if you want to understand a gRPC service, you should start by looking at its definition file. The next section shows the protobuf file that is going to be used in our gRPC service.

Defining an interface definition language file

The gRPC service that we are developing is going to support the following functionality:

- The server should return its date and time to the client
- The server should return a randomly generated password of a given length to the client
- The server should return random integers to the client

Before we begin developing the gRPC client and server for our service, we need to define the IDL file. We need a separate GitHub repository to host the files related to the IDL file, which is going to be `https://github.com/mactsouk/protoapi`.

Next, we are going to present the IDL file, which is called `protoapi.proto`:

```
syntax = "proto3";
```

The presented file uses the `proto3` version of the protocol buffers language—there is also an older version of the language named `proto2`, which has some minor syntax differences. If you do not specify that you want to use `proto3`, then the protocol buffer compiler assumes you want to use `proto2`. The definition of the version must be in the first non-empty, non-comment line in the `.proto` file.

```
option go_package = "./;protoapi";
```

The gRPC tools are going to generate Go code from that `.proto` file. The previous line specifies that the name of the Go package that is going to be created is `protoapi`. The output is going to be written in the current directory as `protoapi.proto` due to the use of `./`.

```
service Random {
    rpc GetDate (RequestDateTime) returns (DateTime);
    rpc GetRandom (RandomParams) returns (RandomInt);
    rpc GetRandomPass (RequestPass) returns (RandomPass);
}
```

This block specifies the name of the gRPC service (`Random`) as well as the supported methods. Additionally, it specifies the messages that need to be exchanged for an interaction. So, for `GetDate`, the client needs to send a `RequestDateTime` message and expects to get a `DateTime` message back.

These messages are defined in the same `.proto` file.

```
// For random number
```

All `.proto` files support C- and C++-type comments. This means that you can use `// text` and `/* text */` comments in your `.proto` files.

```
message RandomParams {
    int64 Seed = 1;
    int64 Place = 2;
}
```

A random number generator starts with a seed value, which in our case is specified by the client and sent to the server with a `RandomParams` message. The `Place` field specifies the place of the random number that is going to be returned in the sequence of randomly generated integers.

```
message RandomInt {
    int64 Value = 1;
}
```

The previous two messages are related to the `GetRandom` method. `RandomParams` is for setting the parameters of the request, whereas `RandomInt` is for storing a random number that is generated by the server. All message fields are of the `int64` data type.

```
// For date time
message DateTime {
    string Value = 1;
}

message RequestDateTime {
    string Value = 2;
}
```

The previous two messages are for supporting the operation of the `GetDate` method. The `RequestDateTime` message is a dummy one in the sense that it does not hold any useful data—we just need to have a message that the client sends to the server—you can store any kind of information in the `Value` field of `RequestDateTime`. The information returned by the server is stored as a `string` value in a `DateTime` message.

```
// For random password
message RequestPass {
    int64 Seed = 1;
    int64 Length = 8;
```

```
}

message RandomPass {
    string Password = 1;
}
```

Lastly, the previous two messages are for the operation of `GetRandomPass`.

So, the IDL file:

- specifies that we are using `proto3`.
- defines the name of the service, which is `Random`.
- specifies that the name of the generated Go package is going to be `protoapi`.
- defines that the gRPC service is going to support three methods: `GetDate`, `GetRandom`, and `GetRandomPass`. It also defines the names of the messages that are going to be exchanged in these three method calls.
- defines the format of six messages that are used for data exchange.

The next important step is converting that file into a format that can be used by Go. You might need to download some extra tools in order to process `protoapi.proto`, or any other `.proto` file, and generate the relevant Go `.pb.go` files. The name of the protocol buffer compiler binary is `protoc`—on my macOS machine, I had to install `protoc` using the `brew install protobuf` command. Similarly, I also had to install `protoc-gen-go-grpc` and `protoc-gen-go` packages using Homebrew—the last two packages are Go-related.

On a Linux machine, you need to install `protobuf` using your favorite package manager and `protoc-gen-go` using the `go install github.com/golang/protobuf/protoc-gen-go@latest` command. Similarly, you should install the `protoc-gen-go-grpc` executable by running `go install google.golang.org/grpc/cmd/protoc-gen-go-grpc@latest`.

> Starting with Go 1.16, `go install` is the recommended way of building and installing packages in module mode. The use of `go get` is deprecated. However, when using `go install`, do not forget to add `@latest` after the package name to install the latest version.

So, the conversion process requires the next step:

```
$ protoc --go_out=. --go_opt=paths=source_relative --go-grpc_out=.
--go-grpc_opt=paths=source_relative protoapi.proto
```

After that, we have a file named protoapi_grpc.pb.go and a file named protoapi.pb.go—both located in the root directory of the GitHub repository. The protoapi.pb.go source code file contains the messages, whereas protoapi_grpc.pb.go contains the services.

The first ten lines of protoapi_grpc.pb.go are as follows:

```
// Code generated by protoc-gen-go-grpc. DO NOT EDIT.

package protoapi
```

As discussed earlier, the name of the package is protoapi.

```
import (
        context "context"
        grpc "google.golang.org/grpc"
        codes "google.golang.org/grpc/codes"
        status "google.golang.org/grpc/status"
)
```

This is the import block—the reason for having context "context" is that context used to be an external Go package that was not a part of the standard Go library.

The first lines of protoapi.pb.go are the following:

```
// Code generated by protoc-gen-go. DO NOT EDIT.
// versions:
//      protoc-gen-go v1.27.1
//      protoc        v3.17.3
// source: protoapi.proto

package protoapi
```

Both protoapi_grpc.pb.go, and protoapi.pb.go are part of the protoapi Go package, which means that we only need to include them once in our code.

The next section is about the development of the gRPC server.

Developing a gRPC server

In this section, we are going to create a gRPC server based on the api.proto file presented in the previous section. As gRPC needs external packages, we are going to need a GitHub repository to host the files, which is going to be https://github.com/mactsouk/grpc.

The code of `gServer.go` (located in the `server` directory) that is related to gRPC (some functions were omitted for brevity) is the following:

```
package main

import (
    "context"
    "fmt"
    "math/rand"
    "net"
    "os"
    "time"
```

This program uses `math/rand` instead of the more secure `crypto/rand` for generating random numbers because we need a seed value to be able to reproduce random number sequences.

```
    "github.com/mactsouk/protoapi"
    "google.golang.org/grpc"
    "google.golang.org/grpc/reflection"
)
```

The `import` block includes external Google packages as well as `github.com/mactsouk/protoapi`, which is the one that we created earlier. The `protoapi` package contains structures, interfaces, and functions that are specific to the gRPC service that is being developed, whereas the external Google packages contain generic code related to gRPC.

```
type RandomServer struct {
    protoapi.UnimplementedRandomServer
}
```

This structure is named after the name of the gRPC service. This structure is going to implement the interface required by the gRPC server. The use of `protoapi.UnimplementedRandomServer` is required for the implementation of the interface—this is standard practice.

```
func (RandomServer) GetDate(ctx context.Context, r *protoapi.
RequestDateTime) (*protoapi.DateTime, error) {
    currentTime := time.Now()
    response := &protoapi.DateTime{
        Value: currentTime.String(),
    }
```

```
    return response, nil
}
```

This is the first method of the interface named after the `GetDate` function found in the `service` block of `protoapi.proto`. This method requires no input from the client, so it ignores the `r` parameter.

```
func (RandomServer) GetRandom(ctx context.Context, r *protoapi.
RandomParams) (*protoapi.RandomInt, error) {
    rand.Seed(r.GetSeed())
    place := r.GetPlace()
```

The `GetSeed()` and `GetPlace()` get methods are implemented by `protoc`, are related to the fields of `protoapi.RandomParams`, and should be used in order to read data from the client message.

```
    temp := random(min, max)
    for {
        place--
        if place <= 0 {
            break
        }
        temp = random(min, max)
    }

    response := &protoapi.RandomInt{
        Value: int64(temp),
    }
    return response, nil
}
```

The server constructs a `protoapi.RandomInt` variable that is going to be returned to the client. We end the implementation of the second method of the interface here.

```
func (RandomServer) GetRandomPass(ctx context.Context, r *protoapi.
RequestPass) (*protoapi.RandomPass, error) {
    rand.Seed(r.GetSeed())
    temp := getString(r.GetLength())
```

The `GetSeed()` and `GetLength()` get methods are implemented by `protoc`, are related to the fields of `protoapi.RequestPass`, and should be used in order to read the data from the client message.

```
    response := &protoapi.RandomPass{
        Password: temp,
    }
    return response, nil
}
```

In the last part of `GetRandomPass()`, we construct the response (`protoapi.RandomPass`) in order to send it to the client.

```
var port = ":8080"

func main() {
    if len(os.Args) == 1 {
        fmt.Println("Using default port:", port)
    } else {
        port = os.Args[1]
    }
```

The first part of `main()` is about specifying the TCP port that is going to be used for the service.

```
    server := grpc.NewServer()
```

The previous statement creates a new gRPC server that is not attached to any specific gRPC service.

```
    var randomServer RandomServer
    protoapi.RegisterRandomServer(server, randomServer)
```

The previous statements call `protoapi.RegisterRandomServer()` to create a gRPC server for our specific service.

```
    reflection.Register(server)
```

It is not mandatory to call `reflection.Register()`, but it helps when you want to list the available services found on a server—in our case, it could have been omitted.

```
    listen, err := net.Listen("tcp", port)
    if err != nil {
        fmt.Println(err)
        return
    }
```

The previous code starts a TCP service that listens to the desired TCP port.

```
    fmt.Println("Serving requests...")
    server.Serve(listen)
}
```

The last part of the program is about telling the gRPC server to begin serving client requests. This happens by calling the `Serve()` method and using the network parameters stored in `listen`.

> The `curl(1)` utility does not work with binary data and therefore cannot be used for testing a gRPC server. However, there is an alternative for testing gRPC services, which is the `grpcurl` utility (`https://github.com/fullstorydev/grpcurl`).

Now that we have the gRPC server ready, let us continue by developing the client that can help us test the operation of the gRPC server.

Developing a gRPC client

This section presents the development of the gRPC client based on the `api.proto` file presented earlier. The main purpose of the client is to test the functionality of the server. However, what is really important is the implementation of three helper functions, each one corresponding to a different RPC call, because these three functions allow you to interact with the gRPC server. The purpose of the `main()` function of `gClient.go` is to use these three helper functions.

So, the code of `gClient.go` is the following:

```
package main

import (
    "context"
    "fmt"
    "math/rand"
    "os"
    "time"

    "github.com/mactsouk/protoapi"
    "google.golang.org/grpc"
)
```

```
var port = ":8080"

func AskingDateTime(ctx context.Context, m protoapi.RandomClient)
(*protoapi.DateTime, error) {
```

You can name the `AskingDateTime()` function anything you want. However, the signature of the function must contain a `context.Context` parameter, as well as a `RandomClient` parameter in order to be able to call `GetDate()` later on. The client does not need to implement any of the functions of the IDL—it just has to call them.

```
    request := &protoapi.RequestDateTime{
        Value: "Please send me the date and time",
    }
```

We first construct a `protoapi.RequestDateTime` variable that holds the data for the client request.

```
    return m.GetDate(ctx, request)
}
```

Then, we call the `GetDate()` method to send the client request to the server. This is handled by the code in the `protoapi` module—we just call `GetDate()` with the correct parameters. This is where the implementation of the first helper function ends—although it is not mandatory to have such a helper function, it makes the code cleaner.

```
func AskPass(ctx context.Context, m protoapi.RandomClient, seed int64,
length int64) (*protoapi.RandomPass, error) {
    request := &protoapi.RequestPass{
        Seed:   seed,
        Length: length,
    }
```

The `AskPass()` helper function is for calling the `GetRandomPass()` gRPC method in order to get a random password from the server process. First, the function constructs a `protoapi.RequestPass` variable with the given values for `Seed` and `Length`, which are parameters of `AskPass()`.

```
    return m.GetRandomPass(ctx, request)
}
```

Then, we call `GetRandomPass()` to send the client request to the server and get the response. Finally, the function returns.

Due to the way gRPC works and the tools that simplify things, the implementation of `AskPass()` is short. Doing the same using RESTful services requires more code.

```
func AskRandom(ctx context.Context, m protoapi.RandomClient, seed
int64, place int64) (*protoapi.RandomInt, error) {
	request := &protoapi.RandomParams{
		Seed:  seed,
		Place: place,
	}

	return m.GetRandom(ctx, request)
}
```

The last helper function, `AskRandom()`, operates in an analogous way. We construct the client message (`protoapi.RandomParams`), send it to the server by calling `GetRandom()`, and get the server response as returned by `GetRandom()`.

```
func main() {
	if len(os.Args) == 1 {
		fmt.Println("Using default port:", port)
	} else {
		port = os.Args[1]
	}

	conn, err := grpc.Dial(port, grpc.WithInsecure())
	if err != nil {
		fmt.Println("Dial:", err)
		return
	}
```

The gRPC client needs to connect to the gRPC server using `grpc.Dial()`. However, we are not done yet as we need to specify the gRPC service the client is going to connect to—this is going to happen in a while. The `grpc.Insecure()` function that is passed as a parameter to `grpc.Dial()` returns a `DialOption` value that disables security for the client connection.

```
	rand.Seed(time.Now().Unix())
	seed := int64(rand.Intn(100))
```

Due to the different seed values generated and sent to the gRPC server each time the client code gets executed, we are going to get different random values and passwords back from the gRPC server.

```
client := protoapi.NewRandomClient(conn)
```

Next, we need to create a gRPC client by calling `protoapi.NewRandomClient()` and passing the TCP connection to `protoapi.NewRandomClient()`. This `client` variable is going to be used for all interactions with the server. The name of the function that is called depends on the name of the gRPC service—this allows you to differentiate among the different gRPC services that a machine might support.

```
r, err := AskingDateTime(context.Background(), client)
if err != nil {
    fmt.Println(err)
    return
}
fmt.Println("Server Date and Time:", r.Value)
```

First, we call the `AskingDateTime()` helper function to get the date and time from the gRPC server.

```
length := int64(rand.Intn(20))
p, err := AskPass(context.Background(), client, 100, length+1)
if err != nil {
    fmt.Println(err)
    return
}
fmt.Println("Random Password:", p.Password)
```

Then, we call `AskPass()` to get a randomly generated password. The length of the password is specified by the `length := int64(rand.Intn(20))` statement.

```
place := int64(rand.Intn(100))
i, err := AskRandom(context.Background(), client, seed, place)
if err != nil {
    fmt.Println(err)
    return
}
fmt.Println("Random Integer 1:", i.Value)
```

Then, we test `AskRandom()` with different parameters to make sure that it is going to return different values back.

```
	k, err := AskRandom(context.Background(), client, seed, place-1)
	if err != nil {
		fmt.Println(err)
		return
	}
	fmt.Println("Random Integer 2:", k.Value)
}
```

With both the server and client completed, we are ready to test them.

Testing the gRPC server with the client

Now that we have developed both the server and the client, we are ready to use them. First, we should run `gServer.go` as follows:

```
$ go run gServer.go
Using default port: :8080
Serving requests..
```

The server process does not produce any other output.

Then, we execute `gClient.go` without any command-line parameters. The output you get from `gClient.go` should be similar to the following:

```
$ go run gClient.go
Using default port: :8080
Server Date and Time: 2021-07-05 08:32:19.654905 +0300 EEST
m=+2.197816168
Random Password: $1!usiz|36
Random Integer 1: 92
Random Integer 2: 78
```

Apart from the first line, which is the client execution from the UNIX shell, and the second line, which is about the TCP port that is used for connecting to the gRPC server, the next line of the output shows the date and time as returned by the gRPC server. Then we have a random password as generated by the server, as well as two random integers.

If we execute `gClient.go` more than once, we are going to get a different output:

```
$ go run gClient.go
Using default port: :8080
Server Date and Time: 2021-07-05 08:32:23.831445 +0300 EEST
m=+6.374535148
Random Password: $1!usiz|36N}DO*}{
Random Integer 1: 10
Random Integer 2: 68
```

The fact that the gRPC server returned different values proves that the gRPC server works as expected.

gRPC can do more things than the ones presented in this chapter, such as exchange arrays of messages and streaming—RESTful servers cannot be used for data streaming. However, a discussion of these is beyond the scope of this book.

Exercises

- Convert `gClient.go` into a command-line utility using `cobra`.
- Try to convert `gServer.go` into a RESTful server.
- Create a RESTful service that uses gRPC for data exchange. Define the REST API you are going to support, but use gRPC for the communication between the RESTful server and the gRPC server—in this case, the RESTful server is going to act as a gRPC client to the gRPC server.
- Create your own gRPC service that implements integer addition and subtraction.
- How easy or difficult would it be to convert the Phone Book application into a gRPC service?
- Implement a gRPC service that calculates the length of a string.

Summary

gRPC is fast, easy to use and understand, and exchanges data in binary format. This chapter taught you how to define the methods and the messages of a gRPC service, how to translate them into Go code, and how to develop a server and a client for that gRPC service.

So, should you use gRPC or stick with RESTful services? Only you can answer that question. You should go with what feels more natural to you. However, if you are still in doubt and cannot decide, begin by developing a RESTful service and then implement the same service using gRPC. After that, you should be ready to choose.

The last chapter of the book is about **generics**, which is a Go feature that is currently under development and is going to be officially included in Go in 2022. However, nothing prohibits us from discussing generics and showing some Go code to better understand generics.

Additional resources

- gRPC: `https://grpc.io/`
- Protocol Buffers 3 Language Guide: `https://developers.google.com/protocol-buffers/docs/proto3`
- The `grpcurl` utility: `https://github.com/fullstorydev/grpcurl`
- Johan Brandhorst's website: `https://jbrandhorst.com/page/about/`
- The documentation of the `google.golang.org/grpc` package can be found at `https://pkg.go.dev/google.golang.org/grpc`
- Go and gRPC tutorial: `https://grpc.io/docs/languages/go/basics/`
- Protocol buffers: `https://developers.google.com/protocol-buffers`

13

Go Generics

This chapter is about *generics* and how to use the new syntax to write generic functions and define generic data types. Currently, generics are under development, but the official release is pretty close and we have a good idea of what features generics are going to have and how generics are going to work.

> The new generics syntax is coming to Go 1.18, which, according to the Go development cycle, is going to be officially released in February 2022.

Let me make something clear from the beginning: you do not have to use Go generics if you do not want to and you can still write wonderful, efficient, maintainable, and correct software in Go! Additionally, the fact that you can use generics and support lots of data types, if not all available data types, does not mean that you should do that. Always **support the required data types**, no more, no less, but do not forget to keep an eye on the future of your data and the possibility of supporting data types that were not known at the time of writing your code.

This chapter covers:

- Introducing generics
- Constraints
- Defining new data types with generics
- Interfaces versus generics

- Reflection versus generics
- Concluding remarks: what does the future look like for Go developers?

Introducing generics

Generics are a feature that gives you the capability of not precisely specifying the data type of one or more function parameters, mainly because you want to make your functions as generic as possible. In other words, generics allow functions to process several data types without the need to write special code, as is the case with the empty interface or interfaces in general. However, when working with interfaces in Go, you have to write extra code to determine the data type of the interface variable you are working with, which is not the case with generics.

Let me begin by presenting a small code example that implements a function that clearly shows a case where generics can be handy and save you from having to write lots of code:

```
func PrintSlice[T any](s []T) {
    for _, v := range s {
        fmt.Println(v)
    }
}
```

So, what do we have here? There is a function named `PrintSlice()` that accepts a slice of any data type. This is denoted by the use of `[]T` in the function signature in combination with the `[T any]` part. The `[T any]` part tells the compiler that the data type `T` is going to be determined at execution time. We are also free to use multiple data types using the `[T, U, W any]` notation—after which we should use the `T, U, W` data types in the function signature.

The `any` keyword tells the compiler that there are **no constraints** about the data type of `T`. We are going to discuss constraints in a while—for now, just learn the syntax of generics.

Now imagine writing separate functions to implement the functionality of `PrintSlice()` for slices of integers, strings, floating-point numbers, complex values, and so on. So, we have found a profound case where using generics simplifies the code and our programming efforts. However, not all cases are so obvious, and we should be very careful about overusing `any`.

But what happens if you want to try generics before the official release? There is a solution, which is to visit `https://go2goplay.golang.org/` and place and run your code there.

The initial screen of `https://go2goplay.golang.org/` is presented in the next figure. Just like the regular Go Playground, the upper part is where you write the code, whereas the bottom part is where you get the results of your code or potential error messages after pressing the **Run** button:

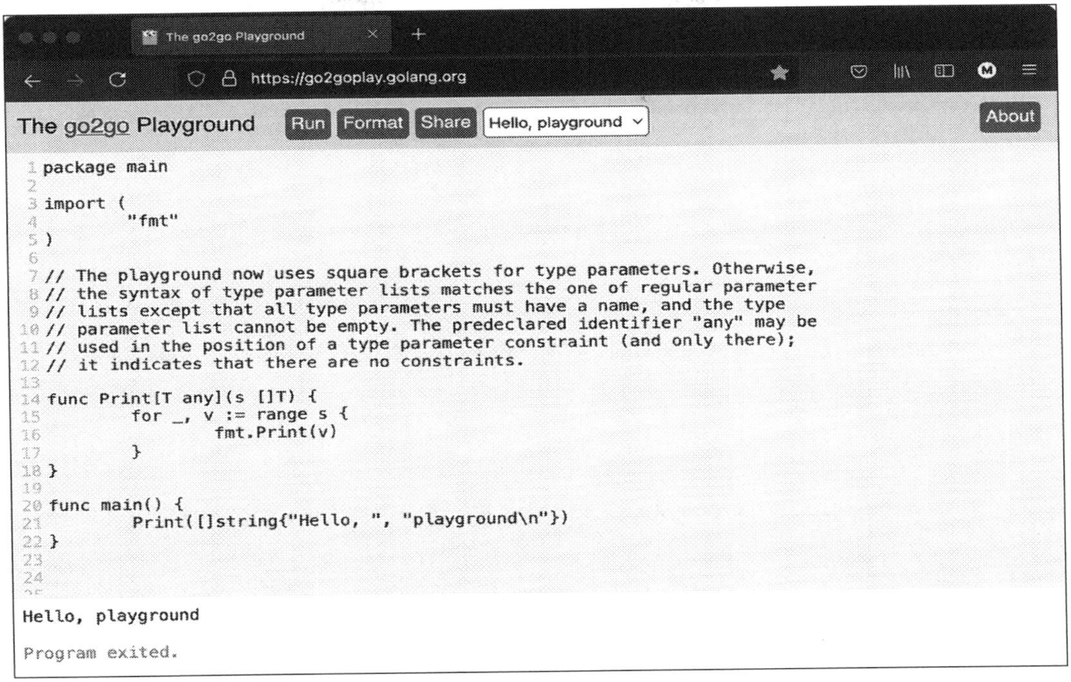

Figure 13.1: The Go Playground for trying generics

The rest of this chapter is going to execute the Go code in `https://go2goplay.golang.org/`. However, I am going to present the code as usual and the output of the code by copying and pasting it from `https://go2goplay.golang.org/`.

The following (`hw.go`) is code that uses generics, to help you understand more about them before going into more advanced examples:

```
package main

import (
    "fmt"
)

func PrintSlice[T any](s []T) {
    for _, v := range s {
```

```
        fmt.Print(v, " ")
    }
    fmt.Println()
}
```

`PrintSlice()` is similar to the function that we saw earlier in this chapter. However, it prints the elements of each slice in the same line and prints a new line with the help of `fmt.Println()`.

```
func main() {
    PrintSlice([]int{1, 2, 3})
    PrintSlice([]string{"a", "b", "c"})
    PrintSlice([]float64{1.2, -2.33, 4.55})
}
```

Here we call `PrintSlice()` with three different data types: `int`, `string`, and `float64`. The Go compiler is not going to complain about that. Instead, it is going to execute the code as if we had three separate functions, one for each data type.

Therefore, running `hw.go` produces the next output:

```
1 2 3
a b c
1.2 -2.33 4.55
```

So, each slice is printed as expected using a single generic function.

With that information in mind, let us begin by discussing generics and constraints.

Constraints

Let us say that you have a function that works with generics that multiplies two numeric values. Should this function work with all data types? Can this function work with all data types? Can you multiply two strings or two structures? The solution for avoiding that kind of issue is the use of **constraints**.

Forget about multiplication for a while and think about something simpler. Let us say that we want to compare variables for equality—is there a way to tell Go that we only want to work with values that can be compared? Go 1.18 is going to come with predefined constraints—one of them is called `comparable` and includes data types that can be compared for equality or inequality.

The code of allowed.go illustrates the use of the comparable constraint:

```
package main

import (
    "fmt"
)

func Same[T comparable](a, b T) bool {
    if a == b {
        return true
    }
    return false
}
```

The Same() function uses the **predefined** comparable constraint instead of any. In reality, the comparable constraint is just a predefined interface that includes all data types that can be compared with == or !=. We do not have to write any extra code for checking our input as the function signature makes sure that we are going to deal with acceptable data types only.

```
func main() {
    fmt.Println("4 = 3 is", Same(4,3))
    fmt.Println("aa = aa is", Same("aa","aa"))
    fmt.Println("4.1 = 4.15 is", Same(4.1,4.15))
}
```

The main() function calls Same() three times and prints its results.

Running allowed.go produces the next output:

```
4 = 3 is false
aa = aa is true
4.1 = 4.15 is false
```

As only Same("aa","aa") is true, we get the respective output.

If you try to run a statement that includes Same([]int{1,2},[]int{1,3}), which tries to compare two slices, the Go Playground is going to generate the following error message:

```
type checking failed for main
prog.go2:19:31: []int does not satisfy comparable
```

This happens because we cannot directly compare two slices—this kind of functionality should be implemented manually.

The next subsection shows how to create your own constraints.

Creating constraints

This subsection presents an example where we define the data types that are allowed to be passed as parameters to a generic function using an *interface*. The code of `numeric.go` is as follows:

```
package main

import (
    "fmt"
)

type Numeric interface {
    type int, int8, int16, int32, int64, float64
}
```

In here, we define a new interface called `Numeric` that specifies the list of supported data types. You can use any data type you want as long as it can be used with the generic function that you are going to implement. In this case, we could have added `string` or `uint` to the list of supported data types.

```
func Add[T Numeric](a, b T) T {
    return a + b
}
```

This is the definition of the generic function that uses the `Numeric` constraint.

```
func main() {
    fmt.Println("4 + 3 =", Add(4,3))
    fmt.Println("4.1 + 3.2 =", Add(4.1,3.2))
}
```

The previous code is the implementation of the `main()` function with the calls to `Add()`.

Running `numeric.go` produces the next output:

```
4 + 3 = 7
4.1 + 3.2 = 7.3
```

Nevertheless, Go rules still apply. Therefore, if you try to call `Add(4.1,3)`, you are going to get the next error message:

```
type checking failed for main
prog.go2:16:33: default type int of 3 does not match inferred type
float64 for T
```

The reason for this error is that the `Add()` function expects two parameters of **the same data type**. However, `4.1` is a `float64` whereas `3` is an `int`, so not the same data type.

The next section shows how to use generics when defining new data types.

Defining new data types with generics

In this section we are going to create a new data type with the use of generics, which is presented in `newDT.go`. The code of `newDT.go` is the following:

```
package main

import (
    "fmt"
    "errors"
)

type TreeLast[T any] []T
```

The previous statement declares a new data type named `TreeLast` that uses generics.

```
func (t TreeLast[T]) replaceLast(element T) (TreeLast[T], error) {
    if len(t) == 0 {
        return t, errors.New("This is empty!")
    }

    t[len(t) - 1] = element
    return t, nil
}
```

`replaceLast()` is a method that operates on `TreeLast` variables. Apart from the function signature, there is nothing else that shows the use of generics.

```
func main() {
    tempStr := TreeLast[string]{"aa", "bb"}
```

```
    fmt.Println(tempStr)
    tempStr.replaceLast("cc")
    fmt.Println(tempStr)
```

In this first part of `main()`, we create a `TreeLast` variable with the `aa` and `bb` `string` values and we replace the `bb` value with `cc`, using a call to `replaceLast("cc")`.

```
    tempInt := TreeLast[int]{12, -3}
    fmt.Println(tempInt)
    tempInt.replaceLast(0)
    fmt.Println(tempInt)
}
```

The second part of `main()` does a similar thing to the first part using a `TreeLast` variable populated with `int` values. So `TreeLast` works with both `string` and `int` values without any issues.

Running `newDT.go` produces the next output:

```
[aa bb]
[aa cc]
```

The preceding is the output related to the `TreeLast[string]` variable.

```
[12 -3]
[12 0]
```

The final output is related to the `TreeLast[int]` variable.

The next subsection is about using generics in Go structures.

Using generics in Go structures

In this section, we are going to implement a linked list that works with generics—this is one of the cases where the use of generics simplifies things because it allows you to implement the linked list once while being able to work with multiple data types.

The code of `structures.go` is the following:

```
package main

import (
    "fmt"
)
```

```
type node[T any] struct {
    Data T
    next *node[T]
}
```

The `node` structure uses generics in order to support nodes that can store all kinds of data. This does not mean that the `next` field of a `node` can point to another `node` with a `Data` field with a different data type. The rule that a linked list contains elements of the same data type still applies—it just means that if you want to create three linked lists, one for storing `string` values, one for storing `int` values, and a third one for storing JSON records of a given `struct` data type, you do not need to write any extra code to do so.

```
type list[T any] struct {
    start *node[T]
}
```

This is the definition of the root node of a linked list of `node` nodes. Both `list` and `node` must share the same data type, `T`. However, as stated before, this does not prevent you from creating multiple linked lists of various data types.

You can still replace `any` with a constraint in both the definition of `node` and `list` if you want to restrict the list of allowed data types.

```
func (l *list[T]) add(data T) {
    n := node[T]{
        Data: data,
        next: nil,
    }
```

The `add()` function is generic in order to be able to work with all kinds of nodes. Apart from the signature of `add()`, all the remaining code is not associated with the use of generics.

```
    if l.start == nil {
        l.start = &n
        return
    }

    if l.start.next == nil {
        l.start.next = &n
        return
    }
```

These two if blocks have to do with the adding of a new node to the linked list.

```
        temp := l.start
        l.start = l.start.next
        l.add(data)
        l.start = temp
    }
```

The last part of add() has to do with defining the proper associations between nodes when adding a new node to the list.

```
func main() {
    var myList list[int]
```

First, we define a linked list of int values in main(), which is the linked list that we are going to work with.

```
    fmt.Println(myList)
```

The initial value of myList is nil, as the list is empty and does not contain any nodes.

```
    myList.add(12)
    myList.add(9)
    myList.add(3)
    myList.add(9)
```

In this first part, we add four elements to the linked list.

```
    // Print all elements
    for {
        fmt.Println("*", myList.start)
        if myList.start == nil {
            break
        }
        myList.start = myList.start.next
    }
}
```

The last part of main() is about printing all the elements of the list by traversing it with the help of the next field, which points to the next node in the list.

Running structures.go produces the next output:

```
{<nil>}
* &{12 0xc00010a060}
```

```
* &{9 0xc00010a080}
* &{3 0xc00010a0b0}
* &{9 <nil>}
* <nil>
```

Let us discuss the output a little more. The first line shows that the value of the empty list is `nil`. The first node of the list holds the value `12` and a memory address (`0xc00010a060`) that points to the second node. This goes on until we reach the last node, which holds the value of `9`, which appears twice in this linked list, and points to `nil`, because it is the last node. Therefore, the use of generics makes the linked list able to work with multiple data types.

The next section discusses the differences between using interfaces and generics to support multiple data types.

Interfaces versus generics

This section presents a program that increments a numeric value by one using interfaces and generics so that you can compare the implementation details.

The code of `interfaces.go` illustrates the two techniques and contains the next code:

```
package main

import (
    "fmt"
)

type Numeric interface {
    type int, int8, int16, int32, int64, float64
}
```

This is where we define a constraint named `Numeric` for limiting the permitted data types.

```
func Print(s interface{}) {
    // type switch
    switch s.(type) {
```

The `Print()` function uses the empty interface for getting input and a type switch to work with that input parameter.

Put simply, we are using a *type switch* to differentiate between the supported data types—in this case, the supported data types are just `int` and `float64`, which has to do with the implementation of the type switch. However, adding more data types requires code changes, which is not the most efficient solution.

```
    case int:
        fmt.Println(s.(int)+1)
```

This branch is how we handle the `int` case.

```
    case float64:
        fmt.Println(s.(float64)+1)
```

This branch is how we handle the `float64` case.

```
    default:
        fmt.Println("Unknown data type!")
    }
}
```

The `default` branch is how we handle all unsupported data types.

The biggest issue with `Print()` is that due to the use of the empty interface, it accepts all kinds of input. As a result, the function signature does not help us limit the allowed data types. The second issue with `Print()` is that we need to specifically handle each case—handling more cases means writing more code.

On the other hand, the compiler does not have to guess many things with that code, which is not the case with generics, where the compiler and the runtime have more work to do. This kind of work introduces delays in the execution time.

```
func PrintGenerics[T any](s T) {
    fmt.Println(s)
}
```

`PrintGenerics()` is a generic function that can handle all available data types simply and elegantly.

```
func PrintNumeric[T Numeric](s T) {
    fmt.Println(s+1)
}
```

The `PrintNumeric()` function supports all numeric data types with the use of the `Numeric` constraint. No need to specifically add code for supporting each distinct data type, as happens with `Print()`.

```
func main() {
    Print(12)
    Print(-1.23)
    Print("Hi!")
```

The first part of `main()` uses `Print()` with various types of input: an `int` value, a `float64` value, and a `string` value, respectively.

```
    PrintGenerics(1)
    PrintGenerics("a")
    PrintGenerics(-2.33)
```

As stated before, `PrintGenerics()` works with all data types, including `string` values.

```
    PrintNumeric(1)
    PrintNumeric(-2.33)
}
```

The last part of `main()` uses `PrintNumeric()` with numeric values only, due to the use of the `Numeric` constraint.

Running `interfaces.go` produces the next output:

```
13
-0.22999999999999998
Unknown data type!
```

The preceding three lines of the output are from the `Print()` function, which uses the empty interface.

```
1
a
-2.33
```

The previous three lines of the output are from the `PrintGenerics()` function, which uses generics and supports all available data types. As a result, it cannot increase the value of its input because we do not know for sure that we are dealing with a numeric value. Therefore, it just prints the given input.

```
2
-1.33
```

The last two lines are generated by the two `PrintNumeric()` calls, which operate using the `Numeric` constraint.

So in practice, when you have to support multiple data types, the use of generics might be a better choice than using interfaces.

The next section discusses the use of reflection as a way of bypassing the use of generics.

Reflection versus generics

In this section, we develop a utility that prints the elements of a slice in two ways: first, using reflection, and second, using generics.

The code of `reflection.go` is as follows:

```
package main

import (
    "fmt"
    "reflect"
)

func PrintReflection(s interface{}) {
    fmt.Println("** Reflection")
    val := reflect.ValueOf(s)

    if val.Kind() != reflect.Slice {
        return
    }

    for i := 0; i < val.Len(); i++ {
        fmt.Print(val.Index(i).Interface(), " ")
    }
    fmt.Println()
}
```

Internally, the `PrintReflection()` function works with slices only. However, as we cannot express that in the function signature, we need to accept an empty interface parameter. Additionally, we have to write more code to get the desired output.

In more detail, first, we need to make sure that we are processing a slice (`reflect.Slice`) and second, we have to print the slice elements using a `for` loop, which is pretty ugly.

```
func PrintSlice[T any](s []T) {
    fmt.Println("** Generics")

    for _, v := range s {
        fmt.Print(v, " ")
    }
    fmt.Println()
}
```

Once again, the implementation of the generic function is simpler and therefore easier to understand. Moreover, the function signature specifies that only slices are accepted as function parameters—we do not have to perform any additional checks for that as this is a job for the Go compiler. Last, we use a simple `for` loop with `range` to print the slice elements.

```
func main() {
    PrintSlice([]int{1, 2, 3})
    PrintSlice([]string{"a", "b", "c"})
    PrintSlice([]float64{1.2, -2.33, 4.55})

    PrintReflection([]int{1, 2, 3})
    PrintReflection([]string{"a", "b", "c"})
    PrintReflection([]float64{1.2, -2.33, 4.55})
}
```

The `main()` function calls `PrintSlice()` and `PrintReflection()` with various kinds of input to test their operation.

Running `reflection.go` generates the next output:

```
** Generics
1 2 3
** Generics
a b c
** Generics
1.2 -2.33 4.55
```

The first six lines are produced by taking advantage of generics and print the elements of a slice of `int` values, a slice of `string` values, and a slice of `float64` values.

```
** Reflection
1 2 3
** Reflection
```

```
a b c
** Reflection
1.2 -2.33 4.55
```

The last six lines of the output produce the same output, but this time using reflection. There is no difference in the output—all differences are in the code found in the implementations of `PrintReflection()` and `PrintSlice()` for printing the output. As expected, generics code is simpler and shorter than Go code that uses reflection, especially when you must support lots of different data types.

Exercises

- Create a `PrintMe()` method in `structures.go` that prints all the elements of the linked list
- Create two extra functions in `reflection.go` in order to support the printing of strings using reflection and generics
- Implement the `delete()` and `search()` functionality using generics for the linked list found in `structures.go`
- Implement a doubly-linked list using generics starting with the code found in `structures.go`

Summary

This chapter presented generics and gave you the rationale behind the invention of generics. Additionally, it presented the Go syntax for generics as well as some issues that might come up if you use generics carelessly. It is expected that there are going to be changes to the Go standard library in order to support generics and that there is going to be a new package named `slices` to take advantage of the new language features.

Although a function with generics is more flexible, code with generics usually runs slower than code that works with predefined static data types. So, the price you pay for flexibility is execution speed. Similarly, Go code with generics has a bigger compilation time than equivalent code that does not use generics. Once the Go community begins working with generics in real-world scenarios, the cases where generics offer the highest productivity are going to become much more evident. At the end of the day, programming is about understanding the cost of your decisions. Only then can you consider yourself a programmer. So, understanding the cost of using generics instead of interfaces, reflection, or other techniques is important.

So, what does the future look like for Go developers? In short, it looks wonderful! You should already be enjoying programming in Go, and you should continue to do so as the language evolves. If you want to know the latest and greatest of Go as it is being discussed by the team, you should definitely visit the official GitHub place of the Go team at `https://github.com/golang`.

Go helps you to create great software! So, go and create great software!

Additional resources

- Google I/O 2012—Meet the Go team: `https://youtu.be/sln-gJaURzk`
- Meet the authors of Go: `https://youtu.be/3yghHvvZQmA`
- This is a video of Brian Kernighan interviewing Ken Thompson—not directly related to Go: `https://youtu.be/EY6q5dv_B-o`
- Brian Kernighan on successful language design—not directly related to Go: `https://youtu.be/Sg4U4r_AgJU`
- Brian Kernighan: UNIX, C, AWK, AMPL, and Go Programming from the Lex Fridman Podcast: `https://youtu.be/O9upVbGSBFo`
- Why Generics? `https://blog.golang.org/why-generics`
- The Next Step for Generics: `https://blog.golang.org/generics-next-step`
- A Proposal for Adding Generics to Go: `https://blog.golang.org/generics-proposal`
- Proposal for the `slices` package: `https://github.com/golang/go/issues/45955`

A note from the author

Being a good programmer is hard, but it can be done. Keep improving and—who knows—you might become famous and have a movie made about you!

Thank you for reading this book. Feel free to contact me with suggestions, questions, or maybe ideas for other books!

Soli Deo gloria

Appendix A – Go Garbage Collector

This Appendix is all about the Go **Garbage Collector** (**GC**). This crucial part of Go can affect the performance of your code more than any other Go component. We will begin by talking about the heap and the stack.

Heap and stack

The **heap** is the place where programming languages store global variables—the heap is where garbage collection takes place. The **stack** is the place where programming languages store temporary variables used by functions—each function has its own stack. As goroutines are located in user space, the Go runtime is responsible for the rules that govern their operation. Additionally, each goroutine has its own stack, whereas the heap is "shared" among goroutines.

In C++, when you create new variables using the `new` operator, you know that these variables are going to the heap. This is not the case with Go and the use of the `new()` and `make()` functions. In Go, the compiler decides where a new variable is going to be placed based on its size and the result of *escape analysis*. This is the reason that you can return pointers to local variables from Go functions.

> As we have not seen `new()` in this book many times, have in mind that `new()` **returns pointers to initialized memory**.

If you want to know where the variables of a program are allocated by Go, you can use the `-m` GC flag. This is illustrated in `allocate.go`—this is a regular program that needs no modifications in order to display the extra output as all details are handled by Go.

```
package main

import "fmt"
```

```
const VAT = 24

type Item struct {
    Description string
    Value       float64
}

func Value(price float64) float64 {
    total := price + price*VAT/100
    return total
}

func main() {
    t := Item{Description: "Keyboard", Value: 100}
    t.Value = Value(t.Value)
    fmt.Println(t)

    tP := &Item{}
    *&tP.Description = "Mouse"
    *&tP.Value = 100
    fmt.Println(tP)
}
```

Running `allocate.go` generates the next output—the output is a result of the use of `-gcflags '-m'`, which modifies the generated executable. You should not create executable binaries that go to production with the use of `-gcflags` flags:

```
$ go run -gcflags '-m' allocate.go
# command-line-arguments
./allocate.go:12:6: can inline Value
./allocate.go:19:17: inlining call to Value
./allocate.go:20:13: inlining call to fmt.Println
./allocate.go:25:13: inlining call to fmt.Println
./allocate.go:20:13: t escapes to heap
```

The `t escapes to heap` message means that `t` escapes the function. Put simply, it means that `t` is used outside of the function and does not have a local scope (because it is passed outside the function). However, this does not necessarily mean that the variable has moved to the heap.

Another message that is not shown here is `moved to heap`. This message shows that the compiler decided to move a variable to the heap because it might be used outside of the function.

```
./allocate.go:20:13: []interface {}{...} does not escape
./allocate.go:22:8: &Item{} escapes to heap
./allocate.go:25:13: []interface {}{...} does not escape
```

The `does not escape` message indicates that the interface does not escape to the heap. The Go compiler performs *escape analysis* to find out whether memory needs to be allocated at the heap or should stay within the stack.

```
<autogenerated>:1: .this does not escape
{Keyboard 124}
&{Mouse 100}
```

The last two lines of the output consist of the output generated by the two `fmt.Println()` statements.

If you want to get a more detailed output, you can use `-m` twice:

```
$ go run -gcflags '-m -m' allocate.go
# command-line-arguments
./allocate.go:12:6: can inline Value with cost 13 as: func(float64)
float64 { total := price + price * VAT / 100; return total }
./allocate.go:17:6: cannot inline main: function too complex: cost 199
exceeds budget 80
./allocate.go:19:17: inlining call to Value func(float64) float64 {
total := price + price * VAT / 100; return total }
./allocate.go:20:13: inlining call to fmt.Println func(...interface {})
(int, error) { var fmt..autotmp_3 int; fmt..autotmp_3 = <N>; var fmt..
autotmp_4 error; fmt..autotmp_4 = <N>; fmt..autotmp_3, fmt..autotmp_4
= fmt.Fprintln(io.Writer(os.Stdout), fmt.a...); return fmt..autotmp_3,
fmt..autotmp_4 }
./allocate.go:25:13: inlining call to fmt.Println func(...interface {})
(int, error) { var fmt..autotmp_3 int; fmt..autotmp_3 = <N>; var fmt..
autotmp_4 error; fmt..autotmp_4 = <N>; fmt..autotmp_3, fmt..autotmp_4
= fmt.Fprintln(io.Writer(os.Stdout), fmt.a...); return fmt..autotmp_3,
fmt..autotmp_4 }
./allocate.go:22:8: &Item{} escapes to heap:
./allocate.go:22:8:   flow: tP = &{storage for &Item{}}:
./allocate.go:22:8:     from &Item{} (spill) at ./allocate.go:22:8
./allocate.go:22:8:     from tP := &Item{} (assign) at ./allocate.
go:22:5
```

```
./allocate.go:22:8:   flow: ~arg0 = tP:
./allocate.go:22:8:     from tP (interface-converted) at ./allocate.
go:25:13
./allocate.go:22:8:     from ~arg0 := tP (assign-pair) at ./allocate.
go:25:13
./allocate.go:22:8:   flow: {storage for []interface {}{...}} = ~arg0:
./allocate.go:22:8:     from []interface {}{...} (slice-literal-
element) at ./allocate.go:25:13
./allocate.go:22:8:   flow: fmt.a = &{storage for []interface {}{...}}:
./allocate.go:22:8:     from []interface {}{...} (spill) at ./allocate.
go:25:13
./allocate.go:22:8:     from fmt.a = []interface {}{...} (assign) at ./
allocate.go:25:13
./allocate.go:22:8:   flow: {heap} = *fmt.a:
./allocate.go:22:8:     from fmt.Fprintln(io.Writer(os.Stdout),
fmt.a...) (call parameter) at ./allocate.go:25:13
./allocate.go:20:13: t escapes to heap:
./allocate.go:20:13:   flow: ~arg0 = &{storage for t}:
./allocate.go:20:13:     from t (spill) at ./allocate.go:20:13
./allocate.go:20:13:     from ~arg0 := t (assign-pair) at ./allocate.
go:20:13
./allocate.go:20:13:   flow: {storage for []interface {}{...}} = ~arg0:
./allocate.go:20:13:     from []interface {}{...} (slice-literal-
element) at ./allocate.go:20:13
./allocate.go:20:13:   flow: fmt.a = &{storage for []interface {}
{...}}:
./allocate.go:20:13:     from []interface {}{...} (spill) at ./
allocate.go:20:13
./allocate.go:20:13:     from fmt.a = []interface {}{...} (assign) at
./allocate.go:20:13
./allocate.go:20:13:   flow: {heap} = *fmt.a:
./allocate.go:20:13:     from fmt.Fprintln(io.Writer(os.Stdout),
fmt.a...) (call parameter) at ./allocate.go:20:13
./allocate.go:20:13: t escapes to heap
./allocate.go:20:13: []interface {}{...} does not escape
./allocate.go:22:8: &Item{} escapes to heap
./allocate.go:25:13: []interface {}{...} does not escape
<autogenerated>:1: .this does not escape
{Keyboard 124}
&{Mouse 100}
```

However, I find this output too crowded and complex. Usually, using `-m` just once reveals what is happening behind the scenes regarding the program heap and stack.

Now that we know about the heap and the stack, let us continue by discussing garbage collection.

Garbage collection

Garbage collection is the process of freeing up memory space that is not being used. In other words, the GC sees which objects are out of scope and cannot be referenced anymore and frees the memory space they consume. This process happens in a concurrent way while a Go program is running and not before or after the execution of the program. The documentation of the Go GC implementation states the following:

> *"The GC runs concurrently with mutator threads, is type accurate (also known as precise), and allows multiple GC threads to run in parallel. It is a concurrent mark and sweep that uses a write barrier. It is non-generational and non-compacting. Allocation is done using size segregated per P allocation areas to minimize fragmentation while eliminating locks in the common case."*

Fortunately, the Go standard library offers functions that allow you to study the operation of the GC and learn more about what the GC covertly does. These functions are illustrated in the `gColl.go` utility, which can be found in the `ch03` directory of the book's GitHub repository. The source code of `gColl.go` is presented here in chunks.

```
package main

import (
	"fmt"
	"runtime"
	"time"
)
```

You need the `runtime` package because it allows you to obtain information about the Go runtime system, which, among other things, includes the operation of the GC.

```
func printStats(mem runtime.MemStats) {
	runtime.ReadMemStats(&mem)
	fmt.Println("mem.Alloc:", mem.Alloc)
	fmt.Println("mem.TotalAlloc:", mem.TotalAlloc)
	fmt.Println("mem.HeapAlloc:", mem.HeapAlloc)
	fmt.Println("mem.NumGC:", mem.NumGC, "\n")
}
```

The main purpose of `printStats()` is to avoid writing the same Go code multiple times. The `runtime.ReadMemStats()` call gets the latest garbage collection statistics for you.

```
func main() {
    var mem runtime.MemStats
    printStats(mem)

    for i := 0; i < 10; i++ {
        // Allocating 50,000,000 bytes
        s := make([]byte, 50000000)
        if s == nil {
            fmt.Println("Operation failed!")
        }
    }
    printStats(mem)
```

In this part, we have a `for` loop that creates 10-byte slices with 50,000,000 bytes each. The reason for this is that by allocating large amounts of memory, we can trigger the GC.

```
    for i := 0; i < 10; i++ {
        // Allocating 100,000,000 bytes
        s := make([]byte, 100000000)
        if s == nil {
            fmt.Println("Operation failed!")
        }
        time.Sleep(5 * time.Second)
    }
    printStats(mem)
}
```

The last part of the program makes even bigger memory allocations – this time, each byte slice has 100,000,000 bytes.

Running `gColl.go` on a macOS Big Sur machine with 24 GB of RAM produces the following kind of output:

```
$ go run gColl.go
mem.Alloc: 124616
mem.TotalAlloc: 124616
mem.HeapAlloc: 124616
mem.NumGC: 0
```

```
mem.Alloc: 50124368
mem.TotalAlloc: 500175120
mem.HeapAlloc: 50124368
mem.NumGC: 9

mem.Alloc: 122536
mem.TotalAlloc: 1500257968
mem.HeapAlloc: 122536
mem.NumGC: 19
```

The value of `mem.Alloc` is the bytes of allocated heap objects—*allocated* are all the objects that the GC has not yet freed. `mem.TotalAlloc` shows the cumulative bytes allocated for heap objects—this number does not decrease when objects are freed, which means that it keeps increasing. Therefore, it shows the total number of bytes allocated for heap objects during program execution. `mem.HeapAlloc` is the same as `mem.Alloc`. Last, `mem.NumGC` shows the total number of completed garbage collection cycles. The bigger that value is, the more you have to consider how you allocate memory in your code and if there is a way to optimize that.

If you want even more verbose output regarding the operation of the GC, you can combine `go run gColl.go` with `GODEBUG=gctrace=1`. Apart from the regular program output, you get some extra metrics—this is illustrated in the following output:

```
$ GODEBUG=gctrace=1 go run gColl.go
gc 1 @0.021s 0%: 0.020+0.32+0.015 ms clock, 0.16+0.17/0.33/0.22+0.12 ms
cpu, 4->4->0 MB, 5 MB goal, 8 P
gc 2 @0.041s 0%: 0.074+0.32+0.003 ms clock, 0.59+0.087/0.37/0.45+0.030
ms cpu, 4->4->0 MB, 5 MB goal, 8 P
.
.
.
gc 18 @40.152s 0%: 0.065+0.14+0.013 ms clock, 0.52+0/0.12/0.042+0.10 ms
cpu, 95->95->0 MB, 96 MB goal, 8 P
gc 19 @45.160s 0%: 0.028+0.12+0.003 ms clock, 0.22+0/0.13/0.081+0.028
ms cpu, 95->95->0 MB, 96 MB goal, 8 P
mem.Alloc: 120672
mem.TotalAlloc: 1500256376
mem.HeapAlloc: 120672
mem.NumGC: 19
```

As before, we have the same number of completed garbage collection cycles (`19`). However, we get extra information about the heap size of each cycle. So, for garbage collection cycle 19 (`gc 19`), we get the following:

```
gc 19 @45.160s 0%: 0.028+0.12+0.003 ms clock, 0.22+0/0.13/0.081+0.028
ms cpu, 95->95->0 MB, 96 MB goal, 8 P
```

Now, let us explain the `95->95->0 MB` triplet in the previous line of output. The first value (`95`) is the heap size when the GC is about to run. The second value (`95`) is the heap size when the GC ends its operation. The last value is the size of the live heap (`0`).

The tricolor algorithm

The operation of the Go GC is based on the **tricolor algorithm**. Note that the tricolor algorithm is not unique to Go and can be used in other programming languages as well.

Strictly speaking, the official name for the algorithm used in Go is the **tricolor mark-and-sweep algorithm**. It can work concurrently with the program and uses a **write barrier**. This means that when a Go program runs, the Go scheduler is responsible for the scheduling of the application as well as the GC, which also runs as a goroutine. This is as if the Go scheduler must deal with a regular application with multiple **goroutines**!

> The core idea behind this algorithm came from Edsger W. Dijkstra, Leslie Lamport, A. J. Martin, C. S. Scholten, and E. F. M. Steffens, and was first illustrated in a paper named *On- the-Fly Garbage Collection: An Exercise in Cooperation*.

The primary principle behind the tricolor mark-and-sweep algorithm is that it **divides the objects of the heap** into three different sets according to their color, which is assigned by the algorithm and can be black, gray, or white. The objects of the **black set** are guaranteed to have no pointers to any object of the **white set**. On the other hand, an object of the white set can point to an object in the black set because this does not affect the operation of the GC. The objects of the **gray set** might have pointers to some objects of the white set. Finally, the objects of the **white set** are the candidates for garbage collection.

So, when the garbage collection begins, all objects are white, and the GC visits all the root objects and colors them gray. The **roots** are the objects that can be directly accessed by the application, which includes global variables and other things on the stack. These objects mostly depend on the Go code of a particular program.

After that, the GC picks a gray object, makes it black, and starts looking at whether that object has pointers to other objects of the white set or not. Therefore, when an object of the gray set is scanned for pointers to other objects, it is colored black. If that scan discovers that this particular object has one or more pointers to a white object, it puts that white object in the gray set. This process keeps going for as long as objects exist in the gray set. After that, the objects in the white set are unreachable and their memory space can be reused. Therefore, at this point, the elements of the white set are said to be garbage collected. Please note that no object can go directly from the black set to the white set, which allows the algorithm to operate and be able to clear the objects on the white set. As mentioned before, no object of the black set can directly point to an object of the white set. Additionally, if an object of the gray set becomes unreachable at some point in a garbage collection cycle, it will not be collected at this garbage collection cycle but in the next one! Although this is not an optimal situation, it is not that bad.

During this process, the running application is called the **mutator**. The mutator runs a small function named the **write barrier**, which is executed each time a pointer in the heap is modified. If the pointer of an object in the heap is modified, this means that this object is now reachable, the write barrier colors it gray, and puts it in the gray set. The mutator is responsible for the invariant that no element of the black set has a pointer to an element of the white set. This is accomplished with the help of the write barrier function. Failing to accomplish this invariant will ruin the garbage collection process and will most likely crash your program in a pretty bad and undesirable way!

So, there are three different colors: black, white, and gray. When the algorithm begins, all objects are colored white. As the algorithm keeps going, white objects are moved into one of the other two sets. The objects that are left in the white set are the ones that are going to be cleared at some point.

The next figure displays the three color sets with objects in them.

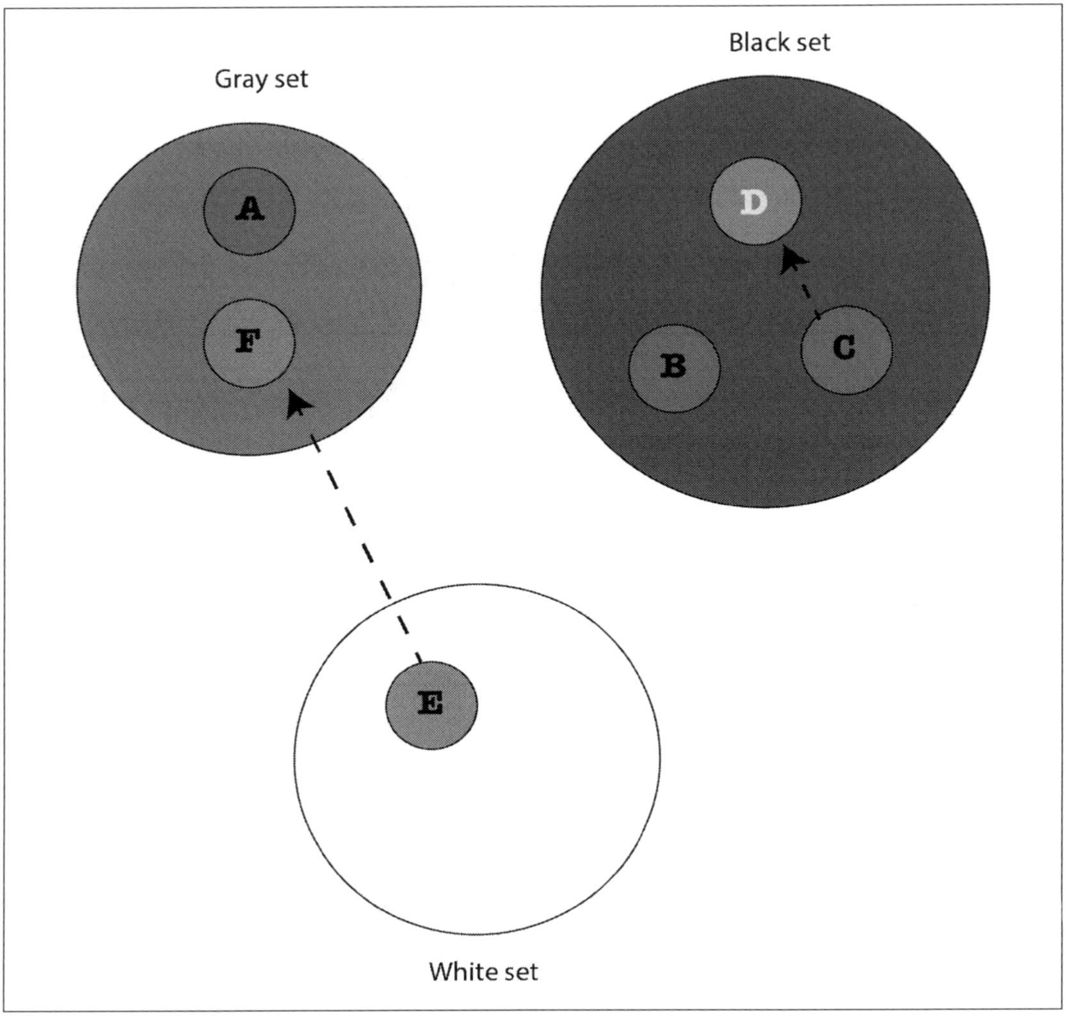

Figure 1: The Go GC represents the heap of a program as a graph

While object E, which is in the white set, can access object F, it cannot be accessed by any other object because no other object points to object E, which makes it a perfect candidate for garbage collection! Additionally, objects A, B, and C are root objects and are always reachable; therefore, they cannot be garbage collected.

Can you guess what happens next? Well, the algorithm will have to process the remaining elements of the gray set, which means that both objects A and F will go to the black set.

Object A goes to the black set because it is a root element and F goes to the black set because it does not point to any other object while it is in the gray set.

After object E is garbage collected, object F will become unreachable and will be garbage collected in the next cycle of the GC because an unreachable object cannot magically become reachable in the next iteration of the garbage collection cycle.

> Go garbage collection can also be applied to variables such as **channels**. When the GC finds out that a channel is unreachable, which is when the channel variable cannot be accessed anymore, it will free its resources even if the channel has not been closed.

Go allows you to manually initiate garbage collection cycles by putting a `runtime.GC()` statement in your Go code. However, have in mind that `runtime.GC()` blocks the caller and it might block the entire program, especially if you are running a very busy Go program with many objects. This mainly happens because you cannot perform garbage collections while everything else is rapidly changing, as this will not allow the GC to clearly identify the members of the white, black, and gray sets. This garbage collection status is also called a **garbage collection safe-point**.

> Note that the Go GC is always being improved by the Go team. They are trying to make it faster by lowering the number of scans it needs to perform over the data of the three sets. However, despite the various optimizations, the general idea behind the algorithm remains the same.

You can find the long and relatively advanced Go code of the GC at `https://github.com/golang/go/blob/master/src/runtime/mgc.go`, which you can study if you want to learn even more information about the garbage collection operation. You can even make changes to that code if you are brave enough!

More about the operation of the Go garbage collector

This section talks more about the Go GC and presents additional information about its activities. The main concern of the Go GC is **low latency**, which basically means short pauses in its operation in order to have a real-time operation.

On the other hand, what a program does is create new objects and manipulate existing ones with pointers all the time. This process can end up creating objects that can no longer be accessed because there are no pointers pointing to these objects. These objects are then garbage and wait for the GC to clean them up and free their memory space. After that, the memory space that has been freed is ready to be used again.

The mark-and-sweep algorithm is the simplest algorithm used. The algorithm stops the program execution (**stop-the-world garbage collector**) to visit all the accessible objects of the heap of a program and *marks* them. After that, it *sweeps* the inaccessible objects. During the mark phase of the algorithm, each object is marked as white, gray, or black. The children of a gray object are colored gray, whereas the original gray object is now colored black. The sweep phase begins when there are no more gray objects to examine. This technique works because there are no pointers from the black set to the white set, which is a fundamental invariant of the algorithm.

Although the mark-and-sweep algorithm is simple, it suspends the execution of the program while it is running, which means that it adds latency to the actual process. Go tries to lower that latency by running the GC as a concurrent process and by using the tricolor algorithm described in the previous section. However, other processes can move pointers or create new objects while the GC runs concurrently. This fact can make things difficult for the GC.

As a result, the basic principle that will allow the tricolor algorithm to operate concurrently while maintaining the fundamental invariant of the mark-and-sweep algorithm is that **no object of the black set can point to an object of the white set**.

The solution to this problem is fixing all the cases that can cause a problem to the algorithm. Therefore, new objects must go to the gray set because this way, the fundamental invariant of the mark-and-sweep algorithm cannot be altered. Additionally, when a pointer of the program is moved, you color the object that the pointer points to as gray. The gray set acts like a barrier between the white set and the black set. Finally, each time a pointer is moved, some Go code gets automatically executed, which is the write barrier mentioned earlier, which does some recoloring. The latency introduced by the execution of the write barrier code is the price we have to pay for being able to run the GC concurrently.

Please note that the **Java** programming language has many GCs that are highly configurable with the help of multiple parameters. One of these Java GCs is called **G1** and it is recommended for low-latency applications. Although Go does not have multiple GCs, it does have knobs that you can use to tune the GC for your applications.

The section that follows discusses maps and slices from a garbage collection perspective because sometimes the way we handle variables influences the operation of the GC.

Maps, slices, and the Go garbage collector

In this section, we discuss the operation of the Go GC in relation to maps and slices. The purpose of this section is to let you write code that makes the work of the GC easier.

Using a slice

The example in this section uses a slice to store a large number of structures. Each structure stores two integer values. This is implemented in `sliceGC.go` as follows:

```
package main

import (
    "runtime"
)

type data struct {
    i, j int
}

func main() {
    var N = 80000000
    var structure []data
    for i := 0; i < N; i++ {
        value := int(i)
        structure = append(structure, data{value, value})
    }

    runtime.GC()
    _ = structure[0]
}
```

The last statement (`_ = structure[0]`) is used to prevent the GC from garbage collecting the `structure` variable too early, as it is not referenced or used outside of the `for` loop. The same technique will be used in the three Go programs that follow.

Apart from this important detail, a `for` loop is used for putting all values into structures that are stored in the `structure` slice variable. An equivalent way of doing that is the use of `runtime.KeepAlive()`. The program generates no output—it just triggers the GC using a call to `runtime.GC()`.

Using a map with pointers

In this subsection, we use a map for storing pointers. This time, the map is using integer keys that reference the pointers. The name of the program is `mapStar.go` and contains the following Go code:

```
package main

import (
    "runtime"
)

func main() {
    var N = 80000000
    myMap := make(map[int]*int)
    for i := 0; i < N; i++ {
        value := int(i)
        myMap[value] = &value
    }

    runtime.GC()
    _ = myMap[0]
}
```

The operation of the program is the same as in `sliceGC.go` from the previous section. What differs is the use of a map (`make(map[int]*int)`) for storing the pointers to `int`. As before, the program produces no output.

Using a map without pointers

In this subsection, we use a map that stores integer values directly instead of pointers to integers. The important code of `mapNoStar.go` is the following:

```
func main() {
    var N = 80000000
    myMap := make(map[int]int)
    for i := 0; i < N; i++ {
```

```
        value := int(i)
        myMap[value] = value
    }
    runtime.GC()
    _ = myMap[0]
}
```

Once again, the program produces no output.

Splitting the map

In this last program, we used a different technique called sharding, where we split one long map into a map of maps. The implementation of the `main()` function of `mapSplit.go` is as follows:

```
func main() {
    var N = 80000000

    split := make([]map[int]int, 2000)
    for i := range split {
        split[i] = make(map[int]int)
    }

    for i := 0; i < N; i++ {
        value := int(i)
        split[i%2000][value] = value
    }
    runtime.GC()
    _ = split[0][0]
}
```

The code uses two `for` loops, one for creating the map of maps and another one for storing the desired data values in the map of maps.

As all four programs are using huge data structures, they are consuming large amounts of memory. Programs that consume lots of memory space trigger the Go GC more often. The next subsection presents an evaluation of the techniques presented.

Comparing the performance of the presented techniques

In this subsection, we compare the performance of each one of these four implementations using the `time` command of `zsh(1)`, which is pretty similar to the `time(1)` UNIX command.

```
$ time go run sliceGC.go
go run sliceGC.go  2.68s user 1.39s system 127% cpu 3.184 total
$ time go run mapStar.go
go run mapStar.go  55.58s user 3.24s system 209% cpu 28.110 total
$ time go run mapNoStar.go
go run mapNoStar.go  20.63s user 1.88s system 99% cpu 22.684 total
$ time go run mapSplit.go
go run mapSplit.go  20.84s user 1.29s system 100% cpu 21.967 total
```

It turns out that the map versions are slower than the slice version. Unfortunately for maps, the map version will **always** be slower than the slice version because of the execution of the hash function and the fact that the data is not contiguous. In maps, data is stored in a bucket determined by the output of the hash function.

Additionally, the first map program (`mapStar.go`) may be triggering some garbage collection slowdown because taking the address of `&value` will cause it to escape to the heap. Every other program is just using the stack for those locals. When variables escape to the heap, they cause more garbage collection pressure.

> Accessing an element of a map or a slice has *O(1)* runtime, which means that the access time does not depend on the number of elements found in the map or the slice. However, the way these structures work affects the overall speed.

Additional resources

- Go FAQ: How do I know whether a variable is allocated on the heap or the stack? `https://golang.org/doc/faq#stack_or_heap`
- The list of available `-gcflags` options: `https://golang.org/cmd/compile/`
- If you want to learn more about garbage collection, you should visit `http://gchandbook.org/`

Packt>

packt.com

Subscribe to our online digital library for full access to over 7,000 books and videos, as well as industry leading tools to help you plan your personal development and advance your career. For more information, please visit our website.

Why subscribe?

- Spend less time learning and more time coding with practical eBooks and Videos from over 4,000 industry professionals
- Improve your learning with Skill Plans built especially for you
- Get a free eBook or video every month
- Fully searchable for easy access to vital information
- Copy and paste, print, and bookmark content

At `www.packt.com`, you can also read a collection of free technical articles, sign up for a range of free newsletters, and receive exclusive discounts and offers on Packt books and eBooks.

Other Books You May Enjoy

If you enjoyed this book, you may be interested in this other book by Packt:

Git for Programmers

Jesse Liberty

ISBN: 9781801075732

- Create and clone repositories
- Understand the difference between local and remote repositories
- Use, manage, and merge branches back into the main branch
- Utilize tools to manage merge conflicts
- Manage commits on your local machine through interactive rebasing
- Use the log to gain control over all the data in your repository
- Use bisect, blame, and other tools to undo Git mistakes

Packt is searching for authors like you

If you're interested in becoming an author for Packt, please visit `authors.packtpub.com` and apply today. We have worked with thousands of developers and tech professionals, just like you, to help them share their insight with the global tech community. You can make a general application, apply for a specific hot topic that we are recruiting an author for, or submit your own idea.

Share your thoughts

Now you've finished *Mastering Go, Third Edition*, we'd love to hear your thoughts! Scan the QR code below to go straight to the Amazon review page for this book and share your feedback or leave a review on the site that you purchased it from.

https://packt.link/r/1-801-07931-5

Your review is important to us and the tech community and will help us make sure we're delivering excellent quality content.

Index

Symbols

A

B

C

D

E

F

N

O

P

R

S

T

U

V

W

X

Y

Made in the USA
Monee, IL
20 May 2022

96759642R10374